Memphis Boys

"For Your Precious Love" session, 1967. Left to right: Don Crews, Reggie Young, Tommy Cogbill, Gene Chrisman, Oscar Toney Jr., Papa Don Schroeder, Chips Moman, and Bobby Emmons (seated). Photo courtesy Erick Crews, © Papa Don Schroeder.

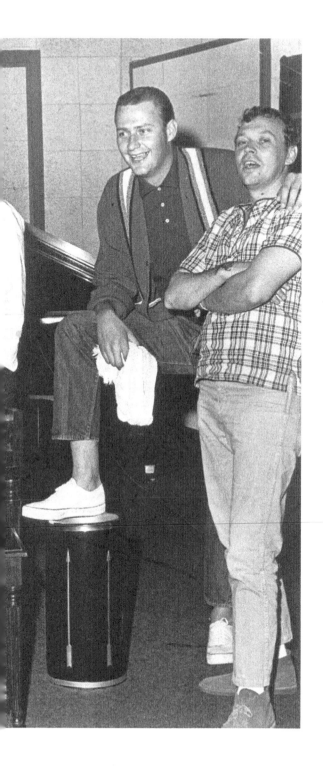

# Memphis Boys

## The Story of American Studios

## Roben Jones

University Press of Mississippi     Jackson

www.upress.state.ms.us

The University Press of Mississippi is a member
of the Association of American University Presses.

First printing 2010

Library of Congress Cataloging-in-Publication Data

Jones, Roben.
 Memphis Boys : the story of American Studios /
Roben Jones.
    p. cm. — (American made music series)
  Includes bibliographical references and index.
  ISBN 978-1-60473-401-0 (cloth : alk. paper)  1.
Memphis Boys (Musical group) 2.  American Sound
Studios. 3.  Moman, Chips. 4.  Musicians—Nashville—
Memphis. 5.  Sound engineers—Nashville—Memphis.
6.  Sound recording industry—Nashville—Memphis—
History.  I. Title.

 ML421.M45J65 2010
 781.64092'2—dc22
 [B]                                    2009031476

British Library Cataloging-in-Publication Data
available

# In memory of Tommy Cogbill

# CONTENTS

||||||||||||||||||||||||||||||||||||||||||||||||||||||||||||||

## ACKNOWLEDGMENTS
||||||||||||||||||||||||||||||||||||||||||||||||||||||||

No one does a book alone, particularly not a first book, and particularly not a comprehensive music history. A music documentarian is by definition enlisting the help of many people and with this one, five years in the writing and two more in the editing, I have had help from the best.

Thanks to Mike Leech, Reggie Young, Bobby Emmons, Bobby Wood, Gene Chrisman, and to later arrivals Glen Spreen, Johnny Christopher, Hayward Bishop, and Shane Keister. Each of them endured many hours of interviews, emails, and questions about what all of it meant with remarkable patience, and each brought his own form of assistance to the table. Mike Leech helped conceive this project, arranged many of the initial interviews, and for much of it worked as de facto editor, all of which made it a better book than it would have been otherwise. He also kept the group informed of new developments in the writing and kept them on board with the project, a task akin to herding cats. Reggie Young and Bobby Emmons shared the session books that each of them faithfully kept, documenting session dates and times and sometimes amounts paid, which was an invaluable help in establishing chronology. Bobby Emmons replaced Mike Leech as de facto editor for the final half of the book, supervising during a critical phase. And Reggie Young arranged the introductions to the musicians from Muscle Shoals, for which I owe him eternal gratitude. Thanks also to Gene Chrisman's stories and fact checking, and the comments, additions, corrections, and suggestions freely supplied by Bobby Wood.

Thanks to Hayward Bishop, Mike Leech, Glen Spreen, Papa Don Schroeder, and Erick Crews (Don's son) for the photos and to Erick an additional thanks for the hand-drawn map of the studio, as well as his enthusiastic cooperativeness in supplying visual material. Thanks also to Hayward Bishop for providing the introduction to John Broven. Spooner Oldham, Glen Spreen, and Hayward Bishop supplied me with CDs by the American group that I did not already have in my collection, adding to my store of knowledge about the band. Johnny Christopher and Shane Keister are to be thanked for the enthusiasm, brilliance, and complete sincerity which they brought to this project.

Chips Moman was unfailingly courteous and gracious when I spoke with him. For his patience in going over material about which he had probably spoken to journalists a hundred times or more, many, many thanks. If there is any accuracy, craftsmanship, and professionalism at all in my writing it is in many ways due to his dedication and determination that I should keep working on the book until I had it right. I am pleased to have been the recipient of his perfectionism and commitment to excellence.

Another special thanks to Billy Burnette, Red West, Richard Mainegra, and Rick Yancey for their perspectives. Wayne Carson deserves extraordinary commendation for having sat through the many interviews he so graciously granted. And a nod to the American group support system: sound engineers Ed Kollis, Mike Cauley, and Stan Kesler, secretary Ima Roberts Withers, and the original business manager Don Crews. Marty Lacker and Bob Moore are the best fact checkers in the world, and thanks to both of them.

To the musicians in and of Muscle Shoals, Alabama, for their participation in this account. Many thanks to all as they recalled the road trips and their memories of Tommy Cogbill. A warm and appreciative thanks to Jimmy Johnson, who organized some of the initial interviews. Thanks also to David Hood, Roger and Brenda Hawkins, Spooner and Karen Oldham, and Jerry Carrigan. Additional thanks to Norbert Putnam, who supplied the project with invaluable background information and insights, enthusiastic encouragement, and good advice. Dan Penn provided many comments about events never previously discussed by historians, such as his official photographs for the Elvis sessions. Special thanks as well to Donnie Fritts for his insights and encouragement.

Others who contributed to this book and deserve commendation include studio clients Quinton Claunch, Fred Foster, and Papa Don Schroeder, recording artists Brenda Lee, B. J. Thomas, and Sandy Posey, and musicians Larry Butler, J.R. Cobb, Jim Davis, Wayne Jackson, the late John Hughey, Gary Talley, Bobby Dean Stewart, and Ron Oates. Dan Penn's wife Linda and Tommy Cogbill's widow Shirley were inspirations throughout the writing of this book—when I grow up, I want to be like them.

Special thanks as well to Buddy Spicher for his encouragement and understanding. For other assistance and various kindnesses I would like to thank Kittra Moore and the late Bobby Thompson and his widow Judy.

Thanks to Craig Gill and his staff at the University Press of Mississippi for their interest in and commitment to this book, and for their editorial suggestions that made it stronger and better. Thanks also to John Broven, who introduced me to the world of book publishers, to John Ridley for the American Group discography, and to Joe Bageant for literary advice, for understanding exactly what it took to write, and for the invitation to the 2007 Southern Festival of Books in Nashville.

And then there are the others who gave me so much, and who are indirectly responsible for this book in ways large and small. Many of them are no longer living: grandparents Thomas and Alice Cantley, who provided me a home for many years; mother, Natalie Cantley Jones, whose sacrifices and ambition made me a writer; father, Charles Jones, who put up with me; godmother Clarice J. Lawson, who first sensed that I could become a writer, and godfather, Mannie Klein, who always knew it would happen and said so. My first mentor, Hugh McPherson of West Virginia Public Radio, and his wife Myrtle, would have loved to have seen this book, as would my best friend, the late Spiegel Willcox, and his wife Helen. Dwight Wetherholt's passion for history helped incite within me a similar devotion to facts from the past. Additional family members no longer living to whom I owe much are Sara Cantley Jones; Jack, Johnny, and Terry Jones; Thelma Cantley Marshall; and Abby Adkins, as well as family friends Bernie Privin and Gladys Fox.

More than anything, I wish Joe Martin had lived to see this book. Joe died in the fall of 2007, as the final drafts were being written. I will miss his encouragement, thoughtfulness, warmth, and gracious spirit each and every day of my life.

To those still living, thanks to Patrick Harold Jones and to family friends Rosalea J. Poland, Mary Helen Cobb, and Victoria Babick. To two of the best "best-friends" a person could have known as a youth, Joseph T. Hardy and Rob Prichard. And thanks to Susan Coleman for standing by me when I needed a friend back there in 1969. Thanks also to Howard Farber, whose used-record business gave me many of my favorite American group recordings over the years. Additional support and encouragement came from Joan McInerny, Evan and Carolyn Roderick, Gladys Lawson Price, Billy Edd Wheeler, Rebecca Williams, Natalie Green, Helen Lanier, Julie Martin Ezell, Madhu Graham, Linda Bowles, Dave and June Conner, my kindred spirit Dottie Dillard, and Tommy Lovelace.

Two others no longer living deserve some of the deepest thanks of all. Thanks to the late Lovell Webb, whose radio show from WKAZ and later WXIT in Charleston, West Virginia, featured the work of the Memphis Boys and instructed the listening audience in who these magnificent musicians were. And especially to Tommy Cogbill, who was the heart and soul of the Memphis Boys. Tommy's productions captivated my heart and my imagination and thus began the long, sometimes arduous, journey that eventually led to this book. So perhaps in a strange way the book is also his creation.

And thanks most of all to James Earl Fetterly, the wind beneath my wings, who knows exactly what I am and endures me anyway, and without whose kindnesses, assistance in ways too numerous to cite, understanding, and almost unconditional love this book would probably not have been written.

They were a band without a name for a long time. In the late sixties, when they began an unprecedented streak of hit records, no one called the band anything at first. In 1968 they released a few instrumental recordings as the American Group. After that they were occasionally billed as the 827 Thomas Street Band, after the address of the Memphis studio where they worked. By 1972 they began the second phase of their careers, as freelance session players in Nashville, and established musicians in town would say of them, "Oh, you know . . . that's some of those Memphis boys." With the release of a 1991 album produced by Allen Reynolds, they made that phrase the title, and the Memphis Boys they officially became.

This book is the culmination of a forty-year journey, for them and for me.

In April 1969 I was the typical rebellious fourteen-year-old of the time. I wore wire-rimmed glasses, denounced the Vietnam War at every opportunity, and was in the process of being expelled from my West Virginia junior high school for "insubordination" and "failure to show proper respect to school officials." At my hearing before the county board of education, I was declared an "unreachable child" and told I could not attend school anywhere in West Virginia. My family would have to move, and at the time, we did not know where. All of us were going to suffer because of the stand I had taken.

I was out of school for most of that year, which allowed me to pursue a better kind of education. The radio was always on and I was developing a passion for all kinds of music. My family was slightly concerned that I spent so much time listening to the radio and seemingly caring about nothing else—in those days such things just were not done—but they sensed I needed it and more or less left me alone. I stayed in my room and did not bother them with my music. And that was how, one Saturday morning, I heard a song that literally changed my life.

Drifting out of my speakers was Alex Chilton, at the time one of the Box Tops but whose recordings were solo performances with session players accompanying him, singing something called "I Shall Be Released." It was a Dylan tune, but I did not know that then. I could certainly relate to the words, about a man in the lonely crowd who remembered "every face of every man who put me here" and swore that he was not to blame. But even more than the song itself, what got me was the music.

It opened with a resonant grand piano, then continued quietly with the piano and an acoustic guitar underlining the verses. But the anguish implied in the lyrics burst forth in the choruses, with a horn arrangement building and building to screams of bewilderment and pain. Bob Dylan may have been writing about a literal prison, but these musicians, these producers and arrangers—whoever had gotten that sound—had built and woven around Dylan's words to describe a prison of the spirit. These people knew something about agony and loss and bleak empty roads stretching endlessly before them.

It was the most musically creative thing I had ever heard; the production embellished the song to create a completely personal statement. There was nothing else on the air to compare with it.

My family made our weekly trip that afternoon to Montgomery, the largest town near us, and there in the old wooden record bin at G.C. Murphy I found that single. Along with it I bought an album, Merrilee Rush's *Angel of the Morning*, because I loved that song and her sweet, hurt-sounding voice. I took the records home and looked at the credits, because I was especially interested in who had gotten that particular sound on the single. The production credit on the single, I discovered to my surprise, was the same as that for the album: Tommy Cogbill and Chips Moman. I had never heard of either of them before, but I knew they were on to something. I absolutely had to hear more. That day I began my life as a record collector.

There was a lot of work from the American

Studio group to collect that summer. Dionne Warwick's *Soulful.* Herbie Mann's *Memphis Underground.* Neil Diamond's "Brother Love's Traveling Salvation Show" and, later, "Sweet Caroline." Hearing "Windmills of Your Mind" on the radio sent me to the *Dusty in Memphis* album, and from there on to Aretha's *Lady Soul.* B. J. Thomas's single, "It's Only Love." And finally Elvis Presley's famous comeback sessions. Through it all, I discovered, the producer whose work I had so admired was also an astonishing bass player.

Before CMT, before *Rolling Stone* was widely distributed, before MTV and VH-1, listeners had to puzzle out alone what was happening with their favorite kinds of music. I deduced that the creative leadership of the group was coming from Cogbill and Moman, and that there seemed to be a third voice named Dan Penn who operated slightly independently of the other two. I avidly read the credits on the back of the album jackets—particularly those from Atlantic, a label that was good about assigning proper credit—to learn who the other musicians were and what they did. Musicians: Gene Chrisman. Reggie Young. Bobby Emmons. Bobby Wood. Bobby Womack. Spooner Oldham. String arrangements by Mike Leech or Glen Spreen. And the writers whose work was also making such an impact: Mark James. Wayne Carson. Billy Burnette. Richard Mainegra. Johnny Christopher. Donnie Fritts. All these players and writers, with their country outlook and strong melodic sense, spoke directly to me. Their very Southernness, their sense of themselves, resonated with me.

As I delved into the world according to these session players, writers, and producers, I found a philosophy more coherent and mature than anything most rock bands were serving up. Both lyrically and musically, many of the songs seemed to be about pain, suffering, hard times, and hard choices. The sound was intricate and textured, with a deep, full tone. The basic rhythm was strong and spirited; the keyboard-driven midrange gave the records complexity; the string lines ranged from somberly contemplative to anguished or despairing.

I did not know it, but I had been captivated by a way of making music that was different from anything a casual listener could have imagined. What I was hearing was an interpretive art that had nothing to do with formal training, composed notation, planned preproduction, or note-reading musicians. It had everything to do with the soul and skills of the producers and players. "I've always found that studios need musicians and vice versa, and producers need musicians and vice versa," said the legendary songwriter and keyboard player Spooner Oldham, who wrote many of the Box Tops hits and who occasionally did some producing.

"The outside has no real clue about the recording process," said Glen Spreen, one of the two arrangers for the Box Tops record. "In ninety-nine percent of the recordings the producers, arrangers, and musicians were the decision makers and in control. . . . The producer and musicians were the center of the sessions. The singer, for the most part, had little participation in the process of which songs were recorded and how those songs were interpreted. The producer and the musicians (mostly the musicians) decided on the interpretation, the arranger worked alone and no one heard his interpretation until the day it [the string and horn overdubs] was recorded."

Bobby Wood, who played the resonant piano introduction to "I Shall Be Released," explained that freeform recording method simply. "We were basically artists," he said. "We were all producers."

Had I been right in my assumption that these record producers and session musicians drew on their own experiences as they embellished existing tunes to describe the dark night of the soul? Were they making statements about what their own lives had been? For Bobby Wood, the question was so obvious it did not even need to be asked. "Oh yeah, everybody does that," he said matter-of-factly.

It was equally obvious to Shane Keister, the keyboard player who replaced Bobby Wood in 1972, knew Tommy Cogbill well, and who himself became a producer. "We all do that," he said, echoing Bobby. "I guarantee you, there's not a musician alive, whether they are playing in a studio or onstage, who doesn't draw on his own experiences." As he outlined the process, it sounded close to the way an actor uses sense memory to interpret a scene. "I don't know how it is with other people, but I have always been conscious of the lyric," he said, noting that this was one of the skills he learned from this group of musicians. "Sometimes, while I am in the studio and running down my chart, key words or phrases will leap out at me. I don't consciously do this, but I draw from my own experiences. If the lyric is about an unhappy love affair, I place myself in the memory of someone I loved I broke up with. Even if there's an up-tempo funky groove, I tap into the excitement it creates. I'll think about things as far back as my childhood, my children, my grandchildren, my parents, my cousins, my friends. I don't consciously do this, but the reason I know is that when it is over, I remember not only the lyric, but the scenes, the pictures it suggested. And we all remember pictures more easily than we do words." He recalled Chips Moman suggesting ideas to the band in the form of pictures the music should paint. When Shane began producing during the late seventies and early eighties, he often asked Tommy Cogbill about sounds or key effects; the advice he got was to notice the song's meaning. "He listened to the lyrics. . . . He really, really dug into what a song was all about," said Shane.

"All of the people are emotionally interpretive people," said Hayward Bishop, who became the studio percussionist a year after the Dylan song was recorded and who also spent much time with Tommy. "It's the emotion that connects with the people who are buying the record. The producer himself is an artist, the musicians are artists. It's artistic people creating a commercial structure.

"[Chips and Tommy] chose that song because they could relate to it. Why would somebody pick a song they don't relate to? . . . What most people don't realize about record producers like Tommy Cogbill, for instance, is that they involved their own emotions from the time they would choose which songs would make the cut. Good producers like Tommy knew the emotional value of the songs they

were choosing as well as the emotional interpretive and enhancement skills of our band. Their job and purpose was to look for that combination of emotional and commercial-sounding performance in the song-choosing stages and then be able to mechanically break it down while producing it with the musicians and put it all back together again as a polished, finished work that sounds like the vocalist was thinking out loud! . . . It's the producer's emotions that would steer and temper the musicians' emotions so that the final product would stir the emotions of the listener."

Reggie Young, who played lead guitar on the Alex Chilton (Box Tops) session as well as on everything else coming out of the studio, said that he had given the matter a lot of thought over the years and that geography may have been one influence on the highly personal way the songs were interpreted and played. "For all of us, it was the area of the country we lived in," he reflected. "It's the dead center between Delta blues and Nashville country. Some of the things we cut could have been country. All the club bands played that way. If you blindfolded me and took me into a club and I heard somebody play that way, I'd know I was in Memphis."

The musicians, writers, and arrangers at this studio were a literal cross-section of the American South: several from Alabama and Tennessee, two Georgians, an Arkansan, two from Mississippi, two Texans, one each from Louisiana, Missouri, Virginia, and my own home state of West Virginia. Since the players, writers, and producers all had the same regional and musical background, establishing a sound from that common pool of sense memories was easy. To Chips Moman, the co-producer of the Box Tops song, it was essential to distill those experiences and see that they reached the largest possible audience–but first came the record's acceptance by the studio band. "I want everybody to like it. I think that's important," he said.

Marty Lacker, the former Elvis associate who became office manager for the studio at roughly the same time the Box Tops session was done, offered a perspective that in many ways was the mirror opposite of mine. He had grown up in the North and his family had come south when he was fourteen. He knew from observing at close range what I had sensed from listening. "Chips is the one that put these musicians together one by one as a band, so he must have recognized that southern breeding that gave each one of the guys their life experiences that translated into their style of playing and the feel they each brought to a song. That might be because he shared that same kind of upbringing and the South's lifestyle of hills and valleys."

"People in the South have a way of living true to life," observed Johnny Christopher, the acoustic guitarist and songwriter who was the newest musician on staff at the studio when the Box Tops session was done. "Whenever a society or a civilization perishes . . . do you know what the preconditions are? People forget where they come from." The recordings of the American Group are a stunning reminder of roots—that the South was originally a land of impoverished, neglected people who, in the case of sharecroppers, textile workers, and coal miners, at times were little better than serfs.

Spooner Oldham described the process of creating music from this pool of memories as so intuitive that "little instruction needed to be given" from the producers. "You rarely have to verbalize the feeling or the mood. They're just such learned musicians, they pick up on the mood and go with it." "We analyzed music by playing it together," added Hayward Bishop. "It's a thing jazz musicians do when they get together and jam. We don't read music, so how else are we going to do it?" "We weren't like five egomaniacs, you know," Reggie Young continued. "Instead of five players, we were like one band."

"I heard theories somewhere that people think from different quadrants of the brain and that affects your decision-making," said Bobby Emmons, the studio organist who played on the Box Tops session. "It was rumored that corporations gave psychiatric tests on job applications for executives to determine what quadrant they were thinking from and then make an effort to evenly distribute the type thinkers they had in production groups and so forth. I

often wondered if we lucked into such a combination with our band.

"You're a product of all the music that you've ever tentatively listened to and you're programmed subconsciously to a certain extent by everything that's playing, whether you're listening attentively or not," Emmons added. "To go on, everything you've ever really liked or really disliked makes a lasting impression that you carry with you. When you need to make a decision musically with something you've been working on, those things become guidelines. They program you in the direction you're wanting to go. They push your mind away from the bad and toward the good."

"It really boils down to who you are," Glen Spreen elaborated. "If you have had a lot of sadness in your life, it never leaves you and you will respond to that. We were all products of our environments. Our music worlds were all influenced by our personal histories. Our opinions and styles were a product of the lives to which we were subjected. Our personal experiences were the major and central driving factors in the music we liked and played. I think that was referred to as 'soul.' It was our way of communicating and talking with the listeners," he continued. "We had no choice. It let us survive with our sanity intact. This brought us together and gave us a common bond and meaning."

Their main message seemed to be about stoicism, about triumphing through simple endurance. It was a message that resonated to a young girl coming from an Appalachian family plagued with both bad luck and bad judgment, a girl who never fit into her own household because she did not seem to her elders to be reserved and stoic enough. Years later, it was suggested to me that perhaps that was the secret of the music's appeal: I turned to the American Group for guidance on how to fit into my family, and for lessons on how to be strong. If so, I was not disappointed. The group, and especially Tommy Cogbill, never failed me in that regard.

My records accompanied me to my family's new house in Ohio, and as a Southerner in exile, a wallflower at school, and increasingly isolated from my family, the recordings of the American Group became more important to me than ever. They were letters from home, telling me what was happening in the South and how that region was changing. Before there was southern rock, there was the American Group, writing and commenting like a living newspaper on everything that was happening back there, and keeping me connected to my roots. I wandered away for awhile; there was a period of extensive jazz listening, discovering the big bands and small groups of the Roaring Twenties. But that music was too frivolous to help me face the challenges of a family life that careened from one misfortune to another, one tragedy to another. And so I returned to the American Group.

Night after night, for more years than can be counted, I sat in my room and listened till long into the morning, playing the records of the American Group over and over, searching for nuggets of meaning like a prospector panning for gold. What other people my age seemed to get from rock, I got from these musicians—a context. I got a sense that the lives and experiences of people like me and my entire embattled, luckless family had some significance, and that truth could be learned even from meaningless suffering. In good times and some absolutely horrific ones, the music made by these people gave me hours of inspiration, thought, and sheer pleasure. It was the most real thing in my life.

And through it all I kept coming back to where it began for me. Tommy Cogbill, especially as a producer, was a beacon in the dark. I felt as if I was not listening so much as I was conducting a dialogue with him through music; I came to Tommy bearing a young girl's questions, and he answered them. His productions taught me how to see and interpret; he showed me the importance of structure and form, whether in a song or a paragraph. After his photo appeared on the back cover of *Aretha's Gold* in late 1969, I would go down to the local five-and-ten and pull the album out of the bin and stare at it for hours, trying to see into the soul of the man who made that beautiful music I loved. And, two years after the fact,

when I read that he had died the words rushed up at me like a freight train. I think I cried . . . but I don't remember.

Fast forward to the new century and the Internet. A chance online encounter with the then-extant website of Mike Leech led me to do further research on the careers of these musicians. I began corresponding online with Mike, and asked him so many questions about the group and about working with Tommy that eventually we began talking about my doing a book—the story of American Studios. Immediately I knew that telling their story would be my thank-you letter to all of the people whose work I so deeply respected.

Gradually, by email and then phone, I began contacting present and former members of the group, asking them questions about specific songs and sessions. One question or story led to another, and another, and another; one person referred me to another who might have something to contribute. It was a big wheel that never stopped rolling. People who had fallen out of touch with colleagues from long ago wanted to know how old friends were doing; people who were still working together gained insights about one another they had never had before. It was a learning experience for everyone involved, most of all for me.

What emerged from these talks and emails was a collective memoir, a sort of group biography that took shape as the writing progressed. Gradually it became apparent that their story could be told almost exclusively from the viewpoint of these studio musicians who brought the songs to life, rather than from the more commonly sought perspective of the stars. The American players never felt they had gotten proper credit for their work anyway; it had always been a sore point with them that other Memphis studios like Sun and Stax had gotten the press. In fact, one of the most remarkable things about the American Group was its sense that they were a band of renegades battling the entire music business because of their differences in recording methods as well as content (it is no accident that later, when the group resettled in Nashville, they became the prominent backing band for the Outlaw movement). That clannishness was extended even to the way they treated one another; musicians who came into the group later on were only half tolerated. The fact that one and all spoke as freely as they did for this book is astonishing in itself.

Not every interview I sought came off, but I was able to speak with all of the American group save three. Mark James, one of the studio's most important songwriters, said he would think about speaking, but never got back to me. Every effort to locate Darryl Carter, one of the studio's longest-lasting sound engineers and Bobby Womack's frequent songwriting partner, was fruitless. Bobby Womack, who occupied a unique position as both studio musician and one of the best-known artists who recorded at American, was writing his autobiography at the time and could not be reached. I am sorry that I never had the pleasure of talking with them. Apologies as well to Albert "Junior" Lowe, whom I was unable to locate in time to get his recollections. It is to be hoped that his memories of the Wilson Pickett and Aretha Franklin sessions in Muscle Shoals can appear in another book I hope to write.

I am also sorry I did not get to speak with the staff from Atlantic, the record label most closely associated with the Memphis Boys during the years of this study. The gifted producer and engineer Tom Dowd died in October 2002, as the book was getting under way; Arif Mardin and Ahmet Ertegun died within five months of one another, midway through its writing. It is the deepest regret of all my experiences with this book that I was unable to talk to these extraordinary gentlemen; from what the American musicians and others told me of them I know I missed something. The last member of the Atlantic crew, Jerry Wexler, told his story often and through many forums, cited in the bibliography; his version of events seemed to be already well documented. He died in August 2008, as the book was in its final stages of editing; he had been ill for some time, although he kept in touch by phone with several of the people cited here (Chips Moman, Bobby Wood, and the Muscle Shoals songwriter Donnie Fritts all spoke to him regularly).

The Box Tops' lead guitarist, Gary Talley,

attempted to put me in touch with Alex Chilton; given Chilton's reportedly prickly personality, it is not surprising that he did not respond to a request to rehash his early recordings one more time. I also never spoke to Toni Wine, the New York songwriter who came to American in its waning days and who eventually married Chips Moman; her career as Brill Building writer, singer, and musician during the 1960s is worthy of a biography in itself. So I decided to tell the story almost exclusively through the eyes of the players, writers, and engineers who made the music at American Studios so special, with an occasional comment from a friend or colleague who witnessed the magic.

As I talked to these musicians and to many of their friends, it occurred to me that the great story I was hearing was even greater because so much of it has never been talked about in most music books referring to the time (therefore causing me to rely on sources never cited before: the participants themselves). It is the story of a group of studio players who remained colleagues and lifelong friends. It is the story of how working together created such a profound brotherhood that even former members remain affected by and identified with those recordings of so long ago. It is the story of some of the most creative decades ever in pop and country music. Above all, it is the story of some fascinating human beings; their old patron Papa Don Schroeder was right when he described them as "men of character." Dan Penn was right, too, when he said of the group's journey: "It really is the Untold Story."

This is their history. This is their music.

## PROFILES

||||||||||||||||||||||||||||||||||||||||||||||||||||||||||||||

(along with ages in 1970)

### The Leader

LINCOLN WAYNE "CHIPS" MOMAN (33)

Farm boy from LaGrange, Georgia. Came to Memphis at fourteen and played guitar for Dorsey and Johnny Burnette. Owner of American Studios, which he established with Seymour Rosenberg as his first partner in 1962; producer, arranger, songwriter, guitarist, occasional background singer. Played lead guitar on the first Aretha Franklin session for Atlantic Records. With Dan Penn, wrote "Dark End of the Street" and "Do Right Woman." Produced the Gentrys' "Keep On Dancin'," Sandy Posey's "Born a Woman" and "Single Girl," B.J. Thomas's "Hooked on a Feeling," and the Elvis comeback sessions of 1969. His vision and view of the world strongly influenced the group and the kind of recordings they made.

### The Partner

DON CREWS (40)

Farmer from Lepanto, Arkansas. Partner in American Studios with Chips Moman beginning in 1964. Served as original business administrator and office manager for the studio. Left in 1970 following a lawsuit by Chips Moman; acquired Onyx Studios, where he later produced some of T.G. Sheppard's early hits.

### The Core Group

TOMMY COGBILL (38)

From Brownsville, Tennessee; family moved to Memphis when he was a child. Bass player, guitarist, producer, occasional percussionist. Soul of the band in the same way Keith Richards exemplified the Rolling Stones. Originally a steel guitar player, then played jazz in small clubs before going into studio work. Best known for having played bass on Aretha Franklin's recordings and on Dusty Springfield's "Son of a

Preacher Man." Produced Merrilee Rush's "Angel of the Morning" and Neil Diamond's "Sweet Caroline" and "Holly Holy." Co-produced King Curtis's "Memphis Soul Stew" with Tom Dowd and the Box Tops' "Soul Deep" with Chips Moman. Left the group in early 1972 and resettled in Nashville; there he produced Carl Carlton's "Everlasting Love" with Papa Don Schroeder in 1974. Died of a stroke in December 1982 at the age of fifty.

REGGIE YOUNG (31)

From Osceola, Arkansas; family came to Memphis when he was thirteen. Lead guitarist, sitar player, occasional songwriter. First came to national prominence with the Bill Black Combo in 1959. Played electric sitar on the Box Tops' "Cry Like A Baby" and B.J. Thomas's "Hooked On A Feeling." Also known for the lead guitar line on "Son of a Preacher Man."

BOBBY EMMONS (28)

A farm boy from near Corinth, Mississippi. Organist, piano player, songwriter, occasional backing vocalist. A charter member of the Bill Black Combo along with Reggie Young, and later worked extensively on freelance sessions at Hi Records. Probably the member of the group closest to Chips Moman, with whom he later wrote "Luckenbach, Texas."

GENE CHRISMAN (27)

Memphis native. Drummer, percussionist. Also filled out the official forms documenting the sessions for the Musicians' Union. Worked for awhile as drummer for Jerry Lee Lewis, then joined Bobby Wood's band the Starlighters, playing in a local club. Recommended for the group by Tommy Cogbill.

MIKE LEECH (27)

Another Memphian. Bassist, string arranger, occasional producer, occasional percussionist. Joined the group in 1967, shortly after its original formation. Studied for a time at Memphis State University. First string arrangement appeared on the Box Tops' "The Letter." Played bass on Elvis's "Suspicious Minds" and on Bobby Womack's "Woman's Gotta Have It."

## BOBBY WOOD (28)

A farm boy from New Albany, Mississippi. Pianist, background vocalist, occasional songwriter. Worked as a part-time group member practically from the band's inception; became a full-time member in late 1968. Had some success as a solo singer, placing one hit ("If I'm a Fool") on the pop charts in 1964. Later collaborated on songs with Johnny Christopher.

### Additions

## DAN PENN (29)

Originally from Vernon, Alabama. Songwriter, singer, producer. Worked in bands from his mid-teens, came to Muscle Shoals, Alabama, in 1960 and became part of the scene coalescing around the studio and central figure of Rick Hall. Introduced to Chips Moman by MGM label head Jim Vienneau in 1966; left Muscle Shoals later that year to work at American Studios. Produced the Box Tops hits "The Letter," "Cry Like a Baby," "Choo Choo Train," and "I Met Her in Church." With Chips Moman wrote "Do Right Woman" and "Dark End of the Street." With Spooner Oldham wrote "Cry Like A Baby," "Sweet Inspiration," "I Met Her In Church," and "A Woman Left Lonely." Left American in late 1968 to open his own studio. Produced Ronnie Milsap's first album and served as official photographer for the Elvis sessions in early 1969.

## LINDON DEWEY "SPOONER" OLDHAM (27)

Pianist, organist, songwriter, occasional producer. Originally from Center Star, Alabama, near the Shoals. Attended Florence State College in Florence, Alabama; was on hand at the beginning of the Muscle Shoals scene. Replaced David Briggs as studio keyboardist when Briggs left for Nashville in 1964; played organ on Percy Sledge's "When A Man Loves A Woman" and on Aretha Franklin's first hit "I Never Loved A Man." Came to Memphis in early 1967; while there, wrote "Cry Like A Baby," "Sweet Inspiration," and "I Met Her in Church" with Dan Penn. Left in late 1968 and resettled in Los Angeles as freelance studio

keyboardist; wrote "A Woman Left Lonely" with Dan Penn after that. Also wrote "Roadmaster" and "Lonely Women Make Good Lovers" with Freddy Weller.

## BOBBY WOMACK (27)

Singer, songwriter, guitarist. Came to Memphis in 1967 following time in California working with his brothers in a group called the Valentinos, mentored by Sam Cooke. Also played on sessions in Muscle Shoals for Wilson Pickett and in New York for Aretha Franklin. Wrote "I'm in Love," "Midnight Mover," and "Woman's Gotta Have It" with soundman Darryl Carter. Left Memphis and returned to California in mid-1968, but recorded his first two albums at American Studios; returned again in 1972 for the recording of "Woman's Gotta Have It."

### Late Arrivals

## GLEN SPREEN (29)

Native of Houston, Texas. String arranger, pianist, saxophonist, woodwind instruments, occasional songwriter and producer. Worked with B.J. Thomas in Houston. Introduced to the group by his and B.J.'s songwriter friend Mark James. Began working with the group full-time in late 1968 following his discharge from the army. Produced B.J. Thomas's "Most of All" and "No Love at All." Left in late 1970 and relocated to Nashville; during his tenure there, wrote string arrangements for Dan Fogelberg and produced Dave Loggins's "Please Come to Boston."

## JOHNNY CHRISTOPHER (27)

From Atlanta, Georgia. Songwriter, acoustic guitarist, background vocalist. Came to Memphis in late 1968 as bass player for Ronnie Milsap's band, backing the singer when Chips Moman found for him a residency at a club called T.J.'s. Placed "Mama Liked the Roses" with Elvis and, on the strength of this demo, was hired as acoustic guitarist on sessions. One of three credited with writing "You Were Always on My Mind"; later wrote successfully with Bobby Wood. Left in early 1972 and resettled in Nashville.

### HAYWARD BISHOP (25)

Native of Norfolk, Virginia, and veteran of the beach-music scene. Drummer, percussionist, occasional background vocalist, producer. Came to Memphis in early 1969 following time in the air force. Hired at American Studios as assistant engineer; first contributed occasional percussion to records, then replaced Gene Chrisman on drums in early 1972. Discovered the three-man singing/writer's group Cymarron and produced their early demos. Played drums on "Woman's Gotta Have It" and "Good Time Charlie's Got the Blues." In Nashville, played drums on recordings by the pathbreaking country group Alabama.

### SHANE KEISTER (19)

Synthesizer player, pianist, songwriter, producer, arranger. A native West Virginian whose family moved to Portsmouth, Ohio, when he was seven. Attended Marshall University and North Texas State University; while at North Texas State joined a band called Southwest FOB with Dan Seals and John Ford Coley that recorded for Stax. Came to Memphis in 1970; replaced Bobby Wood in 1972 following several years of session work and club appearances. Later became the most prominent synthesizer player in Nashville.

### Writers

### WAYNE CARSON (THOMPSON) (28)

Songwriter, singer, occasional background vocalist and guitarist. From Springfield, Missouri; protégé of Springfield music impresario Si Siman. Wrote Box Tops hits "The Letter," "Soul Deep," and "Neon Rainbow," and B.J. Thomas's "No Love at All." Main composer of "You Were Always on My Mind." Successfully operated his own studio in Springfield for several years.

### MARK JAMES (27)

Songwriter, singer, occasional producer. Native of Houston, Texas. Vietnam veteran who came to Memphis in 1967 through the auspices of a friend from Houston, Scepter Records promotion man Steve Tyrell. In turn, brought B.J.

Thomas and Glen Spreen to Memphis in 1968. Wrote "Eyes of a New York Woman," "Hooked on a Feeling," and "Suspicious Minds": one of three who wrote "You Were Always on My Mind."

### RICHARD MAINEGRA (27)

From Slidell, Louisiana. Singer, acoustic guitarist, and aspiring writer who came to American in 1969. Wrote "Let's Give Adam and Eve Another Chance" and "Separate Ways" with Red West. With friends Rick Yancey (Memphis native who also came to American in 1969 following staff writing for Hi Records) and Sherrill Parks (a farm boy from near Jackson, Tennessee), was a member of Cymarron, a vocal trio who had a hit with "Rings" in 1971.

### BOBBY "RED" WEST (35)

Memphis native. Songwriter, producer. Brief tenure at American Studios from 1969 through 1970; discovered Richard Mainegra and Rick Yancey. Best known for his work as bodyguard for and close friend of Elvis Presley and his work as actor and stuntman on Robert Conrad's TV shows *Wild Wild West* and *Black Sheep Squadron*. Wrote "Let's Give Adam and Eve Another Chance" and "Separate Ways" with Richard Mainegra; made sure that Elvis got a copy of "You Were Always on My Mind." Later co-author (with Dave Hebler and cousin Sonny West) of *Elvis: What Happened?*

### DONNIE FRITTS (27)

Singer, songwriter, organist from Florence, Alabama. Along with Dan Penn and Spooner Oldham, a key contributor in the early days of Muscle Shoals. Wrote "Choo Choo Train" and Dusty Springfield's classic "Breakfast in Bed" with Muscle Shoals guitarist Eddie Hinton and "Rainbow Road" with Dan Penn. Later played in Kris Kristofferson's backup band for many years and wrote "We Had It All" with Troy Seals.

### BILLY BURNETTE (18)

Songwriter, singer, guitarist. Son of legendary Memphis songwriter Dorsey Burnette; nephew of Johnny Burnette and cousin of

Rocky Burnette. Signed as a writer by Chips Moman when Billy was just out of high school in 1971. Later worked as guitarist with Fleetwood Mac, replacing Lindsey Buckingham.

### TONI WINE (23)

Songwriter, piano player, backing vocalist. A native New Yorker and child prodigy who was classically trained and gave her first recital when she was ten. At sixteen she was a successful songwriter working out of the Brill Building; wrote "Groovy Kind of Love" with Carole Bayer Sager and "Candida" with Irwin Levine; sang backup on Tony Orlando's recording of the latter tune. Also wrote "Black Pearl" for Sonny Charles and the Checkmates; that same year she sang on the Archies novelty hit "Sugar, Sugar." Began working in Memphis at the beginning of 1970; embarked on a complicated affair with, and later marriage to, Chips Moman.

### *Sound Crew*

### ED KOLLIS (27)

Engineer, harmonica player. Native of Madison, Wisconsin, and graduate of the university there. Came to Memphis in 1967 and played harmonica on Joe Tex's "Skinny Legs and All"; also contributed harmonica to "Stranger in My Own Home Town" from the Elvis sessions. Left American Studios in early 1970 to become staff engineer at Columbia Studios in Nashville.

### MIKE CAULEY (22)

Arkansas native. Engineer, aspiring producer and songwriter. Replaced Ed Kollis in early 1970; left American for good in 1971. Worked subsequently at Onyx Studios with Don Crews, then for many years as a professional gambler.

### STAN KESLER (42)

Engineer, songwriter, producer, steel guitarist. From a farm near Abbeville, Mississippi; came to Memphis after World War II. Knew Tommy Cogbill in the late forties; worked as songwriter and steel player at Sun Records in the fifties; while there, wrote both "I Forgot to Remember" and "I'm Left, You're Right, She's

Gone" for Elvis. Wrote "If I'm a Fool" for Bobby Wood in 1964. Produced Sam the Sham's novelty hits "Wooly Bully" and "Little Red Riding Hood." Developed the band the Dixie Flyers and the Sounds of Memphis studio. Came to American in 1971. Later engineered at Pete Drake's studio in Nashville.

### *Office Staff*

### MARTY LACKER (35)

From what is now the South Bronx in New York, his family moved to Memphis when Marty was fourteen. Worked as a radio announcer and then foreman of Elvis Presley's Memphis Mafia from 1961 until 1967; from there worked at the jingle company Pepper-Tanner. Joined American Studios as promotion man in late 1968; became studio manager, replacing Don Crews, in 1970. Left in 1971 to operate his own promotion firm and to work on the Memphis Music Awards. Later did two books about his experiences with Elvis.

### IMA ROBERTS (LATER WITHERS) (21)

Secretary hired by Don Crews to help handle the workload in late 1967. Left the studio in late 1970; eventually became a key executive at BMI in Nashville.

# Memphis Boys

III

# Sun Days and Hi Times

In 1960 the Memphis music scene, for all intents and purposes, looked dead. By decade's end, with the Stax and Hi record labels, independent studios including Ardent, the Pepper-Tanner jingle company, and the remarkable comeback of Elvis Presley, the recording scene had come roaring back—only to finally and spectacularly fall in the middle seventies.

"Memphis was primarily a pop market," observed Bobby Wood, one of the young musicians playing clubs in town. Many of the artists who had made Memphis that way in the first place—Elvis, Johnny Cash, Roy Orbison, Carl Perkins, and even lesser-known Sun discoveries like Conway Twitty and Ed Bruce—were no longer recording in town by 1960. Charlie Rich had just broken through, and he would be the last great Sun discovery. Elvis, of course, maintained his mansion, Graceland, in the Whitehaven suburb outside Memphis, but many of the others had moved to Nashville, near where they were recording. Even the great blues players like Ike Turner and Howlin' Wolf weren't Memphis-based anymore. B. B. King was still around, and that was about it (and he spent much of his time touring). Small wonder it looked as if Memphis had had its time in the national spotlight.

There were still some optimists around who seemed to think Memphis had a future. Sam Phillips had just completed a new recording studio complex, named for himself. His old associates and former Elvis accompanists, Scotty Moore and Bill Black, each had set up studios and record labels of their own (Fernwood and Lyn-Lou, respectively) which gave them incomes now that Elvis was in the army. Another former Sun musician, the steel guitarist Stan Kesler, was doing small-scale recording at his Echo Studio. Jerry Lee Lewis was blacklisted by radio, but his concerts were still packing them in. And Jim Stewart and Estelle Axton, with help from a young Georgia guitarist, Chips Moman, were just beginning Stax Records.

There were others out there too, younger players whom nobody had bothered to inform that Memphis music was officially dead. Some of them were already there—native Memphians like Gene Chrisman and Mike Leech.

"Gene is a brilliant drummer," said Monument Records president Fred Foster, who would hire Chrisman many times over the years for sessions. "He plays just behind the beat enough to make it soulful." Gene was more modest. "I was just self-taught. Never took any lessons, just tried my best to do what I could, and went from there. I first liked music when I was in the ninth grade and going to sock hops and so forth at Whitehaven School in Memphis. I enjoyed Fats Domino, Little Richard, Chuck Berry. I would listen to their records and play along with them on cardboard boxes and pots and pans. My mother later got me a set of old used drums at a pawn shop. I began to play along with the records on the drums, and later found a few guys that did about the same thing I did." He formed a band in high school that featured another future Memphis music legend, the Johnny Cash soundalike Tommy Tucker, on vocals; Tucker later recorded a few singles for Hi.

Mike Leech had a similar story to tell. He grew up in the same neighborhood as Steve Cropper and Duck Dunn (both of whom became members of the racially integrated Stax house band Booker T. and the MG's), and first picked up a guitar in their presence when he was fourteen. Shortly thereafter he joined a high school rock and roll band, switching from guitar to bass. The highlight of his career at that point, he recalled, was his group's audition for Sam Phillips's right-hand man, Jack Clement. "He was dating someone who lived a block or two from where I grew up. Anyhow, the audition was a total disaster. We could never get in tune. Not just 'out of tuneness,' I mean we didn't know what we were supposed to tune with, so we were like, at least, a whole step out. Our sax player got embarrassed and began packing up."

Undaunted, Mike continued with music, playing trumpet in his high school marching band. "That trumpet paid my way through college," he observed, for on the advice of a friend he applied, following his graduation, for a music scholarship at Northwest Junior College in Senatobia, Mississippi. "At Northwest Junior College, I had a little rock and roll band, and we were playing around Memphis, Arkansas, Mississippi. We were also under full scholarship at Northwest, for books, lodging, tuition, everything."

While playing weekend gigs at roadhouses and clubs, Mike had his first experience of working with a star. "Somehow I was hired to play the C&R Club in Truman, Arkansas, on several occasions. A fellow named Curly owned the club, with Curly's Motel across the street and Curly's Liquor Store next door. The club was a Quonset hut and always jammed with customers." Charlie Rich, just coming off his first hit, "Lonely Weekends," played regularly there, and Mike's band backed him at the club. "Charlie was always laid back, easygoing. I always enjoyed working with him," Mike remembered with pleasure. "We would start out the gig playing old songs to a full dance floor. 'Big Boss Man' was one of Charlie's favorites. Drinks were cheap, and although I was underage I was allowed to participate. Charlie did too, and he would usually get drunk and get on a jazz and blues kick later on. Those were some wild nights. On at least one occasion I took Charlie's Cadillac and drove like a bat out of hell to West Memphis to get something— seems like Curly's liquor store closed early and Charlie had me go get more booze. I was so snockered one night I had to close one eye to keep from seeing double lane lines."

The conflict of interest between formal music and rock and roll was not without repercussions, he discovered. "Ben Rackard was our band director, and we got involved in doing some musicals. We explained to Mr. Rackard that we wanted to do the musicals, but we

also had jobs to make to have spending money. We gave him ample notice that one weekend we had a gig in Memphis. He purposely kept us late during rehearsal one night, knowing we wouldn't make our gig on time. We were quite upset, and we kept reminding him that we needed to leave. He blew his top and told us to get out 'and bring your out-of-state tuition on Monday.'"

"Our big mistake was that next day we took the problem to the school president. I learned a big lesson that afternoon when I was summoned to the president's office. There sat Rackard, and the president said (something like), 'Mr. Rackard tells me you have been very uncooperative on this project.' (I had already told the prez what went down.) He followed that with, 'If you don't repair this attitude I think you should make plans to leave Northwest Junior College.' Rackard just sat there grinning. It scared me to death so I apologized and told them I would cooperate from now on."

Unbeknownst to Mike, the script of a Frank Capra movie was being played out behind the scenes. "Half the faculty knew about this and, depending on the outcome, were ready to turn in their resignations on my behalf. There was also a town council meeting on my behalf, discussing a possible ouster of Northwest's president, also depending on the outcome. You see, most of the faculty liked me and my band, as did folks in the city of Senatobia, and my possible expulsion caused quite a stir. Had I known all that, it would have made a big difference in my meeting with the prez."

Mike finished his junior college years without incident and continued his music studies at Memphis State, also with the aid of a scholarship, joining a student body which included such future luminaries as the guitarist Charlie Freeman and the trumpeter/sound engineer Kenneth Laxton. He married and resumed his junior-college routine of studies by day and playing local clubs at night, getting around town in a British-model Ford.

"My wife and I, newly married, rented a small apartment above a doctor's office on Cooper Street in Memphis. We were both still in school. Every morning I would have to crawl under the car (sometimes in the snow), take the transmission out, haul it upstairs, lay it on spread-out newspapers, take it apart, reset the pin bearings, put it back together, back downstairs, back under the car, reinstall it, then go to school. I finally traded it for something I don't remember, but it had to be better than that thing."

According to Mike, "If I could say one individual was responsible for my career as a musician, it would be an old pal, Ronnie Coletta. Ronnie played baritone horn in the high school band [the same Catholic high school Mike attended] and he also played guitar. We became friends and he taught me some chords on the guitar. We eventually formed a little band and began playing sock hops, CYOs, things like that."

The band played a local talent show and backed a singer on the bill who had had a local hit with a song called "Please Please Little Girl." After the show, the singer, Kimball Coburn, was so impressed he asked the group to be his regular backup band. "And that's a book in itself," chuckled Mike.

Around that same time Mike met another guitar player, Ralph Floyd, who was then a member of B. B. Cunningham's band. (As a member of the Hombres, B. B. would have a hit with a parody of psychedelia called "Let It All Hang Out"; his brother Bill would play guitar for the Box Tops.) Mike and Ralph spent many late hours together, hanging out in clubs, bars, and at each other's houses, where they sat and listened to records together all night long.

"Ralph and I remained friends but he didn't pursue the recording career as I did," said Mike. "But he is definitely worth a mention as being a tremendous influence in my life, not only musicwise, but as my confidante."

Some of them were from other places originally, but had come to Memphis as children with their families, like Tommy Cogbill and Reggie Young. Tommy's family came from Brownsville, Tennessee, about sixty miles just east of the city. "His father worked for Armour and Company," recalled Shirley Cogbill, Tommy's widow. He discovered steel guitar at an early age—in those days it was still the "Hawaiian"

or lap steel, without the pedals—and by the time of his senior year in high school, in late 1948 through early 1949, he was playing with a country group broadcasting over WDIA (not yet the famous R&B station it would become). There he met another steel guitar player just up from a cotton farm near Abbeville, Mississippi: Stan Kesler.

"I was with Rex Torian, Tommy was playing with Mel Allen, who sang and played rhythm," Kesler remembered. Torian's band and Allen's had back-to-back fifteen-minute shows at noon over WDIA. "He came down to do that program on his lunch hour from high school. I was probably twenty years old, he might have been sixteen or seventeen." Already, Cogbill was demonstrating to those he met a remarkable dedication and maturity. "He seemed just a mild, laid-back teenager," said Kesler. "Of course, he was laid-back all his life, but he had a little wild streak."

Following his graduation from high school, Cogbill went to Hollywood, Florida, with a piano-playing friend named Leon Knowles, and the two of them played clubs in that area. He returned to Memphis, joined the air force (where he worked on ground crews as a fireman), and it was during his service hitch that, through mutual friends, he met the woman who became his wife. Once out of the service, he took several day jobs, including selling sewing machines for the Singer company, working for A. B. Dick, the furniture outlet, and for S. C. Toof, a printing firm (the Toof family were the original owners of Graceland). Wayne Jackson of the Memphis Horns recalled selling Electrolux vacuum cleaners with Tommy in 1962. "We got seventy-five dollars a week, and at the time, we needed the money," said the trumpet player, who was just beginning his own career as a featured player with the Mar-Keys. "It was canvassing neighborhoods, selling door-to-door."

"He did that 'cause it was better'n choppin' cotton," said the songwriter Wayne Carson, who worked extensively with Tommy. "He told me a story, it sure as hell was funny—He was in this woman's house, demonstrating the cleaner, and he threw the shit on the rug—feathers and cat fur—and then he asked the lady, 'Where do I plug this in?' She said, 'I don't have no electricity.'"

"He was searching for something to do," said Shirley Cogbill. "They try everybody on those jobs, seeing who can measure up to these things, who can do it and who can't. Eventually, he decided that he would just rather work in clubs at night playing music." By then he had switched to acoustic guitar, seemingly never giving the steel a second thought. "He never played steel guitar the whole time I was with him," Shirley said.

Reggie Young's family came to Memphis from Osceola, Arkansas. His father, Reg Sr., had played a little guitar on a radio show there, along with Reggie's uncle, and not long after the family's arrival in Memphis the thirteen-year-old became enamored of the instrument. He devoted himself to music, listening to Chet Atkins and Les Paul, and looking to a local player for further inspiration. "I used to chase B. B. King's bus up and down Beale Street," he told *Guitar Player* magazine in 1986. He began playing lead guitar at the Eagle's Nest with Eddie Bond's band, and they became mainstays at the Clearpool complex, a teen hangout in town where Elvis had played some of his first local shows.

Eventually Eddie Bond's band landed a recording session in Nashville—the first of many for the young guitarist. The session resulted in a hit, "Rockin' Daddy," which in turn led to the big time—a stint on the Louisiana Hayride. Shortly after Reggie's arrival in Shreveport, where the radio show was based, he went from Bond's band to the road band of another Hayride star, Johnny Horton. "This was 1958 and Marshall Grant [Johnny Cash's bass player] had recommended me to Johnny," Reggie said. "We traveled, it was just the three of us, me and Horton and Tillman Franks, his manager. We would drive to someplace like Phoenix, Arizona, and do a show, then have to come back for the Hayride. I was gettin' paid by the job, I think it paid twenty-five dollars." This was in addition to his pay for appearing on the Hayride. "I think it paid thirteen dollars. I was living in a hotel in Shreveport and every dime I

made I spent on my hotel room and expenses." To him it was worth it, though—"I didn't know I was starving"—because of the caliber of musicians with whom he was working, not only Horton himself, but others. "David Houston was my best friend down there, and we'd play some local places around town. The guys with the Newbeats were around there. Jerry Kennedy was around, and Billy Sanford," both of whom would make their names as session musicians in Nashville a few years later. Reggie liked working with Johnny Horton. "He was quite a gentleman, a very nice man." Reggie might have stayed in Shreveport longer, but he received notice that his home draft board in Memphis might soon be calling him up. "I left Shreveport around Christmas, New Year's of 1959." He was back in Memphis when Bill Black put together his own unit. Black remembered Reggie from around Memphis, and Reggie became the featured player in the Bill Black Combo.

Some of them came from the country into the city to try their luck, like Bobby Emmons and Bobby Wood. Bobby Wood grew up on a cotton farm near New Albany, Mississippi. He came from a large family, and he learned responsibility early. "When I was about twelve years old, my daddy would let me drive a wagonload of cotton to the gin," he recalled. "My mother'd say, 'He's too young to be doin' stuff like that,' and my father'd say 'No he's not, let him go.'" Bobby recalled with affection the area where he grew up. "I went to a country school, Ingomar. There were two hundred students there, first to twelfth grade. We all knew each other, our families knew each other, we had all visited each other's houses."

Church was a large part of the family's life, and they all played music and sang gospel—Bobby's father was a song leader, had done a gospel radio show at WELO in Tupelo, and he taught singing schools using the old "shape-note" style of sight reading. When Bobby was a teenager, he and his sisters sang hymns at local churches, and his father took them to Memphis in hopes of getting them a record deal with Sun. "That was the first time I met Elvis," Bobby remembered. "He was sitting at a desk out front. We talked awhile, and he was a real gentleman." Another Sun artist, Jerry Lee Lewis, provided direct inspiration, and from the time of Jerry Lee's first records Bobby adapted his piano playing and singing to that style. His family did not approve. "They said I was going to hell," he remarked, and then, unconsciously echoing Huckleberry Finn, "And I said all right, I'll *go* to hell." Bobby began playing piano with a Future Farmers of America group. They had a half-hour Saturday afternoon radio show, recorded one single for a man Bobby remembered as "the biggest crook in Memphis," and competed in a "battle of the bands" with another FFA group from Corinth, Mississippi, whose keyboard player was Bobby Emmons. Emmons's band placed first in the contest, Wood's group came in second. "Who would have thought it?" laughed Bobby about the rival keyboardists becoming colleagues later.

"If I could pick one person to carry with me on a session and guarantee that the session would yield a hit record, it would be Bobby Emmons, "said American Studios drummer/percussionist Hayward Bishop. Emmons came from a farm near Corinth. His early influences were Joe "Fingers" Carr and Bill Doggett but, other than emulating what his heroes had done on records, Bobby had practically no formal training. "I learned to play 'by ear' as far back as I can remember," he said. "Mother sent me to two different private teachers over the years but I just never did pick it up. Still can't read music." By Bobby's late teens he was good enough to work local clubs, and he was "playing piano in a honky-tonk" when he met Chips Moman, who was passing through town. Later Chips temporarily moved to Corinth, and he and Bobby worked together several weekends at the club where they had first met. Bobby continues the story from there.

I stayed with a cousin in Memphis during the summer of 1959 and, ironically, sat in with Tommy Cogbill at a jazz club, Reggie Young at a little club in Arkansas, and auditioned for Ray Harris at Hi Records who showed an interest in signing me as an artist singing and playing piano. I finished out the time until school started playing solo at a club four nights a week and went back to Corinth to start the eleventh grade.

Chips called and offered me a tour with Gary Stites and the Satellites, plus Charles Hines, up through the Midwest starting January 15, 1960. The tour ended in a car wreck.

Chips broke his leg in the accident, and while he was recuperating he and Emmons shared the rent on a house in Memphis. Together and separately, they played the tough dives near the naval base in Millington, just outside of Memphis, and at "clubs all around the Memphis area." By day, Chips was working at Stax Records, serving as guitarist, talent scout (he led them to William Bell), engineer, producer, arranger, and Jim Stewart's second in command.

By then the Bill Black Combo was just getting under way, having had a hit record with "Smokie, Part Two." "The 'wonka wonka' rhythm was created by Reggie hitting the guitar strings with a pencil," said Mike Leech. "We mention him playing the 'pencil lick' sometimes." "It was an old gimmick from the bebop days where the drummer took a pencil and put it on the bass strings," Reggie Young explained, referring to the Bob Crosby hit "Big Noise from Winnetka," which had featured the drummer banging on everything at hand, up to and including the strings of Bob Haggart's upright bass. "I tuned my guitar down two whole steps. And we cut this crazy li'l tune."

It was a tossup whether the group would be named for Reggie Young or Bill Black, but Bill's name had slightly more weight with the general public because of his work with Elvis. "Reg said when they cut 'Smokie' a question was brought up, did they want to share in the royalties or get paid for the session," said Mike Leech. "I think he said that everyone but Marty Willis [sax player] wanted royalties." "We cut that first record in 1959, it came out in September," remembered Reggie Young. "I didn't even have a car then, Bill would pick me up; he drove an old Studebaker, I believe. If we were out after dark, we had to stop two or three times and he'd kick the fenders to get the headlights to come on." "Smokie, Part Two" was one of the first rock and roll instrumentals, inspiring bands like the Ventures and Johnny and the Hurricanes. But shortly after the recording was released, Reggie was drafted. "It was around my birthday, the twelfth of December—I got sworn in on my birthday."

Success meant that a touring band had to be quickly organized, even if Bill had to do without the group's mainstay. "Reggie said he was on a bus headed for boot camp, and he looked out the window to see a Cadillac passing them, with 'The Bill Black Combo' on the back," related Mike Leech. However, Reggie was there for the group's most important performance.

"I took a thirty-day leave and we did the Dick Clark show. That was a real trip," he said. This was not *American Bandstand*, based out of Philadelphia, but Clark's larger-budget, more prestigious Saturday night show, broadcast live. "The Saturday night show, from New York, was at a place called the Little Theater, where Johnny Carson was doing *Who Do You Trust*," said Reggie. On the program with them that night were Jackie Wilson, Toni Fisher (the lady who sang "The Big Hurt"), and "the Four Preps or one of those vocal groups." The group Bill put together for the event was Reggie Young with Johnny "Ace" Cannon, Jerry Arnold (nephew of Eddy), Jerry Lee Lewis's keyboard-playing cousin Carl McVoy, and the leader on bass. As was the custom on all of Clark's shows, the musicians mimed their hit single, but McVoy played "Jingle Bells" live, in honor of the holiday season, as the closing credits rolled—and got paid extra for it too, Reggie remembered. "That was, like, big-time."

Some changes still had to be made. McVoy was recording solo on Hi and was needed for keyboard work on other sessions at the label; Bill had to find a replacement. "Bill Black called Chips looking for an organ player," Bobby Emmons remembered, "and Chips recommended me. I worked the NCO club at the Memphis airport with him a few times, and he hired me to go on their first tour, April 1, 1960. We were on the road about eighty percent of the next three years, mostly one-nighters playing forty-seven states, Jamaica, Nassau, and Canada. Reggie came to the NCO club one night before

we left on tour. He had finished basic training in the army, and was being shipped off to the other side of the world." Reggie spent almost his entire tour of duty in Ethiopia, working as a specialist in Morse code.

With Emmons replacing Carl McVoy and with "Hank" Hankins added on guitar, the Bill Black Combo hit the road. It was obvious that Ace was the group's drawing card. He was with the Combo "from early 1960 until his own records hit in '62," said Bobby Emmons. "Everywhere from a Wildwood, New Jersey, showbar to one-hundred-percent black Texas blues clubs, he just played Ace Cannon until they were hanging over the rail calling for more. He put a band together after his second single went Top Forty pop, and for about two years both groups stayed on the road most of the time. We should check, Ace may have been the first 'spin-off.'"

After Reggie's hitch in the army, he returned to Memphis. "I'd been in Ethiopia so long, I was lost. When I got out of the army, I had all these record royalties I hadn't spent. I took my money and bought a white '61 Pontiac Bonneville convertible." He rented a house with several other aspiring musicians, all four sharing the rent—they called it the Haunted House. He also rejoined the Combo, becoming a road warrior along with the rest of them. "He had people over the front of the bandstand all the time," Emmons remembered of Reggie's playing. They were doing long tours up and down the East Coast by now.

"Bill moved Hank Hankins over to bass and stopped going out with us," Bobby Emmons continued. "We were staying out longer and longer each time. Finally, six weeks into a scheduled four-week tour, we got word that it had been extended for two more weeks." For Emmons (newly married to his high school sweetheart Dot) and the others, this was the last straw. "We one by one waded through knee-deep snow to the pay phone outside a Scottsbluff, Nebraska, motel to tell Bill no."

In order to stay home more, Emmons recounted, "Me, Reggie, Jerry Arnold, and a bass player named Bobby Stewart signed on to work days at Hi, trying to come up with something, in addition to sessions." "We finally were getting like fifty bucks a week," Reggie remembered. Bobby added, "And fifteen bucks a side"—but only if Ray Harris and Joe Cuoghi, who owned Hi, used the side. In those years Hi had a more varied clientele than is remembered today. "We in various combinations played on albums by Bill Black's Combo, Ace Cannon, Willie Mitchell, Jerry Jaye, Charlie Rich, Narvel Felts, Charlie and Inez Foxx, Chuck Berry, Thumbs Carlisle, Murray Kellum, Gene Simmons, and Lord knows how many I've forgotten," said Emmons. "I know of one session of Willie's I didn't play on, but I think Reggie played on everything! We spent a world of time in the studio for Willie with Ray Harris at the board, putting together original instrumentals, trying different rhythms on old stuff, and cutting tracks on various young singers."

"Reggie was a perfectionist," recalled Larry Dean Stewart, cousin of the Hi staff bassist. "I remember Hi had built a separate room and the walls were concrete and we called it the 'echo chamber.' I would sit for hours and listen to Reggie practice with a 'cat-gut' guitar in the doorway of the chamber and the sound was awesome. At first I didn't realize he was hard at work striving for perfection on some new lick and he would do it over and over, a million times it seemed and once I said 'Reggie, play something else.' He just looked at me and laughed, played a few bars of something else and just when I thought it was another song, he began practicing again. I think he slept with a guitar."

The perfectionism brought dividends in February 1964. When the Beatles toured America for the first time, they specifically requested the Bill Black Combo as their opening act. "The Beatles tour was incredible," stated Reggie Young. Bob Tucker, who had purchased the group name from an ailing Bill Black, organized the musicians for the tour and for a followup tour of England and the continent in a musician's union exchange. (Bill Black died of a brain tumor in 1965; the Combo continued recording for Hi and touring for several years, utilizing many of the aspiring musicians on the Memphis scene.) There was no question

but that Reggie would go. "I figured, well, that's a free trip to Europe, and I was single," he shrugged.

Mike Leech was originally scheduled to make the trip. "When the Beatles tour came up, Bob called and asked me if I wanted to do it. I said yes, then he changed his mind. He was a bass player also, and apparently he had decided to do it himself. Piano was Bubba Vernon." Sammy Creason, later of the Dixie Flyers and Kris Kristofferson's road band, was the drummer, and "I think a singer named Bill English did the tour—not sure," offered Mike. All of them were Reggie Young's compatriots at the Haunted House. "We caught a Greyhound bus and went from Memphis to San Francisco. We rode that thing, it seemed like forever," Reggie chuckled.

The first night at the Cow Palace, he knew he was hearing a phenomenon in the making. He was standing backstage after the Combo's opening set and a short intermission, and all of a sudden "I thought it was the end of the world. I heard this . . . screaming." The cacophony never let up, he remembered, from the time the Beatles took the stage till they left. He was once mistaken for an English dignitary. "Back then you played in dark suits and ties. We had dark suits that said BBC on the lapel." Standing around outside, he learned what a mistake those uniforms were. "They had barricades eight to ten deep. We were standin' around, the crowd thought we were from the BBC and had touched one of them." The crowd tried to rush the barricades. "I'd never witnessed anything like that. Ever. I had no idea in my wildest imagination." He was also amazed at the Beatles' then-new technology; he told *Guitar Player* about the "big old Vox amps; it was the first time I had ever seen amps that big." Standard procedure during the tour was for the Bill Black Combo to open, play two instrumentals, and then remain onstage for an hour or so backing the Righteous Brothers, the tour's second act. Mike Leech related a story Reggie had told him. "He said that at the shows, there would be a huge promo beforehand, that the announcer would say to the one hundred-thousand-plus crowds, 'Are you ready for the Beatles?' And the crowd would go nuts. Then he would say, 'But first, here's the Bill Black Combo.' Wonka wonka wonka . . ."

The Beatles were as impressed with Reggie's musicianship as he was with theirs. "George Harrison sought me out after the first night. We were on a plane going someplace; I was in the back of the plane, in the cheap seats. And George was asking people, 'Which one is the guitar player for Bill Black?' They told him where I was, and he came back to me and said, 'What are you playing through?' I had this little tube Standell amp; it had a fifteen-inch speaker. He LOVED those Standell amps." This led to a discussion of amps and guitars, with Reggie giving tips all through the tour to George about the "string bending" technique for which both guitarists would become known. Reggie had fond memories of the Beatles. "They were super-nice guys, all four of them," he said. "We was in Key West for about three days. We just sat up and jammed all night long. We got to know them really well. George Harrison said that it was just soaking in that there was no place on the planet now where they could go and not be recognized. They had nowhere to hide."

Occasionally things on the tour got rough. "Cincinnati was one of the dates, I guess midway into the tour. Jeane Dixon had predicted that the plane carrying the Beatles and all of us would crash, and that they would all be killed. They called her and she said that no, she didn't say that, but it was a rough landing. We flew out of Seattle on our way to Vancouver and they called us back, there was a bomb threat. We were onstage in Las Vegas and all the electricity went out during our part, and these guys were crawling under that stage, looking for bombs. It was a little hair-raising at times." The tour featured several other acts along the way, and Reggie had a brief romance with one of the other artists, Jackie DeShannon, with whom he would work again years later, and for whose talent he always held the highest regard.

On the British leg of the tour, Reggie said, "Billy J. Kramer was the headliner. Other acts on the bill were the Yardbirds with Eric Clapton, Lulu, the Kinks, and the Ronettes." He recalled vividly his first impression of England. "I remember seeing these signs saying 'Down with Guinness'" (a popular advertisement at the time for ale). "I thought it was a politician they were trying to kick out of office." While the band was there, they all splurged and bought pegged pants and Beatle boots, and wore them onstage at night. On one occasion, Reggie remembered, the band came out to play their two instrumentals and then were supposed to back the Ronettes. The girls raced out, the group struck up the familiar intro to "Be My Baby," and "Sammy just quit!" Nobody could figure out why he had stopped playing. "The girls were wandering around on-stage. He had got his bass drum pedal underneath his pants leg!"

While Reggie Young was touring, the Hi staff band worked nights at a club on South Third called, appropriately enough, the Hi Hat. "In that two-year whirlwind of people and events I can't really sort out, we helped build the Hi Hat club into a packed house seven hours a night, seven nights a week with Ace Cannon," remembered Bobby Emmons. The Hi Hat eventually burned down—"I lost a brand-new acoustic piano, Hammond organ and all the trimmings," Emmons noted—and reopened "at some place on Brooks Road," said Mike Leech, who by now was occasionally filling in for Bobby Stewart on bass. The Brooks Road club band sported a slightly different lineup. "That was Jerry 'Satch' Arnold, Emmons, Reggie, erstwhile horn players Joe Arnold and another guy—friend of Reggie's—can't remember his name," said Mike Leech. "Charles Hines was the vocal. We did some Righteous Brothers songs, Satch and Charles singing blues. Satch had some drumsticks painted with fluorescent paint that would glow in the dark. We did 'Caravan,' which always featured a drum solo, and they would turn down the lights."

The club work had other consequences, Mike remembered. "We played a club in Memphis together where Reggie met Diane. She worked there." At the close of 1964, Reggie Young and Diane were married.

And it was here, in the Memphis clubs, that the musicians began to mingle, sitting in here, landing a recording date there. "We was all young and spry, ten feet tall and bulletproof," laughed Bobby Wood. "They was all just kind of driftin' around, we were all tryin' to find our place," said Stan Kesler.

Tommy Cogbill was finding his place in the jazz clubs. "He played out on Highway 51, near what is now Elvis Presley Boulevard," said Shirley Cogbill. "That is one of the old, old places." "I first worked with Tommy at different clubs where he played guitar, and he could burn one up," said Gene Chrisman. "He played jazz guitar, he wasn't quite as commercial as R&B or pop," remembered Stan Kesler. "The first time I ever heard of Tommy was when he was playing a gig at a little joint in Southeast Memphis," said Mike Leech. "A buddy told me how great a guitar player he was, so we hit it one night. I was disappointed because he was playing bass and switching off to steel. I had no idea what I was hearing. Wish I could do that one again." "The first time I guess I ever saw him, he was playing with Ray Jaffee on a little side street down in a basement, in a club under a hotel," said Reggie Young. "It was just the two of them. I just remember he was playing bass and sometimes, guitar. From the time they started playing, I was lost, I could not tell where one was."

"I had the same experience," added Bobby Emmons, about his meeting Tommy in 1959. "The club he was playing was the Keller Club, which was downstairs over the Rebel Room, on Bellevue. My uncle took me up there to sit in with people. It was Tommy on upright bass and Ray Jaffee on clarinet and Ray Stitham on piano. I just remember these three. And I *never . . . found . . . one . . . chord*," he emphasized slowly, in his deliberate manner. "All the way through the song, I never found a place to touch the keys."

Bobby Wood also had found a following in the clubs. "I met Bobby in '58 or '59," Stan Kesler recalled. "His brother Billy was older. They came to Memphis and got in the music scene." "My dad wanted me to stay on the cotton farm and I said no thank you, I'd seen enough of that," Bobby said ruefully. He was living with his brother while he played piano and did some singing in local clubs; he wanted to be an actor,

but he did not have the money to get to California and try his chance in the movies. With Billy on bass, a friend from the FFA band on lead guitar, and Bobby on piano and vocals, a group established itself at the Starlight Club, taking the club's name for their own. "I remember the Starlighters, going to hear them," Mike Leech reminisced fondly. "I loved that band. They did an old tune, Bobby 'Blue' Bland's I think, 'Cry Cry Cry,' that just blew me away." Soon the Starlighters became one of the most popular bands in town, allowing Bobby to give up his day job pulling auto parts for the chain that later became NAPA. "We had the North Side covered and Willie Mitchell had the South Side," Bobby recalled with delight. One night Jerry Lee Lewis and his road band came to the club to sit in—a defining moment for a young piano player. "I mean, I looked up to him like he was Jesus Christ or something," Bobby remarked.

Gene Chrisman was Jerry Lee's drummer. "I was playing at a place called the Five Gables when I found out that Jerry Lee needed a drummer. He came by the club one day and set in, and I got the job with him. I got to see a lot of the country when we only traveled by car. It was myself, Jerry Lee, and his father-in-law on bass, J. W. Brown. I played with him for about two years." He was with Jerry Lee on the night the band went in to the Starlight Club. "Gene liked what he was hearing so much that he gave his notice to Jerry Lee on the spot," recalled Bobby Wood, a detail Gene confirmed. "I liked the music they were doing, and quit Jerry Lee not long after that and went to work for Bobby. We used to do all those old songs, 'Cry Cry Cry' and 'Turn On Your Love Light' and those people loved it! I think I enjoyed that more than anything, working with Bobby." The two musicians became fast friends almost immediately. "I actually lived with him at his grandmother's house for about a year," Bobby Wood recalled. "We was young, and single, and fancy free."

Not for long, though. Gene Chrisman, like Reggie Young, met his wife at the club where he was now based. "Charlie Chalmers was in the band with us. He played sax. My future wife-to-be and her sister would come out there, and later in 1962 Charlie and I married the two sisters. What a coincidence, but that is the way it happened. We got married in March of 1962, two weeks apart. He got married first." Gene's oldest child, a son named Ronnie, was born that December.

The years in the Memphis clubs and on the road with Jerry Lee had indelibly honed Gene's playing. He had become a blunt, emphatic, no-nonsense drummer with an ingrained rhythmic sense; his sound was never formless or muffled. It didn't always translate, Mike Leech remembered. "When I was at MSU, our tiny (pseudo) music fraternity threw a party at a hotel once, and the band was Gene, Reggie, Stan, and can't remember who else. This was before I had ever really worked with these guys. We all knew each other but barely. Anyhow us music snobs took note that Gene wasn't playing his sock cymbals, like what is a must on uptown gigs like that." Gene did not need to; his crisp rhythms got the dancers out on the floor, and he was a welcome addition to the Starlighters.

Through Bobby Wood's friendship with Stan Kesler, the Starlighters did some recording at his studio, and again later when Stan resumed working for Sam Phillips. "Me and Stan just kind of hit it off the bat," said Bobby Wood. "Stan's a nice guy. Too nice for his own good, sometimes." Stan Kesler was equally complimentary about Bobby. "He was so talented, he picked up on things real quickly," Stan observed. Stan was drawn to the music of the Starlighters because they sounded fresh.

"After the rockabilly days, everybody was tryin' to get away from that, tryin' to do somethin' different," said Stan Kesler. "We did a lot of demos and a lot of custom recording—we did one on Bobby Helms, I believe." Gradually it became apparent that the band's main strength was its piano-playing lead singer. "Billy was a good guitarist, he just wasn't all that serious about it," Bobby Wood said of his older brother. "He just wanted to get out and do other things, and eventually that's what he did. Wound up back in Mississippi, driving a truck." Stan began experimenting with recording the young singer as a solo act.

Mike Leech by now was working out of the Nitelighter club as a member of Marty Willis's band, having dropped out of college in 1963 to do music full-time. Regarding his employer he observed, "In retrospect, he wasn't a great player, but he did have a good band. Before I was hired for that gig, I used to haunt that club quite often to listen to the band."

Several club residencies, sitting in, going all over Memphis to hear one another: a joining of forces was inevitable. There seemed to be no grand design, no one person responsible for putting the combination together. Certainly Stan Kesler, who is usually credited with assembling them, had a lot to do with it—"I used one from here, one from here, two or three over there"—but so did Ray Harris and Willie Mitchell at Hi, and so did Ace Cannon, who would go out on weekends through Alabama and Mississippi with Emmons, Cogbill, and sometimes Reggie Young. Gradually the musicians found themselves drawing closer and closer.

The next step would be a recording.

The musicians do not really remember what was the first recording made with all of them present. Everyone had his own candidate. Gene Chrisman and Bobby Emmons both recalled it as a James and Bobby Purify session. Mike Leech seemed to feel it was the Sandy Posey sessions cut just after the band had begun working as a unit for Chips Moman in 1966. Bobby Wood and Stan Kesler, with some justification, nominate a different work—Bobby's solo album for Joy Records, done at the Phillips studio on Madison and released in late 1964. "Even Chips was there for that one," recalled Kesler. "He played guitar." Chips's most successful composition up to that point, "This Time," also appeared on the album. "It was Gene, Mike, and probably Reggie." Kesler recalled the rest of the lineup. He had used Mike Leech on bass, he said, because "Mike was the only one who could play true notes on the upright bass." "Tommy played second guitar," Bobby Wood added, "and Emmons was there for some of it" (although the organist did not recall).

The album features Wood as a light crooner

in the Bobby Vee mold. The back cover photo shows him wearing a continental cardigan and slacks, cigarette between his fingers and his head cocked in a Dean Martin pose. "That photo was taken on the set of the George Klein TV show, *Talent Party*," he said. The material is a mix of standards and new compositions. "I had songs, and a lot of 'em I wrote myself," said Stan Kesler. His songs on the album seemed aimed at the Eddy Arnold "countrypolitan" audience of the mid-fifties. Bobby, who considered himself a "Charlie Rich type of singer," had mixed feelings about the album's direction. "That stuff like 'Lavender Blue' that you hear on the album wasn't really me," he said. "I didn't know any better, my producer didn't know any better; he let them talk him into it." Stan, the producer, agreed. "That was Joy Music's ideas, some of 'em. I think 'Lavender Blue' was one they suggested. Nothing wrong with that, it's a good old don't-make-too-much-sense song. But it has a nice melody."

But the last cut on side one, "How Could Anybody Be So Cruel," is unlike anything else on the record. The track opens with a booming, bottom-heavy piano, and the musicians settle into a loping groove that they slightly smoothed out for the Sandy Posey sessions a year or two later. The drums battle the strings (arranged by New Yorker Al Hamm) and Bobby's voice, telling the tale of a rejected lover, for prominence on the track, and the mood conveyed is one of *suffering*.

The sound of the Memphis Boys was born. "It was a good track, sure was," Stan Kesler noted laconically.

The album was done following the release of a hit single, Stan Kesler's composition "If I'm a Fool for Loving You" (reportedly Vernon Presley's favorite song). "This was a big pop record in several cities," Bobby Wood noted. "I think in Cleveland it was number one for about eight weeks. We were top-20 pop for about six months." He went on several grueling rounds of one-nighters to support his hit. "In Cleveland I had my clothes tore off me," he recounted. "The teenagers were comin' after me with scissors and stuff. They wanted a lock of my hair, a scrap off my shirt, anything."

He summed up the teen-idol experience in one word: "Frightening."

The tours were exhausting. "We was rippin' up and down the country," said Wood. "I didn't have a band backing me. Most times I'd just use the house band wherever we played." He did one package tour with Murray Kellum, Travis Wammack, and J. Frank Wilson, of the hit "Last Kiss." The song's grisly scenario was nearly repeated. "We were five days into a tour at 500 miles a day, tryin' to make it to Lima, Ohio, after a stop in Wheeling. We left after the show. "Bobby had been driving, but at some point that night he pulled over and let J. Frank's manager take over.

"That's the last I remember," he said. "I woke up in the hospital." J. Frank's manager had fallen asleep at the wheel, and "We plowed into a semi, head-on. We were in a station wagon and had stuff loaded on top, in back, in the trunk, everywhere. Me and J. Frank was in the front seat, asleep. I went through the windshield. I was out of it till about three days later. The whole right side of my face was destroyed. I lost my eye. There was some question about whether I would recover, because my brain was swollen. But seven or eight days later, I went home. The insurance company paid for me and my girlfriend and my father to take a private plane back to Memphis. It was on the national news, everything."

Back in Memphis, "I just laid around and recouped. I had to go and get fitted for a glass eye. They just fish around in a bin till they find one that looks reasonably like yours, and then they shape it and try to fit it. I also went through about three plastic surgeries." The complications from the wreck and the scheduled surgeries caused Bobby to receive a medical discharge from his National Guard unit, where he had been serving for almost a year. "I was in the Army in '63 for a six-months' National Guard training. I was in the medics. When I was finishing basic training they were already sending people off to Vietnam," he noted sadly. "I received a 1-Y honorable discharge." But having to leave the Guard so soon "knocked myself out of VA loans and stuff like that," he continued regretfully. During this time he married his girlfriend Janice, a backup singer from Ohio whom he had met at Echo when he was playing piano on a recording date Stan Kesler produced for her and her sister. "This was around '64, '65," Bobby recalled. "I spent about a year in limbo."

While Bobby Wood recovered from the wreck, the other musicians stayed busy doing club work and moving into session jobs all over town. Bobby Emmons's experience was typical. "I chopped a used Hammond down to a portable and played some great shows in the new monster-style ballroom clubs out in Texas, Arkansas, and Louisiana, and one banquet for the London Records [Hi's parent label] promotion men that got me the deal for *Blues with a Beat and with an Organ*" (his 1965 solo album).

The band was coming together. They were beginning to record. Their sound was falling into place.

All they needed now was a studio.

### CHAPTER 2

# Chips, Goldwax, Sandy, and the Garage-Band Sound

The studio that became almost a literal home to the group was a one-story, flat-roofed, red-brick, boxlike building that was part of a five-store strip mall located on the corner of Danny Thomas Street and Chelsea Avenue in North Memphis. In its previous life it had been a grocery store; it had been owned at that time by a Memphis policeman who lived just back of the building. Also out back was a parking lot. There were no signs on the building to mark its purpose; it was low-profile and everyone liked it that way. Most people, musicians and visitors alike, did not even use the front entrance.

To an observer the place had little to recommend it. It was in a run-down part of the city, in a mixed neighborhood slowly changing to black; it shared a wall with a barbershop (later a print shop) next door, and on the other side of it was the Ranch House restaurant, one of those small places that served "home cookin'" back in the days before fast food was everywhere. The studio was no more prepossessing inside than was the exterior; Reggie Young remembered the sound of rats in the rafters.

"We had echo chambers that were just rooms, burlap over newspaper, bare rafters," recalled Ed Kollis, who worked at American in the late sixties as sound engineer. "And it was a natural room—what a rarity."

Hayward Bishop did some engineering at American at the turn of the decade. "I read in these electronics magazines about how a room is supposed to be symmetrical to get the best sound, and I laugh. That was the most *unsym-metrical* studio and control room!"

"It was actually taller than it seemed," remembered Dan Penn, who saw the studio in its earliest days as a going concern. "It was pretty spread-out, and it was pretty roomy. The acoustics were good." Bobby Wood remembered that the studio walls, from the earliest days, were covered with Celotex insulation as a primitive form of soundproofing.

The recording equipment was basic—"two Ampex mixers for a board, a mono machine, maybe two mono machines, and that was about it," said Dan Penn.

"There was a mixing board, an old radio board, a monaural Ampex machine and an old piano there," added Don Crews, an eventual partner in the studio.

But the place had one important resource that no other studio in Memphis could match: the talents of Lincoln Wayne Moman.

Chips Moman (the nickname deriving from his longtime fascination with gambling, particularly poker) had already accomplished a lot by the time he set up his studio. He came from LaGrange, Georgia, in an area of the state that produced many important country music figures (Doug Stone, Alan Jackson, Trisha Yearwood, Travis Tritt, the songwriter Pat Alger, and the humorist Lewis Grizzard). "Me and my mama and daddy were just dirt farmers / Growing from the land the things we'd eat," he wrote with simple dignity in his 1978 autobiographical song, "Dusty Roads." He had sought a life in music against his father's wishes but with the total support of his mother. At fourteen he dropped out of school and went to stay with an uncle and aunt in Memphis (this uncle reportedly taught him the rudiments of shooting pool). He worked odd jobs, mainly as a house painter, and played guitar in clubs; went on the road with the Burnette brothers (later Dorsey's son Billy would work for him); and got as far as California, where he was welcomed into the crowd of younger session players working mainly out of Gold Star Studios, Phil Spector's

recording home. But he was first and foremost a Southerner, and he returned to Memphis, where he met Jim Stewart and Estelle Axton.

"I was a guitarist. Jim called me to play on a session out at Brunswick," said Chips, remembering Jim's initial operation just outside of town. He stayed on after that, helping Jim and Estelle put Stax Records together. It was here that he began his career as a producer, overseeing the recording of Stax's three earliest hits, all of which indicated his future artistic direction—"Last Night" by the Mar-Keys, with its garage-band rhythm; the passionate, overwhelmingly emotional melancholy of Carla Thomas's "Gee Whiz"; and the homespun simplicity and pride of William Bell's "You Don't Miss Your Water." In 1961 he had a further triumph: a song he had left behind in California, "This Time," became a hit for the teen idol Troy Shondell. The song bears examining, as Chips's first important cut as a writer. It is a lovelorn ballad about a breakup, with the chorus reflecting the despondency which would become a Moman trademark: "My heart is broken now / It doesn't matter much anyhow / Since you have gone away / I only live from day to day."

What a difference a year makes. By 1962 Chips was unemployed, ousted from Stax by Jim and Estelle over how much of Stax's increasing profits he should have. "I had twenty-five percent—I thought," Chips said sadly. "They owed me my share of a million dollars they'd made that year—'61, '62."

Wayne Jackson was sitting in the hallway at Stax the day the final blowup happened between Chips and Jim Stewart, and he overheard the whole thing. "It was over money, and you can quote me," he said firmly. "At some point, royalties came down from Atlantic [Stax's distributor]. Chips didn't feel he was getting paid his share of the royalties. They exchanged words, and Jim said, 'If I fucked you, prove it.' Chips stormed out of there and into his TR-6 and never came back." Did Jim Stewart mind? "Hell, no," shrugged Jackson. "He just got rid of another hillbilly."

Others offered different reasons for the break. Jimmy Johnson, who worked extensively with Chips in Muscle Shoals and who was also familiar with all of the Stax musicians, said that there was a personality conflict between Chips and Steve Cropper, upon whom Jim Stewart was coming increasingly to rely. But Chips had helped make Stax a player among the independent Southern studios, had been in the studio all day while Jim and Estelle held down their nine-to-five jobs (he was a bank clerk, she a former teacher who now also worked in banking), and had helped develop all of Stax's homegrown talent thus far from Carla Thomas to Booker T. He had invested so much time, and so much of himself, in the company, and just when it was beginning to do well, he was out. And it hurt.

For the next few years, Chips was like a man caught in a revolving door. Wayne Jackson recalled that Chips did some work at the Phillips studio immediately following the break with Stax. Eventually Chips wound up in Nashville, playing guitar on demo sessions for aspiring writers such as Roger Miller and Dottie West and making a few friends, but he was despondent over how Stax had treated him and he was drinking too much to kill the pain. And then a Memphis music lawyer named Seymour Rosenberg approached him.

It apparently never occurred to Chips that he had a right to sue, but Rosenberg persuaded him. "I found out later he was working for Jim Stewart," Chips told Peter Guralnick. And when Rosenberg pressured him to settle for three thousand dollars, Chips accepted (three thousand dollars, a pittance compared to what he might have gotten, sounded like a fortune to him). Not content with that, Rosenberg, who had always wanted to be in the music business, suggested they open up a recording studio together. Chips had a knack for finding great old buildings—Peter Guralnick noted in *Sweet Soul Music* that Chips discovered Stax's famous movie theater—and the location for his new place was found the same way, while he was "out drivin' around." The spot seemed to have been chosen out of proximity to Rosenberg's law office, a one-man operation located next

door to his father's auto-parts store, one block further down on Chelsea.

But Chips, still caught in that revolving door, could not hang on to what he had. "I was young and learned all my lessons the hard way," he said. Before much time had passed the business was entirely in the hands of Rosenberg, who allowed Chips to have continued access to the building as a sound engineer. Records had been cut there since the studio opened in late 1962; Isaac Hayes, not yet at Stax, had done a demo there with Tommy Cogbill on bass, and a local rock band named Tommy Burk and the Counts had cut a single (the future Box Tops drummer Tom Boggs was part of that group). But it was not doing much as a studio, and Chips sold his half to Seymour, who quickly realized that the business was becoming a losing proposition.

He approached Wayne McGinness, an aspiring singer, and Wayne mentioned the idea of owning a studio to his uncle, Don Crews. "Wayne and I had kind of a record company when Seymour and Chips started American," Don said, remembering that there was not much activity at this point. "They was kind of shade-treein', most people in the Memphis music business had day jobs at that time in the early '60s." His own company, Santo, was a typical Memphis small-scale operation; he remembered that it featured "basically some local acts, and I bought some Thomas Wayne tapes from Slim Wallace over at Fernwood. We had the follow-up to 'Tragedy.' We put out one thing on Ace Cannon, 'Sugar Blues.' Seems as though we signed a lease deal with Vee-Jay Records out of Chicago, we put out a couple of things on Harold Dorman." Dorman wrote and had the hit with "Mountain of Love," which became something of a standard, and Thomas Wayne (Perkins, the equally ill-fated brother of Johnny Cash's guitarist Luther) was a crooner with a tuneful voice. But nothing happened with any of the Dorman and Perkins releases, and by 1964 the Santo label fizzled out.

Don Crews's day job was farming—"beans and cotton"—across the river from Memphis, in the flat country of Arkansas. He had always farmed; he always would. "I knew Reggie Young from Osceola," Crews said laconically. "Reggie's uncle was the deputy sheriff. I went to school with Narvel Felts there."

"He was an ol' country Arkansas guy, matter-of-fact guy," said Bobby Wood admiringly. "Don was a straight-shootin' guy."

"Don Crews was a silent, in-the-shadows figure," observed Ed Kollis. "But he's got some rock-and-roll in him, or he'd never have done what he did. You should see where he lives on the farm in Arkansas—the damn tractor's worth more than the house."

"Wayne and I kind of bought it [the studio] as a partnership," Don said. As best he could remember, he and his nephew together paid a thousand dollars to take the whole thing off Seymour's hands. "I bought Wayne's interest out about a year or so later, back in '63. Chips called me late in December '64 and asked what I was gonna do with the old studio and if we could work in partnership." Don agreed, and the studio—christened American from its inception because "I wanted to be the first in the phone book," said Chips—was on its way. "The thing wouldn't have happened without Don Crews," Ed Kollis stated succinctly.

The early fortunes of American were closely tied to those of a new record company in Memphis. Quinton Claunch, a former Sun musician, and Rudolph Russell ("Doc" because of his pharmacy) had launched Goldwax in late 1963. "I saw the success of Jim Stewart," Quinton remembered, and his ambition was to do something similar, with "anything that was good, mostly soul and rock and roll. You can't hardly cut country in Memphis, the musicians don't understand it, neither do the engineers." Quinton had played country fiddle all his life and loved the Nashville Sound, but he bowed to the inevitable; in the home of soul, you cut soul records. The arrangement called for Doc to be the financial backer—he put "six hundred dollars on the front end"—while Quinton provided the musical expertise. "He didn't know a

guitar from a bull fiddle," Claunch said of his partner. Their first discovery, O. V. Wright, was prevented by previous contractual obligations from working with them further, but they had found a black singing group, the Ovations.

The choice of where to take the group to record was easy. Quinton had American and Chips in mind, being familiar with his work at Stax. "Chips had a good reputation, and a good ear for a song. I remember now how I met him. He walked into Pop Tunes [Hi owner Joe Cuoghi's record store] with a guy he was working with. He said, 'Man, if you ever need to work with me, call.' It was an honor to have met him that night." Quinton refuted the story, told by Chips in *Sweet Soul Music*, that a man named Leroy Daniel had told him Quinton and Doc wanted to work with him because they knew they could give him the old "ten bucks and a bottle of whiskey" treatment. "Now, Leroy Daniel may have said that to him," mused Quinton. "It sounds like something he would say. But it wasn't true. I respected Chips. The man, shoot, what you talkin' about?"

They cut the Ovations singing "It's Wonderful to Be in Love" at American, with Chips engineering, and several of his future group (Gene Chrisman on drums, Bobby Wood on organ, Tommy Cogbill on bass). "They wanted me to engineer and then do whatever else," Chips said of his role. Reggie Young was not there. "There was an old black guy on some of the early records, Clarence Nelson," remembered Wood. "They wanted Reggie to play that Nelson style." The piano player recalled that Clarence's bluesy playing had been a considerable influence on Chips's guitar sound. Claunch also recalled Nelson's presence there.

Production was very low-key. "I'm kinda like Chet Atkins—if you leave 'em alone, they'll cut you a hit," said the aspiring producer. "Quinton was a musical person," recalled Bobby Wood. "I was never sure of Quinton's ear for music," said Mike Leech, who would become familiar with the Goldwax style later on. "He didn't seem to know what he wanted, but was happy when he got it." Quinton categorically denied Jim Dickinson's contention in Peter Guralnick's *Sweet Soul Music* that if he did not like what someone was playing, he would walk up to them and chink the change in his pockets. "I might have jiggled the change, but not for that reason. That remark was embarrassing, and I didn't appreciate it."

"Doc usually stayed in the control room while Quinton would mingle around the studio," Mike Leech recalled. "Most arranging was done on the floor, and they depended on us to come up with things, and usually liked our ideas."

Quinton was impressed enough by what he saw out of Chips and the musicians to know he would have to work with them again. They liked him too. "They was good guys, both of 'em," Gene Chrisman said warmly of Quinton and Doc. "Doc and Mr. Claunch were always friendly and enjoyable for me to be around," said the writer and keyboard player Spooner Oldham, who became part of the group several years later. "He was always appreciative of what we'd done," Bobby Wood remembered of Quinton. "Doc reminded me a little of Fred on the old *I Love Lucy* show," observed Mike Leech. "He had very thick glasses, seemed nervous, an always-moving sort of character. He was tall, not particularly skinny. He had a nervous grin almost all the time." Gene Chrisman remembered Quinton's stammer whenever he got hung up on a word, and their affectionate nickname for the bibulous Doc: "Rudolph the Red-Nosed Russell." "I think Doc Russell was his calming partner," Mike Leech observed further of Quinton. "I remember Doc as a short dumpy jolly old man with a red nose, sort of like Santa Claus. Yeah, everybody liked Doc."

One of the distribution deals made by Goldwax would have an impact on the group's future. "It's Wonderful" was leased by Tollie Records, a subsidiary of Chicago's Vee-Jay. "Man, Vee-Jay was one of the premier labels of the day, super-big," Quinton remarked in awe. When Vee-Jay went broke nearly a year later, in 1965, Goldwax distribution was handled by the New York label Bell. "Bell sought us out," Quinton remembered. "Our first deal was for four years with the option for four more." It

was the first that Bell Records president Larry Uttal had heard of the new sounds coming out of Memphis, and it would not be the last.

With Goldwax signing and bringing in new artists, a certain amount of work was guaranteed, but sporadic. The musicians still needed more sessions to tide them over.

For the time being, there was Hi.

By early 1965 Bobby Emmons and Reggie Young were firmly entrenched at Hi, and Tommy Cogbill increasingly joined them. As recordings made nominally under the Bill Black banner from that time reveal, Reggie had become a forceful lead guitarist with a commanding, twangy blues style. "He terrorized that thing," Bobby Emmons said affectionately of Reggie's guitar. "People talk about the difference between live and studio players, they should have seen Mr. Young with his big 330 Gibson and those Standell amps. They were on the same frequency and he'd do twelve solos in a row and you'd say, 'No way he's gonna get out of this.'"

Reggie remembered feeling slightly intimidated at first by the newcomer on the Hi scene. Tommy Cogbill was becoming a formidable jazz guitarist, setting standards a musician as talented as Reggie had to recognize. "He knew all those standards, 'Stardust,' every standard song there was in the key that it was written and that's what they did back then, you didn't play 'Stardust' in E, you played it in the key that it was written," said Reggie. "His sense of groove was incredible. If it was a little too slow or a little too fast, Tommy would be the first to spot it." Reggie got over his sense of intimidation when it dawned on him that "I'm not a jazz player, so when I got that out of my head, I just do what I do." From then on there was no sense of rivalry between the guitarists ever, with each being quick to commend the other's work.

There was much to commend. On the weekend trips into the Mississippi clubs with Ace Cannon, no one who heard Tommy play ever forgot it. Fred Hester, an aspiring musician in Tupelo, heard him when Ace Cannon brought him down for a gig and hired Fred's high-school group to back the two of them.

"Tommy was playing a Gibson hollow-body jazz guitar at the time, Byrdland, L5 or something like that," Fred remembered, "and I could not believe the way he could drive that rhythm section on those honky-tonk blues shuffles. Then, after the gig, we'd lock all the doors of the club and get down to some serious playing, jazz standards like 'All the Things You Are' and 'Green Dolphin Street.' My jaw would drop once again as Tommy would close his eyes, turn his head to the side and play some of the most incredible jazz guitar I've ever heard in my life . . . I've played with many great musicians, like Ira Sullivan, Joe Dorio, George Coleman, as well as great blues-rock players like Duane Allman and Charlie Freeman, but Tommy Cogbill still stands out in my mind as one of the best all-around musicians I've ever heard. When he played rock or blues, it was the real deal; when he played jazz you'd swear you were on the bandstand with Tal Farlow or Howard Roberts, although Tommy had his own individualistic approach . . . Tommy was one of a kind." Put simply, Tommy's guitar playing slashed; as a rhythm player, he was one of the first to utilize power chords; as a lead guitarist, he was interesting, intricate, subtle. This mix of understatement and fire would be the key to all his future work, and those who were there at the time it emerged counted themselves lucky to have borne witness.

Bobby Emmons said it best. "I held the highest respect for Tommy Cogbill as a musician and as a person, and loved him like a brother. Tommy had a wonderful feel for life that carried over strongly into his music. To me he knew the right amount of every ingredient available a situation could stand to get the job done right and still push the envelope. The balance of seriousness to fun, funky to slick, busy to solid, was easy for Tommy. He was a dear friend and an inspiration."

This, of course, was praise from an equal, for Bobby Emmons was revealing considerable talent not only as a musician but as a songwriter. Early compositions, among them "86 More Miles" and "Mattie Ree," were cut by Hi artists Narvel Felts and Jumpin' Gene Simmons, respectively, and though Emmons did not remember the circumstances that caused these songs to be written, they revealed a thoughtfulness rare for the Top Forty of the time. "86 More Miles" is a considerably more realistic treatment of a man thumbing a ride, "cold and tired and feeling low," than, say, Marvin Gaye's hitch hiking song at Motown, and "Mattie Ree" is about a stalker, who receives this pertinent message: "If you need a helping hand, look on the end of your arm." His keyboard playing was rewarded with Hi's offer to do a solo record, and work began on *Blues with a Beat and with an Organ* in early 1965.

Jerry Arnold was along on drums, as he still was for nearly every Hi recording at that point. Reggie Young played guitar. Ray Harris engineered, supervised by Hi label head Joe Cuoghi. All agreed that Emmons could best be heard in an understated format, with the fewer musicians the better, so a trio backing seemed logical. They had the drums and the lead guitar. Who would play the bass? Bobby Stewart was still on staff at Hi, but "Emmons wanted a little funkier player for his debut album, so he begged the producer to hire me," said Mike Leech. "'Blues with a Beat' I think was my very first experience as a session player. Emmons fought the establishment to get me on that album. I'll never forget it."

The material was also easily chosen—a mix of standards ("Cotton Fields" and "Corrina" were already staples of the Hi sound) and hits such as "What'd I Say" and "I Got a Woman" ("E has always been a Ray Charles fan, so we did some of his things," remembered Mike Leech) and three Emmons originals, "Sittin' Home," "Blue Organ," and "Cherry Blue" (the titles made up, Bobby recalled, by Joe Cuoghi).

The opening track, one of Bobby's preferred Ray Charles numbers, "What'd I Say," is a fine introduction to his style. He is sharp, compelling, authoritative; his fills and runs (approximating the Raelets' call-and-response lines) echo the normal phrasing of a lead guitar, and Mike Leech deftly follows.

Mike introduces himself to the listeners on the second track, "Corrina Corrina." His playing is thunderous, rhythmic, straightforward, with phrasing similar to Cogbill's. Reggie

Young is heard in the middle of the song, playing a jangling, Chuck Berry–influenced solo. Emmons is joyful but cautious here, happy to give the song over to his friends—a restraint for which he would soon become noted.

His melodic gifts are emphasized on the third song, "Sittin' Home," the first and best of his three tunes on the album. The organ lead adds to the mournful bluesiness of the melody, and Reggie's sympathetic chord changes provide solid support. After two uptempo songs, a listener is likely to be pleased at the new mood, and amazed at the musicians' versatility. It's surprising this was never released as a single.

The last song on Side One, "Peg o' My Heart," is a landmark. The song has been done many ways since its initial appearance in 1913; never had it been given this sort of treatment. The loping groove that had been fighting to climb out of Bobby Wood's album is finally released here; Mike Leech and Reggie Young speeded up the rhythm until it sounded like a romping, stomping, raucous garage band. The group had now found, and would securely latch onto, an identifying trademark; the raucous sound would remain theirs for the next several years.

Side two offered up more of the same, with two Emmons compositions, as well as a bluesy "Sentimental Journey," and the now-patented stomp of "C. C. Rider." The album has a very spontaneous feel, which is surprising given the way it was recorded. "Seems back then, at least when working for Ray Harris, we would do take after take before he was satisfied. Sometimes thirty or forty if I recall," noted Mike Leech. For a session novice, this amounted to a lot of pressure. "I also remember trying very hard to please, because of my pursuit of becoming a professional session player. I was on edge because I wanted Bobby Stewart's job. Well, not his job exactly, but I wanted to work with the guys on a regular basis." During one point in the recording, he noticed that Ray Harris was talking to Willie Mitchell in the control room, and that the two of them were looking at him. "Ray hit the talkback and said something like, 'Bear down on that bass, boy.' I did, and noticed he and Willie grinning. Wasn't long after, I was booked on some sessions for Willie. I became

staff bassist at Hi and worked on almost everything that came through there."

Hi was located in an old movie theater, the Royal, and it had acoustics all its own. "The sound at Hi left much to be desired from my standpoint," said Mike Leech. "Everything had a dry, bright sound to me—very little reverb, if any. Any distortion was unacceptable. I think that's noticeable on *Blues with a Beat.*"

Not that it mattered. Mike was now a session man. Full time.

The others were not exactly idle. Gene Chrisman had been breaking into studio work with Stan Kesler at Phillips and Roland Janes at Sonic since the dissolution of the Starlighters, and Bobby Wood, recovering from his auto accident, was doing a lot of soul searching. "I'd gotten real tired of the road, and I said, 'Why am I doing this, beatin' my brains out for peanuts?' I just had a decision to make and I decided to hang the star bit up." Once he had sufficiently recovered, he went back to playing piano in the clubs, working strictly locally, accompanied by one of the most respected steel guitarists in Memphis. "John Hughey and I worked the naval base out at Millington—that was when a different kind of country music was comin' on strong," Bobby recalled. He grew interested, noting the way the new-style country songs were being put together.

His and Gene's mentor had launched a project of his own. Stan Kesler had discovered an aspiring blues-rock singer with the imposingly Latin name of Domingo Samudio. "He came from Dallas, he's strictly Mexican—Mexican Gypsy," said Stan. "He talks good, and he's just a good entertainer." Stan had first seen Sam (as everyone called him) on George Klein's Saturday afternoon TV show *Talent Party*, where Sam performed the R&B classic "Haunted House." Sam had recorded it, and the master was scheduled to be picked up by Hi, but "Joe Cuoghi wanted to cut out the guitar solo and shorten the song; Sam wouldn't agree to it. He's a weird dude. Sam is a character." "It was a *seven-minute* guitar solo," noted Bobby Emmons with dry precision. Cuoghi cut a version with someone already signed to the label, Gene

Simmons, with Emmons and Reggie Young backing him; it went Top Ten. (Sam's version eventually appeared on an MGM anthology album.)

Shortly after he had lost "Haunted House," Sam came into the Sun studio. "We had a lathe-cutting machine," said Kesler, "and Sam wanted an acetate dub of a tape. Right after I'd seen him on the show." Stan told Sam that he was interested in recording with him, and soon afterward Sam showed up with his road band, the Pharaohs. Their first release was a blues classic that had been circulating among blacks for years, most recently in obscene variations; it had been Stan's idea to do Willie Dixon's "The Signifying Monkey." The record went nowhere, but Stan and Sam decided that recording would be worth another try, so Sam came in to the studio again.

"We come in the studio, we didn't have nothin' to record," Stan remembered. "I asked them to just play for me, stuff they'd been doing in the clubs. They started playing this song." Stan asked Sam to come up with something that had the same sound and feel as what he had just heard and "He came up with 'Wooly Bully' in a matter of thirty minutes. We did it in two cuts."

"Uno, dos! One, two, tres, quatro!" Sam shouts at the beginning of the record, and one of the ultimate party songs went straight to Number One. "That record was so in left field," said Stan Kesler. "Stan told me when I first heard it, 'If this ain't a hit I'm hangin' it up,'" Mike Leech added.

"We released it on our own label," Stan continued, "but we had a distributor that really believed in it. Howard Allison kept talkin' to these guys." Every label head approached turned it down. Finally, MGM's Jim Vienneau decided to give it a chance. "The rest is history," said Stan.

The success of "Wooly Bully" was a mixed blessing. It typed Sam, and Stan Kesler to a lesser degree, although Stan maintained that he could have become a high-profile producer had he so chosen. "I turned down a lot of offers. I had a chance to go to New York. I had four artists working on MGM at that time. We

produced the records and gave them to the label." The combination of Stan Kesler and Sam the Sham (as the label billed him) lasted several more years, with Stan occasionally using the musicians he already knew, especially Tommy Cogbill, instead of the road band This gave Sam's records the trademark garage-band effect. The material was usually good; notable for their quality are numbers such as "I'm in with the Out Crowd" (a takeoff on the Dobie Gray hit of the time). A song on the album *On Tour* was credited to Tommy Cogbill (though Reggie Young said "I don't ever remember him having a desire" to write songs), and the Texas writer Bob McDill placed some of his first songs with Stan, including a telling number about high living versus a virtuous life, "Black Sheep–White Sheep." "I remember Tommy working very hard on 'Black Sheep,'" said Stan, referring to the song's guitar line.

"I played organ on 'Black Sheep,'" recalled Bobby Wood, who was also recording again for Stan as a solo artist on MGM, though his records never became hits due in part to his refusal to tour. "Sam was a nice guy. I enjoyed working with him." He remembered an occasion just after a session when he was going on an errand and Sam offered him a ride downtown in the vehicle he used for his gigs—an old hearse with "Sam the Sham" painted on the side. "This was shortly after the wreck, and I still had a lot of bruises and was wearing an eyepatch and walking around on crutches, and Sam was wearing his turban. People were coming out of buildings to stare at us as we rode by, like we were some kind of carnival or freak show or something."

As time went by, Kesler noticed that Sam became increasingly tired of the stereotype. "To start with, Sam was all right, but he wasn't happy doin' the novelty stuff. I told him, 'I'll keep you on the charts every year,' but he wanted to be a soul singer or a Frank Sinatra. Sam was more of a character; he had a style that was quite different. It was hard to get him to do the things that he could do. And there's no way of making somebody do something, music isn't made that way, it comes from the heart and soul." In Bobby Wood's recollection, Sam became increasingly eccentric. "He was into some kind of weird religion, and he carried around this sack of chicken bones. The bones would tell him what to do." Bobby vividly recalled the day it all blew up. Stan had booked a session and the players, including Bobby, had been sitting around the studio waiting for Sam to arrive. He got there late, Bobby remembered, and "he threw these chicken bones on the desk and said 'The bones say I can't record today, it isn't right.' Man, Stan was as mad as I've ever seen him. He was hot"—a telling comment about the usually mild-mannered Kesler. Sam would go on to times good and bad; an album with the Kesler-created Dixie Flyers, a movie soundtrack with Ry Cooder that brought almost unanimous critical praise, and lows low enough that Sam wound up as an itinerant street-corner preacher in Memphis.

Chips Moman cut a party record too, with a local rock group, the Gentrys. "They were just high-school fellas," Don Crews remembered. "They were having what they called talent shows around town and they had already won a talent show. Chips was aware of the group, more so than I was." George Klein, who had emceed many of the talent shows, told Chips about them; in Robert Gordon's book *It Came from Memphis*, the group elaborated about meeting Chips for the first time after a show. To them he probably looked like anything but a studio owner—tall and round-faced with a laconic Georgia drawl—but several weeks later, after their invitation to appear on *Talent Party*, they decided to give him and his studio a try.

Two singles were released on Chips's Youngstown label (the first of many attempts at a label of his own, because a custom label was "a good way to start happenin'"). The A-side of the first single, "Sometimes I Cry," had originally been recorded by the Everly Brothers. The title sums up the song; it is about sorrow, emotional pain, and despondency, subjects to which Chips seemed increasingly drawn. Though none of his future group was there for the session, the organ lead and understated guitar were a further refinement of the sound that Emmons and friends were creating over at Hi.

"It was a good local record, about six thousand copies were sold locally," Don Crews noted, which would have made it a fairly substantial regional hit. A follow-up was needed. They had the A-side, a song whose potential Chips believed in strongly, "Make Up Your Mind," which sounded vaguely like the Beatles' "Please Please Me" slowed down and gone country. "We tried two or three times to get a B-side because we needed the release," said Don.

He and Chips remembered a song, "basically a ballad," that Chips had cut with the Avantis (one of several groups in Memphis, including Chips's own Triumphs, that were named for cars) and leased to Chess. "We made two or three takes, trying to get something," Don recalled. "Chips and I were just sitting at the old control board." Nothing was working, and the bass player, Pat Neal ("He was some kin to Stan Kesler," offers Don Crews), got tired and went home early. "We just EQ'd the piano until it was bass-y-sounding," remembered Chips, who was determined to get something down even without a crucial instrument. "We left it up to the fellows to come up with something," remembered Don, and somewhere along the way the band speeded up the song's tempo. "Chips said, 'Let's put it down and see what happens,'" Don continued. "We made one run to get a level, about half the tune, and then we recorded it. It came out at about a minute and thirty seconds. I said, 'That's just too short,' and he said, 'I'm not gonna cut another damn lick.' So, we just faded it out and spliced the first verse on again. We just faded it out plumb to the last drumbeat." "I had cut it without using the monitor so I cut it off too soon," Chips explained.

The song, "Keep On Dancin'," was as fresh and infectious a debut record as "I Want to Hold Your Hand." Even more than "Wooly Bully," it became a party classic. The lyrics exhort everyone within earshot to have a good time; the music is garage-band stomp with a touch of class. Above all, it's *fun*, a quality that was only in part at a premium in 1965. The Beatles, and by extension the young people for whom they sang, seemed to have taken over the world; all was youth and laughter, bright clothes and optimism. This trend was lost on Nashville, which had settled into a fog of gloomy ballads following the deaths of Jim Reeves and Patsy Cline, as if the town were still in mourning. And for all the joy and energy of the Beatles, the pop charts were full of bands, both British and American, who were mainly second-string, wimpy-sounding imitators. "Keep On Dancin'" was an open window, admitting light and air and space to a pitch-black room.

Don Crews knew they were on to something; he could not wait to get the record pressed. "We were doing the whole thing, there was a pressing plant in Memphis that belonged to Buster Williams," he said. "An old Quonset hut was Buster's first plant. It wasn't far from American, over on Chelsea." The record, on Chips's label, was pressed there and quickly taken to the Memphis radio stations. "A couple of jocks uptown done literally wore the A-side out," Don said, "and then Paul White and Jack Grady turned it over and 'Keep On Dancin'' turned out to be the side." Jack Grady had written "Make Up Your Mind," and Chips said that this was why the record had been flipped over, to avoid giving the appearance of promoting a record in which Jack had an interest. "The radio station jumped on him because he had written it and, you know, you're not supposed to do that."

Conflict of interest for a local announcer was one thing; getting the record out to a national audience was another. Don Crews found a way. "I knew a jock in Nashville, at one of the pop stations, Noel Ball. Noel Ball was *the* number-one jock in Nashville. We sent it to Noel and he put it on the air. He called me back and said, 'We're getting all kinds of action on this thing. We need to lease it to somebody.' I said, 'Y'know anybody to lease it to?' He had leased previously a pop tune to MGM Records." The Gentrys were signed to the label, and MGM label head Jim Vienneau became Chips's patron and benefactor as he was Stan Kesler's, especially after the record's success. "It was Number Four in the nation," Don stated proudly.

For the followup single, they repaid Noel Ball by letting him pitch them a song written by an act out of New Mexico that he sponsored. "Brown Paper Sack" isn't much of a song,

although it probably expressed Chips's feelings about Stax very well; "You treated me so bad I might as well have been a brown paper sack." The A-side, "Spread It On Thick," Don Crews called "a new Tree tune," written by company staffers John Hurley and Ronnie Wilkins. Its bouncy organ-driven lead is so close to the sound of the Sir Douglas Quintet that at first hearing some listeners must have thought it was Sahm and company. The DJs could not decide which of the songs had the most potential, so they played both, diluting the success of the single. "That's where we made our mistake," said Crews. "We put the wrong side out. 'Spread It On Thick' was too slick. 'Brown Paper Sack' should have been the one." "Brown Paper Sack" appeared on the Gentrys' first album; "Spread It On Thick" did not.

The record is for all practical purposes Chips Moman's debut album, his first one made entirely without Jim Stewart looking over his shoulder. In addition to "Brown Paper Sack," "Make Up Your Mind," and "Sometimes I Cry," Chips chose songs old and new to present himself to the world. None of them were selections he had written. "Everybody to Their Own Kick," a new song by Stan Kesler's buddy Stacy Davidson, is a Moman manifesto: "I just want to be left alone / And not to conform / Or reform / But to be left alone." Another Everly Brothers standard, "So Sad to Watch Good Love Go Bad," is immersed in melancholy, and the old Johnny Otis hit "Hand Jive" is prophetic in its declaration, "I know a cat named Way-Out Willie." And two songs are almost joyfully defiant; the Motown classic "Do You Love Me" and a tune by local writer Donna Terry (later Weiss): "Don't Send Me No Flowers" ("'cause I ain't dead yet"). Clearly, Chips was sending a message; the revolving-door ride was over. Jim Stewart had not defeated him. But not without lasting effects. "That put a thing in me that made me never really trust anybody ever again," Chips said, looking back at the Stax experience. "I got the impression," said Hayward Bishop, who worked for Chips later, "that almost everything he did was motivated by a desire to show them at Stax."

Chips had had a hit with a party record; so

had Stan Kesler. At Hi, they threw themselves a party for the recording of *Ace Cannon Live*, done "in a studio that I am 99.999 percent positive is not Hi Records, the Royal, in a setup I am 100 percent sure is not for master recording," remembered Bobby Emmons as he looked at the album cover. "That was fun," Mike Leech recalled. "They set up tables in the studio and invited a small crowd in for the effect." Mike played bass, Tommy Cogbill and Reggie Young were on guitars. Emmons believed he was not there for the recording, but Mike Leech placed him at the scene, and though the piano player visible on one of the cover photos has his back turned he distinctly resembles Bobby. Tommy Cogbill is also pictured in the album cover's two photos, playing his blue Hagstrom electric guitar. In one photograph he is the model of dignity, serious and quiet. In the other, he's open-mouthed, wide-eyed, clearly enjoying himself. "That laughing open-mouthed look is what I remember," said Mike Leech. Perhaps the camera had caught one of his trademark mannerisms: "'*Whooo!*' he'd holler to the top of his lungs," chuckled Bobby Wood. The whoop was reserved especially for when things were going well; apparently Tommy was happy at the "concert."

"A lot of the songs were stuff we were doing with Ace in the clubs," Emmons remarked about the album's selections. "Girl from Ipanema" and "Stranger on the Shore" seem particularly suited to a club setting, even if faster numbers like "You Can't Sit Down" would have challenged the dancers. There are ample solos from Reggie Young; Tommy Cogbill and Reggie both are heard on "Honky Tonk," and Ace seemed to be at a clear advantage playing to an audience's response. The highlight of the concert is Ace blowing "Yakety Sax" while behind him the two guitarists gleefully play in a repetitive pattern vaguely reminiscent of the Stringalongs' "Wheels." For those not familiar with his playing, the album is a good way to begin. "Ace Cannon is a whole damn book by itself," observed Bobby Emmons.

By this time the musicians were making records on a regular basis. Chips Moman had produced one successful hit single. The players were proving themselves almost every day; Chips had to find another artist and prove that he was not, as so many were, just a one-hit producer.

He would find his second artist, literally, at his door.

Sandy Posey was the secretary at American Studios, "basically answering the phone," remembered Don Crews. "I did that to be able to be around the music business," she said, echoing the words of many aspiring singers who worked as secretaries, from Lynn Anderson to Lee Ann Womack. She'd already been doing some backup singing around Memphis with Herschel Wigginton's group (later to become the Nashville Edition), but "Every session singer and musician will tell you, it's either feast or famine, and it was famine right then!"

She had come from Jasper, Alabama, the daughter of a mechanic. "Most of my relatives were singers and musicians. My daddy's side of the family and my mother's side both played music. My older sister wanted to sing; my brother could have been a country singer, but they both married young and started raising families." At sixteen she moved to West Memphis, Arkansas, finished high school there, and went straight into singing with Wigginton's group when, in the time-honored showbiz manner, a girl booked for a session with them at Sonic did not show. "There was a man, I call him my first manager. He worked for a local television station. Herschel called and asked if he knew of anyone who could sing and he recommended me. Then we were called to sing for Rick Hall. I found out later that Rick Hall had recommended that I stay in the group."

She was at the front desk of American the day that Gary Walker, a song plugger for Painted Desert Music in Nashville, came by to play Chips some songs he wanted the Gentrys to record. He talked briefly with Sandy, and she told him, "I'd be recording myself if I could find a good song." Gary had one in his stack of demos; "Born a Woman," written by Martha Sharp (later the Warner Brothers executive who discovered Randy Travis). "He asked me if I'd demo the song. We cut it down in Muscle

Shoals." Although Sandy recalled that "Chips thought it was a hit immediately," Don Crews said that the demo lay around the studio for several months. "And I finally said to Chips, 'Somebody else is going to cut this thing, if we don't.'"

Sandy was eager to record the master session, and from the beginning, there was no doubt with whom. "I'm an instinctive person," she mused. "Chips hadn't produced that many hits, but instinctively I knew that he would be the best producer." Chips had been certain all along that Sandy should sing the master— "Absolutely!" he said, without a moment's hesitation. They cut the song at Hi because "Chips was just getting started and was having problems with his studio," Sandy remembered. Don Crews added, "Hi had a multi-track machine, they had three-track. We used a little pickup band"—Scotty Moore on lead guitar, Tommy Cogbill on second guitar, Mike Leech on bass. Ronnie Capone (Al's nephew, who became a sound engineer at Stax) played drums (and, according to Mike Leech, endured much kidding about his notorious relative). And on piano, there was a friend of Chips from Nashville by way of Pensacola, Florida (where he had been a music prodigy and later a DJ), Larry Butler.

Larry's life was in flux at this time, and he welcomed the chance to get away from Nashville for awhile and work with Chips, whom he had met at Tree Publishing. He loved being part of the Memphis scene. "It was very vital as far as the knowledge I gained as a producer," he observed. "I brought back to Nashville what I had learned in Memphis. If you let yourself do it, you could absorb all sorts of knowledge." What he had learned was difficult to describe, he said. "It's more or less a feel of music, just a style of playing, that R&B feel. I still use some of it today." He placed Chips alongside his Nashville mentor, Billy Sherrill, as an influence on his own production style. "Sherrill and Chips were both kind enough to let me sit in the control room and watch how they did it. Number one, simplicity; number two, the ability to get the very best out of the musicians. I don't see how producers who don't know music can communicate with the musicians. Sherrill

and Chips had the ability to communicate with musicians immediately." He also learned the strength of a good song. "Chips was a genius," said Larry. "He knows songs, he knows great songs. He can hear one the masses will like." "Chips didn't look for a pop song, he didn't look for an R&B song, he didn't look for a country song, he looked for a great song," elaborated Sandy Posey.

The recording of "Born a Woman" went well. "I remember thinking that the studio sounded better than I had ever heard it sound, with Chips at the controls," Mike Leech observed. Sandy was easy to work with—"laid-back, a quiet girl," Don Crews remembered; "very timid, kind of shy," said Larry Butler. "She was such a sweetheart, we were all pulling for her to make it." She had a good rapport with Chips and took pleasure in seeing her instincts borne out. "The number one reason I enjoyed working with Chips was that he was creative," she said. "He didn't just call the musicians in and say, 'Play me something,' he was creative, he had ideas of his own. The second thing that impressed me about Chips: he does not try to inhibit the singers or the players in any way. He never told me how to sing. Working up here in Nashville, I've seen producers come out and literally tell the musicians the lick to play. Chips never did that. That's inhibiting. And when you inhibit somebody, it destroys their creativity."

Larry Butler also emphasized the way Chips relied on the input of musicians. "He doesn't come in there with a preset concept. He has a ballpark idea of where he wants to go. He's not a weak producer by any means. But it's a melting pot of emotions, so why not get everybody's emotion? I think a producer who walks in and tells the musicians what to do is relying on just one man's ideas." Shane Keister, the keyboard player who worked for Chips during the final days of American Studios, observed the same thing: "So many times, his directions would be deliberately vague, because he didn't want to interfere with someone's creativity. He's a master of that. I remember several times we'd be counting it off and he'd come up with a scene, a picture of something" that he described for the players to convey what he wanted the music to express. Chips, in discussing Sandy's gifts and the contributions of the musicians, explained his philosophy simply: "Songs are the most important things, and then you have to have people who can interpret them."

He could seize the moment if a player came up with something. Larry Butler recalled the way the song's arrangement was constructed: "We were trying to get the feel for 'Born a Woman.' I sat at the piano and went 'bom, bom-bom.' That's how that feel came alive. When you're searching for that feel, it's not an accident. We were just trying to see what would happen. It was my concept to use that sort of a pattern. Chips was down there, scratchin' his head, saying, 'What do you think, Larry?'" "Larry takes credit to this day for the bass line I played on 'Born' . . . Not true," said Mike Leech. "It was my idea and he jumped on it." The opening lick referred to is one of the great hook lines of recorded history, leading the way into the music's loping groove, somewhat softened for the occasion. The understatement catches the ear; "it's subtle, it's not overplayed," said Larry.

When the track was finished, and taken as a matter of course to MGM, Don Crews stated that "The MGM crew said 'If you have strings, it'll be so much better.' At that time, money wasn't all that plentiful so we used a steel guitar and an organ. We put the steel guitar on and mixed it with the organ—John Hughey and Larry Butler. We put each one down, low and high, and then we reversed it. Know what we came up with for 'Single Girl'? Same thing!" Don whooped gleefully. "That shows you that the brain system don't always work." Chips Moman remembered that it was Pete Drake, not John Hughey, who had done the steel part on the session; Hughey concurred. Sandy liked the effect, remarking that strings on those records "would have been too pretty." The song was released in the summer of 1965 and became an immediate pop crossover hit, for which Sandy totally credited Chips. "If I had recorded that song with any other producer, what I would have gotten was just a country hit record," she said.

Despite having a hit record, Sandy did not tour. "That was one of her downfalls, she wasn't much of a stage act," said Don Crews. Sandy felt in retrospect that not touring was "a big mistake," but she did not want to trade her studio gig for the uncertainties of the road. "We were poor, and singing on sessions was the most money I'd ever made in my life." By now she had moved to Nashville and was singing regularly with Herschel Wigginton's Nashville Edition backup group (though she would return to Memphis occasionally to sing backup for Chips), and it was in Nashville that her first album would be recorded.

The monologue is, or was, a Southern female art form. It flowered during the era just after *The Feminine Mystique* was written and before women's rights had national impact; it was the venting of women bright enough to grasp the idea of liberation but too mired in the traditional lifestyle of husband, home, and family to seize it. Dan Kiley, in the followup to his classic book *The Peter Pan Syndrome*, described it as a form of female narcissism. "When the complaints reach a certain level," he wrote, "the [woman] starts to believe any complaint she thinks of, simply because she thought of it." Loretta Lynn made history around the same time setting these monologues to music, but Sandy's first album establishes her as another credible voice for all the desperate housewives lost in a maze of their own circular thinking. "The verbalization of her complaints may have been more important than the complaints themselves," wrote Kiley about one of his patients who wandered about her house all day long, complaining to herself out loud. "She needed to hear herself talk, if for no other reason than to reaffirm that she was who she thought she was."

"If you're born a woman, you're born to be hurt," Sandy sang in a bitter tone. "You're born to be stepped on, lied to, cheated on, and treated like dirt." An angry woman? No, because in the final chorus we learn that the speaker has only been letting off steam: "I was born a woman / I didn't have no say / And when my man finally comes home, he makes me glad / It happened that way." That ending, said Sandy, came from a suggestion by Chips. "He said to her,

'Martha, this is just so negative; it'll never sell, go back and rewrite it.'" The added final verse not only softens the song but gives it complexity, and Sandy's voice rides with the conflicting moods in a tone so experienced it is hard to believe that it is coming from a soft-spoken twenty-one-year-old girl. Though Sandy dismissed her recordings as "bubblegum stuff, not the kind of depth and soul I could have been doing," her signature hit addresses complicated emotions, and Chips's down-home production gives the monologue a regional flavor that not even Loretta herself, mistress of the form, could match.

Sandy triumphs again in the female version of Bobby Vinton's "Mr. Lonely," playing the part of a soldier's wife, "forgotten, yes, forgotten," and as an unhappy rich woman in "Satin Pillows." Her own "Blue Is My Best Color" is Nashville Sound "countrypolitan" in its approach, but wistful in its heartache. "Her voice had so much feeling, you talk about sad, man, she could sing a sad song," enthused Larry Butler. Sandy thought she knew why. "I think it's because of the pain that many of us go through. And I have had a lot of pain." This was perfect for Chips's style; "He can wring every bit of tears out of a song that need to be done," Larry Butler remarked.

Additional cuts included "Just Out of Reach" (a song that Chips came back to time and again), "It's All in the Game," and Chips's own "This Time"—"I always liked that song," said Sandy. Her gentle, romantic side is expressed in "Caution to the Wind," and "You've Got to Have Love" is straight-ahead rock.

The album musicians are the same ones who performed on her single; it was recorded "on the second floor of the old Life & Casualty Tower, the Foster Monument studio," said Don Crews. "We cut the first and second albums on Sandy there." "The first album was recorded in Nashville because that's where Jim Vienneau wanted it to be recorded," added Sandy. "He thought the greatest musicians were in Nashville, but he had a lot to learn." Strings were used on several of the selections, also at the request of Vienneau, and were arranged by Bill McElhiny, Owen Bradley's (later Billy

Sherrill's) string man. Mike Leech mentioned McElhiny as an influence on his own string writing. "The hook to Sandy's recordings was when Chips doubled her vocals in unison on most tracks. That was sort of 'her sound.' She was very good at it, as she was also good on backup," he added. "We had Herschel Wigginton and the Nashville Edition doing the backup," said Don Crews. "She did all her harmony parts herself, her unison parts."

For Chips the success of Sandy's record was a complete vindication. The financial windfall from Sandy and the Gentrys enabled him to arrange a trade with Don Crews. "I just told him I'd give him half of my acts"—that is, half of the producer's royalties on his two hits—"and he'd give me back the studio." This was done, and Don remained at American as business manager and, for the time being, de facto secretary, freeing Chips to concentrate on writing and producing, the aspects of the business he preferred.

Jim Vienneau was pleased with the results of Sandy's album. He became even more of a Moman booster. "He was a nice guy," said Mike Leech. Something of a musical matchmaker, Jim liked to put artists and writers together to see what creative results would happen (in the early nineties, he was trying to get Tracy Byrd and Tracy Lawrence to collaborate on some songs). And Jim knew just the person Chips ought to meet. Shortly after the work on Sandy's album was completed, Jim introduced Chips to a young songwriter from Muscle Shoals, Alabama.

The writer's name was Dan Penn.

||||||||||||||||||||||||||||||||||||||||||||||||||||||||||||||||||

### CHAPTER 3

# The Road, the Tree, and Its Branches

The success of the Hi label and Stan Kesler's work with Sam the Sham were blips on the radar screen. They could easily be dismissed as novelties—Hi for its instrumentals and comic songs of the "Haunted House" variety, Sam's records for their nonsense verses and the occasionally bizarre subject matter that reflected the interests of the singer. Chips Moman's work with Sandy Posey and the Gentrys had drawn some notice, but he had not attained national significance. This changed when Jim Vienneau introduced him to a sound engineer/aspiring singer/recently successful songwriter who was on staff at Fame Studios at Muscle Shoals, Alabama. Directly and indirectly he would introduce Chips, a fledgling studio, and some incipient ideas to the attention of the entire South and then to the larger world.

He was born Wallace Daniel Pennington in Vernon, Alabama, one of that state's typical county-seat towns, not far from the Georgia border (on a longitudinal line with Chips's hometown of LaGrange). He had a typical working-class Southern childhood and adolescence that he seemed to remember as nearly idyllic. "In my time, there was such a sweet period between '58 and '64," he recalled longingly. Much has been written about the soft, ruminative quality of Dan's voice (captured for all time on his live-in-concert CD, *Moments from This Theater*); not enough has been said about the content of his conversation, which mixed Southern inflections and good-ol'-boy aphorisms with sudden flashes of poetic elegance. If ever a man's occupation could be discerned by his speech patterns, it would be Dan Penn's; if

ever a man could be described as a born writer, it was he.

He was surrounded all his life by music; his father, like Bobby Wood's, was a song leader in church and a singing-school director. Like many Southern teenagers of his era, he discovered black music from the late-night broadcasts of WLAC in Nashville, and he identified his favorites early on. "Ray Charles had my attention all his life; Ray Charles was the one who took all us white boys into the blues. He was the one we all emulated when we were all in our hometowns." Bobby "Blue" Bland, based out of Memphis, was his other hero. "He was my second in line behind Ray Charles, and he's awful close to it." Between Ray Charles' down-home melancholy and the sassiness of Bland is where the songs he was beginning to write would fall, and along the way he was developing a rare sensitivity to R&B. "I used to have an affinity for the black race, I really did," he reflected. "Everything out of N'Orleans I just loved. I used to, I wouldn't even listen to you if you weren't black, I'm sorry." At the age of fifteen, he joined a band that alternated between rock and roll and square-dance music, which meant that he inevitably absorbed some of the formula for traditional country, despite his open dislike of it. "My heroes all come from the funky side of the tracks, there wasn't too much country music that seeped into my soul," he said. By the age of eighteen, he had been invited up to North Alabama by his former bandmate, Billy Sherrill; by the age of twenty, he was an integral part of, and founding member of, the Muscle Shoals recording scene.

The story of Muscle Shoals is often told, but it bears repeating. Two songwriters, Rick Hall and Billy Sherrill, began noticing that North Alabama was becoming a magnet for musical and songwriting talent from all over the state (and since both of them were dance-hall veterans, they already had a line on who most of them were). Why not, they reasoned, let the players and writers work on demos close to home, instead of having to go all the way to Atlanta or Nashville to record them or find a publisher? Their idea of a demo studio did not get far until they found a backer in Tom Stafford, a local pharmacist's son and town eccentric who already ran the movie theater in Florence and was looking for someplace to put his extra money. He staked Hall and Sherrill and let them build their first studio in an office over his father's drugstore; it was this building to which Dan would come after graduating from high school in 1960. "After Dan saw what was going on there, the writing, the songs, the players, he liked what he saw," said his collaborator, Spooner Oldham. It is also worth noting that Muscle Shoals was never intended to be the recording center it later became; everyone made it up as they went along, one thing led to another. Dan's take on it was direct: "Everybody in the South at that time didn't know nothin'. Memphis didn't know nothin'. We were cornball, just doin' all kinds of crazy stuff to make a sound. Rick didn't know nothin', he'll tell you his self he didn't know nothin'."

With the exception of a three-month layoff later in 1960, for the next six years Muscle Shoals was Dan's point of reference, his only world. He had his first hit, "Is a Bluebird Blue?" recorded by none other than Conway Twitty, then a big name in rock and roll, shortly after he came to the Shoals; he cut a record of his own that became a small-scale local hit; he married his high-school girlfriend Linda and brought her to North Alabama; and when Rick Hall broke with Stafford and started Fame Studios, Dan was there, a staff writer whose initial salary was twenty-five dollars a week. He wrote songs and engineered sessions at Fame by day; nights and weekends he joined musicians Norbert Putnam, David Briggs, and Jerry Carrigan in a band originally called the Mark V's and later Dan Penn and the Pallbearers because they traveled to their gigs in an old black hearse (shades of Sam the Sham). "They'd bring him into the show in a casket," remembered Muscle Shoals rhythm guitarist Jimmy Johnson, "and he'd come out of the casket and sing." Jimmy remembered that the band included a three-piece horn section, and that they could play perfect duplicates of R&B hits like the Mar-Keys' "Last Night." Eventually the horn section

was scrapped, and the group became a quartet, renowned in the area for playing "lots of Ray Charles, Dinah Washington, Bobby 'Blue' Bland," remembered Norbert Putnam.

Jimmy Johnson recalled being embarrassed when his band, the Del Rays, saw Dan's group onstage. "Boy, we thought we were hot shit till we saw the Mark V's. We came home wanting to quit! I'd never seen a Wurlitzer electric piano, just heard it on records like Floyd Cramer's 'Last Date' and 'Mood Indigo.' David Briggs had one and was playing it onstage and I said 'What the hell is that?' Boy, you oughta seen the tail between our legs." Their gigs were mainly the fraternity circuit of Alabama and Mississippi, the infamous "Animal Houses." Dan noticed the reactions of the frat boys and their dates. "In Mississippi they were very quiet and listened; in Mississippi we were two steps from the blues. They listened and they watched. In Alabama they'd come up and try to take the microphone away from you. I'd get drunk and lay on the floor. The audiences in Mississippi were kind of like English audiences now."

The Animal House years came to an end when Norbert Putnam and friends moved to Nashville to become session players in 1964, taking the hearse with them. Dan did not go. "Number one, I wasn't asked; number two, I wouldn't have done it." Their move prompted a period of soul-searching and reassessment for Dan similar to what Bobby Wood had been going through that same year. "It was kind of a very here-it-is moment," remembered Dan. "Here they go, they've got the whole world open to 'em; my compadres were fixin' to go. 'What do you really want to do, boy?' That's the question I asked myself. Here I am, y'know, a cold fish." He apparently tried doing a few Pallbearers gigs with Spooner Oldham and some of the other second-unit Shoals players (a photograph from this period exists showing Spooner and the drummer Roger Hawkins among his backing musicians), but when he thought about it, he admitted to himself that he was tired of the frat circuit, being away from home on the weekends and drinking too much. He could have found other musicians and formed another band, remaining a hot local attraction for another few years, but "getting a new band is painful. I don't like pain; I never did." The answer for him, then, was easy; he would write and remain in the background. "That's what I'm gonna be; I'm gonna be a studio cat."

He applied himself more than ever to his writing, collaborating extensively with Fame regulars Donnie Fritts and Spooner Oldham, despite the fact that the odds of becoming successful from where he was looked to be against him. "It just seemed impossible that you were gonna cut a hit out of Muscle Shoals, Alabama; it wasn't New York, it wasn't LA, and it wasn't London." He continued engineering sessions for Rick Hall and began to think about producing records the way he had witnessed Rick, and Otis Redding, doing. "Me and Spooner wrote day and night. I felt like I was in the right place, even then." The diligence paid off when Vienneau, who had followed his work since the initial Conway Twitty cut in 1960 (when Conway had been an artist on MGM), introduced him to Chips. "We was just downtown in an office," Chips said about the circumstances of meeting Dan in Nashville. "That was the night we almost hit a dog taking Linda to the hospital. That was more conversation than I could handle at that time," he cackled. Despite this auspicious beginning (or maybe because of it), Vienneau had fulfilled his intent. Chips and Dan became friends immediately.

To those who knew them both, it was not hard to understand why. "Chips and Dan were actually kind of alike," said Reggie Young. "Dan and Chips were so much alike they could be twin brothers, they both have that little snarl; they could sit in a room for two hours, look at each other, and never say a word," observed Larry Butler, who met Dan shortly thereafter, when Dan began coming up to Memphis on a regular basis to write songs and hang out with Chips. Chips's casual, thoughtful speech patterns were similar to Dan's; so, too, was his determination. And it was most clearly in the company of Dan that another one of Chips's talents began to reveal itself: the ability to command the abiding friendship and fierce loyalty of many of the people around him. Chips and Tommy Cogbill were fast friends by now, and Larry Butler, still living in Memphis, drew extensively on his closeness to Chips. "He was a lot of fun, the best; I remember one night there was a little place across the street, a diner; Chips said go get some ribeyes, he and I finished—it was real late, no knives and forks, we ate it with our hands. It was one of those magic moments." Bobby Wood recalled riding motorcycles with Chips at about this time; it was a hobby they later shared with many of the group.

Dan had a realistic appraisal of his new friend. "Talented people, they have both sides," he observed, reflecting that much could be said for Chips either way. "He's world-class. There was one thing that he was, he was never publishing crazy. That's important"—referring to the practice among producer/publishers of imposing bad songs on their artists for the sake of royalties. "He was never petty. He was always generous, in many ways. He's complicated, we all are; I'm complicated myself."

The first Dan Penn song recorded at American was cut by the Goldwax group, the Ovations; "I'm Living Good" has a slow, elegant, casual feel, and the Ovations' lead singer, Louis Williams, evokes Sam Cooke—a phrasing and delivery Quinton Claunch viewed as a tribute. Its message was one of quiet contentment, spoken from the point of view of an old boy who hasn't much money—he lives in a shack, his car does not run right—but nevertheless is happy, because he has the woman he loves. In 1966 this was a reassuring reminder of what is really important in life; when heard in the midst of the new century's consumer mania, it is a revelation, a quiet voice murmuring beneath the clamor. "I still like that record," mused Spooner Oldham, who wrote the song with Dan.

"Sunshine Girl," a song Dan and Spooner had already written, was the next one accepted by Chips, for an upcoming album he'd be working on that spring for the Gentrys. The song is a portrait of a type of woman idealized at the time, a freewheeling, lively, somewhat kooky, but always loving sprite—the personality also immortalized in the Association's "Windy" and Wayne Newton's "Sunny Day Girl." When asked how such an enchanting vision came to be written, Dan answered, "To get a cut."

He had already evolved a philosophy of songwriting, a code he would honor for years to come. "People ask me how I write my songs, and my answer is always, I write straight ahead. I'm one of those beeline persons, don't look to the left, don't look to the right." He had made up his mind early on to have no references in his songs to anything that was going on in his personal life at any time, a reticence he shared with Don Williams and John D. Loudermilk, among other writers. "We always made up stuff. I don't write no true stories; I don't believe in 'em. You can't write songs that way." There was more room for imagination in his method, he believed: "You put yourself further out in the atmosphere and you say 'Hmmm . . . let's dream awhile,'" he murmured thoughtfully, and one could almost see him drifting off into space, considering ideas.

This approach differed from the realistic, slightly autobiographical concept Chips Moman was developing, ideas he tried out in expanded form as he recorded the Gentrys' second album, *Gentry Time.*

Theoretically, the album should not have worked. There were problems with it from the beginning. Many of the cuts were tracks left over from the group's first session. Some of the earlier musicians in the band had quit; several more would leave during these sessions. Chips was still having trouble with some of the unreliable monaural equipment in his studio; for that reason, they recorded at Hi, a studio that Don Crews liked no better than did some of the regulars there. "The studio at Hi was a dull studio," he said. "You couldn't hardly hear the vocal." Nevertheless, from the first cut, the album has a coherent authority; it's the closest thing to a joyful album that Chips would ever make.

The first cut, "I'm Gonna Look Straight Through You," practically leaps off the turntable; it's New Wave before the style was officially invented. "Let's Dance," the Chris Montez hit, was given the garage-band treatment, and there's a reference to Mick Jagger in the chorus. Both songs move the album along at a foot-stomping pace, which Chips interrupts for the third cut, "(Don't Let It Be) This Time," a ballad he wrote with Larry Butler. "I remember I was in Nashville when I started writing it," Chips said. "I can't remember if I was living there then or just visiting. But I started it and Larry Butler finished it." The song refers directly to the earlier hit; it also evokes the Everly Brothers and nostalgic songs such as "Sweetheart of Sigma Chi," along with a sudden burst of agony in the middle: "The pain is greater now." Why the sudden lapse into melancholy three songs into an up-tempo album?

"He's a melancholy-type person," Dan Penn shrugged.

Chips restores the groove with the Arthur Alexander composition, "Every Day I Have to Cry Some." Like "I'm Living Good," it explains the good old boy's attitude about the world and money. It is Chips making self-references out of a song he never wrote; this one, like many on the first Gentrys album, can refer indirectly to the Stax experience and the ways in which his life fell apart thereafter. It is also a cautionary tale, as if Chips were trying to convince himself to beware of the seductive power of lucre; the song suggests that it is nothing but a hassle that gets in the way of true love. (Of course, it is easy to express such an attitude when you're operating on a shoestring, as Chips still was at the time.) Larry Butler had suggested that one; "Damn good track!" he exclaimed, and one notable for a voicing that would soon become familiar—the unstoppable groove of an intricate bass line. Larry laughed and would not comment about Chips's use of session players other than himself to augment the Gentrys' sound, but both Chips and Don Crews remembered the bass player—Tommy Cogbill.

Many of the tunes are centered around Tommy's bass lines, a technique Chips relied on more and more over the years. Then there was his subdued temperament—"a very nice, gentle man," observed Mike Leech; "the kindest man I ever worked with in the business," said Hayward Bishop. Unassuming and cooperative, Tommy nonetheless projected strength. This too gained the admiration of the more mercurial Chips. Bobby Emmons had called Tommy an inspiration; this term was increasingly being used to describe the bassist.

The guitar leads that also became familiar on Chips's recordings were by Reggie Young. He brought to the Gentrys session a folk-style ballad he had come up with called "I'm a Ramblin' Man" (no relation to the later Allman Brothers hit). In this defiant song, a hard-travelin' man announces to his prim and proper woman that he is not about to change his way of life for her; like its writer, it projects that elusive quality called "cool." "The progression for that song came from Jackie DeShannon," Reggie remembered. He had heard the Kentucky girl singing the traditional ballad "Sweet Betsy from Pike" when he had gotten to know her on the Beatles tour, and he wanted to create something with a similar chord structure and feel. To his astonishment, the song was seized on as authentic; several folk singers and groups recorded it, as did Jumpin' Gene Simmons. The song did reasonably well, but Reggie never profited, since it had been done under the auspices of Hi. "Ray Harris told me, he said, 'We'll cut it but we'll get the writing and publishing, and put your name on it,'" recalled Reggie. The song was a harbinger of the strong writing that became another trademark of the American Studios sound.

There was Dan's and Spooner's "Sunshine Girl," and a pretty but slight Larry Butler ballad, "I Wanna Be In," which Chips arranged with plaintive acoustic guitars to emphasize the wistful melody. "Gimme Love Now" utilized fuzz-tone guitar over a rhythm pattern that lapsed into near-minstrel show overtones at the end, and on the ballad "Givin' Love Never Hurt Nobody," Chips gradually increased the rhythm content, building and building the song until the listener becomes aware of nothing but the groove and the stomping beat.

The tape came out with the vocals too low for Jim Vienneau's taste; he sent it back for a remix, which mortally offended the producer. "Chips didn't mess with it," remembered Don Crews. "Chips was a fella that if he got his feelings hurt, he wouldn't do anything. Stan Kesler and I remixed it at the Phillips studio and sent it back to MGM." Stan didn't remember the details, but he did recall Don Crews bringing something in for a remix; the Phillips studio on Madison was state-of-the-art for remastering, and it was common for other labels and studios to take tapes there.

When the album came out, the Gentrys were scheduled to tour and needed a keyboard player. Larry Butler stepped in. "I became a Gentry, went on the road with them, grew my hair down over my ears and just went crazy," he remembered. The tour won for his newfound colleagues a great deal of Larry's respect. "Larry Raspberry [lead singer] was a really talented guy," said Butler. "He had such a rapport with the audience in those days. Jimmy Hart [second lead vocalist, later to become Hulk Hogan's manager] was a great entertainer. We played the Whiskey A-Go-Go in Hollywood, everybody else was wearing T-shirts and man, we dressed up in blazers and white pants. Lloyd Bridges was in the audience one night. Lloyd Bridges loved our music."

Something was happening, all right, by May 1966. Chips had cut two of Dan's songs, and now he was going to be doing his friend another favor. He and Tommy Cogbill were going to Muscle Shoals to play on a session for one of the hottest singers in the country.

They were going to be working with Wilson Pickett.

The Memphis invasion of Muscle Shoals was never as cut and dried as history has made it sound. Reggie Young was going down for sessions as early as 1963. "They had a guitar player named Terry Thompson, he had passed away and I just sort of filled in for him," he recalled, discussing the circumstances of his accompanying Quinton Claunch (a native Mississippian who had lived in the Shoals and was close to Rick Hall) and Doc Russell to Fame for some of their early Goldwax recordings. Reggie was included at the request of Rick, who had met him at Hi while he was working on a session. Dan Penn remembered them well. "Sometimes I would go for food in Doc's 1964 Cadillac," he said, noting the vehicle with the precision of a classic-car enthusiast. "They didn't cut records like everyone else; they just sat back and said 'Yeah!'" (Chips, he added, "was like a *real* smart Doc and Quinton.") Sandy Posey sang backup there on a regular basis with Herschel Wigginton, who was from the Shoals; sometimes their vocal group rode down with Reggie Young.

Reggie's recollections of the early days in Muscle Shoals, and of Dan Penn, were vivid. "The first time I ever met Dan, he came up to me and he said, 'You must be a really good guitar player.' I said, 'And why is that?' And he said 'Because of your guitar case.' It was battered and beat-up and looked as if it had been around the Horn several times." Dan's work, and in particular his singing, won Reggie Young's admiration. "He was such a soulful person," Reggie recalled fondly. "The demos I heard when I first went down, he sounded like a black guy. He didn't sing anything at all like he looked"—an accurate assessment, if one contrasts Dan's gritty singing with his laid-back drawl and his eternal habit of slouching. Reggie also recalled Rick Hall's perfectionist production style. "Rick was at that time like most of the Memphis producers—you'd just play a song over and over and try to change it. He would have suggestions—he would get out on the studio floor, where we were, and play a guitar or a mandolin lick or something." He noted that "there wasn't any time limit there." The marathon sessions he had already done for Hi had gotten him used to working at that pace—a habit that stood him in good stead later.

Even Chips Moman's involvement with recording in Muscle Shoals was varied. He had gone down in late 1964 at the behest of his boosters at Tree in Nashville to participate in the session that had yielded Joe Tex's first hit, "Hold On to What You Got," and had been on a couple of other sessions since then. "Cogbill didn't show up exactly with Chips, Chips came down by his self once, maybe twice," said Dan Penn. "I loved that studio," Chips recalled with warm enthusiasm. Of Rick Hall, he remarked admiringly, "He had a great set-up. Those guys we worked with were fun, and he had some really great musicians. They're good guys, too."

He took note of Rick Hall's recording machinery and, he said, "Fact is, I liked it so well that when I got my new board at American I got one just like it. It was a Universal Audio." Others recall the machine as a United Audio 610, designed by studio technical whiz Bill Putnam. "When Pickett was there we used mono gear, one-track mono cut on quarter-inch tape," Jimmy Johnson said authoritatively. "They've never even had a stereo version" of the first Pickett album. On later sessions the tapes recorded by Rick Hall at the Shoals were taken to New York, where engineer Tom Dowd remixed to stereo on the state-of-the-art Atlantic equipment.

Chips remembered that Jerry Wexler, who had known him from Stax and who had always respected his ability as a musician, had requested that he be on the Pickett session, since Rick Hall had only a rhythm guitarist; when the New Yorker asked if Chips knew of any other musicians, Chips immediately recommended the one who had been doing some work for him. "We were big friends and we needed the money," Chips said, explaining his reason for taking Tommy. "Before me, they were brothers, so they were old brothers," said Dan Penn. "Chips was trying to promote his boys." He also wanted to work with Dan; he was hoping that this would be an incentive to get Dan to move to Memphis and become part of a master plan he was formulating.

It worked. "When the road trips started, I thought two people who could really play were there," said Dan. "They were very talented and we had a lot of fun with them," said his writing partner Spooner Oldham. "I think Chips is a musical whiz." Spooner had not really heard of Chips before, he recalled, but "once it was said that he had engineered at Stax, that told me volumes." "It was just a time of getting to know each other," said Jimmy Johnson. "We all became great friends." "I thought Chips was a wild guy," said the Shoals trombonist (later bassist) David Hood. "He comes driving up one time in a XKE. He was a gambler, he played cards and stuff. He seemed like a real slick, sharp guy."

The musicians were also impressed by Wilson Pickett. "He and I hit it off real well,"

Spooner Oldham said of the singer. "I knew him as Mr. Energy, I had loved the Stax records that he'd done." "I do remember me and Rick picking him up at the airport," Dan said, referring to the well-documented occasion when a reluctant Pickett almost refused to work after looking out the airplane window and seeing cotton fields, then meeting Rick Hall, whom he thought looked like the stereotypical Southern sheriff (actually Hall resembled the country singer Doug Stone). "When Wilson sang, he stomped," Dan continued. "He was one of them guys that just went after it!"

Pickett had plenty of opportunity to go after it, with the empathetic work of the Southern musicians behind him. The sessions began with Tommy Cogbill playing his blue Hagstrom, which Reggie Young remembered as "the loudest-sounding guitar I had ever heard." "He didn't even bring down another guitar," recalled Jimmy Johnson, who played rhythm guitar to Tommy's second and Chips's lead, with Junior Lowe on bass. This configuration recorded "Land of a Thousand Dances," a song that had been written and recorded first by Chris Kenner in 1962. More recently, it had been revived by a one-shot studio group called Cannibal and the Headhunters, which had been assembled in California by a young arranger named Glen Spreen. "Land" was not much different from the garage-band sound Chips had been doing on his recordings or that Tommy was cutting at Hi—but Pickett's harsh vocal and Chips's stinging guitar asides gave the record an aggressive edge—was this a party, or a riot? No one was sure, and its ambiguous message, in a summer of racial tensions, went to Number Six on the national charts.

There were a few problems at first, Jimmy Johnson remembered, due to "the stumbling Junior Lowe did." The descending-note fast intro of "Land" was particularly difficult for him. Jimmy remembered, "Junior was fumbling on the intro, it took him about five minutes to get it. It took him about twenty passes" before a take could be completed. This did not sit well with the New Yorkers, who were used to recording songs in one or two takes; they were prepared to endure it for this session, but no

longer. The singer continued to do what he did well, and this earned further respect from the musicians. "It was fun to work with Pickett, little intimidating at first," noted the Fame drummer, Roger Hawkins. "From reading him at first, you knew he had a short fuse. Pickett showed me what to play."

A group photo survives from that monumental first afternoon in Muscle Shoals. Jimmy Johnson recalled, "I think they might have been pitching pennies just before that was taken. Chips, he was a real gambler. He would actually try to talk anybody into betting on anything with him, and he usually won." "I learned a couple of gambling things from him," remembered Roger Hawkins. "He was trying to get Charles Chalmers to bet him on anything." They noticed some steer horns up on the wall of a restaurant, Roger added, and Chips was asking Charles, "What about these longhorns? Are they real or plastic? What if one side is plastic and the other one is real? How much do you want to bet on that?" Finally, said Roger, Charles took the bait. "Chips told him, 'I'll bet you I can smoke a cigarette without lighting either end,' and Chalmers said, 'You're on.' Chips lit up the center of the cigarette." A similar trick was played on Roger himself, and he laughed appreciatively at the memory. "Chips said, 'Stand right here. Here's an imaginary circle, I'll bet you five dollars when I walk around you three times you'll be out of the circle.' I said, 'Yeah, go on, you're gonna push me, right?' He said, 'No, I'm not gonna touch you, I'm just gonna walk around you three times and you'll be out of the circle.' So he walked all the way around me, twice. In the middle of the third walk he stops and says, 'I'll see you later—I didn't tell you when I was gonna walk around you the third time.' Boy, he knew all the tricks. That circle trick amazed me. He was a good hustler, fantastic hustler, in a good way."

In the photo, taken just after some of Chips's betting escapades, Tommy Cogbill is on the very edge of the frame, holding up a carton of chocolate milk in a celebratory toast; his expression is alert, bright, inquisitive. Chips Moman stands next to him, in the center of the photo, dominating it; a half-eaten hamburger and a bottle of orange soda are clutched in his hands. His head is cheerfully cocked and he is smiling, revealing his ease with his surroundings. Behind him stands Spooner Oldham, who played piano on the session and is beaming with delight, and next to him, Roger Hawkins, solemnly holding a sandwich and a milk carton. Down front are Junior Lowe, gazing seriously into the camera; Wilson Pickett in his dark jacket, the epitome of city cool compared to the casually dressed musicians, and a naive-looking Jimmy Johnson. The photo revealed the attitude everyone seemed to have about the session; elation that something great had been accomplished, but at the same time a determination to take it in stride, as befitted the pros they all were by now. "It was a good day, musically," said Spooner with quiet satisfaction.

The treat of the album from these sessions, *The Exciting Wilson Pickett*, was Chips Moman's edgy lead guitar. The sound revealed another facet of his personality—tough, hard-boiled, raw, experienced. He follows Pickett's graceful vocal effortlessly on another Chris Kenner tune, "Something You Got," and on Don Covay's "Have Mercy," the cynical, put-upon tone of the lyrics is perfectly echoed by the guitar. Were it not for Reggie Young's presence on so many of his records, the evidence here states that Chips would have been a volcanic force as lead player. "He's an excellent guitar player—the licks he played on those sessions are still identifiable today," was Reggie's considerable judgment. The thick drumming of Roger Hawkins sets up a solid foundation from which Chips and the two other guitarists can fly. To the great frustration of the listener, Tommy Cogbill's rhythm lines seldom emerge due to the mono mix; his presence is felt rather than heard. But on "You're So Fine" and "I'm Drifting," two songs inconsequential in themselves, it comes together. Tommy's rhythm lines are slightly audible, and they blend almost instinctively with Chips's lead and Hawkins's drums to set up snapping, relentless grooves. On the latter song, while Pickett sings of searching for "a place where there's a party going on" in the same tones as if he were seeking the Heavenly Kingdom, Tommy and Chips imply musically

what that party will feel like—a joyful, uninhibited romp of pure sound and exhilaration that dares the listener not to join in the fun. Maybe that party is taking place in heaven after all.

The album was filled out with some tracks left over from Pickett's previous sessions at Stax, and the difference between the work at the two studios is telling. The Stax material had stronger songs ("In the Midnight Hour" is even recycled from Pickett's previous album), but the Memphis and Muscle Shoals musicians are playing in a more versatile style than much of what had been placed on records by Stax at that time. "The songs were picked during the sessions," Chips Moman remembered. "He and Jerry would do that, and sometimes me."

To Chips Moman, Tommy Cogbill, and the Muscle Shoals rhythm section, it had been just another session, but a record that was a national hit put their playing in demand, especially to the people at Atlantic. "I just think the world of those guys," Chips said warmly of Wexler and Dowd. "I learned some things from Dowd—I learned the different ways of miking a bass drum, for example. He was a good electronics man." "Tom was . . . well . . . seemingly organized, congenial, talkative, obviously a great engineer," said Spooner Oldham, searching for the exact descriptive phrase. Chips liked the creative freedom the Atlantic people gave musicians who played on their records. "They don't necessarily tell you what they want you to play. Sometimes they'd bring in a demo they wanted you to copy, but for the most part every record I was involved in was just head arrangements." Dan Penn admitted that they all admired the New Yorkers. "I thought they were smart. I thought, 'These guys are my heroes.' I'd been listening to LaVern Baker on Atlantic . . . I thought the world of how they did in the studio. I didn't emulate 'em in any way but I learned how to approach somebody and I learned from their enthusiasm. I don't talk like them, but I learned from them. They had finesse in the way they approached a musician. They didn't insist, but they did." "They were always focused on the task at hand, they didn't waste time," said Roger Hawkins with obvious admiration.

Spooner Oldham remembered Jerry Wexler somewhat differently. "I think Jerry may have been a little nervous about us—he hadn't a clue who we were," was the piano player's observation. "I don't know what had made him want to come down to the Shoals in the first place—I don't know what rang his bell. I thought maybe this man was going to be a little abrasive, maybe this isn't gonna work, because he got on the talkback and said something, it was very loud. I wasn't sure it would work. I'm not sure I wanted it to work. It was a weird opening step. I thought we were gonna be corralled like a bunch of horses." Very likely what Spooner saw was Wexler establishing priority, a way of letting the musicians know that he was the boss; once that had been made apparent and the players began to take direction from him, Wexler seemed less insecure. "It was just a continuation of good work—just a continuation of their lives and their work," Spooner said of the Atlantic attitude toward them from then on.

The New Yorker's dominance stunned the younger Muscle Shoals staffers, according to Jimmy Johnson, who remembered that "we were all kinda petrified" of Wexler. "He was the epitome of the New York record man. He was It, he was the Guru, y'know? The way he talked, it commanded respect. Oh man, if the president of the United States had come in it wouldn't have been as important to us." Perhaps because of this awe due to their relative inexperience with the big time, the younger musicians became close to Wexler in a way that Chips Moman, Tommy Cogbill, Dan Penn, and Spooner Oldham never were; the four of them kept their dealings with him cordial but professional.

Regarding their new guitar-playing colleague, the Muscle Shoals musicians had strong impressions from the beginning. "Tommy is and was, I thought, a wonderful human being," said Spooner Oldham warmly. "He was a real quiet, kind of a good-natured guy," said Jimmy Johnson. "His talent never ceased to amaze us. All of us." Dan Penn was somewhat puzzled by him. "Tommy was harder to figure out as a person. For one thing, what an intricate player, to

start with," he recalled. His memories of Cogbill, even after working with him extensively, would remain enigmatic. "He had a terrific smile and there was always something going on behind those eyes," Dan noted, referring to Tommy's intelligent expression. "As far as saying 'Did you know him very well?' I didn't. He was also mysterious; he was kind of self-contained. He'd share a joke with you, pull a lot of stuff."

There was no puzzlement in Dan's or anyone else's estimation of a writer friend of Pickett's whose song, "She's So Good to Me," the musicians heard on a demo at this session and recorded. Bobby Womack grew up in Ohio; under the tutelage of his father, a man with the endearing name of Friendly, he and his brothers formed a gospel group. Their singing drew the notice of Sam Cooke, a former gospel singer himself, and, as others had done for him, he eased their transition into the secular music world, renaming their group the Valentinos and steering them through a moderate hit, "Looking for a Love." The Womack Brothers sang backup on Cooke's sessions. Bobby contributed a moody guitar solo to one of Sam's last records, "That's Where It's At." Bobby had married Sam's widow an unseemly week after Sam's death, making him persona non grata in Sam's hometown of Chicago and his and Bobby's adopted base of Los Angeles. This ostracism occurred even though people had been aware for a long time that Sam's marriage was troubled. "Sam and his wife weren't really married, if you know what I mean," said Jimmy Johnson.

Bobby was now in exile. He tried Detroit, where he met an aspiring singer named Darryl Carter; they collaborated on a jaunty boy-meets-girl tune for Tamla, "L-O-V-E," featuring Bobby's guitar and Darryl's hoarse vocal, but their work was probably a little too blunt for Berry Gordy. The Rolling Stones had just had a hit with Bobby's "It's All Over Now," an angry and prideful farewell to a woman who was always "playing her half-assed games." To the rugged individualists on the Muscle Shoals sessions, a left-handed black guitarist with a controversial song and an equally controversial marriage was their kind of renegade; they all agreed that they would like to work with him in the studio during some future road trip.

It was a foregone conclusion that there would be another one.

||||||||||||||||||||||||||||||||||||||||||||||||||||||||||||||||||||

### CHAPTER 4

# Walking Through an Open Doorway

When Tommy Cogbill returned from Muscle Shoals and resumed work at Hi in the early summer of 1966, it was increasingly more of the same old thing. Ray Harris and Joe Cuoghi had hit upon a successful formula for the label, with lots of help from Willie Mitchell. "I always liked his horn lines and ideas," Mike Leech said of Mitchell in those pre–Al Green days. "He was a funny, interesting man to work with in the studio. Plus, he had a regular gig at the Manhattan Club where Reggie and I would haunt quite often, and usually sit in." "Willie was a very nice man. He was always together," said Reggie Young admiringly, speaking of those days when he, newly married and starting his family, worked extensively on records with Mitchell. "I had an apartment over in East Memphis, and he helped me move my furniture. I learned a lot from Willie, especially in the R&B world. He would find that little magic spot and he would not go to the left or the right of it."

Willie Mitchell was universally respected and trusted by the Hi musicians, but there were a few slight reservations about Ray Harris. "Ray was a very country person, a rural person," Reggie Young observed. "He was like a horse trader. He would work us to death. I liked Ray, but he was always trying to get something for nothing." "He was boisterous," remembered Mike Leech, who also noted that Harris didn't have "a good command of the language. He was buck-toothed, with gaps. Very 'rednecky.' But funny, and fun, at times. Terms he used with an artist; 'Crowd that mike, boy!' To Reggie, 'Clean that guitar up, boy!' . . .

Ray could hear a hit, which was a plus, him being a simple carpenter." "Although Ray Harris and Willie Mitchell had different styles of communication with you during a session, both were fine to work for as far as I was concerned," said Bobby Emmons equivocally. "I can't really draw any hard lines except to say I think Willie gave me a little more freedom in finding something on my own than Ray did, although Willie was cool in letting you know he didn't like what you were doing. Ray would describe his suggestions with comparisons to familiar sounds or images (waterfalls, beautiful, shots, strong, light) and Willie would refer to musical landmarks (players, songs, styles, era)."

Album sales at Hi, the label already billing itself as "The Memphis Sound," were steady and respectable, and the results were always musical, even if listeners did not notice that on every Hi cut, one could hear the same dominant lead guitar. "Gosh, back then . . . Ray would cut, it would be kinda dry," Reggie Young said about one of the most notable aspects of the Hi sound. "I can't say it was bad because it was good for what it was. You didn't get any reverb, everything would be real flat." The flatness came from the layout of the studio, said Hayward Bishop, who visited the place around 1969. "Hi had a very dead sound." Bobby Emmons recalled that the walls were covered with Celotex and that "they used portable baffles for isolation." He remembered the slanted floor: "Royal Recording was carpeted (beige, I think), slanting uphill from the front door to the control room. I wondered if somehow the entrance wasn't once at the control room since you didn't go into theaters at the screen end back then, and the front as we knew it was on South Lauderdale, same as the address."

The recording space was known as "the killing floor" to all the regulars at Hi. Bobby Emmons described it as "one big room with the high ceiling except for later on, two very small booths in the far right corner from the front." "I remember Hi as, walking in the front door to an entrance area with some chairs, then through another door to the main studio. I remember it as being fairly large, rectangular, sloping slightly upwards," said Mike Leech,

with a precise eye for detail. "Just through that door you looked straight ahead to the far end, to the control-room glass. With an entrance on the left. When you walked in and turned around facing the back, upstairs was another glassed-in booth. Not sure if recording equipment was up there or not. Hardly ever went up there. Seems some of Willie's 'family' hung out there a lot. Perhaps [it was] a writing room of a sort." Mike also remembered the Celotex on the walls. Hi's control board, powered by vacuum tubes and hand-built by the company's founder, Bill Cantrell, was famous. It would not take a sound technician to realize that great records were often made there under adverse circumstances.

Ray Harris's concept of sound seemed to be an inhibiting factor. The muffled, hesitant quality he got was evident on the album of Hank Williams standards Charlie Rich cut at Hi that winter. With Reggie Young, Bobby Emmons, and Tommy Cogbill along, the album should have worked, but Harris mixed the musicians very low. "I think Ray might have been a little slower about recognizing a good take," Reggie Young observed. "We were in there once and Tommy was playing bass and, as a joke, Tommy turned his bass off and just pretended he was playing for the whole take. Harris got on the talkback and said 'Yeah! That's it!'" Reggie Young was given the freedom to arrange some of the sessions, and he took advantage of the chance, experimenting with new sounds in the studio and taking the records away from the increasingly constricted formula. His contributions made 1966 the peak year for the early Hi in terms of quality. "At Hi we'd just go in and start doing stuff," said Reggie. "It was an over and over thing, partly because of the limited equipment they had."

His fuzz-tone is heard on many of the Hi records from this period, from Gene Simmons's garage-band stomper "Bossy Boss" to Ace Cannon's version of "Hang On Sloopy" (which also features some intricate interplay with Mike Leech's bass). His guitar line on Ace's "Funny How Time Slips Away" is acerbic, bitter; and Bobby Emmons's organ weaves a line throughout that glistens like a metallic thread, illustrating why Hayward Bishop later dubbed him "the King of Licks." Reggie arranged the definitive version of "Ram-Bunk-Shus" on Ace's *Sweet and Tuff* album, cut shortly before Chips Moman and Tommy Cogbill went to Muscle Shoals for the first time; "Listen to the Mockingbird," from the same sessions, even features a tenor banjo! "Clear Days and Stormy Nights," written by Mike Leech and the Willie Mitchell protégé Don Bryant with the intention of pitching it to Percy Sledge (though Mike's name was inadvertently left off the credits), is an impassioned, deep-soul ballad underscored by Reggie's equally passionate, eloquent guitar work in the background. Then there is the jaunty, swaggering run accompanying Gene Simmons's monologue about a drunk at a bar, "Listen to Me Lie," and the way Reggie and Mike Leech romp, stomp, and tear to pieces the old Ray Price tune "Invitation to the Blues," also sung by Simmons. Some of these cuts can be heard on a CD called *The Hi Records Story: The Early Years, Volume Two.* Both volumes of these Hi CDs are essential for anyone who wants to know what the musicians were up to. Reggie's finest recording of the time, "Down in the Alley," with Gene Simmons, features a blistering blues guitar line; it remained unissued for thirty years. "Reggie Young can play about anything," remarked Stan Kesler.

Though Reggie said of himself, "I was always a player instead of a writer," a few of his songs drew notice. Many of them were thought up while he was just sitting around the studio at Hi; this was the case with a composition cut by Jumpin' Gene Simmons that fall. Its hook line, Bobby Emmons said, "came from a guy named Gene Parker; he's a saxophone player that worked with Bill Black. If he had a good-looking pair of shoes, he'd sit and look at 'em and say, 'Go on, Shoes!'" Reggie turned this feet-don't-fail-me-now phrase into a stark, desolate song reminiscent of Porter Wagoner's classic "Cold Dark Waters"; the singer, tormented by a woman's betrayal, urges his shoes to keep on walking, from the lonely side of town down to the river, "where it's cold and it's dark and it's mighty, mighty wide," and to see if they could walk him into the river, "all the way

to the other side." Though Emmons believed that "the progression was the main thing on 'Go On, Shoes,'" it is the absolute despair that rivets the listener, the sense that one is literally eavesdropping on the thoughts of a suicide.

The song did not do well in the charts, which disappointed Reggie. Equally disheartening, he said, was Hi's system for session payments. "At Hi there was no time limit; when we'd get four songs, they'd turn it in to the union. Union scale was sixty dollars, they'd pay us fifteen dollars a song. If all we got on a session was two songs, we still got union scale but had to kick back thirty dollars to Joe Cuoghi." The custom in Memphis—and Muscle Shoals—was to pay the musicians for the completed song, no matter how many hours were spent working on it, and fifteen dollars "was the going rate around town," said Reggie. He remembered the turning point, when he realized that something had to give. "This is strictly personal from me," he said about his moment of disillusion. "Ray Harris called me. I'd just found out that my wife was pregnant with my son. Ray called and said, we'll cut you back to ten dollars a side. I said, well, I'll have to quit. Five minutes later the phone rang again. It was Joe Cuoghi. He said, 'I'm sorry about that. Ray's just horse tradin', and we'll keep you on at fifteen dollars a side.'" But the damage was done. After that, said Reggie, "I didn't feel as loyal as I had. That was the beginning of the end for me."

Fortunately, it was looking more and more as if he had a way out. Chips Moman was in a position now to unveil his plan. He would have a hand-picked band, consisting of the best musicians in Memphis, to be available on call twenty-four hours a day, seven days a week for sessions. He selected the musicians in the same way that a casting director chooses actors for a play. There was no question but that Tommy Cogbill would be part of his plans, as close as the two of them were; Tommy suggested Gene Chrisman. Reggie Young, of course, was already considered in some quarters to be the finest lead guitarist in town, and Chips definitely wanted to hire him. Reggie was agreeable, having already made up his mind to leave Hi at some point. "I said I'll get out one of these days and Chips was the vehicle to do it," he said. "I really felt that I was moving forward."

Then there was the matter of acquiring a keyboard player. Larry Butler had left Memphis following the Gentrys tour earlier that year and returned to Nashville, working sessions there. "Chips was disappointed," he remembered, "but he had a couple of other keyboard players so it wasn't life or death." But did he? Bobby Wood was reluctant to commit himself when approached, because he did not want to tie himself to one studio but also out of loyalty to Stan Kesler, for whom he was still doing sessions and solo recording at Phillips. "I needed to make up my mind," he said. He was even occasionally touring again, although never at the pace he did before the wreck. Scotty Moore had left Memphis to pursue a full-time studio career in Nashville, and he occasionally asked Bobby if he would like to do the same. The piano player thought about it but decided, "I wasn't ready." Bobby Emmons and Chips had been out of touch for awhile; it was Reggie who asked him, on behalf of Moman, if he would join. Though Emmons was not unhappy at Hi, he welcomed the chance to be working again with his old friend. He didn't even need to break a contract to do so; "All I was doing at Hi at the time . . . was freelance sessions, so there was no hiring away from anyone in particular," Emmons noted. Chips now had an organist but still wanted a piano player; since Bobby Wood had indicated that he would only do sessions at American on a part-time basis, Chips had in mind another keyboard player whom he hoped to hire.

"I'm from Center Star, Alabama," said Spooner Oldham. "It's about twenty miles from the town of Muscle Shoals . . . a small little place."

He was originally christened Dewey Lindon Oldham, Jr. (Many of the American musicians bore the names of their fathers—in addition to Spooner, there were Tommy, Reggie, and later arrivals Johnny Christopher and Hayward Bishop.) The nickname by which Dewey would forever be known came about when, as a child,

he accidentally poked out his right eye with a spoon. Like all of the others, he came to music quite young.

"I first learned a few chords on guitar, then mandolin," he recalled. "My dad had played mandolin, he and his brothers had had a band." The senior Oldham, a partially paralyzed World War II veteran who had been injured in the Battle of the Bulge, still kept his old instrument close by, and, when Spooner was around eleven or twelve, "One day on the sofa I asked him if he'd show me some chords on the mandolin." His father obliged, and rather than pester him further about the finger positions, Spooner said, "I just, like, took a photograph in my mind because I didn't wanna beleaguer the thought. He said, 'You learn these three chords and you can play almost any song,' and that is still true today."

He kept on with the mandolin for a year or two, until one day when he was in the eighth grade at Killen Junior High. "A friend, Ronald English, saw a piano in an otherwise empty room. He liked to sing, but I thought he'd grow up to be a sports announcer because he had the voice and the love of sports." Impulsively Ronald and Spooner went for the piano and decided to try out a song, "something that was ringing daily on the radio airwaves. He sang and I played 'Whole Lotta Shakin',' we did a fair rendition. . . . Somehow I just transferred the information I knew from guitar and mandolin. I was surprised that I could play it as well as I did. I said, 'Why don't we start a band?' . . . and then the following week we began practicing at my cousin Bruce Oldham's house. I had just recently met Roger Hawkins, who joined our band. We were learning a few songs, and thought we needed a bass player. Albert 'Junior' Lowe drove over one day, with his upright bass strapped to the top of his car . . . what a wonderful sight and sound. There are some good memories of that first band." Hawkins, Lowe, and Spooner would become members of Rick Hall's second studio band, replacing Norbert Putnam and friends. All three had been part of the Muscle Shoals scene virtually from the beginning, when Spooner enrolled as a student at Florence State College (later to become the University of North Alabama) in the fall of 1961.

He lasted a year and a half before he quit college in frustration. "You go there and you sign up—'What's your major?' I hadn't a clue, they try to intimidate you into choosing a major." Naturally, he picked music, but studying it formally was not quite what he had expected. "One day I'd be learning the scales on a clarinet, which is a woodwind instrument; then learning the scales on a trumpet, which is brass. Then I'd be singing in a choir. It was all Greek and Arabic to me. I think my two favorite subjects were my electives—Social Dancing and Art Appreciation; they show you a bunch of pictures and you sit around and discuss them." Outside of school, he was already acquainted with the musicians at Rick Hall's demo studio, having seen some of them on the circuit when he played with his high school group. "That's where Dan and I met, when we were teenagers," he said. Spooner had experimented with writing songs before, composing them on the old upright piano in his parents' basement and playing the results for his first audience, his sister. But one evening in Muscle Shoals, he and Dan had free time and decided to try something out.

"It was at James Joiner's studio, we borrowed a piano for an evening." (Joiner had actually opened the first Muscle Shoals demo studio in the late fifties.) "We realized that the chemistry was probably okay." In fact, the chemistry was ideal; Spooner's contemplative temperament matched Dan's sharper-edged one in the same way Tommy Cogbill balanced Chips. "Spooner, him and Dan were like two peas in a pod," observed Reggie Young, who knew both of them well by then and had seen a great deal of their approaches to life and music. The aspiring writers began taking their finished demos to Rick Hall. It was this growing involvement with writing and studio work that led Spooner to drop out of college, following one of those soul-searching epiphanies common to so many of this group. "I was workin' ten hours a day, making records and getting

paid . . . sometimes," he commented dryly. "I just stopped myself in my tracks one day and said, 'What do you want to do?' 'I want to write songs and make music and play piano on sessions.' 'What're you doing now?' 'Writing songs, making music, and . . .' They didn't have a good class in any of them," he chuckled.

Upon dropping out, he played Wurlitzer electric and upright piano for a short time with another one of the fraternity-circuit bands, this one belonging to Hollis Dixon, a band that also featured the aspiring songwriter Donnie Fritts on drums. "That was sorta interesting in hindsight, in a lotta ways," said Spooner. The band played fraternity houses "all over the Southeast. Tommy Couch [who later ran Malaco Records out of Jackson, Mississippi] used to book us." He remembered the frat circuit for the audience reactions: "It was undetectable how they liked it because most of 'em were half-drunk. They could've put robots out there and they wouldn't have noticed—'Give the robot a beer.'" As for the music: "You'd take a break and go outside during intermission, you could hear Slim Harpo playing in a frat house next door. Screamin' Jay Hawkins might be playing down the street." In addition to the frat circuit, he continued to play on demos at Rick Hall's studio; when David Briggs left the piano chair vacant in 1964, Spooner took his place, becoming an indispensable part of Hall's organization. He came to prominence with the record-buying public through his intense, mournful organ line on Percy Sledge's "When a Man Loves a Woman," which had been a hit in the spring of 1966; it was this record that fully brought Muscle Shoals to Jerry Wexler's attention.

Oldham would also, like Tommy Cogbill, become one of the most universally respected musicians ever, not only for his playing but for his temperament. "Spooner is one of the sweetest, non-assuming guys you will ever meet," said Mike Leech admiringly. "I've never heard him raise his voice or get angry." His absent-mindedness would also become legendary; Spooner himself laughed about the time he bought a house on a lake near the Shoals, then, when trying to show the house to a woman friend, couldn't find it. She married someone else anyway, he shrugged. "Spooner can't be categorized," said Mike Leech. "He has an unusual personality that's hard to describe. He likes to maintain a low profile and if he entered a room with a group of people, you might not even notice he came in. . . Has an unusual sense of humor, but funny. He always seemed a little sad."

His infinite patience came in handy on the second Pickett session in October 1966, a session that must at times have seemed like the recording date from hell. Part of the master tape was eaten by the machines, just after they had finished what Spooner recalled as an almost letter-perfect take of one song. "The song that I remember positively that it happened on was 'Mustang Sally,'" he said. "It was sort of scary. Everybody was recording live out there and you get a sense of sort of, 'Well, that was a good one, I think.' The hub on the tape recorder was too loose and threw bits of tape, thirty pieces, which Tom Dowd spliced together and played back to us, after a thirty-minute break. Wilson was cussing. Wilson had little faith—O ye of little faith." "The song was up and somehow the reel just came apart, tape was flyin' all over the control room," remembered the Muscle Shoals guitarist Jimmy Johnson, awestruck at Dowd's ability to reconstruct the recording flawlessly from "little slivers" of tape.

Junior Lowe's difficulties working with the songs on the previous session had been ill received by Atlantic, and, observed Jimmy, "it appeared that because of that struggle, they wanted another bass player. When we started the next session, Junior wasn't booked." Spooner Oldham remembered Junior being there at first and having been jettisoned shortly after the sessions began (and his name appears on the album credits, giving credence to the recollection). "They had a breakdown with the bass player," said Don Crews, who wasn't there but who got the full story later, "and Chips said, 'You got the best bass player in the country, right here.'" Crews believed that Wexler asked Chips if he knew a bassist, and Chips recommended Tommy Cogbill. "I talked Jerry Wexler into letting Tommy play the bass," Chips

recalled, although he thought the occasion had happened several months later, at the first Aretha session.

Junior Lowe never played on another Wexler-supervised recording, though he remained part of Rick Hall's studio band for the next several years. His having been replaced so abruptly struck fear into the hearts of the remaining session men—as, perhaps, it was meant to do. Everyone quailed at the possible consequences of not taking direction from Wexler. Jimmy Johnson recalled an occasion during this session when he was playing and the fear kicked in. "One time Wexler came up to me and said [Jimmy slipped into a Yiddish-accented voice, affectionately imitating Wexler], "*Jimmy*—can you give me a little gingy-gingy-gangy-gongy?" I thought, Oh, Jesus, I've had it. I'm sittin' here, Lord, what does that mean? I thought he was speaking another language. I'm sayin', Jesus, help me through it. I had another lick in mind that I knew would work, and I played it. He said [slipping into his Wexler voice again] '*Jimmy*, I like it.' I said, whoa, thank you, Jesus. I stayed afraid of him for many years."

From this session on, the bass became Tommy Cogbill's instrument, which came as a surprise to everyone who was aware of his passion for jazz guitar. "I didn't really know he was playing bass till somebody mentioned it to me," commented Stan Kesler, who knew Tommy as well as anyone. Though Tommy, with characteristic reserve, didn't say anything that anyone recalled about the changeover, it was apparent that with his permanent assignment as bass player, he had found his musical voice. His playing on the tracks from the Pickett session has a resolute authority; it is the work of a responsible man who was handed a job to do. To the Shoals musicians, who had never heard him as a bassist, the results were astounding. "I was like a big question mark," said Jimmy Johnson of his first impression, "but I knew Chips didn't work with anyone who wasn't superior." That superiority was evident from the first note played. "It was like hearing Aretha play piano for the first time," Jimmy said of Cogbill's musicality. "He was so gifted, and he locked in with the drummer like I'd never heard before. It was sorta like your mouth'd be wide open. It was like, 'What has God wrought?'"

Jimmy was even more amazed to discover that Cogbill displayed no outward sign of time-keeping. "From where I was sitting, I couldn't see his fingers, I could just see his chest and the bass around his neck. . . . He would just sit still and look down at the bass. Then you'd hear the playback and say, 'Lord, is he doing all that? Whoa!'" What Tommy did was, in effect, play bass as if it were a jazz guitar, with driving, complicated runs and riffs that bore some resemblance to what James Jamerson was doing at Motown, but with completely different results. "He had such a deep knowledge, too, just having a real deep jazz background is immeasurable. . . . I imagine he just transferred what he knew [on jazz guitar] to the bass. His lines to me were like horn lines. He had a sound in those fingers most bass players wish for," Jimmy said admiringly. "His sound in his fingers was shocking. He'd play a line that when I'd play it, it would sound mushy. When he played, it had a spunk and a bounce, a bite. You could hear those strings, the full tone of a wound string. I learned to love his bass better than anything. There was something so special about him as a bass player. I could hear the personality when he played."

Tommy's sensitivity to other musicians was noticed by Roger Hawkins, who was just beginning to make the transition from playing clubs and frat parties to session work. "I'll always say that Tommy taught me time, straight time," said Roger respectfully. "Tommy taught me a lot about not rushing. When he played he would rock back and forth, to show me"— something he did not normally do. "He was really the first Southern bass player I'd played with who played syncopated. He could be playing his thing and still supply the bass line. I felt like he was the foundation and I'd better pay attention to him. He could get to the bottom of [musical] problems quickly."

Personality was the other half of this equation, for it was Tommy's personality as much as his playing that made him so revered by his colleagues. It is probable that no one else could have taken Junior Lowe's chair on orders from Atlantic without being resented, but Tommy was so highly regarded that he managed to soothe any potentially ruffled feathers. "We just all took to Tommy real well," Spooner Oldham said warmly of Cogbill's new role. "Junior was a friend, and Tommy was a friend, so I would have noticed if there were any weird vibes going on." "I hated it for Junior, but his chops were not up, and Tommy's was never down," said Jimmy Johnson. And everyone remembered that Tommy's presence made work go smoothly. "Tommy projected a seriousness, which was good," said Roger Hawkins. "He was one of those kinda guys that never gave anybody a hard time," remarked Jimmy Johnson. "I was not of his caliber, but he never made me feel that way. Most people with that kind of talent will stick it on you." "Tommy would reserve his comments, his suggestions, to the level of people he was working with," said Roger Hawkins. Nor does it seem that Tommy ever lost his love for the guitar. Stan Kesler remembered Tommy coming in to the Phillips studio and getting a guitar and just sitting there, playing for himself; Chips Moman said that he and Tommy would play together at American as a way of unwinding: "When we didn't have anything to do we'd just sit over there and play guitars." Tommy later captured some of this improvised relaxation on tape; for now, it was enough to have a good friend to work with, and with whom to exchange ideas and share the discoveries of recording.

The set of songs Tommy and Chips had to work on were stronger than those on the first session. "It was just a joy to me, the material has stood the test of time," said Spooner Oldham. "Mustang Sally" was admittedly a novelty, but a good one, and the car theme would have appealed to automobile enthusiasts such as Cogbill, Dan Penn, and Chips. Wilson Pickett had brought in the song, and Spooner remembered, "Seems like the demo singer was Sir Mack Rice—seems like the demo didn't have a keyboard. In my mind, I was thinking, how can I play a part in this? I just dreamed that I was driving a Harley-Davidson motorcycle through the studio," resulting in the honking, revved-up effect on the organ. "What is it, the mother of invention?" Spooner laughed. (Roger Hawkins amusedly recalled journalists asking him many years later, "What were you thinking when you played on this song?" His reply was prosaic: "I was thinking that I'd better play well or they're going to replace me.")

Jesse Hill's "Oo Poo Pah Doo," the New Orleans classic, expressed succinctly what Chips was hoping to do, and what Dan intended to accomplish as well; "I won't stop trying till I create disturbance in your mind." A song that had recently been a hit for the Rolling Stones featured a thoughtful guitar solo by Chips and served notice about the musicians' faith in the groundbreaking work they were doing: "Time Is on My Side." Pickett's friend Bobby Womack contributed "Nothing You Can Do," a song about the search for contentment; "I'm gonna get a fine apartment / Where the water runs hot and cold / And a good little girl / To satisfy my soul." And "Three Time Loser" expressed impatience with hard times and suffering, wondering when the payoff for all of that pain would occur.

But the strongest writing came from Dan Penn and Spooner Oldham, who brought some of their finest songs to the session. "Uptight Good Woman" is a masterwork, a shopping list of qualities for the perfect wife. "It just sounded like somebody in search of true love," Spooner said modestly of the narrator's stated wish for a "downright, uptight, good woman— or no woman at all" (a line partially supplied by Jimmy Johnson, who got a third of the writer's royalties as a result, though his name was not on the credits). "'Uptight' was slang at that time, I never knew what it meant for real, I just made up my own meaning," chuckled Spooner. Female listeners were heartened at the declaration that a woman "don't have to have a pretty face" as long as she possessed other virtues, including two not often cited on such lists— "courage and pride"—but obviously important qualities to the writers; and breathed there a woman with soul so dead that, after hearing this song, she was not inspired to mold herself to this pattern?

Though Dan avoided autobiography in his songs, it is difficult to believe that his wife Linda did not at least partially inspire this prototype. "Linda's the best thing that ever happened to Dan," said Mike Leech. "She's a good lady." Perhaps, too, the fact that Dan was fortunate in his choice of a wife contributed to the considerable respect for women (rare in Southern music), and compassionate understanding of a woman's point of view, that emerges in so many of his songs. "She Ain't Gonna Do Right" is the flip side of the coin, the description of a gold-digging bitch who would never change. And then there is the standard that Dan Penn wrote with Rick Hall and that was originally demoed by Otis Redding: "You Left the Water Running." This is Dan at the top of his game; a simple phrase with layers of wordplay going on underneath, a flowing melody line, and a vague hint of vengeance at the end of the song, when Pickett promises the woman who left that "you will get your water bill to pay."

Chips was more impressed than ever with Dan's writing, and all the more determined to hire him away. His task was made easier because Dan, like Reggie Young, had been frustrated in his present position for quite some time. "Dan was getting anxious to produce records by 1966," Spooner Oldham recalled. Rick Hall had other ideas. He wasn't letting go of the control he had fought hard all his life to obtain. "He didn't particularly want nobody fooling around in his area," Dan remarked. "I think the producing opportunity may have been more available," Spooner continued.

Then too, by this time Muscle Shoals was doing so well that not even Dan Penn was indispensable anymore. Young producers, eager and hungry to make hit records, were booking time at Fame Studios in hopes of obtaining some of that North Alabama magic. It was obvious that Rick Hall was going to do just fine—and did anyone ever doubt it? After all, his business had survived the departure of his first group of players. "He went through three or four rhythm sections, I'd have been scared to death," Dan Penn said admiringly.

Typical of the young producers now booking time at Fame was an intelligent, aggressive impresario from Florida, Don Schroeder. He came from Pensacola, Larry Butler's hometown, and had already spent a short time in Nashville pitching songs he had written. But he had not liked the intrigue and the politics of Music City and had returned to Pensacola, where he had become a successful disc jockey. "Papa Ding Dong Daddy Schroeder," laughed Larry Butler, referring to the on-air nickname Don had given himself to seem older. "He and I were DJs on competing stations." They were on the air at the same time of day, and "We would play the same records at the same time, just to screw people's minds." Papa Don went from there to becoming a successful business-man. "I'll never forget—I had a restaurant, a beautiful, wonderful restaurant in Pensacola," he said, his voice soft with nostalgia. "One day a guy walks in the back, says, 'I'm Oscar Toney Jr., and this is Mighty Sam.'" Sam McClain and Oscar Toney would both sing in another one of Don's properties, a club he owned in town. Papa Don was impressed by Sam's husky voice; he wanted to record him, quickly, and the near-est place he knew of was Muscle Shoals. "Rick Hall and I got to be friends when I was a DJ in Nashville," he recalled. "Rick and I met through Shelby Singleton."

He took Mighty Sam to Fame Studios and there he cut the standard "Sweet Dreams," fea-turing Spooner Oldham's piano and a blaring, Stax-style horn arrangement. "Great record. Wonderful record," said Don with enthusiasm. He and Dan Penn mixed the track and Don took several copies to his friends in Nashville. One of his contacts there, the publisher Buzz Cason, told Papa Don, "Wow, what a record. You need to get this to Larry Uttal at Bell Re-cords. He's in town right now." "I think he was at the Spence Manor," Papa Don remembered. Papa Don played him the track and, he contin-ued, "He said, 'What'll you take? What'll you give?' I said, eight hundred dollars and eight percent."

They agreed, on the basis of a handshake deal. Papa Don continued; "I had a call when I got home, from Jerry Wexler. Man, I had al-ways wanted to work with him. He said, 'Man, I want this record.' He said, 'I'll give you eight hundred dollars and ten percent.' I said 'Oh, Lord.'" Wexler reasoned that since Uttal and

Don had not signed anything, the agreement was not binding. Don protested to the execu-tive that he did not want to go back on his promise. "He said, 'Papa Don, this isn't the way business is done.'" Papa Don said he would talk to Uttal and see if there was any way he could get out of his agreement; when he did so, Papa Don remembered with amusement, "Man, Larry Uttal hit the roof. *Hit . . . the . . . roof.*" Papa Don decided to go ahead and honor his verbal agreement with Uttal; when he apprised Wexler of this, "Wexler said, 'Papa Don, are you crazy? Are you nuts? Do you realize this is *Atlantic Records?*' I said, 'I may be a fool, but my mama raised me, all by herself, and she told me your word is all you have.'" Mighty Sam's record made the charts, though Papa Don felt that its impact was blunted by the simultane-ous release of the Tommy McClain version, and that he had come out for worse in the deal. "I had to pay the act," he said. "None of us made any money. It was a joke. Everybody took advantage of everybody back then." Nonethe-less, he had made the charts, and Mighty Sam trusted him enough to bring another act to his attention.

"Mighty Sam brought me James and Bob-by," he said, referring to the cousins James Pu-rify and Robert Lee Dickey, who had worked together in one of Oscar Toney's groups, the Dothan Sextet. "We went to Tom's Tavern," said Don, where he heard James sing and Bobby play guitar. He liked what they were doing, and booked time in Muscle Shoals, where, he said, "I was gonna cut a couple of sides on James and a couple on Bobby."

Once he got there, in October 1966, "Seems to me he didn't have any songs for 'em," Spoon-er Oldham mused. "It sounds too strange to be true." Papa Don was led to an upstairs of-fice where the demo tapes were filed, given a Wollensak tape recorder, and left alone to lis-ten to whatever he thought would be good. About half an hour later, he came downstairs with one of Dan's and Spooner's songs, one that Dan Penn had started from a simple guitar riff. "I'd got a little twelve-string Stella guitar; if you went to a certain string, you could go ding-ding-ding. Spooner started playing this thing, blong-blong-blong, against it." An idea had coalesced around the melody and countermelody and "I'm Your Puppet" was born. Papa Don was already familiar with the song. "Dan told me that 'I'm Your Puppet' had been cut thirteen times before I ever cut it," he said. "Dan had cut a version on MGM, it wasn't a hit. Dan had sent me a copy when I was a DJ." Papa Don suggested the song for Bobby Lee Dickey; the cousins were not singing together yet. Bobby Lee was having trouble with it, and Don recounted, "James said, 'Here is what he means.' When I heard them sing together, I was just amazed." "Once they got into it, it was like honey and butter and biscuits," Spooner Oldham said with pleasure.

The ethereal harmonies were stunning. "James Purify was one of the greatest gifted singers alive," said Papa Don. He intended to sell them as a "brother" duo from then on, and he billed them under James's name because "I thought Purify was the funkiest name I'd ever heard in my life!" Dan Penn engineered the track; Spooner Oldham played chimes. Other backup musicians were from Papa Don's club in Pensacola, including his keyboard protégé, the Alabama native Barry Beckett. James Purify narrates the story of a man so besotted by love that he will do anything the woman asks, underscored by Bobby Lee's soft harmonic echoes and some mellow trombones (courtesy of David Hood) near the fadeout. Some of the horn players came in straight from their ordinary jobs, Spooner Oldham recalled: "We had to wait till the midnight shift was over at the factory to get the horn players in to do their part." Spooner stopped by the Howard Johnson's, where Schroeder was staying, the next morning, and he noticed Don's excitement. "He said something that pretty much floored me—I'm pretty slow to get excited when somebody tries to sell me on a song, I usually wait for the check—but Papa Don said, 'You wanna hear a hit?'" Schroeder turned on the Wollensak tape recorder and played the finished recording, and the keyboard player was amazed. Other participants had apparently not been; "James Purify never liked it," said Papa Don of the singer's reaction.

Papa Don's excitement about the recording did not dwindle after he left the Shoals. He called Larry Uttal in New York and asked for fifteen hundred dollars for his new master, unheard. Wexler was calling, too, and the tape was in a bidding war that ended when Uttal agreed to Don's terms and told him the fifteen hundred was on the way. "He had a damn good ear," Schroeder said of the label head. Uttal signed the Purifys to Bell and Schroeder to a production deal. The investment paid off; "Puppet" went to Number Six in the nation (although, Papa Don emphasized, that was on the *Billboard* chart; *Cash Box*, the other industry publication, ranked it at Number Three, he said proudly). Most important of all, it gave Dan Penn and Spooner Oldham national prominence as writers and became a standard, with even Papa Don cutting a second version of the song in 1974, released in early 1975. By century's end, it had become a favorite among Latino listeners. "It's still going on out there in a current way," said Spooner Oldham. "It's just one of those things that won't go away, and you're grateful."

Soon enough Papa Don was back in Muscle Shoals, recording the Purifys' first album. Chips Moman was there, playing guitar. Don remembered, "Chips pulled me aside when we were smoking a cigarette, he said, 'I've found a band and I want you to be the first producer to use them.'" Chips said it did not happen that way, that it was Papa Don who approached him. Don wanted to bring up Mighty Sam and the Purifys.

From there it was on to the DJ Convention in Nashville, where Papa Don met up again with Moman and Penn. "We had a hotel room rented—I did, I think," said Schroeder. "I think it was the Capitol Inn, not sure. I can remember the hotel room like it was yesterday." The visitors indulged him in a poker game one night. "Chips never lost at gambling," remembered Papa Don. "If he played poker, he won. If he pitched pennies, he won. I used to think he was the luckiest person I'd ever met. I found out it wasn't luck," he chuckled. "I'd lost a little money, Quinton Claunch had lost a little money. I'd lost three or four hundred dollars, but that was a lot of money for those days. Dan confessed a little later that he and Chips were cheating. Dan took a break and said, 'Listen, I can't do this to Papa Don anymore.' I won my money back." Dan also admitted to Peter Guralnick, many years after the fact, that he and Chips had been cheating on that occasion.

In the middle of the game, inspiration hit. Chips and Dan needed a room to complete work on a song they had been thinking about for a long time. Quinton Claunch had the hotel room across the hall. "They just came in and kinda took over our room, talking and playing poker at the same time," Quinton remembered, though he did not recall Papa Don being there. "They'd play poker, take a break, and go write a little of the song. They was having a little toddy along, you might as well throw that in. . . . I told Chips, 'I don't mind if you stay here but you've got to give the song when it's done to James Carr.'" The two agreed, and emerged from Quinton's room roughly thirty minutes later with arguably the greatest cheating song ever written: "Dark End of the Street."

So many years later, Quinton Claunch still sounded awed at the creativity he had witnessed in that room. Although he said of the song, "At that point in time you didn't think how big it was going to be," he was still amazed at the piece itself. "Oh Lord, it just knocked me out." To him, it was a song that had everything: "It had all the ingredients, a good melody line, it just flowed, and the lyric—*um*!" "Oh, man—*flipped*," said Papa Don as he recalled hearing it that night. "It's fun to be there at the beginning of a new song." "Best I can remember, I had that little thing starting it off, 'at the dark end,'" Chips Moman recalled of the collaboration with Dan. "We wrote good together, and we always both contributed a lot to the song."

Dan Penn remained forever dismissive of his accomplishment. "Songwriters get things in their minds, like 'I'd really like to write a great cheatin' song.' Every songwriter worth his salt at that time was tryin' to write a cheatin' song." He preferred an earlier effort along that line, the Jimmy Hughes number "Steal Away," from the early days of the Shoals. "'Steal Away' is kind of the father of 'Dark End,'" he said.

"'I've got to see you' is an immediacy—*now*!" Though "Steal Away" is a good song and a great record, there is nothing quite like the pain and paranoia, the impending awfulness of the fate implied should the lovers be found out, and the utter fatalism that nothing can be done, of "Dark End." "We're not pleading; we're just statin' facts," said Dan. "People love a little doom and gloom," he added with relish. "I'd say fifty-percent of the time most people are depressed about something, unless you're 21 years old." That sentence would become the philosophy behind the deep melancholy of the American Studios sound; the belief that adult life is full of pain and in the pain lies wisdom, and in the wisdom lies salvation. It would color almost every recording made by the musicians from then on.

The writers collaborated on the production of "Dark End" in the fall of 1966. It was Dan Penn's first project following his departure from Muscle Shoals to throw in his lot with Chips. The parting from Fame Studios was amicable. "I have nothing negative to say about Rick Hall," Dan avowed loyally. "He was like the Wall of Gibraltar." Contrary to most impressions, Dan Penn did not come to American Studios as a partner; Chips never shared ownership of the operation with anyone except Don Crews during those years. "I liked Dan, he wasn't no problem," Don Crews said of the newcomer. "We gave he and Spooner five hundred dollars each to come up and sign with Press [Chips's publishing company, which he had started in the Rosenberg days and in which Don Crews still owned a half interest] as a writer." Spooner Oldham did not leave right away, wanting to remain in Muscle Shoals until Rick Hall could find a replacement keyboard man. He did not officially join up until the following spring. After trying out Carla Thomas's brother Marvell for awhile in that spot, Rick hired Barry Beckett to occupy the piano bench.

Chips kept his promise to give the song to James Carr, with whom Chips had recorded since the beginning of James's signing with Goldwax in 1964. In an interview with British writer Barney Hoskyns for the liner notes to a CD reissue of James's work, Chips praised the "emotional power" of James's voice; this force interested him the most as he put James through his paces singing the contemporary soul equivalents of old-time "sorrow songs." This pairing, orchestrated of course by Quinton Claunch, had already yielded two masterworks of autobiography, one for the recording engineer and one for the singer. "Pouring Water on a Drowning Man" had been brought to Quinton after the first road trip. "Chips found that song for me, he was down in Alabama, he said 'This'll be good for James Carr.' . . . somebody brought that song in, he said, 'I know somebody you can pitch that to.'" The composers were the Shoals writers Drew Baker and Danny McCormick, who wrote for QuinIvy's publishing company. Ostensibly the complaint of a lover, the song also holds obvious references to the way Chips was treated during his ordeal with Stax and Rosenberg ("You push me when I'm falling and you kick me when I'm down / You stab me in the back every time I turn around"). It is a portrait of Chips as victim, which became a recurring theme in the music. And few recordings are as riveting as Carr's "You Got My Mind Messed Up" from April 1966; written by the future country singer O. B. McClinton, who was then a student at Rust College, it is a piece that descends from stateliness at the beginning to the splintering disintegration evoked by the stammering vocal and Reggie Young's guitar, with many of the same runs created on the Don Bryant ballad "Clear Days and Stormy Nights" used for a different effect here, as it literally sounds like a mind shattering beneath tormenting thoughts. It is a horrifying record, one in which we witness the descent into hell, watch the deterioration happening before our very eyes. It would be the epitaph for the singer's life and career.

"James Carr was a very soulful person," remembered Reggie Young. "Brook Benton and Joe Simon were his main influences," said Quinton Claunch. "You couldn't get him to admit he was as talented. His timing was impeccable. He just had that little technique." From the beginning, James liked the song, and Quinton was eager to have it recorded, due to what Mike Leech remembered as the Goldwax

emphasis on quality. "'Dark End' and other songs [that appeared on the label] apparently were cut because of their strength as great songs," he noted. "I guess [Quinton] was smart enough to recognize that fact and record them for the hit possibility and lose publishing, unlike what is done today—record crap so the labels can retain publishing."

Chips Moman was, yet again, having trouble with the machines at his place. "We started out over at American, the equipment was out so we called Royal," Quinton Claunch remembered. "It was kind of at the beginning of the session. I know James was late getting there, all the musicians were set and ready to go. Finally his ride brought him." Chips recalled the vocal coaching James received. "Dan sang it for James, and he really showed him how to sing it," he said. "The rest of the time I remember him sleeping on the couch"—a remark followed by an amused cackle. The lineup of musicians was Chips's basic group—Reggie Young, Tommy Cogbill, Bobby Emmons. "I did not play on 'Dark End of the Street,'" said Gene Chrisman. "I can't for the life of me remember anything about the 'Dark End of the Street' session except I played my chopped Hammond on the track going down, and over-dubbed acoustic piano fills from the second verse out," Emmons said of his contribution. "I recall being at the James Carr session when 'Dark End of the Street' was recorded at Hi studio," said Spooner Oldham. "I was thinking maybe I played organ and Bobby Emmons played piano . . . on the other hand, maybe I was just watching and listening. I probably wasn't firmly planted there at the time."

Reggie Young's trembling guitar, Carr's depressed, smoky vocal, along and the sparse production make this a record to remember. The spareness of the sound probably owes more to Dan's input than to Chips's, and Carr sings with a direct eloquence worthy of his heroes and none of the improvisations common to his style or even the signature stammer "I–I love you!" that he used on the fadeout of many of his records. "Chips engineered the session," noted Quinton Claunch, "and Dan was sitting in the control room behind him.

Chips was a great engineer for that kinda stuff. Man, he just smiled all over himself when that big voice came out of the speakers singing his song. He said, 'We got one. We got the right man to sing this one.' I think it was about two or three takes," Quinton added, before they got a version that was satisfactory. Dan Penn told Barney Hoskyns, "When James sang it, he did it exactly how Chips and I heard it in our minds."

The song went on to become a country, soul, and rock standard, with versions done in all these styles. "No telling how many times that song's been recorded, maybe a hundred times," said Quinton Claunch admiringly. That probably would not even include the number of artists recording at American who cut the song (the most notable versions being Joe Tex's, from the spring of 1968, featuring Tommy Cogbill's relentless bass line, and Bill Medley's brooding, tortured version produced by Chips in the summer of 1970). "It was almost funny because in the middle of an album we— Chips or Dan—would run out of good songs, and here would come 'Dark End' again," remembered Mike Leech with amusement. Although (just to name one of the outside covers as an example) Linda Ronstadt's version on her 1974 *Heart Like a Wheel* is melodic, romantic, desperate-sounding, and inspired, "everybody seems to like James's version best," said Quinton Claunch. "Perfect song for James Carr," said Papa Don Schroeder. "It's still the best record on that song ever." That opinion holds for one of the writers as well; Dan Penn's oft-quoted comment from his live CD is, "People ask me what my favorite version is, as if there were any version other than James Carr's." Chips Moman said of the covers he had heard, "I think everybody's made a good record," though he added that his favorite version was the unreleased demo done by Dan, with himself singing a harmony line.

Mike Leech, who would either play on or arrange the song in the other versions recorded by the group over the years, offered a trained musician's analysis of why the composition was successful. "The progression, if it were in the key of C, is, C, B minor, A minor," he explained.

"What makes that unusual is, that is a popular progression, and the normal or usual way a writer would more than likely play it is, C, G/B (C chord with a B bass), A minor . . . You can hear a very slight difference, being only one note different. That one nuance made it a black song, almost like it was a mistake, dark." "I guarantee, it's made them a bunch of money," said Quinton Claunch. Even more than the money it obviously brought him, Chips Moman took a great deal of artistic satisfaction in the results. "A lot of people seem to like the song, and that makes me very happy," he said. "Dan and I are proud of it." "All the same, I'm *tired* of that song," protested Dan Penn.

Interestingly, Chips and the group saw none of the mental and emotional problems that plagued James Carr later and derailed his career; they recalled him as quiet, talented, absolutely cooperative, and very hard-working. He was, in fact, so understated a personality that Emmons and Spooner, masters of understatement themselves, scarcely remembered anything about him at all. "He was his own worst enemy," Quinton Claunch said of his troubled protégé. "One of the nicest guys you ever met, never spoke ill of anybody. He was just a good person. If he did hear somebody talking about someone he'd say 'You shouldn't be talking that way.' It's been written that he was the world's greatest soul singer, and I wouldn't argue with them one minute." Reggie Young remembered a few problems with the session, but none of them were the fault of James. "We cut 'Dark End,' it was a Top Ten R&B and we had never gotten paid for it. They wrote us a fifteen-dollar check. Emmons was so mad he didn't cash his check—he still has it." Par for the course, in that town: "The Memphis musicians were really abused," Reggie sighed matter-of-factly. "You never got paid for your creativity." Emmons confirmed the story. "I can always find a way to waste money, so I still have my 'Dark End ' check. It is just another way of answering the question, 'Is fifteen cool with you, man?' It was back when you could get several big sacks of groceries for that."

They had done a recording for the ages, and other monumental moves seemed to be in the making. Don Crews recalled that the company made several important business decisions to close out the year. The first and most pressing decision was the realization that something had to be done to upgrade the studio equipment. "It was a necessary-type trip," Don Crews explained. Jerry Wexler claimed to Peter Guralnick that he loaned Chips five thousand dollars to purchase new recording machinery, a claim refuted by Chips, who did not recall Wexler having had a great financial interest in American. Don Crews revealed the real source of the money. "There was an electrical shop across the street from the Phillips studio," he recalled, a shop owned by a woman named Cora Wooten and run by her brother. "Leon Sides was kind of an electrician and he was going to do the upgrading for us. She got all our equipment for us. We went to the bank and she co-signed a loan for $15,000. Seems like it started in the fall of '66, seems like he couldn't get around to finishing it." Chips remembered that he had also contributed some of the money for the renovation out of his own recording and publishing royalties. Eventually arrangements were made with the man who had built Rick Hall's studio, Paul Kelly (not the songwriter the group recorded later), to come up and install the same kind of sound equipment as was already operational in Muscle Shoals, a project that did not see completion until early 1967. "Basically, our studio was similar to Rick's," Don Crews observed about the finished product.

The second decision with important consequences was the administrative deal made for Press Music with Buddy Killen's Tree Publishing in Nashville, Chips's longtime boosters and supporters. "Chips and I signed an agreement with Tree, they got half for forty-five thousand dollars, which we well needed at the time. I first thought that they would be placing our material in Nashville. It was just before Christmas of that year," Don Crews remembered. "Each one of us got a check for $25,000." It was an unmistakable triumph for a man whom everyone in Memphis had written off as finished four years previously.

Chips and Crews had wanted a conduit to Nashville. "That was one of the programs we thought would happen, but it didn't," Don remarked. They did gain access to Tree's catalogue; Roger Miller's songs had made Tree one of the most profitable and adventurous publishers in town, though Don Crews recalled that it still took a few years for the company to come into its own: "Tree wasn't all that big then." But it was a door that swung only one way. The executives at the company did not return the favor. Songs from Press, with their uniquely down-home slant, were never as widely circulated around Nashville as they could have and should have been. "The only tune I'm aware of that Tree even published in Nashville was 'Do Right Woman,'" said Crews, referring to the famous song Chips and Dan wrote the following year, which became one of Barbara Mandrell's early hits and inspired the name of her road band, the Do-Rights. The executives at Tree seemed to have seen their role as strictly administrative. "Tree basically did all the bookwork," Don explained. "We would just send those people a copy of the song that we were doing and they would get it copyrighted." Even the material sent to them by Tree was, in the beginning, not work from A-list writers. "They had a buncha ol' junk that nobody would fool with," Don said dismissively. "I talked to Jack Stapp [head of the company] one time and said, 'What are you doing with those ol' crappy songs?' and he said, 'Volume, son, volume.'"

John Hurley and Ronnie Wilkins were the best-known of the full-time Tree staff writers (Roger Miller, though his songs were published by Tree, was a writer-performer). They had a demo studio in the basement of Tree, and Don Crews recalled that he and Chips sold them the old radio board from American to use at their studio. "They bought it for fifteen hundred and they were supposed to give us another thousand, but all we saw was the fifteen hundred," he noted with precision. "They gave us a cashier's check and part of that went to pay on the new board. Chips put it [the old board ] in my truck and we drove it to Nashville." The writers also contributed a new song for the Gentrys, who were cutting a single.

Jimmy Johnson remembered coming up from Muscle Shoals to play rhythm guitar for a Gentrys session; this may have been the session that closed out the year with a landmark song from Hurley and Wilkins, though forgotten now on grounds of political incorrectness. "A Woman of the World" is a good old boy's look at a girl, perhaps a classmate and certainly a peer, who seems to have been bitten by the nascent feminist bug. From her sentiments and philosophy, as quoted by the song's narrator in the dramatically paced, slowly building music of the verses, she emerges as the kind of driven personality that in later years would become a politician or TV anchorwoman. It is, in fact, impossible to hear the song today without calling to mind biographies of the late newswoman Jessica Savitch. But Savitch was an ambitious Northerner; the song describes the price the girl will pay in the Southern scheme of things, from being seen as a showoff to being completely cut out of the mating herd: "All of your phony sophistication won't do nothin' but ruin your reputation / And I couldn't hold my head high and walk with you again." The chorus, speeded up and featuring a romping bass line by Cogbill, offers the solution to the girl's discontent: "She needs a big strong man to help her understand / And a great big heart to make her toe the line / And she'll be fine." It is a sentiment that probably would have appealed to Chips, who was nothing if not traditional; though his female acts were never the Stepford wives of Billy Sherrill's imaginings, they presented typically feminine personas on record—from Sandy Posey's monologues and Merrilee Rush's wistful flower child to Carla Thomas's unabashed romanticism and Petula Clark's consoling thoughtfulness.

"Two Sides to Every Story," the B-side of the record and a composition by Gentrys lead singer Larry Raspberry, features Cogbill's bass lines changing patterns several times through the motif of the song, a man defending himself against the derogatory remarks of his former lover: "If she was acting all the times we were together she should win some kind of an award / And the story I could tell about the real her would be a loss she could never afford." This was a sophisticated pair of songs from a band that most people remember as the epitome of

garage rock; the subject matter served notice that Chips and company would not be purveying teenage fodder. It is probably no coincidence that the teen-oriented Gentrys saw their national popularity diminish at about this time, although they remained a benchmark for aspiring groups in Memphis through 1967, when even their local influence began to fade.

Bobby Emmons remembered the latter half of 1966 as basically a blur. He recalled a few sessions having been done at that time over at Sun, presumably as a result of Chips's chronic trouble with his recording machinery. "I do remember feeling honored when Tommy Cogbill asked me to play on an album he was starting on himself there," he remarked. Tommy's solo album, featuring his inimitable jazz guitar, got as far as two cuts having been finished; increasing demands on the group's schedule regrettably caused the project to be shelved. Other sessions done at the Sun studios within the following six months, Emmons said, included one that "I try not to remember, for some producer who was said to know how to 'really cool a groove.' Yeah, he cooled it right out. And one when Dan Penn had a pack of Harley-Davidsons in the studio for sound effects. You might say, session-wise, that those three were the low and the high with The End in the middle."

Lows and highs, lows and highs—a good description of the way things were going to be for the group from then on.

||||||||||||||||||||||||||||||||||||||||||||||||||||||||||||||

### CHAPTER 5

# Grabbing the Pie and Biting the Apple

Politically and socially, early 1967 was not an experimental time. The country was still basically in support of the Vietnam war; mainstream public opinion did not tip in the opposite direction until the Tet offensive one year later. Integration in the Deep South was progressing slowly due to white resistance, while up north the issue was evolving from a matter of basic civil rights to Congressman Adam Clayton Powell's cynical but accurate term, "the gut issue of who gets the money." In San Francisco, college students, local musicians, and disaffected dreamers had begun to cobble together an alternative society, but the hippie movement and what it represented had not yet gone national.

But the music business is a world unto itself, and in this world it was a time for experiments. In Los Angeles and San Francisco, the Byrds, the Doors, the Jefferson Airplane, and Big Brother, and the songwriters John Phillips, Brian Wilson, and James Hendricks (Mama Cass's husband, who wrote many of the middle-period Johnny Rivers hits) were creating a new kind of rock music. In Detroit, Norman Whitfield and Holland-Dozier-Holland guided the output at Motown, placing strings, synthesizers, oscillators, and anything else unusual they could find over the jazz-based Motown backbeat. In London, the Beatles were still on the cutting edge; their albums *Rubber Soul* and *Revolver* had people from every field of music listening, and rumor had it that they were working on an album that would surpass anything they had previously done.

In Nashville, Chet Atkins updated the smoothness of his trademark production sound to embrace a style he called "folk-country," signing up Bobby Bare and Waylon Jennings to deliver music with realistic lyrics and slightly more aggressive playing. Within a year, folk troubadours flocked to Nashville in droves. Even easy-listening music was not just for elevators anymore. Herb Alpert and the Brazilian-born Sergio Mendes in Los Angeles, Burt Bacharach in New York, and Paul Mauriat and Raymond Lefevre in Paris were all rewriting the rules for music's softer sounds, with a livelier beat and more intricate instrumentation; soon Ray Conniff and Percy Faith would have to follow, filling their albums with songs like "Sounds of Silence," material that was in some cases ill-suited to their style.

And in the middle of all this experimentation was Memphis. With its sparse production and gritty-voiced singers, Stax seemed to be leading the way, but the success of the records on which Chips Moman and Tommy Cogbill played had alerted the powers that be, particularly at Atlantic, to the fact that Memphis was worth further investigation. With Chips in the process of upgrading his studio, it looked as if he was going to have a permanent base of operations when the work was done—a fact that also did not escape the notice of the people in New York.

Goldwax and Hi still paid most of the bills, and with American under renovation many of the sessions done for Quinton Claunch at this time were recorded at Phillips with the engineering usually handled by Stan Kesler. A photo taken around this time, which shows Stan seated at a control board with Quinton leaning on the console beaming benignly and Doc Russell listening intently, is credited by many to have been taken at American, but was identified by both Quinton Claunch and Stan Kesler as having been taken at the console in the Phillips studio. James Carr did a few sessions there and so did Spencer Wiggins, Goldwax's other long-running success at that time. "My first memory/impression of Stan was that he was very patient, methodical, unassuming . . . He listened to ideas carefully, considered a lot of them. Was always open to suggestions, a good sense of humor," remembered Mike Leech, fondly looking back at those sessions.

The Goldwax recordings done at Phillips were augmented by players from Stan Kesler's stable of musicians, among them Bobby Wood. Reggie Young, Bobby Emmons, Tommy Cogbill, and Mike Leech could not help but notice how well Bobby's sound fit in with what they were doing. They noted his gift for finding the perfect opener to a song—"I was the Intro King," Bobby Wood chuckled about his specialty—and for his lighthearted playing that carried the rhythm along as effortlessly as a summer breeze. They were aware of his longstanding association with Gene Chrisman, and the way he could adapt to any groove the drummer established. Chips Moman noticed, too; he repeated his offer to make Bobby a permanent part of his group. Wood was unsure. Stan Kesler was putting a band together to play on demos, a group that included Charlie Freeman on lead guitar, Tommy McClure on bass, Sammy Creason on drums, and Donna Rhodes on rhythm guitar and backing vocals; Bobby wanted to see what would happen with this venture. Stan was so committed to the idea that he was thinking about leaving his job at Phillips and setting up shop with the band in an independent studio. It seemed worth a try.

And the others still had commitments to Hi. Reggie Young remembered that sessions for this label comprised the bulk of his work in early 1967. He did recordings for the Hi stalwarts Jumpin' Gene Simmons, Charles Hines, and Don Bryant, and several sessions for Charlie Rich. Two of these sessions yielded recordings that are now considered to be among the Silver Fox's masterpieces; "I'll Shed No Tears" and "Who Will the Next Fool Be." He had recorded the latter in 1960 at Sun, but it is the Hi version of this song that everyone remembers.

And no wonder. To those who know of Charlie Rich only as the mellow-voiced balladeer of the seventies, these records are startling; here he is revealed as a blues singer in the Ray Charles mold. "I'll Shed No Tears" in particular has a Ray Charles feel to it, accented by

the background vocalists who respond to the lead in the manner of the Raelets. Rich wrote both of these songs, so it is not surprising that he sounds at ease; he seems more comfortable with the driving sound of these musicians than he did placed in Billy Sherrill's somewhat more stilted settings. The songs also display the group's instinctive knowledge of R&B; Reggie Young makes brief, economical statements on guitar, Bobby Emmons plays powerful sustaining organ lines, and Tommy Cogbill's bass notes slip and slide through the songs, adding not only propulsion but forward momentum, an outreach that Tommy carried over into his work as a producer.

At one point during the bridge of "I'll Shed No Tears," everything falls away to reveal Charlie's jazzy piano, Reggie's bluesy guitar, and Tommy's bass, only to have the music build back up again in the final verse—perhaps the earliest notable example of what would become one of the group's trademarks, the use of dynamics, accentuating the built-in rise and fall of a song's structure to completely enthrall the listener. It is a technique originating in classical music, and one that the core group could have been led to in several ways: Tommy Cogbill with his expertise in jazz (which borrowed heavily from its supposed opponent), Bobby Emmons and Reggie Young through their knowledge of call-and-response song structure. It may come as a surprise to many people that Chips Moman was and would remain a devoted listener of classical music, and though it s not as surprising to learn that the American string arrangers Mike Leech and the later arrival Glen Spreen each had some formal training, they utilized the dynamic and harmonic lessons they had learned in ways that would surprise—and possibly please—Johann Sebastian Bach. Mike Leech offered a look at the breadth of his classical influences: "I especially love the big symphonies, Stravinsky, some of Tchaikovsky, most of Brahms, Mahler . . . Not Mozart . . . not Beethoven. Mozart and Beethoven do not have the substance I enjoy, the depth . . . Schubert (or Schumann—always get them confused) has a concerto that is one of my all-time favorites. *Concerto #1* I think. It's from his stuff that I get my 'build' sense of making records."

"We usually always treated a ballad like building a house," said Bobby Wood regarding dynamics. "Start from the ground floor and go up from there. First verse would be fairly empty. . . . Uptempo songs sometimes were either the same or full band from the get-go; just according to whatever we thought fit the groove best."

The dynamic pace and hard-edged backing on the Charlie Rich material drew attention in music circles, even though the records did not sell. Buddy Killen at Tree requested Tommy's—and Chips's—presence in Nashville for preliminary work on a Joe Tex album he was starting in late January; they could not go and sent Reggie Young instead. They were already booked in Muscle Shoals for a session that sounded as if it was going to be monumental. Jerry Wexler seemed to have big plans for this artist he had just signed.

A woman with a curious first name: Aretha.

"Boy, you better get your damn shoes on. You're getting someone who can really sing," Dan Penn told Rick Hall when Rick had notified him about the session. Dan may have been one of the few people to recognize this at the time. Even among the musicians, he recalled, "nobody really knew who she was 'cept me. I'd been listening to these people on WLAC for years and I didn't forget nothin'."

Aretha Franklin was unforgettable; ever since she had been signed to Columbia by John Hammond in 1960, she had been the best-kept secret in the music business. She had released singles and albums regularly on Columbia, but the company had cast her as a sedate vocalist in the manner of Nancy Wilson. "She had jazz albums out," explained Jimmy Johnson on the subject of why he and his cohorts had never heard of her, "and we were not listening to the jazz file." Though several singles, most notably 1964's "Soulville" ("Show me the way to get to Soulville, y'all"), showed hints of the Aretha the world would come to know, and would have made an impression on R&B fans,

she had never had either material or record sales commensurate with her talent. When she and Columbia parted by mutual consent in late 1966, Jerry Wexler and Atlantic were waiting in the wings. Wexler knew that Aretha—who was born in Memphis, let us remember—had never really been recorded properly. And he knew how to fix that problem.

This session was deemed so important that a new board was installed at Fame. "The first stereo session [in the Shoals] was Aretha," said Jimmy Johnson. "Dig this, Rick buys a three-track. Never understood why, but he had got a three-track . . . it was in stereo. Tommy Dowd helped put that in. Dowd came down early and rewired some of the console" for the new Scully machine. The lineup of musicians was sound and proven—all of the Fame group minus Junior Lowe and including Spooner Oldham; and of course, Chips Moman and Tommy Cogbill.

Dan Penn came down too, bringing with him the demo of a new song he and Chips had written in Memphis. "I went over to Chips's house for dinner one evening, just us and our wives," Dan said. After dinner they got a guitar and began developing an idea that Dan had had in mind for awhile. "Anybody who's been writin' for a long time, they write and they write and they write some more and then they carry stuff around with them they don't even know," Dan observed. He had been playing around with the phrase "do right"—"It's kinda like a thing people were sayin' at that time," he noted. "Me and Spooner had done a couple of do-right songs in Alabama, 'She Ain't Gonna Do Right,' 'Uptight Good Woman' . . . Uptight, do-right, good-night." The result: "Do Right Woman," another instant classic composed by Dan and Chips, ready for Aretha's hearing except for some work on the bridge of the song. They specifically hoped she would use it on this session, because from the moment the song was written they believed in it. "There wasn't no doubt about that one, that was a smash," Dan said authoritatively.

"I think I'd heard of her, but I didn't have any preconceived notions," said Spooner Oldham of his thoughts before the session. "They know they've got a black woman, which is good," said

Dan Penn of his colleagues. "I don't think too many people knew what was fixin' to hit 'em." He told Peter Guralnick that he had raved to the others, "Man, this woman gonna knock you out." With his love of R&B and appreciation of its great singers, he prided himself on being ahead of the curve. "I was with-it, I was pretty street, I was street-smart about music." It would not take long for him to see his instincts about Aretha confirmed.

"I think the real key thing they did was to let her play piano," Jimmy Johnson observed. Spooner Oldham was under the impression that this had not been Atlantic's original intention, although Jerry Wexler eternally maintained that it was. "I walked in the studio and there's a microphone in the corner and Junior Lowe said, 'She's probably gonna sing back there.'" If that had been the original idea, the plan was altered when Aretha sat down at the grand piano to run through a meandering composition by the Detroit writer Ronnie Shannon. "Everybody was like flies buzzing around the queen," Dan Penn described the reaction to Peter Guralnick.

"I suggested to Jerry that I play electric piano," said Spooner, who otherwise declined to talk about the decision to feature Aretha, much discussed by historians as pivotal. "It doesn't make a hill of beans, I don't want credit and I don't want to sound like a idiot"—something about which Spooner need never have worried in any case. Dan Penn gave him credit for figuring out the tilting, lurching groove that made the other musicians fall in on the Ronnie Shannon song, "I Ain't Never Loved a Man (The Way I Love You)."

"You're no good / Heartbreaker / You're a liar / And you're a cheat," Aretha complained in the opening verse, and people in the music industry sat up and took notice, for it was well-known in New York and Detroit that her marriage to the Detroit businessman Ted White was stormy. But even if listeners knew nothing about Aretha's private life, they were compelled by her intense, aggravated vocal; this was a real woman talking about real emotions. And changing emotions, at that—she moves from the anger in the verses to a testifying gospel shout on the exclamation "I ain't never!" and when she follows with a lingering sigh as she murmurs "loved a man . . . the way that I . . . love you," the reason is apparent why she stays. All the while, Tommy Cogbill's bass thuds ominously behind her and Roger Hawkins's drums are sharp as a cracking whip. If that were all, it would be a superb recording. But near the end of the song, there is more.

"I can't sleep at night," Aretha confesses, to which Chips Moman responds with an angry guitar line. "And I can't eat a bite," she adds, and a furious, stinging guitar passage blazes as Chips answers her. Those lead lines save the final verse from sinking into complete self-pity, and seem to be giving Aretha the heart to fight back as Chips duels with her impassioned shouting on the fadeout—a prime example of how a good musician can bring additional flavor to an already masterful lyric reading. Aretha had finally found the road to Soulville. And she would not lose her way again.

It was a classic recording, but after the playback it was time to put that behind them and press on to the next song. Jimmy Johnson explained the mental process, standard operating procedure for any session player: "We had to clear our brain. You had to almost brainwash what you did on the last song." Dan and Chips brought out their composition and Aretha wanted to try it. "Jerry suggested that it needed a bridge," remembered Spooner Oldham. "The chords were there, but there weren't no words," Dan recalled. "We worked on the bridge in the cloakroom, under the stairs at Fame. Every once in awhile, Wex'd peep in and say, 'Have you got it? Have you got it?' Some of those lines, he came up with, 'But you can't prove that by me.' Aretha stuck her head in and I ran it down to her, her and Wex are both standing in the door."

When the bridge was finished and all was ready, "she wouldn't commit to the song," said Dan. "We just had a skeleton crew working on it," added Spooner Oldham, who contributed organ to a backing track that was little more than what would have been used on a demo, with Chips Moman playing a slight lead and Tommy Cogbill providing what Dan called "a little ticky tick of bass." Dan sang a guide vocal on the track, because "Aretha didn't have an opportunity to learn that song," said Spooner. "You talk about something pitiful," Dan said dismissively. "At the end of the day I thought, 'Boy, that's some wasted effort.'"

Though they weren't in evidence on the just-completed track, Rick Hall had gotten a horn section for the sessions—unfortunately, not the one he wanted, due to a scheduling conflict. He had to settle for a section assembled at the last minute by the former Starlighter, Charles Chalmers. "Charlie put together the group and brought in this guy," said Jimmy Johnson, referring to the trumpet player, Kenneth Laxton. "This new musician was somebody nobody even knew." Even David Hood, the trombonist who had worked with Chalmers for many previous sessions, had not met Laxton before. "He was always—he had a kind of arrogance about him," Chips Moman remembered of Laxton. "I tried to keep my distance."

The trumpeter got out of line with Aretha somehow, making either an overly flirtatious or a bigoted comment—exactly which, even many of those present were not sure. "It was not anything outrageous that I remember, and I was sitting nearby," observed David Hood. "He had been drinking and that did the problem," said Jimmy Johnson. "It was not a thing in the world but liquor, you know?" Chips Moman added sorrowfully. "He was just tryin' to be cool and drink out of the same bottle" as Ted White, who had brought out some booze in impromptu celebration. At the time it happened, many of the musicians, including Chips, didn't even catch it, due to the way the baffles were placed around them in the studio, which made it difficult for them to see one another. Nor did they notice any displeasure from Aretha's husband: "Ted was wearing what I call Alabama State Trooper sunglasses, they had mirrored lenses," Jimmy Johnson said. "You can't see what they're lookin' at, he was lookin' at everybody and never said a word. He thought Laxton was doing his number, he never said anything, he didn't make a move." White did complain to Rick Hall, and Rick fired Laxton, allowing work to continue on "Do Right" until something

had been captured on tape, at which time the session ended for the day. The musicians departed, the local ones to their respective houses and Tommy, Dan, and Chips to their rooms at the four-story Downtowner in Florence, where Wexler and Ted White were also staying. As far as the players were concerned, that was it.

What came next has been partially outlined, although David Hood commented, "Nobody really knew what happened on that session for sure." As Southerners so often do in cases of misunderstanding, Rick Hall attempted to explain himself, and what had happened with the horn section, to Ted, with the usual consequences of such explanations. "He was trying to mediate," said Jimmy Johnson. "He meant well, but it went bad. I'm sure it got to the point where they were just wall to wall." The resulting dispute led Ted and Aretha to (separately) leave Muscle Shoals, canceling the week's worth of scheduled sessions. Jerry Wexler would dine out on the events of that evening for years, telling both a British film crew making a documentary about Aretha and a *Rolling Stone* reporter about "footsteps running up and down the hall, loud noises, I thought I heard shots going off." Wexler had always wanted to be a journalist, and in keeping with contemporary journalistic techniques he left much open to interpretation, planting a question in the minds of the listeners and readers about exactly who it was that ran up and down those hallways, making noises and firing those shots. One thing can be determined—whatever he heard, it came from none of the supporting cast.

The musicians knew nothing of the trouble between Rick Hall and Ted White, and Wexler's subsequent disagreement with Rick. They weren't even aware that the next day's session had been canceled. "In the beginning," said Jimmy Johnson, "they didn't tell us nothin'. They may have told Tommy and Chips." The visitors found out what had happened "the next day, like everybody else," Chips Moman said with a chuckle. "I think Wexler told me, and I told Tommy. We just drove back to Memphis." The session's cancellation left Tommy characteristically unruffled. "I remember him sayin' a little somethin' about it but it didn't really bother him too much," Chips observed. He himself thought the whole situation had been mismanaged: "You don't really supposed to let sessions get out of control. They ain't but two people to blame for it, the musician and Jerry. When you see somethin' happenin' that might destroy the session, you need to replace that musician. It wasn't like he was one of the regular guys." He and Tommy both felt that something of this kind would not have happened if they had had the authority to deal with it: "Sessions at that time, [there] were not a lot of, and you had to protect your session."

Jimmy Johnson learned that the session was off when he reported to the studio. "Rick's car was outside, but the doors were locked. We waited outside for an hour. Rick came to the door, he looked very tired—he'd been up all night. Said 'There won't be any session' and he basically shut the door in our face. We were like, 'What?'" At least Spooner Oldham was allowed into the building when he heard of the cancellation. "The only time I knew there was any difficulty was when I came in at ten o'clock as scheduled, and no one was there, except the cleanup person. About ten minutes later I said, 'Where is everybody?' and they told me the session was cancelled." "I went to the studio next day to work and there was a sign on the door," David Hood said about how he got the word. None of them knew why, and not until Peter Guralnick pieced together the story of the dispute in *Sweet Soul Music* did they find out. "We were like pawns, y' know? Musicians have always been pawns," said Jimmy disgustedly.

Aretha never went back to Muscle Shoals, preferring from then on to record in New York. Jerry Wexler grew reluctant to work with Rick Hall, and he began casting around for another studio as his Southern base of operations. And Kenneth Laxton wound up in Nashville, first engineering at Columbia Studios for the former Muscle Shoals musician Billy Sherrill, and later at a smaller studio in Nashville's Berry Hill district; from there he vanished into history.

When he returned to New York, Wexler overdubbed Aretha's piano and some background singers on "Do Right Woman," and

guided Aretha through her dignified vocal. Then he had the two songs from Muscle Shoals pressed and released. The 45 was practically an overnight hit, and a two-sided one at that, offering further vindication of Wexler's decision to sign Aretha. An album was inevitable. Though Aretha didn't want to go South again, she had no objections to working with those same musicians; Ted White told Charlie Gillett that he paid out of his own pocket for them to be there. Most of the Muscle Shoals musicians were asked to participate; even Charles Chalmers from the horn section came up, but not the trombonist David Hood, and of course not Laxton. Getting Chips and Tommy there was easy; Wexler simply called and asked them to fly up, and Dan went, too. Getting the musicians away from Muscle Shoals took some subterfuge on Wexler's part. "He called us under the auspices of doing a King Curtis album," said Jimmy Johnson. "That's how he got us there. Rick Hall would have fought it."

Work began the week of Valentine's Day, 1967. "Jimmy and I went up to Memphis and flew up with Tommy and Chips," said Roger Hawkins. "Small-town guys go to New York City, don't dare take a taxi into town 'cause it's gonna cost too much money, you'll ride a bus into town. Then we were in midtown, we'd been dumped off and there was this sea of people. We go through the turnstiles, this guy hands me a ticket. This bunch is moving a little more and I start hearing this guy holler '23! 23!' They give you tickets to get to the taxis, my ticket said '23.'"

"They put us up at the West 57th Street Holiday Inn," Jimmy Johnson said. "We walked to the studio, it was only three blocks. There was so much to see within one block that my mind couldn't manage it all. I was gettin' migraine headaches going to the session." Spooner Oldham also remembered the three-block walk but said he enjoyed it: "That was fun because you could take in the sights and sounds of the city." Dan Penn would have been outwardly indifferent, slouching as usual, yet inwardly registering everything he saw, and if he was impressed, said Chips, "he wouldn't have let on." In this situation, as in all of the others Jimmy

Johnson had the opportunity to observe, Cogbill was handling himself exceptionally well. "Tommy kinda took New York in stride," he said. "He was cool. Yeah! But he was older than us, he was more mature. We kinda looked up to him and Chips. They were kinda showin' us the ropes." "Tommy's so laid back, he didn't pay much attention," was Chips Moman's recollection. Chips had been in New York before, but he was doing his best to be as calm as his friends. Spooner Oldham had also been in New York before, on his senior class trip in high school.

Not only were these country boys dealing with the big city, they were awed by the recording technology in the Atlantic studios on Broadway. "It really did impress me," noted Chips thoughtfully. "To me, just the fact of being in a New York studio was big time." "Atlantic had the second eight-track in the world," Jimmy Johnson said, referring to the console. "They had to get something that would deal with a wider tape." "I knew it had some history," Spooner Oldham said about the studio. "I knew, in my own mind, Ray Charles had been there. I was anxious to hear what we sounded like with that kind of equipment." Spooner's interest led him to examine the entire layout of the Atlantic building. "On my breaks I would go introduce myself to the guys in the offices. I'd get in on what they were doing. I met the accountants, the guy who did the liner notes for the label. I wanted to see what they were doing, I was just curious." "Here's what I really thought: Not as nice as I expected," Roger Hawkins observed. "That one—it didn't have all the beautiful sound baffles, it didn't have mood lighting, everything was white and spare. I really wasn't thinking much about the eight-track machine sitting in the corner. It was real clinical."

During this week in New York the musicians met the third member of Atlantic's production team, the producer/arranger Arif Mardin, whom everyone immediately liked. "Arif [was] kind of an articulate kind of guy . . . a pleasure," Chips Moman said respectfully. "Arif Mardin was congenial and appreciative of our talents," added Spooner Oldham. "I enjoyed being around him. He played vibes on a song or two, and did the string arrangements on 'Natural Woman.' . . . He was always willing to be helpful if needed." As admirable as the players found Arif to be, and as awesome as the recording equipment was to musicians used to two- and three-track machines, even more formidable was the caliber of artist with whom they had initially been asked to work.

Curtis Ousley had been around. He had been a standby on Atlantic since the 1950s, when his yakety sax had enlivened the Coasters' recordings. He had played on Waylon Jennings's first single, which had been produced by Buddy Holly; his big band, the Kingpins, was well known in New York and featured the top R&B musicians in the city. "A ray of light," said Roger Hawkins of Curtis. "A guy comes in—everything's cool, everything's fine. He just walked in, you could feel talent. He came with open arms. It was never a feeling like 'let's see if these white boys can play.' I don't like to bring up the racial issue, but there was a racial issue, back then. [But] he was one of us, we were one of him." It was hardly a stretch for Curtis to do an album of hits made famous by Stax, but the work of the Southern musicians took his playing to new heights—and gave him wider popularity. *King Curtis Plays the Great Memphis Hits* was the first step in his becoming a national figure.

The album opens with Eddie Floyd's "Knock on Wood," taken at a relaxed-sounding pace set by Tommy Cogbill. The Otis Redding ballad "Good to Me," which immediately follows, finds Spooner Oldham playing sustaining organ lines behind a melancholy repeating blues figure by Chips, and the horn phrases introducing the song and featured at several intervals throughout add to the somberness of the piece. Tommy is finally unleashed on the third cut, "Hold On, I'm Comin'," and he and Roger Hawkins offer an illustration of the way drums and bass can function as a single rhythmic entity. "Tommy Dowd, I think he coined it—in his mind, the drum was the engine," said Roger Hawkins. "Tommy kinda dictated the beat, Tommy would almost make Roger play with him," observed Shoals bassist David Hood, who cited Tommy as an important influence on his own style. Chips Moman is audible around and over the voices of the Sweet Inspirations in the chorus and Curtis sounds exhilarated by the talented instrumentalists inspiring him. The blues figure first heard on "Good to Me" is used again on "When Something's Wrong with My Baby," as is Spooner's mournful organ line, but in the middle of the first verse, Chips takes the song to a different place by way of his string-bending guitar riff, giving it an almost psychedelic effect (and this was fully three or four months before that style became well known).

But Chips would never become a truly successful studio musician. The very things that made his work both distinctive and underrated—the raucous bite, the jagged edges, the scattershot phrasing—would work against him on sessions. One suspects he knew it, too; he surrounded himself with some of the best guitarists anywhere—Reggie Young, Tommy Cogbill, Bobby Womack, Johnny Christopher—and although he occasionally played rhythm on some of the records he produced he could seldom be induced to take a lead. "From time to time in Memphis he would try and play a lick on a recording but to my knowledge the things he would try never made it to the final mix," Mike Leech commented regretfully.

The funky side of Spooner Oldham's playing is heard to advantage on "Last Night" and especially "Green Onions," and as he recreates Booker T's organ lead on the latter song, Tommy Cogbill is with him every step of the way. When Tommy and Roger Hawkins quicken the pace on "Fa-Fa-Fa-Fa-Fa" and "Midnight Hour," neither sacrifices the easygoing mood they established earlier. But for those who love Tommy's playing, "Jump Back" is the treat. Roger Hawkins seizes the listener's attention with one of his trademark intros, then Tommy enters with the rest of the band. From the beginning, he is stunning; no matter how many times one listens, one is likely to gasp in awe. One wonders, not only here but on so many of the recordings Tommy made, why the other musicians did not simply stop playing and stare in open-mouthed wonder at the flurry of notes booming from his amp and 1959 Fender Precision bass. ("We actually did stand around with our mouths open," said Mike Leech about

the Memphis players' reactions. "He amazed us all. Never got used to it.")

Musical quotes turn up in several places on the album; there's the horn section's reference to "I'll Fly Away" in the intro to "Fa-Fa-Fa-Fa-Fa" (ironic in light of the eventual fate of the song's composer, Otis Redding), and then there is Tommy's adaptation of "Baby Elephant Walk" in the middle of "Walking the Dog." It's easy to imagine Chips looking over and grinning as he realized what his running buddy was up to. "Tommy was a part of Chips's thing, the two of them together was hard to beat," said Jimmy Johnson. "They both had the magic, but when they worked together, there were no egos. It was wonderful to be around them." Chips is very much a part of the proceedings on "Walking the Dog." His stinging lead work is among his best ever; he is as incisive as he was on "I Never Loved a Man," proving again what a good rhythm and blues player he was. "Chips had that R&B thing, even though he had a country background, he really had a black feel," noted Jimmy. In the end, the King Curtis album is as much a vehicle for the backing players as it is for Curtis himself—and the saxophonist played as if he did not mind a bit.

The King Curtis album was done in about three days, Jimmy Johnson remembered. "And then one day before we were leaving, Wexler said, 'You know, we've been getting a lot of airplay on the single [for Aretha]. Why don't you stay over and play on the album?'" This, of course, the Muscle Shoals players were more than happy to do, and "we worked about two or three more days" on her epochal first album for Atlantic (for all practical purposes her real debut album). Two classic albums recorded in roughly three days each—effortless work for these pros.

"Aretha and Jerry found material, and she brought her own, too," Jimmy said about the song selection. "It all had to be centered around Wexler." "They probably found every song in the world they possibly could," added Spooner Oldham. "We basically sat down and played them from scratch. We'd just record 'em out of the dirt." "It really should have been a Wexler-Aretha production, she was big into it," said

Jimmy Johnson (a point she conceded in her memoirs, saying that she should have pressed for a production credit). It was even she who decided the final vocal takes. Work on the sessions began early and ran late. "We'd start around ten or eleven or something, eat supper at six and finish at midnight," Jimmy remembered. "Food was brought in. By the time we got back to the hotel, we were wiped!"

"I think she was comfortable with us," Spooner Oldham reflected, and that ease is evident from the first track on the album. The biting introductory guitar line by Chips Moman leads the way into the album and an instant classic to start things off: Otis Redding's "Respect."

"'Respect' was, again, street and carrying things with you; respect was very big in the black community," explained Dan Penn, the observer on these sessions. The thinly disguised plea for racial equality in the line "All I'm asking is for a little respect" is obvious, and Jerry Wexler thought Aretha carried it one step further, that her version was also a demand for "sexual attention of the highest order." But respect has a class connotation also, and the presence of working-class white Southern boys on the record raises the stakes; it is also a plea by them not to be depicted as rednecks or hillbillies, what would now be called trailer trash—to have their personal and economic grievances seen as legitimate. And for one of the participants, "respect" had a specific meaning: Chips had not won the acceptance of the music-business executives he scorned, nor would he; this would never stop him from wanting their regard even as he disdained it and refused to do the back-scratching he would have had to do to win it. The backing parts, done by Aretha and her sisters, Spooner Oldham was sure had been worked out at home. "I don't know how you could not smile when you hear it on the record," he chuckled about the "sockittome, sockittome" line. He was not the only one listening and loving it; Tom Dowd always claimed that he fell off his chair at the perfection of the line.

"Drown in My Own Tears," the Ray Charles hit written by Henry Glover, probably would have appealed to Chips, since its title referred to suffering. He is not featured, however; after Aretha's strong gospel piano, the dominant instrument is Tommy Cogbill's bass, providing a deliberate anchor for the impassioned testimony of Aretha and the Sweet Inspirations. His reliable timekeeping gives Aretha the freedom to take off and wail, here and elsewhere. But he can also follow her lead, rising with her magnificently on the song's soaring bridge.

In a way, "Soul Serenade" is a continuation of the King Curtis session; it was Curtis's composition, his theme song, and the biggest hit he had had to date. He was also in the horn section for Aretha (he is featured on "Respect"). Aretha handles the Luther Dixon lyrics with sensitivity and grace, punctuated by some shimmering guitar asides by Chips Moman as Tommy Cogbill eases the rhythm along at a tempo not only comfortable for her, but for them, due to reasons that will soon become apparent.

"Don't Let Me Lose This Dream," with its bossa nova feel, is unlike anything else on the album or anything that Chips would record at his own place. It is one of Aretha's compositions, and though the lyrics refer to a love affair, in this context they can possibly refer to her recent signing with Atlantic; "If I lose this dream, I don't know what I'm gonna do . . . Everything all of my life I wanted to do / Has made me blue / Help me hold on to this dream, 'cause sometimes dreams often come true/And they'll come true, they'll come true, for me and you." Roger Hawkins is particularly effective here; he comes to the fore as a skilled, versatile drummer.

"Baby, Baby, Baby," written by Aretha and her sister Carolyn, who sings backup, is reminiscent of Carolyn's later "Ain't No Way," particularly in the chorus and in its intimate mood accented by Spooner and by Chips's mellow, melodic asides. Tommy Cogbill is the gray eminence behind the pyrotechnics, keeping time flawlessly, as he also does on the next cut, Aretha's slow blues tune that seemed to be written for and about her husband, "Dr. Feelgood."

Sam Cooke's classic "Good Times" is

nothing less than Chips's and Tommy's equivalent of Bob Wills's "Stay All Night, Stay a Little Longer." In their hands it is less a party song than it is an expression of the way Chips would run sessions at his studio: "We gonna stay here till we soothe our souls, if it takes all night long." It is his show all the way, as he answers Aretha's good-humored vocal with twangy, jubilant guitar lines.

"Do Right Woman" is next, read with all of Aretha's quiet power, and the chorus emphasizes a rejection of the double standard: "A woman's only human, and this you should understand / She's not just a plaything, she's flesh and blood, just like a man." The idea that men and women were equal in needs and desires, and that a man should not expect behavior in his wife or lover he would not live up to himself, was a progressive view for women in 1967 (or even now). The difficulties recording the basic track in Muscle Shoals caused Dan to second-guess himself on the song, and to refer to it as "the dog of the century"; he changed his mind once he heard the New York overdubs, rightly knowing that he and Chips had written a standard. "I think Jerry was happy that we had cut that song," commented Chips.

As astounding as all of the songs on this album have been, the stunners are about to come. They begin with Aretha's composition about helpless love, "Save Me," in which she invokes solidarity with others in her position: "Those who love always give the most / We're crying together from coast to coast." It was the era of Marvel Comics and televised superheroes, and she calls on both Batman and the Green Hornet to help her. Chips's lead locks perfectly with Jimmy Johnson's rhythm guitar and Tommy Cogbill's bass, and between verses the horn section quotes from their earlier version of "Walkin' the Dog." Even in those pre-sampling days, quotes often inspired other quotes; later in the year, working with Etta James, Rick Hall based "Tell Mama" on this recording, and he asked Jimmy Johnson and Roger Hawkins to repeat the rhythm pattern used here.

Aretha honored her friend Sam Cooke by recording his masterwork and his epitaph, "A Change Is Gonna Come." Like Dylan's "Blowin' in the Wind," its inspiration, this song can be applied to every stride toward freedom from the civil rights movement to the fall of the Berlin Wall. Chips Moman's guitar shimmers as gracefully as ripples on a pond, and Spooner Oldham's organ lines whirl through the final bars of the recording. "Tell you 'bout the changes," Aretha sings on the fadeout, and after listening to the album you feel she has done just that; you have heard the story of one woman's life, and the physical, emotional, and even societal changes she has been through.

The musicians knew more than ever that they were in the presence of a formidable talent. "When she got it, everybody in the building was happy," said Jimmy Johnson. "We would start cuttin', she would sing in the 'phones. Soon as she got the track, she would get up from the piano and stand in this one place right in front of the control room." Here she recorded the master vocal, to the delight of the players. "We looked like a caterpillar, all the musicians gettin' up," Jimmy continued. "We would march in to the control room and listen and watch her freeze us to death, which she never failed to do. She'd chill-bump us. Tommy loved it, we all did." The musicians found her to be kind but somewhat impersonal. "She loved Tommy Cogbill, oh yeah, absolutely," said Jimmy, adding, "She was very introverted. She was not a hugger. Most people in the music business, if they don't see you for awhile, they gon' hug you. She was not a forward person. . . . In some ways I understand why she wasn't too warm to us. I think early on she wasn't too sure of us. She was just real introverted. We didn't take it as an insult or nothin'."

"I remember thinking I had a connection with her," Roger Hawkins said softly. "She came from the Pentecostal music and I did, too. She was shy, but she wasn't shy when she started playing and singing." Ted White, Jimmy Johnson remembered, "was the other way around. He gave us gifts for playing on her sessions, he gave us a watch engraved. He was always very nice and intelligent-acting. . . . Even up there [in New York] he was nice to us." "I think we found that level with her," Spooner Oldham said of Aretha. "Things were going so quickly, so fervently with the music, we had very little down time to sit and chat. She'd ask me for a Kool cigarette if she ran out."

It was during one of the breaks in the session that Chips Moman finalized the plans to bring Spooner Oldham to American, pulling out five one-hundred-dollar bills to seal the deal. From then until May, Spooner had one foot out the door at Fame, exempting him from the reaction when Rick Hall found out that his pickers were up in New York recording Aretha. Claiming that they were needed for sessions at home, an enraged Rick contacted Atlantic. "We lacked one day, Rick called up and demanded that Roger and I return," Jimmy Johnson said. "That's how Roger and I missed the session Gene got."

Wexler still had several songs to record and needed a drummer. Tommy Cogbill called Gene Chrisman and Gene was up on the plane from Memphis that same day, despite his emphatic dislike of crowds, cities, and especially New York, which he had seen for the first time in his Jerry Lee Lewis days. Gene can be heard on "Soul Serenade," "Dr. Feelgood," and on a Carole King composition recorded then but not released until late 1967. "To this day, Roger and I go *rrrrgh* that we never got to play on that song, 'Natural Woman,'" said Jimmy Johnson. "I got politically taken off a thing that was out of our control." Roger Hawkins was more accepting of the circumstances. "I didn't come home brokenhearted, I didn't come home excited," he remembered matter-of-factly, and he praised his substitute. "I don't think Gene ever got his due PR," he accurately observed, speculating that it must have been because of Gene's unassuming manner. For example, he said, when he and Jimmy Johnson went up for the Gentrys session, "We really didn't know anybody. My eyes just went right past Gene, my brain didn't even consider that he was the drummer."

Jimmy Johnson also regarded Gene highly. "I'll tell you the thing that blew me away about Gene Chrisman. Gene was writing his own chart by the numbers, I'm going, 'Now

that's unusual.' . . . As a drummer, Gene is an amazing timekeeper. He had knowledge of music that most drummers don't have—notes, chords, everything." "I just picked that up by listening," Gene Chrisman said about that accomplishment. "There are still some chords that I don't hear, but they have to be pretty rough for me not to hear them. I just find out from the players that do know them, put them where they should be on my chart, and say, 'Let 'er go, boys.'

"That was a good session, I enjoyed it," he added cheerfully. He, Spooner Oldham, and Tommy Cogbill are all understated on "Natural Woman," letting Aretha's voice and piano primarily carry the song. Chips Moman is not audible at all. "There's no guitar on it," offered Jimmy Johnson. "He probably said, 'I don't hear no guitar on this one.'" Actually, the reason there was no guitar is that Chips was not there; he flew back to Memphis the preceding evening following the session, the same day that Roger and Jimmy left. (Dan Penn had gone midway through the week's work.)

Had Chips been there, the results might have been the same; he would not impose his playing on an artist if it did not fit the song. This willingness to underplay or even to drop out of the lineup for the sake of an effective recording was a characteristic shared by all the American musicians. "I have never tried to be or care about overplaying, I think it needs to be the song and the singer and let the guitars do whatever they want to do," Gene Chrisman remarked. "If you've got a ballad, I'll lay out on that sucker in a minute! You don't need a lot of flashy stuff. . . . I won't play on nothin' if it don't need drums. I will play around the artist." That philosophy added much to the confiding mood of "Natural Woman."

"What a great record, see, we would have been on it," said Jimmy Johnson. "I have never forgiven Rick Hall for that. We got home and there was no work. It was pure political bullshit." He had longed for Spooner's chance to work on a song of such quality: "I remember he came back and told us, we went 'Wow.' It blew our minds." Jimmy was never again completely happy at Fame, and successive journeys to New York for Aretha sessions only fueled his discontent. He began to weigh other options. Chips Moman had his own studio, after all, and that way he could call the shots to a great degree. Maybe that would be the answer for Jimmy.

Gene Chrisman, Tommy Cogbill, and Spooner Oldham finished the session in one afternoon. "We did those songs and then went out to eat, then we went home," Gene remembered. "It was a bumpy ride back"—so bumpy that Gene couldn't concentrate on the book he was reading for being jostled. No matter. Sessions were booked back at American. Papa Don Schroeder was wanting to come in, and Sandy Posey needed a follow-up record.

It was time to go home. Memphis was waiting.

### CHAPTER 6

# Soul Dance Number Three: Keeping It Real

The importance of the New York Aretha session to Chips Moman and his friends cannot be overstated. It had proven that their backup work could be as effective behind a new star as it was with an established performer; it solidified their professional relationship with Atlantic; and, most significantly of all to Chips—who still kept the perspective of the Georgia farm boy he would at heart remain—he had proven that he and Tommy Cogbill and Dan Penn could take on New York and meet its challenges on their terms. In addition, the success of "Do Right Woman" showed that his and Dan's collaboration on "Dark End" was no fluke. From now on they would be boutique writers, with their names on a composition automatically garnering respect and prestige, even if the ensuing cut did not sell many records.

Having hits was what the record business was all about, however, and the hitmaking potential of American Studios was beginning to be discussed in the industry. Because of the Wilson Pickett and Aretha sessions, R&B was considered the fledgling studio's specialty; it was this side of the group's music that had begun to interest both established producers like Fred Foster—who began sending some of the acts signed under the SS7 division of Monument to Memphis under the supervision of the famous WLAC disc jockey John Richbourg, better known as "John R"—and some of the newer producers upon the scene. Chief among the newcomers was Papa Don Schroeder.

Papa Don, of course, was making his reputation primarily with R&B acts. To Chips Moman, Papa Don seemed at home with the relaxed, easy Sam Cooke groove that Chips himself liked. To some of Chips's musicians, Papa Don seemed to be, like many producers, a frustrated artist, and in fact Don had once recorded some singles for Vee-Jay under his given name of Gerald Schroeder. Hayward Bishop, who later worked extensively with Papa Don in Nashville, felt that Don's radio background—a background he shared with Hayward—made him sensitive to good material and kept him in touch with what the public wanted. "There was one thing Papa Don could do," Hayward reflected. "He could hear a good singer and a good performance." Others simply remembered him as an amusing character, in a business not lacking in those. "He was always kind of a loud, flamboyant-type guy. Good guy," said Stan Kesler, who later engineered a few of Papa Don's collaborations with Tommy Cogbill in Nashville. "He'd get so excited when he was cuttin'," remembered Jimmy Johnson, who had witnessed Papa Don's enthusiastic reactions in Muscle Shoals. "A high-powered guy," observed Dan Penn. "Very enthusiastic guy," said Roger Hawkins. "He was always groovin' with whatever was goin' on," noted the reticent and reserved Bobby Emmons about Papa Don's behavior. Papa Don admitted that music, particularly R&B, was his passion, and throughout his intermittent career as a producer he would remain as thrilled as any fan about the sound of a great recording.

Others recalled his cultivated charm—"a salesman," both Bobby Wood and Hayward Bishop would say of him. "He seemed like he borderlined not being honest with you, but still he was a lot of fun to be around because of his enthusiasm," observed Jimmy Johnson from his vantage point in the Shoals. "He was a smart guy, but you could see through it." Others remembered the radio patter he would never quite shake. "I met Don at Fame Studio, when he was producing Mighty Sam [there]," said Mike Leech, who was not yet an official part of American but was somewhat enviously watching the studio's progress from the sidelines at Hi. "Chips and Tommy landed me that gig. He hit the talkback at one point with the comment, 'Man, that bass is warpin' my mind.'" Hayward Bishop said vexedly, "He couldn't even call you on the phone without saying"—lapsing into a flawless imitation of Don's dulcet, unctuous tones—"'This is the ol' Papa Ding Dong Daddy Doo-Dah Don Schroeder.' I mean, come on." "A strange character," Chips Moman, who himself was often described that way, said of his studio's first outside client. "He was Mr. Ego, Mr. Flash," said Bobby Wood, summing it up; like Hayward, Bobby would work with Papa Don later in Nashville and not find the experience pleasant. Eventually, Don's size— "like Baby Huey," Mike Leech would say—and his bounding enthusiasm earned him a nickname based on the Sesame Street character: Big Bird.

Papa Don brought James and Bobby Purify to the American Studios in mid-March 1967, almost a month to the day from the Aretha sessions, with Oscar Toney Jr. agreeing to meet them there. It was not an ideal time to start recording. Paul Kelly from Muscle Shoals was rewiring and reconfiguring the control board as the sessions were getting under way, and Don Crews remembered that the studio did not become fully operational even with the new equipment until mid-July of that year. But Papa Don was banking on Chips's recommendation of the band. "Moman says, 'Pop, I'm almost finished with the studio. I give you my word, they're the best musicians in America.' . . . He said, 'If you don't like it you don't have to pay for the session.'" Papa Don was intrigued by this offer despite his closeness to Rick Hall and his love of the Muscle Shoals sound: "I couldn't screw up my deal with Larry Uttal, so I said I'd try it, just once. I never went back to Muscle Shoals, because I met my best friend, Tommy Cogbill." Papa Don's departure from the Shoals ruined forever his friendship with Rick Hall, but he explained his decision to work with Chips: "I took a chance because he was so talented."

Tommy's calm seemed to attract emotional

personalities such as those of Chips Moman, Papa Don, and later, Hayward Bishop; they drew strength from his steadiness, they valued his judgment, and he in turn seems to have appreciated their spirit. There is no doubt that he and Schroeder formed some sort of immediate alliance when they met. "Tommy Cogbill and I were closer than grits," said Papa Don. Chips was Tommy's closest friend and main collaborator at this point; a few years later he would befriend the Monument staff writer Johnny McCrae, but Tommy was essentially a loner. For now, though, he and Papa Don were taking one another's measure as they began working together, and both seemed to like what they saw.

Thus began a session that became legendary in the annals of the American musicians, partly due to the quality of the material presented. "I had this song by the Five Du-Tones that I found in St. Louis," explained Papa Don of the James and Bobby Purify session. "'Shake A Tail Feather' was the only song I had in my back pocket. We really, literally, rewrote the song on the floor. I always produced records from the floor." "Don isn't a control-booth producer," agreed Mike Leech. "He's out on the floor often with ideas, comments, suggestions, which was sometimes not too cool." "Don was . . . quite particular in what he wanted," observed Reggie Young with a diplomatic chuckle. "Papa Don was a charmer at times, but he could be a bit of a tyrant, working the musicians until he got what he wanted," added Mike Leech. Papa Don leaped out of his chair and leaned over the control board so often, inadvertently readjusting Chips's settings, that eventually Chips installed a special switch just for Don to use as a talkback—a switch that connected to nothing. The musicians believed that Papa Don never learned the secret, but "there was always a joke about Moman disconnecting my switch," he said with evident good humor.

Papa Don came to the sessions already having great respect for Chips. "Chips Moman is one of the greatest talents that ever lived in the record business," he said. "I learned so much from Chips and Tommy; they had the best ears

in the business. [Chips] was the best at whatever he wanted to do. *Whooo!* Chips Moman, are you kiddin'? Chips Moman . . . one of the greatest record men who ever lived. But he's crazy, like all of us."

Chips was a known quantity, but Papa Don was astonished at the developing interplay he saw among the musicians. "There was Cogbill, there was ol' Gene Chrisman, there was Reggie right under the window of the control room," he recalled. "And Bobby Emmons—that li'l ole groovemaker . . . that's what Cogbill always called him. Chips recognized that quality about him [Emmons] and kept him close." Mike Leech reconstructed what Papa Don would have seen. "[There was] Reggie, always messing with his guitar, amp, working on a certain tone, practicing licks, quiet. [It's] hard to get his attention when he's in that phase . . . Emmons [was] always looking in the control room for approval on his playing. If he got a grin or a nod from Chips, that's what he worked for . . . Gene [was] waiting patiently in the drum booth for everybody to get their parts together. Nothing to say, ready to roll . . . Cogbill? A bit shy, especially about his playing. Accepted compliments shyly. You never knew what he was thinking . . . He had a comrade in Reggie, because he played great guitar." This in-studio behavior would solidify as the years went on, leaving others as well as Papa Don amazed to see that these unassuming people could, when placed together, create powerfully authoritative music.

The session was also memorable for its length. "That's the longest session I ever played," said Reggie Young. Some of the time consumed was due to the usual run-throughs and to the perfectionism of both Papa Don and Chips, who was engineering. "When I think of Papa Don, I think of take after take after take after take, he'd just work us silly," said Reggie. "It was like over and over and over and over, I don't know what he was listening for." But far more of the delays were due to the fact that the studio was a mess. Paul Kelly was installing the new board even in the middle of the session. Don Crews despaired of the chaos, and so did a recent arrival, looking on—"Dan said, 'What in the world have I got myself into?'" Crews remembered. "We had this great thing going and Chips wasn't ready," groused Papa Don. Chips, though, was seemingly above the confusion; an onlooker might have suspected that he thrived on it.

"They put the board and the new console in and they still had to prop it up at times," commented Gene Chrisman. "We mixed 'Shake a Tail Feather' upside down, the board lifted up so the engineer was down there working on it," said Papa Don, a seeming bit of improbability confirmed by Chips, who recalled the upside-down mixing with amusement.

"It was a *tank*!" Bobby Emmons exclaimed of the new half-inch Ampex tape machine. "A custom board built from modular pieces. There were eight [microphone] inputs. We had a stereo mix bus, mono (still the money mix of the era), and four echo returns. It was maybe ten or twelve modules lined up. I know we had one Universal Audio limiter, maybe more. . . . I don't think the talkback was rigged up yet. Their voices would come through a spare guitar amp with a mike plugged into it." Emmons also remembered Paul Kelly's technical crew. "They were there to stress-test the board, they realized some things weren't right so we took lengthy breaks while they rewired," he said.

"We worked and worked on 'Shake a Tail Feather,'" said Papa Don. "We'd cut awhile and sleep awhile and cut awhile," said Reggie Young, who remembered everyone falling out where they could on the floor. Legend has it that they never left the studio for nearly sixty hours, though Bobby Emmons debunked the myth. "I think we actually left the building and maybe went home," he said matter-of-factly. "My session book shows two days for the Purifys." Why did they remain in the studio for so long, working in between the console rewiring? "We kinda had 'Tail Feather' hemmed up and we didn't want to lose the groove," Emmons explained. "We would do a take, they would rewire the equipment, do another take, another rewire, for a reported fifty-two hours (it was hard to find out much about time or sound equipment back then). They finally got it wired right. We had a studio."

"[Chips] got most of the bugs out on *our time*," said Papa Don with annoyance. "To tell you the truth, I was so pissed because he [had] promised not to call me until American was finished . . . but I kept my mouth shut because I was loving what I was hearing and was having fun even though we were all dead." Accounts of the number of hours actually spent vary; Papa Don estimated that "it took twenty-seven hours" to complete the basic track, but Gene Chrisman thought it took longer—"We were in there for forty, forty-five hours"—and Reggie Young put the estimate closer to fifty-eight. The time frame apparently increases with legend—"Everybody talks about how long the sessions were; fifty-two hours, now they say it's fifty-four," Emmons noted with skeptical amusement.

To keep everyone going, Papa Don handed out a supply of Am-bars—diet pills, uppers. Bobby Emmons, a teetotaling non–drug user always, declined, preferring his usual potion for staying awake, cup after cup of strong black coffee (at one point he was consuming thirty cups a day). Chips Moman and Dan Penn were no strangers to pills; neither differed in their amount of consumption from many songwriters of their era, and neither of them had any misgivings about the uppers. Pills were a new experience for Gene Chrisman, a surprise given his former association with Jerry Lee Lewis; coffee and cigarettes had seen him well enough through his touring days. Now, he decided that the effects of uppers were not to his liking. "I'd get home at five-thirty, six in the morning and then you get in bed and stare at the walls with your eyes open. You're like on jet lag," Gene said disgustedly. Reggie Young and Tommy Cogbill had been around; they did what they had to do, in this instance, to stay awake and to get the job done, but pills had never been a big factor in either of their lives, nor would they be. "I promise you, none of the five of us were druggies," Papa Don said emphatically, and the proof is in all of the music made by the core group; it is completely professional, absolutely without self-indulgence or sloppiness of any kind, focused as a laser and clear as a mountain stream. "I have nothing but wonderful things to say about these people," added Papa Don. "Quality human beings. Men of character, I'm telling you. The sanest, the finest, the straightest." Well-brought-up Southern boys all, the musicians were too busy making a living and creating to waste time behaving like the hippies from that era; their high then was work, and the sound and feel of a good groove.

Mike Leech's experience with uppers was closer to that of most musicians of his day. He first encountered them in his days backing Charlie Rich at the C&R Club. "One night I was tired and yawning onstage. During a break, one of the waitresses came over and gave me a small, matchbox-sized box and said, 'Here, honey, these will keep you awake.' Those were the first 'bennies' I ever saw—benzedrine. I took one and felt awesome the rest of the night. The bad part, after all was over, when I finally got home I couldn't sleep. I finally crashed some time the next day, and the awesome feeling was replaced by big-time depression." Here, during the crash, is where many people pop another pill just to avoid the depressed feelings. Mike was already given to somber introspection, and though he decided at the time that pills were not for him, he would, like Johnny Cash, struggle with addiction for many years.

And the results of that session, those hours in the studio, that amphetamine-hyped madness? "Shake a Tail Feather," one of the great party records of all time, sounds as spontaneous as if it had been captured on the first take. Reggie Young commands the intro and, propelled by Emmons, the rest of the group falls into a rocking, lurching groove that never lets up and seems to inspire James and Bobby as they exhort the girl in the song to have a good time, get down, and get with it. "The main challenge there was just focusing and physical, because that song has a fiery groove," commented Bobby Emmons. According to Papa Don, the inspired call-and-response riffing by James and, particularly, Bobby Lee Dickey on the fadeout is completely improvised; one can imagine how much fun they must have had with this in live performance. For the musicians, it was one of their most famous party records ever. For Chips Moman it was a triumphant finale to

the stomping uptempo sound he had made famous with the Mar-Keys and the Gentrys. The sound of American Studios would increasingly be given over to Chips's sorrowful visions, a change apparent in the next recording the group would make.

For Oscar Toney Jr., the singer who had met up with the rest of Papa Don's crew in Memphis, was still there in the studio, waiting for Papa Don to fulfill his promise and let him do a demo or at least give him an audition. Papa Don recalled the event: "Chips is sittin' there with me and Cogbill, the band is packing up," he recalled. "Oscar said, 'You told me, "if you come up I'll listen."'" Schroeder had forgotten all about him, but now he asked Oscar to go on out onto the studio floor while he and Chips rolled a tape. "I said, 'Toney, go to that microphone over there and pick the greatest old song you know.' I said, 'What's the song that best illustrates your talent, that tells who Oscar Toney Jr. is?' He said, there was that old Jerry Butler song, 'For Your Precious Love.' I said, I *looooove* that song! It was ten years later, I said, shoot, there's a lot of record buyers who have never heard this song. He said, 'I wrote this recitation . . .'" Oscar went over to the microphone and began talking. "Cogbill said, 'Whew, I'm likin' this.' Chips and I looked at each other," Papa Don remembered.

No wonder Chips was riveted. Oscar's opening lines, "Into each life a little rain must fall / Every day can't be Sunday / Every smile isn't a smile of happiness / And every tear that's shed is not a tear of joy," were straight from Chips's own philosophy, and Oscar's earnest delivery increased the impact. The musicians scrambled to their places; Chips dialed up the echo, always a favorite effect of his, for Gene Chrisman's drums. "Moman's got the damnedest little slapback echo," said Papa Don. "He said, 'This sounds like a blankety-blank smash!' We cut it in fifteen minutes." The result is a record both somber and passionate, less a statement of love than a declaration of sorrow at missing someone, and the musicians let Oscar have center stage with the story. Over twenty-four hours for one cut, fifteen minutes for another; the last party record and the first of what

Chips, in a later composition, self-mockingly called "those sad, hurtin' songs."

Amazingly, the story does not stop there. Papa Don continued the chain of events. "Moman said, 'Let's play this stuff for Larry Uttal.' We couldn't wait to tell Larry Uttal. Uttal had said, 'Call me. I know you stay up late but if I'm asleep, call me when you get something.' We called him at his penthouse around two, two-thirty in the morning. I played him 'Shake a Tail Feather' and he went bananas! I said, 'We've got the basic track,' and we told Larry, 'We've got another one.'" Papa Don thought that at that time he had also pitched to Uttal a solo production of Dan Penn's called "The Letter," but the group, Don Crews, and Chips all remembered this as happening several months later; Dan had not begun flying solo yet. But Uttal was so impressed with what he did hear that he wanted Papa Don to come up to New York with the tapes right away.

"Now listen to this story, because it's very interesting," Schroeder instructed. "I always finished my records back then in New York, because I had Melba Moore, Doris Troy, and Ellie Greenwich—they sang backup on all my records. I tried my best to sign Melba!—but she was 'committed to her husband,'" he mocked bitterly. It was this formidable trio who are contributing both the partying shouts in the background on "Tail Feather" and the soft, sorrowing backup lines on "For Your Precious Love." There was also an engineer in the city whom Papa Don trusted. "George Schaller—big, heavyset, wonderful engineer," he remembered. "Schaller did the basic track, I did the background voices, we mixed the track together. [The Oscar Toney, Jr. track] was the first time I put violins on in my life! Three violins, overdubbed." Now it was time to take the tapes to Uttal. "I went up there in my cutoff jeans and my London Fog hat and my London Fog raincoat," said Papa Don.

Bobby Emmons recounted what happened next. "Papa Don took off . . . with the huge half-inch three-track master tape (Wow!) and told us later he jumped out of a taxi in the rain, dropped the tape box, and the reel popped out and went unwinding down the street. "Reggie

Young added that Papa Don sank to the curb, his head in his hands, almost crying." He gathered it all up in a wad and the record survived," said Emmons. Somehow, rewinding it inch by inch, he had been able to save the tape, and when he played it in Larry Uttal's office, the Bell Records head "just absolutely said, 'Oh my God, what have you done, Papa Don?' Larry Uttal had one hell of a week."

Once the records were released, both of them charted, and they are now viewed by many as among the era's classics, their prestige increasing with time. Bobby Emmons noted that "'Tail Feather' went at least as high as #25 in the Billboard Hot 100, and we were told it was a million seller (damn the glory, it was hard to find out anything about music or money back then)." Even Papa Don did not really know how many units were sold: "To this day, I have never gotten a statement." The Oscar Toney record, Emmons added, would go to #23.

"Tail Feather" had production credits assigned to the entire group as well as Papa Don, and Chips got an engineering credit placed prominently on the label; they had all been promised a share of the proceeds. "I did say that I would pay Reggie Young, Bobby Emmons, Tommy Cogbill, and Gene Chrisman one percent of my eight percent on the net royalty of those two records because I felt guilty that they had to work so long to get it all done," remembered Papa Don." By the time Uttal screwed us out of a fair count and deducted for session cost of a crappy, rushed LP, there was zilch left." "It was a strange deal," Chips Moman mused. "We cut several records with him [Papa Don] and I don't think we got a nickel from him." "Every time we worked with him, something was not paid," added Bobby Wood. "We'd work and work and work our fingers to the bone and it'd be his deal."

"We all remember things differently, don't we?" Papa Don said ironically. "I wish I still had the canceled checks where I paid the musicians extra money after 'Shake a Tail Feather' and 'Precious Love' became hits. . . . I gave 'em all two hundred bucks apiece." He was deeply hurt and angry that anyone should have even remotely considered him less than honest. "I did many arrangements for Papa Don, and I was always well paid," Mike Leech said supportively on Schroeder's behalf.

Some of the comments may have stemmed from Chips's annoyance at Schroeder's cutting hits with a band he already thought of as exclusively his. On the other hand, neither Chips nor Bobby Wood witnessed Papa Don's struggles to pry money from the wallets of reluctant executives. "I am sure that no one back then realized how badly the producers were screwed by the record companies when it was time to get paid," Papa Don reflected. "We only had an eight percent royalty rate and had to pay the artist half of that. And then we got paid only *half* of that, if we were lucky. And, as soon as you had a hit, they rushed you to spend most of your eight-percent royalty on a follow-up crappy album that didn't sell but 15,000 copies. I think that is exactly what Larry Uttal said that the first Purifys album sold. . . . We were all underpaid." Chips himself had trouble getting money from many of the executives with whom he dealt, but he seemed to see this as a vendetta directed at him, rather than standard practice within the industry (especially regarding the Southern producers and players, whom many in the New York music business doubtless regarded as hicks). Papa Don explained why it was difficult for anyone to recover the money owed them: "You can say, 'Well, why don't you do something about it?' If you're broke, it costs money to sue, and they know that."

Nevertheless, the buzz was out—Papa Don had been recording with a Memphis session band and it was obvious where the musical direction on these singles was coming from. It was obvious to Papa Don, most of all. "I found out a long time ago—I had the number-one band in the world," he said proudly. "And we did a good job. We really did. And that's all I have to say about that."

Two weeks after the Oscar Toney record reached its highest chart position, a new one from American's own Sandy Posey went Top 12.

She was already having a good year. By the beginning of 1967, her second hit, "Single Girl,"

had placed Top Ten on the charts. It was another Martha Sharp monologue, brought to her by the former song plugger from Painted Desert, Gary Walker, who was now managing Sandy on a part-time basis. She had recorded it in Nashville with Chips and more or less the same supporting cast from her first album and single, and the same organ-and-steel effect substituting for strings. Don Crews remembered that they had held the song back for awhile— "After we cut and finished 'Single Girl,' we waited six months before it was put out." But when it was, once again both country and pop audiences related to her message. Typically for Chips's recordings, no one was really quite sure if this was a pop record that had crossed over to country or a country record that had crossed over to pop.

In some ways this monologue was superior even to her first hit, since this was written straight from the experiences—and feelings— of "girls" like Martha Sharp and Sandy herself, young women from small towns who had flocked to the cities in search of work, adventure, and romance. This song could have been written for and about the young women on the research staff of *Time* magazine Jack Olsen interviewed five years later for *The Girls in the Office*. It could have been written for the secretaries on Music Row, for the girls clerking in travel agencies, in banks, or waiting on tables, selling dresses in stores. It could have been written by Sandy about her own life.

The single girl as Sandy describes her is a far cry from the type Helen Gurley Brown was making a fortune portraying. She has her rent to pay and everyday concerns and problems, all the while trying to fight off the phonies, avoid the predatory men in the dating scene, and find true love. It was another American Studios classic—autobiographical material that would have resonance for listeners going through the same experiences. The musicians follow the same formula that had yielded Sandy's first hit; Mike Leech's bass, playing the same rhythm figure as the intro of "Born a Woman," points the way for the rest of the players, especially Larry Butler's Floyd Cramer–influenced piano. The party-band stomp is again softened, cushioning Sandy's voice; her vocal is spunky and assertive, with just a hint of her deep vulnerability appearing here and there.

It was a rousing success, and recording was going on intermittently for her second album. Much of it was still being done in Nashville, with Reggie Young now replacing Scotty Moore; the MGM head Jim Vienneau, watching the proceedings, seemed to be having second thoughts about Chips's players, despite the success of the two singles. At one point, both Reggie and Sandy remembered, Vienneau had some of the top Nashville session crew—the fabled A-Team—on standby, waiting in the studio. "Seems like Jim Vienneau wanted [Chips] to use the Nashville musicians," Sandy reflected. "Chips wasn't happy about that. It never happened again. It probably was some political move." Sandy disliked the political maneuvering in Nashville, and she had her own ideas by now about what constituted the successful formula for a hit recording. "It's the combination of the songs, the singers, the musicians, and you can't leave out the musicians."

She felt that the creativity of the Memphis musicians was worth leaving Nashville for a while to obtain. "I wasn't really impressed with the Nashville musicians because I'd already heard the Memphis players," she said. "When you're picking musicians, you have to be so careful." She liked the freedom and spontaneity she heard from Chips's Memphis band, so she returned there for a singles session. The results were basically monologues, again—John D. Loudermilk's "What a Woman in Love Won't Do" is about a woman who is overly solicitous of her cheating husband, because she is doing the same thing herself; the track features an almost deliberately "hokey" upright bass line, adding to the joke. There was also a new monologue, "Are You Ever Coming Home," written by Dan Penn and Spooner Oldham under the auspices of Press. The new song had Sandy musing that she was waiting for word from her lover, even though she knew she "should be out tonight, having a party." The tension between the condition of her yearning heart and conventional wisdom gives this monologue a special appeal, and one can imagine it getting played on a thousand lonely nights by the wives of men who are often away on the road.

Mike Leech was there, playing a bouncy, intricate bass on Dan's tune. Bob Taylor, a trumpet player who had lived at the Haunted House with Reggie Young, was partially responsible for that. "When I first worked for Chips, he would call me for demos that would last all day, and the pay was very low," Mike said. "This was . . . just some thrown-together groups. I did this several times till I was fed up, and I told Chips I didn't want to do that anymore. He told me fine, that he would never call me again. It wasn't too long afterwards that he and the group started turning out hit records, sans me. I was very jealous and wanted very much to be a part of that group. It was Bob Taylor who, on my behalf, talked Chips into calling me . . . It was at this point that I became an official member of the group, and was welcomed in. We also recorded 'I Take It Back' during those sessions, so I proved myself a worthy sub for Tommy, and will never forget Bob Taylor."

The monologue to which Mike Leech referred was one of Sandy's most affecting. Half song and half recitation, the work concerns a girl who would like to walk out on her man, but every time she tries he looks at her so helplessly and pitifully that she apologizes: "I take it back / I didn't mean it / Please forget the things I said." A subtext seems to imply that the girl is announcing her impending walkout to bring herself to the man's attention. After three tries, the girl realizes that she is powerless to walk away, and the song ends with her concluding sensibly, "Sometimes it's better to be loved . . . than it is to love." It features not only Mike Leech's bass but Tommy Cogbill's snappy, jangling lead guitar, a solo turn identified by Mike as having been played on a Gibson Super 400 that had originally belonged to Scotty Moore.

The song had been brought to Chips in the middle of the sessions, pitched to him in person by the writer, James R. Cobb Jr. A Birmingham native, J.R. first came to prominence with a band in Jacksonville, Florida, where he had spent his high-school years; following his graduation in 1962, he joined another local group. "At the time, I was an apprentice welder making $47 a week and I could make a hundred dollars a night playing guitar," he recalled matter-of-factly. "I felt like I was kinda stealin' that money." Originally, it was a true soul band, with horns and all, but gradually the extraneous players fell away and it was down to four people. J.R. played rhythm guitar and was experimenting with writing songs, often in collaboration with Buddy Buie, who had ties to the publishing firm run by Bill Lowery. "Bill was the Godfather at that time; Bill Lowery was Mr. Music in Atlanta, Gee Ay."

Eventually J.R.'s band, the Classics, moved to Atlanta, where Lowery recorded them for Capitol in 1964. Their first record, "Pollyanna," was a Joe South composition about a woman who uses relentless optimism as a defense against her fear of life, and the flip side, "Cry Baby," written by J.R., is an expert blend of Four Seasons vocal harmonies with a beach-music shuffle. The Classics seemed to be on the verge of something big; frontman Dennis Yost had a voice that could slide up to a full Frankie Valli falsetto wail at a moment's notice. His soft, confiding midrange made him a good interpreter of J.R.'s romantic ballads, and it was on this that Lowery urged them to concentrate. "He convinced us that the world already had a Four Seasons," J.R. said of the changeover.

"I Take It Back" was one of the first songs J.R. and Buie had completed, and a demo sent to Chips by Buie, who knew him slightly, resulted in a phone call telling them to come up to Memphis and play it in person—a traditional style of song plugging that Chips continued to prefer. Sandy remembered, though, that her "manager," Gary, had also sent it to her in a demo, because Gary was acquainted with Bill Lowery. Whichever way it got there, the song launched J.R. on a long career as a writer. With Dan Penn already there and J.R. having made his acquaintance, Chips now had sources of solid writing talent other than his own.

"I Take It Back" reached number 12 in June 1967. By then new recordings from Wilson Pickett were also on the charts, drawing even more attention to the musicians. Don Crews recalled that the band had recorded two albums' worth of material on Sandy Posey by

the time her third single became a hit, though most of it would not be released in album form until after J.R.'s song made the charts. Bobby Emmons was elated at their success. "The band had it wired right too," he said, referring to the ordeal of the console reworking.

Great ventures seldom get off to a smooth start, and these early days were not without tension. Mike Leech recalled receiving a certain amount of initial hazing. "I was the 'college boy' who could read and write music, and I felt a lot of resentment from the guys. I got slammed a few times by Chips for the same reason, but I think deep down he respected my 'talent.'" J.R. Cobb, he recalled, was also fond of needling him about his higher education. "I was usually the fall guy who was the recipient of most slams. I think that was because even back then I would make a feeble attempt at a comeback, whereas the others wouldn't. . . . These were all high-school dropouts making it the best way they could [actually, only Chips and Bobby Emmons had never graduated] and I fell in right out of Music Theory class to assume a position in the studio that they had struggled to find through a back alley. Tommy was the only one who never caused me to feel ill at ease. I think he respected my abilities and I felt he even looked up to me sometimes because of my education. I've brought that up before and don't mean to dwell on it, but it happened."

Of course, when one is putting five disparate personalities in a studio for hours at a time, there is bound to be some slight contention until the players are used to one another. Mike Leech, Reggie Young, Bobby Emmons, and Tommy Cogbill had already become fairly close to one another because of their work together at Hi, but there were initial personality clashes with some of the others, as Mike recalled. "There was a certain individual I felt (I knew) didn't like me, for some unknown reason. This went on for quite some time. One day I went to him and told him what a good musician he was, how much I enjoyed working with him, and that I valued our friendship. You should've seen him light up. That particular person is now a dear friend and would (and has) taken up for me on several occasions. That was Gene Chrisman, many years ago."

For better or worse, Mike and the others were there to stay. And, as Al Jolson could have told them, they hadn't seen nothin' yet.

Chips and Tommy were getting their act together, and they were still taking it on the road. Shortly after the sessions with James and Bobby Purify and in between the intermittent ones for Sandy Posey, they returned to Muscle Shoals for the third Wilson Pickett album. It was here that they finally met Bobby Womack; Bobby had come down with Wilson, and he contributed three songs for the album. He also took Tommy's former chair as second guitar, uncredited, on several cuts. A photo of him and Jimmy Johnson, working on "Funky Broadway," with Pickett looking on, shows Bobby in his element: seated across from Jimmy to watch him closely, and grinning with merriment. "He was a sight to look at, 'cause he was a left-handed guitarist and he strung his strings upside down," remembered Spooner Oldham. Bobby became an immediate favorite, someone the Memphis and Muscle Shoals players were always happy to see. "He was very receptive to meeting us; he was very friendly," said Jimmy. "We loved working with him; we were just blown away by Bobby." "I don't think there was an adjustment period," mused Spooner. "He was just a team player . . . he just fit in like a regular guy."

The friendliness Bobby Womack exuded seemed to set the tone for the kind of music being made; it's rhythmic, soulful, and easily accessible to a listener. The first two tracks, "Soul Dance #3" and "Funky Broadway," both adhere closely to the "Mustang Sally" groove; Tommy and Spooner establish the pace, Roger Hawkins nails down a firm backbeat, and Chips's leads lope along good-naturedly. The Stax-inflected horn lines are due to the presence of Memphis Horns stalwarts Wayne Jackson and Andrew Love (though Wayne and Andrew were primarily working at Stax, they had no exclusive contract there, which enabled them to take other session work when possible). On "Funky Broadway," the song's bridge belongs

exclusively to Roger Hawkins and Chips, whose twangy guitar notes are reminiscent of Reggie Young. Dan's and Spooner's "I Need a Lot of Loving" is casually paced, relaxed; Pickett's vocal sounds effortless, and Chips carries the tune's easy groove. It is much more laid-back than the somewhat frenetic version of the song cut at American by Mighty Sam under the supervision of Papa Don; the Memphis version features Tommy, who is restrained and low-key here.

Spooner Oldham directs the way on Wilson's two-part, gospel-steeped freestyle ballad, "I Found a Love," and once again Chips's lead rings with Reggie-influenced string-bending lines. He's more fluid and terse here than he was on the Aretha album or on any of his previous work at the Shoals, and it suits him. He rides Roger Hawkins's scrambling beat with professional, accomplished ease.

"You Can't Stand Alone" is the track Tommy Cogbill fans had been waiting for. He and Spooner Oldham thunder a solid sheet of sound behind Pickett's commanding vocal. Though Spooner cuts loose on a rocking organ solo in the instrumental bridge, the song really belongs to Tommy, as it always did when he turned up the heat. "He killed us all. The lines and that touch," said Jimmy Johnson in amazement. "His time was immaculate. There was no rushing within the riff, no dragging within the riff. He would play it in a personal Tommy Cogbill way." Though Hawkins is not immediately in evidence, his rhythm is the implied underpinning for the whole track; he rises to Tommy's inventiveness and matches it. "Tommy brought out the best in every drummer," said Hayward Bishop. Jimmy Johnson echoed and expanded the thought. "He had a special way of getting the best out of every musician," Jimmy said. "I'd always feel comfortable. He was more of a schooled player than the rest of us. . . . People that really get into progressive jazz, you have to be a special person to want to play it in the first place." Nonetheless, everyone agreed, Tommy was genuinely humble about his talent. "He never flaunted it. Ever. He never stuck it in anyone's face," Jimmy said firmly. "You never heard him say a bad word about anybody. He accepted you, he would accept you for what you were." Some of that cordialness is audible in his genial but forceful playing on this track; it became one of the identifying characteristics of his unique bass style.

"Mojo Woman," the following track, offers a taste of specifically Southern atmosphere; it is one of the first regional genre paintings by Chips and his friends. The opening bars of the tune were later slightly adapted by Motown for Edwin Starr's "25 Miles"; New Yorker Bert Berns situated his story line "thirty-two miles out of Waycross" on the suggestion of Jerry Wexler, who thought Waycross, Georgia, was the most rural, backward-sounding place he could think of (though, as Gram Parsons's hometown, Waycross may have had the last laugh). The mojo woman in the song is apparently possessive of her only daughter, who plans to elope on the evening train to Atlanta with the narrator; "Let your baby go! Mama!" shout the Sweet Inspirations (overdubbed in New York), who also appear throughout the album.

The three Bobby Womack compositions are next, and taken in order, it is possible to hear them as a unified suite of songs about love in all of its complex moods. The first, "I Found the One," is a predecessor of the later "I'm in Love"; in this song Bobby, speaking through Wilson's voice, expresses his gratitude to the woman (Barbara Cooke?) for giving him peace of mind and improving his life. Her affection seems to be at least partly maternal (not surprising, given that Bobby was scarcely out of his teens); she reassures him, offers him money (which he declines) and tender understanding. Spooner's Fifties-style piano underlines the story and sets up a heartfelt background for the feelings expressed.

Womack's second song, "Something Within Me," is presented as a classic slow-drag blues. Musicologists have noted its resemblance to the old gospel song "Something Within Me," written by Memphis's own Lucie Campbell; it is likely Womack was rewriting a classic from his world, in the Ray Charles tradition of turning church songs secular. The recording features Chips's strong lead lines; the opening verse sounds as if it were written specifically for and

about the visitor from Memphis. "Something within me I can't explain / Something within me makes my heart in pain / Lord, I don't know what it is / But it just won't let me be." His scattered guitar lines, tough and bluesy, dominate the record's fadeout.

The third and final selection in Womack's suite about the vagaries of love, "I'm Sorry about That," is a classic weeper; so laden with guilt, contrition, and apologies to the woman for sins real and imagined that if it had been covered by a honky-tonk singer there would not have been a dry eye in the bar when it came on the jukebox. Chips is prominent, calling attention to the song's expression of regret with a gently understated guitar line beneath the vocal, and Tommy Cogbill's intricate, sliding bass line and Spooner's harmonic line on organ continue the feeling of brooding, tortured misery.

The album's finale, "Love Is a Beautiful Thing," was written by two of Atlantic's newest protégés, Felix Cavaliere and Eddie Brigati, from the New York white-soul band the Young Rascals. It gives Tommy Cogbill the chance to play a more subtle, jazz-inflected bass part than anything else he has done on the record; the call-and-response between Wilson and the Sweet Inspirations is also a treat. It ends the album on a happy note and its mood would be sustained in many of the records Tommy did on his own as a producer. It seemed to be a comfortable place for him musically, making much of his work a contrast to the despondent-sounding recordings more typical of the American Studios sound.

Tommy and Chips had done another classic album, with the help of Spooner and their friends from the Shoals; the record yielded three hit singles and continued the high opinion Atlantic already had of them. In addition, Bobby Womack was now considered a friend; it was possible, very likely probable, that he would join them for work on another project soon.

Nor was Chips planning to leave his new friends from the Shoals lost in the shuffle. He and Dan Penn were still writing together extensively. "It was a different style, fifty-fifty writers, nobody bullied anybody," said Bobby Emmons with awe. "Chips and Dan were a good match; they wrote well." Their confidence in themselves was at an all-time peak due to the success of the two hits they had already written; still, Dan wanted to do more producing, and he and Chips lined up another session on which they would collaborate, to record a spicy little song written by Dan and Spooner called "Cheater Man."

They recorded it in April 1967, and the voice chosen to sing their message was a woman of near-legendary status—"Little" Esther Phillips, a recent Atlantic signee (one can imagine how delighted Dan would have been to be working with her). The production would be the first American Studios project for Atlantic, done with the studio house band: Reggie Young, Gene Chrisman, Tommy Cogbill, Bobby Emmons, and on piano, the newcomer to Memphis, Spooner Oldham.

Dan and Spooner, so alike in many ways, had formed different impressions of Memphis. "Race relations in Memphis had always been exceptional," Dan said warmly of the pre-1968 river city. "That was just a delightful town as far as race relations were concerned. It was so friendly, such a friendly place. There was so much respect in the air in Memphis. I never saw so many black people with smiles." Spooner Oldham, who had lived in Memphis for three months as a boy while his father was undergoing physical therapy at the V.A. hospital there, had a slightly different take on the city. "It was an odd feeling, to me it was just so spread-out, I didn't know anyone. I approached it with a good attitude." What he remembered best was the live-music scene, which he caught when his writing and recording schedules permitted. "We'd go to the Thunderbird Lounge and hear Flash and the Board of Directors" (a Memphis rock band featuring Tom Boggs, who would later work for the Box Tops; the band recorded several singles at American over the next year). "They were new and refreshing sounds." T.J.'s, a new club run by an old friend of Chips named Herbie O'Mell, also quickly became a hangout for Dan and Spooner (Tommy Cogbill continued to prefer the Thunderbird).

"Spooner's a talented keyboard player," Bobby Wood said of the new man on the scene. Chips used Spooner on sessions but now basically wanted him around as a full-time writer with Dan; he was still hoping to hire Bobby Wood, and to that end was calling Bobby more and more to play on dates. Bobby, even more unsure that working for Chips would be completely the right move, was still playing local clubs and recording occasionally at the Phillips studio for Stan Kesler. Stan was becoming more committed to his part-time rehearsal band. Bobby wondered whether to accept the keyboard chair with Stan's new group or to work for Chips; for the time being, he did nothing, knowing he would have to decide sooner or later.

Mike Leech recalled that Bobby Emmons seemed initially intimidated by Spooner; the new musician's noncompetitive personality was enough to defuse any rivalry, and the keyboardists soon developed a mutual admiration society. Spooner had never worked with another keyboard player, and he recalled with pleasure. "That was a lot of fun; I don't get to do it much since then, and I miss it." He attributed the success of such a lineup to the experience both he and Emmons had developed: "We had both been at it a while, doin' what we do. . . . I liked the way he played." There was also a growing respect for Bobby Wood, who would soon reap the benefits of the keyboard players' regard for one another.

Benefits were also reaped by Dan Penn, who watched Chips carefully as they worked together. "Really, what he was doin' was tryin' to get me started," Dan said gratefully. "I think he had me around because he liked me." Dan was making a study of his friend's production methods. "I can't particularly pinpoint what I learned from Chips," he said in retrospect. "I learned something from everybody along the line." His biggest influences in record production before working with Chips were Rick Hall, whom Dan described as "a heck of an engineer and a great record producer," and Otis Redding, who had recorded Arthur Conley in Muscle Shoals. "I mean, I was sitting right there when Otis produced 'Sweet Soul Music,'" Dan remembered joyfully. "This man had a smile on his face when he woke up in the morning. Otis Redding was one heck of a record producer. Anybody could [record him], ain't gotta be no genius to get something from him. Record producing is about communication, and revving people up for their enthusiasm."

At this Dan thought Chips was exceptional, even though he did not handle the sessions in the manner Dan was used to. "Rick Hall was working in a different way, a little more dictatorial in getting what he wanted," Dan observed. "Chips might give directions from the booth, but he'd never come in and take a guitar and play a break. He hardly ever told the musicians what to do. He stayed off the talkback all he could. He mostly sat and listened for the band to hit that sweet spot. Chips had a great way of listening for the cut. He was always looking up at the speakers like he's praying or something, like he's fixing to get it and you know, it always would happen, every time."

Of Chips's perfectionism, Dan expressed amazement. "Chips's patience runs endless; he'll do forty-three cuts," Dan said. "When I got to Memphis it was this cut-all-night business." But even more than the hours, he was astonished at the band's willingness to work as hard as Chips could drive them. "When they start cuttin', they could go for about sixty-two hours!" he marveled. "That gang of boys right there, they wanted to make better records than Stax. They had an affinity with Chips. They fit him, he fit them. He was in with 'em real thick and he never got 'em mad. It was all a big party."

The musicians, of course, had to have a good song with which to work, and Dan and Spooner had handed them one. "Cheater Man" is infidelity sung from a woman's point of view. "I don't think it's necessarily based on life, or truth," Spooner Oldham mused. "It was just a little blues song. It was our attempt to write a blues; we didn't care for blues much. It was depressing, too depressing for me. I can stand it for about fifteen minutes, then I gotta leave. That's not a popular viewpoint." Nonetheless, the song is one that Bessie Smith could have sung; any woman with a philandering husband

or lover for whom she still cares will understand the sentiments of a lady saying, "I'll be here when your wild oats are sown," threatening to incinerate his little black book, and saying she will be a better woman for him, learning how to cook so she can feed him "cornbread and peas," thus giving the song a specifically Southern context. "Lucky man!" chuckled Spooner about the devoted-woman lyric content. "I was daydreamin'; escapism, that's what that song was."

Esther Phillips had recorded country-tinged material before; it was no problem for her to attack it now, and Janis Joplin for one learned much from her flamethrower vocal. "I always liked her singing, even before I met her," Spooner Oldham said admiringly. "I don't remember what her personality was, but I'm sure she had one." The session, he recalled, was "sort of uneventful"; apparently things went very smoothly, for Emmons, Gene Chrisman, and Reggie Young had only the vaguest memories of the recording. That is ironic in light of the session's importance—the first session with Spooner participating, the first where everything, even the string arrangement, was done with the American players—and even more ironic because the band was at their best. Bobby Emmons's domineering organ line and Gene Chrisman's brisk drum taps on the intro pave the way for the other musicians to completely take over the track, with Reggie Young's fierce, sputtering guitar line and an incendiary bass track that the Esther Phillips compilation album credits to Tommy Cogbill but that Mike Leech recalled as his (proof positive that Mike could play as scorchingly as Tommy).

His bass line offers an illustration of what musicians mean when they say that they have "found the groove." "I once was asked to describe a groove," Mike reflected. "That was one of the toughest questions ever asked of me. And I still don't think I can explain it, but it is what a musician captures during a song that can't be taken away by any external disruption, whatever it may be. I've struck a groove many times in the past—mostly live—where I was almost in a trance—didn't know or care where I was. Those are few and hard to come by, but if you catch one, you better have tape rolling." Similar to what athletes call "the zone," it seems to be most accessible when the entire track is catching fire and the players are almost thinking as one. This happened on "Cheater Man," and the result was a recording that was not quite R&B, not quite pop, and not exactly country; it was a style that seemed to take the best elements from all these fields and combine them into something all the musicians' own, a sound that Chips had begun to approach in his work with Sandy Posey. Mike Leech, as perfectionistic as all the others, second-guessed himself at first. "I remember the playback on 'Cheater Man' in the control room and how I thought my bass line could have been a little busier, but then discarded the thought. It worked well."

The musicians further explored their new style on the single's flip side, a remake of the old Brenda Lee country-pop hit "I'm Sorry." Spooner Oldham, Bobby Emmons, and Reggie Young make a tightly woven harmonic line behind Esther's vocal, and a stately, thoughtful string passage glides through the song. The string line is attributed to Tommy Cogbill; his ideas were written down and conveyed to the players. Those ideas were some of the most unusual ever placed on a record from Memphis; he set up long, trailing string lines that filled in where a steel guitar might go on a conventional country recording. This treatment of the strings, and eventually of all the instruments, as if they were a steel guitar eventually became a trademark of Tommy's work, as if he were remaining loyal in his own way to the instrument where for him it had all begun. But here he was reluctant to put himself forward. Mike Leech recalled that Tommy deferred to practically everyone else's ideas; one gets the impression he may not at first have had confidence in his ability to be out front. To whom much is given, much is expected, and Tommy seems to have expected a lot of himself. Nonetheless, "I'm Sorry" was a good beginning and an artistic triumph.

Dan Penn was certain that the results of the band and of Chips's production technique yielded wonderful effects. "Before Memphis, there was just a whole lot of crap going on between the talkback and the musicians," he said, making it clear that he preferred the way things were done at American. "I learned something at American I'd have never learned anywhere else. I call it the Memphis way, leave the band alone and have some great expectations. Stax, they were more kin to Alabama; they wouldn't just sit and cut till the walls caved in. Stax was also the Memphis way, but it wasn't *my* Memphis way." He continued years later to be a partisan of this approach. "It worked better than anybody ever knew. And they still don't know. And they still don't care."

Chips Moman was a fan of horse racing. He liked to be around the races and gambling people; later, when he could afford it, he had stables and horses of his own. As a racing man, he knew thoroughbreds when he saw them; he had an eye for the ones who could really go. And by the end of only three months' time from where he sat in the control room at American, two of his thoroughbred musicians would make a run for the roses.

# CHAPTER 7

|||||||||||||||||||||||||||||||||||||||||||||||||||||||||||||||

# New Voices, New Visions, Wayne's World, and a Letter

The summer of 1967 depended on your perspective. If you were a soldier in Vietnam, particularly a grunt, you were just praying you would get home alive. If you were a hippie, especially in San Francisco, you would have felt validated; 1967 was the Summer of Love, the pinnacle of the movement. Monterey Pop, the music festival of that spring, had focused worldwide attention on the psychedelic sound and had pioneered a new style of rock concert. Hippie music was all over the airwaves that summer; the Jefferson Airplane had scored a huge success with "Somebody to Love" and the album *Surrealistic Pillow*, and beginning in June, the drones and blares of *Sgt. Pepper's Lonely Hearts Club Band* seemed, temporarily at least, to have united the world. The Beatles made the theme of unity even more explicit with their call for peace and harmony, "All You Need Is Love."

For African Americans, especially in the cities, it was the year of the long hot summer. Detroit went up and so did Newark, Roxbury, Portland, Wilmington, and Toledo, among other places. Lyndon Johnson authorized a commission chaired by the Illinois governor Otto Kerner to investigate why these riots were happening; the report was written, suggestions were made as to the causes (an increasingly two-tiered society, based on race and economic class); the recommendations were noted and promptly forgotten. It was back to business as usual.

In Memphis, "business as usual" meant cutting hit records. It was turning out to be one of Stax's best years, but American was gaining ground. The musicians at these studios had no idea of the impact their records were having; Stax was an assembly line, and if American was not quite that yet, it was evolving from the ragtag operation it had been several months before.

Some of that was due to the business sense of Don Crews, now the office manager who scheduled sessions. The success of the records done that spring under Papa Don Schroeder's direction attracted more accounts. "We were cuttin' a lot of rhythm and blues for different people," Crews remembered. Quinton Claunch continued to bring in Goldwax artists on a regular basis and Fred Foster in Nashville was becoming more and more of a patron and booster.

But much of the success American enjoyed that summer was due to a concept Chips Moman had held from the beginning: the notion of the recording studio as an experimental laboratory where anyone who had an idea and wished to put it on tape was free to try it out. "The deal was, I gave everybody in the band a chance," Chips explained. "They could use the studio free. Tommy was the only one who seemed to want to do that. . . . I encouraged everyone to get involved." This was almost unheard of in an industry that regarded pickers as the low men on the totem pole, but to Chips it was a matter of treating them fairly. "I was a session man before I got that deal and I would have *loved* to have had something like that." He thought he had found it at Stax, but circumstances had intervened; now he was planning to play benevolent patriarch to a new generation of musicians, a role that he obviously felt suited him.

The idea applied to songwriters, too. Dan Penn had been interested in production from the moment he got there; his whole impetus for leaving Muscle Shoals had been to produce records . He had crafted his own demos for years, finding out through trial and error what sounded good; now he had taken the next step by way of his co-productions with Chips. The results were invariably excellent, but the collaborations heightened the differences between the two. "Dan was gonna do it his way, Chips would do it his way," observed Reggie Young. "The difference between me and Chips is, I like funk and he doesn't," noted Dan. There were other differences as well; Dan's solid grounding in R&B and traditional country (all those square dances he'd played as a teenager) made him seek a sparer sound than some of the pop-crossover productions of Chips. And Dan found himself contributing only a secondary opinion to Chips's decisions; this did not sit well with someone as strong-willed as he. "He was a dreamer of a producer, he didn't need no help," Dan said of Chips. "That's what producing is; you're driving. That's what I loved about that era." Now he had been given the keys to a brand-new sports car, and he could hardly wait to get behind the wheel.

"Myself, I had to kind of insist on producing," he reflected. "I finally told him, 'Hey look, I don't wanna produce with you no more. You don't understand. I'm not gettin' my licks in. I wanna produce somebody myself. I don't care who, gimme your worst artist.'" Chips "mulled it through in his mind," said Dan, and then decided his protégé was ready. Chips suggested that Dan begin working with a local rock group he had recorded in 1964 and did not want to again. Since then they had been performing around the city at teen dances and taken on an extraordinary lead singer, a sixteen-year-old R&B devotee named Alex Chilton. At the time, they called themselves the DeVilles. To get an idea of how they sounded, Dan gave them a tape and suggested that they familiarize themselves with the songs on it, all of which were the work of an Ozark-based songwriter whom Chips and Dan by now knew slightly. The writer's name was Wayne Carson Thompson, and the last song on the tape Dan had given the group was a fast little number called "The Letter."

Wayne Carson Thompson (he would later drop the surname) was young, but in terms of the amount of experience he had and the legends he had already known, his qualifications

in the music business reached back half a century. His father, using the stage name of Shorty Thompson, had led a western swing band and then formed a smaller unit with Wayne's mother and aunt. It was called the Tall Timber Trio, and Chet Atkins played backup guitar; "My dad fired him four times," Wayne chuckled. If Wayne was not born in a trunk, it was close; the family had migrated to Denver, where the trio had a successful radio show, and Wayne had met famous people from the time he could walk. "Chet and Leona [Chet's wife] used to live behind my house, in the caretaker's cottage," he remembered. "Two doors down, Babe Zaharias lived." The Tall Timber Trio were frequently on the road, and when Wayne was six his father bought a farm in Walnut Grove, Missouri, and played music in and around the Springfield area. "My dad invented the Ozark Jubilee," said Wayne, referring to the famous nationally televised music show of the 1950s. "He did it locally, it got taken away from him. He didn't really get it stolen, but my dad was not a good businessman."

It was hardly surprising that Wayne began playing guitar in his teens, inspired by the rock and roll he loved: "I grew up on Little Richard, Fats Domino, all that business." (According to the Springfield impresario Si Siman, Wayne's younger brother Gary was an equally talented guitarist, though Gary chose to make a living outside of music as a concert promoter.) Wayne's songwriting was "just somethin' that kinda came on me," he reflected. "I got tired of singin' the same old Top Forty—'Oh yeah, Sugar Shack.'" Just like that, he started writing things of his own, occasionally featuring them in the rock bands with which he played on the road. "When I was a kid, I was 17, 18, workin' with bands," he said. "My dad wrote me a postcard, 'You need to come to Springfield and meet Si Siman.' I was just coming to a full head of steam. I would have probably ended up in California, pickin' fruit." Instead, he went back to Springfield, played his songs for Siman, and "I formed a friendship with Si that lasted forty years."

Si arranged for Wayne to work with another Siman protégé, the slightly down-on-his-luck country legend Red Foley. "I worked eight or nine years for Mr. Foley," Wayne said respectfully. "I played for Red . . . on the road. I was his valet. Every human being on this planet should be like him. Red taught me how to be a professional." Since Red's experience went all the way back to the 1930s National Barn Dance on WLS, he would have had much professionalism to teach; recordings of his radio shows even today reveal his charm and his way with an audience. But performing out front did not seem to be what Wayne had in mind, although Si had other ideas. "Si kept trying to make me a record star; I didn't have the stomach for it," remembered Wayne. "I couldn't listen to somebody tell me what to do daylight till dark. 'Wear this shirt, don't cut your hair.' I'm too independent."

Songwriting seemed to be a way of keeping his autonomy, so occasionally Si and Wayne traveled to Nashville to pitch Wayne's compositions for Si's contacts there. It's possible Si hoped that the strength of Wayne's songs plus his easy, slightly Ozark-inflected croon (reminiscent of a smooth Roger Miller) would land him a recording deal. "I went and auditioned for Chet one time; I sang in one key, played in another," Wayne chuckled. In a tape of reminiscences made for the Nashville songwriter Billy Edd Wheeler, Si remembered another time when they had gone to Nashville and Wayne, frustrated at the lack of progress they had made, went storming out of the motel room into the snow, wearing no coat heavier than his unlined denim jacket. But the persistence eventually paid off; Chet Atkins got some of the songs to his friend and client, Eddy Arnold, and Arnold chose one called "Somebody Like Me" to record. It went Top Ten country in the summer of 1966.

Wayne's first hit was different from any of the you're-gonna-lose-that-girl songs that had been recorded before. Seldom had any song featured the jaunty directness of Wayne's memorable tune and colloquial speech. "Wayne was the most unusual songwriter I'd come around," said Reggie Young. "[Each of his songs] had a little twist to it, something you wouldn't usually hear in a country song." Jim Vienneau

must have thought so, too; he signed Wayne to a recording contract with MGM, and, musical matchmaking again, suggested that Wayne begin working with Chips Moman in Memphis instead of with the more traditional Nashville musicians. "Jim said, 'He's got a little rock and roll band that'll be more your thing,'" Wayne remembered. Wayne went to Memphis, met Chips and immediately liked him, and they did a session together. He spent that Thanksgiving holiday of 1966 in Memphis with Chips, Dan, and their wives. Overjoyed at having placed his second hit song, "Do It Again (Just a Little Bit Slower)," Wayne sat and played them most of the things he had written. "Dan said, 'You're the only guy I ever saw I could stand to hear sing more than two or three songs. You just don't write a bad one.'" Wayne gave Dan the tape of his work that featured "The Letter," a song Wayne had been inspired to write by his father, who was fascinated with the word "aero-plane." Wayne was not sure about the song; no one seemed to be.

The DeVilles were not sure of the song, or for that matter, the whole recording process. In a 1990 interview with the record collector's magazine *Goldmine*, the band members expressed their sinking disappointment. They had expected to be working with Chips; instead, they had been foisted off on this novice producer who slouched and wore old plaid Bermuda shorts, taped-up sneakers, and kept a pack of cigarettes rolled up in the sleeve of his baggy T-shirt. They had hoped for state-of-the-art professionalism; instead, they arrived one Saturday morning to find the studio littered with dirty dishes and ashtrays and leftover food from the previous night's session. To make matters worse, Alex Chilton, who would be responsible for interpreting the song, was tired and hung over from celebrating the night before. But somehow, Dan managed to get something down on tape that he liked. Alex had been uncertain at first how to phrase the song, but due to Dan's vocal coaching he delivered the lines with passion and conviction.

After the basic track had been cut with the group, Dan still felt there was a "hole" in the track somewhere and began thinking up ways to fill it. "Dan's a good producer," reflected Mike Leech. "If something came along that he liked, whether it be during writing, producing, whatever, he would go with how he felt. If a steamboat whistle was called for or if he wanted a sound for any reason, it would be there." It was Mike Leech to whom Dan turned for help on finishing the track.

"My very first string arrangement was 'The Letter,' and the only reason I did that was because I knew how to write music notation," Mike reflected. "Nobody else in the group did or I'm sure someone else would have gotten the call.

"Dan called me to come in the studio and play some things on the [Hammond B3] organ while he listened in the control room. When I played something he liked he would tell me to 'write that down.' Interesting side note, after he was satisfied with the arrangement he asked me if I had other ideas and I suggested the two trombones. He liked the idea and said, 'Do it.' The string section consisted of two violins and one viola."

Mike's sweeping string melodies, carrying forward the ideas implicit in the basic tracks, became a trademark of the American Studios sound, and the stateliness of his arranging style was there from the beginning. A string section from the Memphis Symphony was contracted, "something I dearly loved, which was being in the position to hire Noel Gilbert [and his group]," Mike said of the concertmaster and violinist. "Noel was one of my instructors at Memphis State University. He taught a piano class that was required for music majors." "I liked the Memphis Strings of that era better than any string section," Dan Penn added enthusiastically. "They just had this barbecue sound, it was great." "The Memphis Strings were a little sloppy," Mike Leech admitted. "Downbeats were a matter of opinion. But they had a soulful sound. Dan Penn loved them. The very first time I heard of a violin using a mute came from Dan. I didn't know about that but it is a very nice mellow sound. I've used it many times since." "I just heard somebody say 'mute' and I heard a very nice hum," Dan explained.

As Mike would do on every string session he arranged at American thereafter, he was in the studio when the overdubs were added to Dan's basic track. "Strings were always an overdub because of mike sensitivity," the arranger recalled. "Although the room had great acoustics, separation was always somewhat of a problem. Hence isolation booths being a primary factor in the construction of new studios." Folding shutters along the side walls were opened to allow more depth in the sound.

He explained the process further. "It's standard operating procedure for the arranger to always conduct the sessions," he said. "Seldom is an arrangement written that doesn't have mistakes that have to be corrected out on the floor.

"Back when I was doing a lot of arranging, the standard operating procedure was, write a score, which has all the voices. Turn that over to a professional copyist who is told how many violins, violas, horns, etc., and he or she transcribes from the score to individual parts. At American, I didn't have that luxury, and wrote out all the parts myself. Pretty big job, because once the arrangements were written, I still couldn't rest until all the individual charts were done."

The DeVilles must have wondered if Dan was ever going to put the record out, he was taking so long to perfect it. He decided that it needed a literal illustration of the story, so he borrowed a sound-effects record from the library and played the track on the tape machines while Bobby Womack's pal Darryl Carter, who had begun hanging around the studio a little in the interim between the recording of the track and the overdubs, ran the sound of a whooshing jet engine on the turntable. Although Dan remembered Darryl as "a nice guy," he remained adamantly dismissive about the engineer's credit Darryl received on some of the later records coming out of American. "Darryl Carter was no engineer," he scoffed. "He was a gofer. He never did any engineering for me, I wouldn't let anybody near my records! I just can't put up with an engineer, they'd wanna go left, I'd wanna go right. I didn't even know people were comin' in and doing that! I decided they were the Enemy."

With the airplane overdub, the tape was finished, and Chips tried to talk Dan out of keeping the sound effect. Dan told Peter Guralnick his response: "That's my record, and I'm gonna get a razor blade and cut this tape up into a million pieces if you make me take that airplane off." Chips conceded the issue. Dan played a rough cut for Jimmy Johnson and Spooner Oldham when Jimmy visited in Memphis; Jimmy remembered driving home feeling happy because he was certain his friend had done something that was going to be really big. Wayne Carson was not so sure. "I got there right after they did it," he remembered. "Dan called me and said, 'You need to hear it.' I said, 'I'm not impressed.' Dan was the only one that thought it was a hit. The day it came out, I went on a USO tour. We were gone seven weeks, touring the Caribbean."

It was now a matter of where to place the song. "Dan asked me, 'If I do this, can I sign this with a label of my own choosing?' and I said, 'Sure,'" Chips recalled. Papa Don Schroeder was in the studio at the time when these discussions began, recording the Purifys' second album. (That LP featured the lighthearted hit "Let Love Come Between Us"; a jokey song called "Goodness Gracious Chile," written by Papa Don and Spooner; and a remake of the R&B standard "I Love You, Yes I Do," with some relentlessly propulsive bass from Tommy.) "Dan Penn had been up for a week before I got there, he didn't even know where he was," snorted Papa Don. "[He] was out of it. [He] came in and he said, 'I've got this little record I did just before you got here. I sure would like it if you'd help me get a deal on it. Man, if I could get eight hundred dollars and eight percent [for the producer's royalty]. I knew I could get him that. Cogbill said, 'It's a nice record, Pop.' Moman said, 'Yeah, it's really nice.'" With recommendations like that, Papa Don knew he could not go wrong, so he picked up the phone and called Larry Uttal in New York. "I think he paid us nine hundred dollars for the master, it was a lease deal," remembered Don Crews, who placed Uttal in the studio at the time the deal was made (though Mike Leech believed the label head came down later in the year).

As had happened in his deals with Quinton Claunch and Papa Don, who had first familiarized Bell Records with American, Uttal now had rights to any independent or spec recording done at the studio. Dan had thought in terms of placing one master and now they were, in effect, officially signed to a label. American Studios would be, for all practical purposes, the Southern division of Bell Records until the three-year deal with the label ended in early 1970. "Dan Penn doesn't even remember it," huffed Papa Don indignantly, "but that's the way it happened."

Papa Don was not the only indignant one. So was Jerry Wexler, when he found out that American product was now signed to his label's archrival. "Jerry Wexler was always on my behind about 'The Letter,'" Don Crews stated. "Wexler said, 'Why didn't you give that record to me, Don?' I told him, 'It's no slight to you, he just happened to be there.' Jerry had an old saying that Larry came and picked up the crumbs after him."

Other New York labels were interested in what was going on at American. Steve Tyrell, an aspiring singer and promotion man at the time for Scepter Records (Dionne Warwick's label), turned up occasionally, inveigling Chips to work with some of his company's artists. "I think I met Steve when he was eighteen or nineteen; he would sit in and do 'Stand by Me,'" remembered Glen Spreen, like Tyrell a veteran of the Houston music scene. Tyrell was still in touch with many of the musicians in that area, and he sent a friend of his, a songwriting hopeful whose career he had been managing, to pitch some material.

"Mark James came up from Houston around '67," Don Crews remembered. "Mark had just gotten out of the military and Steve Tyrell pointed him our way. He'd been in the army—I think he went to Vietnam, but he didn't get into anything." Mark had served with a communications team, working in advance of the grunts; although, typical of those who have actually been in combat, he was reluctant to discuss what he had seen, Glen Spreen recalled a vague reference to "a sniper and one of Mark's team members." Chips Moman recalled that Mark had just gotten back to the States, and that Mark's wife was pregnant. "I met him at the airport and tried to find him a place to stay," added Crews. Upon hearing a few of Mark's songs, Chips immediately put Mark on a writer's salary with Press Music. "We paid him seventy-five dollars a week, best I remember," said Crews. Chips said that he had hired Mark partly because he knew Mark's songs would be hits and partly because he felt that Mark was a talented young man who could use the break.

Chips's new staff writer had grown up in a securely middle-class family from a good neighborhood in Houston. Ed Kollis was under the impression that Mark's father owned a lumberyard, but in fact it had been a flooring company; the tiles in the Houston airport had been laid by his firm. "Mark's mother was my third-grade teacher," added Glen Spreen. Mark's middle-class background—which set him apart from the predominately working-class musicians and from Chips—gave his songs an ironic air reminiscent of Paul Simon (the quintessential bard of the American middle class) and a sophistication rare in Southern music at that time. The musicians at American recognized Mark's talent as quickly as Chips had. "I always enjoyed working with him," Reggie Young mused. "Mark's songs were probably the most difficult [to play] because of the chord changes." "He was good-looking, young, eighteen or nineteen, very smiley and cheerful though I could tell he had a brooding side to him," observed Spooner Oldham. Hayward Bishop, who met Mark later, remembered Mark's sidewise, faintly smiling expression, with an intense gaze and an uptilted head; the pose can be seen on the cover of Mark's 1973 solo album for Bell. "He had that long-tall-Texan kind of look," added Spooner. Mark's attitude was pure Texas, too, and so was his voice, a sly drawl that slipped into a pleasant, slightly sardonic tenor when he sang.

As he did with everyone who came on the scene, Chips encouraged Mark to get involved in all aspects of the studio, so Mark played his twelve-string guitar on a few sessions and occasionally contributed harmonies to the loose, ragged-sounding, whoever's-in-the-studio

aggregate of musicians doubling as background singers that was irreverently dubbed "the Moman Tabernacle Choir." "Chips liked home-grown backing vocals," observed Bobby Wood, another frequent contributor of background harmonies. Mark also hung around the studio and watched while recording occurred, which is how he came to be there during the first week of July, shortly after his arrival, when the Atlantic crew descended upon American en masse.

They were all there: Wexler, Dowd, Mardin, and King Curtis, accompanying Wilson Pickett for a week of recording, signaling to the world that Atlantic took American seriously enough to make it their new Southern base. Atlantic had done what had amounted to a trial run that spring, flying the entire band up to New York City for a session with Solomon Burke; the results, produced by Chips and Dan, had yielded one single thus far. They had also recorded Patti Labelle and the Bluebelles, singing a song Dan had written called "Dreamer." "It wasn't no big deal," remembered Don Crews, who also went along. "I don't even remember where we stayed at. That old building [the Atlantic studios] was a cold old building. We had to go downstairs to this rental place and rent some drums and instruments. [The studio] was one story above their offices . . . kind of a corner studio. Tom Dowd, he was the engineer so we did the picking." Crews had originally questioned Chips's selection of a collaborator. "I told Chips, he wanted Dan to come up and help him produce—I said, 'You need to have Tommy come up and do this, not Dan, because Tommy should be the man, because he's been with you through thick and thin.' Chips didn't see it that way." Tommy did contribute his deep, rumbling bass to the two songs released at that time, giving the music a texture that enhanced its moods.

The A-side of the record was one of Chips's and Dan's sorrowful, stark compositions. Structured like a traditional story-song, "I Stayed Away Too Long" sounds like a gospel tune recorded in the shadow of Clinch Mountain. Solomon narrates the tale of a man going back to see his old lover, only to discover weeds grown up around the now-dilapidated house and the neighbors telling him that the girl had gotten married to "a tall, handsome guy" and moved away. The Sweet Inspirations cry out the title line with passionate sadness, and Solomon sounds like a lost soul, burdened forever with the fact of his negligent regret. The adherence to strict ballad and gospel form is obviously Dan's touch, but the portrait of a man almost blind with pain is pure Chips. It is the audio equivalent of an Edward Hopper painting: realistic to the smallest detail, capturing loneliness in an unsparing way.

And that was just the first side of the single. Traditionally, the B-side of a record is not as strong, but Dan's and Spooner's "Take Me (Just As I Am)," in which a good old boy admits that he does not have a lot of money but does have a great deal of passionate love for his woman, became a soul-music standard. Quinton Claunch recorded it with several of his artists for Goldwax. They had brought the song with them from Muscle Shoals; Dan had recorded it there for Rick Hall's Fame label under the name of Lonnie Ray. Dan's ideas seem to be slightly more prominent on this side of the record, and he tilts the production heavily toward the gospel-styled "testifying" at which Solomon excelled. "It's an odd little song," Spooner commented thoughtfully. "It's definitely a mood of the times; it's not a mood of the times today, but it's a good song. It's one of those I hope will resurface again, in a good way."

As with so many of the American Studios works, this two-sided hit was a recording for people who had endured the harder sides of life. Some of that could have been due to the fact that, although their songs were beginning to reach the Top Forty at a predictable rate, these musicians hardly thought of themselves as kids. "We was young, but we wasn't teenagers," said Dan Penn. "I was twenty-six when I cut 'The Letter,' that made Moman about thirty-one." Tommy Cogbill was four years older than Chips; he was rapidly becoming the father figure, the one to whom even Chips and Dan deferred because of his experience and perspective on the business. "Tommy was knowledgeable about what should or shouldn't be,"

remembered Don Crews respectfully. "Tommy had a maturity and wisdom and you knew he was there," said Johnny Christopher, who met the American musicians for the first time later in the year. "I looked up to Tommy." The Atlantic group admired Cogbill also. It was mutual, as was the admiration of the others who had previously worked with the New Yorkers; the rest of the group soon discovered why this was so.

"I always liked Tom," Don Crews said of Dowd. "He was a good engineer and a good electrician. He was a nice fellow, one of the nicer people in the music business I was associated with. He was really the man they depended on at Atlantic." Gene Chrisman echoed the sentiment. "Tom and I and Duck Dunn and Steve Cropper, we played golf all the time," he recalled (a memory Dowd spoke fondly of in his interview for the book *The Record Producers*, noting that the musicians used their 9 A.M. tee time as a warm-up for going into the studio one hour later). "I enjoyed working for the Atlantic crew most of the time, but in retrospect, those guys emitted jive," shrugged Mike Leech. "Tom Dowd always engineered, and spent a lot of time underneath the console with a soldering gun. Arif had an air of shyness, I thought at that time."

"He was *very* easy to work with," Reggie Young said respectfully of Dowd. "I can still see him moving his hands around. He'd kind of draw you a picture mentally. . . . I remember Wexler would usually give it direction, Dowd would concentrate on the sound. He used the word 'marriage'—'The marriage of the keyboard and guitar isn't right.' He was very professional. He was very careful not to kill any grooves or throw a blanket on anything. I don't know if that was his natural way, but that was how he was with us. . . . As I look back, I guess our little place, our studio, was quite unique, slightly different than what they were getting in New York."

"I always looked forward to sessions with Atlantic Records," said Bobby Emmons. "At American we worked the most with Tom Dowd and Arif Mardin, but everyone from that label was a pleasure. They brought great songs and all their artists had a jaw-dropping talent to try to complement musically. Tom and Arif's relaxed professionalism I believe helped create the atmosphere that allowed us to get into some of those fine grooves." Bobby Wood, who played piano on this session, remembered the Atlantic staff respectfully, although he said, "Frankly, I didn't have a clue who Wexler was or what he did. I do remember Wexler as being a fairly laid-back person. Don't remember ever talking to him. Arif was always the same. A mild-mannered person and kind of laid-back."

Chips Moman was also delighted to have the Atlantic people there, for slightly different reasons. He had been practically living in the studio at that point, doing all of the engineering, and he was happy to have Tom Dowd come in and run the board, "so I could *leave*," he said emphatically. He had developed other interests by now; he had gotten to be fond of horse racing, and had discovered water-skiing and golf, a game to which, like Gene Chrisman, he became devoted. The presence of the Atlantic group allowed him to have some valuable time off.

By default, then, the ranking presence in the studio for the Pickett/King Curtis session was Tommy Cogbill. To observers, it was apparent that his confidence had grown in just the two months since the "Cheater Man" sessions, when his ideas had first influenced the direction of a record. Photos of him taken during the interim, on a vacation in Arkansas with his family and that of Reggie Young, show a relaxed man with a joyfully sunny smile. He would take another step forward for these sessions, as he was slated to co-produce along with Tom Dowd.

Tommy never talked much about how he arrived at momentous decisions, so it is not fully known how or why he got interested in record production. Even Chips didn't seem to be clear on this point, beyond a vague "I guess he just got interested after working with me awhile." Nor is it clear why he decided he would begin by collaborating with Dowd. Perhaps it was simply the desire of a talented musician to expand creatively. "All musicians that get involved with studios want to get involved with production; it's like the guy coming in to shoot

pool eventually wants to open a pool hall," said Jimmy Johnson. Tommy's suggestions on this session were not well remembered by the rest of the group, so it is likely that he called a few of the shots from his place out on the studio floor and mainly served in an observer's capacity, watching carefully how Dowd achieved the smooth sound that Tommy admired.

What is known is that he was pleased to see again a new acquaintance that Pickett had insisted on bringing to the sessions. Bobby Womack brought his guitar, a few new songs, and his writing partner Darryl Carter, all of whom were warmly welcomed. "I admired Bobby Womack as a musician and as an artist, too," Reggie Young remembered happily. "He influenced my playing from the time I met him. I was blown away by the way he played. Him being left-handed, he sat across from me and it was like looking in a mirror. He could take my guitar and turn it upside down and play it without changing the strings. We'd sit in front of each other, and I'd have my head cocked.

"He had a hollow-body electric, that old guitar he had was handmade in New York. I don't know why he got rid of it [later].It had such a sweet sound. It was a hollow-body, more of a jazz guitar."

"I loved him, man, he was a super guy," said Bobby Wood enthusiastically. "Him and Reggie worked well together. We all really enjoyed those times, that was a learning experience for me." "Very talented guy. I learned a lot from him about what was hip and what wasn't in his style of music," offered Bobby Emmons. "He was very cocky and confident. Well, you know how musicians are. You try to impress somebody if you've got the horsepower to do it."

"He was writing songs on the spot," said an awestruck Reggie, and in fact the first song on the Pickett album was one of Bobby's; the intro features his sharp, twangy lead. "Jealous Love" is about an obsessively controlling woman who apparently goes everywhere with her man, tries to catch him looking at other women, and rifles his pockets looking for phone numbers. Bobby's position regarding this behavior is that it is degrading to both the man and the woman. The song has a brooding, almost paranoid tinge in the verses, bursting into a gorgeously expansive chorus accented by Arif Mardin's soaring strings. Pickett cries, shouts, screams, and pleads for help in the fadeout, while Womack's guitar skitters nervously and Tommy Cogbill's walking bass strolls nonchalantly away, mirroring his habit of vanishing at the slightest sign of discord.

The second song, "Stagolee," had been a hit for Pickett's friend and mentor Lloyd Price, and Pickett gives a conversational reading of the story; his phrasing and his timing are faultless, and Arif's nine-piece horn section blasts the emphasis out even further. "I thought Wilson was a little nervous and uptight, until we got into the music, and he seemed to relax," observed Bobby Wood, and the easy, natural quality with which Pickett sings on this track makes his eventual comfort with the musicians clear. Reggie Young remembered, as had Dan Penn in Muscle Shoals, Wilson's habit of stamping his foot when he sang, perhaps a timekeeping technique; whatever it was, it worked, for his singing at American was some of the best in his career.

"That Kind of Love," introduced by Womack's blunt, attention-grabbing lead line, continues the uptempo mood, and then comes the album's stunner, Womack's song for and about Barbara Cooke, "I'm in Love." He had written it after an evening spent griping to some friends about the way his marriage was perceived, and about how no one seemed to understand the depth of his love for her. His friends suggested that he put his thoughts down in a song, and the result was what the critic Jon Landau, writing in the liner notes, called "a beautiful synthesis of several different types of songwriting—gospel, soul, and pop."

The track was something of a synthesis as well. Womack's guitar introduces the song and establishes its groove. "I loved Womack because that song 'I'm in Love' had such an unusual rhythm," Bobby Wood remarked. "I had to count every stinkin' bar on that thing. Womack was a Floyd Cramer fan, he wanted me to play those Cramer licks. On a lotta things we did I'd try to get real funky because his stuff was funky, but he'd want to hear them Floyd

Cramer licks." Against this background, as the music swells and builds, Wilson, speaking as Bobby in first person for the duration of the song, explains that he truly is in love and that this woman makes him happy. He compares his joy to that of a child on Christmas morning, and says his friends do not know what to make of it, or him. And at the end of the song, Pickett tosses off a graceful reference to another longtime friend. "I can knock on wood now," he says, quoting the Stax hit of earlier that year, "Just like Eddie Floyd did"—Floyd being the writer and singer who had made that song successful.

King Curtis's "Hello Sunshine" features Tommy's jazzy descending bass line, and the lyrics about emerging from darkness and finally finding happiness are a good metaphor for a man like Tommy who had been scuffling around in the music business for years and was now becoming established: "I can't explain what I've been through." As with much of the material produced by the American group (especially by Chips and Tommy), the ostensible lyrics of a love song provide an autobiographical framework; the listener does not even have to read between the lines to understand the references.

Another autobiographical work would be recorded later in the session. "Don't Cry No More," the old Bobby "Blue" Bland classic, is astonishing. Wilson's wild, passionate shout as he counts off the song leads to Tommy's incredible repeating figure on bass (one wonders how human fingers can possibly play the notes that fast). Gene Chrisman is featured alone behind Wilson in the chorus, and the ferocity of his drumming illustrates why King Curtis called his style "fatback." The track has a classic New Orleans rhythmic feel, seemingly an odd style for a Memphis producer to adapt until one learns of a conversation Tommy had with Hayward Bishop in the summer of 1970. Discussing musical influences, the drummer said that he had always loved and tried to emulate New Orleans music. "Tommy's eyes got as big as saucers," Hayward remembered, "and he said, 'Me, too. Me, too!'" Bobby Wood was another New Orleans devotee, not surprising in light of the fact that the Crescent City had always been a piano man's town. "I was trained by ear, listenin' to those players," he said. "I liked Frogman Henry, Allen Toussaint." Though Bobby isn't a featured soloist here, his piano emphasizes the rhythm, and the song flashes like a comet. The listener scarcely has time to register the lyrics, but play that track once and it will be listened to over and over and over again.

Reggie Young had a hand in putting together the next song, based on a fragment Womack had already begun. "He only had one verse written, he was singin' it over and over," Reggie recalled. "I said, 'What is it?' 'Something I'm writing.' He told me, 'Help me fix this song for Pickett, I'll give you half.'" Reggie contributed an additional verse and part of the chorus, and "We've Got to Have Love" was done. The opening verse is practically an American Studios position paper: "Some folks think they got the world on a string, but we know better / Some folks think that money is everything, but we know better." The chorus speaks of "a voice crying out in the wilderness," and the final verse mentions what is needed to help get through it all: "I found me a real true love" (which Reggie thought was the song's title). "I didn't hardly remember what I'd done," he added. "The early records had my name on it [as coauthor], the later ones had Pickett's name." Bobby saw to it that Reggie got the royalties, though.

Pickett delivers a heartfelt version of Sam Cooke's classic "Bring It On Home to Me," featuring some emotional call-and-response work with Womack that echoes what Cooke and Lou Rawls had done on the original. The piano flourishes Bobby Wood plays on the fadeout emphasize the song's gospel roots even further. "I played stuff right out of the church, the Baptist church," said Wood. "Now, I don't care for the sound of the white church, I'm tired of funeral music." Bobby's playing was hardly dirgelike (of the American keyboardists, Spooner Oldham's work most closely fits that description), but there was a spiritual component to it that enhances the proceedings here. "In those days I was just learning to get into the groove of R&B, which was on the other end of the

spectrum from hair-on-fire rock and roll," the piano player explained.

Bobby Womack's "I've Come a Long Way" is the album's closer, and listening to it is like gazing into a hall of mirrors; one is not sure if it is the singer (Wilson), the writer (Womack), or the co-producer (Tommy) who is predominately speaking, or all three at once, since the song's message can be applied to the lives of each. Womack and Reggie Young play an intertwining guitar part to open the piece; they separate briefly and then reunite for the rest of the song, demonstrating their meeting of minds. Bobby Emmons comes in with a sustaining organ line as Pickett sings, "I've come a long, long, long, long way / Since I found a love." Here, finding a beloved becomes symbolic of finding one's place in life, and resting after an uphill struggle: "It was so hard, day by day." The chorus acknowledges all the years spent drifting with no end in sight: "I used to run / Here and there / Here, there, and everywhere." It is the summary both of Wilson's and Womack's journey from gospel to soul, from Prattville, Alabama, and Cleveland, Ohio, to Detroit and Los Angeles, and of Tommy Cogbill's wanderings through several styles of music. Acknowledgment is paid to the woman who "smoothed out all the rough roads" this could apply to the apparently maternal Barbara Cooke or the reliable gentleness of Shirley Cogbill. We are left at the end of the song, and the album, with Wilson seemingly shaking his head in astonishment at how far he has come, with Bobby Womack's determined guitar and Tommy's walking bass implying that further trudging lies ahead. Tommy in particular seems to be echoing Robert Frost's "But I have promises to keep / And miles to go before I sleep."

Womack's virtuosity stunned the group so much that Chips came in to record him; "What Is This" would be Bobby's first solo single. The dominant phrase of the song may again have been Womack borrowing from a gospel song of the same title. With Tommy's intricate bass filling in the melodic line, Bobby cries out with the passion of Pickett and the ferocity of Levi Stubbs; he has not found his own vocal style yet, but his admiration for his heroes is touching. Mike Leech colors in the verses with a descending string line similar to the one he used in "The Letter"; though countermelodies were not a usual trademark of his writing, the muted violins hum across the melody effectively, and in the chorus they become the respondent to Bobby's gospel calls.

Bobby Womack had made a decided impression on the group, but their freewheeling style of recording made an equally powerful impact on him. "Gosh, Bobby just fell in love with the place," said Reggie Young. "He rented a cheap old apartment in downtown Memphis. He hung out there writing, trying to get his writing chops back. He wanted to hang out in Memphis to get his soul back, he said he'd been living in too fine a house in L.A." Chips Moman improvised a position for Bobby as songwriter and second guitarist, and he and most of the musicians said that Womack was a part of the group for the duration. Bobby Emmons offered a clarification. "Womack was *not* part of the core group, he was a *guest artist*," the organist declared emphatically, through gritted teeth. Chips also created a place for Darryl Carter, signing him on as a songwriter and giving him an additional assignment as assistant engineer, the first of a long succession of talented sound-crew laborers. Womack and Carter now had unlimited time to craft songs, learn more about studio techniques, and of course occasionally sing backup in the Moman Tabernacle Choir.

In five months Chips had taken on a number of remarkable writers. The list of artists recording at American was becoming formidable too, thanks to Atlantic's patronage. King Curtis had been impressed with Tommy Cogbill and the other Memphis musicians when he worked with them on Aretha's and his album there; now he wanted to try putting a few things down on tape for his next project, experimenting as he went along. According to Tom Dowd in *The Record Producers*, Curtis asked him how much of the players' soulfulness was theirs, and how much due to Atlantic's coaching; Dowd replied, "The way they play and write is the way they live" (foreshadowing Willie Nelson's line from years later, "We write what we live, and we live what we write," but giving it a slightly different emphasis). When Curtis met all the musicians, he was overwhelmed; he could not believe that wiry little Gene Chrisman was the powerhouse drummer he heard on the records. (Presumably he had gotten over the shock of seeing the equally wiry, somewhat frail-looking Tommy, and contrasting his appearance with those thundering bass lines, up in New York.) He had been there only a day or two when he and the musicians were sitting in the Ranch House restaurant eating lunch; Curtis looked at the menu and exclaimed, "Today's special is Memphis Soul Stew." Immediately he knew he had the theme to hold together a little rhythm piece he had been working on in New York. Reggie Young remembered everyone racing back to the studio in haste to capture it.

From the beginning, "Memphis Soul Stew," appropriately, belongs to Tommy Cogbill. His bass underlines Curtis's spoken introductions as, one at a time, the other musicians enter. Bobby Emmons creates a whirring line on the organ to simulate stirring and blending as Curtis announces the recipe's ingredients and directions. But when Curtis shouts "Now *beat . . . well!*" and begins playing his saxophone melody, Tommy's bass rumbles good-naturedly beneath, and keeps pace throughout the rest of the record. It is as if Tommy is introducing himself directly to the listener, and letting us know what he is all about. He also brings a sense of exhilaration to the table; no other producer at American ever sounded as if they were having as much fun in the studio.

"Gosh, Tommy was a sweetheart to work with," Reggie Young reflected on Cogbill's production style. "He didn't have a problem explaining anything. Usually, things would fall together quicker [on his sessions] because he was a musician. You'd be on your toes, because he was listening with different ears." A photo of Tommy taken during these sessions shows him doing just that; listening with his head down, apparently during a playback. An empty Coke bottle with a cigarette butt dropped inside it sits on the ledge in front of him. Beside him stands Gene Chrisman, who apparently moved just as the picture was being taken; he looks blurred, but he brandishes his cigarette with a flourish. Directly opposite Tommy, visible through the control-room glass, is Curtis, who looks rumpled and tired, but game; if you can stay up, I can stay up, he seems to be saying. Dowd, seated in the producer's chair, looks exhausted; he's obviously counting the seconds till he is out of there. And we get our first glimpse of Mark James, seated at the assistant engineer's chair to Dowd's right; with his thatchy pompadour he already looks more Memphis than Texas, and his eyes have the keen, intent gaze of a watchful observer.

If Mark was learning a lot from watching King Curtis, he was not the only one. "I think we all learned a lot from the New York people coming down," observed Reggie Young. "King Curtis was the best musician I had ever worked with at the time I met him. He kind of made the mark a little higher. I had never worked with a musician who was as quick as he was. He was real quick where we would take all day doing a take.

"I found out that the best-feeling solos are the ones you do right off the top of your head. Your first idea is usually the most soulful. I'd play a solo again and again and get picky picky picky. Usually, the first time you start running it down is the best you're ever gonna get. After the first few takes, there's no more creativity. A lot of producers didn't know when it was going downhill. A lot of times, they'd let it go by them.

"King was—man, he was always right there. I remember when 'Memphis Soul Stew' came about, King would ask us, 'What key you wanna do this in?' He didn't mind playing in guitar keys. That's not the usual key for a horn. . . . The first time he played, it was absolutely wonderful. That rubbed off on me, to where I thought, you don't need to be so picky, picky. I was *very* impressed with him. I like to think he rubbed off on us."

"King was my favorite of all," echoed Bobby Wood. "He seemed to be one of us and easy to know. Guess we had the musical thing that tied us together. I already had a ton of respect for him from the Coasters records that I grew up on." Bobby Emmons, too, was honored to have Curtis there. "I was crazy about 'Soul Twist' and 'Soul Serenade,'" he said. "I showed my enthusiasm by playing something that would support him. He was friendly and sensitive to remarks, he didn't cut you down, no jive." The friendliness comes through even on the slow-drag version of "C. C. Rider," featuring Reggie Young's intense guitar line and Emmons's sparkling piano fills. "I think I must have not been there the day 'Soul Stew' was cut or just laid out," Bobby Wood said of his compatriot's presence on piano. "I did that a lot, but I do remember playing on some of the album [when Curtis returned later in the year to finish the project]." On the final verse, Curtis and the band make the tune tilt and sway back and forth, giving a relaxed sound to even the deepest emotions the song evokes.

"When a Man Loves a Woman" was a showcase for Curtis's intensity, and a perfect opportunity for Memphis to pay tribute to Muscle Shoals. Bobby Emmons's organ line is both less despondent and more restrained than Spooner Oldham's on the original, perhaps because he plays a supporting role. Curtis interprets the song both passionately and thoughtfully, and Reggie's lead guitar lines show how much he had already learned from Womack; he embellishes each bar with the graceful curlicues that henceforth would be a trademark of his style. At times the string arrangement almost seems to battle Curtis for prominence (a conflict Mike Leech never created with his supportive string lines), giving the song a sense of someone struggling with the knowledge of how hopeless his feelings are. Tommy adds what he needs to but no more. All those elements, pulled together, create a strong, emotion-filled track, though perhaps more dramatic than it would have been had Tommy had complete control; in his solo productions, he made a point of avoiding melodrama and abstraction. Atlantic was obviously satisfied with the results of the experiment, for they booked Curtis to come down and finish his project at American in the following month.

One album for Wilson Pickett, the beginning of a new project for King Curtis, and an additional few sides cut for Don Covay—by the time the Atlantic crew left American at the end of that monumental Fourth of July week, they must have felt they had been treated to a display of fireworks like none other.

Those summer months were the turning point.

### CHAPTER 8

# A Place in the Sun

American became a success before the musicians fully had time to realize it. One minute they were a struggling studio with only a few outside accounts, most of whom, like Quinton Claunch and Papa Don Schroeder, were themselves in the aspirant category; the next, seemingly overnight, they were the Southern recording base for two New York labels (Atlantic and Bell) and were welcoming artists of worldwide renown. Once everyone became aware of what was happening, there was a tremendous sense of accomplishment, a feeling that they were all part of something creative, vital, and growing. "I just remember the early days of American being a fun time," Bobby Wood reminisced happily. They were learning about each other, about themselves, and about working together; and they were delighted at having proven that they could work with established artists, create quality recordings with them, and have hits— the success of Atlantic's first batch of records made with the group had proven it.

Jerry Wexler knew a hitmaking team when he heard one, so Tommy Cogbill and Spooner Oldham once again joined their friends from the Shoals in New York that summer for work on Aretha's second album. The sessions were slightly delayed due to the singer's having broken an arm while she was on tour; she was determined to play piano, however, so she simply worked with one hand throughout the week of recording.

The mood and character of this adventure differed slightly from the first New York road trip six months earlier. Tommy and Spooner had been up again for the Solomon Burke sessions, and even the Shoals musicians, back in New York for the second time, were more at ease. Though they had all mostly played close to home until they began doing work for Atlantic, they were growing accustomed to being in a large city, and running on and off planes. "Our first jet was a 727, we used to call it '727, gonna take us to heaven,'" laughed Jimmy Johnson. They had gone home from the first road trip with a sense of pride: "We said well, by golly, no one can ever take this away from us, we've done it once. By the second trip, I was out there flaggin' the cabs. We Alabama rednecks, we adapt!" (Perhaps, but another dimension can be heard on the old Cecil Gant wartime ballad, "I Wonder," in which all of the musicians paint a heartfelt, moody portrayal of homesickness.) Jimmy Johnson recalled a different hotel this time. "They moved us up to Central Park South. They'd give us our own private room. It was like, *wow*. We wound up goin' to little old restaurants right around the studio there. Once they heard us talkin', we were the Rebs. The better the places got, the nicer they treated us. That's why we knew we had to make it!"

The musical lineup was different, too. Chips Moman had the studio going fulltime now and could not get away as easily, so Atlantic hired Joe South, who was developing a reputation as an incisive guitarist and interesting songwriter, to come up from Bill Lowery's in Atlanta (where J.R. Cobb was now ensconced as a studio player and composer) and replace Chips on lead guitar. Joe had already written his famous crosstown romance, "Down in the Boondocks," which had been a big hit for fellow Lowery artist Billy Joe Royal; "I Knew You When," a treatise on snobbery, had also been successful. In addition, he had the cachet of having worked with Bob Dylan for the Nashville *Blonde on Blonde* sessions. He was musically adventurous enough to fit in perfectly with these players and with Aretha, who seemed to willfully defy categories on this album, presenting listeners with unusual reworkings of "Satisfaction," "You Are My Sunshine," "That's Life," and even the novelty song "96 Tears."

Among those category-defying selections was Willie Nelson's classic "Night Life," which Joe and Tommy transform into a slow blues dialogue. It is ironic in light of the fact that Tommy, for all of the long hours spent recording at American, was never really at his best late at night. Most of the other musicians at American were temperamentally and artistically inclined to be nocturnal. "I definitely think music is for night," Bobby Emmons observed thoughtfully. "Unless there's no windows in the building, music has too much treble in sunlight." "Tommy was more of a day person, around ten o'clock he'd start to fade," said Bobby Wood. "He would get tired; he'd go to sleep on you," chuckled Chips Moman. Bobby Wood agreed. "We weren't day people, we just about wore Chrisman out because we'd get [out of the studio] at three A.M." Gene Chrisman cheerfully acknowledged it. "I have *never* been a night person. It was frustrating to me. Stayin' up all night just don't get it."

Tommy and Gene handled the problem of operating on different clocks from everyone else by disappearing as soon as their work on the basic tracks was done, despite Chips's preference that everyone stay there so they could be available for overdubs or repairs if needed. Tommy would seize a chance and slip out the back door so quietly that none of the musicians even realized he was gone. "I always said that Tommy could find a hole in the wall at Fort Knox," laughed Bobby Emmons. "I was glad to see Tommy go 'cause there'd be no more need for the session," said Reggie Young. Mike Leech remembered everyone confronting Gene Chrisman about his refusal to stick around one minute longer than the demands of cutting the rhythm track required; he recalled saying to Gene, "Well, we're all here and we are all willing to stay here, why can't you?" and they tried to persuade him for over an hour. Gene was adamant: "I'm *not* gonna work all night." And that was that.

But then, Gene prided himself on his differences. "I kinda stayed out of the way," he said. "I was kinda the lone wolf of everybody. I was the one that stayed on the back burner. I just laid low, did my part, got the heck out." "He does his thing the way he wants it and nobody, but nobody, is going to change him," observed Mike Leech. Gene's serious attention to detail made him the perfect person to handle the paperwork documenting sessions for the union. "I'd type out the contracts so I memorized everybody's address and Social Security number," he said. When he was not working, he played golf or spent time with his family. Tommy Cogbill went fishing or, occasionally, squirrel hunting (Mike Leech went with him once, killed one squirrel, and sadly resolved never to do that again), and he also worked on cars—hardly the hobbies of people inclined to keep late hours.

For the others, the night shift was their idea of paradise. Mike Leech and Reggie Young thrived on it, relishing both the work and the group camaraderie. Bobby Wood found it stimulating. He spoke of going home and lying down while his mind was still going over a particularly exciting track they had cut in the studio; he called it "a music hangover. And those are the best kind." Bobby Emmons was also eager to put in late hours; frequent sips of black coffee saw him through the grind. Rarely did Chips even schedule day sessions; the later the better, as far as he was concerned. He borrowed a page from Phil Spector's book in working with one song till the musicians were almost exhausted, then recording the results, apparently believing that this was the best way to capture the weary, dispirited sound that was becoming his trademark.

"We had good times and bad times and I think that time in the studio aged us all," said Gene Chrisman, which made Tommy Cogbill's New York recording of the blues classic "Going Down Slow" with Aretha a further irony. Though no one seemed to be aware of it at the time, the pressure of being a day person in a night person's world was rapidly affecting Tommy; photos taken of him in New York early the following year would show a tired, careworn man with deep lines on his face. He was thirty-five, but seemed ten years past that; for the rest of his life he would look worn, exhausted, and old before his time.

The Sweet Inspirations, New York's most successful backing vocalists, had sung on both of Aretha's Atlantic sessions. They began as the nucleus from the gospel group the Drinkard Singers, led by the powerful voice of Emily "Cissy" Drinkard Houston; others who had passed through the group at various times included Houston's relatives Dionne and Dee Warwick and Judy Clay. As background session singers, they took over from the earlier Atlantic-featured group the Cookies when the Cookies left to work as the famous Ray Charles Raelets. It was only a matter of time before they got their own record deal, and in August 1967 Tom Dowd brought them to Memphis where he and Cogbill would be collaborating on the production of their first solo album. Ironically, Margie Hendricks from the Cookies/Raelets had cut some solo sides at American earlier in the year; Reggie Young, who knew as much on this subject as anyone who has ever lived, pronounced her "very cool." Mike Leech remembered her as every bit the pepperpot shown in the Ray Charles biopic; although her life and career were in the downward spiral that would end with her death in July 1973 (rather than circa 1965 as the movie stated), she was still capable of turning on some sass. Mike remembered, "She rolled in the studio . . . 'hey baby, whas happenin'?' 'We gonna rock some tonight, yeh baby, whatcha got goin'?' 'Count it off, honey—we be groovin.' I'm truly sorry she's gone, and happy that she left a legacy behind."

Chips Moman and Darryl Carter were there at varying times to do some of the engineering for Dowd. Mike Leech called Chips "a master mixer and engineer. I loved to hear his playbacks and I loved to watch him mix. He would play the console like it was an instrument. A cigarette between his fingers and manipulating the faders as the track went by. I learned a lot from watching and listening." "He was a great engineer," said B.J. Thomas; Hayward Bishop, no admirer of Chips, called him "an expert engineer, the best tape splicer ever," and described him as knowledgeable and authoritative on the matter of sound. Tom Dowd had been formally trained as a physicist and he had relatives who worked in classical music, so the combination of a schooled electronics man and a self-taught guitarist and songwriter made a good (and interesting) balance in the control room. "He really knew what he was doing," said Chips appreciatively, with the respectful tone characteristic of all his reminiscences about working with the Atlantic staff.

To the American group, who had come to

admire the Sweet Inspirations when they had all worked together in New York, the vocalists getting an album of their own was an honor long overdue. "They were just such a great group, you know, and Cissy Houston has one of the greatest voices in the world," said Chips Moman with warm enthusiasm. The Drinkard Singers had recorded a gospel album that remains a critical favorite, but this was their first solo album since going secular, and that alone would have made it a monumental occasion. "I was really up about their chance to record," said Spooner Oldham. Everyone wanted to make this project go well; they approached it with the attitude they were beginning to bring to every session, an approach described by Bobby Wood as "making every song that we cut have the potential to be a Number One hit record. Not Number Three, not Number Two, Number One."

Though they were not really aware of what sort of people the audience for their work might be, they all wanted to make recordings that were accessible to the public—at a time when popular music, especially that influenced by psychedelia, was becoming fragmented and at times incomprehensible. "After all, [the general public] are the reason we became session musicians," Mike Leech reflected. "We want them to purchase a record we played on, so we play what we think they would like to hear—that thought should be in the 'session man's bible.' I think a lot of players forget that and play for themselves. If that's the attitude, then they should just become jazzbos and play for themselves. And that's not meant to be a slam of jazz players. I love jazz and studied it for several years. But being a 'commercial' session player is second nature to me (and most successful session men) now. This is a good subject and should be extrapolated on by musicians who want to be session players."

It was precisely the lack of commercial potential, and of quality, that dismayed Spooner Oldham as he and Dan Penn watched the beginning of the session from the comfort of a huge sofa that had been placed in the control room. He was there strictly as an observer, although with his typically delightful vagueness he could not remember why he was not playing. Nonetheless, as he heard the vocalists running down the two songs Atlantic had suggested, he felt that he and Dan could come up with something better, and he proposed that they write a song. "As we walked out [of the studio], up the steps to where Chips had his offices, Dan said, 'You got any ideas?' I said, 'What's wrong with 'Sweet Inspiration'?'" Spooner recalled. They were upstairs writing, in a room with just a guitar, for "maybe an hour and a half, half an hour."

When they came back downstairs, they ran through the new tune for the singers and the delighted musicians. (Chips Moman, in the control room, remembered being delighted too, and proud of his friends for having come up with something. He too had felt that the New York–selected songs lacked quality, but that it was not his place to say anything, since he was only the engineer for this session.) "I'm playing guitar, Dan is singing," Spooner said. Spooner had come up with a rolling guitar riff to introduce the song and it was decided that this, too, was a keeper. The singers were already learning the words when Tom Dowd called a lunch break, much to Dan's exasperation. He later told Peter Guralnick, "Spooner had this damn lick down so good the musicians wouldn't go eat, they wouldn't leave because they knew by what was happening we could just cut it." They did, with Dan seated at the controls engineering: "I did my mix on the first take," he told Guralnick.

It is a remarkable song, full of intensity, rising to a grand soaring bridge. Apparently the Atlantic staff was resigned to Dan's fait accompli, presenting them with a finished track by the time they got back from lunch, because the song was released as a single; it became a big hit the following spring. "We basically gave 'em a gift," said Spooner Oldham, reflecting on how successful the song had been. "It was fun to see a creative idea come to full fruition in about three hours' time. I really haven't had that sensation since." The immediacy of "Sweet Inspiration" seems to have energized the entire session; the singers sound totally committed to the material, and the group plays with power and pride.

Another Penn-Oldham song, "Oh What a Fool I've Been," leads off the album. "I wonder if we may have written it with those girls in mind," said Spooner Oldham. "I don't remember writing the song from experience. We were very spontaneous with that stuff." It is a more complex song than it seems, with its mood going from angry to melancholy to a self-mocking aside in the bridge, but in the end the dominant mood is resignation, a shake of the head at one's own stupidity; when you have deluded yourself, set yourself up for a fall, Dan and Spooner imply, it is nobody's fault but your own.

"Blues Stay Away From Me," the second song on the album, was recorded at Spooner's suggestion: "I remember Tom Dowd and I walking across the street to go have lunch and I mentioned the old Delmore Brothers song. My dad and his brothers used to sing it. It just popped out of my mouth. We walked over to Tom Phillips's [Sam's brother's] record store and found a recording" so that the Sweet Inspirations could learn it. A black gospel-based group singing a traditional country standard exemplifies the blend for which American Studios was becoming known. This type of recording was already attracting notice in Nashville, despite the fact that the musicians at American did not consider themselves to be country players, then or ever. "Back then, Stax was the Enemy, then Nashville," Dan Penn declared, revealing the siege mentality which overtook the group at times. "They cut in all that ol' stupid thin country music. No funk, I always liked a little funk." This version of "Blues Stay Away From Me" is nothing if not funky; Cissy Houston's powerful voice allows for some down-home gospel shouting above Tommy Cogbill's bouncy bass line and Reggie Young's sharp guitar notes. The musicians play sparingly, but every note counts, and any song with the line "Life is full of misery" would also have fit the evolving studio formula of stoic sorrow—a tribute to the accuracy of Spooner's ear. "I'll take credit for that, even though I'm a songwriter and I'm supposed to pitch my own stuff," he chuckled.

In the context of the musicians' progress by August 1967, "Don't Let Me Lose This Dream" could have applied as much to Tommy Cogbill and Dan Penn as the first version could perhaps have applied to Chips. Having just begun their experiments at production, they were both bringing something to the Moman dream of a musicians' collective, and they might well have wondered if they had "the heart or mind to make it come true and help it grow." The American group plays the song straightforwardly, with no trace of the bossa nova rhythm in Aretha's version; that style probably would not have been to the taste of Tommy, who denounced an Antonio Carlos Jobim record Mike Leech owned and liked because "the tempos sounded phony." The R&B listener that Tommy had always been left him preferring straight, unornamented rhythms; although he enjoyed it when a drummer cut loose, the drums had to do so within a solid groove, to which Tommy could—and did—embellish with as much intricacy on the bass as he thought fitting.

"Do Right Woman" is given a fervent reading, and Cissy Houston's call and response shouting on the fadeout turns the whole thing into a sanctified sermon. "Knock on Wood" and "Don't Fight It" both sound perfunctory, although Tommy's loping bass provides a focus on the former tune. "Don't Fight It," more than any other cut on the album, displays the smooth veneer of a Tom Dowd production. But on side two, beginning with "Sweet Inspiration," the varnish begins to wear off, and the rough pine wood of the American sound shows through. It is as if Tommy is finally becoming confident, after having introduced himself on "Memphis Soul Stew," and he emerges from the shadows to place his personal stamp on some of these recordings. Chips Moman remembered Tommy's expanded role: "He was there to help all he could," observed the engineer.

"Let It Be Me" employs a specific musical strategy, with the Sweets beginning the song in soft, bell-like unison and then increasing power and volume until the end of Cissy's solo turn on the bridge, when the song softly descends and the voices chime in unison once more. The musicians were developing a patent on this style; the musical peaks and valleys of their recordings were among the trademarks for which their audience would avidly listen. And "I'm Blue" is a romp, transforming what would have sounded like a threat coming from Tina Turner (who had originally recorded this composition from her then-husband Ike) into an exhilarating call-and-response from the Sweets, with Cissy Houston being especially creative.

The real Tommy Cogbill begins to be heard on the Burt Bacharach "Reach Out," the Dionne Warwick hit on which the Sweets had originally sung backup and now made their own. Tommy sets up the song with production flourishes similar to those he would use to introduce the Masqueraders' "I'm Just an Average Guy" almost a year later, building the song to a fierce, bursting gospel chorus that Cissy Houston does not sing as much as she attacks. The lyrics of encouragement and comfort are addressed to someone who feels put upon by the world (Chips, perhaps?), and Tommy offers a reassuring presence—a thread that ran through all of his life and work, and that was given even stronger emphasis on the next-to-last cut from the album.

The Isaac Hayes–David Porter tune "Here I Am (Take Me)," completely unrelated to the Al Green song of the seventies with the same title, can take a listener's breath away. Here, Tommy Cogbill sets up a piece of soulful material not for apparent self-justification (as Chips would do all too often), but as a cry from the heart.

While Bobby Emmons plays a crawling organ line behind her, adding to the tone of intimate somberness, Cissy Houston declaims lines stating that, though poor both in spirit and in fact, one can give what one has and never think of it as sacrifice. If this is foolish, the song continues, so be it; later on she sings, "I just want to be the reason for everything that's good." The chorus is basically one line—"Here I am, take me" (and, it is implied, make use of me in any way you see fit)—and if this piece is a reflection of Tommy, as it seems to be, the line

could have conceivably been addressed to his family, Chips, the Almighty, or all of the above. Listening to this song is like eavesdropping on a late-night prayer. It was the first of a series of Tommy Cogbill's productions whose titles read, in retrospect, like a litany, or the story of a spiritual journey.

The album closes with Roebuck "Pops" Staples's "Why Am I Treated So Bad," and it is impossible not to imagine Chips in the engineer's chair nodding in identification with that sentiment. Reggie Young again reveals the influence of Bobby Womack upon his playing, contributing a terse, bitter lead line. "We all stole from Bobby Womack," Reggie admitted. He also spoke glowingly of the Sweets themselves: "I thought they were outstanding, really outstanding," he remarked. "It was really a pleasure doing those sessions. They just blew me away singin'." Despite their regard for the talent of the Sweets, the band did not socialize with the singers outside of the studio; as if it comprised a conflict of interest, the musicians made it a point of honor not to hang out with the singers with whom they worked or to know them in any capacity other than that of clients. But American would soon welcome an artist who broke through that wall.

Even in the midst of doing the Sweet Inspirations album, other sessions went on (though Chips and Don Crews seemed to prefer only working with one act at a time when possible). They did demos for some of Dan Penn's songs and some of Darryl Carter's, and were also working on the third album for Sandy Posey, which was released late in the year. The album was progressing well, although Sandy's rapport with Chips at that time was so intense that everyone else on the scene felt left out of the proceedings. It seemed to them that Sandy was concentrating on the opinions of, and relying on feedback from, Chips to the point that their creative input was no longer sought or desired, a lapse that they were quick to add was only temporary with her. "She's really a sweet person, she really is," said Reggie Young empathetically. "I think she might have been influenced by the way things were done in

Nashville." Music City, of course, was becoming as much a producer's town as it was a town for writers and musicians, and the connection between producer and artist was often emphasized on recordings made there. Sandy was still very young, and naïve, and extremely vulnerable, and she poured out all her tender fragility into the songs on the two albums she released in 1967.

Her heartfelt romanticism can be heard on her warm reworkings of the Ovations' "It's Wonderful to Be in Love" (one can imagine her smiling radiantly as she sang) and the Fleetwoods' gentle "Come Softly to Me" (taken at the old breakneck stomping pace so as not to sound too gooey). She brings to "Love of the Common People" an autobiographical touch; John Hurley and Ronnie Wilkins could have been writing about her own poor-but-solid Alabama childhood, and she delivers the lyrics with the quiet conviction born of experience. Best of all were two songs from Dan Penn and Spooner Oldham. "Standing in the Rain" is the lament of a jilted lover, and Bill McElhiny's arrangement on the fadeout seems to have been deeply influenced by Dan's concept of the "barbecue sound" and the placement of the strings. "I don't remember ever being caught out in the rain that long," chuckled Spooner. And with "Bread and Butter," no monologue this time but the reflections of a working-class woman content with her lot and happily respectful of her husband, Chips Moman explores a state of mind he had never before attempted to describe: serenity at the end of a long day's labor, feeling at peace with the world. It was a view of life that Chips evidently admired but, with his chronic restlessness, could never manage. Nonetheless, for the first time Chips offered a possible antidote for the pain he was so good at describing: happiness may not be attainable, he (and by extension, Dan and Spooner) seems to suggest, but contentment is, and he implies that the latter state of mind is accessible to anyone—perhaps, eventually, even himself.

This emotional range, even more interesting than the monologues that first made Sandy's reputation, is reflected not only in the songs she was then recording, but in the album she already had out, which sold well in the late summer of 1967. The *Single Girl* album was released on MGM in the United States, but, perhaps due to new contractual obligations, released on Bell abroad.

The album features the title tune, but its delights do not end there. To the eternal credit of the group and Chips, the albums they worked on feature no filler, and unlike, say, the Nashville Sound, did not have a predetermined formula that worked more or less the same way on every song. Nor were the songs themselves formulaic; Wayne Carson contributed the well-written "Shattered," about the end of a love affair and its resigned conclusion "I guess I never mattered." "See You Round on the Rebound" is a contrast; here Sandy is not grieving but happy to be rid of her demanding, troublesome, immature lover, leaving him with a parting shot: "When you treat someone like dirt, you're going to get hurt."

Except for the title song, only one other number, the Penn- Oldham ballad "Hey Mister," could properly be called a monologue. Mike Leech's bass signals the listener like a semaphore, and Sandy is completely convincing in this Carter Family–style tale of a young woman stranded in Chicago without money, family, or friends, far from her native South after having been seduced and abandoned. Bobby Emmons enhances the mood, playing a bewildered-sounding organ line that follows Sandy like her own inescapable confusion; she pleads, "I want to talk to Mother," then adds as an aside, "dear mother," and her voice takes on an unusually sardonic quality that tells the listeners why she would have been ripe for the picking by a sweet-talking man. (One can imagine the interminable lectures the prodigal daughter will receive if she ever gets back to the Carolinas.) If the craft of singing involves some acting, Sandy would have been believable on the silver screen; she infuses each role she is given in this set of songs with compassion and wisdom beyond her years. That understanding is revealed again in "Patterns," a reflective song about the deterioration of a hollow marriage, and in Larry Butler's "Last Day of Love," with the opening lines that must have delighted

Chips: "It's raining / Dark clouds descending / Down on this gloomy day."

Rain seems to be a hidden metaphor throughout the album. One can imagine the homeless Southern girl of "Hey Mister" panhandling on a Chicago street in a drizzle. Larry Butler's light piano intro on "I'm Your Puppet" evokes images of Sandy wearing the dark turtleneck and light trench coat in which she was sometimes photographed, dodging rain-splashed puddles in downtown Nashville; her vocal gives the song a tender intensity, revealing her complete willingness to remain "hanging on a string" for the sake of love. "Twelfth of Never" also allows us a glimpse of her sweet romanticism, here suggesting flowers and old-fashioned music boxes.

Midway through the album is the Stevie Wonder hit "A Place in the Sun." Since Southern working-class whites outline the story here, a song originally meant to describe the struggle for racial equality can (as in the case of Otis Redding's "Respect") also be viewed as a call for social and economic equality, and the hope of some end to all of the constant struggling. Compared to Stevie's hopeful delivery, soaring with youth and optimism, Sandy's voice is tempered with restraint and the full knowledge that neither she nor anyone she knows may ever find what they are looking for—but they are all determined to keep trying. It is an emotional masterwork that displays both the Moman philosophy that life is an uphill battle and Sandy's abilities as a thoughtful, interpretive singer.

Other singers began coming around at this time. Steve Tyrell brought in a friend of his and Mark James's from Houston, who at the time was going through a career slump after having had several Top Ten hits the year before. Mark had been encouraging the singer to come up and give Memphis a try. "First time I saw B. J. Thomas, he was with Steve Tyrell and that ol' boy who became the president of Universal Records," Don Crews remembered. "B.J. was there to try and find a song to record," added Spooner Oldham. "We were just kinda lookin' for the right combination," said the singer.

There was no doubt that he had found it, for in B.J. Thomas, Chips Moman and the musicians had discovered *their* singer—the man who embodied the integrity, craftsmanship, versatility, originality, and refusal to be categorized that typified the American group. For this reason, he became the artist more closely associated with them than any other (with the possible exceptions of Waylon and Willie in the seventies). Like them, he would experience bad luck, bad judgment, and monumental success; and like them, he traveled a circuitous route to get to the top.

Billy Joe Thomas grew up in a working-class family from the Houston area, with the main constants in his life being his love of music and the protective devotedness of his older brother Jerry. Much of his story was told in his 1978 once-over-lightly memoir, *Home Where I Belong* (the as-told-to writer was the *Left Behind* series co-writer Jerry Jenkins). Like many singers, he was also interested in athletics but abandoned that preoccupation over several years; music became a priority when, during his junior year of high school, his brother arranged for him to audition as a singer with a local band called the Triumphs.

From then on he was serious about singing. He and the Triumphs played local clubs and made two small-time records, and he met and became friends with Steve Tyrell, Mark James, and Glen Spreen—"We just bumped into each other through that music scene," he said. The Triumphs were making their third single when B.J.'s father suggested that they do an old Hank Williams song he admired. It wound up as the B-side of their next single, but a few disc jockeys played it and "I'm So Lonesome I Could Cry" was picked up for national distribution, thanks to Steve Tyrell at Scepter. Radio listeners immediately paid attention: here was a singer who had an effortless, unpretentious voice with immense range and a perfect sense of pitch, capable of conveying the sorrow of the song with a lonely wail that still never sounded remotely "hillbilly." "Music to me has always been about emotion, about feeling," said B.J., and his ability to convey these was unmatched.

Hard-country music was making something of a last stand on the charts, with Ernest Tubb, the Wilburn Brothers, Johnny Wright, Loretta Lynn, and Porter Wagoner all scoring hits. B.J.'s sound appealed to record buyers preferring the more melodic approaches of Jim Reeves, Don Gibson, and Eddy Arnold. Interestingly, though the record found favor with country audiences, B.J. was also invited to sing at Harlem's famous Apollo Theater; the bookers for that venue thought he was black.

All ears were now on a basically shy young man who had yet to grow into that magnificent voice. He was deluged with requests for personal appearances, and when the Triumphs refused to travel, a road band was quickly assembled. Glen Spreen has been credited for completely hiring the band, but B.J. remembered, "I think I put the band together and Glen helped me a good deal." "I'm not quite sure, but I think I hired the trumpet player that skipped out on us in Canada, the bass player that never showed for the tour, and the young drummer (still a friend so I won't mention his name) who kept showing off and stepping all over B.J.'s singing with drum breaks in the middle of songs," chuckled Glen, offering an object lesson for anyone who thinks assembling a backing band is easy. B.J. and the new road band worked everywhere, even doing a Dick Clark tour (James William Guercio, later the producer for Chicago, Blood, Sweat and Tears, and the Buckinghams, was playing bass on the Clark tour for Chad and Jeremy at this time, and he backed B.J. onstage). And the hits kept coming: "Bring Back the Time," an underrated ballad about love gone wrong; another contemporary update of traditional country with Ernest Tubb's "Tomorrow Never Comes"; and "Billy and Sue" a Vietnam song with a subtle antiwar message: "This is the story of Billy and Sue / They were as in love as were any two / But then Billy had to die / And when you hear the reason why / You'll hang your head and cry." But by the end of the year, it began to look as if B.J., for all his talent, had played out his string. He was still based in Houston, where it was difficult to launch a national career; the material

became lackluster; and the draft had caught up with Glen, who had played on and arranged some of the hits. And then Mark James told B.J. about Memphis.

Chips was encouraging, too, B.J. remembered. "Chips said hey, if you move to Memphis, you'll be around close to what's happening. My brother and I moved up there in 1967." He recalled in his memoirs that he had relocated shortly after he had met Gloria, his wife-to-be; in Don Crews's recollection, later confirmed by both B.J. and the session books that Reggie Young meticulously kept, Mark James came on the scene during the summer of 1967, and B.J. quickly followed. He and Jerry took an apartment in the same complex as Mark (Spooner Oldham was also one of the building's tenants). And beginning in mid-August, he started going to American to rehearse, sort through demos, and look for material to record.

He was astonished when he began working with Mark's newfound friends. "Chips is a genius and each one of these guys is a master in his own right," he said admiringly. "When I went in there and first saw those guys, they astounded me, they don't look the part [of successful studio musicians]. These guys looked like they had come off the couch watchin' a baseball game. Unpretentious to a fault. Sweet, genuine people. None of 'em play that role." To B.J., still shy and ill at ease with his new success, no environment could have been guaranteed to make him feel more comfortable. The group also welcomed Jerry, who spent a great deal of time there watching over his brother; they were not intimidated by Jerry's toughness or irritated at his slight speech defect caused by a childhood hearing loss, so that he pronounced words the way his hearing impairment distorted them. To paraphrase the title of B.J.'s memoir, when he walked into American he knew that he was home where he belonged.

The musicians were not overly given to superlatives, but they brought out every adjective of praise in their collective vocabularies to describe their admiration for B.J.'s talent. "We really hit it off with him," said Reggie Young enthusiastically. "He was an excellent singer, he was one of the few people who really filled up the speakers." "He really sang good, and always did," Gene Chrisman remarked. "He was an exceptional artist and still is in my book. One of the finest if not the finest artist I have ever worked with. His voice is so unique, his pitch is so good, phrasing on songs, and the way that he delivers the songs." "I always thought that he could sing well because his reputation preceded him," commented B.J.'s new neighbor Spooner Oldham. "I knew he was a talented singer because I'd heard 'I'm So Lonesome I Could Cry.' I knew he could sing the kind of songs I like to hear. Every time he stepped up to the microphone or opened his mouth he sang like a bird. . . . He's like any other what I call great artist, you don't have to think about helping him. He was a stalwart thing, a stalwart person." "When B.J. Thomas came in, I didn't have a clue who he was or what he'd done," said Bobby Wood. "I personally had never heard of B.J. first time he rolled in the studio," added Mike Leech. "But he and Jerry, his brother, quickly became good friends. Somebody made a comment, that while the band is kicking ass during a track recording—that is, the singer would be the last to get in the groove, so to speak—we needed to be careful, because B.J. would outsing the band." "The first time I heard B.J. Thomas sing, in person, in the studio," reminisced Wayne Carson, many of whose compositions were recorded by the singer, "I said, 'Imagine that, a guy who sings perfectly in tune, with beautiful phrasing and clear as crystal . . . shit! . . . he's gonna give rock and roll a bad name!'" "Clear as a bell," Hayward Bishop remembered warmly about the quality of B.J.'s voice. His voice apparently affected people profoundly even in his earliest days onstage; the outwardly unemotional Glen Spreen called his friend "an inspiring singer," and said that he got cold chills the first time he had heard B.J. sing.

B.J. and Jerry introduced the American group to corkball, a game that got them through endless evenings and nights as they waited around to do overdubs or for Chips to show up. "It's a wonder we didn't break the windows out of the studio because we played inside most of the time," Reggie Young said ruefully, momentarily forgetting that the studio had no windows except for the one between the studio and the control room. This window served as home plate. "The cork was a thermos jug cork," Reggie continued. "It had to be the old thermos cork," Mike Leech added. "The ones made today won't work. Also the old cloth-type adhesive tape. You would put a coin on one end of the cork for balance, wrap it entirely with adhesive tape. The bat was a sawed-off broomstick. You would pitch the cork sort of like a 'knuckleball' and if you were good, you could make it rise or fall, curve up or down, slow or fast. If the batter hit the cork and it was caught, you were out. If the batter swung and missed, and the catcher caught it, you were out. It was great fun. We would play all day. Gene was very good, of course. I wasn't too shabby." "I loved that thing, I'd pitch," echoed Gene Chrisman enthusiastically. Reggie Young also remembered the daylong games with delight. "They don't make those corks anymore or we would still be playing," he said. Chips Moman seldom played. Dan Penn and Spooner Oldham also kept a distance from the games. Tommy Cogbill and the three Bobbys also preferred to observe, but the musicians who joined the staff later were eager corkball players.

The first of these late arrivals began turning up on the scene at about this time. To the musicians, it was beginning to look as if Mark James, who had only been there several months, was running a one-man employment agency. He had just brought B.J. into the picture, and now he was inviting Glen Spreen to observe the proceedings when Glen could get leave from the Aberdeen Proving Grounds in Maryland, where he served as piano player and arranger for the Army band (arguably making him the original 101st Fighting Keyboardist). He was also playing electric bass in a jazz trio on weekends. He joked that he was at American so much on his frequent leaves, and calling in sick so that he could stay longer, that he was almost court-martialed for going AWOL. He first heard of the group from "Memphis Soul Stew," and had been impressed by Tommy's bass playing; he loved the musical creativity and freedom of what he was now seeing, and immediately made plans to join the American staff when his hitch was up. American was the place to be, and he had made a deliberate, conscious decision to become part of it.

His working-class background was similar to that of B.J. Thomas. "Glen came from a funky, funky neighborhood in Houston; I've seen it," said Ed Kollis. Such a neighborhood was an incongruous place for a man who wrote string arrangements based on and inspired by baroque classical music, but he was a self-taught saxophonist and keyboard player who had won a music scholarship to college, tired of it after a year, and gone on the club circuit in Houston. He had been in California for a time, going at the request of Kenny Rogers's brother Lelan, and while there had put together the studio group Cannibal and the Headhunters. It was they who had had the hit with "Land of a Thousand Dances" before Chips and Tommy had recorded the Wilson Pickett version at Muscle Shoals. Glen had returned to Texas, written and arranged some small-scale recordings in Houston, and was informally working with B.J. when the draft had found him. The Memphis musicians, watching Mark's friend calmly studying everything and not saying much, could not help but wonder if they were going to be inundated with Texans, despite their immediate liking for B.J.

One Texan whom the musicians had no reservations at all about was King Curtis, and he was joyfully made welcome when he returned to finish his album. To Reggie Young especially, the return of King Curtis (with Tom Dowd in tow) signaled complete acceptance from pros in the music industry. "Here's this guy from New York, worked with every big act there was, and he treated us with the same respect, as I look back I really appreciate that," said Reggie gratefully of the Atlantic sound man. "I was interested in his mixes, because he recorded everything basically flat, unlike what we were used to hearing from Chips," commented Mike Leech. "That was probably smart though, because the effects weren't locked in, and more could be added later."

In his interview for *The Record Producers*, Tom Dowd recalled that these sessions went

unusually well, with some of the songs having been recorded in a single take. One he remembered as having been done that way was "Ode to Billy Joe," the Bobbie Gentry hit that had everyone talking that summer. Mike Leech remembered Ray Harris, for whom they were still doing occasional sessions though they were phasing out their involvement with Hi Records, playing him Bobbie's record in the Royal control room. On the American version, which was released as a single, Tommy Cogbill's bass line creates an ominous mood behind the hushed tones of King Curtis, the mood building to the point of tension and suspense through Arif Mardin's gritty string melody. This is the soundtrack for a Southern Gothic horror movie starring Tommy Lee Jones; it is the music Erskine Caldwell and William Faulkner must have had in their heads when they wrote.

The remarkable synchronization between Tommy's bass and Gene Chrisman's drums is exemplified on the B-side of "Billy Joe," a soulful march called "In the Pocket" which did not appear either on the album or on the CD reissue. It is Mongo Santamaria's "Watermelon Man" as filtered through John Philip Sousa in a Mississippi roadhouse. The smoothness of Dowd's production is nowhere to be found; the booming, heavily echoed roughness (one can imagine Chips being instructed to dial up the echo) is Tommy's all the way. His bass is commanding and precise, and the biting solo by Reggie Young in the second bridge is an effect Tommy used again and again over the years. And Tommy and Gene Chrisman seem to be playing and thinking as one. "The team of Cog and Chrisman was unbeatable," said Mike Leech admiringly. "He played with Gene much better than I did, and I know why. If you lead Gene, he will follow, and that's how he and Cog worked together. I am more of a follow-the-drummer player, which works well in most situations, as it did with me and Gene. I have, on occasion, developed a bass line that required everyone to follow, drums included, and it usually turned out to be pretty funky. That approach, though, is difficult unless you come up with something strong enough to follow, such as the 'Memphis Soul Stew' bass line was. You seldom hear bass lines like that anymore, that dominate the track. Shame, because they were really exciting tracks."

If "In the Pocket" was strong and rough, "Whiter Shade of Pale" is strong and melancholic. Bobby Emmons handles the famous organ intro with ease, and Curtis twists the melody. The string line sounds as if it had been suggested to Arif or Ralph Burns by Tommy, for it sweeps grandly along only to trail off quietly, like the sound of a tired man sighing. Chips Moman and Dan Penn each cut good versions of the song: Dan's production for the Box Tops featured a sheet-of-sound string line from Mike Leech; Chips's 1982 version with Waylon and Willie was simple, mysterious, and dark; but for sheer moodiness and power, Tommy Cogbill's version is the best of the three. "For What It's Worth" returns to chilling ominousness, with Gene Chrisman's conga drum taps like relentless footsteps and Reggie Young's bluesy playing.

With "Don't Let Me Lose This Dream" Tommy slowly began remaking a few of the songs he had done for the road trips, and "I Never Loved a Man" was next for revision. Tommy kept his original bass line, but Reggie Young's guitar fills were placed differently from those Chips had done on the original, with Reggie choosing to play his brittle, blaring lines in the second verse and letting Curtis wail away unopposed on the ending. It is raw, unpolished—and compelling. "Nashville was such a perfectionist place," reflected Reggie about the competition. "We weren't perfect, that was what made it soulful. That's why King Curtis impressed me so much. He would start it, from the top to the bottom, it was perfect. And he could do it so quick!"

The Stevie Wonder hit "I Was Made to Love Her" offered a perfect chance to salute the Motown sound (Chips Moman's "Place in the Sun" had been more about the song, and perhaps his own inner restlessness as reflected in those lyrics, than the Motown style per se). It was an evenly matched contest. Reggie Young could match the Motown lead guitarist Robert White phrase for phrase and twang for twang (White, a Northerner from Pennsylvania, played with a more "country" inflection than did the Southern, blues-based Reggie). Tommy's bass lines, while not as pulsating as those of James Jamerson, were even more intricate. "The people who were on the same musical wavelength all found it at about the same time—Tommy, Jamerson, and Jerry Jemmott," said Bobby Emmons. "Tommy struck everybody dumb, he brought so much to the game."

The album yielded three charted singles, two of which were enormous R&B hits; it was validation for Tommy Cogbill, proof that he had an ear for what people liked. Hayward Bishop, who himself harbored ambitions of becoming a record producer, expressed it succinctly. "The first time you produce a hit record, it's a fluke. The second time, well, maybe you just hit it lucky again. The third time, you've proven you can record a song in a way that people want to hear. You're really a producer then." He further elaborated on the producer's role. "The producer is the director, if you put it in a movie anthology," he explained. "The producer is responsible for the context. He's the one that tells the musicians when to stop creating. When they're there."

By that definition, Tommy was on his way—and by extension, so were the rest of the American group. Their style was taking shape. In their own words, they had found a groove.

### CHAPTER 9

# Chill of an Early Fall

The American group had been recording steadily throughout the summer of 1967, but the pop music world, consumed as they were by the Beatles' long-awaited *Sgt. Pepper*, paid their records little critical heed (despite the fact that many of them had been commercially successful). But by the early fall of 1967, when the chill had set in and the Summer of Love already seemed like a distant illusion, it was time to search for something new—something tougher, more realistic, more in keeping with the times. And here was Memphis, quietly doing its thing.

That autumn, Memphis music enjoyed a spectacular comeback. The studios maintained their pecking order, as they always had, and among the Big Four the results were varied. Sun was almost completely out of the picture, and two years later Sam Phillips would sell the catalogue of incomparable Sun masters to Shelby Singleton. Hi was in transition as the musicians who had contributed so much to that label concentrated on marathon sessions for Chips. Willie Mitchell slowly replaced each man with protégés of his choosing, and eventually this new group became Hi Rhythm.

That left Stax and American. There was a sense of respect between American and Stax, but also a sense of rivalry; the competition may have fueled some of the creativity at both studios. Much of the local attention and that of the worldwide music press was focused on Stax, to the American group's eternal annoyance. "In Memphis, all you ever heard was Stax, Stax, Stax," groused Dan Penn. "They didn't care about nobody but Stax, and they didn't care really about them." Mike Leech felt

that the amount of publicity given to Stax was somewhat unfair, since Stax had made its reputation with R&B alone while American from the beginning was more diversified. Gary Talley, the Box Tops' lead guitarist, thought that the American studio band, particularly Reggie Young, should have been better known to the general public and that Reggie should have been seen along with Steve Cropper as the embodiment of Memphis guitar.

Stax, of course, automatically had a higher profile than American because Stax was a record label, with the studio and the house band only a part of its magic. Though Chips tried several times with custom labels distributed by larger companies, he never became an independent entity in that sense. Stax's product was clearly identifiable as R&B; much of American's output fell into a gray area between soul and country music, and the industry executives themselves—with the notable exception of Atlantic—often had no idea how to market the recordings. "We bumfuzzled the label heads," said Bobby Wood amusedly. "They'd say, 'That don't sound like anything else [you've done],' we'd say, 'It sounds like a hit.'"

The scope of American's approach showed up best in August 1967, when the little rock band nobody wanted to bother with, the novice producer, the commuting songwriter best-known for his country efforts, and a first-time string arranger scored the Number One rock record in the land for four weeks in a row. "The Letter" generated an incredible response, first on the local scene and then across the country. "It was a hit in Memphis long before it went national," said Mike Leech, reflecting on his first arrangement. "So Memphis played the hell out of it, then stopped. Then it went national so the Drake stations [among them WHBQ, the Memphis station where Elvis associate George Klein worked] started playing it. I'm sure the public was sick of it after awhile."

But it seemed the public could not get enough of it. Wayne Carson's simple song had resonance, in part because he left the story line fairly vague. We know the boy in the song is planning to fly back to the woman he loves, because she wrote and said she cared, but that is all we know; it is up to the listeners to create the back story. It had a great deal of meaning to soldiers coming back from Vietnam: to them, the airplane noise at the end of the record (the very thing Chips had not liked—"I thought it was the hit clincher," said Mike Leech, and Chips Moman admitted, "I was wrong") was the Freedom Bird, taking them back home to their loved ones. It could have personal significance for couples en route over long distances to be married, and for lovers reuniting after a quarrel. It was perfectly possible for a listener to read into the song his or her own personality and experience in addition to those of Wayne Carson, Dan Penn, and Mike Leech, all of whom are so prominent throughout. The brevity of the song was a crucial hook also, and many DJs waited until shortly before the station IDs to play it. "It was just such an interesting thing, it was a minute and fifty seconds; it sort of defies gravity rules," mused Spooner Oldham.

Wayne Carson was still on his service tour, unaware that he had scored his biggest success to date. "Those were all naval installations with Marine detachments," he remembered about the bases he played. "We were down in the Caribbean, down in Guantánamo Bay in Cuba, in the Canal Zone—we played all those damn things. I went through three days of training exercises. They didn't have these satellite TVs then; I remember guys asking, 'What's the new styles in the States; new music?'" Upon finishing his tour, he and the other members of the troupe checked into a hotel at a naval installation in Florida. "It was the first time I'd ever seen a TV with a console between the beds. I turned on the radio and the announcer was saying . . . 'number one for the second week in a row, The Letter.' I came off that bed like a flyin' saucer; I was levitating."

Back in Memphis, a triumph of that scale seemed almost to go unnoticed. "Dan didn't change, nor did I," reflected Mike Leech. Dan Penn took his success in the best I-knew-it-all-along manner straight from the Shoals: "I just patted myself on the back and poured another drink." But beneath the surface, there were currents: Chips Moman, who was already having to deal with the possibility of Tommy Cogbill's success as a producer, was faced with the fact that the studio's biggest hit had been produced by another of his protégés. His reaction, Dan remembered, was "kinda dark and gloomy. Following that, it seemed like he moped around for months. The kid had upped him." Dan also told Peter Guralnick that during the four weeks "The Letter" was Number One, Chips did not even come to the studio. Apparently it had never occurred to Chips that, in allowing his friends the chance to express their creativity, the record-buying public might like their efforts just as well as they liked his. "There was a lot of competition on the high-end side of this deal," remembered Bobby Emmons. "When Dan became the number one producer, that became a competitive thing with Chips."

Chips was loath to claim anything but pride in the success of his protégé, saying that he had been happy for Dan. "I was happy for us all," he added thoughtfully. Tommy Cogbill was also struggling with it, according to Dan Penn: "He was competitive, but he was subtle. You had a lot of pride runnin' around in those days." The rest of the American musicians emphatically contested that, saying that Tommy was never anything but openly encouraging to all. "Tommy was always happy for someone else's success. If he liked it. And his commercial ear allowed him to like most everything we did," said Mike Leech. "He never sulked over someone else's product. Ever." Probably the least shortsighted of the whole group when it came to the future, Tommy seemed to realize that the success of another producer could reflect favorably on the entire studio. Chips Moman agreed. "Any time you have a record that big, it helps," he observed, noting that though the studio was doing well before that song hit the top, there were more bookings afterwards.

Dan did not find himself besieged with production offers yet, but Mike Leech quickly learned that he was now being considered an arranger more than a musician. "I still didn't consider myself an arranger. It was a little frightening for me because after 'The Letter,' everybody just assumed I was a good arranger, which I was not. . . . You see, to the powers that be at American, just the fact that I could even write the notes down made me the arranger," he noted with some frustration. "No matter about ideas. So immediately after 'The Letter' hit, I was arranging stuff all over town. And horrible arrangements they were." The turning point came when he was asked by Chips to conduct the re-recording of a Bill McElhiny string arrangement for what was most likely one of Sandy Posey's songs. Chips attended the overdub session, Mike remembered, "set the charts down, I handed them out to the string players and conducted the session. I was the star! And I didn't do a goddamned thing! I got pats on the back, grins, 'good jobs' . . . Funny." In studying McElhiny's score, Mike learned what to do. "Up until then I had my scores way too complicated—till I saw his—very simple. . . . From that point on I basically wrote like he did voicing-wise, not idea-wise. After that, my arrangements got better, and I developed confidence in what I had written."

In many ways it was a dream come true for Mike, who had always wanted to be a symphony conductor, but he too was struggling with some implications of the record's success. "My sad part of it was, I didn't charge for the arrangement, so I not only didn't get paid, I will never see any royalty when it's used in other media, like movies. Too bad . . . my fault. But since that was my very first arrangement, I was so naïve and felt I would be taken care of. . . . I thought that since I was the new guy on the block, that I would be taken care of, that the bosses would see that I was duly paid and that all I had to concentrate on was my ability to arrange. I sincerely thought Dan would see to it that I was paid and that any future use would be taken care of. . . . I guess that's youth and naïveté combined but I sure was wrong, wasn't I? Man, that was a blow to me to find out that nobody really cared." As a novice producer, Dan may have not yet understood how the royalties were divided on a record, and in any case Mike did not discuss it with him then. It was a small thing, but Mike noticed and filed it away in his mind, creating a slight distance between him and the rest of the American group that would widen over the years.

At the time, the distance was imperceptible. Dan Penn was full of admiration for Mike's work as both arranger and bassist. He described Tommy as "one of the best fanciest bass players," stating the obvious, "[but] as good as Tommy Cogbill was, I gotta say a few words for Mike Leech. Mike is world, world-class." As an arranger, Dan continued about Mike, "he's kind of a nonchalant guy. If he ever thought about what he was doin' it'd scare him to death." Mike actually put a great deal of time and worry into his arrangements; he was by no means as matter-of-fact as his outward attitude led the rest of the group to believe. To Tommy Cogbill, it may have seemed as if Mike was not even taking the success or its demands all that responsibly; he felt it necessary to tell Mike, in a few private conversations, to keep his eyes on the brass ring. "I was a young pup jumping around and having a great time, not caring about anything, and Tommy was there to slap me down, to tell me to 'cut that shit out and get down to business.'"

Mike also contributed the string line to the B-side of "The Letter," a Penn-Oldham rock tune called "Happy Times," which featured an explosive bass track from Tommy Cogbill. Though the lyric ostensibly expressed sorrow at a lost romance, what one comes away with is the feeling that for all the pain, there was considerable joy; the speaker reminisces about holding hands and making love by the river while the birds sang overhead. "I can forthrightly tell you that it wasn't from personal experience," chuckled Spooner Oldham. He speculated that they had gotten the premise from his and Dan's combined unconscious: "Growing up in the South, the river is so prevalent in our lives." The song does evoke a specifically Southern sort of romance, as Tommy Cogbill's bass races like the engine of a finely tuned sports car. "Everybody has a happy time, somewhere in their lives," reflected Spooner; from this lyric, it is apparent that if they don't, they should. Mike Leech's string accent pushes and sustains the track almost as much as does Spooner's Hammond organ; here he utilizes his trademark sound, an unbroken line accentuating and emphasizing the lyric, building in crucial spots like the classical music so many of the group loved.

The single was still Number One on the charts when Bell Records pressured Dan Penn to do an immediate album. That deadline pressure, as well as the difficulties of getting a young band to work efficiently in the studio, led Dan to the solution he had tried with "Happy Times." The American group did most of the playing on subsequent Box Tops records, reducing Alex Chilton's group to the status of a road band. (Dan tried to record them in Muscle Shoals, and, along with Shoals guitarist Eddie Hinton filling in for a hospitalized Gary Talley, they appear on "Break My Mind"; Chips went ballistic when he found out and ordered Dan and the Box Tops back home.) It was standard practice throughout the music business at that time to augment rock groups with studio pros; country performers were never allowed to use their road bands on records. It still goes on today: Alabama, the leading country group of the eighties, were always sensitive about the fact that their recordings were augmented by session players, including American's Hayward Bishop. Alex Chilton and his group were no less sensitive about it, especially since the Monkees' use of studio pros automatically rendered a rock band dependent on such things "not serious," fit only for the bubblegum Top Forty.

Several of the American musicians themselves were a bit puzzled at the custom. When Spooner was asked to play keyboards on the album, his first response was, "I'd love to, but why would you do that?" Reggie Young said that, all things being equal, he would have preferred that the Box Tops play on the album: "I always kind of encouraged it, if guys have road bands they should come in. They do the hard work, we have the easy part." To Alex Chilton, who always prided himself on being in touch with the cutting edge, it was anathema, but he and his band swallowed their pride and went along, partly because they enjoyed having a hit record and also partly because they liked Dan. Gary Talley said that even then he understood perfectly why studio musicians would be doing most of the work on the album: "Compared

to those guys, it was gonna take us ten times as long to do a cut." For his part, Dan would have been less than human had he not viewed Alex Chilton as clay to be molded; seeing this young, passionate teenage singer was like reliving his adolescence.

It was with this set of customs and expectations that Dan and the American group, with members of the Box Tops in supporting roles like backup vocals, went into the studio to begin work on the album in late August 1967. Also in secondary roles: Bobby Womack and Wayne Carson, both of whom contributed guitar and songs. Wayne's "She Knows How" came from his back catalogue, and he was laughingly dismissive of it, but Gene Chrisman's firecracker drum intro, Tommy Cogbill's walking bass, and Mike Leech's unbroken melody line on the strings behind Chilton's bemused vocal make it a fun recording. Almost anyone can identify with the story line of the girl who "knew how"—to charm her man, make him want her. (An implicit subtext is that the narrator feels manipulated by the girl's knowledge but enjoys the game.) Even more memorable was a composition Wayne brought to the session and sang for Chips as Moman was experimenting with the placings of new microphones: a song about a city by night.

As is the case with most writers, ideas came to Wayne from practically anywhere, and he was constantly priming the pump with new information; a conversation with him was inevitably peppered with "Did you read this? Did you see this movie?" "Neon Rainbow" came to him that way. "I wrote that based on New York City, especially since I'd never been there," said Wayne. "Somewhere in there, I saw an aerial view of New York City at night." But it could have been written about the magic and mystique of any nighttime city, especially as seen from the windows of a passing car or a moving train. It evokes Nashville as much as New York, and the recording has a forward, propulsive rush, guided by Spooner Oldham's Hammond organ, Mike Leech's flowing string line, and Wayne Carson's lead guitar. ("That was a little ten-dollar pawnshop guitar that Gary Talley had brought in and was fooling with," said

Wayne. "I was playin' it and Dan heard me." Gary remembered that the guitar may have been brought in by John Evans, another member of Alex Chilton's band.) There is a sense of wonder in it, too, as could have been conveyed only by country boys like Dan Penn and Wayne Carson who had recently arrived in the big city.

It was also unlike any pop song on the radio, grabbing attention with its sound and its well-written detail. "Wow, this is the most different song, almost like a psychedelic song, like a Beatles song," Gary Talley remembered his first reaction being when he heard it. "I don't remember thinking it out that well," Dan Penn shrugged, but he obviously tapped deeply into his subconscious to create the sound of the record. He always said he tried to make images with his productions; he tried to visualize what the song was saying and then convey that picture. "Neon Rainbow" was the beginning of the American group's impressionism, exactly comparable to that famous French movement in painting in which scenes and details of everyday life are depicted with imaginative use of light and color. Both as an audio painting and as a tone poem, it is a record for the ages. En route to the BMI awards in New York that December, the plane carrying Wayne and Si Siman touched down at night, and Wayne finally saw the skyline of his imagination.

The success of those two Box Tops singles established Wayne Carson as a writer, and his advanced subject matter and song structure inspired other writers to imitate him. "Spooner told me, 'Between 'The Letter,' and 'Neon Rainbow,' you started something, every song now has got to be filled up with these interesting chords.'" Jim McBride later borrowed Wayne's metaphor and extended it for Alan Jackson's "Chasin' That Neon Rainbow," an extension Wayne nonchalantly shrugged off. "Hell, everybody's gonna rewrite everybody, you know? When you're the first one, it just lends itself to imitation." He was open about the writers whose work he liked: "I always admired Neil Diamond, I still admire Randy Newman, Bacharach and David, and of course, all the older writers." Starting out as a Nashville-oriented

writer had led him to spend some time among the other Music City tunesmiths, and their fraternal bond was not for him. "I watched what they were doing, all of them, Harlan Howard, Ronnie Self, Willie . . . I thought, hell, I don't need to do this, I need to get off by myself and think." Ever the guarded loner, he chose to stay in Springfield without a music scene to distract him, commuting to Memphis and Nashville when he needed to. He could also remain close to Si Siman. "I wanted to be around Si. We played so much golf together, hunted and fished together. I didn't move to Nashville because I didn't want to leave my best friend," he said with a that's-that air of finality.

Under Si's guidance and advice, Wayne became the foremost writer in a style Nashville was just beginning to call "advanced" or "progressive"—going beyond the classic drinking and cheating songs (though in the seventies Wayne's work for Gary Stewart would prove him a master of that form as well) and discussing all aspects of life through music. Wayne was one of the first to place hits on the rock, pop, easy listening, and country charts all within a single year. "I guess the thing I always had, that a lot of writers didn't have . . . Ever seen a turret on a tank that goes 180 degrees instead of 360?" he explained. He composed in bursts of spontaneity, agreeing with Jack Kerouac that "first thought, best thought." Unlike Kerouac, mercifully, he would go back and make changes. "I've always believed that great songs were written, hit songs are edited," he said, emphasizing his words carefully. "When you write, goddammit, stay with it. I see these goddamn writers, and I've written with several, they wanna stop and say, 'Should we say "if," "and," or "but" here?'—Who gives a damn!" he snorted explosively. "Worry 'bout that crap later. You lose the spontaneity of the damn thing, it gets too clinical. That's just pissin' in the wind, as far as I'm concerned."

Bobby Womack's writing also had a casual air, and his contributions to the album were as remarkable as Wayne's. "Gotta Find Somebody" features Womack's lead guitar, and it emphasizes the importance of true love as a safety device, the siege mentality coming through again:

"This is a mean world to try and live in all by yourself." The line is another of Bobby's gospel borrowings, and it also appears in a blues classic by Little Walter and by T-Bone Walker, both of whom had hits with the song. The other Womack tune, "People Make the World," is nothing less than an explanation of how a man gets character, and Bobby is specific about the things that shape a person: ". . . the friends we have, and the books we read." Character is also created "by the pity we show / in the hour of care / by the loads we lift, and the souls we share." Mike Leech's string line comes in beneath Bobby's words about compassion; the string placements always indicated which details of a song the American musicians wanted to emphasize. Dan Penn is heard almost vehemently shouting "People make the world what it is" on the fadeout, sounding partly resigned and partly disgusted.

Dan and his usual collaborator, Spooner Oldham, contributed several strong songs to the album. There's a solid remake of "I'm Your Puppet," featuring Spooner on chimes and Tommy Cogbill's emphatic bass. "Happy Times" is on the album also, and two newer songs from this team glow like jewels in a crown.

"Everything I Am," the love song that closes out side one of the album, shines with beauty. It is a letter of appreciation for a woman's love and loyalty, set to a tune slightly reminiscent of the old ballad "Annie Laurie" (though Spooner Oldham maintained that neither of them were consciously aware of that older song). Although Dan Penn avoided open autobiography, it is impossible to understand this song without seeing it in the context of the novice producer scoring his first success; he is thanking his steadfast wife Linda for all she has done to help, encourage, and inspire him. "It's a joy to watch she and Dan together," Mike Leech remarked. "He will walk up to her for no reason and give her a big hug. They'll look at each other and grin . . . They've always been that way." Spooner Oldham interpreted the lyrics as a possible thank-you letter to God, as well: "Everything I am, I am because of you." Dan had already won a reputation among R&B fans

as their kind of writer: with this song, based on a classic tune, he was exploring territory that only a few intrepid Nashville writers were beginning to work, re-tailoring elements of traditional ballads to contemporary themes. Dolly Parton and Tom T. Hall were content to simply reshape old storytelling methods; Dan carried the approach further, throwing out everything that did not seem useful and leaving the basics of the form.

"I Pray for Rain" continues the updated approach: in just a few words, Dan sketches a complete picture. One can see a Southern boy much like himself, slouched before a window checking the sky, praying it rains on his former girlfriend and her new love as they go for a picnic. It is right up there with the song Flatt and Scruggs had recorded several years previously, "The Train That Carried My Girl from Town"; when Lester Flatt snarls meanly, "I wish to the Lord the train would wreck, kill the engineer and break the fireman's neck," the impulse is the same as Dan's. Justice was served for the boy in his tale by using sound effects to reproduce the sound of thunder and a downpour; the rain in this atmospheric piece was coming down so heavily the lovers might well be soaked before they can get to a safe place. One could imagine the boy at the window, watching the downpour, chuckling to himself and smiling—revenge is sweet. Spooner elaborated further on the use of rain as a metaphor. "Rain, in one sense, is depressing, or can be, because it shuts down your outdoor activities," he said. "But it draws you more into yourself. A lot goes on with rain, emotionally, I think." (J.R. Cobb was another writer who used rain as a motif; his rain songs symbolized intimacy, as in his Classics IV ballad "Rainy Day" and the later, stunningly tender "All Night Rain," which reads like a primer of romance.)

The sound-effects record was put to further use at the beginning of the Burt Bacharach "Trains, Boats and Planes," as Dan mixed and blended the sounds of those methods of transportation. Appropriately for the work of a piano-based composer, Spooner Oldham is predominantly featured, although he, Tommy Cogbill, and Gene Chrisman enjoy several wonderful moments of romping, stomping interplay during the instrumental breaks. "It was probably the knowledge of the song that gave us the freedom to experiment a little," Spooner said. It was also the chance for him to pay homage to someone he had admired since the Shoals, when Bacharach's hits with the Shirelles and Dionne Warwick were on every jukebox and turntable. "At that time, he was delving into rhythm and blues himself, [although] he may not have known it," said Spooner of Bacharach's effect on him and many of the original musicians at Fame who cited the New York–based pianist as an influence. "He was speaking to us at that time; he lost me a little later, because he got into show tunes, pop—that isn't my forte." "Trains" is an effective song to begin with (Mike Leech named it as one of his all-time favorites), delivered passionately by Alex, who was still being coached to become an R&B belter with Dan's own mannerisms and phrasing. Chilton had misgivings about that practice, wanting to display the pop and rock sides of his musical personality more; but nobody can deny he reached his biggest audience, and had his most successful records, while working at American with Dan. "He would say, 'That doesn't sound like me,'" recalled Mike Leech about Alex's reaction to the vocals. "I personally think any artist with the success he had would be delighted to ape someone else's style. I certainly would shove my ego back and go for it."

Everyone at American liked Alex, wished him well, and took pride in his success. "He was a quite talented young man," said Reggie Young thoughtfully. "I liked him from the get-go. For a young guy—he was still in high school—he was soulful, very soulful." "Alex back then was a real energized youth; I thought he had more depth of mind than I would associate with someone that young," remembered Spooner Oldham. "He and I always got along," said Mike Leech. "He would ask me for advice from time to time, mainly about money. I advised him to be very careful, that his career might be short-lived as most artists' are, and to save as much as he could for the present."

Alex's intelligence and talent contributed to

the ease of the sessions; another factor was the unaffected style in which Dan Penn conducted them. As a producer, Bobby Emmons judged admiringly, "Dan was the best there was"—a particularly interesting comment given Bobby's lifelong respect for and closeness to Chips. "He was *very* very very picky about what he wanted, more so than Chips," said Gary Talley, who worked with both. "Dan's a character," laughed Gene Chrisman. "He used to smoke like crazy and he'd leave ashes in the fader." "Dan projects the old country-boy image, which he likes to portray," observed Mike Leech, remembering Dan coming into the control room for sessions barefoot or wearing bedroom slippers, propping his feet up on the console, and placing a case of Falstaff beer, to which he often repaired as the proceedings continued, on the floor beside his chair. He had not discovered his sartorial trademarks of overalls and plaid shirt yet, but the basic style was there. Gary Talley remembered a time when Dan was sitting on the control-room sofa drinking a beer and John Evans's mother brought her son in to the studio, since Evans could not yet drive. "And this could only happen in the South," Gary chuckled. "He kicked the beer back under the couch so Evans's mother wouldn't see him drinking."

Behind the good-ol'-boy manner was that racing motor, kicking in now to overdrive. Dan had always been more ambitious than anyone could have suspected; now he was in a position to make so many of his dreams come true, even though he outwardly shrugged off his new role: "Production is nothing more than one man's opinion." His own opinions, however, were typically strong. He never felt his records were done properly unless he had a hand in both the engineering and mixing, and he was right. "I miss the days when the producers mixed. There was a difference. [Back in those days] there was no plan, there wasn't a designated engineer or producer sittin' thinkin' up one cool thing to do. I don't know what I'm doing as a producer. I don't want to know. I lay hands on my board, I'm there, I'm home. [Sometimes] I put somebody behind me watching tracks. Sometimes I don't *want* a decent sound, and that's what these engineers don't understand."

He loved engineering almost as much as he did producing, bringing his sense of what he wanted to both skills: "When I sit down at the board, I can produce from that perspective and I'm not afraid of what the guy might do, cause I'm the guy. They teach 'em . . . now, they say, 'This is a producer and there's an engineer, they do different things, it's wearing two hats.' Well, we don't wear hats, we wear caps, and you can wear caps on anything."

Besides the visual impact he wanted his records to have, Dan was striving to catch emotion. "The worst thing that was ever said in a studio is 'What do you think?' We ain't thinking, we're feeling. . . . I try to think, 'What would my heart feel?' Everybody that's ever cut a record or wrote a song has put their heart into it. In Alabama, we didn't skip that part; we worked with our heads as well as our hearts. "Having musicians like the American players, people aware of the implied feelings and ideas in a song, was a bonus. The American band could take a piece of junk of a song and they'd work with it and find a groove that you couldn't live without," he said with obvious pleasure. "They're the most underrated band in the country. I mean, these are *the* guys!" To him, the joy of producing lay in propping his feet up on the console, sitting back, and listening as the band worked through a tune, forgetting the clock or any other distractions, going for itself. "To me, it don't get no better 'n that."

It didn't get much better than that for Jerry Wexler, either, so once again Spooner Oldham, Tommy Cogbill, and Bobby Womack joined their friends from the Shoals to work on an album for Aretha that may be her most consistent and best. *Lady Soul* is a triumph from beginning to end, incisive, emotional, and focused; it is as if even the previous two years of work with these players was only a preparation for the masterwork to come.

Joe South also returned to New York for these sessions, and his guitar intro to Don Covay's "Chain of Fools" begins the album in a compelling way. "He loved Pop Staples," Jimmy Johnson said of the riff's inspiration, "and he tuned that E string down to a D. That

great guitar was unbelievable. He had three or four styles people tried to copy"—though the "Chain" opener established his sound as a guitarist. "Jerry Wexler would say, 'Joe, woulja tune that guitar?'" recalled Spooner, who played Wurlitzer electric piano on the song. "He had to tune it two or three times."

Joe South was less than a year away from recording the songs that made him nationally famous—"Games People Play," "Rose Garden," and all the others which told the entire world that he hated everything and everybody in it, including, perhaps, himself. To Jimmy Johnson, his longtime colleague (they had known each other since the days when Felton Jarvis brought his Georgia-related acts like South, Jerry Reed, and Tommy Roe to Fame), Joe seemed to be dealing with many interior conflicts. "Joe was a different duck," Jimmy observed. "He may have been slightly older, like Tommy or Chips. He'd been to the farm a time or two." Later there would be other difficulties—"Joe always had a slight problem taking care of Joe," said Jimmy—but nothing affected his music. "He was always very upbeat, and whatever he played always turned me on," Jimmy added. "He was a super talent. Joe and us always had a great time together. He and I were playing the same kind of guitar. It was an orange single-cutaway, Chet Atkins Gretsch model. The only difference was, mine had Sho-Bud pickups."

They learned "Chain of Fools" off a demo Don Covay had submitted; the atmosphere around an Aretha session by now, Jimmy Johnson said, was electric. "There was some big famous songwriters comin' in there trying to get a cut. Carole King and her husband, Gerry Goffin, were around. It was just an umpteen number of writers." "It was so much fun to hear those new songs come up in your face," Spooner Oldham recalled joyfully. Jimmy Johnson elaborated further on Wexler's song selection. "Wexler preferred to deal with writers rather than the publishers. I know this was smart because [when the players at Jimmy's later studio were producing sessions] I've never gotten a song I liked from a major publisher. I got *crap*! I don't call 'em B-sides, I call 'em a Z-side!" "Chain of Fools" was anything but that;

released as a single that fall, it went onto the charts almost immediately, and even people who had never thought about soul music before found that they could not get the "chain chain chain" chorus out of their heads. The story line of the song, about a woman trying to break what seems to be an unhealthy codependence, is almost beside the point. Much more relevant was Tommy Cogbill's bass line just before the last chorus: the downshift, a flurry of descending notes, would be one of his signatures forever.

Most of the songs on the album, beginning with James Brown's "Money Won't Change You" and ending with the Ray Charles classic, "Come Back Baby" (which Charles had learned from the Walter Davis version of 1940) are taken at a mid-tempo pacing perfect for Tommy; it was a groove he could ride endlessly, leaving plenty of space for Roger Hawkins, who played at his most explosive level on this record. The Atlantic crew knew how to get the best from everyone, but so did Tommy. And he was doing it his way. A scrap of film, possibly taken by Spooner Oldham, survives to document that session; it has surfaced in a recent film about Tom Dowd, and watching the snippet one is stunned at Tommy's self-assurance while taking direction and his ease when he played. He looks the part of the slightly seedy jazzman; clad all in black, with sunglasses making him look even more impenetrable, he gives a little half-smile at nothing in particular while Dowd, on the studio floor, waves his hands about to instruct the players. "When I saw that film," said Hayward Bishop, who later teamed on many records with Tommy, "I knew exactly what he was thinking. 'What the hell is this???'" There is a bit of amusement in Tommy's manner, as if he is thinking, "Okay, do what you have to, then stand back and let me do my thing." When he does, launching into the easy pattern of "Come Back Baby," he is leaning forward a little, his right elbow jutting out at an odd angle as he casually plays, not moving with or to the beat or the other players, but locked into his own world, enjoying the ride. Fred Foster, one of the American group's most loyal clients, knew his sessions were sounding fine if Tommy was

seated that way; if Tommy was slumped back in his chair, not seeming to care, something was wrong. Very little went wrong on an Atlantic session, and Tommy was energized, carrying that delight into songs like "Nikki Hoeky" and "Since You've Been Gone."

Some of the reason things at Atlantic went right had to do with the continuing skill of the company's staff—Wexler, Dowd, and Arif Mardin—at making a relaxed atmosphere. "Arif was always humble, eager. I could tell he was learning because he had never worked this way before; we would play on what we called head sessions," said Jimmy Johnson. Down South nothing was written out, but the number system—where numerals were used in place of chord changes as a road map to guide the musicians—was in standard usage. The same custom was followed in New York, since Wexler could see it got results far ahead of what written parts could have yielded. His antics continued to amuse the musicians too. "Wexler was cool," said Jimmy Johnson, thoroughly used to the executive by now. "His vocabulary would scare you to death. I used to bring a dictionary with me every time I went to New York, I'd be in the hotel room at night phonetically trying to learn what he was saying. He had a lot of vigor. He would totally, with that accent, would totally get you. We all learned to talk like him—'Can ya dig where I'm comin' from, *baby*?' . . . Even though Jerry was not musical as far as educated-wise, he didn't have to be. He knew feel. He knew when a record felt good. He'd get up and dance, do the boogaloo or somethin'. If a groove hit him, he'd get out on the floor and just get it." Besides, any technical insight Wexler might have lacked could always be supplied by Tom Dowd. "Dowd was good on trackin'," Jimmy recalled. "He was a brilliant guy. There was nothin' you couldn't ask him that he wouldn't know. I used to sit and ask him things, just to get him goin'. . . . I mean, there was a lot of talent on those sessions."

Some of it was even added later. In one of his first ventures for his new American label (his group Cream were on Polydor in Britain), Eric Clapton overdubbed a blistering guitar line for Aretha's slow blues, "Good to Me As I

Am to You." She gives this self-composed wail a performance worthy of Bessie Smith, and Clapton matches her line for line and note for note throughout most of the song. But after her shrieking chorus, which gets louder at each line and almost threatens to go over the top, another virtuoso leaps out. Tommy Cogbill's playing on the final verse is nothing short of breathtaking; one does not even notice Aretha's vocal swoops and flights as he digs in, and Dowd has the Clapton overdub mixed low enough not to overpower the bass. It is one of Tommy's grittiest, bluesiest lines ever, and to those who love what he could play at full power, this is an astonishing illustration.

Bobby Womack, who is glimpsed in the abovementioned film, was every bit as amazing as the others. "He's the reason I began to play a Telecaster," said Jimmy Johnson. "He had rented one at Manny's [the famous New York music store] and he said, 'Y' know, this is what you need to play.'" He contributes a jaunty lead line to Aretha's version of "Groovin'," the Young Rascals song which in the hands of the Southern players becomes less a celebration of young love than a celebration of the big city, its easy sound capturing the pleasure of newcomers to the Apple as they go exploring its delights on a Sunday afternoon in spring. This was accurate; the muscians had all grown accustomed to New York and, according to Tom Dowd in *The Record Producers*, when there was free time left over from the week's recording the musicians trooped around New York looking for some typical city experience in which to participate. "Once you get used to a studio, it's just a matter of where you're eating and sleeping. I knew my hotel, the studio, a place I could eat; it set a pattern where I didn't feel estranged. It got more and more familiar," Spooner Oldham said of his acclimation. "It was like a little playground, there were things to do if you chose. I went to see *Hello Dolly* with Barbra Streisand and walked out in the middle; I just thought it was too weird to be there by myself." Joe South apparently spent time hanging out; when the sessions were over he vanished with a coterie of friends, not to be seen again until the next day. Tommy Cogbill, of course, remained laid-back and quiet. "Tommy was a family man and a father—he was something else. He didn't gallivant and whoop around," Jimmy Johnson said respectfully. "That says volumes about a person."

It also speaks well of a person if he knows when to take the lead and when to be in the background, and Tommy proved that he knew this as the musicians worked on the most classic and most heartfelt track from these sessions, the song penned by Aretha's younger sister Carolyn: "Ain't No Way." It is not a song to be played by the blaring light of day, but at midnight when the room is dark, the world is quiet, and all things are possible and everything can be said. Aretha's vocal is impassioned but controlled, with few pyrotechnics or shouts; the background vocals of Carolyn and the Sweet Inspirations sound haunted with memory and feeling. Tommy Cogbill and Roger Hawkins are only slightly audible throughout, with Aretha's piano given the lead; Spooner Oldham is not heard at all. "I'm not sure if I played on 'Ain't No Way,'" he reflected. "There was one song I chose not to play; I didn't feel they needed me. I just set in the control room." The performance he witnessed was one of stunning beauty; the ethereal, wordless vocals of Carolyn Franklin and the Sweet Inspirations as the record fades out remain in a listener's mind long after the song is heard.

It was a touch that Tommy Cogbill began bringing to his own productions; a lingering, lonely sound that settled in the heart and soul of whomever might choose to hear.

# It Looked Like a Family

The American group were only dimly aware of it, but they were developing a reputation beyond the city limits. Musicians were learning from their records, with Reggie Young and Tommy Cogbill especially being widely copied; the jazz bassist Jaco Pastorius and the Muscle Shoals bass player David Hood, both of whom were just starting out, openly acknowledged Cogbill's influence. The studio was filling up with hangers-on, as more and more people wanted to be part of a hitmaking scene.

American was becoming a way station for record-company executives like Bell's Dave Carrico, who spent a lot of time hanging out with the group, backslapping them and taking them out for expensive dinners on the company's tab. (Carrico was and would remain one of Quinton Claunch's favorite people as well—years later, Quinton was still wondering how to reestablish contact with him.) Publicists like Jack Grady, who had moved on from radio announcing, were on the periphery. George Klein, from WHBQ, was there a great deal, badgering Chips about why he could not be the one to "break" new records on the air, since Klein was bound by the Bill Drake "boss radio" playlist. Producers and publishers, especially in Nashville, were interested in the cheap Memphis union recording rates.

"Everything in Nashville was done in three hours; you had to pay 'em. . . . At American I think we were doing five, six-hour sessions," said Reggie Young. "We'd get whatever the scale was, roughly $65 a session. . . . If we'd logged our sessions we would have been quite wealthy." If they had been working in Nashville, where the musicians' union rode herd on sessions more strictly than in Memphis, their sessions would have been divided into three-hour segments, with the musicians being paid for each three-hour block of time; as it was, Chips could pay them scale and no more if they sat there for ten hours (something not unheard of in his sessions). Chips's complete one-stop of a studio was also a strong drawing card, and he knew it. "I had good equipment, I had a good band, and I got a good sound out of the studio," he said proudly. Dollar for dollar, producers could not have gotten a better bargain, and that fall several from Nashville began bringing their acts around.

Fred Foster had been issuing rhythm and blues for awhile under his subsidiary Sound Stage Seven label, which was still under the supervision of the Nashville DJ John Richbourg. "Fred goes back so far in the business," Bobby Emmons said with awe. "He recognized talent in the rough, long before Monument. Fred always treated me way better than I deserved, every time I was around him. I always considered him a friend outside of the studio. He's a good man."

"Fred's such a nice man," said Reggie Young respectfully. "He knew songs, he was a good song man." The producer was equally admiring of the guitarist: "If you were going to have one guitar player to play on your records for the rest of your life, it would be Reggie Young," he said warmly. Fred occasionally came to Memphis to look in, and liked what he saw. "It looked like a family, y'know?" he said of the ambience. "The studio was sort of magical. The echo chamber was stuck up on the roof somewhere and it had water when it rained, the roof leaked. That gave it a really different sound." (Fred's memory did not serve him well here: actually, there were two echo chambers, placed back to back on the north side of the studio. A third echo chamber was added later.) When sessions in Nashville took up Fred's time, he left the recording supervision to "John R." "John Richbourg was a nice man but he did not know much about recording at all," said Bobby Wood, who was spending more time recording with the group as work at Phillips slacked off. "He would just say that's good or whatever. He was completely at our mercy. I remember one day I asked him if he wanted some Ray Scott piano on the song we were about to record and he said yes, that would be good. Ray Scott was a local singer and not much of a piano player. The other guys looked at me trying to keep a straight face." (Bobby developed a reputation as one of the group's most celebrated pranksters; the tricks involving his glass eye became legendary. "That eye turned up in a lot of interesting places," Bobby chortled mischievously.)

Richbourg brought several people in to American, none of them as closely associated with the studio as the Louisiana native Joe Simon, whose deep, rich voice and unconventional phrasing may have made him the most underrated soul singer of the era. "There was never a doubt in my mind that they could make a hit record with him," said Fred Foster. "He was definitely a certified great soul singer, I know that I was inspired every time I worked with him," agreed Bobby Emmons.

To many of the musicians, Joe was a surprise. Mike Leech remembered that the singer talked in a rural, ungrammatical way not consistent with his intelligence. Reggie Young laughed at Simon's terrible memory for names. "Joe, he never got Chips's name right," said the guitarist. Simon referred to Chips as "Skip Morris"—which provoked delighted cackles from the control room. "And lordamercy, it took him all week to get to 'Skip Morris,'" Reggie continued. (Chips got good-humored revenge years later; in a chance encounter at the Nashville airport, he shouted, "Joe Tex! Joe Tex!" at the singer.) "Wilson Pickett was bad about that Skip thing, too," noted the producer in a bemused aside. Joe also never bothered to learn the names of the musicians, said Mike Leech; he addressed them as "guitar boy" or "drummer boy." Once he walked up to Tommy Cogbill and called him "guitar boy," apparently not knowing the difference between a guitar and a bass, causing Tommy to stop playing and erupt in his characteristic sputtering laughter. "Joe was nice to everyone, though, and we like always gave it our best," Bobby Wood said of the resulting album, the somewhat mistitled No Sad Songs.

Seldom had a singer with a deep, expressive voice been showcased so well. "You Keep Me Hangin' On," a song written by the Bakersfield scene founder Billy Mize, sketches through understatement a complicated romance; the voluminous echo and Joe's weary vocal depicts a man adrift in a sea of bewildered, resigned despair. It's probably Chips's most impassioned production since "Gee Whiz"; he did not write the song, but he produced (and arranged) it as if he had. "Very, very good record, we were all pleased when we made that record," said Reggie Young with quiet pride.

"My Special Prayer," the song that became a hit that fall, is also classic Chips. Though the song does not say where the church is that the narrator stumbles into and prays for his lover's return, Chips gives the background music a slightly Spanish feel, a precursor of the Western-flavored material he recorded later, including "Pancho and Lefty" and "South of the Border." We are in the same Southwestern territory occupied by Brooks and Dunn in the video of "My Maria," when Kix Brooks wanders into an adobe mission church and lights a candle; but in Chips's dark vision, the narrator is trapped in an endless hell, the sadness unresolved as the record fades out.

It is ironic that a studio known for despairing music would have sponsored the uptempo writing of Darryl Carter; even more ironic that during his time at American, he should write a selection called "No Sad Songs" that became something of a group standard for awhile (that fall alone, not only Joe Simon but Oscar Toney Jr. would record it). Chips always kept the basic arrangement for the song that he used here; a horn figure to introduce the number and a string line countering each verse, with a blaring horn section competing in the choruses. The story line expresses gratitude for the woman who took away all the pain and made the speaker stop listening to sad music. (One assumes Chips would not have wanted the entire record-buying audience to follow suit, because there would go his livelihood.) On the album, after the proclamation that there would be "no sad songs," one immediately follows: "I Worry About You" features light piano fills and a mellow, saxophone-laced groove reminiscent of the fifties (an era that Chips, with his rough jeans and James Dean manner, seemed in a fundamental way never to have left). All is prelude, though, to the first song on the second side of the album.

"Nine-Pound Steel" sums up all that is best in the art of American Studios—excellent songwriting, innovative playing, quality production, and a consistent theme emphasizing reflection, loneliness, sorrow, and anguish. It is stark, going directly back to the old ballads for its theme: the narrator is in prison for theft, having stolen to buy things for his woman. He now repents of his crime and agonizes over his regrets; although he speaks of hope and of his eventual release, the implication is that only death will free him. So ancient is it in its sorrow that contemporary Nashville, anxious to live down the "hillbilly" tag, would not have gone near it. For Chips Moman, who produced the recording, it was a dress rehearsal for another song of the same type he later recorded with Tommy Cogbill: "I Shall Be Released" has many of the same elements of remorse and despair. This was music for those who had been left behind by life. It was music for the forgotten.

It originated from a marathon staged by Dan Penn and Wayne Carson; in an amphetamine rush, they stayed up for nine days writing the song. "Penn said, 'Pound a day,'" Wayne chuckled. "That was when we jumped in the car and drove across the river and got to ol' Dr. Duck—that *quack*—and got some Am-bars." Amphetamine-driven writing sessions were the norm in Southern music, particularly in Nashville; virtually every songwriter of distinction was flying on them. "I tell you what, you get into another plane of thinking on those," Wayne reflected. Robert Gordon described Wayne and Dan at this session as having sat in the same spot facing each other for hours as they traded ideas; at one point Wayne, overcome with exhaustion, slid off his chair, only to have Dan lash him to the chair with his belt and exclaim, "Oh, no you don't—you're not quittin' on me now!" Completely accurate, Wayne said, offering a postscript of his own: "I was stayin' with Dan and when it was over I went there and

fell asleep in the bathtub. Linda was goin' out to work, and when she came home, I was still there. When the water cooled off, boy, it was cold."

The tune had been inspired by the Merle Travis classic "Nine Pound Hammer"(which the group would record with John Prine in 1973). "Penn said, 'Let's don't call it a hammer; let's call it a steel, what it is,'" Wayne remembered. They cut the record at Hi with Dan contributing a sparse, spare mix that added the element of Clinch Mountain shadows and grimness. Why were they at Hi? The studio was undergoing another major equipment overhaul, said Wayne: "We went from two-track to four-track to sixteen-track in a year, literally." (It may have seemed that way, but members of the sound crew recall the 8-track going in later; most of the records at American's peak were cut on four-track.) Joe Simon's stately delivery gave the tune a dignity far beyond what an Appalachian bluegrasser would have made of it, bringing to the narration a sorrowful stoicism. "Joe kinda played with the lyrics," said Wayne. "Dan looked over and said 'He ain't gettin' none of the songwriters' licks in there.'" "Joe's timing, it took us awhile to get that," said Reggie Young. "I remember his timing, it would be different each take. I thought that was kinda strange, because he was such a soulful guy."

"Joe Simon, when he did it, he had made many great changes," Dan Penn said admiringly. "We sounded like rednecks compared to him. Emotion means everything. He tilted it this way and that way." The sound of a hammer on an anvil runs as a leitmotif through the song; it was inspired by the background on Sam Cooke's "Chain Gang." "I was always enthused with the sound of a chain being recorded," said Dan, who had already proven himself partial to sound effects.

As often happens when these appear on a recording, what the listener hears is not literal. It was actually a Coke bottle, struck with a stick by Bobby Emmons. Emmons recalled that originally they tried getting the effect by banging two hammers together. "Don't try that at home!" the organist laughed. "Too much recoil." "I always wanted to do something [different on a record], even if it meant opening the piano and raking the strings," said Bobby Wood, who did not play on this session but whose observation in this case spoke for the entire group. "Let's show some new colors. History's been written, let's write some more history." With "Nine-Pound Steel" they certainly had, and everyone was proud of the finished work; even Dan Penn, who tended to shrug off his accomplishments, felt that he had given the world an underrated masterpiece. "It's like a hidden gem or something, nobody ever talks about it," he said with some puzzlement, wondering why the record has not become more widely known.

The recording of masterworks, neglected and otherwise, was becoming standard operating procedure at American. "We just kinda took it for granted, oh, we were in the charts all the time, "said Reggie Young. "It was quite a feat, we didn't know what we were doing. We thought that's what you're supposed to do, be on the charts and make hit records." "That's the best record Joe Simon ever had," Wayne Carson said authoritatively, noting that this song went over better among African Americans than the efforts of a writer from Bakersfield. "Them country boys tried to say 'Hangin' On' was bigger. A lot of that's *hype*," he added, giving a special emphasis on the h-word to indicate his distaste for it. "You can look at this business two ways, the way you wanna see it or the way it really is."

Several of the uptempo songs were showcases for Tommy's by-now-patented romping style, but Chips seems to have recorded them in an oddly dismissive fashion, perhaps finding them not in agreement with the mood he wanted to display. Much more to his taste was something like "In the Same Old Way," from Dan's and Spooner's back catalogue, or the Charles Chalmers ballad, "Can't Find No Happiness" (the title alone would have delighted Chips). Joe Simon declaims it in a way that would not have been out of character for Otis Redding, and the presence of Wayne Jackson's horn section from Stax adds to the emphasis. "Worries on my mind / Trouble at my door," Simon announces simply. "Your love is hard to find, and I can't take it anymore." The confusion in the lyrics is underscored by Chips, and the record fades to a Stax-style ending as the singer concludes that he will "never see the light." It's not a record to play on a good day; but when life and love have one completely up a tree, one could not possibly do better.

The same applies to the recordings the group was doing with Oscar Toney Jr., who was back at American to complete his album. Once again, the musicians enjoyed seeing and working with him. "I liked that album, I liked him," said Reggie Young thoughtfully. "What you heard was what you got, he didn't try to be anything other than himself." Papa Don Schroeder insisted that photos of the American musicians appear on the album, just to let people know that white players could back a black artist and still have the music sound soulful.

Several tracks on the album stand out. The Bobby "Blue" Bland classic "Turn On Your Love Light," with the background voices overdubbed in New York, catches the sound of every great Southern party or family reunion; not even the rollicking version the group recorded with Conway Twitty in 1978 (with Jerry Carrigan sitting in on drums and contributing one of the finest performances of his career) can equal this sense of fun. The spoken introduction Oscar uses on "Without Love" would be later used almost line for line on more bombastic recordings of the song, most notably that of Tom Jones, who had a hit with it in 1970. And "Moon River," seemingly an odd choice of song for a soul singer and a Southern band, is magnificent. There is only a slight comment now and then from Reggie Young, and the rest is Tommy Cogbill's brooding bass and the ascending strings dubbed in New York. It paints a picture in sound; one can almost see a full moon rising over the dark Southern waters. It takes longer to realize that the recording unwittingly refers to the collaborations between Tommy and Chips. The Johnny Mercer lyric accurately describes the "two drifters . . . after the same rainbow's end." By the finale of the song, we are left recalling the photographs of Tommy as he began to look more and more worn, and the recording fades him out as if he were a cowboy riding off into the night, making one of his celebrated exits.

An exit is nowhere apparent in the album's second-best song, "Down in Texas," written by Dan Penn's new acquaintance Eddie Hinton, who was developing a reputation at the Shoals not only as a writer but as a formidable lead guitar. Hinton was young, but he had talent; he was already collaborating with established writers Donnie Fritts and Marlin Greene, and it was Greene with whom he wrote this tough, realistic ballad about a worker stranded in Texas, wanting to ride the train back to his home in Washington, D.C. The song features a couplet worthy of consideration in any list of great blues lyrics: "I've been up Broadway, high as you can see / they pay you like you're half a man, and they work you like you're three"—a line that would have had great resonance for the overworked musicians sitting there for hours at a time taking direction from Papa Don. The record features a wild "burping" saxophone line and Tommy Cogbill's bass suggesting the sound of train wheels—a sound that had been featured in Memphis music since the days when Luther Perkins had simulated a train for Johnny Cash's recording of "Rock Island Line." American continued to put this signature of Tommy's to good use.

Through Dan Penn, Eddie Hinton was visiting the studio now and then, watching how things were done and pitching new songs, as was his collaborator, Dan's old pal Donnie Fritts. "Dan was our Alabama connection," Mike Leech remembered, and because of Dan the Shoals musicians, past and present, were now becoming well known to the American players, even those who had never been there. "The Muscle Shoals players were like our brothers in music," Bobby Wood said warmly. Actually, they were more like distant cousins; Mike Leech thought them a real contrast, finding them for the most part slightly more rural in outlook than the Memphians. This was understandable in terms of what much of their experiences had been thus far (although the ones who moved to Nashville developed a great deal of sophistication). "They were almost as tight as the Memphis bunch," Mike added.

There were other differences as well. The young Shoals musicians held an almost idolatrous worship of visiting executives like the Atlantic crew which the American players, with their fierce commitment to egalitarianism, did not share, despite their respect for Wexler and Dowd. (The American musicians viewed every person with whom they worked as equal, but as their leader, Chips was "more equal than others.") The American musicians preferred to work from intuition; the Shoals players were analytical. The American group seemed to take their musical and philosophical outlooks to a certain point and no further; the Shoals players allowed their minds free rein. The groupthink forming at American was never a factor in the Shoals; not even Rick Hall, by all accounts a dominating figure, was the reference point for his musicians that Chips would be to his. Those of the group who remained closest to the Shoals were Dan Penn and Spooner Oldham, both loyal to the place where it all began for them; Reggie Young, who had admired the Shoals players since his earliest visits there; and of course Chips Moman and Tommy Cogbill, whose schedules increasingly kept them away from their friends but who remained as closely in touch as they could with developments in Alabama.

In fact, it may have been at around this time when Chips stunned Jimmy Johnson and Roger Hawkins by making them an offer: he wanted to sell American to them and let them run it. Years after the fact, Jimmy continued to be puzzled at Chips's invitation. The motive remained unclear, apparently even to Chips, but the evidence suggests that the pace, which was rapidly picking up during the fall of 1967, was frightening him a little. The studio was beginning to move beyond a group of old boys picking on the front porch, the atmosphere in which Chips was comfortable. For the time being, Jimmy and Roger were also more comfortable there, which is mainly why the idea fell through. "He scared us," Jimmy Johnson remembered. "We didn't know anything about Memphis, 'cept that it was a big ol' town. . . . We never got to price, he just kept talkin' about 'I wanna sell you the place.' We just weren't ready." Roger Hawkins gave the offer so little credence he scarcely remembered it later. In the end, Jimmy also rejected the idea as frivolous; he thought Chips was perhaps having trouble with someone or that Chips's chronic restlessness was overtaking him.

Jimmy may have been closer to the mark than he knew. "I didn't want to be gone from home," Chips explained. Having made his point and triumphed over his dismissal from Stax, he now wanted to take some time off. "I spent most of my life in a little ol' control room with no windows in it, and I'm such an outdoor person," he observed with some amazement at himself. He had purchased a farm at Raleigh, north of Memphis, and he wanted to be there among the animals and in the fields he loved. Unable to get rid of the studio, he began absenting himself more and more, immersing himself in his hobbies; also, "I spent a lot of time sleeping," he cackled. At least one client found it more than they could take: Papa Don Schroeder had scheduled a session with R&B legend Chuck Jackson, only to discover that Chips did not even show. An infuriated Schroeder vowed he had seen the last of the studio—not quite true, as he would return with Mighty Sam McClain the following spring, but Schroeder retained respect for the musicians and sorry that it had all blown up as it did. "We could have had such fun," he said regretfully. Perhaps the ambitious, goal-oriented Papa Don was missing the point: when everything began to morph into a professionally-run studio and sessions, that was when it stopped being fun for Chips.

The workload was becoming enough that Don Crews could no longer function as de facto secretary, as he had since Sandy Posey's departure for Nashville. To help out in the office he finally hired a young woman named Ima Roberts (later Withers). "It was a one-girl office there for a long time," she said thoughtfully. Her job was mainly clerical, handling much of the forms and paperwork from the union and from publishers. "I did the musician's contracts, all of the single-song contracts for Tree. Press Music was administered by Tree, we paid them a fifteen-percent administration fee. My everyday contact [there] was Joyce, who was Buddy [Killen's] and Jack [Stapp]'s right-hand lady. I did book sessions," she added. "Don was signin' checks, tryin' to keep everybody on an even keel."

Everyone coming to American Studios had a favorite, almost the way everyone had a favorite Beatle, and for Ima it was an immediate decision. Then and forever, her highest regard was for Tommy Cogbill. "He was *fabulous*," she said emphatically, her warmth and respect still evident after many years. "He was very special, he was one of a kind. You know, when they said they broke the mold, it was true. He was a man of not many words . . . as laid-back as they come. He was a thinker, and it showed in his face. He was kind and gentle; he'd help anyone. He wasn't a very big man in stature, but boy, he was a *big* man inside." Throughout her tenure at American, she remained protective of Tommy, conducting her tasks with his interests foremost at heart. Tommy rewarded her loyalty with unfailing kindness, letting her know how much he appreciated it. Dan Penn was another favorite, she said, but all of "those guys were like my brothers. Reggie Young is one of the most incredible guitar players I have ever heard in my life! They don't have egos, not as we know of egos today."

Ima soon had a chance to observe the people from Tree Publishing at close range, since Buddy Killen was interested enough in what the American group was doing to see if they would work well with his R&B act, Joe Tex. The decision had its roots earlier in the year, when Chips Moman and Tommy Cogbill had sent Reggie Young to Nashville in their place to record with Killen; the session had yielded the Joe Tex–penned "Show Me," which also became the first big hit for Barbara Mandrell. Killen asked Reggie to come back and finish the album, but by now, Reggie recalled, "we had just bound ourselves together in that little brotherhood of whatever it was" and he would not go without the others. Presented with no other choice, Killen came to Memphis for a project he supervised and Chips engineered.

Everyone at American looked back at Joe Tex's sessions with fondness. "There's a lot to remember about Joe," Bobby Wood observed. "First of all, he was more like one of us than most. . . . Out of all the artists I've worked with in over forty years, Joe Tex was definitely a highlight and I miss him." "I loved Joe, he was such a talented man," Chips Moman reminisced with delight. "He was an absolute pleasure to be around. I always loved it when Joe Tex came in." Spooner Oldham said they had been looking forward to working with him from the beginning, because "Joe's reputation preceded him. He was one of those, in my mind, who was a classic soul artist." "I remember Joe Tex was one of my favorites," Gene Chrisman added joyfully. "Ol' Joe'd come in with his Kentucky Fried Chicken and a quart of orange juice." (Bobby Wood added that Joe did not stop there; he often brought in a whole watermelon!)

"Joe Tex was such a pleasure to work with," Reggie Young said warmly. "He'd have his songs written down on a Kleenex or a paper towel. He didn't know music, he didn't know chords. Me or Emmons would sit with him and try to write a chord chart, we'd do it with the number system. It was totally amazing, the first verse was exactly the same as the second would be—same chord changes, everything. He knew exactly what he was doing and what he wanted on the record."

Bobby Wood also remembered working with Emmons on occasion to find the chord changes for Joe's songs. "Joe would start singing and try to communicate the rhythm and we would work one bar at a time," recalled the piano player. "He would say that chord is not right or just say no and we'd keep looking until he'd say that's right. It would take about half an hour to an hour usually to get the whole song on paper with what he wanted. He would also communicate the groove and bass lines to everyone. He did the same thing with horns." Bobby Emmons recalled seeing Joe perform in a Texas club during the days of the Bill Black tours: "He had as much fun on stage then as he did on sessions later, and was the best showman I had ever seen. His microphone sleight of hand and other stage moves rival anything I've seen since." And everyone remembered

Joe's habit of wearing bedroom slippers to the studio. That casual, "party" atmosphere was perfect for the funny, down-home records Tex liked to make. "Joe always seemed to be one of the guys and never seemed to get the ego that a lot of artists get. He just wanted to have a good time recording and I think that showed on his records," Bobby Wood observed. They immediately got down to work with the track for which he is remembered, "Skinny Legs and All."

In lesser hands than those of the American group, the song might have come off as a minstrel show; Joe's gleeful country-inflected voice seems to be announcing a beauty contest, an auction, or a little of both. The exchange between him and Bobby Womack (who just happened to be standing beside Joe in the studio, Reggie Young recalled) is completely impromptu. The descending guitar lick almost "chicken-picked" by Reggie in the bridge was added at the request of the singer. "He asked Reggie to do him a funky intro and Reg worked for awhile on it," said Bobby Wood. "Joe then asked him to play something like a chicken lick. Reggie did something like what is on the record and Joe fell on the floor laughing. He said do that again and he fell on the floor again." "'Skinny Legs' was in A-flat, I tuned my guitar a half step," said Reggie Young. "Joe just fell out, fell on the floor! He was kicking his feet up." Buddy Killen thought the lick so innovative that when he was overdubbing voices and audience reaction to the song to simulate a live performance, he cued the "audience" (actually a busload of tourists he corralled en route to the newly opened Country Music Hall of Fame) to applaud after Reggie's bit, alerting listeners to the fact that the guitarist had done something remarkable. An impromptu gesture from Killen also found its way into the record—when he opened the control-room door and mumbled something, Joe Tex seized on it and made Killen's voice the character of "Leroy," the bumbling fool who was supposed to take the girl.

Killen may have been the nominal producer, but there was no doubt among the musicians that Tex really called the shots. "He asked me to do the rhythm that I played and the same for everybody including bass," said Bobby Wood.

"We had to write down or listen for key words he was singing to go to a different section, chorus, or hook of the song." The spontaneous style evolved on this occasion carried over through all of their sessions for Joe Tex in Memphis and later in Nashville.

Playing a wild, fluttering blues harp on the record was one of the American group's most rugged individualists in a studio already brimming with them, a Wisconsin native who looked like Davy Crockett and acted like Lenny Bruce. Ed Kollis came from a long line of Upper Midwest eccentrics—his father had finally secured a post office job after a Depression youth spent riding the rails, and he passed some of that instinct for hard traveling on to Ed, as well as a talent for the harmonica. Ed never took the harp seriously until he was in college at the University of Wisconsin in his home town of Madison, when a friend of his suggested that if he learn it, he could be in their band. The White Trash Band was there at the beginning of the Wisconsin blues scene in the early sixties, the training ground for Boz Scaggs, Steve Miller, and Tracy Nelson. "We were going from folkie to electric, like Dylan did at that time," Ed recalled in his gentle, spacey voice. "We played a bar off-campus called the Glen and Anne. It was fun till we hooked up with a local booker named Ken Adamany [who later became the first manager of the Boz Scaggs band]. He'd do dumb things, rig talent contests, stuff like that. He just didn't have the touch." Prior to Adamany's involvement, Ed himself had been handling the bookings. "One summer, I played music, trimmed trees for a living, and rocked all night," he recalled joyfully. While visiting Tulsa to find a bass player for his group, he fell in with all the prominent Oklahoma musicians—Leon Russell, J. J. Cale, Carl Radle, and others, and for several years went back and forth between Wisconsin and Tulsa, slipping easily into the bohemian life of both places.

It could have gone on forever, but it ended in late 1967, when "Otis Redding's plane crashed in my hometown. I thought to myself, there's a big void in Memphis"—a void that a blues harmonica player could fill. Otis's plane crashed

in December of that year, but Ed was already in Memphis by September. The first place he worked was at Stax, backing Jimmy Hughes on a session; he then heard about the upcoming Joe Tex session and talked his way in. During recording hours, the back door at American was never locked; many sessions were interrupted by people wandering in directly off the street, so it was easy for someone like Ed to slip in. "Ed came in there and I thought he was from another planet," said Chips Moman, with the amusement typical of all his recollections. Chips had a liking for characters anyway, the more authentic the better; when he heard Ed's bluesy harmonica playing, he rather diffidently asked Ed if he would like a job as one of the sound engineers. Ed looked at Chips for a moment, grinned, and said, as if he were revving up a motorcycle, "Vroom." That was all Chips needed to hear, and from then on Ed became one of his favorites.

Ed had never even thought about sound engineering, let alone about making it his career, but just once behind the board and he was hooked. "There have been two times in my life when I've been illuminated: one time when I talked to a lady I'd been dating, we were talking about life and relating to people—I can still see the hallway we were standing in—and then the other time when I was taking a raw song and putting it together, like a chemical mix. And to be part of that is illuminating." As Darryl Carter had already discovered and Hayward Bishop later would, engineering at American was not a job for the uncommitted: "I was there twenty-four hours a day, got there first and left last," Ed remembered. "I'd fill in the blanks for Chips" whenever the studio head was gone—an increasing occurrence. Being at the studio also gave him a chance to contribute harmonica work to records. "I love his harp playing," enthused Reggie Young. "He had this microphone, it's an old Shure mike and this funky ol' amp. It was just down-home, ol' gutbucket blues. He fit in perfect." Besides "Skinny Legs and All," Ed's harmonica work from this period included an appearance on Joe Simon's "I'm a Traveling Man," in which Joe recites a tour schedule seemingly arranged by throwing darts at a map (Gary Talley, surviving almost three hundred days a year on the road with the Box Tops, vouched for the accuracy of such a schedule.)

Surprisingly, Chips did not feature Ed's harmonica on many of his productions, compared to Tommy Cogbill and Dan Penn, both of whom relished having a new sound with which to experiment. "I wasn't as crazy about the blues as everyone else—the blues came from pickin' cotton and I don't need that," said the Georgia farm boy. "Every one [blues] sounds just like the other one. Playin' blues is not my idea of a good time." Riding motorcycles was, however, and Ed soon joined Chips and Tommy Cogbill in frequent trail-bike outings. Ed also won an ally in Mike Leech, who appreciated the outsider's perspective Ed brought to the table.

The outsider's perspective was particularly useful in their dealings with Nashville producers such as Killen and Roy Dea, who had worked with some of the musicians at Hi and who brought the fading jazz vocalist Gloria Lynne in for a Motown-style session engineered by Chips that was intended to revitalize her career. The musicians and Chips found Roy to be agreeable, always one of their favorites, and they remained close to Fred Foster. Reggie Young offered his view of their other prominent Nashville client, Buddy Killen. "Buddy had paid his dues, he'd played bass on the Grand Ole Opry," he said. "We used to joke, we'd always ask Killen if he'd had a bath to wash the country off him. Everybody thought Nashville was really rural. What you'd see on TV was the Wilburn Brothers or Porter Wagoner, with all due respect to them." Reggie liked the new patrons for their willingness to think outside the assembly-line mentality. "In Nashville, you'd go in for a three-hour session and you'd leave. . . . Music was more structured here," he said, from the perspective of having established himself in both cities. "Buddy Killen and Fred Foster weren't that way, they didn't want four songs in three hours, they wanted a hit song!"

Perhaps the fact that both Foster and Killen had publishing companies (Combine and Tree, respectively) made them as song-oriented as were the Memphis players. In any case, just as

the musicians did, the producers loved the creative atmosphere—and the fact that the band was giving them hit records. "The whole group had great ideas," said Fred Foster enthusiastically. "They had the same good idea at the same time, or something. It was like it was supposed to be."

The staff at Tree did not always show as much appreciation as did the head of Monument Records. "I'll tell you how one-sided Killen was," complained Bobby Wood. "We'd given him a Top Ten record on Joe Tex. That Christmas, he gave all the secretaries at Tree in Nashville color TV sets. You know what he sent to us? One bottle of wine, to be divided among all of us. Tommy was so mad he ordered the thing crated right up and sent back. It wasn't even very expensive wine. It's a wonder it didn't have a screw top!"

But with Buddy Killen's help, and the additional support of Fred Foster, Quinton Claunch, and the people from Atlantic and Bell, the studio was becoming better known.

|||||||||||||||||||||||||||||||||||||||||||||||||||||||||||||||||

### CHAPTER 11

# Standing on the Verge of Getting It On

This famous George Clinton phrase accurately describes where the American group stood at the beginning of 1968. In a year and a half they had become one of the most versatile recording teams in the music industry (even though they still flew under the radar, getting less worldwide attention and press scrutiny than their contemporaries at Stax and Motown, or even in Nashville). Chips Moman, in his understated way, had established himself as a producer, and Dan Penn and Tommy Cogbill were making important contributions to the studio. Wayne Carson, Chips, and Dan were gaining recognition as writers. Even friends of the group were doing well: in early 1968 J.R. Cobb's Classics IV entered the Top Ten for the first time with Cobb's composition "Spooky," a song that anticipated both the Eagles' "Witchy Woman" and Stevie Nicks's entire persona by several years. "I was trying to write a standard," J.R. said of the work he was doing at that time. He had not gotten there yet, but he, like the writers at American, was en route.

The George Clinton quotation is apt in another way: by early 1968 it was apparent that Chips had the potential—one he would never fully realize—to become one of music's great bandleaders, on a par with Clinton, Jerry Garcia, Bob Wills, or more to the point, Duke Ellington. His productions, and those of the rest of the group, captured the mood of the contemporary South in the same way Ellington's music described 1920s and 1930s Harlem, or

that of Strauss described nineteenth-century Vienna. Also like Ellington, Chips's lineup of strong individual voicings seasoned the music; his greatest instrument was the band. Night after night, Chips sat in the control room at American, running the musicians through their paces, offering suggestions or comments in tones so unassuming an onlooker might have thought he was not giving any direction at all (sometimes it even seemed that way to the musicians), but sculpting the sound as if working with wet clay, shaping and molding it to the pattern in his mind.

If Chips was the Ellington of Southern music, who would be his Billy Strayhorn—his sounding board, collaborator, best friend, and alter ego? To observers, it looked as if Tommy Cogbill, Dan Penn, or both were in line for the role. They were close to Chips, hung out with him away from the studio (much more than Gene Chrisman or Mike Leech did) and they collaborated with him on records and on the development of new ideas for the company. Yet there was an independent streak in them, obvious in Dan's case and more subtle with Tommy, that prevented them from existing completely in Chips's shadow. For the role of alter ego, it became increasingly obvious, Chips had chosen Bobby Emmons.

There was an almost mystical dimension to the friendship between the Fifties rebel and the bookish intellectual. It was a connection never fully understood by the rest of the group, or for that matter, Chips and Bobby themselves. They never analyzed it; they were too busy in the first place, and not temperamentally inclined to examine the tradeoffs in the second. Certainly Bobby's musical perfectionism, a perfectionism shared by Chips, played a part; the keyboard player often spent time alone in the studio, developing new sounds on the Hammond B3, experimenting with runs and riffs he would later insert into songs. Chips was also aware of Bobby's development as a writer. After a relative lull, Emmons was composing again; interesting songs such as "Just You and Me," with its somewhat psychedelic effects, displayed his quirky intelligence. "I felt a lot of encouragement from Chips to pursue my writing,"

Emmons said warmly. "I always admired his melodies and his uncanny ability to predict what to write about. We usually didn't have to go very far with one of Chips's ideas before a lot of people really liked it." Even more to the point, Bobby had no desire to produce records, and thus would never be in direct competition with Chips. With Emmons, Chips had found one of the things he had always been looking for; a colleague whose loyalty would not, even for a second, be in doubt.

Not that he had reason to wonder about the others. "Loyalty with a capital L was the main thing for most of us back then," said Mike Leech. The result of all those hours spent together in the studio was exactly what Chips had hoped it would be: they could now read each other's musical moves and moods—and those of Chips—without hesitation. They were getting a sense of one another's personalities, locking into each other's minds, creating a thought collective (to the frustration and despair of the later arrivals, shut out from the groupthink). "One of Chips's reasons for liking us is that we share some of the same abilities," observed Mike Leech. "That is, to be aware of what the other is thinking or trying to say. Communication between us and the control booth is uncanny sometimes, like we are all part of one brain." "I think the main thing is, we're involved in it as a team, I think that's the best thing I can say about it," added Chips.

There were nicknames now, a sure sign of familiarity with each other. Tommy was "Cog," especially to Mike Leech, and he was also called "Super Clark" because Clark was his middle name. Mike's nickname came about when, the arranger recalled, "Reggie hit me with 'Lurch,' which I hated but which stuck for a long time." It seems to have been coined because of the similar-sounding last name. (Ironically, Mike's rawboned Irish features, his height, and his short, sandy hair gave him a resemblance to Ted Cassidy, who immortalized the role of Lurch on television's *Addams Family*.) Reggie Young was "R" or "Reginald," the others finding it amusing that such an unaffected man should have been saddled with such a dignified first name. Spooner Oldham, who had started

out with a nickname anyway, quickly became "Spoon," and Bobby Emmons, partly for reasons of efficient speech and partly to avoid confusion with the other two Bobbys who were increasingly around the place, became known as "E."

If anyone following the group's work had any doubts about the increasing importance of E to Chips, the speculations were allayed with one of the first recordings placed in 1968. "I Don't Want Nobody to Lead Me On" by the Masqueraders, is a strong song with a biting vocal attack from one of the song's composers, a pounding figure from Mike Leech that could have been mistaken for one of Tommy Cogbill's bass lines, and some especially emphatic swirls on the Hammond organ from Emmons.

The Masqueraders were a soul group out of Dallas who had originally sought their fortune in Detroit. Speculating about Memphis, they seem to have showed up at American while simultaneously hoping they could get on at Stax. As they reported in an interview for their compilation CD, when they first arrived at American in late 1967, Chips was not there, but Bobby Womack and Darryl Carter were, and Womack's encouragement convinced them to stick around. They quickly became favorites at American. "The Masqueraders, I thought were a good act, kinda like the Four Tops," said Don Crews, noting the similarities between the gritty voice of the lead singer, Lee Jones, and that of Levi Stubbs. He also noted their talent as writers. "They were a very nice group; they had some pretty fair songs." "I loved the sound of that group," said Spooner Oldham. "I loved those guys—the sincerity of their talent," Mike Leech said. "Their vocal arrangements were great, and all we had to do was play along. We spent a lot of time with them and got to know them fairly well."

"It was a mystery at first and a frustration later that we couldn't get a big record on those guys because they had *everything* it usually took," said Bobby Emmons. "They definitely worked hard enough throughout to deserve one." "They were fun, just a fun bunch of guys," Bobby Wood remembered enthusiastically. When he heard them, Chips liked the contrast of raw lead vocals with the gentle backing harmonies led by Sam Hutchins (whom he also recorded later as a solo act). "Sam Hutchins—a nice guy," Mike Leech remembered. "He was doing a vocal overdub one day when a huge hailstorm sounded like the roof was coming off. When it stopped Chips was ready to resume recording and Sam had disappeared. They found him hiding [somewhere]." The combination of rough and smooth voices that made the Masqueraders so unique inspired Chips to create with them some of his most compelling work.

"Let's Face Facts" was the B-side of "I Don't Want Nobody," and facing facts was the key to the song. Also composed by members of the Masqueraders, it described the thoughts of a draftee about to go off to Vietnam, concerned for his safety but trying to reassure his girl. Not until Green Day's famous song about the Iraq war, "Wake Me When September Comes," would the thoughts of an embarking soldier again be musically so well documented, and it drew on the by-now standard American Studios theme of stoicism: "I don't want to go, but it must be this way." Mike Leech's string line hints of agony at the danger and separation but quickly settles into sad resignation, while Reggie Young's gentle string-bending and Bobby Emmons's prominent organ line emphasize the stress inherent in the soldier's immediate future.

"On The Other Side," a ballad written by Dan Penn, Spooner Oldham, and Mark James, is both one of Chips's most sparse productions and one of his most effective. It is easy to imagine how receptive he would have been to the song when his friends premiered it; the opening line, "You left me cryin'," would have been enough for him. The song, seemingly addressed to a discontented, searching person, wonders what they will find "on the other side," though exactly where that is never gets fully explained; Dan and Spooner were becoming masters of the well-placed mysterious line. "My tears are falling down," Lee Jones bellows with pain, "and the loneliness is on the rise." The other Masqueraders offer a sort of Greek chorus, humming in assent like friends nodding sympathetically, and only a cutting guitar line from Reggie Young or a swirl of keyboard work from Emmons intrudes now and then. We hear a man grappling with something—unhappiness, destiny—concluding "What's the use" in the chorus, and returning to his tears in the song's final verse, railing against his fate but surrendering to it. Interestingly, the lyric seems to offer a look at the emotional price paid by those closest to a restless soul like Chips—a price of which the writers, especially Dan Penn and Mark James at this point, were fully aware, although Spooner Oldham said that he had never intended the piece to be "a reflection on Chips's work ethic." Mike Leech remembered Mark spending time sitting in the control room, muttering darkly about things he was beginning to suspect were not to his liking. Glen Spreen recalled that the majority of Mark's complaints had to do with the way Chips chose to interpret his songs.

Chips placed the first Masqueraders single with Scepter and the second with Bell, using his contacts at both labels to get them released. (Don Crews thought the Scepter single was the ballad "I Ain't Got to Love Nobody Else," but that was recorded later in the year.) Not surprisingly, these bitter songs did not do well in the charts—hippie optimism and brotherhood were still getting a run for their money, with songs like Chet Powers's "Get Together" (already a standard among musicians before the world discovered it a year later) and Jim Post's "Reach Out in the Darkness," recorded in Nashville roughly around the same time as the Masqueraders' singles. Chips tried one more time, then, irritated at the lack of immediate response, behaved as he increasingly did when he no longer wanted to work with an act—he turned the group over to Tommy Cogbill. "It didn't bother Chips at all," Mike Leech said about the producer's relinquishing the Masqueraders. "Now he could fly his airplanes, race his horses, make tons of money for studio time, and not work." "Chips wasn't no ball of fire about stuff he didn't want to fool with," said Don Crews regretfully. "If he didn't have any money comin' in it he wasn't interested." The new assignment was fine with the bass player, who still loved R&B although he was recording rock groups such as the local Flash and the Board of Directors; it was like handing him on a plate the chance to experiment. "I Don't Want Nobody to Lead Me On," however, was deemed such an important song that it became an American Studios standard for awhile. Several acts recorded it, all of them following the same original fiery arrangement, and none more effectively than the half-country, half white-soul version done by Paul Revere and the Raiders practically simultaneously with the Masqueraders' recording (and Mike Leech's bass playing is even more incisive on their version than it was on the original).

The Raiders' arrival at American was another sign of how important the studio and its staff was beginning to look in the larger world. The Raiders had started in the Pacific Northwest, specifically Idaho, where the keyboard player Paul Revere Dick had met a young saxophonist and aspiring singer named Mark Lindsay. The group first came to prominence in the Seattle-Portland area but were now based out of California, where they had been headliners on a Dick Clark afternoon TV show called *Where The Action Is.* In Mark Lindsey, the band had a lead singer who was willing to tackle anything from soul to rock to country. At the time, the Raiders were a band in transition; their drummer, bass player, and lead guitarist had all left the group and Revere and Lindsay were breaking in replacements.

"We had admired their records," said Bobby Wood appreciatively. "I was already sold on the Raiders before they had arrived," echoed Bobby Emmons. "It was different, a different kind of music than we'd have been doing, the bubblegum pop of the day," Reggie Young observed, although the desire to do something different from "bubblegum pop" had motivated the band's decision to come to American. Mike Leech remembered that his two nieces were "blown away" when he arranged for them to come down to the studio and meet the Raiders. The band had first heard of American from their business manager, Jerry Williams, who was from Memphis; the more they spoke to Chips and Don Crews about recording there, the more they liked what they heard and so,

complete with some new songs Mark Lindsay had written on the plane heading south, the Raiders came to town.

Well, some of the Raiders. In the usual road-band/session player divide, the new bassist Charlie Coe and the new drummer Joe Junior Correro were left at home. Revere, Lindsey, and their lead guitarist, Freddy Weller (who had grown up with Joe South and Tommy Roe in Atlanta) booked the session at American under Jerry Williams's name, and even the musicians did not know they would be backing the Raiders until work began. The resulting sessions were remembered warmly; Reggie Young in particular was pleased to see Weller there, because having another guitarist on hand "made my job easier." All the musicians were there for the session save Spooner Oldham— he would never remember why Bobby Wood, and not he, played keyboards on the session. "That's another one of my missing memories," he laughed. Interestingly, although Freddy Weller and Spooner did not meet during the guitarist's time in Memphis, within two years they became songwriting collaborators.

The Raiders session was the first time the group found themselves with some equipment that the Vox company sent the studio in apparent hope of wangling an endorsement. "They sent music stands, shaped like old dance-band stands, with lights on them," said Reggie Young, who also remembered a trumpet, a saxophone, and several guitar amplifiers. "The amps weren't really good at all. I don't think I ever used 'em; I don't like 'em, I always used a Fender." Bobby Wood remembered an electric piano he rated little better than a toy. "The keyboards were awful," he said. "Bobby E wired our Wurlitzer piano to the Rhodes suitcase-bottom and that gave us a stereo Wurlitzer sound."

One album was recorded with the new equipment: the work of the Raiders' protégé Merrilee Rush, done during the same time as their session, appeared with the credit "Amplification by Vox." The sound of the album is small and tinny in a way the recordings had never been before; after the work on the album was done, Chips had an acoustics expert come in and examine why the room sounded different. The problem was traced to the boxes of Vox equipment stacked along the walls in the studio, and the boxes mysteriously disappeared shortly thereafter. "All of 'em were there and gone, I don't know what happened," chuckled Reggie Young. "Emmons thought somebody in-house sold 'em." "I think all that stuff wound up down on Beale Street in the pawnshops," Emmons laughed.

The Vox items may have been in the custody of the American group's unofficial mascot, an African American neighborhood kid named J.P. who sneaked into the building one day and became the pet of the studio. "J.P. was about fourteen, fifteen, sixteen when he hung out," said Bobby Wood. "We tried to help him, gave him tips and things. Nearly everybody there gave him money and tried to take care of him. We felt sorry for him, we kinda took him under our wings." "I thought he was the official gofer for awhile there," said Bobby Emmons. "If you needed something, like a pack of cigarettes, or a can of breakfast drink or something like that, J.P. would go and get it for you. I thought he was also supposed to be helping Gertrude with the cleanup." "All the recording artists that ever came in, they *loved* J.P.," Chips Moman reminisced fondly.

There was a problem with him, however, which the group would not discover for years. "J.P. would carry them asbestos gloves because he would steal red-hot stoves," Chips said amusedly. "J.P. wound up with about half our equipment—microphones, instruments," added Bobby Wood. "He [later] got in trouble for something, a robbery, and the police found all these instruments and equipment at his house. We'd had the deal with Vox and they sent us a lot of amplifiers and stuff, they were all over the studio, Mike had his trumpet down there—I think most of it wound up with J.P." J.P. had free run of the place and was an observer at many of the sessions, so it would have been easy enough for him or some of his friends to have walked off with something. Chips was extremely relaxed about security. Even for the Raiders' session, which under comparable working conditions in LA would have been heavily guarded, no special arrangements were made other than

adherence to the studio's usual late-night policy. "Our security was, Fire three times and say, 'Who's there?'" Bobby Emmons chortled.

Emmons's keyboard work is prominent on the first several tunes from the Raiders album. "Boogaloo Down Broadway" establishes the mood of the entire project—fast, fun, and funky. Emmons skates through his solo spot in the bridge and the ending slides into a garage-band riff appropriate for Rufus Thomas, with Mark Lindsay making a joking reference to the already famous "Skinny Legs and All." On "Every Man Needs a Woman" the organist comes into his own: working off a thumping riff from Tommy Cogbill, Emmons employs every specialty run in his musical vocabulary for his solo turn, as Mark Lindsay comments in an unlikely Southern accent. It was definitely Bobby's show, but it could just as well have been a moment seized by Tommy or Reggie. "It was good having more than one head in the studio because some days when some of us might not feel creative there would always be one or two of us that would come up with something fantastic," remarked Bobby Wood. The album showcases Emmons and Tommy throughout, as the songs are mainly hard, aggressive R&B delivered in Lindsay's approximation of a Wilson Pickett–style shouter.

Also featured are Wayne Jackson and the Memphis Horns, who were quickly becoming regulars at the studio in their spare time from Stax, contributing brassy, blaring arrangements outlined for them by Mike Leech. It was a challenge he enjoyed, although he was aware that some of the others did not always share this enthusiasm. "Emmons didn't like horns, because they were brash, usually out of tune, and mostly held an attitude," he observed. "If there was a horn overdub E would probably hide out somewhere. I do think he liked horns in a live studio situation though. It sparked the track." "I thought they had a little too much attitude for people that it took four of to play an A7," laughed Emmons, who added, "No, I'm kidding. I love horns." Wayne Jackson described the horn section's participation on sessions at American: "The horn overdubs were done mostly in the daytime, from eleven AM to five or six PM (usually, although anytime would do if we didn't have a gig). Many times the producer and an engineer would oversee, sometimes only an engineer. Chips might be there or decide to go to lunch while we did our thing."

The group, without the horn section, also recorded the theme music for the Raiders' soon-to-be-launched Saturday TV show, *Happening '68*. Although the program was nominally a rock show, the Raiders used it to feature virtually every act in West Coast country music, from Linda Ronstadt to Buck Owens and the Buckaroos (whom they undoubtedly remembered from Buck's years on the Pacific Northwest circuit). The mere act of using Southern musicians to record the theme song indicated the Raiders' refusal to draw lines with their music, mirroring that of the American group and making the sessions go especially well.

Even more chance-taking was in store, for those sharp enough to perceive it. The album's ballad, "One Night Stand" (written by Mark Lindsay, according to George Klein's liner notes, while the group had taken a "dinner break" around four-thirty in the morning), features the kind of swooping string arrangement Mike Leech was writing for Dan Penn's productions; his string line sometimes overpowers the lyric. It is easy, in concentrating on Mike's contribution, to forget exactly how pathbreaking the song is. By 1968 it was understood that women were sometimes going to be broken-hearted at the consequences of the emerging sexual revolution (and within weeks the group would record the ultimate musical example of this), but no one thought of the effect casual sex had on a man. Lindsay's lyric offered a role reversal comparable to Shania Twain's later "Honey I'm Home"; in his story, it is the *man* who is sad that his lover is leaving in the morning and that the relationship is apparently not to go any further. He is distraught that his lover intends to act as if their night never happened at all, but he promises that he will honor her request and just "smile and walk on by." It is a brave song on many levels, paving the way for an even more beautiful song of love and farewell. Mark's vocal is half-muttered, half-wailing, an effect from which Mike Leech said

he learned. "Mark liked mixing at a very low level, and preferred the vocal to be just audible above the track," said the arranger. "I've used that method a few times since and [it] seems to work very well (on certain projects)."

Mike Leech noted that Chips had "a quick wit and will sometimes throw fun without you realizing or catching it," although he usually punctuated his hijinks with his trademark cackle. Several tracks on this album seem to emphasize Chips's ability to laugh at himself and at his tendency to lose instead of win (or perhaps, to win when he lost; with Chips one could never be sure). "My Way" has no relation to the Sinatra/Elvis declaration of pride; in echoes of Willie Nelson's later "The Last Thing I Needed," it is about a man who suffers one small mishap after another following the departure of his wife (he can't make the coffee properly, his shirt button falls off after he sews it back on, his friends congratulate him instead of sympathizing). He concludes resignedly, "There's a right way, there's a wrong way, and there's my way" (a sentence that could have been Chips's motto). "I'm a Loser Too" is even more explicit, three verses narrating a repeated propensity for misfortune, and the incidents involved—inviting a friend who turns out to be a freeloader to crash at his place; loaning out his truck and the driver getting in a wreck, resulting in a lawsuit—are things that could plausibly happen to Chips. (The exception is the narrator's "gambling friend," Dirty Dan, who swindles the narrator out of his share on a winning bet—that likely would not have occurred to Mr. Penn.) "I'm just a gullible character, I think," Chips would say, ruefully but without further explanation.

Gullible he may have been, and he often came out on the losing end in his dealings with record executives, but at this point in his life Chips was riding high. Always a dreamer, he was now consumed with a new idea—one that, if he managed it properly, would give him and the group an empire, a Motown on the Mississippi. It had not even originally been his idea, although he recalled that it was (Don Crews and Ima Roberts remembered it differently). Larry Uttal had first suggested that Chips form a custom label, but once the suggestion had been proposed to him, with his typical enthusiasm for any sort of innovation he leaped at the chance. Custom labels were beginning to be discussed as an alternative to the corporate record industry; the Beatles started Apple, the best-known of these, later that year. Eventually the Rolling Stones, the Jefferson Airplane, Led Zeppelin, and the Beach Boys would try running them. In all cases, the idea was the same; the musicians themselves would make artistic decisions (such as signing acts) and administer the plans cooperatively, and there were profit-sharing goals. Distribution and promotion would be left to the parent labels underwriting the ventures. There was a budget for production, administered quarterly—"I'm giving you a figure, I think it was $75,000 a year," said Don Crews. This was an extraordinary amount of money at a time when albums could be produced at an average cost of three thousand dollars; it was like handing Chips and the group a blank check. It was the first time such an idea had been floated about Southern music circles. "That was when I had made a request to the record companies that all the musicians should receive royalties," Chips said. "That was a thing I've always been proud of." He'd been thinking along these lines anyway, and the suggestion from Bell made it official; Bobby Emmons remembered, "We got production percentages from some of the acts even before we became AGP."

The musicians were energized at the new development; everyone was excited about the label's possibilities. "It was just such a buzz going on," said Ima Roberts, keeping track of everything from her secretary's desk. Tommy Cogbill in particular was eager, from most accounts: he saw it as the very thing the studio needed to make further progress. "I think he was [excited about it] but I don't really know what he was thinkin'," said Chips. Tommy's contributions were obviously going to be welcomed, and with his stability and experience he was the logical second-in-command. The only sticking point was a name: no one could figure out what the label should be called, until Don Crews discussed the matter with Uttal

and the label head suggested that they go with the name they were already beginning on occasion to use—American Group Productions.

Ed Kollis drew the logo; the initials AGP as a blockish pyramid, with the A triumphantly perched above the bottom two letters (eventually the pyramid letters would be slanted and flattened out). The first recording on which the new logo appeared would be on Bell, and it established Tommy Cogbill's reputation as a producer once and for all. It was the record for which he would be remembered. Fourteen years later, it would be his epitaph.

"Angel of the Morning" was not even a new song. Evie Sands had recorded it shortly after it was written, the preceding year. Her version had gone nowhere, though Reggie Young remembered Tommy listening to it. A British singer named P. P. Arnold attracted a little attention with her version. The composer, Chip Taylor, just coming off the success of "Wild Thing," was a hot writer, better known at the time than was his brother, Jon Voight. Accounts differ as to who got a demo of the song to American: in an early-nineties interview on the Ralph Emery *Nashville Now* program, Tony Orlando, who was then a song plugger for Blackwood Music, said he had been responsible for getting the song to Memphis. Chips believed it had gotten there more directly—"Chip Taylor was a friend of Jack Grady"—and Don Crews echoed Chips's recollection, though noting that Orlando had apparently seen some merit in the song and had managed to get the demo tape to Jack. However it got there, it grabbed the immediate attention of Tommy, who was apparently struck by its gentle beauty; from the minute he heard it, he knew he had to record it with someone. Mike Leech remembered Tommy carrying the demo tape around with him in his pocket for several months, waiting with infinite patience for the right time, the right person, to deliver the message.

The right person came through Paul Revere and the Raiders, who brought her with them to Memphis. Merrilee Rush also came from the Pacific Northwest, where she had grown up studying classical piano; charmed away from serious music by rock, she had been singing her own blend of rock and country in local clubs for years. "She had her own band, Merrilee and the Turnabouts," said Reggie Young. "We thought that was so cool. That was the first woman I knew who had her own band. . . . I admired her as a bandleader, she seemed to be the boss." She still played the piano, and her keyboard work was featured on a few of the cuts she recorded, but for the most part the instrumentation was done by the American musicians.

"We had a great time, she was like one of the guys, she would laugh and kid around, we all had a ball," said Bobby Wood about recording with her. Although her session was to have been a collaboration between Chips and Tommy, Chips absented himself while Tommy handled the basic tracks; this became the standard procedure when they worked together. The musicians always loved doing Tommy's sessions: "They were just seamless, effortless," said Spooner Oldham joyfully. "It was like a removal of all impediments"—a different method of recording from the endless interruptions and retakes of sessions run by Chips or Dan. "It was just like he was a player," Spooner added about the mood when Tommy ran a session. "He was just a joy to be around, that's what I remember. He wasn't wearing a badge that said 'I'm a Producer' or anything. He was a treasure trove of activity." On all of the collaborations with Tommy, Chips supervised overdubs and they conferred on the best effects, kicking ideas around until the two of them were in agreement. The tension between Tommy's upbeat quirkiness and Chips's melancholy created a whole new color in the American production palette, a "third way" that was greater even than the sum of its parts.

"He'd want me to mix," Chips remembered, and several of the others noted that Tommy was not technically oriented. He could engineer a little if he had to and mix, but his main interest was in capturing the sound as it happened with the players on the studio floor. Mike Leech thought that Cogbill's disinterest in technical matters influenced the kinds of sounds he wanted, since he did not automatically dial up the echo when recording as Chips

did. "Tommy relied on a lot of outside help with his mixing, myself included," Mike noted. "I would occasionally help Tommy with EQ [equalization], track selection, things like that. That was okay, gave him a break to think about other matters. . . . We mixed a Joe Simon tape at the old Ardent Studio on National one night. He mixed for several hours, then invited me to mix for awhile. He liked what I had going, and finally between us nailed a good final. . . . I almost nailed a perfect mix but had the strings a little loud at one point. Tommy liked the mix though, and he sat down and did another with what I had basically set up."

Merrilee, like the Masqueraders, became a group favorite. Her voice conveyed sophisticated emotions in spite of its small range. Don Crews had his own perspective on it: "Merrilee was not a real good professional singer, she had a sound of her own," he noted. "That's all I ever looked for, was something different." Technically, her sound had many of the same characteristics as her British contemporary Sandie Shaw, whose voice was described by Nik Cohn as "an ache that worked just right, a beautiful creak." Merrilee read music and could play amazingly down-home-sounding piano for a woman who was classically trained; those studies gave her knowledge of dynamics the equal of many at American, including Chips Moman and Mike Leech, who listened to classical music for pleasure.

Then there was her considerable beauty. "I just remember her appearance and her music; she had that long hair and that smallish build," remembered Spooner. "Not every lady I knew had long hair back then. She was a sweet-looking lady." "This gorgeous girl," said Ima Roberts glowingly. "She was real pretty, sang in a real different voice," said Wayne Carson, who wrote several of the songs she recorded. Merrilee seemed to be the epitome of a flower child; her dark hair fell almost to her waist and her large wistful eyes peered out from beneath her long thick bangs. Dressed in psychedelic-print pantsuits and Indian kurtas she often designed and sewed, she was a visual role model for young women who loved her ethereal, free-spirited recordings. In her televised performances, even in comfortable venues like the Raiders' TV show (where she was a frequent guest) she either hid behind a piano or rocked and swayed as she sang, looking down at her feet and clutching the microphone like a woman in a wind tunnel holding on for dear life. Listeners sensed vulnerability from her body language onstage and from the exquisitely timed creak in her voice. Nor was any of it an act: "I found Merrilee to be pretty and a little shy," said Mike Leech respectfully. Ima Roberts agreed, and added that the singer's shyness made her a little aloof: "She wasn't the kind you just sit and chat with." "A few of the guys had a crush on her," Mike also remembered.

None of this was lost on Chips, who was very aware of her looks and gentleness, according to the singer's later accounts. A photograph taken at American shows Merrilee, colorfully dressed and with a ribbon in her hair, seated at the upright piano while Tommy authoritatively hands her a manuscript; Chips is leaning on one end of the piano, eagerly looking on. "I really enjoyed working with her, I really did," he said admiringly. And Tommy? Did her stunning appearance have an effect on him? If so, he remained proper about it; everyone recalled his behavior toward Merrilee as exemplary. "Tommy and Chips were like daylight and dark," Bobby Wood observed. "Tommy was Mr. Gentleman and Chips was the gambler type."

Merrilee's first session, Reggie Young wrote in his account book, was "free"; he was unsure, years after the fact, whether that meant that the studio time had already been paid for or whether she was recording on spec. But from the beginning, everyone knew it was going to be an extraordinary six hours. "Angel" was a big reason why. "That was a magic moment, when we did that song with her," Reggie remembered, his voice still soft with wonder and awe. "That was one of the few times I played acoustic," he added, noting that he was using "an old guitar that Tommy had around the studio, it was just another cheap guitar. The strings were a mile high off the neck, it was really hard to play." "They put the trombone on

as they mixed it because they had run out of tracks," remembered Don Crews, referring to the song's memorable dirgelike intro. "If you'll notice, toward the end of the song, right after the breakdown section, where she comes back in with 'Baby, baby, Just call,' leading toward the fade, the vocal jumps *way* out in the track," observed Mike Leech. "That was an accident, but the rest of the mix was so good, they kept it."

From the droning trombone and organ line to Reggie Young's gentle guitar, to John Hughey's overdubbed steel that sounds like falling tears ("overdubbing the trombone part I had written," said Mike Leech), to Merrilee's quavering delivery of the unusually poetic lyrics about the regrets following a one-night stand, it is impossible to hear this record and not be emotionally stirred. The feelings expressed cut to the heart, and exemplified the higher spiritual mood Tommy seemed to be seeking. The record is especially poignant now, since it was played at his funeral. With the passage of time, it is not Merrilee speaking to a lover we hear, but Tommy's dry, quiet voice, accepting responsibility for anything he might have done that would lead him to die of a stroke in 1982 at the age of fifty ("And there's no need to take a stand, for it was I who chose to start"). One of the things he had "chosen to start" were the cigarettes he was often photographed smoking (the group all held recollections of him recording, mixing, and playing with one ever-present in his mouth). Nothing is demanded, not even that he be remembered; he requests no farewell but one last look and a slow turning away. It is first and foremost a brave record, and a beautiful way to say goodbye.

Not that any of this was apparent at the time. Tommy's mood was up, he had unlimited access to the candy store, and he was determined to make good use of the creative opportunities the AGP setup would allow. Nevertheless, the spiritual search, and perhaps a strong sense of eventual consequences, are there on the recording. "Angel of the Morning" is perhaps the strongest of Tommy Cogbill's litanies, conveying so much more than the mood and the lyrics of a simple love song.

The group was not about to stop with one killer song or one astonishing production. Most of the collective's best writing talents were marshalled to contribute, and the ones that Merrilee, Chips, and Tommy chose were stunning.

An example: the B-side of "Angel," Mark James' "Reap What You Sow." If "Angel" was a premonition, this was rooted in the immediate; it is an uncharacteristically blunt and angry song from Mark, who usually preferred to sheathe his barbs. Merrilee snarls the lyrics, to the accompaniment of her own down-home piano; Tommy's bass pounds out a descending line that evokes a picture in the listener's mind of stairsteps. Interestingly enough, though the A-side is attributed to both Chips and Tommy, this raging work is credited to Tommy alone—proof that there was more to this gentle-looking man than anyone would have thought. On the surface, Tommy remained quiet, soft-spoken, mild-mannered, but this record is evidence that there was a hurricane inside him.

Mark James contributed two more songs. "It's Worth It All" is part of the standard American Studios preference for songs about being bewildered by love rather than happy. Here Mark describes a relationship with limits; the speaker knows that it cannot go any further, but she lives for her moments with her lover anyway, at whatever cost to her heart and her pride. "Sunshine and Roses," which cuts George Klein in as co-writer (perhaps in the hope that he could air it despite the Drake playlist) concludes Merrilee's album and though it outwardly refers to a failing love affair, it could possibly be read in part as Tommy Cogbill's gentle protest against the late hours the musicians were required to keep and a subtle mention of the toll it was taking on him: "Out in the garden, there's a rose dying / Just because it can't get enough sunshine." The song is interpreted like a folk ballad, accented by one of Mike Leech's more memorable string parts—a muted, rising hum that alternates with Reggie Young's tender guitar line and gathers momentum as the record fades out. Though more famous tunes established Mike's reputation, his work here demonstrates his greatest skill as an

arranger: underlining the existing mood of the track, building on it, and giving it a new inflection with thoughtful lines that spoke directly to listeners.

Chip Taylor's writing is represented more than that of anyone else save Mark. "Billy Sunshine" is a standard rock tune, notable mainly for Tommy Cogbill's bass line (although Mike Leech was the main bassist for the project when the producer sat in the control room). "Working Girl" is a neglected masterpiece, like "Angel" an intelligent blend of traditional and modern country music, with just a hint of pop. Such songs were perfect material for a musician who had started out playing a traditional instrument—the steel guitar—had gone on to acoustic jazz guitar, and who was now one of the most innovative bass players. On this cut, Tommy fulfills the promise of all these genres: it features pitiless, almost mocking lead guitar from Reggie Young, with a strong lyrical story line about a secretary subjected to a topic seldom discussed in those days, sexual harassment. Here, the autobiographer is Merrilee, who in interviews years after her time on the national stage said that she felt victimized by people she had met in the business who tried to take advantage of her. It was a surprise to the American musicians, who were unaware of that side to her story. "I was surprised to read the remarks about sexual harassment many years later," said Bobby Emmons. "Unless she was counting what we wrote about later in a song, where 'we let our eyes do the talking.'" "I remember reading on her website, it was like she was being thrown to the lions, I never knew," mused Bobby Wood in amazement. As with "Angel," Tommy chose to show the woman's view of an exploitative situation; he placed the emphasis on Merrilee's vulnerable, pleading vocal, making it clear that he understood and agreed with her.

Two more of the cuts came from Merrilee's pals, the Raiders. "Observation from Flight 285 (In 3/4 Time)" is Chips's and Tommy's road-trip song, the summing-up of their journeys to New York. It is obviously one of the tunes composed on some tour or another by Mark

Lindsay, who was well-known for writing while he traveled, and is probably the most accurate description of an airplane flight for those who have never experienced one. "Do Unto Others" was another litany, a plea for brotherhood and understanding coupled with the knowledge, more true in the twenty-first century even than in 1968, that mainstream media was never going to provide those answers. "You won't find it in the morning paper," Mark Lindsay had written, "and the television is just for fun." Tommy Cogbill's spiritual search is apparent here, since the song begs for unity.

On Joe South's "Hush," Tommy turns a simple rock tune into a hoedown different from any hoedown put on record before, with stomping piano, Ed Kollis's wavering harmonica, and emphatic, intricate bass. "Hush" is typical of the upbeat sound Tommy characteristically wanted on his records; his productions are propulsive and compelling, though at work Tommy was matter-of-fact. "He was one of the most somber people you ever met in your life when he was producing," said Bobby Wood. "I think most of the guys will tell you, he was a hard person to read." To Mike Leech, Tommy "looked like he always had a secret he wouldn't tell." "I never did get on to just what made him tick as a record producer," added Dan Penn, who also found Tommy to be elusive. "I didn't see him as a record producer, but that's how people always see record producers, nobody saw me as one until I cut a hit. Looking back on it, he was a *great* record producer."

But there was Chips's melancholy to consider as well, and from the depths of his seemingly endless sadness he, Dan Penn, and Spooner Oldham had composed another masterpiece, partly one of Dan's reworked Clinch Mountain ballads, part litany and part lamentation: "Sandcastles." Spooner called it "an odd little beach song." It's the forerunner of Garth Brooks' cowboy epic "Beaches of Cheyenne" (whose themes of sudden death and never returning home also evoke Tommy Cogbill's eventual fate). Here, the distraught woman is not walking the beaches but standing still; haunted by her lover's disappearance—or death, it is never made clear which—the footprints leading to the sea

keep inviting her to join him. It is what happens after "Angel of the Morning": grief and a young girl's tender regret. "We must have been chasing that elusive butterfly of love," chuckled Spooner Oldham. His funereal-sounding organ line and Merrilee's soft vocal underscore the sorrow, and the deliberate vagueness of the lyrics leave several possible interpretations to consider. "We get a lot of compliments on that song," Spooner noted with quiet pride. "I always liked that one a lot, to be honest," adding that although he could not recall who came up with the story line, he could vividly remember them writing it. "I can see Dan and Chips and I in American Studios just walking around, talking one evening," he said.

Dan also wrote "Handy," with Darryl Carter; a song about a woman who feels like a convenience—perhaps she is a girlfriend, perhaps a mistress, but certainly a refuge for her lover, who can do as he pleases with her. Merrilee's version is soft, accepting; the version Sandy Posey recorded with Chips several weeks later is pure autobiographical monologue, made clear by the fact that she substitutes her name for the title on the fadeout (one can picture her glaring into the control-room glass as she sang that line). Merrilee's version is heightened by a sympathetic piano; Sandy's features a jangly, almost-out-of-tune guitar lead from Bobby Womack. This is a good example of how Chips could use one song to convey two completely different meanings, and he frequently used this technique in the years ahead.

One song could convey several meanings, but there was no mistaking the meaning of all the group had accomplished with just a few important sessions. And January 1968 was not even over yet. If the first month of the year was starting off this well, with the promise of a developing empire all their own under way, what on earth would the coming months bring?

|||||||||||||||||||||||||||||||||||||||||||||||||||||||||||||||||||||||

### CHAPTER 12

# Songs for Young Weepers: Crying Like a Baby and the Death of a Dream

As the American group laid plans for their empire, Chips Moman, Dan Penn, and Tommy Cogbill were all scheduling sessions regularly and accounts such as Atlantic and Goldwax filled in the remainder of studio time.

Life at 827 Thomas Street fell into a pattern of sorts. The first person to arrive at the studios every morning, at around nine o'clock, was Gertrude, the black cleaning lady, who lived in the neighborhood. She had her work cut out for her, as she invariably had to empty numerous overflowing ashtrays (the entire group, from Chips to the sound crew, were chainsmokers) and toss out the remnants of food left over from the previous night's sessions. Seldom did any of the musicians actually see her cleaning, but everyone praised the results, and those who came in early enough could catch a glimpse of her moving efficiently through the building. Mike Leech scared her once while he was working with a theramin, the wandlike instrument creating the eerie sound on the Beach Boys' "Good Vibrations." She rarely spoke, as she had a cleft palate that made her difficult to understand (although Gene Chrisman could, without malice, imitate her perfectly).

Ima Roberts arrived at ten when the studio officially opened, and immediately went to her upstairs office to take calls, answer and

send out mail, and handle all essential paperwork. By noon Don Crews was usually up in his office also, having spent much of the morning working on his farm. The business ran efficiently enough, he remembered: "We had a list of what we were going to do, which kept it going fairly decent." Occasionally he still looked in on the proceedings downstairs, but by and large the evolving division of labor between him and Chips suited him: "I wasn't a musician. Didn't claim to be."

The hours scheduled for sessions varied. Atlantic preferred to begin work as soon as the studio opened for the day, so the musicians could count on the New Yorkers observing fairly normal hours. Tommy Cogbill was a day person, as has been noted, and preferred to start sessions around noon and get everyone out of the studio by ten at night, to the relief and delight of his colleagues—except on the nights Tommy was finishing up and Chips, who as a matter of course stayed away while Tommy was working, "just happened" to stroll in with a casual, "Boys, I've got a little idea I'd like to get down on tape." (Dan Penn did this too, but never to the same extent as Chips.) Everyone looked at each other in dismay when that happened, because by now they all knew the outcome.

"Lotta times I'd walk outta there and it'd be daylight," said Reggie Young. "If it was Moman we'd work later and later and later." "We would stay there probably fifteen, sixteen hours a day," added Bobby Wood. "That's the reason Bobby Emmons said, 'I'm gonna call home sick'"—a phrase that became an inside joke for the musicians.

"We'd been in there eighteen, twenty hours [when he said that]," Wood continued. "Oh gosh, we'd do about forty takes [of the same song] and you can't get a feel for anything that way." Reggie Young noted that Chips often put them through endless takes on a song and then chose the first or second take, recorded while the musicians were still fresh, as the one to be released. He could find no logical explanation for it and thought that Chips may have preferred that approach for his own reasons: "Moman might have been a little superstitious, he might have cut a hit or two that way," he reflected. And then there was the endless ordeal of trying when the music did not seem to jell. "When it started going down, man, it was the pits, but Moman didn't give up," Reggie sighed. Bobby Wood concurred, adding that he thought Chips's perfectionism was the main reason for the grind. "Chips kinda wanted his patent on everything," Wood observed. "Lotta times he was looking for something on the board. Man, from our side of the wall it was really tiring. Once you've done a song thirteen or fourteen times, it kinda gets a little mechanical." (In Nashville, seldom did a song go over two or three takes; the musicians got something down on tape with a minimum of experimentation.)

It bears reiterating that the group was not paid extra for all this overtime. Chips counted all the hours spent as a single session, so the players got scale for their efforts, nothing more. And because they were not on retainer, they did not even get that if no sessions were booked (a moot point at the time, but it would matter later). The overwork and underpayment of the musicians at the Southern independent studios such as American has been, in the eyes of many of the players from that era, one of the most neglected aspects of this story. "It would have been really nice if we had gotten paid for all the hours we worked," said Reggie Young. "The biggest year I ever had [in Memphis] was around thirty thousand dollars. The first year I came to Nashville, it tripled." "The biggest year moneywise I ever had in Memphis was twenty thousand dollars," said Mike Leech (and he was paid separately for his bass playing and arranging chores).

"You'd think Chips would have put the musicians on salary," observed Norbert Putnam, who along with his friends contended with the same kind of long hours and low pay in the early days of the Shoals. Why did Chips not keep the group on weekly retainer as he did his writers, especially since he viewed the musicians as his house band and they functioned as such?

"Didn't see any need to; they were makin' the big money by gettin' scale," Chips said

blithely. Reggie Young's account book noted that in early 1968, union scale was sixty-five dollars, and sessions were frequent. Even so, the American group never saw in Memphis the kind of money that their contemporaries did in Nashville. That was true for musicians all over the city. Wayne Jackson of the Memphis Horns, who were still primarily affiliated with Stax though they did additional work for others studios, said that, in New York, Atlantic paid people five times what the horn section could earn in Memphis. "*Five times.* That was sort of amazing to us."

It was true that by the beginning of 1968 everyone at American was doing well enough to own houses (even though their families benefited more than they, since they were seldom home except on weekends). Gene Chrisman still lived in his hometown of Whitehaven, the South Memphis suburb best known as the site of Graceland; Bobby Emmons and Reggie Young were there also, and Mike Leech moved to the same subdivision, in a twenty-thousand-dollar ranch house (Mike remembered that Emmons and Reggie both paid slightly less for theirs). Tommy Cogbill lived in North Memphis, fairly near the studio, in the Fraser district (later he too moved to Whitehaven). Bobby Wood, by now a part-timer, was in Bartlett, a suburb of Memphis (Stan Kesler moved there when he retired). Bartlett was practically in the countryside, which delighted Bobby: "It was pretty out there," he said nostalgically. Chips Moman had his farm north of Memphis in Raleigh, where he was installing a professional-level dirt track for horse racing. The only renters now were Bobby Womack, enjoying his ratty little apartment downtown; Spooner Oldham and Mark James, still ensconced in their apartment complex, along with B.J. and Gloria Thomas. Several months later when he joined the staff, Glen Spreen also lived there, staying with Mark in the beginning. Spooner described the place as "very modern . . . sort of a rambling motel-style double-decker." Within the year, Spooner and Mark would also buy houses and settle in; Mark found a two-story townhouse in the same Whitehaven subdivision as Mike Leech,

Bobby Emmons, and Reggie Young. Dan Penn lived in the Audubon Park area, another quiet neighborhood east of downtown.

Like Chips, Dan was known for his marathon working hours. "If Dan was doin' somethin', he'd call it for eight at night but it would likely be ten or later when he got started," said Don Crews, who was usually leaving the building when Dan's sessions began. "Sometimes [Dan] stayed for three days and never went home," Ima Roberts remembered fondly. In a classic blend of Shoals and Memphis, his sessions were informal but exacting. "Dan was a very hands-on producer," said Gary Talley of the Box Tops. "Dan enjoyed a good time but when it came down to recording he was dead serious—no shenanigans," added Mike Leech, accurately attributing this no-nonsense attitude to the "Muscle Shoals mentality." Dan had been used to so many nights in the control room at Fame, running the board as assistant engineer to Rick Hall or producing his own demos, that he seemed more at home in a studio than he did anywhere, with the possible exception of fishing or fixing one of the vintage cars he restored when he had free time. Such an occasion was rare by then; he was recording demos of his songs and placing them all over the country, and Bell wanted a follow-up single to "Neon Rainbow" and a new Box Tops album. "They're always wantin' product and you've always gotta be scrapin' it up," said Don Crews philosophically of the executives' demands. Dan was too independent to let the suits pressure him, but being in the studio had pleasures of its own—he was in control now, with a full production budget courtesy of Bell and the freedom to take the recordings in any direction he wanted. He was the first of the musicians from Fame to gain that kind of freedom—and the Muscle Shoals musicians with similar ambitions were paying close attention.

As with many American group projects, the Box Tops album didn't start off auspiciously. Dan had scheduled a session for ten in the morning, and he and Spooner Oldham had stayed up all night trying to write something. "We spent a lot of hours and a lot of focus on writing for the Box Tops," Spooner said of their collaborations during this period. This particular night was one of those heartbreaking times familiar to every writer, when the well of inspiration seems to have suddenly gone dry and it appears the spark will never return. The two exhausted composers adjourned to the Ranch House for breakfast, where they talked about the difficulty in coming up with a song. Spooner sighed, "I'm so discouraged, I could just lay my head on this table and cry like a baby." Dan perked up immediately, and they raced back to American to complete the song. Within half an hour, they had it, and between them there was the instantaneous sense that they had created a classic. When they played it for Alex Chilton just before the session, he knew it too: "He stuck his hand out and said 'Thank you,'" Spooner remembered. Gary Talley felt the same immediacy: "I thought the minute I heard the track it was something good," he recalled; Gary named "Cry Like a Baby" as his own all-time favorite Box Tops recording.

The writing was half of how the recording came together. The other half came about because of a gift Jerry Wexler sent down to Tommy Cogbill—a Coral electric sitar. "Reggie showed up, there was a box in the corner, nobody knew where or how it had got there," said Spooner Oldham. "The electric sitar was in the box." Tommy had taken the sitar out and played it a time or two, but Reggie Young now began noodling with it, partly out of curiosity and partly because of Dan's casual interest. "Nobody had ever seen anything like it," Reggie remembered. "Dan said, 'Whyn't you play that funny-lookin' guitar over there? Try it out and see what it sounds like.'"

The result was one of the most stunning lead lines on a song that year: it was impossible for a listener to get it out of his mind. "I remember thinking, 'Oh, man! How'd he do that??'" said Gary Talley admiringly. "I'd never even seen an electric sitar before. I got myself one and started playing it." From the time George Harrison had used the unamplified sitar on a pop record with the Beatles' "Norwegian Wood" a few years before, the instrument had been an accent piece, suggesting either dreamy, drug-induced trances or Indian mysticism. Reggie Young's straight-ahead playing gave the sitar a country inflection, twanging along with the lovelorn story line to create a jukebox standard. An essayist for Time-Life Records, discussing the inclusion of "Cry Like a Baby" in a CD repackaging of Sixties hits, called the recording and others like it "songs for young weepers." That is not a bad description of what the American group was doing, describing sorrow in melodic, innovative ways unknown to either country music or rock but increasingly influencing both fields. That fall, several months after the first appearance of Reggie Young's lead sitar, musicians long established in Nashville began experimenting with the instrument: the better sidemen were beginning to get restless in Music City, longing for the Memphis players' creativity and freedom.

Reggie Young added that the prominently mixed sitar lead took the place of the airplane sound effect Dan Penn used on "The Letter." "Moman said, 'You got that sitar cranked up a little loud doncha, Dan?' So, Dan would turn it up louder!"

The musicians knew the recording had something the minute a take was done: "I told Dan Penn, I said, 'Dan, that's *got* to be a big record,'" Gene Chrisman remembered. His relentless drums and Tommy Cogbill's walking bass line pushed the song, and the two of them might have carried the track and gained more attention from listeners had it not been for Reggie's magnificent sitar lines. Gary Talley felt that, as daunting as it was to try to duplicate Reggie's sitar playing onstage, the Box Tops bassist Bill Cunningham had the more difficult task. "The challenge was for the bass player to do Tommy's part, and very few bass players were capable of it," Gary noted. "I remember Cog assuming the bass chair on 'Cry,'" said Mike Leech, whose mournful string arrangement also contributed so much to the track. "When they started running the song down Dan liked it immediately and began recording right away. I don't think he changed the arrangement at all. The horn riff just before the bass solo was a result of a mistake made by

Spooner on the organ. Instead of repairing the mistake, we added the horns." The horns were courtesy of Wayne Jackson and Andrew Love, augmented by a few players from Pepper-Tanner, the huge jingle factory in Memphis which occasionally hired some of the American group, particularly Reggie Young, to add a bit of originality to their product. The burst of sound used to cover Spooner's flub also added something to the record: "We had good mistakes," Dan observed.

And then there was the B-side of the single, also written by Dan and Spooner, a masterwork no one could call a mistake. Had it been written and recorded there, "The Door You Closed to Me" would have been seen as classic Nashville. It features an anguished vocal from Alex Chilton, sparse instrumentation from Spooner Oldham, Tommy Cogbill, and Gene Chrisman, and production from Dan evoking a dark and stormy night. The echoing emphasizes the singer's complete desolation, as he narrates being locked out of the house in the cold and dark while a party is going on. "It sounds like somebody got their feelings hurt, doesn't it?" Spooner said amusedly. The high lonesome sound lurks in the melody, stripped of the twang and whine, leaving nothing but raw and total emotional agony: pain so deep that one is past any knowledge but that of pain. You would do anything, absolutely anything, to be free of this kind of suffering. Alex Chilton yells, wails, and slurs the vocal with a maturity far beyond his years and Spooner's dominant keyboard work is funereal but strangely reassuring.

According to Spooner Oldham, it was easy to create memorable licks on a record when working with Alex Chilton. "Like all good artists I've had the opportunity to work with, say, great artists, let's notch it up a bit, they all can sing their song and just let you play your instrument." By now, the keyboardist emphasized, the creative vision was coming from Alex: the young man was more assured in the studio and there was no need to be coached by the producer. "Dan told me years later, 'I never told Alex anything except [to say] 'aero-plane,'" remarked Spooner, correcting the impression partly given by Alex in interviews over the years that all of his singing on the Box Tops records was the result of Dan's detailed instructions. And Spooner saw for himself how well the two were working together. "It was a wonderful relationship, I thought," he said of the rapport between Dan and Alex. "There was no negativity in any form or fashion. . . . We'd just go in there and interesting things might happen."

That spirit of experimentation was thoroughly alive as Dan began work on the second Box Tops album. Once again, the Box Tops became the supporting cast, with the American musicians as the prominent players. "We seemed to get it together a little quicker than they did, nothing against them because they had had the Record of the Year," observed Reggie Young. Gary Talley remembered that the Box Tops played on the album's last cut, a note-for-note replica of the Vanilla Fudge's slowed-down version of "You Keep Me Hangin' On," a hit the previous summer; the track reveals the band as raucous but game. It starts with a bit of audio verité: Dan shouts to the band, "On yer mark . . . git set . . . ," and then the keyboard comes in before he can say "go," which he then mutters disgustedly while someone else yells "Whaddaya mean 'on yer mark, get set, go' anyway?" Gary Talley said that, given the group's relative studio inexperience, it was an easy recording to do. "I don't remember us doing a whole lotta takes on it," he reflected. "The one thing I do remember, I thought it was one of the better things we had done with just the band. A lot of people really like that track, and a lot of people mentioned that they liked it later."

If it was an attempt to establish the Box Tops as a more "serious" band, it did not work: the Penn-Oldham and Wayne Carson compositions may have given them credibility with Nashville progressives, but radio programmers of both commercial and underground rock stations pigeonholed the band as Top Forty lightweights, much to the frustration of Alex Chilton, who had had artistic ambitions from the beginning. Some of his ideas would have taken the Box Tops into even grittier blues-rock:

"Alex and I wanted to cut 'Wang Dang Doodle,' that old Willie Dixon song [later a hit for the Pointer Sisters]," noted Gary Talley. "Dan said, 'Oh, no, we can't cut that, that's about razor totin' and carryin' guns.'" Dan continued to have definite ideas about what should and should not be included in music, and he looked for songs that sent another kind of signal, as he made clear. "Music is something that's supposed to soothe you; I wanna hear about love and happiness."

"Love and happiness" did not quite cover the spectrum of American group recordings, which usually emphasized sorrow, loneliness, hard times and hard luck (especially in the productions done by Chips Moman). "Cry Like a Baby," was a perfect example, the startoff song on this album: it established the dark-and-stormy-night feel that Dan continued through all of the album's tracks. "Deep in Kentucky," the second song on side one, was written by Stan Kesler's buddy Stacy Davidson: Chips recorded his own version with Sandy Posey several weeks later, even featuring some whistling buried beneath the elaborate string line. On Dan's production, Mike Leech's contemplative arrangement follows the song's melody closely, painting a sound picture of the old boy escaping on "a train bound for Paducah," heading for the countryside where his previous life will never catch up with him. In keeping with Dan's—and the group's—experimental approach to making music, this song features an oboe, a contrast against Alex Chilton's gruff voice. No one seems to remember who the oboist was (Gary Talley thought it may have been a woodwind player from the Memphis Symphony).

An oboist—or anyway, somebody who could play one if needed, even if that was not his primary instrument—was there, but only in an observer's capacity at that point. Glen Spreen was still coming to Memphis when he could, hanging around the studio with Mark James and making plans to get a job there when he would be mustered out of the army later in the year. He made his unofficial first appearance with the group on this album as composer of a song he worked on with Mark during one of the visits to Memphis. "Lost" is a tune with a simple storyline; the narrator has failed at love and wants a second chance, but the undertone is pure desolation, as he wanders about bewildered and suffering.

The song originated with the chorus, structured around the title, and Mark James borrowed a phrase from his Vietnam years not in common usage then, which to Glen conveyed a universal message: "We're all lost in a world of hurt." The song has a somewhat irregular tempo, slowing down slightly in the chorus and then returning full bore, gaining speed and volume as the song's title phrase is repeated. Dan chose to give the ritard an instrumental interlude, with Mike Leech's accelerating string line and Tommy Cogbill's thundering bass bringing the melody up from a waltz to pounding rock and roll—"As I recall, Dan was big on dynamics," Glen Spreen observed. He was present while the recording was done and upon hearing the finished product had second thoughts about it: "The verses let that song down; specifically, the melody (or lack of)." He and Mark rerecorded the song in November 1968 shortly after his official arrival at American; it appeared as the B-side of an AGP single under the name Butterscotch Caboose, but the "Land of a Thousand Dances"–style production of the remake did not improve upon the first version. "I thought it was real interesting, I thought it was kind of spooky," said Gary Talley of the Box Tops' version, and it does accurately describe a haunted interior wilderness. If Dan had not quite created a classic with Alex's version of "Lost," he had drawn on his sense of originality to make a record worth hearing.

"Lost," however, was an experiment. Two Mickey Newbury tunes are more typical of Dan's musical inclination and direction. Newbury was a hot writer in Nashville at the beginning of 1968. He had written the parody of psychedelia, "Just Dropped In (To See What Condition My Condition Was In)" that became the first big hit for Kenny Rogers. Even Gary Talley, who did not follow country music that much at the time, had heard of him. Spooner Oldham remembered that his writing partner was very impressed with Newbury's

writing and his approach: "Dan would have Mickey Newbury come in and sing some of his songs," the piano player said.

From the group of songs by the Texas writer, Dan chose two of the best. "Weeping Annaleah" is a treasure, from the woman's name with its Civil War overtones to Reggie Young's mandolin playing to the grand sweep of the arrangement, loosely based on the traditional arrangement of the 1939 classic "Last Letter" (which Glen Campbell was remaking in California at around this same time). "Good Morning Dear" is also a slow waltz, featuring the oboe and the thundering of Tommy's bass with Gene Chrisman's punchy drums at the end of the song, transforming the softness of the melody into something more assertive. Though Newbury's songs were seen as the height of progressive country then, both the songs and Dan's production seem respectfully traditional, the most adventuresome thing about them being their appearance on a supposedly Top Forty rock album.

There were, of course, several songs by Dan and Spooner that would not have been out of place on a Top Forty station: "If You Need" features a shouted backing vocal from Dan, intense keyboard work from Spooner, and a sliding string arrangement from Mike Leech as the song fades out; "Every Time" is Tommy Cogbill's show all the way, with the bassist repeating a fast descending figure that astounds the listener with its speed and force, especially evident since Dan mixed the song with Tommy's contribution in the foreground. "I can understand Cog's bass lines being up and emphasized," said Mike Leech without envy, despite the fact that his own work was often mixed down. "They were great lines, innovative, and needed to be."

Tommy Cogbill's second showcase was on one of the more memorable songs written by Dan and Spooner for the album, "Fields of Clover." His Motown-like bouncing bass line carries the entire melody, as Alex Chilton narrates the story of a man talking to an old flame who had "finally made it to the classy side of town." He does not begrudge the fact that she is now "steppin' high, like a lady should," but rejoices in her success, is resigned to being in her past, and just hopes she will wave to him from across the tracks someday. Just after he finally tells her "I know you're sleeping warm tonight," Tommy Cogbill's stomping bass line carries the entire song to the fadeout, with some help from a bright trumpet solo by Wayne Jackson.

For Wayne it was a welcome break in the routine. "I'm a *great* trumpet player, and I play *great* solos, but that's not what I do. I don't guess I played more than ten or twelve trumpet solos during that whole time. . . . It was rare that I got to play the solo, because trumpet was passé at the time," he observed. "Saxophones were sexier than trumpets in the Sixties." The horns for the album were recorded at Ardent, a studio that had just opened a year or two before but that was beginning to be in demand for string and horn overdubs, despite its somewhat distant location. "Ardent had a brighter sound that was good for horns and strings," Mike Leech remembered. "It had a wonderful floor," Wayne Jackson said with pleasure at the acoustics. And, unlike Chips Moman, who often left horn overdubs to Ed Kollis or Darryl Carter to set up, Dan was always there for an overdub session. "Mike used to write out some horn arrangements, but not for Dan Penn," the trumpet player continued, noting Dan's fondness for improvisation. "[Dan and I] stayed up a week on that second album [for the Box Tops], having fun. It was in the name of rock and roll and partying and carrying on. . . . We didn't care about tomorrow. There was always something going on, some reason to be there [in the studio], even if we had to make up one. I don't know how our wives put up with it, but they did."

When it came time to do the solo, Wayne remembered, it was completely left up to him what to play. "I'm a *great* spontaneous soloist. I don't think about it too much. I'd say, punch the red button and let's do it, *bang*." He could read and write notation, and often did when he played clubs or jingle sessions at Pepper-Tanner, but he particularly liked coming up with the head arrangements that he dictated to his partner, Andrew Love, and to the other horns augmenting the duo. It was all part of Dan's "Memphis way": spontaneity as a matter of course.

There was a demand in other recording centers for that kind of spontaneity by now, and "727," the road-trip song, summarizes that. Dan and Spooner take the phrase used by the musicians from the beginning of the New York visits and turn it into a travel piece with deliberate overtones and echoes of "The Letter," particularly in Mike Leech's swooping string arrangement.

"All the arrangements were done under Dan's supervision," Mike noted. "I wrote them just like I did on 'The Letter'; playing the parts on the organ until Dan heard what he liked." Gary Talley was present for the recording of "727," though he did not remember playing on it. "It was a time when I was hangin' around the studio a lot and watching what was going on," he said. He recalled the endless number of takes Dan put the musicians through—"I don't remember how many takes they did, somewhere around fifty"—and his astonishment at the fact that Reggie Young sat patiently throughout the whole thing and never played a lick or a line the same way twice.

Gary had no way of knowing that, despite Reggie's outward cool, the guitarist had already spent so much time working on endless takes that it would never be the way he liked to record: "You wind up trying to copy yourself and all the soul goes out the window." That wasn't the way it looked to Gary. "I thought, 'There is no end to this guy's creativity,'" he said, still amazed. "Being a guitar player, I always noticed what Reggie was doing. . . . I remember it was ninety percent of what he did on a white Telecaster and a super-Fender twin amp." Gary added that if Reggie felt the track needed something different he would walk over to an adjoining closet that held an array of guitars owned by Chips and Tommy, select one, and walk calmly back over to his place and play. "Reggie did all this brilliant stuff," said Gary. "He does things that fit the song so perfectly." "Reggie's a database," said Roger Hawkins of the Shoals in praise of the guitarist's musical knowledge. Reggie wound up using the electric sitar on this recording also: he's audible right after the song's second chorus.

The time would come when the American players were far too busy at home to take that 727 to the Apple, let alone be gone for a month as the song stated (they were never gone for a month at a time, but to homesick Southern boys it probably felt that way). For now, though, Wexler needed Tommy Cogbill and Spooner Oldham for another Aretha session, so off they went as usual.

The veteran music-business photographer David Gahr was at Atlantic to do pictures of Aretha for the album cover, and he also took a memorable group photo. Dominating the photo is Atlantic's arranger, the late Arif Mardin; he is smiling, looking gentle, alert, and happy. According to Roger Hawkins, that is exactly the way he was: "A very enthusiastic gentleman, absolute *gentleman*," Roger said of him. "Very diplomatic. He didn't seem to have a bad moment. . . . He was a Turkish gentleman that knew music, loved music. . . . You didn't feel intimidated by him at all, he sought *you* out, he really wanted to know everything about you, and he wasn't just schmoozing you. It was like he wanted to absorb anything and everything about music."

Standing next to Arif in the photo is Tommy Cogbill. One notices immediately how small he is compared to the others: he has a little half-smile and his eyes glint mischievously. He is assuming what Hayward Bishop recalled as a characteristic stance, with his thumbs tucked in the belt loops of his slacks, in the style of the early fifties, quiet but cool. "Tommy had slightly rural good looks, an infectious smile or laugh," Mike Leech said warmly. "And he always dressed impeccably, even though Style Magazine might not agree with his choices." Though Tommy is dressed casually, his clothes fit well. His hair has begun to recede and his face looks serenely thoughtful, qualities even more evident in closeup photos of him from that same day. The definitive photo of him was taken then: it appears on the back cover of the greatest hits compilation, *Aretha's Gold*, and shows Tommy at work, wearing headphones, his head inclined slightly toward the guitar he played on this session, a weary but gentle expression softening his appearance. To those who had heard Tommy's work without knowing what he looked like, this picture, along with the group photo taken that day, is like the Rosetta Stone: everything meaningful about the American group is here.

Next in the photo is Roger Hawkins, looking relaxed, which by now he was—the Memphis and Muscle Shoals musicians had gotten thoroughly used to the city. Hawkins described the road trips as "fun, it was like going to another planet and meeting alien people. In many ways, Northern people are more hospitable than Southern people," he added thoughtfully. He emphasized, as did all the road-trip players, the warmth and graciousness of the Atlantic group, and the ease with which the musicians are standing with them in the studio portrait proves that true.

Between Roger Hawkins and Aretha, who is seated happily in the center of the photograph, is a musician who was loosely affiliated with Atlantic through King Curtis but whom none of these players had met before. Jerry Jemmott was working with King Curtis's Kingpins around New York, along with the drummer Bernard Purdie and the guitarist Cornell Dupree: they were viewed as among the best of the city's young studio players. He had been recruited for the bass chair on this session, switching Tommy Cogbill over to lead guitar; no one was sure exactly how or why that change came about. "I never understood why [Wexler] took Tommy off the bass," said Jimmy Johnson. Roger Hawkins was sure the switch had not been done for any significant reason. "If something had happened, there'd have been a bunch of big talk between us," he reflected. "Usually if somebody's being relieved, hard ol' words and shit like that get around." Jimmy Johnson conjectured that Aretha may have been under pressure to hire more African Americans for her studio recordings: another possibility is that Curtis suggested the change. The musicians remembered Jemmott as a good player, with more of a Motown feel than Tommy (although his work on this record is more subdued than Motown bass, and on some selections identical to anything Tommy might have played).

On the other side of Aretha is Spooner Oldham, his head turned slightly as if he is looking at Tommy, laughing at something that has evidently just been said: and on the other side of him, Jimmy Johnson, looking directly into the camera. Jimmy, too, was more comfortable in New York and with the increasingly lavish way the musicians were being treated on Atlantic's tab: "They moved us up to Central Park South. They'd give us our own private room. It was like, *wow*. The better the places got, the nicer they treated the rednecks." They were discovering the delights of the restaurants, good food and elegant wine. "Wexler turned us on to Chateau Lafitte Rothschild," chuckled Jimmy. "Y'all oughta seen all our faces frown. After about two or three trips, we was all guzzlin' that stuff."

Spooner Oldham remembered the entire week as a combination working road trip and holiday. Sometimes when the sessions ran over into the weekend, the musicians stayed in New York, and Wexler took great delight in inviting them all out to his place on Long Island for supper and just to hang out with him and his family. "We'd have a really nice dinner, china and silver, the whole bit," the piano player said enthusiastically. They never knew whom they might run into there; the previous summer, they had found Wilson Pickett swimming in Wexler's pool (the singer even loaned Spooner a spare bathing suit). Wexler's family was interesting, too, Spooner remembered, chuckling about an exchange he had had with Wexler's son. "I said to Paul, 'What're you gonna be when you grow up?' and Paul said, 'I wanna be a model'" (a contrast to the decidedly macho Wexler).

Tom Dowd rounds out the photo. He bears a striking resemblance to Spooner, since he too was tall, thin, and bearded, but he carries an unmistakable air of authority signaling to all who viewed the photograph that he was one of those in charge. The gloss and elegance Dowd preferred is much in evidence on this album;

this may have been one of Aretha's most accomplished recordings.

*Aretha Now* is a tone poem about all the aspects of involvement with a difficult, unpredictable man (reports surfaced later in the year that Aretha was a battered wife). She begins with "Think," one of her strongest compositions, in which she challenges her lover to stop playing with her mind; then notches it up from the personal to the political with her rallying cry in the chorus of "Freedom, freedom, freedom!" Wexler noted in his memoirs that the guitar line Tommy Cogbill plays underneath the second verse is vaguely reminiscent of "Dixie," and interpreted this as a political statement; more likely, Tommy is simply saying he wishes he were home. The song, and the entire album, is a showcase for Tommy's guitar (not heard often enough on records), and there are times as a lead player every bit as much as when he was on bass that he could take a listener's breath away.

One of those times is a version of the Burt Bacharach hit "I Say a Little Prayer" that is so different from the Dionne Warwick recording it is practically a new song. "What we did to it is our version of what it was," said Roger Hawkins, who cited this track as an example of dynamics. Tommy Cogbill's skills as a jazz guitarist and the subtlety of Roger Hawkins's drums provide a supportive background for Aretha as she reworks the melody, turning it sideways and embellishing it with intricacy. She narrates the story of a woman who, as she goes through the day, can't stop thinking of her beloved no matter how far away from him she is, praying that he thinks of her too, and the background music accentuates the mood of passionate longing. "I know one thing, it happened fast, it was within one or three cuts," the drummer remembered. "When they said that's it, I said shit, I could have played that a lot better." How he could have improved on it is hard to see; his intricate drum pattern reveals a jazz sensibility in tandem with Cogbill's—one of the reasons they as a rhythm section worked well together. It is worth noting that almost a year later, when the French orchestral leader Paul Mauriat arranged a version of "I Say a Little Prayer" for one of his albums, it was not the Dionne War-wick version he chose to follow, but Aretha's; her version had eclipsed the original. In a famous poem about the singer, written later in 1968, Nikki Giovanni wrote: "aretha sings 'i say a little prayer' and dionne doesn't want to hear it anymore." Aretha supposedly made a comment around this time that Dionne was not soulful; it was this offhanded remark that led Dionne to her own encounter with the American musicians later in the year.

Don Covay's "See Saw," a sassy, elegant song to begin with, is given a rousing treatment at full power from Aretha and Tommy Cogbill, who contributes stingingly ironic lead lines. Jerry Jemmott's bass line also romps through the song as Aretha discusses the moods of a man who will "change just like the wind." "Jemmott had that bouncy feel," said Jimmy Johnson. "It was similar to Tommy's but different. Black guys play different than white guys. They would be busier." If anyone is busy here, though, it is Tommy: his sharp asides are hard to hear over the vocal, but wonderful when picked out. "He was the consummate ultimate musician," said Jimmy.

"I think he had to dig a little deeper because he wasn't working with his buddy Gene," observed Roger Hawkins, commenting on how well Cogbill and Chrisman worked together and noting that the Memphis and Shoals musicians played in totally different styles. The American players developed a series of signature riffs and licks that surfaced on almost every record they made; the Shoals musicians adapted their sound to fit the style of the artist. Typically, in Muscle Shoals one musician functioned as leader on all the sessions. "In our band, we didn't have that," said Reggie Young, emphasizing the collective nature of the American group. "Tommy would make a lot of suggestions, but we all kinda pitched in," and the musicians took turns functioning as session leader. A chart on the studio wall documented the rotation. The Memphis players were more self-contained than were the Shoals group, Reggie continued: "They might have used more outside influences coming in and mingling with the band."

The methods of making music reflect differences in outlook; the Muscle Shoals musicians were less reserved. The ones who fit in at American (Dan Penn, Spooner Oldham, Donnie Fritts) had somber temperaments closer to that of Chips. "I think the American band played a little more pop than we did," observed Jimmy Johnson thoughtfully. "A lot of ours were records that made the R&B charts that crossed over. Everything they played had a real polish to it, ours had more of a funk sound." Reggie Young preferred to emphasize the musical similarities between the two groups rather than the differences, noting that they were all committed to quality. "There's a little what they call the pocket, and that's what makes soul music so good," said Reggie, referring to the relaxed sound common to both recording centers. "When we intermingled, we'd talk about it."

Aretha's playing was also exceptional, and her piano work is heard for a small interval on "Night Time Is the Right Time" and the intro to "You Send Me," which, along with "You're a Sweet Man," provides the listeners with positive reasons why she still cared for her difficult lover. The mood of these songs is warm and affecting. Roger Hawkins taps lightly on the drums as her lilting piano comes in on the Sam Cooke tune; her voice is a little too raucous, but she sounds good-humored and happy, and Tommy Cogbill's guitar comments on her obvious euphoria. Hawkins has a commanding solo turn behind Aretha on the first verse of "Sweet Man": then the overdubbed horn section (Wayne Jackson and the Memphis Horns, along with King Curtis and the other New York stalwarts) blazes in, followed by Tommy's incisive, string-bending lead lines. The effect is dazzling, in part due to the horn arrangement courtesy of Arif Mardin. "Arif, a lot of times it seemed to me, he was having to work on the fly," said Roger Hawkins, observing that Arif seemed to be thinking far ahead when he talked to the players; perhaps in his mind, Hawkins thought, he was already hearing the places where the overdubs should go.

Aretha also sounds dazzled on King Curtis's "Hello Sunshine"; she comments, again with emphatic help from Tommy Cogbill, on what it is like when her man stays away for awhile and then returns: all is well again, all is right with her world. She shouts and screams so joyously that she all but drowns out the instruments, except for the horns, mixed to bursting in an attempt to keep up with her. But this record makes clear that Aretha could keep up with anybody.

She proves it in "I Take What I Want" and "I Wanna See a Change," announcing to her man and to all who might be listening that she is no doormat; however much she loves him, she is not willing to be treated as anything less than equal, in this context a statement not of assertion but of outright defiance. The lead guitar on "Change" is equally fiery; perhaps that is the reason Wexler and Dowd mixed it more prominently than they did Tommy's lead lines on any other track. It is a bold statement, determined without being bossy.

The album ends with her final conclusion: after taking herself through all the feelings and changes associated with her love for a difficult man, Aretha sighs quietly, "I can't see myself goin' away to stay . . . I can't see myself leaving you." Tommy Cogbill underscores her reflections, his guitar line curling upward as gently as an April mist. Her comments and his graceful playing fade the album out to what should have been a satisfying conclusion—but in music as in life, things sometimes do not end with happily ever after.

Two songs that never made the album but that were released as singles later in the year tell the rest of the story. "The House That Jack Built" is the story of the man leaving Aretha for good; it is prophetic, because by late 1969 her marriage to Ted White was over. Tommy Cogbill makes occasional biting remarks on guitar and the horn section again blends with Aretha. Jerry Wexler retained a vivid memory of the lady singing her heart out on this one in the studio; her cries are agonized but strong, as if she knows she will get through it, whatever happens. But with her remake of Johnny Ace's "My Song," all bets are off.

This is her most intimate recording since "Ain't No Way": tenderly cushioned by organ lines courtesy of Spooner Oldham, she and her piano plead with a sound like worn velvet for her lover to come back so they can "be together for eternity." As with the earlier song, it is best experienced late at night, in a darkened room; if you are missing someone and hurting about it, it will be all you can do not to reach for the phone. "Please tell me . . . tell me what is wrong," she begs. Tommy Cogbill is not audible here, but the group, after all, was famous for not intruding into a song when their presence might not be necessary. Aretha had let it be known that she was still happy recording with these musicians and would even like to go back South; though her time in the Shoals had ended badly, she was ready to try again and planned to do her next session at American.

She would have been in good company had she gone. Though the studio had just done some songs that would become pop-rock standards, they were still recording R&B as much as ever. In the weeks following Aretha's New York session with Tommy and Spooner, Wilson Pickett was at American, along with Bobby Womack, accompanying Wilson on guitar for a few tracks slated to appear on an album later in the year. Rosey Grier, predating Terry Bradshaw in his ambitions to be a country singer of sorts, came in for some singles released on AGP and earned the affection of everyone at the studio; Reggie Young called him "a gentle giant." The Masqueraders were always around. Arthur Conley was there with Tom Dowd from Atlantic; Dowd had promised Otis Redding before the plane crash that he would take Redding's young protégé to American. If the results were good, Redding had hinted, he just might have worked there himself (which would have been a wonderful coup for Chips, snatching the heart and soul of Stax Records away from under Jim Stewart's very nose). And on April first, Arif Mardin brought King Curtis down for a project on which Tommy Cogbill would be working as sound engineer.

Three days later, Memphis exploded.

It happened on the evening of Don Crews's birthday. Martin Luther King Jr., in town to help with a garbage collectors' strike, stood on the balcony of the Lorraine Motel where he was staying and called out to Ben Branch and

Jesse Jackson standing below. A second later he was dead, killed by a sniper's bullet. As the news spread over Memphis the city went first into shock, then rage.

Many of the American group forever remembered where they were that day. Gene Chrisman was sitting in the Ranch House having dinner, he thought perhaps with Bobby Emmons, when the news came over the TV. Immediately he knew he had better get home. Bobby Emmons did not remember being at the Ranch House, but he remembered watching the horror on television. Upstairs in the office, Ima Roberts's father called and told her; she left the building immediately. Don Crews was just returning to the studio from somewhere when he got the word. "The Masqueraders were in the studio and said, 'Can you take us to the hotel?'" They were staying at the Holiday Inn Rivermont, and on the way there, Crews remembered, "the policemen stopped us."

Reggie Young was driving to the studio when he heard the news on his car radio. "It was really eerie," he said. "When I knew that, I knew something was wrong. . . . I remember we got a call from a friend of ours, he was a police dispatcher, he told us we should probably go home." Mike Leech did not remember where he was when he heard, but "I remember Chips advising us all to stay home until things blew over." Spooner Oldham was at home, he said, and the news took him aback: "Totally surprised, for sure." Bobby Wood offered slightly more detail: "I'm pretty sure I was at home, probably asleep," he said of his whereabouts when it happened. "We didn't know who had shot him at first. Everybody was kind of gutshot. Everybody was afraid there was gonna be a racial war. They ended up burning their own end of town, which I thought was strange."

Chips Moman was horrified at the nightmare into which Memphis quickly descended: "I remember it was chaos everywhere, people in the streets." Reggie Young echoed the thought. "There was looting, there was burning, there was curfews," he said, shock and sorrow still evident in his voice. "I think we knew, oh gosh, we could get hurt. We were in a very black part of Memphis, where the studio was. There was a

lot of crime in Memphis but we never thought it would affect us. . . . I couldn't believe that it had happened there. I knew there was going to be repercussions." Chips and Tommy Cogbill chose to stay at the studio for several days, guarding it in shifts with some weapons from Chips's collection and a mean-looking 45-caliber Apache machine gun Tommy had purchased from a gun dealer who came in through the back door at American one night (Mike Leech had bought one too, never intending to use it but just to say he had it). Mike called the studio every now and then to check in, and got Tommy telling him everything was all right. One of the later arrivals was also affected by the assassination: a communications detachment from the Air Force base at Blytheville, Arkansas, was sent into the city that night to keep order, and it was one of Sergeant Hayward Bishop's first glimpses of Memphis.

It falls to Dan Penn, the most racially sensitive of the group always, to best tell the story, and to sum it up. "I was in the control room messing around with the tapes," he remembered, working on one of the Box Tops tracks just recently cut (ironically, "Cry Like a Baby" was premiering on many small radio stations around that time). "Chips called and said, 'Dan, get outta there, they've shot Martin Luther King.' I could see what was coming. It was a hateful, messy day. When I [left there and] turned the corner, I could see that things were . . . *awfully* awry. When I got outta there and went away, I *went away*. I might have gone to Alabama for a few weeks, I don't know, I don't remember." As with Reggie Young, his voice became softly sorrowful as he contemplated what had happened. "It was just that one shot that stopped everything," he said, referring to the integrationist dream to which he had devoted his musical life. "It just spilt the blood that day. It actually changed the whole world that day, and not for the better."

Reggie Young concurred. "That changed *everything* in Memphis," he said emphatically. Spooner Oldham agreed. "I felt like it was different; I felt like the mood changed, but I don't know from whence it came." Mike Leech also believed that "Memphis was different after that." Bobby Wood was not so sure. Disputing Dan's contention that "race relations in Memphis had always been exceptional," he thought the picture was more subtle. "To be honest about it, Memphis has always been strange," he mused thoughtfully. "There has always been a hatred between black and white. A lot of white people hated Martin Luther King. You had a different breed of people from the old school to the younger school. . . . The staunch people that hated the guy were gonna continue to hate. I guess it got really more uptight."

The question of race was one that nobody had considered a problem before, despite varying attitudes from the group on the issue. For Chips Moman, Dan Penn, Spooner Oldham, Tommy Cogbill, Bobby Emmons, and Reggie Young, the issue would never arise; before the assassination, their judgments had been made and friends were chosen solely on content of character, and for all of them that would continue to be the case. Mike Leech admitted that at first he had had to struggle with some racism he learned earlier in life, but in keeping with his usual reasonableness he confronted it and pushed it away. Gene Chrisman, too, was still learning, and even the usually race-conscious Bobby Womack was patient with him as his attitudes adjusted. Bobby Wood, from rural Mississippi, had a more difficult time. "I was born with racism all around," he said. "I think my dad had a great influence on me. He was always kind to everyone and didn't seem to see color. I didn't realize I had any animosities toward anyone until I made a decision to surrender to the Lord," referring to his recommitment to Christianity some years later. "Whatever was there was gone in a second." He was quick to emphasize that, in the music business, racial typecasting was not good form anyway: "From my Sun days to the American days we all worked side by side and black and white wasn't in the picture." Black and white musicians always got along well at American, he recalled: "We were all brothers. Al Jackson was one of my best friends, along with Booker T, Bobby Womack, King Curtis, Joe Tex, and the list goes on and on. The Masqueraders were from Texas and I thought they were cowboys." "Always it was

respect on everybody's part, whether you were black, orange, green, whatever," Reggie Young said emphatically. "I thought, musicianwise, there was no segregation in music circles that I experienced, until after the assassination," observed Bobby Emmons. "After that, it seemed like everybody felt an obligation to divide down racial lines for one reason or another."

The values of the American musicians were fairly advanced for their time and place, but they did not live and work in a vacuum. The tragedy in Memphis had lasting consequences for the city, and some ramifications for the studio as well, despite Mike Leech's contention that when they reopened "we continued to record as if nothing had happened." "It got violent, and it never was that way before," Reggie Young said of the city. "Who could blame 'em?" shrugged Dan Penn rhetorically about the new mood among Memphis blacks. "Their man got assassinated, and it ruint the business I loved." "A lot of wariness set in, that all was not so well in paradise," Spooner Oldham said of the reactions he sensed. "We still did black acts, Joe Tex came in for a week, Bobby Womack came in," said Reggie, but he added, "I sensed a lot of the acts didn't wanna come to Memphis. We had Aretha booked and she decided she didn't wanna come there and we were like, 'We didn't do nothin'.' . . . Maybe I was paranoid, maybe I was thinkin' maybe they don't like us. It was a shame that it had to happen in Memphis. You just mention Memphis and you had that negative thing." Ever since then, Mike Leech thought, his hometown was "under a spell." "I don't think the scars healed from the riots in the streets for days after," Bobby Emmons reflected. "I was basically scared and worried about my family, in an area that seemed to be a war zone."

All over the South, a generation of musicians who had grown up playing R&B and recording with blacks shared the sorrow and horror felt by the American group. Roger Hawkins, his voice sounding as devastated as Dan's and Reggie's, remembered the reaction in Muscle Shoals: "When that happened, we all looked at each other and we were shocked. Sadness. Sadness." In Atlanta, Dr. King's hometown and the site of his funeral and burial, the Classics IV guitarist and songwriter J.R. Cobb thought the mood was comparable to the time of President Kennedy's assassination and described it as a period of "uncertainty and shock, for black and white alike. It was a pretty traumatic moment, as I recall." Nonetheless, Memphis was the city most affected, and it was appropriate that Chips later produced the Kris Kristofferson song about Martin Luther King (among others Kris praised for having sacrificed their lives to benefit mankind), "They Killed Him," with background harmonies by Chips's friends in the Memphis Policeman's Chorus.

The studio was shut down for six days. Everyone stayed home and tried to deal with what had happened. When they returned, the building was intact, but much had changed. Dan Penn was more affected by the assassination than anyone; he told Peter Guralnick that while he was away, he discovered marijuana (an unknown quantity to the rest of the musicians then). It served as a sedative for his stunned, bewildered pain. He also told Guralnick that he thought it had affected his writing, that he lost his focus. "From '68 to '70 I had two years when I didn't hardly write nothin'," he said many years later. "It took me a pretty long time to get my feet back under me." The routine of Ima Roberts was also upset; for several months after the assassination, Gertrude the cleaning lady walked into the building with her each morning in case of trouble. Everyone remembered hearing footsteps occasionally running on the building's flat roof; nobody knew what was going on. There was more concern for the safety of the musicians while they were working. "Lieutenant Russell would have the dispatcher send cars around periodically to check on things," said Reggie Young. But within the studio, life went on. Sandy Posey was working on a new album, and the black performers who had been recording there at the time of the assassination continued with their projects.

The American group struggled on despite the sorrow—and that, after all, is what their music was about.

### CHAPTER 13

# Memphis Goes On

Memphis was never the same after the King assassination. The American group found it easy to get back to work, but some unpleasant overtones remained. The Masqueraders went home to Texas during the troubles, and stayed away for a month or so until it was time for another session. When they came back, there was still some edginess. Mike Leech remembered a certain attitude on the part of Lee Jones, the lead singer (who later became a Muslim, as would Joe Tex). "He resented the white boys a little," said Mike dispassionately. Once Gene said, 'Lee, sing that part again.' Lee responded, 'Yassuh, massa!' But we still got along. . . . I think he just had to get it out of his system. Gene said to me, 'What was that all about?'" Mike thought he knew. "This was during a time when we were all tired and Gene's question was taken the wrong way," he observed.

But with other R&B acts, who perhaps knew the band a little better at that point, there were no problems. King Curtis worked on his project, came back later in the year to finish it, and was rewarded with a warm and sympathetic sound mix from Tommy Cogbill. Joe Tex did one album of country standards featuring Tommy's freight-train simulation and another album of novelties, and the group found him to be as much of a joy as ever. Solomon Burke, whom everyone had last seen in New York, did a session at Sun with all the group sitting in, and Reggie Young remembered a comment from the presiding producer, Artie Butler: "I can tell you one thing," Butler said. "That drummer is certainly no R&B drummer." "We used to joke with Gene about it," Reggie laughed. "It was the famous session where I thought I'd do something workable," added Bobby Wood. "And I said, when do you want me to come in and [Solomon] said, last eight bars of the fadeout. . . . in other words, lay out . . . thank you very much. I guess he was trying to be funny at the time but I didn't take it that way."

The Arthur Conley sessions with Tom Dowd also went well, said Spooner Oldham, who remembered Arthur from his first hit, recorded at Fame. Although to Spooner, the singer "seemed to be a little bluer in Memphis . . . he was fine wherever he was." Perhaps Spooner sensed Arthur's depression over Otis Redding's death, from which the singer never really recovered. Nonetheless, he cut some fine tracks at the studio, most notably "Funky Street," which would be a hit that summer (his album's back cover features a scholarly Bobby Emmons and a somewhat sulky-looking Dan Penn). Nor were the R&B acts from Quinton Claunch's Goldwax label affected; several of them recorded with the group (as well as with Stan Kesler's new band, the Dixie Flyers) and no incidents occurred.

Yet a sad, angry feeling lay like a pall over the city, which made Bobby Womack's recording of a song he had written, "Love, the Time Is Now," especially poignant. It is a passionate, reasoned plea for peace and equality—"Freedom for all," he wrote, "and not just for some." Bobby Emmons holds the recording together with his intricate organ lines, and an occasional swooping flight from Ed Kollis's harmonica is the only touch of elaborate filigree. Mike Leech's strings never sounded more stately or sorrowful, and Chips's production was deliberate, measured, steady. Bobby's voice is gentle, stoic, impassioned, as if he feels more than he can say. Listening to it now is to weep. It is the sound of a man's heart breaking for his country.

The song's plea for tolerance and understanding from both races held special irony in that both Womack and Darryl Carter seemed to exemplify the new militant mood. "Carter was a bit of a jiveass," Mike Leech recalled acerbically, noting further that Bobby and Darryl used "dap" handshakes and ghetto slang to accentuate their identity in the midst of the white country boys. They were in their element when another of their buddies, Wilson Pickett, came to town, and Bobby Womack recorded his first album with Chips immediately following sessions with Pickett for Atlantic. There

was inevitably some duplication, since Bobby presented Pickett with new material from his catalogue that Chips also liked; this explains why there are two similar versions of Bobby's famous "I 'm a Midnight Mover," a song that has as much to do with the studio preference for late hours as it does with sexual bragging. The bass riff Tommy Cogbill played on "Midnight Mover" was inspired by Bobby Wood. "I played this riff to him when we were fooling around in the studio and he loved it," said the piano player. The Pickett session also features Womack's and Reggie Young's second writing collaboration, a charming, highly charged tribute to a lady named Magnolia entitled "I Found a True Love" (which Reggie originally thought had been cut with Tommy Cogbill several months before).

Womack and Darryl Carter also collaborated on some material. Their "I've Been Good to You" features the snap and crackle of Bobby's guitar and is full of great lines and similes: "I feel like a lost ball in tall weeds," the second verse begins. The third verse has a couplet that reads like another position paper from the group: "Shiny things walk hand in hand with trouble / You think you're getting something for nothing, and you wind up paying double." The fast piece, "Let's Get an Understanding"— a catchphrase Bobby inserted into several songs—featured blurry, hissing feedback guitar, and a shouted exchange about it from Pickett and Bobby.

Womack also recast "That's Where It's At," the song Sam Cooke created shortly before his death on which Womack had played backup. Here he changed the title (to "It's a Groove") and tempo but kept the emphasis, still choosing to describe that magical time when the lights are out, good music is playing, someone you love is near, and the two of you are communicating without words. This, Bobby implies, is both temporary escape and permanent redemption, the moment when one is most fully alive. The American group seldom did songs about infatuation: in their somber world, contentment was the most one could hope for, and Bobby's mood piece was one of its best depictions.

Janis Joplin later made "Trust Me" famous.

Womack, whose guitar would also grace her version, is mixed higher here by Dowd than the way Paul Rothschild recorded him later, and Tommy Cogbill's thoughtful walking bass illustrates the special attention the American players could give to a great song. Chips Moman produced two equally good but neglected works for Bobby's album: "You Ought to Think It Over" is a strong song to begin with, but Mike Leech's soaring string and horn lines and Tommy Cogbill's solid anchoring both command attention. It is propelled entirely by mood and feel, which the group felt was their specialty. "We were all feel players, we weren't Juilliard grads," Reggie Young stated. "We were rhythmmeisters, groovemeisters," echoed Bobby Wood. "We had to pat our feet, so if we did, somebody else could, too. You didn't dare watch Bobby Emmons's foot, 'cause he was always pattin' his foot to some other rhythm!" The tension between Chips's melancholy and the musicians' eternal search for the groove (a holdover from all their years listening to and playing rhythm and blues) defined the sound of the studio; the effect was a mood that had not much to do with sitting in a corner weeping, and everything to do with marching on bravely and smiling through one's tears.

"Money in My Pocket," the second memorable new Womack composition, is a list of complaints that would have delighted Chips with its opening lines: "How long . . . will trouble last / Won't somebody tell me, when the ol' hard times pass"—although he faded Womack down in mid-recitation, as if he could not abide even a friend reciting more troubles than he had. He delighted in Bobby's expert reworking of standards—"California Dreaming" never sounded as intense as when Bobby did it, and it would become prophetic autobiography when the singer moved back to Los Angeles for good later that year. And the crackling versions of "Fly Me to the Moon" and "Moonlight in Vermont" created by Womack and Chips are uptempo, imaginative—and different from anything else on the radio.

This, of course, was the idea; Chips had obviously been influenced by Phil Spector's directive to "create a sound nobody can copy or cover." "The thing about it, Chips never really knew what he wanted," Mike Leech recalled. "He was impulsive, like on a nice ballad he would suggest the most off-the-wall idea for an overdub, like putting a tuba solo (extreme, but you get the point). Then he would leave it up to the musician to make it work, and it usually did." "He knows what he wants but he don't know what it is till he hears it," said J.R. Cobb, who would become as close to the American group as anyone could who was not in the immediate "family." "Sometimes he doesn't know exactly how to say what he wants."

"We'd beat the song to death a lot of the time," Bobby Wood said cheerfully about Chips's quest for the perfect recording. "Not to take anything away from Chips, but it took him forever to get his act together with the band. That's the old school of playing, where you play it till you're blue in the face. You can beat a dead horse to death. . . . I hated the times I had to sit there and wonder, should I play to please Chips or play to please the band? I'd sit in a cold sweat and go, 'God, what does he want?'" They put up with the long hours and endless retakes because they knew Chips wanted to do something creative. Although Mike Leech recalled that Chips could sometimes be "intimidating," he added, "Chips had the ability to make someone think the direction is their idea. When we [were] all in the studio with Chips, he [could] suggest or coerce direction in a way that's not offensive." By this time the dark, despondent, melodic sound, heavily overlaid with echo and emphasizing the dynamics available with strings, had become the Moman formula; from here on out he would refine the style but never go past it. In commercial terms, it worked, and by the end of the year anyone buying a record with Chips's name on the production credits knew exactly what they were getting.

That was not true with Tommy, who was still experimenting in the studio. There would never be a recognizable Tommy Cogbill "sound" on his productions. Listeners who found their way to his records, most of them AGP singles at this point, were discovering something even more wonderful—the innermost workings of Tommy's mind. "Tommy just did everything from feel and soul," said Bobby Wood admiringly. His work runs the gamut from a recording Reggie Young named as a personal favorite, the Masqueraders' moody "I Ain't Got to Love Nobody Else" (in which Mike Leech's string lines bring the extravagant claims of the singer back down to reality), to Gene Simmons's reflective "Home Again"—the mirror opposite of Paul Simon's "Homeward Bound," because in this song the bars and the road are the only life the singer longs for. There is the drive of the Flash and the Board of Directors rock music and the wild punning humor of Gene Simmons's "Don't You Worry 'Bout Me"—the record didn't sell very well, but Reggie Young's sarcastic lead line in the bridge was discovered and widely copied by other guitarists. It began showing up intact on rock records by the following year.

Chips Moman was not about to be outdone by any of his friends, not even Tommy, and his 1968 work with Sandy Posey shows how much he had evolved even from the records he had done with her the previous year. The album—and the summer's single, an elegant Martha Sharp meditation on compromise called "Ways of the World"—featured fewer monologues and more thought pieces.

"Shades of Gray," a social commentary from Barry Mann and Cynthia Weil, exemplifies this approach. It is about remembering a time when "the answers seemed so clear" and about mourning that loss of clarity: "Today there is no black and white . . . only shades of gray." The garage-band groove, slightly cushioned by Mike Leech's string line, makes the song less gauzy than the way others have recorded it; the piece catches a moment in time between two assassinations, a moment both of innocence and chaos, when it seemed the country would either heal itself of its divisions or completely tear itself apart. "Chips liked that song," Sandy remarked, and it is easy to see why. It would have been a baffling era for a Georgia farm boy (Lewis Grizzard, another farm boy from Chips's home turf, famously said that he

never understood anything that happened in the world after 1962), and "Shades of Gray" reflects discomfort as much as the earlier Bobby Womack song revealed idealism (although Chips seemed to consider himself a hard-boiled realist). It also indicates how important he was becoming within the industry; established writers were now besieging him with songs, and he would have even more of a pipeline when Bell Records merged with Screen Gems early the following year, giving him unlimited access to Brill Building compositions. "We had access to the 'A' material when we were hot," said Mike Leech. "Most good writers hoard their material until a chance for a hit cut arises."

Up until now Chips had relied mainly on his friends for songs, which was not a bad idea with friends like Wayne Carson and J.R. Cobb; both of them contributed beautiful works to Sandy's album. Wayne's "Meadow of My Love" provided a peaceful alternative to the chaos described in "Shades of Gray"; his vision is idyllic and Sandy's voice is sweeter than the hard-edged monologuist of the earlier recordings. J.R.'s "Something I'll Remember," about a girl reciting events most likely forgotten by her lover, who is not "the sentimental kind," features an elegant, cello-driven string arrangement wrapping Sandy's modern voice in rose-point Victorian lace. It was all an attempt to create standards, said J.R., who from the beginning of his career had aspired to the mantle of the great songwriters. "I thought Burt Bacharach and Hal David hung the moon," he said of those he admired. "And who could have heard Lennon-McCartney and not been amazed? Paul Simon's an outstanding writer." He and Buddy Buie had deliberately crafted the song for Sandy, he recalled: "We'd had one hit with her and we were trying to get another. We were definitely trying to write another song for her; you don't get that many vehicles, that many artists. To tell the truth, mostly that don't work. Nine times out of ten it's accidental." Their other composition, "Out of Tune," features dissonant, off-center playing and echo shrouding the warmth of Sandy's vocal.

The two songs should have drawn notice;

after all, J.R.'s new song for the Classics IV, "Soul Train," was attracting some interest and getting played on the radio, though ultimately it did not do as well as its composer felt its mellow groove deserved. Choosing something worthy of airplay was dicey to begin with, and many artists felt that they did not have as much input about releases as they would have liked. Sandy remembered a set-to about the single release that summer. "I liked 'Ways of the World,'" she remembered, "but what I really wanted to be released was 'Handy'" (the semi-autobiographical monologue featuring Bobby Womack on lead). "I played it over and over for Vienneau. We didn't always get our way back then. Vienneau was a nice man, but I guess he had a different ear than what we had. That's why we didn't record more songs after that."

Dispirited at her choices having been ignored, Sandy withdrew from the scene, continuing as a studio singer in Nashville, the Shoals (she and Jeannie Greene can be heard wailing sorrowfully on Percy Sledge's "Take Time to Know Her") and Memphis. She moved back to Memphis and at a party she discovered another manager, Stan Schulman, whom Chips considered an intrusive presence in the studio. "He wasn't—he really wasn't qualified to be a manager," Chips reflected. "He wanted to concentrate on songs that she had written. I'm not gonna record anyone who wants to pick the songs. It was annoying because he didn't really know how. Nowhere near it."

She also married Billy Robinson, a Vietnam veteran good-ol'-boy type with only a peripheral interest in music sparked into further curiosity by his marriage and the time he spent at American. "I really enjoyed going over there," he said warmly. "I knew what I was listening to was history in the making. They seemed to give it their own kind of feel." He immediately befriended Tommy Cogbill, and the two of them spent time hanging out. Billy's presence in the studio and his role in Sandy's life further strained the ties between her and Chips. The stress revealed itself in disagreements over material, differences of opinion that Sandy later regretted. "Sometimes I wish I'd listened to his suggestions more," she said of Chips, her voice

still softly respectful after all that had passed between them. "He wanted to record 'The Chokin' Kind' on me and I didn't hear it. He wanted to record 'Angel of the Morning' but I didn't hear it and I didn't like what it said."

The collaboration became so difficult for both of them that Sandy finished the album with Joe South producing two songs (although neither can be classed with his best work—the arrangement on "One-Man Woman" is embarrassingly dated). Nonetheless, Sandy had good memories of her session with him. "He was a real easygoing fellow, easy to work with. I'm really mad at him because he didn't cut 'Rose Garden' with me," she added teasingly. Joe in fact had just written "Rose Garden" and recorded it for his own album, a collection of philosophical pieces meant to be slightly different from his usual style—it was no accident that he titled the record *Introspect*. Still, Sandy occasionally sang backup on recordings made at American from this period. (Memphis seemed to have been a background singer's town as much as it was a musician's town: in addition to Sandy, other singers working there at one time or another included Janie Fricke, Judy Rodman, Rita and Priscilla Coolidge, and three of the backup singers for Lynyrd Skynyrd—Jo Billingsley and Cassie Gaines from the original three-voice choir and Carol Chase from the band's second edition.)

The only one of Sandy's songs to make the final cut of the album was a piece called "Silly Girl," a story of lovers' bad timing emphasized by Reggie Young's gentle-sounding acoustic guitar. The album featured two monologues: the aforementioned "Handy" and another Mann-Weil tune, "It's Not Easy," which Chips gave an unusual touch by having Sandy speak over her sung part in the manner of Rosemary Clooney's hit "Hey There." "The Wonderful World of Summer" was a John D. Loudermilk descriptive piece that really should have been the A-side of the single; one listens and can almost feel the spray of garden hoses and the sizzling heat radiating up from the sidewalks. The lyrics are vivid enough, but the swirling sounds of Bobby Emmons's organ and the steady, rhythmic beat bring the words to life. "You make that song have its own picture," Bobby Wood explained about the sound-painting process, "and that picture has to be different from anything you've ever seen before." Sandy herself would have preferred a more substantial single: "I didn't want to sound like every other country singer," she sighed.

Her one concession to the limelight was her appearance in ads for Coca-Cola. The print version features a pensive photo of her dressed entirely in red, looking down at the gold of a wheat field. Smaller photos showed her seated on a park bench, writing; dipping her hand in a stream; sitting under a tree, and holding a bottle of Coke in her hands. The copy stressed her gentleness: "She is a serious vocalist and songwriter. She needs time to think things out, to be alone. After all, her songs are of her quiet world. So Sandy insists, despite the interviews, meetings, and rehearsals, that she have time out not to be a star. This is where Coke comes in. Sandy finds her ideas and lyrics go better, Coke after Coke after Coke."

There was also an audio ad. Since 1964, McCann-Erickson, the New York advertising company that handled the Coke account, had been running a series of radio ads that were indistinguishable from pop songs, and could have stood on their own as such (later, one did: Dottie West's 1973 "Country Sunshine"). This innovative approach was supervised by an early Motowner, Berry Gordy's former writing partner Roquel (Billy) Davis. The acts chosen were allowed to write and produce their own material, and Sandy came up with a fresh-sounding song about "talking things over," which Chips obligingly produced and on which the American musicians played. It turned out so well that several other Coke radio ads were done by the American group, most notably the ones Mark James wrote for B.J. Thomas a year or two later.

Dan Penn took the Box Tops to New York to record their jingles; this may have been the occasion when Mike Leech was asked to be part of the proceedings, only to have Chips stun him with "Me and Tommy ain't decided whether you're going to go." "I didn't," Mike said, never once blaming Tommy for Chips's decision. According to Gary Talley, Mike missed an amusing set of events. "You could have done a comedy movie about Dan Penn in New York City," Gary laughed. "We were going into a café in New York with Dan, evidently he hadn't been there very often. He ordered iced tea and they didn't know what it was. They brought out hard rolls with butter and butter with ice on it." The studio recording was just as much of a culture clash. "Some famous studio guitarist came in and did some overdubs," remembered Gary. "They were always lookin' at the clock, and in Memphis you *never* looked at the clock. The strings came in and they wanted string parts. 'Where's the music?' [they said], and he said, 'We ain't got no music.' . . . I never will forget the shocked look on their faces. [They were wondering what to do and Dan] said, 'Awww, you know, put the thang on it.' . . . He ended up hummin' the parts." The band did several jingles there, and "some of 'em sounded very Dan-ish," said Gary. There was one about the road—"Hotels, motels"—and the need to calm down and relax with a Coke. Another had a somewhat eerie production full of (apparently unintentional) menace with Alex Chilton growling leeringly about the "girls in the little town square" drinking Cokes.

Dan was proprietary about his work, even if he was only recording a jingle, Mike Leech noted. "[I have] vivid memories of Dan wrapping up a session, walking out with a couple of multi-track tape boxes. Same with Tommy. They were more methodical than Chips in keeping track of what they had. Or at least they kept their product in their own safekeeping, whereas Chips had a rack on the wall of the control room where all his stuff was placed." To the best of Mike's recollection, none of the tapes done by Chips ever left the control room, and at the time many of them were not even properly labeled, although Chips seemed to have no trouble locating things. "He kept track of which tracks were being used for which overdubs," said Mike. "That's pretty amazing when you consider he is producing at the same time. . . . I've worked with Chips when he kept tape running almost constant, depending on the [production] budget I'm sure. I've seen stacks of 24-track reels piled in a corner. On the other hand, I've seen 'rewind' on many occasions, to save tape. So it just depends." Keeping track of what was needed for Sandy's jingle would have been fairly easy for Chips anyway, since he cut just a simple basic track for that project and let it stand.

Endorsing Coca-Cola was no problem for the American players; the long hours in the studio were made easier by conspicuous consumption of soft drinks—usually, nothing stronger, in part due to the preferences of Chips. "One side of Chips that was a little unfair," Mike Leech reflected. "If he didn't like something, or was unable to do something we liked, it was restricted. He couldn't drink, or at least he said the doc told him he couldn't for some reason, so we weren't allowed to. It was really no problem, because most of us didn't drink while we were working anyway, and what we did after work was our own business.

"I guess we all drank cokes, soft drinks," he continued. "Bob Taylor saw to it that we had a water cooler installed in the studio which was nice to have. My favorite drink, after we were through recording, was bourbon and coke. We didn't have glasses or cups (except for coffee cups), so I would pour about half the coke out and fill it up with booze.

"One of my fondest memories was when, after work, Reggie and I would go to the Three [he could not remember the rest of the name], have a few brandies, go back to the studio and listen to tapes of what we had recorded that day or that week. That was big fun. Sometimes others would join us, which made it even more fun."

American was no longer just a place to work. It was becoming a hangout.

One of those hanging out at American that early summer of 1968 was the young writer from Muscle Shoals who everyone thought was so promising—Eddie Hinton. He was now writing almost exclusively with Donnie Fritts and playing lead guitar on a few of the records coming out of Fame. His musical curiosity seemed boundless; Jimmy Johnson remembered him poring through a small book

about how to write string arrangements, and that within several weeks of having read it he was turning out master-quality demos of his and other people's songs, complete with intricate string lines that worked almost on a parallel with Mike's. One of those demos featured another young songwriter, Paul Davis, out of Jackson, Mississippi. Davis wanted to be in the music business so badly that he was sleeping on the floor of a studio there and working as a janitor just for the privilege of making demos and pitching his songs. For a young writer, his work had strong images; a demo still exists of his song "Rollin' in My Sleep," about an exhausted hobo trying to catch a ride in a boxcar, and Eddie Hinton's string line fills in all the colors and shadings of the freight rain rolling through the lower South in the rainy autumn twilight. When the American group heard the demo during sessions for the Box Tops' third album, Mike Leech, who usually made it a point of honor to do something completely different from what was on the tape, simply followed Hinton's string part, although with a few more intricate overdubs. "We were not good at copying anything from a demo unless it was absolutely great," reflected Bobby Wood. "We would have to make it fit the artist also." Tommy Cogbill's bass, moving steadily beneath the strings, created the sound and feel of the hobo trudging along, looking for another boxcar to leap into so he could rest.

It was yet another classic American Studios sound painting, done this time without any input at all from the Box Tops, who spent most of that summer on the road. "I don't remember playing one note on the [third] album," said Gary Talley. "I 'm not even sure we sang. We might have missed that one entirely." Alex Chilton came in to do his vocals when there was a break in the schedule. Gary said that although the band would have liked to have been more involved in the recording process, "we all knew those guys were better and faster than we were about cutting records, so there were no hard feelings about it at all. We understood."

Dan Penn was apparently looking for songs about trains, as if he originally planned a concept album on the subject. Though typically, he seemed to lose interest in the idea halfway through production, some vestiges of the idea remained; the album was titled *Nonstop* and the band posed for the record jacket in and around some classic locomotives in a freight yard. Even the B.B. King blues "Rock Me," featuring Ed Kollis's harmonica, is taken at a pace suggestive of the swaying motion of a fast freight. And that is where Eddie Hinton and Donnie Fritts came in.

They thought up "Choo Choo Train" during a routine writing session at a room Eddie rented in Fred Beavis's old casket factory out on the Jackson Highway near Sheffield, a place that Beavis was trying to turn into a recording studio. "We'd been up all night writing, we'd went straight to Quinvy Studios and did a little demo," Donnie remembered. The version cut by Alex Chilton is piercing; though the song is simple, the words and sentiments expressed are not. The narrator simply wants to go home, and by implication, be left alone: "All my wild oats, Choo-choo, done been sown," he explains to the locomotive. Tommy's bass line lopes and Reggie's guitar fills leading into the verses are bluesy and incisive. Gene Chrisman is at his most explosive ever on this track, playing a drum fill at the fadeout which leaves one gasping for breath, wondering as King Curtis did how this wiry little man could play with so much strength.

The train theme continues with Dan Penn's reworking of the Hank Snow signature tune, "I'm Movin' On." Dan made the backing under the first verse sparse and traditional, with Reggie Young's guitar line at its most choked and twangy—and then Tommy Cogbill causes hell to break loose in the instrumental passage. "Things like that were Cog's forte," Mike Leech said respectfully. "He could take a simple song and fit the nicest bass part in." Then it is back to the traditional sound for the second verse, with Spooner Oldham providing a rolling, elaborate piano line somewhat out of character for his style. Not until Shane Keister joined the group later would another piano solo be so intricate. Tommy's rambunctiousness again turns the instrumental break into a free-for-all, with Spooner, Reggie, and the Memphis Horns

joining him in a long, exhilarating fadeout. It was Dan's reply to the Nashville system he so ardently disliked. *Sure, we can make traditional-sounding records when we want to*, he seemed to be implying, *and the way we handled those verses prove it; but isn't it a whole lot more fun doing it our way?*

In Nashville, Dan's old bandmates and several other young musicians agreed with him. "We thought they had a better idea," said Norbert Putnam, who by now was established as the most advanced session bassist in Music City. To him and his friends, the very things the American group did not like were the secret of their success; the late hours and endless reworkings of the same cut allowed them to lock into a song and make it their own, which could not be done as easily on the Nashville assembly line of three songs in three hours. "Their heart and soul is behind everything they are doing," Putnam said admiringly of the Memphis players. "We'd listen to their records and just marvel. We'd say, 'I wish we had all day to make records.'" He regretted the lack of time in his own work to develop bass parts, compared to what Tommy Cogbill and Mike Leech were doing. "I never had an hour. I never had a day."

The two versions of Mac Gayden's "She Shot a Hole In My Soul," one in Nashville with Clifford Curry singing and one in Memphis with Alex fronting Dan's production, make the difference clear. The Nashville version is clunky and rote, almost wooden—literally "by the numbers." Dan's version is casual, loping, with Tommy's bass leaping into every available space and Alex Chilton's swaggering vocal. It is loose, relaxed, and could have come from nowhere but Memphis.

Even more relaxed—and even more exhilarating—is Dan's and Spooner's "People Gonna Talk," a simple song about a girl so attractive she drew gossip, which deeply hurt her. "People gone be people and I tell you, people they just gonna talk," is the song's conclusion, as Ed Kollis's fluttering harmonica underscores the track. Gary Talley remembered Reggie Young's fast, reeling guitar break between the verses, because he had to duplicate it onstage and found it the most challenging thing he had

had to learn. "It's a real clean guitar part," he said. "It stuck out there all by itself." But the strength of the recording is in the long instrumental passage, Dan's ultimate, glorious tribute to Bobby "Blue" Bland. Kollis wails away in fine bluesy form, Tommy Cogbill romps and stomps, and the Memphis Horns turn up the heat. By the end of the record the listener is riding the groove, out past any pressure or hardship or pain. And that was exactly the point. Chips may have been content to depict sorrow in his productions; Dan, by contrast, was looking for solutions for the pain.

One solution, of course, is true love, and Dan's creed of love and happiness is well expressed in "I Met Her in Church." He and Spooner Oldham originally wrote this gospel-inflected song for the Sweet Inspirations; when that did not work out, the tune was brought forth for the Box Tops. It is hard to believe today that this was considered a Top Forty rock song then: the stops and starts, Reggie Young's ringing guitar, Mike Leech's solemn string arrangement, and John Hughey's crying steel guitar would place this record within the purest of pure country. The theme, too, of finding a good woman "in a little church just down the street" as opposed to "on a Saturday night" in a bar is more resonant with country listeners than with rock. The American group never veered from traditional themes, because traditionalists is exactly what they were. All of them had offspring by now: Bobby Emmons's two daughters, Reggie Young's son and adopted daughter (from his wife's previous marriage), Gene Chrisman's two sons and one daughter. Tommy Cogbill fathered three sons and two daughters, Chips was the proud father of a little girl named Monique, and eventually Mike Leech's wife Mary Ann would give birth to twin girls. Bobby Wood's oldest son Chris was born later that year, though he joked that it was a mystery how, since he was working so much by then he was seldom home.

Traditionalism is expressed again in an odd little song from Acuff-Rose in Nashville that Dan turned up somehow. "Yesterday, Where's My Mind," features a rough, anguished vocal from Alex Chilton and an almost deliberately crude arrangement, and says more about Southern sexual guilt than a thousand Kinsey Reports. The narrator anguishes over his one-night stand with "a Dairy Freeze queen" and he goes back and forth between hating himself and hating her for being so cheap (Tommy Cogbill's walking bass paints a picture of her hip-shaking strut). The song ends with a complete rejection of technique: Tommy comes to a dead stop on bass and Gene Chrisman's cymbals bring the mood to a crashing conclusion.

Another song from Eddie Hinton and Donnie Fritts, "If I Had Let You In," featuring another bright trumpet line from Wayne Jackson and a grand, sweeping string part from Mike Leech, closes out the original album, but the CD reissue features several affecting pieces that did not make the cut. It must have been for reasons of album length, since the selections reveal no lack of quality. Randy Newman's "Let Me Go" features Spooner's piano and a woozy Dixieland arrangement from Mike; Alex Chilton growls and slurs in a Memphis version of the Texas drawl commonly heard on the premises of American courtesy of Mark James. A stomping Bobby Emmons composition, "Got to Hold On to You," predates the Statler Brothers' "Susan When She Tried" in its recital of girls, but its message is spoken directly to the woman who could make the speaker "fly above my troubles" (apparently an important criteria for a mate in the American book of life). These two songs were later released as a Box Tops single in 1969.

Most beautiful of all is the simple but touching ballad from Alex Chilton himself, "Since I've Been Gone," which turned up as the B-side to the Box Tops' final single, released on Bell in early 1970. Alex was just beginning, with encouragement from Dan, to try his hand at writing; his gritty "I Can Dig It" appears on the album, as he assumes the persona of an older, lustful man leering at a woman he has wanted for a long time. But on this song he makes no attempt to be something he is not: he speaks from a deep place inside himself. We see him as he is, a seventeen-year-old boy out on his own, accidentally meeting an old acquaintance and asking about friends and family, commenting on how his own life and looks have changed. Reggie Young's gentle acoustic guitar assumes a folk-rock style, and Tommy Cogbill seems content to follow along. Mike Leech's string line, soft to begin with, is mixed even lower until it becomes a subliminal presence. Another producer might have tried to add more ornamentation to the sound, taking away from the message and melody, but Dan's emphasis on simplicity allows the strength of the song to stand on its own. It is one of the defining records of the American group, summing up in a little less than three minutes all that was good about their style of music and their particular view of the world.

By early summer another person who would contribute strongly to that vision began turning up at American. The group had met him the previous year, when a singer from the Carolinas named Ronnie Milsap came to American at the behest of Steve Tyrell at Scepter. Ronnie was a blind piano player and singer whose raw-edged voice could wrap itself around any kind of material from the blues to rock to the most traditional country; Bobby Wood thought Milsap's voice "sounded like an old man" because of its experienced, bluesy intonation. Milsap had made records with Huey Meaux in Texas, but nothing had happened with those singles, and he had been content doing club work in Atlanta when Tyrell brought him to American to try recording with Chips. The result was a unique version of "House of the Rising Sun," featuring Bobby Emmons's lean, mean organ playing that in no way copied that of Alan Price on the Animals' recording (all the embellishment came from Tommy). The verse about a dissatisfied gambler could well have applied to Chips, and he knew it. But they had needed a B-side, and Ronnie suggested a ballad written by the bass player in his club band, Johnny Christopher.

"I Can't Tell a Lie" is the sparse, laconic statement of a man who does not care about a woman who apparently is deeply in love with him. The song takes its narrator through many complicated emotions, all the way from pitying her to profound annoyance. He cannot understand why he is not attracted to her, but in a strange way is proud of himself for not exploiting the situation: "She's the kind of girl that I could spend a day with and I'd not be ashamed of what I'd done."

If that line is almost strong enough for poetry, it is no accident. Johnny Christopher read voraciously about almost everything—"I read some of the classics, whatever was around, science fiction forever"—and had been particularly interested in poetry, observing how its structure could also apply to writing songs. He was also interested in athletics for a time, but by the middle years of high school, the guitar had captured his imagination for good—as music had since he was a child in Atlanta, singing harmony around the house with his sister at the age of three. He had learned basic chords on a ukelele (shades of Spooner Oldham's mandolin) at twelve, and the following year his grandmother had bought him a Sears Silvertone acoustic guitar for Christmas. The acoustic guitar would forever be the extension of his voice.

"I was basically just a self-taught guitar player," he said dismissively, although that would never be the opinion of his peers; no less a musician than Reggie Young praised Johnny's sound and the way "he'd slide his thumb over the strings" to create a jaunty, rhythmic effect. Johnny tried junior college in Marietta, Georgia, for a year, but got impatient with it, dropped out, and began playing guitar in local clubs. He had met Ronnie Milsap while he was in high school and Ronnie was hiring a backup band for what Johnny recalled as a pickup gig; he auditioned and got the job as bass player. When Ronnie was selecting musicians for a permanent club band, he remembered Johnny and hired him. "This was 1965, I worked for him through 1968," remembered Johnny. Before long the young bassist was leading Ronnie around and even driving for him; in his memoirs, Milsap recounted a harrowing experience when he himself decided to take the wheel.

Ronnie and the band had a solid engagement every night at the Playboy Club in Atlanta, and the lack of interest in the Scepter single caused everyone to believe that they would probably stay there forever. All that changed when Chips and Tommy came to Atlanta on a road trip late that spring. They stopped at the Playboy Club to hear Ronnie—Johnny recalled that Mark James was also with them—and Chips talked up the possibility of recording again. Ronnie, according to his memoirs, was not sure, but Chips thought the singer could possibly make a go of it if he and his band moved up to Memphis. Chips pulled some strings and secured a residency for them at T.J.'s, the new club run by his longtime acquaintance, Herbie O'Mell.

T.J.'s had become, in only a short time, the major music-business hangout. O'Mell had been on the fringes of the scene in Memphis for years, and one of Elvis's former bodyguards, Richard Davis, eventually became the doorman. "I really liked Herbie. He was a great guy and he made us feel at home," said Johnny. Spooner Oldham recalled the ambience: "I just remember it was a big ol' cavernous-looking place. Dark . . . dark." "It was a nice club, it wasn't a very big club," said Johnny. "It had a downstairs, where we played, and an upstairs. Later on they had entertainment upstairs also; I remember Charlie Rich playing there." Practically anybody might turn up; when famous singers were in town, they usually relaxed at T.J.'s. "We used to take our artists to T.J.'s because they always had great steaks and fries," said Hayward Bishop, who remembered the club from later on. "It got a great reputation as a steakhouse. The fries were hand-cut, in wedges, they were shaped like pickle slices. You could sit there, get a delicious steak, and listen to some great music." "We used to go down quite a bit after late-night sessions to clear our brains," said Reggie Young. "We'd go down, all of us, Chips, Tommy, Mark, all of us," said Spooner Oldham. "We never paid to get in and sometimes would sit in with the band," Mike Leech remembered. And not only Memphis session players came there to unwind. Tom Dowd came to T.J.'s whenever he was in town. And on Friday nights after a particularly rough week's grind, Norbert Putnam and David Briggs often chartered a twin-engine plane and flew over to hang out at T.J.'s and listen to the band till closing time at two AM, after which

they got back on the plane and were home in Nashville by four.

Everyone remarked on the variety of Ronnie's repertoire. "I don't remember him ever doing a country song back then," observed Norbert Putnam. "Milsap's love at that time was R&B and [he and his band] were good at it," said Mike Leech. "There was nothing country about Ronnie and his band—it was blues, it was Beatles, it was strobe lights," said Reggie Young. "He had the coolest band in Memphis. He was a great player, he was a great singer, right on pitch. . . . There was one country song he used to do every night, it was an old George Jones song." And standing right up there near the piano, anchoring the band with his bass playing, was Johnny Christopher.

A hippie in preppie disguise—temporarily, anyway—Johnny began going along to the studio with Milsap. He wound up being amazed at what he saw. "This group—I learned so much from them. . . . I was in the presence of such greatness," he said, his voice still awestruck after many years. "I was so thrilled to be there, it was a golden situation. I can't tell you—it was inexpressible." His first impressions were of "an especially talented, gifted group of people. They had a wisdom beyond their years." Like virtually everyone who observed or listened to them at that point, he was moved by the depth of feeling at which they worked. "They were in the business of creating records exactly the way they heard and felt," he said. "And if they didn't think they needed to be there, they'd rather not play. That's such an unselfish attitude. . . . that kind of fellowship is rare in the world today, human nature really looks out for itself." It was this cooperative spirit that impressed him more than anything else: "I like to be a team man." He was as impressed with Chips as he was with the musicians. "Chips was destined, absolutely ordained by God to make the kind of music he did," said Johnny fervently. "He had gifts most men don't have. He was just so talented musically." It was a compliment Chips returned, naming Johnny as his all-time favorite acoustic guitar player years after the two of them had had their differences and gone their separate ways.

Unlike Glen Spreen's conscious decision to eventually become a part of the scene, it never occurred to Johnny Christopher that he might be one of the musicians someday. "I just thought, I'm gonna learn as much from this as I can . . . This is a rare special group." His respectful attitude was noticed, and he became accepted as a result. "Johnny was an immediate 'like,'" observed Mike Leech. "On arrival [he] looked like the Good Humor man, like he should have been selling popsicles. He had on a white shirt, white pants, white tennis shoes. Medium height, a little chubby, short, neat hair, friendly fat face, nice. . . . Big-eyed, curious, interested, well-mannered." "For some reason, he always reminded me of Paul McCartney," said Reggie Young. "He was always up and enthusiastic about everything," recalled Bobby Emmons. Johnny's enthusiasm immediately connected with Bobby Wood's bounding energy, and the two of them became fast friends. Johnny began spending time at American, observing and occasionally pitching a song. And, of course, he watched as the group experimented with Ronnie's recordings. "They'd find out where Ronnie was at so they could figure out how to get a hit record on him," Johnny said of their method.

The combination got off to a great start with a recording so different that Reggie Young uncharacteristically wrote down the song title in his session book: "The Old Man at the Fair." The group had never tried anything like this before. A Jim Webb composition, it typifies the elegance and grace of his writing; it is structured as a folk-style ballad with a medieval feel and a tune vaguely reminiscent of "Greensleeves." Tommy applies some sliding James Jamerson–style bass beneath the elegant piano melody and Mike Leech's string line utilizes everything he ever learned about chamber music and then some. The lyrics are startling, about an old man returning to the fair after many years in search of the beautiful young woman he left there, only to find an old crone he does not recognize (anybody who ever fell in love with someone whose looks eroded with time can relate). "I love that song," said Johnny. "I loved it when I was there; I tried to learn it on guitar. . . . I wasn't schooled, so my progress on the guitar was very slow."

It was a record as far removed from both garage-band stomping and aggressive R&B as it is possible to get, and if it had gotten more airplay and become known to the general public it would have killed once and forever the consensus that this group could only make jukebox weepers. "Old Man" aimed at an elegant, upscale audience. It would be a direct line from this recording on through the smooth and highly structured B.J. Thomas productions to the version of Jim Webb's "Mr. Shuck and Jive" (with its quotes from "McArthur Park") that Chips cut with Waylon Jennings and the pathbreaking "Highwayman" track of 1986, and is an aspect of Moman's work that even now is not well known. Perhaps it was because of Chips's insistence on remaining a good old boy, unspoiled by success and even unwilling to appear publicly in suit and tie, but the "redneck" image stuck not only to him but to the music coming out of his studio—unfairly.

It was a time for trying new styles and new sounds. Everyone wanted to come up with something different. Mike Leech, for one, relished that particular period of the group's history. "That's what I loved about the old Memphis days, the experimentation," he said. The Milsap record was a departure for the group, but it had worked, and at around the same time, Dan Penn was trying something similar. He had a collaborator for the venture: Spooner Oldham would be with him as co-producer. The piano player was looking forward to giving some of his ideas a try, and Dan gladly used most of his concepts.

"I'm sure except for the technical aspects of me signing the papers nobody would have reason to know that I produced anything," Spooner said. Nonetheless, he enjoyed branching out. "That's what drives my engine, is variety, creativity, a chance to be creative," he explained. He had first tried producing in Muscle Shoals, recording a few singles that appeared on the Don Varner–owned Southcamp label. The crew from Atlantic Records, impressed with Spooner's musicianship and most likely familiar with those pieces, asked him to join them as a staff producer (an uncanny precursor of their later association with another American keyboardist, Shane Keister). "Tom Dowd, in a nightclub in Memphis, said, 'Do you want to come and work with us?'" Spooner recalled. "He said, 'Take your time, take a year to decide.' I never said no or yes, I never got back to him." Why didn't he accept? "I was already doing what I wanted to do, writing songs and playing piano. I would have had more to do, and I had enough responsibility." Spooner was getting to produce anyway; his work with Barbara Lynn was artistically strong but wound up being unreleased by Atlantic. Now he was working with another artist signed to the label.

The client was Steve Alaimo, a singer from Florida who had been featured for the last several years with the Raiders on *Where The Action Is*. He had been a teenybopper star for awhile, but he was now interested in making records for a mature audience. With its emphasis on sorrow and stoicism, the grownup sound of the American group was the logical way to reach adults, even more so because of Alaimo's rapport with Chips. "Steve Alaimo and I have been friends since the day we met," said Chips warmly. "He's a good guy, he's pleasant. All the time." The musicians shared that opinion and Alaimo became a group favorite. "Every time I think of him I get a mental [picture] of him with no shirt," said Mike Leech amusedly. The air in the building was indeed sometimes close, with all the cigarette smoke and the small heater suspended on a corner wall of the studio going full speed ahead in the winter months. When Herbie Mann came in for the first time later that fall, he too preferred to work shirtless.

For Alaimo's session, Dan and Spooner brought forth a classic, both in its writing and its production. "Watching the Trains" is one of Dan's contemporary ballads, placing us back in Clinch Mountain territory. The narrator is a coal miner's son who goes down to the railroad station every day to watch the trains. It is implied that he would like to leave the area but probably cannot afford to, although he has more than enough reasons for going: his mother is ill, his brother is on the county work farm, a prominent lawyer's wife is pregnant after years of sterility (with strong implications that the narrator is responsible). But in the end, lack of money and inertia win out, and he walks down the dusty farm road toward home again, prepared to endure it all the next day. Dan and Spooner use echo more sparingly here than in any other American production of the time, letting the song speak for itself. Steve Alaimo sings softly, almost sighing with the futility of it all, and Mike Leech's string line sounds like a rising autumn wind. There's even a tenor banjo part from Reggie Young, emphasizing the song's kinship with traditional ballads and bluegrass, and in the end the music fades down leaving Alaimo to whisper the title line unaccompanied, as if the narrator is facing for the first time how alone in the world he really is.

It was a work of pure imagination from beginning to end, according to Spooner Oldham. "As usual, when Dan and I write something, I don't know where it comes from. I wasn't there; I wasn't at the train station." But their ability to put themselves in another person's place—similar to what a good prose writer would have— was remarkable, as if they were writing a novel or directing a movie. The production is so understated, and yet so alive with detail, that a listener can see that dusty road and that train station somewhere in the foothills of the Appalachians. "It had sort of nostalgic feeling, a different place and time in my mind," said Spooner about the effect. It is musical Impressionism, as real as a landscape by Monet or Pissarro.

Spooner was justifiably proud of it. "'Watching the Trains,' I really like that record," he said. "That's one of my favorite things I ever wrote, for sure." The record was not a hit when it was released—Southern genre paintings did not catch on in a market still glutted with psychedelia—and it did not do well even a year and a half later, when Tony Joe White recorded it with the Dixie Flyers as a single. Spooner hoped for a revival. "I 'd love to hear it surface again, sung by somebody, some young man could do it, some old one, I don't care which," he offered. "I don't know if it's human nature that wants to be validated; I like to think it's the music, in my case." Though he never boasted about his accomplishments, Spooner was then at his creative best (as was Dan), and on some level he knew it. Life was peaking for him in many ways: he had met a warm, good-natured woman named Karen whom he would marry the following year. He was settling down. "I bought a house, which was sort of nonevent-ful," he said offhandedly.

If the A-side of the record displayed Dan's grim realism (with a lot of help from the contemplative Spooner), the B-side was the best showcase for his Shoals-style optimism. "Thank You For The Sunshine Days" is the ultimate love-and-happiness song: it traces a couple's romance from bemused childhood to contemplative old age, and at each step along the way gratitude is expressed. Alaimo sounds similar to Alex Chilton, perhaps intentionally, and the bursts of sound from the horn section over the pulsing momentum of the basic track convey surprise and delight. It is an uplifting record in the best sense of that word: the lis-teners are told about something to which they too can aspire—one emotional connection that will last forever.

Alaimo made other interesting records with the group that year. Chips Moman's joyfully irreverent production (complete with Reg-gie Young's electric sitar) of the honky-tonk classic "Wild Side of Life" precedes the Ken-tucky Headhunters' similar treatment of stan-dards, and for the B-side Chips cut a somewhat clunky version of a Mickey Newbury song at the time called "Can't You See" that was over-shadowed by Glen Spreen's later windblown string and horn arrangement of the same song for Buffy St. Marie. Perhaps Chips could not completely find what he was looking for in the song; the lyrics are a battle cry, but his pro-duction drifts along letting things take care of themselves. As long as he was making records in a relaxed atmosphere, he was happy, and so was the group.

But the pressure was about to become more intense. The scene at American was going to expand. It would bring out the best in Chips and the group. It would also bring out the worst—in both.

### CHAPTER 14

# Early Departures and Late Arrivals

There was an atmosphere about the studio that everyone could feel, a sense that the pace was quickening. For one thing, there was the al-ready considerable respect the studio had from its peers. "We were in awe of the rhythm sec-tion at American," said Jimmy Johnson, who was still at Fame but making plans to break away and establish a studio with Roger Hawk-ins as partner. "Man per man, it was just invin-cible." "We all looked up to the guys at Amer-ican," said Jimmy's colleague David Hood. "Those guys seemed so accomplished; they played so well." The client roster was becoming more distinguished, especially among the R&B accounts. Joe Tex and Joe Simon, for example, were both hitmakers by now, and Atlantic was sending them established performers like Ben E. King (although Brook Benton, just signed to Atlantic, somehow slipped past their notice and recorded at Fame). Neither Chips Moman nor Tommy Cogbill aggressively went looking for clients; perhaps they were naïve, but they seemed to feel that the quality of work coming out of American spoke for itself. Chips could not attribute the increasing prestige of the art-ists booked at the studio to anything else. "I guess people heard some of the records and knew some of the work we did and they came a-callin'," he shrugged.

That seems to be exactly how Bang Records out of New York approached them to doctor a recording. The track was Neil Diamond's ballad "Shilo." Eileen Burns, widow of the label head, simply brought them the track and let them overdub whatever they wanted to enhance it. Bobby Emmons, the master of special runs and fills, is prominent. "[Bobby] always played in places in the song where you wouldn't expect to hear an organ or a keyboard," Mike Leech said respectfully. Mike also remembered the overdubbing process for "Shilo": "The track was fed to our headphones and we were told to play along," he said. "If you'll notice, some of the drum fills sound a little sporadic. That's because Gene tried to imitate what the other drummer played. It was an interesting track— we had never done anything like that before." "I think all that wound up sticking out of the original track was the strings, Neil, and the toy piano," said Bobby Emmons. "We painted over everything else." The song was released as a single and did well that fall, although the group was not credited on the label. It would not be the last they would hear of Neil Diamond.

Another indication of success was that they were seldom off the charts—several charts at once, because they were having both R&B and pop successes, and if country radio had not been so restrictive at the time they likely would have crossed over into that format as well. "I think all the different backgrounds musically in this group was a major factor in us having such a wide variety of hits in four different charts," said Bobby Wood.

Merrilee Rush's "Angel of the Morning," the ideal pop-country blend, became a Top Ten hit in June. "I was happy as heck about it," said Jimmy Johnson in the Shoals, rejoicing in Tommy Cogbill's accomplishment. The record was Tommy's biggest success as a producer, and in 1981 when Andrew Gold worked on Juice Newton's remake, his arrangement directly followed the pattern of the original, down to the mournful intro and the drum taps and pauses (though his take on all of these effects was less gentle than Tommy's had been), making the setup as much a part of the song as Chip Taylor's lyric and melody. Despite the almost note-for note copy, those who remembered the American version liked it better. "I thought Merrilee's version of 'Angel of the Morning' was better than Juice Newton's," said Gene Chrisman. "There's something about the original that's hard to top."

Paying homage to a producer's concepts was the ultimate triumph, yet nobody mentioned Tommy; Mike Leech, as arranger, was not even thought of at all. The credit went completely to Chips, even among those who knew better: Merrilee, who raised show dogs as a sideline, presented Chips with one of her animals, an Old English sheepdog, as a thank-you gift. (Bobby Emmons recalled that she gave each musician a wristwatch with the Warner Brothers cartoon character Road Runner emblazoned on it; she herself wore an antique Mickey Mouse watch, a fact she discussed once during an appearance on the Raiders' television show.) Chips promptly named the dog Sweets and began spending so much time with it that Sweets eventually seemed to think she was human. "Sweets was very, very smart," remembered Mike Leech. "She was *brilliant!*" Chips exclaimed, his voice tender with memory. "She lived with me for seventeen years. She always knew when I was comin' home. . . . Her big thing was, she opened every door in the house that I'd need to get through, with her mouth. If I needed something from home, I could tell a stranger to go and get it—they'd say 'How do I get in?' I'd say, 'Tell Sweets to open the door.'" He returned Merrilee's compliment by naming one of his horses Angel of the Morning, and it did fairly well for him in the high-stakes races he sponsored on weekends out at his farm. Both Ima Roberts and Hayward Bishop remembered the dimensions of Chips's racetrack, which Ima described as "state of the art." "It was just like you'd see at Pimlico or somewhere," said Hayward with amazement. "It had a photo finish, electric start—everything." "It's something I liked," Chips shrugged matter-of-factly.

Chips filled his life with horses and canines. He already owned a full-blooded German shepherd dog and a blind collie, and Chips recalled, laughing, that the shepherd used to "lead that collie around." Then Chips acquired another German shepherd that Mike Leech described as being "big, bad, slightly off-center . . . a little bit crazy, mean." Its name, ironically in light of one of the future staffers at American, was Shane, and the musicians remembered the animal vividly because Chips brought it in from the time it was a puppy. "Yeah, I was afraid of him," Bobby Wood said about the dog. "We never ever tried to pet him, even though Chips made sure he wasn't unfriendly to us," Mike Leech added. "He walked with his head cocked slightly to the side [a mannerism the dog may have picked up from its owner] and wasn't what you would call a friendly dog. I was a bit afraid to be near him. He was a one-man dog, and would obey only Chips. . . . He loved Chips but nobody else." "He was . . . a great guard dog. He protected me," said Chips with warm affection. "He would climb ladders . . . all the things you'd want a dog to do. I could tell him to stay in one place and he'd sit there all day." "One day, in the front office, Chips and Darryl Carter were talking," Mike Leech remembered. "Chips left the room and ordered Shane to 'watch' . . . Carter while he sat in the front office. Carter was smoking, and every time he would make a move to dip his ashes, Shane would emit a guttural growl. We were watching through a door window, and when the butt was about to burn Carter's fingers Chips walked in laughing and called Shane off . . . [Darryl] was sweating bullets by the time Chips rescued him."

As in any family, such inside jokes were a constant. Perhaps in reference to the guns that some of the group had begun to carry, if anyone uttered the phrase "I'm game," the others immediately made pistols of their forefingers and "shot" the speaker. No one remembered how that routine came about, but Mike Leech witnessed the origination of another phrase. "There was a black artist, a duet, off the street, Chips was recording one time, and their song was about school, about how you should stay in school. Anyhow, part of the lyric, was something like 'Hey, man, you should get into sports, like football.' And the other guy said, 'Yeah, man, football.'

"Well, that hit Mark James's funnybone. Every time anybody said anything we didn't have a comeback for, we would say, 'Yeah man, football.'" It was also used as a conversation closer, or a way to announce one's departure. "Yeah man, football" became an all-purpose phrase, a way of defining themselves as a group and separating themselves from the outside world.

That apartness seemed particularly important to Bobby Emmons. He had initially been uncomfortable both with Womack and Spooner, although Bobby's friendliness and Spooner's gentle ways had quickly put him at ease. "I was always apprehensive about new people, because I had seen the start of this musical boom town," said Emmons. "Mostly based on greed and get-it-while-you-can. Memphis was just getting rediscovered as a place to make records, and higher-paying sessions had been few and far between for most musicians. The general approach that I witnessed was hit 'em for all you can today because they'll be gone tomorrow. Our group tried to give the clients quality product and not just slam anything down on tape, so there would be repeat business. That was in addition to the fact that we all wanted to cut a great big hit record.

"If you've got enough people on the session that you know feel that way, you've got enough to overpower someone who just wants to slop something down and get out of there. There's two ways to record; one way is to just get in there and do a nice polite recital of what the writer brought you, and then there's the way of creating something that will jump out of the speakers and demand your attention when you hear it on the radio. I wondered if new people would see past having a good cut all the way to making a great record just by leaving out all of those old tired familiar lines and fills. It made me a little too careful sometimes." For Emmons, it would become more important than ever to draw lines in the sand—and to establish who was who.

Two singles blaring over the airwaves at summer's end told the group's current story; one was a hit and the other was a brilliant experiment. Clarence Carter's "Slip Away" was done at Fame under the direction of Rick Hall, with Spooner Oldham and Tommy Cogbill sitting in. Spooner remembered that the track had been cut during the last of the road-trip days, in mid-1967, and that "It sat on the shelf for about a year and Bowlegs Miller asked Rick what had happened to it." (Bowlegs Miller was a Memphis bandleader and horn player who often supplied the sections for productions at Fame, and he also cut a stomping instrumental single for Goldwax.) "Slip Away" had originally been intended as the B-side of the single "Funky Fever," but disc jockeys turned the record over (a common occurrence with Rick Hall 's productions). The Shoals musicians had worked with Carter before, when the duo Clarence and Calvin had done a "Last Night"–style instrumental for Atco, produced by Jimmy Johnson, called "Rooster Knees and Rice." It featured odd, gruesome-sounding recitations by Clarence in the pauses (Jimmy could gleefully imitate the sinister mutter at a moment's notice). "They'd come up to a stop and he'd lean into the mike and say, 'Snail sweat and pie' . . . 'Green grass on toast' . . . 'Rooster knees and rice,'" the guitarist chortled. This, however, was far from such fun.

It was a cheating song in the classic mold, owing a lot to Jimmy Hughes's "Steal Away," the classic from the pioneering days of the Shoals. Clarence's vocal is fervent and rough. "We kinda built everything around him and his guitar lick," observed Jimmy Johnson, but even more than those hoarse shouts and that biting guitar lead, Tommy's springing bass line is what listeners recall, even if they do not know who it is. Spooner Oldham recalled that "the session went swimmingly" and both he and Roger Hawkins remembered it well. "Tommy brought a clarity to Clarence's music," Hawkins observed. "Once you heard the bass line that he played, it was a signature bass line. . . . When you hear that record playing, you know it's 'Slip Away.' It's not a part that is beyond an average bass player's ability to play, but Tommy produced that part in his mind and he executed it." Though Hawkins said, "I didn't know it would be a signature part," he did remember feeling amazed at how Tommy's contribution helped the others: "I played a simple part, not anything very hard, but with Tommy's bass it was very easy. I was just playing quarter notes." "The bass, he killed me," said Jimmy Johnson of Tommy's contribution, on this record as well as all the others. "I learned from Tommy," said David Hood. "I was trying to do session work [David was making the transition from occasional trombone player to full-time bassist with the Fame studio band]. When I heard him I said, 'Gosh, I might as well just give up.'

He knew a lot about chords and the way chords were made up on the bass line."

It was while listening to playbacks, Roger Hawkins noted, that Tommy's strengths as a leader emerged. "No matter how good or how bad it was, he would not show too much emotion. It was as if he was listening to it or feeling it. Then he would casually make comments or suggestions. If he just made a comment, it commanded attention." Tommy's own work was often praised during playbacks, as at other times, and Mike Leech remembered how he handled it. "He was very shy accepting [compliments]," said Mike. "Sometimes you would think he didn't hear you . . . no reaction whatsoever. Then if there was a reaction, it would be a blush or a silly grin." In Muscle Shoals, Jimmy Johnson observed the same thing. "He didn't like people stroking him," said Jimmy. "I think he knew what he was doing." Roger Hawkins noticed Tommy's skills as an editor: "If we did a four-bar turnaround, the little space between the chorus and next verse, Tommy would condense it to two bars. He'd be saying, 'What're we doing with those other two bars?'"

Tommy had a succinct production style as well, although Roger Hawkins and Jimmy Johnson both noticed that Tommy never discussed his upcoming projects. "He was never one to boast. I've tried to follow suit," said Jimmy. "He wouldn't command that you be aware of his presence," Hawkins said. "He could transfer knowledge to you in a way without your knowing he was. . . . He knew deeper things." This knowledge of hidden truths was shown in his collaboration with Chips on the Merrilee Rush ballad, "That Kind of Woman," a song written by Donna Weiss and Mary Unobski that got some radio airplay but did not catch on with the public.

"That Kind of Woman" is more typical of Chips Moman's work than of Tommy Cogbill's. The subject matter is somebody who apparently has been the "other woman" in a married man's life for some time, and the lyric runs through several of the emotions in Chips's repertoire, from self-pity to defiance. But the hammering piano at the start of the record is typical of Tommy (who always emphasized strong intros) and so are the small touches borrowed from "Angel": the drum taps and tempo changes are in evidence here, and the song builds to a climactic cry from John Hughey's overdubbed steel guitar. Listening, one first hears the placement of the sound; only after playing the 45 over many times does one realize that the crying steel depicts the anguish at which the lyric only hints. The steel guitar is mixed almost to blend with Merrilee's voice, so that its scream of agony becomes hers; the same can be said of the string line arranged by Mike Leech. The hammering piano is a woman's pounding heart, which is either joyful with anticipation or missing her lover when he goes home and back to his wife. It is a record about highs and lows: there is nothing in between, and since Tommy's vision again seems to take precedence over that of Chips, he implies that such love and pleasure comes at a terrible emotional price. "Tommy had his eye on the big picture," Roger Hawkins said, and his perspective here is not just the big picture of the record and how it would sound, but about the feeling behind the song's story line. A gentler mix of the song, with a rewritten, slightly more elaborate string line and the screaming steel faded down, was featured on Merrilee's album, but the softer mix seems out of character compared with the original's intensity. The song was a practice run for a song on one of the best-remembered records by the group—and also one of their finest.

Meanwhile, they had another challenge to face. The New Yorkers were so delighted with the American musicians that they planned to conduct an experiment. Atlantic had always been as much a jazz label as it had been one for R&B (Ahmet Ertegun, his brother Nesuhi, and Jerry Wexler were jazz buffs) and they had a strong roster of jazz vocalists and instrumentalists (Carmen McRae, Eddie Harris and Les McCann, the Modern Jazz Quartet, and Hubert Laws among them). The flautist Herbie Mann had made a few records in New York for their label, including a much-acclaimed live album, and it was time to give him a slightly contemporary direction, something that might let him cross over to the rock-oriented younger listeners who were buying records by Charles Lloyd,

Don Ellis, and the reinvented Miles Davis. Certainly he had the group for it: two advanced guitarists, Larry Coryell and Sonny Sharrock, the vibraphone player Roy Ayers, and the acoustic bassist Miroslav Vitous. Atlantic was curious: why not take the whole group to Memphis and see what happened when the New York jazzers met the good old boys?

Jazz was Tommy Cogbill's territory, but none of the others knew much about it. "I for one actually hated jazz," said Bobby Wood. "It all sounded alike to me." Yet there they were, scheduled to make an album with some progressive musicians from an entirely different field. Could they pull it off? Some of them were unsure in the beginning. "I knew I wasn't a jazzer," said Bobby Emmons. "Not that I didn't want to be, it was just that it took more time than I had to get into." "I didn't have a clue what I was doin', I never had been a jazz player," said Bobby Wood, who was sitting in on piano for this album. They were surprised to find themselves enjoying the challenge. Bobby Wood described it as "a lot of fun after I figured out we were supposed to do our thing and let Herbie and the jazz guys do theirs." "It was total freedom, it wasn't so structured like we normally did," said Reggie Young delightedly. "[You'd] turn the tape on and just the rundowns are— man, you can't get any better than that." Not only did they enjoy the adventure that doing such an album offered them, but their personalities fit well with those of the jazz players. "They couldn't have been nicer," Reggie said happily. "I was amazed at the musical ability of all of 'em."

The second most knowledgeable person about jazz around the place was Mike Leech, who owned some jazz albums and had done a fair amount of listening to it back in his club days. It is no surprise that he sounds so relaxed and confident on this album, never more so than on the title track, "Memphis Underground," where he and Gene Chrisman drive the sound, never losing the groove or dropping a thread. Don Crews remembered that this was the track they recorded first. "Well, it was fresh," he said, accurately summing up the appeal of the tune. "We cut it in about the second take."

"Herbie was big on first takes," added Bobby Wood. "I think he knew that doing a song over and over loses the groove and just never feels as natural as those first or second takes."

"Guys like Herbie Mann and Roy Ayers, they play so great that they're probably gonna hit on something they love on the first take," said Bobby Emmons. "A lot of mistakes, with an unprepared rhythm section, is something those sessions definitely *didn't* need." Mike Leech in particular liked Herbie and thought him a very nice man. Reggie Young also liked working with the flautist: "I remember Herbie Mann being an excellent, excellent, *excellent* player," he said. "I don't recall his shirt being on the whole time he was there." It was Indian summer in Memphis, the stickiest time of year for a river town, and the building's air conditioner was broken. It should have made for a somewhat unpleasant atmosphere: nonetheless, everyone remembered the sessions going well with a minimum of discomfort.

Larry Coryell's slide guitar on "Memphis Underground" is almost as rollicking as Reggie's, and his personality was notable: Mike Leech, Reggie Young, and Bobby Wood all remembered one peculiarity. "Coryell, after the 'Memphis Underground' cut and we were listening back, started jumping up and down, and hopped out the front door, hopped all the way around the building, hopped in the back door," Mike chuckled. The other guitarist, the African American Sonny Sharrock, was just as memorable, not so much for eccentric behavior as for the buzzsaw distortion he used not only on "Memphis Underground" but even more emphatically for the extended workout on "Hold On I'm Coming." "I think Sonny put his hands over the guitar and raked the strings, *rrrrrr*," Reggie Young remembered. Bobby Wood thought it was "weird": "He'd just slide up and down and make weird noises, I'd never seen anything like it in my life," he said. "Man, this guy ain't showin' me *nothin'*!" Gene Chrisman said emphatically. "I call it 'narcotic music.' It don't mean nothing." Mike Leech chuckled with amused exasperation at Gene's musical conservatism. "Sharrock was just what was needed on 'Memphis Underground.' Sure

it was crazy stuff but it broke the monotony of the cut. It did not, after all, change chords anywhere in the song."

"Hold On I'm Coming" also featured Herbie's bassist, the Czech player Miroslav Vitous, whose intricate fingering on the acoustic bass was intently observed by both Tommy Cogbill and Mike Leech. "Cogbill was eyein' him up and down, man," laughed Bobby Wood. "The story we, Tommy and I, heard about Miroslav is that while he was studying bass he listened to rock radio, not realizing the bass he was hearing was bass guitar, or Fender-type bass," said Mike Leech admiringly. "Subsequently he learned to play stuff he had heard on acoustic bass. He therefore had tremendous chops for acoustic. . . . He was amazing to watch." "Oh man! I remember Miroslav, seems like when he was there the Russians sent tanks into Czechoslovakia and he was really concerned with that," said Reggie Young. "Miroslav was just a super, super nice man; we were sorta in awe at him." Roy Ayers also made a favorable impression, so much that he was warmly welcomed by the group when he returned some months later to do an instrumental solo album there.

The Gary U.S. Bonds classic, "New Orleans," with Tommy Cogbill in his element playing an intricate bass line, is unfortunately treated as a throwaway: one would have liked to hear a little more of him in this setting. "Chain of Fools" features him in a more extended format, one of the few hints of his jazz playing on record; as always, he leads the way, establishing ever-changing tempos and at one point near the end of the song he seems to be calling for another rapid mood shift by means of some intricate bass passages, and the other musicians pull him back, settling him down for the slower pace needed to end the recording.

The album's masterwork is the version of "Battle Hymn of the Republic" which closes the record. It was a fitting requiem to a year filled with assassinations and riots, a year that was one of the most turbulent in the nation's history. Bobby Emmons's introductory organ line sounds as if it is in mourning. Mike Leech's emphatic bass notes and Gene Chrisman's light drum taps further emphasize that this is a song to be taken seriously, and though the pace slowly picks up it never achieves exhilaration. Finally it comes back down to earth after a short flight, anchored once again by Mike's bass and Emmons's organ: the flute dies out as if concluding a prayer.

Once again the group had taken a chance and it had worked. When *Memphis Underground* was released the following summer, it was an out-of-left-field sensation. "That album stayed in the jazz charts for a year," said Gene Chrisman, with evident pride and amazement. "We was playin' soul jazz," said Bobby Wood. To people who were already fascinated with the work of the group, the real delight was the photo on the back of the album cover; it afforded collectors and avid listeners the first glimpse of the studio.

"The picture was taken from an odd place," Mike Leech remarked. "Whoever took it was in the rafters next to the barber shop [on the other side of the wall]. . . . Just to the left of Sonny Sharrock is a door that led to what used to be part of the Ranch House, where private parties or banquets were held." The entrance to the studio from the outside hall is at the upper right-hand corner of the photo, with the infamous heater just above it. "On almost every record cut during the winter, Emmons would shut it off but it would cycle on once more sometimes during the songs," Mike recalled. "I never noticed hearing it but it for sure would come on in the middle of a cut." Reggie Young dominates the photo since he is in the middle of the room where the string sections usually congregated for overdubs, and not in his usual spot, which is where Larry Coryell, in his striped shirt, stood. The control room was located just to the right of Coryell and Sharrock, invisible from the photo's angle.

In the center of the photograph, just behind Reggie Young, is a temporary isolation booth set up for Roy Ayers and his vibraphone. "Sometimes horns would be in that area, such as they were during Joe Tex's stuff," said Mike Leech. "String players sat all over the place. Sometimes we would have twenty or thirty players so we had to make do." It is a great disappointment that Tommy's bass spot is not visible: it was to

the right of Emmons and Wood, who are seen in the picture. Emmons especially is noticeable; he is playing the Hammond B3 and we also see an electric Yamaha keyboard, dubbed "the Jap" by the musicians (in a masterstroke of political incorrectness). Mike Leech preferred a spot just a few feet away from Tommy's, and his space is also not pictured. Tommy's bass amp was draped with an old quilt, for extra padding and muffling, and he kept his workspace meticulously neat, unlike Mike's space, which he admitted was chaotic.

The control room and its setup had changed very little from when the modular board had been installed in 1967. The console where Chips Moman, Dan Penn, and Tommy Cogbill oversaw some of American's greatest records, and from which Tom Dowd, Darryl Carter, and Ed Kollis engineered, remained in place until 1971, when the sixteen-track was installed. For now, they were doing well enough with the Scully 8-track 280, which sat to the right of and against the gray formica cabinet that housed the console. The console had a switch above the EQ knobs that, when it was switched to the left, fed what Hayward Bishop, who later worked as assistant engineer, recalled as "four buses set up to work with the two assign switches to determine the feed to tracks one through four." The remaining tracks were fed by clicking that same switch to the right. "And that's about as technically deep as the setup got!" Hayward laughed. To the left of the mix switch, there was a telephone, "so that songs could be played or recorded through the phone line," he added. Behind the engineer's chair sat the four-track, two-track, and mono machines, and an AG-440 Ampex three-track was stored in a lounge back of the control room. Over in the corner, to the left of the four-track, was the power-supply cabinet, roughly the size of a radio station transmitter. Five McIntosh tube amps sat on a piece of orange-painted plywood to the right of the mixer. Three of those amps powered the two echo chambers as well as a smaller plate echo chamber at the rear of the studio. One amp powered the three A-7 monitors, which stood on a shelf just above the control room window. The remaining amp powered the center monitor and the talkback. Between the console and the control-room window was the by-now-infamous sofa, where the musicians sat beneath the overhead monitors and listened to playbacks. Chips kept the tape boxes off to the side, on a shelf running the length of the south control-room wall.

"I believe that one of the reasons the room sounded so good is because of a bass trap above the control room that had a lattice and fabric grille over the opening on the studio side of the wall and above the control-room window," Hayward observed. The lattice seemed to catch sound, reflecting it as the musicians played. The big, boomy effect of the recordings from American was probably as much due to this as it was to the sound of the tube amps and Chips's extensive use of echo.

Atlantic, of course, was delighted with the results of this project. No sooner had Tom Dowd finished with this one than he came back to Memphis for another—now considered one of the most important recordings ever to have come out of American (so important that an entire book has been devoted exclusively to it), although it was not particularly noticed at the time.

The recording is *Dusty in Memphis*, a title that was something of a misnomer, since she actually did only a few work vocals at American; she and the Sweet Inspirations laid the completed vocals down in New York (the reason being, according to the Atlantic people, that she was terribly intimidated and insecure).

Dusty Springfield was already known in her native Britain as a brilliant pop singer with a special love for American soul music. Atlantic acquired her contract from the European Phillips label, where she had recorded from the beginning of her career in 1964. For all those years, she complained that she had been treated like a puppet in the studio; much of her material, chosen and arranged in advance by Ivor Raymonde, was standard nightclub fare that, given the beauty of her voice, she could deliver but that was not close to her heart. When she had a choice, she much preferred singing the work of Carole King or the latest Motown writers, and she gave Burt Bacharach songs like

"The Look of Love" a rare sophistication and sensuality. She had been wanting to get away from torch songs and nightclub ballads for a while, beginning with her recording of the theme from the movie *The Sweet Ride* earlier in the year. Lee Hazelwood's cynical lyrics are an odd fit with her vulnerable voice, but the pairing stood her in good stead for the type of mood her new album would convey. It was Aretha all over again, as her work with these players gave listeners a sense of the real Dusty for the very first time.

It was not an album "in Memphis" from her choice of writers, either; she was given the run of the finest Brill Building material, and she chose a beauty to start the record off. "Just a Little Lovin'," a gemlike song from Barry Mann and Cynthia Weil, not only celebrates love in the morning, somewhat in the style of the Glen Campbell and Bobbie Gentry duet on Gentry's song "Morning Glory," but is also a joyful celebration of the unconventional, night-owl life the group was leading. Love in the morning was inevitable for people who worked all night, although given their chronic state of exhaustion this too could be chancy. "We didn't have time for sex, whaddaya talkin' about???" whooped Bobby Wood gleefully. "Sex was the number after five!"

This album was Bobby's first as a permanent part of the band. He had chosen not to throw in his lot with the Dixie Flyers at the old warehouse where Stan Kesler and that band had begun working. However, a version of the classic "No Not Much" that he, Dickie Lee, Knox Phillips, and Allen Reynolds (who would later work with Garth Brooks) had co-produced for Allen's group The Smoke Ring at the Phillips Studio became a hit that fall. Recording sessions for Stan's new group were sporadic, and Bobby did not remember doing much with them anyway. American was doing so well that he could be guaranteed a regular income—an important incentive for a young man who had just started his family. The custom label with Bell and the creative freedom to record anything the group liked was also a contributing factor: Bobby could hold out the hope for a solo deal, and that one of his records might catch on. There was an advantage in the fact that, like Dan Penn and Spooner Oldham when they had joined, "I wasn't a greenhorn to Chips and the studio;" and he was especially close to Gene Chrisman (by contrast, the late arrivals were relatively unknown quantities when they showed up). Mike Leech described what Bobby Wood brought to the table: "Good solid player, would carry the ball on tempos, direction." He also brought a wild sense of humor, with sharp verbal skills and a literal eye for practical jokes, since he used his glass eye to get people laughing.

His contributions are immediately evident on the second track, one of the Carole King compositions, "So Much Love." Bobby's piano line anchors the track and carries the melody, sustaining the mood of gratitude for the duration of the song, as he also does for the Randy Newman tunes "Just One Smile" and "I Don't Want to Hear It Anymore." With Bobby Wood in the lineup, the group closed ranks; from then on the two Bobbys, Mike Leech, and Gene Chrisman would see themselves—along with Tommy Cogbill, who did not bother with such classifications, and Reggie Young, who seemed to be above it all—as the core group, the center.

"Son of a Preacher Man," written by John Hurley and Ronnie Wilkins at Tree, is of course the hit from the album, and it was just as memorable for the group as it was for listeners. "The intro on my part came from some kinda Chet Atkins influence—the harmonic influence," Reggie Young said of his commanding announcement at the start of the recording. "To this day, people will say, 'Oh, that's Reggie, he played on 'Son of a Preacher Man,'" the guitarist added. But, as he was the first to concede, this time it was not his show—"Cogbill! That's a Cogbill record!" he exclaimed—and it is true. Tommy's accelerated fadeout is breathtaking: in listening, one imagines his fast fingers sliding over the bass strings.

Gene Chrisman remembered that Tommy greased the strings with Vaseline for a smoother sound. David Hood recalled this, too. "He'd dip his fingers in Vaseline," said the Shoals bassist. "I carried a jar of Vaseline for *years*" in

an attempt to duplicate Tommy's technique—which of course, David admitted, nobody really could. Tommy's work on "Preacher Man" is a touchstone, studied and copied by virtually everyone who has picked up a bass since then. As with some of Jamerson's bass lines from Motown, Tommy's part here freed the way bass players approached a song. David Hood remembered how it changed: "At that time, the bass became a more busy instrument," he said; spurred on by Wexler—who had gotten thoroughly spoiled by Tommy's playing—Hood devoted hours to learning and mastering Tommy's style (though he acquired his own distinctive voice).

Tommy Cogbill and Reggie Young team up again for the Carole King tune "Don't Forget about Me," the autobiographical piece about the end of her marriage to Gerry Goffin. Tommy's overdubbed acoustic guitar slashes through Dusty's pleas and the gospel shouts of the Sweet Inspirations to set up Reggie's vibrating solos. His descending bass lines tumble gracefully into the choruses, slowly preparing the listeners for the maelstrom of emotion they will find there. But though Tommy could play with white-hot passion, when the song called for it he could be a master of understatement. This quieter approach can be heard in the track from the album that listeners over the years seem to have found the most memorable—and the easiest with which to identify—the composition by Eddie Hinton and Donnie Fritts, "Breakfast in Bed."

Here was the song that the Merrilee Rush single had anticipated, another song written from the mistress perspective. "Beautiful song," sighed Reggie Young. It is a loving, sensuous recording, with Dusty's tender vocals and Tommy and Reggie gently accenting the story line. The "other woman" in the song seems to be a refuge for her aggrieved and aggravated lover, who turns to her after having been hurt yet again by his wife. She offers him breakfast and a place to lie down, take off his shoes, and rest awhile; she asks nothing of him and is happy just to see him again.

Dusty got the song from some demos Wexler already had; the writers tailored the tune with her in mind after Wexler told them she would be recording with him. Donnie Fritts came up with the title, and had a little chord progression. "The melody I had in my mind, there was a little chord change from another song of the time—it was like a note from 'Moon River,'" Donnie chuckled. The progression from "Moon River" is the "huckleberry friend" phrase—anyone humming it can hear the similarity to the opening line that Reggie Young states with a bluesy, bitter guitar intro. "We took a lot of time on that song," Donnie remembered, adding that it came together in two or three writing sessions, rare for them as they were used to coming up with something quickly. "Eddie came up with those great first lines," he remarked. "We both kind of talked it out." Dusty Springfield was the most important artist thus far who had recorded something they had written.

"Eddie and I were so honored," said Donnie gratefully. "It was just amazing, that record is one of the greatest honors I've ever received." For two struggling writers to have suddenly been given an album cut among songs by Carole King, Randy Newman, and Burt Bacharach was honor enough; but that listeners, critics, and musicians all considered that song the equal of those done by the established writers was an even greater tribute. And the impact of the song only began with Dusty's recording. It became a standard, especially among jazz vocalists: Carmen McRae, for example, did a version with the Dixie Flyers some years later. "I've met some reggae guys in England, when they found out we wrote that they were on the floor," Donnie remarked. "I've met people from Jamaica who just worshipped the song."

"Windmills of Your Mind" was a song that on the surface would have seemed out of character, not only for Dusty, but for the American group to try; it was the theme from the movie *The Thomas Crown Affair*, and its long phrases and sophisticated outlook hinted at jazz. Reggie Young proved himself equal to carrying the piece, and his acoustic lead was compelling. It is also remarkable because of Bobby Emmons's conga playing: there was no permanent percussionist at that point, and those accents were contributed by anyone who felt that the track needed it. For example, on the Burt Bacharach "Land of Make-Believe," the conga is provided by Mike Leech, who was otherwise an onlooker for most of the session: Reggie's electric sitar is also featured. The electric sitar, Reggie added as an aside, had been developed in New York by the session guitarist Vincent Bell (who later recorded the *Airport* theme). On this album, as with the Box Tops recording, Reggie makes the instrument his own. "Reggie was always experimenting," chuckled Mike Leech. "He once saw an ad in a magazine about a 'magnetic pick,' which he ordered, thinking it could get a different sound. It was simply a pick you could stick to your guitar when not using. We and he got a big chuckle on that one."

"No Easy Way Down" is one of the strongest Carole King songs, and Bobby Wood's emphatic piano underscores the lyric about loss and decline. He is also a big contributor to the final track on the album, "I Can't Make It Alone," another Carole King tune full of soulfulness and pride. His thick, gospel-style chords fill out the sound and give the midrange, previously occupied by Bobby Emmons alone for the most part, additional depth and volume. "I was kind of trying to just fit in to the situation," Bobby said, sounding insecure despite the fact that he had already proven himself on a number of the group's important recordings. "I remember being given some direction from Arif and Tom Dowd and maybe even Wexler."

The musicians found Dusty to be sweet, rather intimidated by them, and very shy. "She was quite a professional. I don't think she was very happy when we started . . . she seemed to be in awe," said Reggie Young admiringly. "She seemed to have a great time; I found out later that she was scared to death." Bobby Wood offered a dissenting view. "I thought Dusty was a little strange at that time but didn't dare to voice my opinion," he said. "Dusty was just withdrawn and appeared to not want to be there, unlike most artists we worked with. She just didn't hardly have anything to say. She seemed to not be familiar with the songs." "She was kind of prim and proper," said Bobby Emmons. "Actually the princess of prim and proper to date at American." Mike Leech agreed with that assessment, finding her to be "a bit stuffy." "I was disappointed to read that she never liked recording with us, or the project," he added. Mike Leech, Reggie Young, and Bobby Emmons all amusedly remembered her rehearsing in the upstairs offices, singing scales before she came down to work, and everyone recalled the wrap party at the Holiday Inn Rivermont which ended, according to a recollection left by Tom Dowd, with one of Dusty's famous food fights, with much champagne sprayed around (Tommy Cogbill's amusement at such a scene can well be imagined).

Her perfectionism in the studio not only matched but surpassed their own. She was by her own admission so awed by being in the same place where Wilson Pickett and Joe Tex had worked that she could hardly concentrate enough to sing. "We kind of have a difference of memory about Dusty singing on the sessions," said Bobby Wood. "I don't think she sang much but it was enough for us to get the recording spots together. I remember Arif or someone doing some of the scratch vocals too." According to Donnie Fritts, that someone else may have been his writing partner; he and Eddie Hinton came up to hear their song recorded and he recalled Eddie doing the work vocal for that track.

To Ed Kollis, who was not doing any of the engineering but who was nonetheless at the studio observing, the most interesting thing about the sessions was the chance it gave him to watch Wexler and Dowd at work. "They were appreciative, well, they made a lot of money off us," he said. "Wexler was as cool as could be, Dowd was enamored of my energy and enthusiasm." Ed also remembered that the New Yorkers took every advantage of the opportunity to sample Southern cooking. "They liked Pyrtle fried chicken. It's a local Memphis brand. It's so greasy it's gotta give you a heart attack within a week—it was wonderful!" laughed the soundman.

"By the time she left, she still wasn't pleased with her performance," Reggie Young noted. "When they left with the tracks, they were pretty bare," observed Bobby Wood. "Just rhythm tracks and pretty dry [no EQ]. Dowd usually recorded everything flat with no echo or anything." The musicians were proud of the album and felt they had really done something important. "I thought it was one of the best projects we'd done in a long, long while," said Reggie Young. "It's held up well over the years." "I was blown away by Arif's horn parts on it," said Bobby Emmons, referring to the work overdubbed in New York. "Have you ever noticed the contradiction between how aggressive the horns are and how subtle everything else is on 'Preacher Man'? Now *that's* a perfect balance!"

"We thought the finished product was great," said Bobby Wood enthusiastically. "When that record came out, I remember everybody in the studio got this funky little record player and was amazed" at the beauty of the album, Ed Kollis said. "That's a great record," Donnie Fritts sighed with quiet satisfaction about the entire project. "I don't see how it kept from being such a huge hit because everybody we knew loved it. As far as people in the music business goes, *everybody* loved that album." Chips Moman was often credited for the record as he was for the Herbie Mann album, even though he had nothing to do with either project beyond having the Atlantic crew come to his studio. "I've told a bazillion people that I didn't do them," Chips said exasperatedly, amazed at the persistence of the myth. "Tom, Jerry, and Arif were doing the production; we was just helpin' 'em get it together," said Don Crews. "Ol' Chippo was jealous of that," Ed Kollis noted amusedly.

Chips may have been slightly envious, but he relished the time away from the studio more than ever; he had golfing, waterskiing, his racetrack, and his animals to keep him busy, and a new hobby, airplanes. He had loved them ever since he was a boy, even going so far as to haunt airports to watch them the way others his age were fascinated with trains; and he had taken flying lessons, qualified as a pilot, and bought his own small plane. The freedom he now had to pursue his hobbies far outweighed the chance to be working on a landmark recording. The irony is that Dusty had always wanted more creative control, what Reggie Young referred to as "getting her involved in her own music"; in Memphis she had it, but she was so frightened by the freewheeling work of the American group that in the end she resorted to the same method she had used before, standing alone in a New York studio and singing to the basic tracks fed her through the headphones.

Glen Spreen observed some of the concluding work on Dusty's album; he was finally out of the Army and there for good, so eager to start working at American that he did not even go home to Texas first. As usual, creating places for people if someone seemed to be able to contribute something, Chips hired Glen at the behest of Mark James and B.J. Thomas, making Glen a staff writer for Press at the sum of seventy-five dollars a week. Seventy-five dollars went a fairly long way in 1968, and Glen was staying with Mark until he could become accustomed to the city and find a place to live.

The group, which had just recently closed ranks after Wood's official entry, could not figure out what to make of the late arrival. They did not know him all that well; they saw him as Mark's friend and were not sure what he could contribute. Even his appearance was off-putting to most of them. They had never been around hippies before: Johnny Christopher was in disguise at this point, and Ed Kollis was at the time more of a beatnik (though that would change). Spooner Oldham, with his gentle manner and his beard, was probably the closest thing to a hippie they had seen, but Spooner was so much himself that he never seemed threatening. This new guy was something else.

He had bright red hair and horn-rimmed glasses: most of the group had sedate brown hair, ranging in color from Mike Leech's sandy shock to the darker brown of Emmons and Wood: only Tommy Cogbill had black hair (which went gray in a few years' time). His eyes seemed almost too watchful; Mike thought they were feral (actually Glen's eyes were an unusual combination of fierce and sad). His hair was long and wooly and he wore sandals, dashiki shirts over jeans, and his Army field jacket. Eventually he grew a beard, and because of it, he remembered later, "the guys called me paintbrush." Mike Leech recalled hearing some

comments: "Who's that freak?" "What's he doing here?" "Who's that redheaded asshole?" Glen remembered no outward hostility despite his awareness that he was different from the group. His year of college set him apart; so did his months in California with all the implications of exposure to that lifestyle, as well as his Army experience and his aloofness. Mike Leech remembered that Glen "appeared a bit nerdy but covered that by being cool. [He] had a trick of flipping a cigarette from the palm of his hand to his lips."

As would all of the late arrivals, Glen had vivid first impressions, of the group, the studio, and Chips. "Every one of those guys is sincere," he said feelingly about the musicians, adding that his favorite of them was and would always be Tommy. Their recording methods, he admitted, took some getting used to. "Previously, I would walk into a studio, meet the engineer, and pretty much get down to business with time as my challenge," he observed. "These guys set around, talked, played darts before and during the session." Glen did not know it, but this good-old-boy atmosphere was driving the musicians crazy: "We'd go in after lunch, after noon and we'd hear whatever was going on in Moman's life, about his horses and stuff, *all day long* and we'd wonder, when are we *ever* gonna cut?" said Reggie Young, remembering how exasperating this could be. And then there were the endless takes and retakes once work began. "All the wives were exasperated by Moman—I mean, forty takes of 'Hooked on a Feeling' can take awhile," laughed Ed Kollis. But Glen was new to it, and he was intrigued: "Chips . . . was self-taught, like me, and he was, in my opinion, creative and unique." Chips was so instinctive in his production and effects that he initially confused the admittedly more technically minded newcomer. "For example, Chips said, 'cross over.' That was his description for phasing." (Glen was no doubt amused by Chips's habit, when giving direction to the group on the floor, of requesting that the rhythm or volume be changed "just a scosh.") "I remember once that Chips bet he could throw a card over the building," added the late arrival, echoing Roger Hawkins's memories of the hustles down in the Shoals. "Everything stopped while he tried."

The group maintained their misgivings about the newcomer, feeling that Mark James had somehow forced him on Chips and, by default, upon them. They did not include him in the teasing that was so much a part of their way of relating to each other, falling back on standard Southern politeness when they dealt with him. Glen responded with his characteristic aloofness (born of shyness, he said) which further distanced the group. It was a vicious circle, and nobody seemed to know how to stop it. Glen was a new kind of person for them, and as if his own hippie ways were not enough, there was the presence of his wife Judy, who had musical aspirations herself—like her husband, she was a keyboard player. She often accompanied him to the studio and perched on the back of the control-room couch, her long legs dangling from her miniskirt, excitably talking in what seemed to the musicians to be a mile a minute—a complete opposite from her husband, who rarely delivered comments or opinions. "We all were a little bit overwhelmed by this invasion of the 'cool hip people,'" Mike Leech observed.

The personalities of the other wives varied, but they had one thing in common—they preferred to stay away from the studio, though they were not officially barred. "I think they realized that by being there, they stifled our creativity," Mike Leech reflected. "Mainly because our ability to create depended not only on our musicianship, but also on our studio attitude, which was much different than our home attitude. We wore one hat for work, another for home, and the spouses could see that. It was almost embarrassing when a wife showed up because the husband had to change hats, and it was obvious. Plus, it was boring for them. . . . You could almost hear the sigh of relief when [one of the wives] left." Thus, to see someone's wife in the studio was jarring, surrealistically out of place. Judy Spreen was the first of a new kind of woman—assertive and aggressive—that the group would see, and they had the same reaction to her as they would later on when Shane Keister brought in his wife Alice

and Chips Moman took up with the New York songwriter Toni Wine.

As could perhaps be predicted, two exceptions to the way Glen was regarded came from Tommy Cogbill and Spooner Oldham. "Tommy was welcoming. He treated all the same," said the late arrival. Spooner did not feel threatened either. "I saw this influx of Texans around as a good thing, there were more writers around," he said warmly. Already the piano player was expanding his horizons, collaborating with Mark James on a few songs here and there, and one of them, chosen by Chips, was a definitive track on an upcoming album.

The album was *On My Way*, the culmination of nearly a year's worth of work with B.J. Thomas (as such, it surely holds the world's record for longest period of pre-production, at least for that time). Already the album had yielded two hits, both written by Mark James: the prophetic (for Chips) "Eyes of a New York Woman"—a title Chips himself had suggested to Mark—and the larger success, both in prestige and chart appearance, "Hooked on a Feeling." "New York Woman" features Reggie Young's sitar and Ed Kollis's harmonica over a propelling basic track that evokes rushing traffic and racing subways; Mike Leech's string line drifts through the sound like leaves swirling in the wind. The lyrics convey the elegance of both the city—"East Side cafes, West Side plays"—and the woman, and Chips adds an element of pure exhilaration. He carried that over into "Hooked on a Feeling" as well.

"Hooked" is the better-known song, not only for its 1974 remake by Blue Swede which used African-sounding chants at the beginning of the record, but for its use to accompany the famous dancing baby on the TV show *Ally McBeal*. The original was about neither African chants nor maternal longings, but about the first dizzying rush of love. Mark James was so clever in his linking of love with addiction that a year or two later the song was dissected, to his amazement, for possible drug references. If there were any, it was only in the mind of the singer, for B.J. was beginning to develop problems with pills, a story he told in his 1978 autobiography. For now he was able to stay more or less together, and everyone remembered how easily these sessions went.

"Hooked on a Feeling" is an elegant record, not only due to the wordplay of Mark James's lyrics and the uncharacteristically euphoric mood from Chips, but from Mike Leech's sustaining string line, Reggie Young's electric sitar, and for the experimental, overdubbed percussion. On the album version, the knocking, clanging sound is only heard after the second line of the second verse: on the single, Chips added it to the first line as well—an example of his perfectionism. It was a completely spontaneous creation, Gene Chrisman remembered. "On 'Hooked on a Feeling,' there was an ashtray lid, tambourine, and tape box. That was the sound. The box and lid were struck with a stick and the tambourine was played by hand. I think there were two of us that did that because one lick was right after the other. I don't remember doing all three of them together," the drummer explained. "As I remember, something delayed Chips's arrival in the studio for the workup, and we had it pretty much together by the time he got there," said Bobby Emmons. "There were a couple of arrangement things he didn't agree with, but he liked the groove and I guess he was afraid we'd lose it in trying to tear it apart and make changes at that point, so he cut it the way it was and then later edited it with a razor blade." Glen Spreen could pinpoint the exact moment of the splice: Reggie Young's sitar solo midway through the recording. Reggie himself delighted in Gene Chrisman's contribution and credited the success of the record to its experimental sounds. "Whatever came natural is what happened there [in Memphis]," Reggie recalled joyfully. "We'd all be sittin' on the floor doin' a tape box or something, you'd never do that here [in Nashville ]."

As was the custom in those days, particularly for country singers (even the ones who were often on the pop charts, like Glen Campbell and B.J.), several cover versions of contemporary songs were featured on the album. The American version of the Ray Stevens classic "Mr. Businessman" is even more biting than the original—Chips was obviously delighted to tell the suits what he thought of them, and Tommy Cogbill's bass and Spooner Oldham's piano (he and Bobby Wood divided lead keyboard chores on this album) stomped and pounded in agreement. Mike Leech remembered problems with the track. "The horns were an integral part of that arrangement," he explained. "They *never* got it right. I became exasperated and walked out of the studio, telling them to do it *their* way, since they couldn't do what was written. They got p.o.'d but I didn't care."

The cover of Jose Feliciano's flamenco-tinged "Light My Fire" (originally, of course, the Doors' classic) went effortlessly by contrast, and again, as on "Windmills of Your Mind," Reggie Young negotiates jazz-style lines. Mike Leech's string arrangement commands attention also, as his melodic passages blend effortlessly with B.J.'s voice. Thus far, Chips had avoided his trademark melancholy, enjoying the fresh sound the new songs called for: with the next few selections, however, he pulled the mood back into familiar territory, a state of mind that the later arrival Hayward Bishop jokingly called "the black hole."

Ferlin Husky's classic "Gone," for example, is one long shout of pain to begin with, and Chips pulls out all the stops to accentuate it, from Reggie Young's screaming lead to Mike Leech's grieving string line. B.J. wails so effortlessly that Chips could not resist the temptation to treat the vocal as another instrument. "Four Walls" offers more of the same, its agony only slightly offset by a swaying, Willie Mitchell–style horn riff. "Smoke Gets in Your Eyes," with its similar swaying horn arrangement, attempts to be more reflective, but in the end Chips steers the production to the side of despondency. Ashford and Simpson's "I Saw Pity in the Face of a Friend" is the suspicious, prideful side of Chips, a side his musicians were all too aware he had. "Chips has got a thing where he doesn't trust anybody," said Bobby Wood. "But you can understand that because of all he went through." The song also describes Chips's usual way of handling anything he felt was a betrayal: "So I'm taking that road away from you, find myself a place to hide / And when people remember, they'll say, He was saving face and pride." All through the track, Tommy Cogbill's bass is imposed like a special effect upon the relentless paranoia.

Wayne Carson's "Sandman" had been recorded before. Dan Penn had cut a version for the Box Tops' third album featuring a sparkling string line from Mike Leech and Reggie Young's feedback-laden lead guitar. Chips chose to do it softly, emphasizing the gentleness of B.J.'s midrange narrating the story of a fiercely independent man (much like Wayne Carson himself, perhaps) laid low by love. Mike and Reggie are both still featured, but Reggie is playing a quiet acoustic guitar, and the string line is entirely new, elegant and understated. The mood is intimate, almost confessional, with emphasis on the vulnerability implied in the melody and the lyric.

If "Sandman" represents a private side of Chips, "I've Been Down This Road Before," a remarkable song written by Mark James and Spooner Oldham, is the greatest American Studios position paper ever—a summation of all that the group and its music stood for, artistically and philosophically. It almost defies written analysis, as it has to be heard—and even more to the point, lived—before it can truly be understood.

Ostensibly, as with many songs they recorded, it is about a love affair—in this case, one that is ending. But the writers, Chips Moman, and Mike Leech use that theme as a starting place to talk about heartache, despair, chronic hard luck, regret, and the inner strength it takes to face them. "I've walked along that road somewhere," B.J. sings in a voice of soaring beauty, "I've learned a lot then and there." Spooner Oldham's piano accents the track delicately and the unbroken line of Mike's string arrangement becomes part of the melody and can even be sung as such. "Time stood still, with darkness at my door / Yes, I've been down that road before," the song concludes. What Mark James and Spooner Oldham do not say, but what is clearly implied, is that having been through so much in the past gives one the ability to meet sorrow in the present—and the fortitude to face more

suffering in the future. And in that fortitude, Mike Leech's string line implies, is strength of character. It is a way of finding meaning and beauty in hard times and a hard life.

Mike was surprised to learn that his string lines could be seen as melancholy. "I never thought of them that way but it sounds nice," he said. "The only thing I can think of that would put my arrangements in that perspective is, I always tried to make the strings and horns fit the song, or the tenor of the song. Some arrangers overwrite and thereby do not complement the song or the artist—just meaningless notes. I always tried to keep my string lines simple. I think that's why the fake strings on keyboards don't sound just right . . . I think simple single-note lines have more of an impact than multiple notation for the most part.

"When I write string arrangements, I play the track over and over, experiment with lines, until one hits me that makes sense and that I like. This process can sometimes take all day or all night. Also while arranging, I will sometimes write the first thing that comes to mind, quickly. Now sometimes that works, sometimes it doesn't. There is something to be said for spontaneity.

"It depended on how quick Chips wanted the strings done where I would write. . . . There was usually no advance time (especially from Chips) and most of the time it was decided as soon as the track was finished. . . . If it was an all-nighter I would stay in the studio, and, depending on if anybody was using it, in the control room. Also, in Memphis, I never wanted to go home anyhow. I liked the studio much better. I seldom wrote at home.

"Recording the strings in the mornings after staying up all night was rewarding, made it worth it. Always a sigh of relief though, when it was finally done and over with."

Spooner Oldham did not remember pitching "I've Been Down This Road Before" to Chips—he guessed that Mark James did, and with Chips's knowledge of songs he must have known immediately what he had, since he deemed it important enough to make it the B-side of "Hooked on a Feeling." "It was put together wonderfully, I think; as a writer, what more could you ask?" said the piano player with quiet pride. He described the session with B.J. as effortless and, as did everyone else, thought the singer a joy to know. He remembered a night when he was out driving in the new '68 Cadillac El Dorado he had just bought ("It was my first new car, white with leather upholstery") and B.J. was with him. Spooner asked the singer if there was anything he would like to accomplish in his career that he had not already done, and the immediacy of the answer startled him. "Yes," B.J. said almost immediately. "Play Vegas." "It seemed so odd to hear that in the heart of Memphis," Spooner mused. "He had a dream, already."

Spooner was developing his own dream. He had slowly become disenchanted with Memphis since the King assassination, and he told his new fiancée Karen some of his misgivings. "I felt like Memphis, our part of the music, was dying," he reflected. "What made me think it was going to happen? I wonder." Then, during the B.J. Thomas sessions, "My shirts got stolen out of the back of my car. I had thirty-three tailor-made shirts from Tom James," he said, referring to a well-known tailor shop in Memphis. "Tom James had bolts of fabric; you'd just go in and pick a fabric, pick a color. These shirts were different colors, solids, stripes, some of 'em even had 'Spooner' embroidered on the French cuffs"—a seemingly flamboyant touch for such an understated man. "The window was broken, it was in the back parking lot at American," he continued. "Why anybody wanted thirty-three shirts that my mom had just washed and ironed, I'll never know." He went on to add that "oddly enough, I 'd never seen any other burglary activity," but he rightly guessed there would be more. Emory Gordy from Atlanta and several others were talking about moving out to California and setting up a collective to work sessions as a group. To Spooner, it sounded like an option worth investigating.

It was all the more worth looking over because Dan Penn was in the process of leaving. The reasons for the break remain unclear to this day, and if anything they have been further papered over by time. Even someone who was as close to both Chips and Dan as Spooner said of the reasons, "I don't know for sure." Dan Penn offered no more thoughts on the reasons why, beyond a throwaway remark about a few "promises made" that were not kept. It seemed to be at least in part due to Dan's view of how much he had done for the studio—given the group their biggest record and by default gotten them signed to a label—and how little recognition and credit he had gotten for it. "He considered he'd done so much he wanted a piece of the company," said Chips. "I said if you want a piece of the company, start your own. When you buy something with your own money," he explained, "you don't wanna share it with just anybody—I mean, I love to share, but . . ." And he faltered, seemingly unable or reluctant to elaborate further.

There was, of course, more to it even than that, although Chips said he never really understood what went wrong. "I still love Dan Penn, for sure," he sighed regretfully. A born leader, Dan wanted to call his own shots and set his own pace at working. He had started hanging around with Jim Dickinson, the piano player for the Dixie Flyers, and Dickinson was at the center of Memphis bohemian life. In many ways Dickinson had replaced Chips Moman and Spooner Oldham as the closest person to him. He knew he could always write, and he signed a short-term deal as an artist with Atlantic (only one 45 emerged, with Dickinson producing). What he needed for his purposes was a studio of his own, and it looked as if he were going to get it. His old bandmate from the Pallbearers, Jerry Carrigan, was willing to back him financially. In the interim, Dan and Spooner took refuge in a small office on Poplar Avenue that they temporarily used as a writing room. When Dan lost interest and they vacated it, Spooner bought from him their office piano.

Dan continued to be an innovator right up until the time of his departure, said Mike Leech, remembering a time when a thunderstorm hit Memphis and Dan wanted to capture the sound of it on tape. "He placed microphones out back under some awnings, umbrellas, what have you, loaded up the two-track machine and hit 'record.' It was a great storm, loud thunder cracks, lasted about an hour. When we went in to listen, Dan discovered he had threaded the two-track tape backwards, inside-out, so all he got was some muffled noises."

Neither Dan Penn nor Spooner Oldham ever regretted the time they spent at American. In many ways it had been even more productive than their years in the Shoals; their work had found a larger audience and their reputations would forever rest upon what they did with the group. "All those old days were great, I wouldn't take nothing for what I been through," said Dan Penn in summation. "All that stuff was fun to play on and be with the guys as we played it," said Spooner Oldham. And the break was by no means total. Spooner rejoined the group from time to time and played on sessions; Dan produced Ronnie Milsap's first album in 1971 using all the American musicians, and by the late seventies, when everyone had resettled in Nashville, he was writing for them again and occasionally taking on production tasks that utilized the group (though he also tried to include his friends from the Shoals— his ties there too remained strong).

Dan's and Spooner's departures (though Spooner did not officially leave Memphis until early 1969) would have been severe setbacks for the American group even a few months earlier; by now, with the core group cemented, one late arrival (Glen Spreen) on the scene, and one more (Johnny Christopher) waiting in the wings, there were more than enough voices to keep the momentum going. And it did not matter where Dan and Spooner went anyway. For the rest of their lives, they would be identified primarily as being from Memphis and having worked for Chips Moman (the four late arrivals would also discover this, each in their turn). Entering the orbit of American Studios was like becoming a guest at the Hotel California—you could check out any time you liked, but you could never leave.

CHAPTER 15

# People Sure Act Funny

The studio was established, the group was acquiring a reputation, and they were even beginning their own label, for which they all had high expectations. *Dusty in Memphis* had just come out and was being praised as a masterwork; several other albums, most notably the Herbie Mann jazz experiment, were either in the can or in some stage of recording.

For Chips Moman, it was amazing. "We were in a situation where we were making a living and feeding our families and payin' our light bills," he said, his voice reflecting the same astonishment he felt back then. "That was such a relief because Tommy and I had had it rough. Rough." His tone became somber at the memory. Though he didn't talk much about what he and Tommy had endured while they were struggling, he dropped just enough hints to a few friends to give them the picture. "They would write bad checks to each other; they'd pay each other," was one story Roger Hawkins heard. "Chips and Tommy would do a poker thing, hustling; they almost got shot once for it," Ed Kollis said. "I've heard stories that when they were struggling, barely getting by, one of 'em had a key, they'd turn on the gas [for each other]," said Reggie Young. "I just couldn't believe I was making a living playing music," was Chips's astonished conclusion. And though Tommy Cogbill, typically, did not talk about it, from all accounts he too was astonished. Not that they were alone; the others were delighted to be getting all the work they could handle, after years of scratching and scrambling to record. "To have four sessions a day in Memphis, Tennessee?—That was unheard-of!" exclaimed Bobby Emmons. "It was usually two a month!"

Now that everyone had a little money to play with, the toys got slightly more expensive. The parking lot in back of the studio was filled with cars like Chips's TR-3, Reggie Young's Pontiac Sunbeam, Mike Leech's Buick Riviera, Gene Chrisman's Chrysler New Yorker, Bobby Wood's 1960 Cadillac, and the Cadillac that was the first of several cars replacing Tommy Cogbill's beloved but beat-up Oldsmobile Cutlass (Mike Leech wanted to buy the Olds from Tommy, but he refused, saying that it was such a piece of junk it would not be worth the trouble to acquire). Though the cars of Dan Penn and Spooner Oldham were on the premises less and less as they weaned themselves from the scene, Dan's classic Duesenberg and Spooner's Cadillac could also still be found there at times. Even the new kid on the block was indulging himself a little: Glen Spreen had gone out and bought a foreign sports car, whose workings tended to mystify him. Mike Leech amusedly recalled one night when the mechanics of the car caught up with Glen. "He pulled up in the parking lot and asked me if I knew how to dim the lights, that he had driven all night all the way from wherever, where everybody was flashing their lights trying to get him to dim his. I got in the driver's seat and flipped a lever next to the steering column which dimmed the lights." Glen's response: "How the hell did you do that?" Only Bobby Emmons continued as ever, tooling around in an unpretentious Ford.

Chips had always loved motorcycles, and had gone riding with Bobby Wood in the early days; now several of the others owned bikes. Wayne Carson claimed credit for that one. "Hell, I'm the one that sold Dan his motorcycle!" he growled amusedly. "I had a 750 Norton before *any* of those guys had motorcycles!" Dan had gone to visit Wayne in Springfield for a week, and so admired what Wayne was riding that the writer took him to the same shop where he had bought his bike. "He bought it right there in Springfield, Missouri, with Box Tops [royalty] checks," Wayne continued.

Trail biking was another favorite pastime, and here Tommy Cogbill led the way. "Trail riding, absolutely," Mike Leech happily remembered. "Cog had trail bikes, Chips also. . .

. . I think [Tommy] also had a Harley." "Tommy had a Honda 750, it was all tricked out," said Ed Kollis. "Gene had a big Honda something. Chips (of course) had about six bikes. I never owned one but was welcome to go riding, which we did many times. I'm surprised I didn't kill myself. We hit a trail through a park outside of Memphis many times," Mike Leech continued. "I didn't get in on the trail bikes," said Bobby Wood. "I had a 450 Honda street bike. We would go cruising late at night either on the streets or take short trips down into Mississippi. It was me, Tommy, Gene, and sometimes Bob Taylor. I think Chips went with us a few times. There would be no one on the streets at three o'clock in the morning. It was a neat way of relaxing after all the long hours in the studio." "We would sometimes ride [our bikes] to the studio, go out together to eat, and sometimes at night some of us would ride down to Sardis Dam, about fifty miles south of Memphis," Gene Chrisman recalled. "We would just take the ride, get there, and sit around and talk about an hour, then come back home. [The bikes] were a lot of fun. I miss having one, but I'm a little scared to have one now in this crazy traffic like it is and the way that people drive."

Now and then they tried other ways to collectively let off steam. Golf was Gene Chrisman's cup of tea, and between his encouragement and that of Wayne Carson, who discovered the game when some friends in Springfield took him out on the course, most of the group tried it, with Chips Moman and Mike Leech becoming the sport's real devotees. Wayne Carson described the appeal of the game. "It's individual, it's a sport of honor, it's man against the elements," he said. "It's just you and a golf ball, the ball ain't goin' nowhere until you do somethin' to it." Chips's reason for golfing was more elemental. "Hell, he loved to gamble!" Wayne whooped delightedly.

"We bowled a few times, but it finally took a backseat to the studio activity," remembered Mike Leech. "We watched racing some. We did find a place on the outskirts we used as a drag strip. I think Cog and Chips took each other on one night. Don't remember the outcome." Bobby Wood did. "Chips and Tommy got to racing on the expressway at 150 miles an hour. I said, 'You're nuts.' [From Memphis to] Nashville was three hours and they made it in half an hour, driving at 130 miles an hour." (Skeptics have commented that they would have had to have driven at 400 miles an hour to have raced over two hundred miles, the distance between Memphis and Nashville, in the amount of time allotted by Bobby's estimate.) "At times there would be bets at the studio of whose cars could win in a quarter mile," the piano player continued. "That was usually between Ed Kollis and his antique Porsche and the . . . cars of Chips and Tommy." "I raced my Porsche against Chips's Cadillac in the fog somewhere in Millington," Ed laughed. "You had to have something to have a little hobby," shrugged Bobby Wood.

There was even time to rejoice in the success of friends. J.R. Cobb was back on the charts now; the Classics IV had another hit with a song J.R. and Buddy Buie had written. "Stormy" had almost a jazz feel, accentuated by a relaxed-sounding saxophone. The subject matter of a temperamental lover was territory Mark James would work later with his famous 1977 "Moody Blue" and definitely not the usual teenybopper fare. It was all part of his desire to write standards, said J.R.: he was still aspiring to leave an entry in the great American songbook. The suits at their label, Liberty out in California, had been pressuring him and Buie to write something similar to their first hit, so they crafted a song with similar mystery but slightly altered the woman's temperament. The end result was a softly sensual work that gained some attention for J.R. as a writer, since many listeners seemed to like his work (or perhaps the way Dennis Yost, singing exclusively now in his midrange whisper, elegantly delivered the lyrics).

Elegance was not a word commonly used to describe the American group's recordings. Dusty Springfield's album and the recent B.J. Thomas work were going a long way toward changing that perception, but to the outer world, Memphis musicians recording sad songs about life's hard choices was marginal listening at best. For example, no one would think

of having a middle-of-the-road vocalist, someone used to working with Marlene Dietrich's former musical director, come to American and do an album. But that's exactly what Burt Bacharach's and Hal David's favorite singer, Dionne Warwick, did in the fall of 1968. She was on the same label as B.J. Thomas and Ronnie Milsap, and her records were also being promoted by Steve Tyrell, so a visit to American was easy to arrange.

Her decision to work there may have been triggered by Aretha's comment that Dionne was not soulful (even though her early work with Bacharach had been considered the epitome of sophisticated R&B pre-Motown, and had greatly inspired the Muscle Shoals musicians). A woman who, like Aretha, had grown up singing gospel in the church, a former member of Cissy Houston's group—not soulful? "She set out to prove she was," said Reggie Young admiringly.

The photo on the album cover indicated that the music inside was going to be different: a cracked and patched stucco wall, with Dionne, clad in a printed tank top, leaning against it, her wig mussed and her expression bleak. It served notice—this would be a message from the other side of the tracks, where every day was a struggle. It was an even more stark image than Diana Ross and the Supremes donning sweatshirts to perform "Love Child" on the Ed Sullivan show: a signal that reality-based music was the way ahead. "Everyone has their own way of doing things, and singing R&B is no different—I had to do it my way," Dionne said in her handwritten liner notes. Doing it one's own way was a concept the American group could relate to, and the end result was one of their most unified works. That's especially surprising when considering some of the circumstances under which the recording was done.

Dionne was pregnant, with all the attendant hassles that can ensue. Chips was absent for much of the pre-production, so most of the songs were selected by Ed Kollis and Mike Leech. "He'd get gung-ho and then he'd get bored," Ima Roberts said about Chips's level of concentration. "Chips was more interested in Florence Greenberg's [the woman who owned and operated Scepter] money," laughed Ed Kollis. By now the arranger and the sound engineer had formed a staunch friendship, almost comparable to that of Chips and Tommy; Mike admired Ed's restless spirit and Ed trusted Mike's reliability. Ed and a Pepper-Tanner executive, Marty Lacker, had already collaborated on a recording, producing the first song ever recorded by Rita Coolidge (whom the group knew from her backup work at Hi and her jingle singing at Pepper-Tanner, under whose auspices the single was recorded).

"I remember Rita being quiet and shy. Loved her voice," said Mike Leech warmly. Marty Lacker chose both sides of the single; Johnny Christopher wrote the B-side, a mood piece called "Walkin' in the Mornin'." The A-side, a Donna Weiss composition called "Turn Around and Love Me," was the lament of an abused (whether physically or psychologically is unclear) woman, a subject that could have been played for sentiment but here is related matter-of-factly. It attracted some notice, going all the way to Number One on the West Coast and cementing Rita's professional reputation there.

"When I brought Rita Coolidge to American to cut, because Chips and Tommy were busy and I also knew that Bill Tanner of Pepper-Tanner wouldn't pay the normal upfront producer's fee, I decided to do it myself and asked Ed Kollis to co-produce because I did not know how to run the board," said Marty Lacker. Mike Leech was supposed to have gotten credit also, but his name was somehow left off the label when the record appeared. "I had no deal with Mike to produce and I am unaware whatever he and Ed discussed which is why Mike's name was not on the credits," added Marty. "I certainly would have given Mike credit if I had made the deal with him. I opted to leave my name off because credit didn't mean that much to me, I just wanted to cut a hit." For Mike Leech, it was another small incident that he would remember and re-evaluate, as he did about the royalty problems from his contributions to "The Letter." "I was sorely disappointed when my name didn't appear on the record as producer," said Mike, speculating that Chips

may have been afraid to give any more credit to someone from the group after Dan Penn and Tommy Cogbill had been so successful.

That's the way it looked to Ed Kollis, too. "Chips . . . didn't share with the group," observed the sound engineer. "Chips would say 'That's my diamond' when they were the ones who mined it." "Chips was complimentary, but when it came to getting what he wanted, if it came to our expense, that's what he would do," added Mike Leech, aware of the conflict between Chips's genuine desire to operate a collective and his equally strong wish to make the studio a one-man show. Ed Kollis wished that the group could have been even more of a collective, with all of the credit, critical acclaim, and press attention shared equally. "I didn't want to be communistic about it but you saw the work put out," he noted. Sitting in the engineer's chair beside Chips and listening to the comments he made while recording, all of the sound crew were aware of a side of their leader that the band out on the floor were not, and their estimates were colored by these observations.

For Dionne's project, Mike and Ed chose material that in the world of rhythm and blues could be classified as standards, offering at least some slight consistency with Dionne's previous style. There were compositions by Otis Redding, Mann and Weil, and Felix Cavaliere and Eddie Brigati of the Young Rascals. Two American group standards—"Do Right Woman" and "I'm Your Puppet"—were featured, as were three Beatles songs, although their music had long since moved past the R&B to which they had once aspired. Surprisingly, there was very little Motown; only the Marvin Gaye and Tammi Terrell hit "You're All I Need to Get By," which was all over the airwaves late that fall, made the cut (and may have been chosen for its immediacy). It was a long way from movie theme music and middle-of-the-road confections. "I remember us sittin' in front of those little ol' speakers copying down words to some of the songs she'd do, 'cause some of 'em were hard to understand," said Reggie Young.

The album starts strong with a recasting of "A Hard Day's Night." The group slows down the tempo and brings out the starkness of the melody, while Dionne soars on the gradually building sound. Their version restates the obvious: John Lennon's lyrics were about an exhausted working-class man and his mate, and "a hard day's night" was all too often what the musicians experienced with the endless hours recording for Chips. There is strength in their version too, an implication that all the work and weariness is worth it in the long run.

"Do Right Woman" is stoic, with Dionne delivering the opening verse in one of the most gently understated performances of her career, gradually building up to the impassioned final chorus. A similar sense of passion imbues "I've Been Loving You Too Long" with fresh meaning, and Mike Leech's string line soars above the singer's deliberate pleading. Reggie Young contributes some emphatic guitar asides, expressing the urgency in the song. "People Get Ready" takes Dionne back to her earliest days singing in church, and she paces through the lyrics with obvious familiarity and affection.

On all of these songs, Bobby Wood is the standout; his gospel-influenced playing embellishes the material. He remembered clowning and joking his way through the sessions, perhaps to put himself at ease as much as to make Dionne comfortable. "We'd get bored and do stupid things, just stupid out," he remarked amusedly. On one track, Bobby was cutting up and decided to play in an unconventional style, striking the keys with an appendage not commonly used for the piano. "I was a little choirboy at that time," he said of himself. "When you're 22, 23, 24, you're still a boy, you do a few things you shouldn't do but I was always in church every Sunday. We were a lot younger back then and there was a lot more we could handle. I gave 150 percent whatever I played on, I don't care if it was Joe Tex or Joe Blow." The pressure in the studio of coming up with music to embellish a song is intense, and he described the way it worked for him. "Whatever comes down from Heaven or out of the air, that's what you do," he explained. "Everybody'd start grinnin' and hollerin', 'Hey, boys, that feels good, let's do it!' That's the beautiful thing about being creative, when that moment happens."

Chips could not have done an album without at least one or two showpiece productions, and Dionne's recording of "Hey Jude" is exactly that. Paul McCartney's song of consolation to Julian Lennon about the breakup of John's marriage seemed on the surface an odd choice for R&B singers, but only a few months after it hit the charts several had tried it—most notably Wilson Pickett, in a version that more or less introduced the sound of Duane Allman's guitar. Of course, it was a logical song for the group to try: "Take a sad song and make it better" was what their recording philosophy was all about. Chips set up the piece with emphasis on the deep minor chords from Bobby Wood's piano. "He liked a two-note thing with the right hand," said Bobby, "and the nice little in-between things." The production is filled out with the horn section and the background vocals by Dionne herself, floating and faint in a sea of echo. "It was hard to record her because she had a delicate voice," Gene Chrisman admitted. But this track pushes her to sing slightly harder than she was accustomed to doing, and the effect is compelling.

"You've Lost That Lovin' Feeling" was the second grand production, and it became a hit the following September. Marty Lacker remembered that this was one of the songs Chips had chosen. "When Chips met Dionne for the first time the day of the sessions, he asked me to go with him to the Holiday Inn Rivermont, which was the first high-rise hotel Holiday Inns built, it was on the banks of the Mississippi River," he said. "We met her in her suite atop the hotel. Her mother was with her because Dionne was pregnant with her first child, her oldest son, David. Along with them, we went in Chips's Rolls to Poplar Tunes Record Shop, which was on the way to American, where we listened to records for Dionne to record and they chose a number of them including 'You've Lost That Lovin' Feelin', which I believe was Dionne's first single from that album."

Chips followed the basic arrangement Phil Spector had used in the famous version with the Righteous Brothers, but he gave Tommy Cogbill more space, which the bassist used to astonishing effect. As with many of the recordings on which Tommy's brilliance especially shone, one could almost picture his fingers flying over the neck of the bass as he shaped the notes. "Cog and I both preferred to, depending on what the song called for, play down on the neck," said Mike Leech. The call-and-response section at the end is set up not only with Dionne shouting in reply to her own overdubbed vocals: Tommy's bass is literally part of the conversation.

Tommy is easygoing on "I'm Your Puppet," ambling along gently beneath Mike Leech's equally amiable strings; this is the most laid-back version of the song, and in some ways the best. It offers a delightful surprise during the final verse: Dan Penn, in a warm valedictory, can be heard singing the lines back to Dionne. His voice blends with the other elements of the production and makes a listener lament that his songwriting overshadowed his singing, though Dan insisted that he could not have made it as a vocalist given his style and the times. "Back then, a white boy couldn't get on a black station; it'd been that way since 1961." Dan did not know it, but he was dropping out of action at the precise minute that white boys singing stylized versions of R&B were beginning to be accepted—at least if they were British, as the careers of Joe Cocker and Rod Stewart would prove. "People Got to Be Free" is a perfect song for both Dionne and the American group; she delivers it with a true gospel feel, implying spiritual as well as temporal freedom, and Tommy Cogbill and the two Bobbys set the pace for her. It is an exhilarated work, promising that both spiritual and actual freedom is not far away—all one has to do is hold on and be strong. The music of the American group is all about holding on and being strong, enduring the bad times patiently; "People Got to Be Free" offers a look at what happens when good times are in sight, and it is as welcome as sun bursting through the clouds.

To anyone familiar with the Ashford and Simpson lyrics of "You're All I Need to Get By," it is no accident that Chips keeps the first section of the verses quiet and turns Tommy Cogbill completely loose on the second sections. "Whenever you lose your will, I'll be there

and push you up the hill," the bass line seems to promise Chips. "Just to do what's good for you and inspire you a little higher." Everyone around the group had already noted Tommy's importance to Chips in the scheme of things. "He was Chips's foil, a real meek and mild guy who got wild every now and then," Ed Kollis remembered warmly. Though Tommy was not quite all Chips needed to get by—not as long as Bobby Emmons was around—this piece does seem to be a way of placing a spotlight upon the man who had been his closest friend for years, much as Chips would do once again after Tommy's death by recording a version of "Wind Beneath My Wings." "Chips is kind of an island to himself," mused Jimmy Johnson, summing up his time working with Chips and Tommy. "Chips didn't have too many close people. Tommy was the closest and a bit kinda Reggie." That was true, especially at that moment in the group's history, but in time Bobby Emmons became the liaison between Chips and the entire group—a role that Tommy, Reggie, and Dan, despite their closeness to Chips, had never wanted to play.

"We Can Work It Out," the album's closer, can also be seen as an indirect reference to the underlying tensions at American due to the presence of the late arrivals. If Chips was aware that the addition of Glen Spreen in particular (Johnny Christopher was better accepted until difficulties later began to overwhelm him) was causing some adjustment problems, he gave no outward sign—easier to just ignore it all and hope that things would straighten themselves out on their own. Again the dominant voice on the song is Tommy Cogbill, at his Jamersonian best; his work on the fadeout is stunning, influenced by Motown but by no means a copy.

Some of the rejected album cuts surfaced later on a 1972 Scepter double LP, highlighting these sessions plus other soul-oriented tracks Dionne had cut with New York and Los Angeles arrangers (the arrangements erroneously credited to Glen Spreen, who had not even begun arranging yet when these tracks were recorded and was only present as an occasional onlooker). All of the cuts are intriguing; even though Chips apparently decided that these were not up to his standard, it is hard to tell what influenced his decision, because the group plays as innovatively on these cuts as they do on the ones that were released. "The Weight," for example, features a cantering, off-center acoustic guitar intro from Reggie Young, and again Bobby Wood's piano becomes the dominant voice. Ed Townsend's beautiful "The Love of My Man," which had been a big hit for Theola Kilgore, is tender, impassioned, and dramatic by turns; Chips patiently leads Dionne through the song, letting her slowly build up to full-throated gospel—or perhaps semi-orgasmic—shouts of gratified delight. The Holland-Dozier-Holland "Loving You Is Sweeter Than Ever" is a far cry from Motown: Tommy Cogbill announces the song with a flurry of notes that sound like a booming cannon, and Gene Chrisman replies with a rifle-shot crack of the snare. The music swirls around Dionne until all the instruments but the bass drop out, leaving her voice to sail freely over Tommy's intricacies. He evokes Jamerson but plays busier and smoother than the Motown bassist, making the song his own. "Tommy was beyond description as a bass player, sensitive to where the song was going," said Ed Kollis, his voice still awed after listening to Cogbill's playing for hours at a time, night after night.

As pleasant an experience as this album is for the listener, it was just as pleasant for the musicians to make. "Dionne was a matter-of-fact person, of a serious mind," reflected Bobby Wood. "I was really impressed with her skills as a singer." "We really had a great time working with her," said Reggie Young enthusiastically. "Oh man, she just fell in love with all of us. She came down for the Memphis Music Awards [a year later] hoping one of us would win." "Dionne did the Memphis Music Awards at my request and subsequently was the host at the second one the following year," said Marty Lacker. "I also got her, a year or so later, to appear with the Memphis Symphony in concert. She and I have remained good friends." "I liked Dionne, she was one of my favorites," Gene Chrisman remembered happily. "She could sing, boy, blew my mind. She'd go out and sing a harmony line and *nail* it . . . she'd nail that sucker on the first

take—I mean, gosh—" an awestruck assertion equally marveled at by Ed Kollis in the control room, Bobby Wood at the piano, and Bobby Emmons on organ. "She sent us all engraved wristwatches," the sound man remembered (the same gesture Aretha had made to the musicians who played on her sessions).

Chips Moman got more out of it than just the watch. "Out of that album, he got a Rolls," chuckled Ed Kollis. "Dionne [then] got Florence to buy her a Rolls." The idea of Chips in his worn denim shirt, faded jeans and tattered sneakers, cruising around in the world's foremost luxury car is quite an image, especially since such cars were not standard for successful musicians in Memphis. Eventually the Rolls-Royce became something of a company car, used to pick up visiting artists at the airport or to appear anywhere Chips needed to make an impression. It may have been fun for him to say he had it, but Chips was just as happy behind the wheel of his TR-6 or riding one of his Harleys around town.

Chips was in an acquiring mood that fall. He hired a new staffer and was considering taking on a few more, bought a private plane and a Rolls-Royce, and began a lifelong career as a collector—of any and everything, a pastime at which he himself would chuckle. He was buying pool tables, classic jukeboxes, and of course investing much of his profit in the horses he raced out on his farm. And as if those things were not enough, he also acquired another studio.

Neither he nor Don Crews remembered how a little out-of-the-way studio in South Memphis called Onyx came to their attention. Its owners had tried to get it going for almost a year and were giving up. Chips liked the idea of having another building on hand for demos, songwriter offices, or anything else that might conceivably arise, and he and Crews began making plans to buy Onyx. "I wasn't really much in favor of it," said Crews, but he went along with the idea. "I told Chips to offer 'em a hundred thousand," he added, but then for some reason he could not recall, he had to go out of town and was no longer involved in the negotiations. "I was gone, he paid a hundred and forty thousand." When he came back, Don Crews found himself co-owner of a new studio, lock, stock, and equipment (which was not much)—"kind of duddy," to use Don's phrase for anything not really working. Just as the American building had been when Crews first took it over, its control room had a rudimentary board, a piano, and not much more. Nonetheless, Chips had hopes for the building's future importance. "I really had a use for that studio because I couldn't keep on with American being as busy as it was and booked," he recalled; he seemed to think that the overflow could be recorded at Onyx. He also half imagined it as a refuge for some of the aspiring songwriters he knew. "I had so many writers and so many people around that I had to come up with something to get 'em out of my hair."

Onyx never worked out the way Chips expected. Few songs were recorded there; the musicians were used to American and preferred it to the new place. "The studio just wasn't never that good," Bobby Wood believed. "Everything recorded there sounded metallic." "Onyx, it was a dead building," said Ed Kollis. "It was lifeless, it was horrible—cold, sterile." Mike Leech agreed. "Never did like that place," he said. "I didn't like Onyx because it didn't sound good to me. It had a cold bright sound like hard linoleum . . . non-soulful. It was a good overdub room for strings though." "Do you suppose it was the name?" Ed Kollis mused dreamily, his inflections reminiscent of George Carlin. "Onyx—black, like a black hole." In his view, the sound in it was almost too clean; there were no bends and curves. "Music needs some distortion, so you can feel it," he said. Don Crews came to see Onyx as superfluous: "We thought we needed it, but we didn't," he said. The only ones who seemed to have a good word for the place were the late arrivals, who adopted the new studio as their refuge. "It wasn't that bad; it had potential," said Hayward Bishop, who engineered a few projects of his own there in the early seventies. Johnny Christopher occasionally wrote songs at Onyx (though he still preferred the upstairs rooms at American). And Glen Spreen used it as a writing room for the string arrangements he was gradually being called upon to create.

Chips said that from the beginning he had hired Glen as a writer only on pretext; what he really wanted was somebody else who could write for strings. The studio was almost overbooked and the recording schedule was crowded; it made sense to think ahead and anticipate that Mike Leech would not be able to handle the load all alone. It also fit in with the American philosophy that anyone who had the ability was free to jump in and do whatever they liked.

Glen's first arranging project was for Ronnie Milsap, a lilting song that he and Mark James had written called "Love Will Never Pass Us By" that they were sure would be a hit. Mark had serious ambitions to produce records and he was more than happy to take the Milsap project off Chips's hands, even though his style of giving direction was different from the perfectionism of Chips and Dan Penn or the relaxed atmosphere created by Tommy Cogbill. "He has so many ideas (at the same time) it's very difficult to zone in on one before he changes his mind and heads off in another direction," said Mike Leech with amused affection. "Mark was a keyboard player and he could play pretty good piano," offered Bobby Wood. "He kinda knew what he wanted, even if it wasn't commercial. I didn't think he had really a good gut for commercial music. He was tryin' to get his own direction, which he should've."

According to Glen Spreen, who probably knew Mark better than anyone on the premises, Mark was just as perfectionistic as the established producers but in a different way. "Mark was very methodical about the way to go about building a song or a record. Everything was thought through and re-examined to the slightest detail (most of the time). . . . I would sometimes grow a bit impatient because the focus, for the larger view, did not seem to be there, just a lot of small details, all very important. I think Mark thought I needed to be more of the methodical type. . . . I wasn't as seasoned as Mark at the time." This approach may have leaned more on Chips's perfectionism than even Mark realized, the difference being that

Mark had every nuance of the production in his mind and Chips allowed some space for the musicians. The ambitious songwriter discussed ways to get a good performance from singers. "Mainly," said Glen, "he would challenge them to do it better than he could"—a difficult task, considering that Mark sang better than most.

Of course, Mark and Glen viewed Mark's production work as a vehicle for the songs they were writing: perhaps they saw themselves as the new Penn-Oldham combination at the studio, since the originals were in the process of walking. A piece they recorded under the umbrella name of Butterscotch Caboose seems to reach for the kind of audience Dan and Spooner would have had: "Sundown Sally," a brooding, deep-Southern tale of a Louisiana woman who lives by night, seemingly an unlikely story for a couple of Texans to tell. The production values are thick and clamorous: Mike Leech remembered that the musicians thought it a bit overdone, and that when he apprised Glen of this, the novice producer "turned as red as his hair" (although when he listened to the piece again forty years after the fact, Glen decided it worked better than he at the time had thought). Glen was aware of the musicians' discomfort with his work but again remembered no open hostility: "However, I am pretty sure most were trying not to pay much attention. I think it was perceived as something to live with and sort of ignore." Another Milsap piece, called "What's Your Game," recorded almost a year later, features some delightful wordplay on the gambling metaphor from Mark James and a built-in tension, as if the two collaborators are tugging the music back and forth between them, a style originally created and perfected by Chips and Tommy.

That later piece used an apt metaphor, since "What's your game?" was a question the American musicians were asking. There was a growing suspicion among the group that the late arrivals were going to come in, ride on the band's already existing reputation, get what they could from the situation, and leave—a suspicion that increased over time (only Johnny Christopher was ever exempted from this doubt). The core group were by now like old war buddies because they had been through so much together, and most of them resented any intrusion on the core. "I don't feel it's an equal situation when one group fights the battles and another group shows up just in time to march in the parade and carry the flag," sniffed Bobby Emmons indignantly. For now, the band was making the best of things with the late arrivals; but if Johnny Christopher was becoming increasingly well-liked and accepted by the group as time went by, it was obvious that Glen Spreen was not.

The situation only got worse when Chips decided, in a pronouncement that seemed to come out of nowhere, that on the basis of his experiments with Mark James, Glen would become the second full-time string arranger for the group. No one is more insistent on enforcing protocol than those who dislike it, and to the musicians Chips's new edict took on all the flavor of a recess appointment, at which they were outraged. "I knew absolutely nothing about hiring another arranger till he was all of a sudden there," said Mike Leech, who was directly affected by the decision. "The Texans had no qualms about hiring another arranger when the idea was first brought to the table. It was never said, 'Let's talk to Mike first and get his feelings.'" And Chips had not told anyone that hiring another string arranger to help with the workload had been in his mind from the beginning. "You see, [the musicians] were supposed to be having stock in American issued to them, so they felt that decisions of that nature should have been asked before done," Mike explained. "Nobody ever said a word. Chips did that all on his own without asking anybody their opinion. . . It wasn't [Glen's] doing. I don't blame him. I would have accepted the offer also. And I can imagine how he felt about being there [in that position] at first—probably very nervous."

He was, but that did not matter to the musicians. It had been different when Dan Penn had assumed some authority in the group; they knew him fairly well, he had spent time there with Chips for awhile before he was officially hired, and even before he had been producing on his own he had done some collaborations with Chips. In other words, he had worked his way up the ladder gradually. All the group could see now was this latecomer who was getting all the plum assignments before he paid his dues. "He took away our toys," said Mike Leech revealingly.

Chips did not handle the situation as well as he might have, but the musicians could not bring themselves to fault him. Mike Leech, who not only heard all the others' complaints but to a certain extent shared them, explained their collective position further. "Here's a total stranger, who's given all the privileges supposedly just for [us]. The party who should be the recipient of our anger was Chips, but given our roles as mere studio dogs we assigned our anger elsewhere." Not everyone was angry. Tommy Cogbill did not let the new assignment affect him any more than Glen's initial arrival had (if he had had misgivings about anybody, it was Bobby Wood, with whom he sometimes differed musically and temperamentally), and despite Reggie Young's doubts he floated above it all as usual, giving credit and praise anywhere it was due. But the majority of the group devised a pecking order among themselves. If Chips was the alpha, and they regarded themselves as betas, Glen was a gamma, and they never let him or anyone else forget it.

The irony is that at least from an artistic standpoint, the decision seemed to work well. There were ongoing projects that needed two arrangers to hasten the process and deliver the tapes to the labels on schedule. The sadness in Glen's eyes carried over to the string lines he wrote, imbuing the records with further melancholy, and, due to his emphasis on baroque lines and countermelodies, even more fullness. "Glen was a good arranger," said Reggie Young matter-of-factly. "Glen is the kind of arranger who could hear a tape of the song for the first time in the car on the way to the studio, write a string line in the car, and it would be perfect," enthused Norbert Putnam, who worked extensively with Glen in the mid-seventies. Not quite, thought Glen amusedly, but he had his methods.

"I try to pick out what people do, and do the opposite," he said. "I like to be extreme from time to time. I learned that I like to do syncopation,

high strings and low cellos, doing things cellos haven't done before." He also developed a weaving technique, letting the strings float in and out and around a song's vocal, building the line dynamically in the already established tradition at American, for he too knew classical music and understood its principles. "That's how I taught myself, listening to classical . . . even John Philip Sousa. My heroes ranged from highly known classical artists to Fats Domino and Little Richard." To him, arranging was all a matter of listening: "Sometimes, you listen to a song, you break out in a cold sweat, you develop different textures for different songs. You can listen to a car engine and hear music if you're thinking about it. The trick is, never use a piano [to develop an idea]. Never. If it can't come out of the head, it's no good." For his purposes, Onyx was ideal: "I was a deeply focused writer of music scores but only when alone. . . . String arrangements, for example, would take an hour or two."

It was almost an assembly-line procedure: the core group cut the basic tracks at night. The next day, Glen would pick up the tape of the project if it was allocated to him, go over to Onyx, and in peace and quiet, sit there and work out string and horn lines (if the horn parts had not already been worked out by Wayne Jackson or by Mike). He also supervised the string overdubs and conducted the sessions he arranged. Mike Leech stayed out of the way while he was working, and he stayed away when it was Mike's turn; this principle of giving space to a possible competitor had been standard at American since Dan Penn and Tommy Cogbill had begun producing. Like so many things that happened with this group, this policy first began as an unspoken feeling and hardened into a custom. And customs developed this way, without much communication or understanding of why the traditions have formed, are often the hardest to overturn.

Ted White, Aretha's husband, had been a name in Detroit for a long time; he made his money in real estate, but his marriage to Aretha and an earlier involvement with Dinah Washington had made him aware of music.

He discovered an old-school vocal group that sounded somewhat like the Masqueraders, who were still recording with Tommy Cogbill. It is likely that their success on the R&B charts led him to see what Tommy could do for his protégés.

The Dynamics began recording at American during that late fall of 1968. Chips Moman collaborated with Tommy on the production of two songs, but the rest were done by Tommy alone. Their album, *First Landing*, was released in spring 1969, the year man first walked on the moon, so the title was timely. It offers a look at the way Tommy's solo productions differed from the material he worked on with Chips; and, as the King Curtis album from earlier in the year had done, it established his credentials as a soundman, even though Chips said "he didn't live for that engineering."

To begin with, the record is joyful. While Chips's productions tended to start from a low place and build within the confines of despair, Tommy's records started out elatedly and took the listener even higher. The songs brought in by the Dynamics, mostly written either by them or by Aretha favorite Ronnie Shannon, are strictly rhythm songs to begin with, which the group loved recording. Tommy accentuated the feel, much to everyone's delight. "Tommy, he recognized when something had a groove and a snap to it," said Bobby Wood happily. He framed the lead vocals with the ethereal harmonies of the background singers in the same style as for the Masqueraders.

Strings and horns on a Cogbill production seem to leap spontaneously into the mix. It was an illusion, because the arrangements were created methodically. "Tommy and I didn't see eye to eye on some of the parts I wrote for his productions," Mike Leech reflected. "We spent many hours in the studio putting things together. He would sometimes 'float' the horn arrangements, in other words, place them back in the tracks buried in echo. I didn't always agree with his thinking but it was his show so I didn't argue. Most stuff came out in the wash pretty good though." Arrangements were as much collaborative as they were completely created by Mike or Glen Spreen. Chips Moman

remembered occasionally playing for them on guitar a string line he heard in his head to fill out the music, and Mike recalled writing down parts that Tommy would hum. In this capacity, the arrangers were secretaries and transcriptionists as well as contributors, making it difficult for even devoted listeners to tell exactly whose influence was most prominent on a recording.

Chips further muddied the situation by deciding, in a move that seems incredible when considering how much resentment already existed over his recess appointment, that to speed up things even further the arrangers should collaborate most of the time. "That was demeaning to me, but I did it anyway," said Mike Leech, adding that he had already wanted to do some writing with the new man, since they were more or less stuck with him and working on arrangements would be a good way to get acquainted. "The good part about writing with Glen is he could play piano fairly well. I could hum a line and he could play and write it down. It takes me forever," Mike commented. "Once while writing an arrangement . . . he became unhappy with what I'd written, and wanted to call it a night. I was persistent, and we finally put something down which made sense. We recorded it the next day, and it seemed to work with the song very well."

It was truly an awful position for Mike, who was having to deal with the fact that both of the slots he filled at the studio were now shared with someone else. Officially he maintained, with stoic reasonableness, that he did not mind and that he had enough confidence in himself both as bassist and string arranger that having others also occupying those chairs did not matter. But it had to hurt him that the label credits from now on read: "String and horn arrangements by Mike Leech and Glen Spreen." And it hurt him professionally as well. It blurred the line between the two arrangers, obscuring the stylistic differences between them (Mike's eloquent unbroken lines, Glen's rich countermelodies, baroque harmonies, and weaving) and making it difficult to determine who contributed the most. Even listeners within the music business did not know how it worked: Norbert

Putnam had no idea that Mike Leech wrote string lines at all until Mike and Glen had both moved to Nashville.

Despite this, Mike maintained that Chips began with a good idea. "I think Chips's whole plan was to get a section together that could not only lay down basic tracks, but could finish the record without enlisting any outside help," he reflected. "Come to think of it, that was quite an accomplishment, to have an in-house group who could do the whole thing, right up until the mastering process. I'll bet if we had stayed together [in Memphis] we would have eventually done that too.

"He had a hit rhythm section, hit songwriters, hit arrangers, right there. The only hiring-out he did was strings and horns . . . having to play what was written by an in-house arranger, except for a few head arrangements done by the horn sections."

The horns were still prominently Wayne Jackson's group, along with some of the formally trained musicians who worked at Pepper-Tanner. Through the group's increasing involvement with that jingle factory and the Rita Coolidge hit, they came to know Marty Lacker. Marty had recently left Elvis Presley's employ following a long stint as foreman for Elvis's Memphis Mafia; in that capacity he had handled the payroll, supervised logistics when Elvis traveled to Hollywood, and eventually helped arrange the details for the famous wedding to Priscilla (up to and including designing the brocaded jacket Elvis wore). But before working for Elvis, Marty had had some experience in radio, taking several stations in Knoxville and New Orleans to number one in the local ratings.

It was mainly this radio background which interested Chips after he met Marty at a BMI awards dinner, and he invited Marty to come over to the studio now and then and take a look at what they were doing. "Chips and I got to know each other really good," said Marty respectfully. The respect was mutual, and Chips hired Marty as a promotion man for AGP. There was a feeling around the studio that an independent promotion man, answerable only to Chips, would be more interested in getting the records out to stations than would Dave Carrico at the parent label. Marty came on board, working mainly out of Onyx, where he had his office.

When he was at the studio, he was overwhelmed with what he saw. "I learned very quickly what the difference was between them and other groups of studio musicians—creativity," he softly reflected. "With Chips's guidance, the little nuances and little fills they'd put in the records. The more I got in with them, the more comfortable I felt." The group welcomed him warmly, except for Bobby Wood, whose personality did not fit with his. Marty liked the atmosphere and the hitmaking track record of the studio so well that he began lobbying his famous friend to consider doing some sessions at American. But for the time being, Elvis was busy with his wife and new baby Lisa Marie, and he would wave the idea off. "Maybe someday," he would say when Marty brought it up, much to his friend's frustration. But there was nothing Marty could do about it then, and so work on the Dynamics sessions continued uninterrupted.

The album begins with the American standard, "I Don't Want Nobody to Lead Me On." Every version of this recorded by the group got better and better; Mike Leech was even more commanding on this one than he had been on the other two, and Bobby Emmons is snarlingly incendiary with his lead organ lines. For Emmons, coming up with something original was the constant challenge. "We was tryin' to find something that didn't sound like the last song you'd just heard," he said with his usual quiet intensity. "That was the thing to put foremost. It didn't need to sound like two minutes of cliché. I mean, you can go to any club and hear a reading of the latest record." It had to be different, it had to be creative, but it had to be something understandable to the listener, he added: "You had to keep it in the realm of reality. You couldn't take a lot of wild side roads and never get back to the highway." Keeping it real, of course, was the American group specialty, and throughout the Dynamics' album, Emmons is at his common-sense best.

Reggie Young leads off the second song,

"Ain't No Love," with a snapping, crisp four-line intro he handles alone except for light taps of the snare from Gene Chrisman. It is a good demonstration of his ability, although he tended to shrug off praise; his standard response to a compliment was an offhandedly cheerful "That'll work, won't it? . . . Fits in with the groove." Nevertheless, the musicians working with him were aware of how awesome he could be. Glen Spreen called Reggie "magical" and added that "he came up with some things that amazed the hell" out of those hearing him. "Reggie drew blood a couple of times, he was catchin' a lot of people's eye," said Bobby Emmons. "Reggie is a great player. The heat was usually on him in the studio, because he would come up with some great ideas," said Mike Leech, who by now was as strongly allied with the guitar player as he was with Ed Kollis. "Chips would manipulate them, bend them to fit what he wanted, which was not necessarily what Reg wanted, but he did it just to please the boss."

Tommy Cogbill created the effects on his records somewhat differently. If someone had a good idea, he was willing to adjust his concept to fit it rather than have the musician alter his creativity. Nor would he spend hours working on one song. If recording was not flowing naturally, not getting anywhere, Tommy would lay the track aside and call for a break or press on to the next song, then go back later and try it once more. If it still did not work after several run-throughs, Tommy shelved the track and never brought it before the group again. "We used to have a saying—if it don't fit, don't force it," said Bobby Wood.

He had as much ability to emphasize key lines as Chips; the production on Ronnie Shannon's "Ice Cream Song" is almost completely structured to underline the exclamation in the chorus, "Great God Almighty!" And "What Would I Do," also written by Shannon, shows off Tommy's mellow way with a soul ballad; he did several pieces in this style over the years, "I'm Just an Average Guy" by the Masqueraders being the best-known. Though the soaring strings are credited to both arrangers, the sweet sound of the unbroken line is unmistakably the mark of Mike Leech.

All the album tracks are a pleasure, but "When I Lost You" is an unmitigated delight. From the whooping of the background vocalists that begins the song to the long, spontaneous monologue at the end as Tommy fades it out, there is a sense that he just turned on the tape machine, kicked back, and let the ideas come rolling out, both from the vocal group and the band. And "Fair Lover," written by Eddie Floyd and the backup vocalist Donna Prater, is another delight. Mike Leech romps and stomps and storms his way through the proceedings on bass, sparking the track and making it come alive.

The two songs Tommy worked on with Chips Moman are a world apart from the relaxed mood he created alone. The tracks are introspective and the songs themselves full of foreboding. Here the production is constantly being pulled back and forth between the two of them in a style smoother than "What's Your Game" but keeping the same tugging feel (and perhaps due to the same reason: two temperamental opposites who were not only collaborators but close friends). "Ain't No Sun (Since You've Been Gone)" an obscure track from a Temptations album, was one of Norman Whitfield's most grim compositions. It is about depression so deep it is almost suffocating, and Chips seemed to leap at the chance to describe it, feeding off the energy Tommy gave the backing tracks to emphasize the words about how "it's a dark, dark world . . . everything around me faded and gray." There are moments in this gloomy production that sound as if the lyrics are a call-and-response dialogue: "There's a big black cloud hanging over my head," one line announces, and is answered by another that is chilling in retrospect; "It's a cloud of loneliness, I feel like I'm dead." "Murder in the First Degree" is more of the same, with the lover mournfully stating that if his lady goes, his grief will kill him and she will be responsible. These recordings are many things, but frivolous they are not; they are imbued with the realism that name artists like Dionne Warwick were coming to American to obtain.

The Dynamics album came out on Atlantic, but the AGP custom label was still distributed by Bell, and being signed to a label meant close involvement with the suits. Larry Uttal himself often came to town to pick up tapes when they were finished, visiting the studio and making himself known to the musicians. "Larry Uttal was in hog heaven in Memphis," Mike Leech remembered. "I remember Uttal in the control room when Dan played [an] album he had just finished on the Box Tops. He was grinning from ear to ear." Chips Moman thought Uttal to be a typical New York record executive. "Larry was an okay guy, but just like all the rest of the companies; he wouldn't pay you," said Chips. For instance, by the end of 1968, both the American group and the Box Tops were owed some money by the company. "I told Alex Chilton, 'Larry owes me about $100,000. Part of that's yours, but he won't pay you until he gets another Box Tops album,'" Chips remembered. "Alex said, 'I'm game.'"

By this time Alex was disillusioned with both the Box Tops and the music industry. "He had never liked the road," said Bobby Wood, who heard him complain about the touring schedule occasionally. "He came in there all bright-eyed and bushy-tailed, wanting to make records, but the more he became a star the more he wanted to talk about women," said Wayne Carson acerbically. In fact, Alex was so disgusted by the road grind and by attempts to turn him and his band into Top Forty teen commodities, when he wanted to make serious music, that he was thinking about getting out of the game altogether. Like Dan, he wanted to explore other sides of life. "Put it one way, he was a hippie," said Reggie Young amusedly. "He beats to a different drum, for sure," agreed Bobby Wood. He did not even have his compatriots to rely on; Gary Talley was the only original member of the Box Tops left by this time. The back royalties from Bell would give him a chance to make a fresh start. And if he wanted to record at American, he had no choice but to work with Chips, since Dan Penn was removing himself from the scene.

Actually, he was working with Chips and Tommy; Gary Talley remembered that, in a departure from their usual custom, they were both in the control room when all the recording was done. *Dimensions*, the final Box Tops album, was one of their finest collaborations, augmented by Gary Talley and Wayne Carson sitting in with the American group. "I was really glad to play for that," said Gary, who was hoping to make the transition into studio work. "I think Chips saw that I had some potential as a session player, and he tried to give me chances whenever he could."

All of the Box Tops, along with by several of the American players, are heard on the extended jam for the album's closer, "Rock Me." In 1968, long free-form cuts were essential to a band's credibility, and Alex Chilton had sung the B. B. King tune before, under Dan Penn's direction, for the third album. Tommy layers multiple guitar tracks from Gary Talley, Reggie Young, Wayne Carson, and everyone else, capturing the mood of those downtimes in the early American days when he and Chips had nothing to do but just sit and play. The bass is like a heartbeat, and the piano sounds like Spooner Oldham, although he said he was in transition at the time and not there for the project. Alex sounds completely caught up in the moment, and the piece becomes even more free-form before he restates the verses and the band brings it to a chugging, crashing conclusion. "I think Chips saw that we had the potential" to take on that kind of challenge, thought Gary Talley.

The album yielded several hits and more than a few underrated masterpieces—not bad for a hastily assembled group of sessions. "We cut that just so I could collect royalties," Chips said gratefully. "I've always thought a lot of Alex for doing that." He remembered that the sessions had been done over a three-day period—"When we did it in three days, we meant *three days*," he chuckled. Reggie Young's session books reveal that the Box Tops were recorded within five days over a relatively mundane two-week period in late October and early November, in intervals from working on Dionne's album. Perhaps it felt like three nonstop days to Chips, for the album has a compressed intensity about it that from then on would be typical of Chips and Tommy's third way of production.

"Cutting with Chips and Tommy there, it wasn't no different than cuttin' with one of 'em," said Wayne Carson offhandedly. "If it didn't rock, we didn't have nothin' to do with it." For Gary Talley, the delight of the session was taking direction from Tommy. "I thought he was probably the most friendly of all the guys, just the nicest guy in the world," he said warmly. "I remember having several good discussions with Tommy. We were talkin' about cars and I had just gotten a '68 GTO and he had gotten a Cadillac and we went out in the parking lot. He didn't have a bit of ego about him at all."

Gary was aware that he still had much to learn about working sessions. "At the beginning of the session, Chips wanted me to do something [on guitar] and I didn't have the timing right," he remembered. "I'd been only playing guitar two or three years. I only started playing in my middle teens, in eleventh grade." He also recalled the way Chips handled his part of the collaboration. "Chips always seemed like he was the guy who was more in charge," he said. "Most of what was said over the talkback was Chips." Wayne Carson remembered that neither one talked much or established direction; they had their ideas and left it up to the players to color in the spaces.

The album starts with a piece that became a runaway hit the following September. "Soul Deep" was one of Wayne Carson's crossover compositions, a song that could—and did—cut across rock, pop, and country delineations. He did not remember the reason for the story line, but he vividly recalled working on it in Nashville at the offices of Fred Foster's Combine Music. "I had this little riff going on," he said. "Bob Beckham [the man supervising Fred's publishing company] came in saying, 'That's a goddamn hit, finish this song!'" Wayne recorded it at American with Fred Foster producing and Chips engineering; the track eventually appeared on his 1972 Monument album *Life Lines*. Tommy Cogbill was so pleased with the results that he asked if he could use the basic track for the new version. Permission was given, and Tommy and Chips stripped everything but drums and bass, starting over from scratch by layering as much as they possibly could—and having a great time doing so. "Tommy would do a lot of those guitar overdubs when everybody went home," said Gary Talley. "Remember the guitar in the second verse of 'Soul Deep'? That was done [by Tommy] on a big fat jazz guitar, plugged directly into the board while he was sitting there." Even the arrangers got in on it. "I wrote parts for piccolos," Glen Spreen remembered. "Tommy walked up, looked at the speakers, and asked, 'What's that?' The whole time I answered him he was looking at the speakers in a curious way. When I finished my answer he just said, 'Okay', still looking at the speakers. Then he walked back into the front lobby."

As much fun as the song obviously was to make, it is just as much fun to hear, as Chips and Tommy toss ideas to one another and tug the track back and forth between them. One gets the impression that, if Alex had stopped singing, they would have signaled to the group to keep going while they got it on tape, just for the sheer joy of it. "I recall a vision of Chips seated at the console grinning up at Tommy, Tommy grinning back," said Mike Leech. That interplay between the two of them strengthens the song and applies its theme not only to matters of love but of friendship, and gives the context a deeper meaning than Wayne Carson originally intended. Other versions interpreting the piece as a love song (for instance, Eddy Arnold's, on his *Love and Guitars* album two years later) seem limp by comparison. Once again the words take on a call-and-response significance; listeners feel as if they are eavesdropping on a conversation. "Soul Deep" describes both the joy and the dependence Tommy and Chips took in each other at that time; it is one of their most immediate-sounding records (perhaps the fact that they were present at the same time for this recording adds to the impression) and had few parallels then (only Skip Spence's "My Best Friend" on *Surrealistic Pillow* and Dobie Gray's later "The Feeling's Right," featuring Mike Leech and Reggie Young, seem to express similar ideas) and even fewer today.

Throughout the album, Tommy and Chips continued to weave around existing works to create their own artistic statements, and they could do so even more powerfully with a ballad than an uptempo song. Alex Chilton brought them their definitive statement when he came in one day singing "I Shall Be Released." "He loved this, it was a Dylan song," said Wayne Carson. "He said, 'This is one of the best songs I ever heard.'" He probably learned it off *Music from Big Pink*, the album Dylan's backup group had out that fall; they use the song as the album's closer and play it in a traditional style. Perhaps the fact that Dylan had written it as an old-style prison ballad influenced the way his backing band chose to interpret it. Bobby Emmons particularly remembered the "from the west down to the east" line of the chorus; with his writer's eye for tying things together, he interpreted the line as reflecting the influence California, in the West, was having on current music, mores, and fashion. Chips and Tommy recorded the song in a style that has little to do with homage to either traditional music or contemporary modes.

In their version, "I Shall Be Released" is a double autobiography; in three minutes' time they wove the music around the song to make the track a summation of every hurt, every heartache, every struggle, the two of them had endured thus far. It is as if they are looking back at their lives and judging themselves with almost pitiless eyes. Chips could take note of every man who put him "there" ( in his endless depression, his prison of the spirit), and he seemed to see himself as the "man in the lonely crowd." It is likely that Tommy heard him shouting all day long that he was not to blame for any of his misfortunes, and here Tommy offers his friend—and everyone listening—the promise that there is hope somewhere, even if neither he nor Chips can see it. What we are left with from both of them is a heartless but stoic truth, the same one the Greek poet told centuries before: "In our sleep pain which cannot forget falls drop by drop upon the heart until, in our despair, against our will, comes wisdom through the awful grace of God." The verses are soft and quiet, but the chorus—which surely must be included on a list of Tommy's spiritual litanies—builds to an unbroken

line of anguished screams from the words and from the horn section. On the original album version, the final chorus simply winds down; when it was released as a single the following April, Tommy had changed it to make the horns scream one final note of both anguish—and triumph—at the end. The single did not do well in the charts—perhaps its message was almost too strong—but it reached into the West Virginia hills to make a permanent difference in the life of a fourteen-year-old girl, to make of her a record collector and the woman who wrote this book.

Tommy chose to follow a dark statement with good news. "Midnight Angel" had been written by Mark James and Glen Spreen expressly for this session; Glen came up with two lines and Mark did the rest, filling the song out around Glen's concept, and he pitched it to Chips, playing and singing it live. "Oh, I *loved* that one," said Gary Talley. It is a song offering consolation and understanding to a woman who seems to have been kicked around by life; Glen said that Mark interpreted the story line as being about "a street person that someone wanted to help." That interpretation brings the song into focus; Ed Kollis's fluttering, bluesy harmonica illustrates the hard life the woman has suffered, and the chorus, taken at a different tempo from the verses, promises not only concrete solutions but affection. "Walk into my sunshine, baby," Tommy's production and bass line tenderly coaxes, underscoring the two lines Glen had written. "Step into the light of my eyes" (an interesting line coming from a man whose eyes revealed so much about him). As much as anything, it is a plea for trust, encouraging someone with the feral skittishness of a wild animal to take a chance once more.

Trust is also a component of Alex Chilton's "Together"; it is supposedly about romantic happiness, but the words seem irrelevant compared to Tommy's startlingly experimental production. Here again he rejoices in layers of overdubbing, as a very traditional basic track, haunting and high-lonesome in the style of the Carter Family, is heard on the right channel of the stereo speakers while a high-pitched whirring from Reggie Young's electric guitar is placed on top, coming out of the left speaker. "That was a really cool, creative use of feedback," said Gary Talley. The almost inaudible muttering is courtesy of Gary, echoing Alex's line about how "everybody should" find a good woman to stay with—"They wanted somebody with a really deep voice," he remarked. But the record evokes most of all an image of Tommy Cogbill in the control room as many of the group remembered him, leaning forward over the console with his hands delicately placed on the faders almost as if he were taking tea, his expression quizzical and intense as he concentrates on what he is doing while out on the studio floor the lyrics go on about "livin' and lovin' our lives away."

"I Shall Be Released" is a song of outreach; so is "Midnight Angel," and so of course so is the Chips Taylor composition "I'll Hold Out My Hand." This song took almost a year to catch on: at the end of 1969 a group called the Clique took it up the charts on the White Whale label, and Gayle McCormick's band Smith did a hard-hitting version on their first album. Both of these productions are dramatic and forceful, pulling out all of the stops and turning on the volume and power. Not the case with the one by the American group. Tommy is stoic, understated, and quiet, and Chips adds a deep, reflective melancholy; their concept makes the other versions of the song seem forced and overdone. The flat, droning horn section (one of Glen Spreen's trademarks) on the long fadeout adds to the mood of patient endurance; the theme seems to be one of waiting it out, no matter how long it takes, and the sound is filled with centuries-old weariness.

"Sweet Cream Ladies" is one of the American group's most controversial recordings. Many radio stations would not play it because of its subject matter—prostitution—although it hardly glamorizes the profession as does Allen Toussaint's later "Lady Marmalade" or Giorgio Moroder's "Bad Girls." Bobby Weinstein and Jon Stroll, the Brill Building stalwarts from New York who wrote it, seemed to see it as a necessary evil, a safety valve for unhappy men. The work assumes a cold realism the writers, mired in psychedelia, never came close to again, as

their own album done two years later with the American musicians would prove. In keeping with the outreach theme, the horn section here takes on the flavor of a Salvation Army band (to have Tommy and Chips directing such an aggregate is quite a takeoff), with its out-of-tune brass line made up on the spot by Ed Logan and the others from Pepper-Tanner, who had been brought in as usual to augment the sound of Wayne Jackson and company.

Tommy stages Alex Chilton's "The Happy Song" as one of his off-center hoedowns, with Ed Kollis's harmonica leading the way, and a strong emphasis on the rhythm from Gene Chrisman and Mike Leech. "It was a very lighthearted kind of song, which was not typical of Alex," said Gary Talley. (It was not typical of the American group, either.) Alex was writing about a rock group on a bandstand, perhaps a local garage band not unlike what the Box Tops had been; here the context could also refer to a studio group, and perhaps most of all to the producers: "Sing us a happy little song and we can do the rest." "We can light the night if we just let feelings flow, just let ourselves go," the lyric assures, and that is the promise of the American group: a collective of musicians doing what they felt and playing it from the heart. As much or even more than "Memphis Soul Stew," this record defines the Memphis way for all time. "That song was fun to do," said Gary, and it shows.

By now there was a lot of curiosity about Memphis and just what the secret was of all those hit records coming out of there, not only at American but at Stax and to a lesser extent at Hi, which was in transition as Willie Mitchell rebuilt his rhythm section. *Billboard* did several articles on the phenomenon; an article in the November 17, 1968, issue announced the formation of Music Memphis Incorporated, a booster group eventually including Marty Lacker as director, that planned to do for the Memphis music business what the Country Music Association was beginning to do for Nashville. Each year that it was in business MMI sponsored the Memphis Music Awards, to call national attention to the studios and musicians of the city. "It lasted five years until I got tired of doing it and because, by that time, the Memphis music industry was diminishing," said Marty Lacker.

In the same article *Billboard* also announced Stan Kesler's latest project, a studio called Sounds of Memphis. Jerry Wexler had hired the Dixie Flyers, so Stan had to get a new rhythm section for the studio. One of the first people he called was Gary Talley, who stayed with the project until about a year later, when Seymour Rosenberg took it over. Gary wanted to stay ("I loved working with Stan. He was the most nice, laid-back guy") but was outvoted, and the musicians wound up employed by the consortium (co-owned by the Chicago singer Jerry Butler) to which Rosenberg sold the operation. In the meantime, Sounds of Memphis cut a couple of songs by James Carr, though nothing happened with them; Stan Kesler saw evidence of James's emotional breakdown when the singer walked out in the middle of the session and climbed up on the studio roof to look around. Stan's new studio was getting a lot of press space, but so was American, and one of the later *Billboard* features on Memphis, timed to coincide with the Memphis Music Awards, showed a full-length photo of Chips himself, posed beside his private plane.

Though Chips said of the publicity, "I didn't pay a whole lot of attention," and he had a well-known distaste for hype, those who knew him as well as did Marty Lacker were aware that he wanted the vindication. That may be why the mood of a song that was not released on the album but appeared as the B-side of "Sweet Cream Ladies" turned out as it did. Alex Chilton's "I See Only Sunshine" is a love song that winds up being not a love song but a moment frozen in time; it seems to evoke the atmosphere and mood of some point past midnight, when everyone has gone home and Chips and Tommy are alone in the control room, playing the tapes back and discussing possible overdubs and anything else that came into their minds. "I could picture them together," said Glen Spreen, "with Tommy standing slightly apart with his arms crossed, Chips seated at the console," perhaps tilted back in his chair with his feet up on the control board, as he often sat when he was in a talkative mood. "I see only

sunshine for you and me, for years to come," says the chorus, and that may have been the attitude when these two friends looked back on how far they had come. Mark James's busy-doing-nothing song, "Turn On a Dream," is classic Cogbill, and continues the mood of triumph. It is exhilarating; the highs have never been higher on an American recording.

But the underlying tension could not be kept back for long. There had already been a few flare-ups over nothing in particular, and it only would have taken one incident to shove all the suppressed hostilities over the line. Everyone was overworked and stressed to nearly the breaking point. The tensions surfaced at Christmas that year. "Chips and Don gave the guys (okay, they were very tacky gifts) an AGP medallion and an early version of a boom box," said Mike Leech. "We were not too excited about the gifts, but felt really good that Chips and Don had thought enough of us to give us something I guess they thought was special until . . . lo and behold! J.P. walked in wearing one and the same medallion, listening to his new boom box!" The group were outraged and disgusted. "Me, Reggie, and I think Bobby Wood—or Gene—met later and tried to see how far we could throw our medallions across the Memphis/Arkansas bridge," said the usually mild-mannered arranger (Bobby Wood did not recall being there for the event.) "I tossed my boom box out the window, don't remember what Reg [and the others] did with theirs. Moral of the story, every time something was done (we thought) specifically for just *us*, somebody stole our thunder, or had a piece of what we otherwise would have *treasured*." It had been the dominant problem since the introduction of the late arrivals, and it was the problem that would never go away.

And the group did not need any more problems. They would soon be called upon to work at the very peak of their talents.

# CHAPTER 16

||||||||||||||||||||||||||||||||||||||||||||||||||||||||||||||

# The Present Is Prelude

The first act recorded at American in January of 1969 was not Elvis Presley, as legend seems to say, but the star of the previous year, Merrilee Rush. Her records had moved from Bell to the AGP label, and this single was her final one with Chips and Tommy Cogbill together due to a personality conflict with Chips. After this Tommy alone would record her. The collaborators had two beautiful songs with which to work this time, both partly the work of Wayne Carson. His and Dan Penn's song "Everyday Living Days" served as the B-side: "Every day's a groovy day," she shouts joyfully, "every day's a makin'-lovely-love-to-me day." The chorus was extremely explicit for the time: "Lay it on me gently," she intones, "but just enough to blow my mind / Take your satin fingers, and walk them up and down my spine."

It was a good song for a free-spirited hippie girl, although its blitheness had nothing to do with the lives of its writers. "I tried to be a hippie, tried to join 'em and couldn't," Dan Penn said amusedly, looking back at his bohemian period. "Didn't like their music, didn't like their garb. I didn't like the way the country was changing. Vietnam, I didn't know nothin' about all that; I thought we were gonna win the war. . . . The hippies of that day, they're still the same, they're still hippies. As far as I'm concerned they are the ruin of this country," Dan added firmly. And hippie optimism was hardly the province of most at American—"I came up in the school of reality," said Wayne Carson. So why did they write it? "Because that's what we do," Wayne growled dismissively. "Writing is a giant game of Scrabble. You got twenty-six

letters of the alphabet, you got three chords, see what you can come up with."

More autobiographical, and more poignant then and now, was the A-side of the single, a moving ballad written by Wayne and Glen Spreen called "Your Loving Eyes Are Blind." It is another one of the songs that evoke a hall of mirrors; one is not sure if it is the two writers (one a hippie, the other a plain-spoken loner), the two producers, or Merrilee herself who is speaking. The lyrics warn anyone who might fall in love with the speaker (or speakers), that this is a free spirit who can never really be tamed. "You say you love me, but you don't know me," Merrilee wails, and then sorrowfully intones, "You don't understand my kind." Wayne Carson remembered working all night on the song and coming up with nothing but the title line; Glen Spreen recalled the two of them throwing the remaining bits back and forth to one another almost immediately before studio time, though it does not sound like a last-minute concoction. On the contrary, Wayne's typically strong melody frames a finely crafted lyric: "Don't hang your dreams on me, in hopes that I might be / What you're looking for / When morning brings the light, the words you say tonight / You might be sorry for." Tommy Cogbill set up the arrangement with the same drum taps and droning trombone line from "Angel" as the song progresses its mournful, stately way. The record is permeated with a sense of unassailable dignity and self-awareness; everyone involved is perhaps a little sad that they can never change, but in the long run accepting it. In the end it is about hard choices, both in the path the speakers have chosen and the path that anyone close to them takes in caring about them.

Hard choices and the limitations of fate were not often discussed in hippie music, which is why some of the later arrivals (most notably Glen Spreen and Hayward Bishop) felt that the American group never interpreted psychedelia well. But it was not for lack of trying. The first genuinely psychedelic record at American was the slowed-down, Vanilla Fudge–style version of Holland-Dozier-Holland's "Reach Out" that Chips and Tommy had done with Merri-lee Rush toward the end of the preceding year. Steve Tyrell was responsible for the studio's second venture into the form.

He heard Joseph Longoria at a blues festival in Texas and somehow came up with the idea that American would be the perfect place to record him. He touted Longoria to the group as a great songwriter, but when he got his client to Memphis, it was discovered that Joseph had no songs ready at all, just the titles. Mark James and Glen Spreen stayed up for two days and nights fitting words and melodies to Joseph's concepts, and even these tended to be fragments and phrases rather than fully developed songs. Everybody remembered one title in particular: "I Ain't Fattenin' No Frogs for Snakes," a phrase that became one of the group's in-jokes. (Longoria apparently borrowed the phrase from the classic blues by Sonny Boy Williamson, although a slightly different version of it appeared as an incidental line in Mamie Smith's 1931 "Don't You Advertise Your Man.")

Chips Moman was credited as the producer, along with Mark James and Glen Spreen, but he stayed away for the most part, engineering a few selections. Ed Kollis, who would have been much more sympathetic to hippie blues-rock, was the primary engineer. Chips treated the project as halfheartedly as he later did the experiment in psychedelia that comprised Billy Burnette's first album. He did not remember the record at all. It was not his kind of music, and he knew it. His touch is there only in a few subtle ways, such as the reworking of his own arrangement of "House of the Rising Sun" and the way Joseph's singing evokes Alex Chilton (on "I'll Build a City") and Bobby "Blue" Bland (on the quasi-soul ballad "Come the Sun Tomorrow").

It was a departure for the group, but some of them liked it. "I remember the Joseph sessions well," said Mike Leech, the primary bassist on the album (although Tommy Cogbill turned in strong performances on "House of the Rising Sun" and "Come the Sun Tomorrow"). "It was our first attempt to play some hard underground-type rock. I really enjoyed it plus Joseph was a really nice guy. Somebody made

the remark that Joseph sounded as if he'd been gargling with razor blades. It was cool, it was a lot of fun, we just broke out of the mold and did it," Reggie Young remembered with pleasure. "Lot of heavy metal and distortion. It was fun. I can't remember if it was enhanced," he laughed. "That was a neat project, it was something we weren't normally into. Joseph was a different person than we'd normally work with . . . he was kind of a white man with a black soul." "Joey was a wild card which was entertaining in some situations," remembered Glen Spreen. "He would push segments of the songs up or back depending on his urge at the time. That was hard on the band."

The group resolved the contradictions of a soul singer doing Hendrix-style psychedelia at a studio specializing in music about pain and suffering by emphasizing, rather than trying to resolve, the contradictions. They slanted their playing toward the kind of swamp-rock Tony Joe White was making in Nashville at around the same time. Glen Spreen was still in his clamorous period as a producer, and the tracks are heavily layered with overdubs primarily from Bobby Emmons and Reggie Young (Bobby Emmons's ghostly-sounding organ, first faintly heard and then clearly audible as if he is emerging from a mist, introduces the album). The first side of the album is devoted to the fragments loosely constructed around Joseph's titles; they are strung together with no breaks between. The second side features strong songs mainly from outside writers (this seems to be Chips Moman's characteristic contribution), with less emphasis on psychedelia—Joseph's vocal improvisations on the fadeout of "Come the Sun Tomorrow" are indistinguishable from what could be heard on many records by black artists cutting albums at the studio.

Lyrically, the songs centered not on the euphoria of typical psychedelic music but the bottomless anguish that the American musicians already knew how to evoke. Hope, in the form of a pipe dream, is offered only on the piece woven around Joseph's titles, "Gonna Build a City," in which Mark James and Glen Spreen evoke both the gospel promise of heaven and of communes all across the country (as well as

Chips's own communal dream for American, of "building a world and letting only my own people inside"). If a theme emerges on the album, it is that of someone trapped in poverty and hopelessness—for example, the country blues of "Cold Biscuits and Fish Heads," and the Hurley-Wilkins song about the projects, "Got to Get Away," which features a third writer, the then-unknown "G. Allman." The speaker longs to escape his existence and get to the place he hears the hippies singing about, that place of euphoria and brilliant colors, but he does not know how to get there, and this depresses him even more. Glen Spreen's thick production captures that suffocating, choking feeling. It is probably a very accurate view of how the hippie movement looked to the underclass: the hippies were dropping out, but this album reminds us that there were many people who did not have that option because they could not even make it in (that the album was primarily produced by one of the studio's resident hippies only compounds the irony).

The record turned out to be a prestige success: like *Dusty in Memphis*, Tommy Cogbill's 1971 recording with Arthur Alexander, and the first John Prine album (done with Arif Mardin at American), its significance has increased with time. It was released almost a year after its creation to virtually no attention, although Glen Spreen said, "At the time we did think it was unique enough to have a chance." Later he discovered something surprising. "Up until a couple of years ago, I would get calls about the album. The calls came from France, Germany, and Switzerland. At first I denied having worked on the album because I didn't remember it. . . . I found out the reason for the calls although at first it was not apparent. They were asking about Joey's contact information. They wanted Joseph to appear in Europe. The album had become popular."

It is considered a cutting-edge classic today, even though Glen characterized the attempt as "false" and regarded it as not what the American musicians did best. "I felt the type of music we did for that album was out of character for the group as a whole," he reflected. "We couldn't 'dummy down' enough [to do psychedelic music], especially Bobby, Bobby, Mike, Gene, and Reggie. Although it was a decent try it just wasn't the real thing." An even later arrival, Hayward Bishop, who was not there for that album but who was present for the other psychedelic records the group made during their time in Memphis, summed it up: "[Hard rock] was a very detached, un-heartfelt music. They were trying to make psychedelia musical. When you have been playing with melody and harmony and feeling all your life, you can't all of a sudden start playing a different way. They couldn't make themselves non-musical [enough to play that style]."

A classic recognized as such in its own time was created in the period just before and immediately after the Joseph sessions. Neil Diamond, intrigued by what the group had done to improve the basic track on "Shilo," apparently inveigled Russ Regan, then the president of Uni (the label to which he had just signed after a few years with Bang) to set up a session at American. At the time, he was better known as a writer than as a performer; he had written "I'm a Believer" for the Monkees and had had a few hits on his own, but he was not a household name. The bitter "Solitary Man" (which the group later recorded with B.J. Thomas in Memphis and in Nashville with T.G. Sheppard) was probably his biggest hit thus far. It was another sign of how important the group had become: Tin Pan Alley performers a world away from Memphis in background and outlook were beginning to seek them out.

Reaction to the new client was mixed. Chips Moman, who along with Tommy Cogbill co-produced a few of the sessions, liked Neil immediately. "He was all right," said the producer happily. "Neil was a nice guy and we talked for awhile," said Marty Lacker (although he added that he was not at the sessions and had no idea what went on during that time). One of the string arrangers agreed with him. "Neil Diamond was a pleasure to work with," Mike Leech recounted. "He was shy, his voice would break sometimes at which time I would smile at him and he would smile back bashfully. No attitude that I saw." "I guess he was a little

New Yorky," said Bobby Wood. "I thought he was a little arrogant when we were in the studio. He seemed to be adamant about what he wanted. I thought he had a lot of talent." "The whole thing, his voice, his guitar, his songs, was like a package deal with Neil," said Bobby Emmons. Reggie Young agreed regarding Diamond's ability: "The thing I really admired about him was, he wrote these great songs with three chord changes, they were very easy to remember. . . . Neil was quite easy to work with." Glen Spreen seems to have immediately disliked the singer, yet conceded that Neil "had a unique timbre which carried him. . . . His best talent was writing but Tommy had to push him to elevate that talent." "Neil Diamond never fit into that [Memphis] groove, he wanted to but he never could," Wayne Carson remarked acerbically.

According to Chips, the only problem that he had with Neil was that Neil wanted to record some of the newer songs he had written. Chips felt that some of the older material Neil had brought with him, including a song about a tent-revival preacher, "Brother Love's Traveling Salvation Show," had more quality and potential, so that is where they began. And what a beginning.

"Brother Love" is a Southern genre painting, with Chips and Tommy at the peak of their form as aural impressionists. The two Bobbys announce with gospel-style keyboards exactly what is going to happen, and Neil's first words are like the opening sentence in a novel: "Hot August night and the grass on the ground smelling sweet." The second line brings the action in closer, like a medium camera shot of a field somewhere between LaGrange and Memphis: "Move up the road to the outskirts of town and the sound of that good gospel beat." The music swells and builds to the chorus and then back down again, setting the scene for the preacher's entrance: "Room gets suddenly still and when you'd almost bet you could hear yourself sweat / he walks in." The next line, describing the preacher, could have applied equally to Tommy Cogbill, directing things in the control room: "Eyes black as coal and when he lifts his face, every ear in the place is on him." The chorus

builds once more to the voice of Neil Diamond himself as the preacher, sermonizing on the need to reach out to God when there is trouble, and then the chorus again, lifting and carrying the listener all the way to the fadeout. It is more euphoric than most of Tommy's spiritual litanies, offering the promise of salvation and joy as one and the same thing. Spiritual matters seemed less important to Chips (although he wrote movingly of them in his later autobiographical song "Dusty Roads"), but here he infuses the song with all the remembered atmosphere of his Georgia childhood.

Even more moving is the ballad Neil brought with him to the sessions, a drifter's reflection called "Glory Road." In Chips's and Tommy's hands, the song takes over where "I Shall Be Released" left off as part two of their joint autobiography, offering another illustration of the way they could turn lines they never wrote into a completely personal declaration. The drifter speaking could have been Chips if he had never opened his studio, still painting houses and picking lettuce: "Wearing my high boots, got all my worldlies here in a sack / Looking for something, knowin' that it ain't here where I'm at." Mike Leech weighs in with his usual somber work on strings, and Tommy Cogbill's voice is implied in the chorus, asking the drifter a question: "Friend, have you seen Glory Road? / Say, friend, I've got a heavy load and I know Glory Road's waiting for me." It's possible to hear this song as a trilogy with "Angel of the Morning" and "I Shall Be Released" as expressions of both Tommy's spiritual quest and the meaning he found. With three memorable productions, Tommy Cogbill established himself as the John Keats of Southern music—committed to both temporal and spiritual beauty, and seemingly aware on some unspoken primal level that he was doomed. In the end the music stops altogether for a conclusion: "Rest my load, now I know / Glory Road / Won't set me free." And the song resumes, only to fade out on the drifter (Chips) as he wanders away into the sunset, chasing another elusive dream.

Perhaps it was Chips's preference for sorrowful music that led this session to have such an emphasis on ballads: "If I Never Knew Your

Name" continues the pattern. It is the essence of bittersweet, striking a balance between the joy and pain of complicated love. By now Mike Leech was accustomed to the inclinations of both producers, and he created an unbroken string line that builds in the first verse and runs beautifully through a chorus that is solemn enough for Chips but that weaves and twists and turns in the intricate ways Tommy liked. The beginning of the track is staccato and choppy, as if churning with emotion; only Bobby Emmons's humming organ line provides any stability as the track builds to Mike's contribution, which in some ways is the most meaningful. It is such a deeply felt arrangement that when Vic Dana did a cover version in California a year later, the string arranger there followed Mike's original line as closely as possible.

"Juliet" is a ballad with a soft melody and a message of awestruck wonder. "Ohhh, yeah," Reggie Young intoned whisperingly when he recalled this completely atmospheric track, which captures that moment of late-night intimacy when a loved one stands before you for the very first time. Not even a string section carries this recording; the musicians lent the song such a hushed quality that Chips and Tommy let the basic track stand as it was, a testament to the power of a woman's beauty and a man reduced to speechlessness at the sight of her. One pictures Juliet, standing barefoot in a dark doorway with a soft light behind her, holding her shoes in her hand as she walks toward her lover, who is too stunned to even think clearly. A woman listening can envision herself as Juliet, walking into the room, gazing tenderly and expectantly at a man she passionately desires. It is not as famous a recording as some from this session, but its power is astonishing.

Simplicity is also a key to the production of "Hurtin' You Don't Come Easy"; Chips and Tommy set this one up with just Neil Diamond's and Reggie Young's acoustic guitars, giving this a folk-country feel. It is another drifter's ballad, voicing the chronic dissatisfaction characteristic of Chips: "I need to find / What I ain't found / I may be looking for it till the last day I'm alive." Emphatic, determined,

almost defiant—the speaker does not want to hurt anybody, but his restlessness leaves him no choice. As with many songs chosen by Chips, a situation is described where somebody, speaker or listener, is bound to lose. Life, in his world, is a zero-sum game.

Despite the artistic brilliance of the recordings, Tommy Cogbill seemed to be having problems with the session. Don Crews remembered a conversation he had with Tommy just after the first night, when Tommy and Chips had already recorded several of Neil's songs including "Brother Love's Traveling Salvation Show." "Tommy said, 'Don, I don't know, I'm not sure I can work with this guy,'" Crews reported. "It was a personality conflict. I said, 'Tommy, why don't you try it for one more night and see what happens.'" And the following night, the group cut "Sweet Caroline."

It was like pulling teeth to get it, remembered Glen Spreen, who along with Mike Leech (on bass) was there to listen to the basic tracks being cut and decide placings for strings and horns while Tommy was in the control booth alone directing the session. "Tommy was sometimes diplomatic with Neil and sometimes blunt," Glen noted. Neil had brought in a new, semi-humorous song about culture clash between Brooklyn and the South, "New York Boy," which Mike Leech recalled, "we worked on all day . . . an okay song, but nobody loved it." Finally Neil finished cutting an acceptable track and was preparing to go. Glen Spreen, Reggie Young, Mike Leech, and Bobby Wood all recounted what happened next: Tommy looked at Neil and said in his dry, quiet voice, "That all you got?" (Bobby Emmons and the sound engineer Mike Cauley, who at that point was only hanging around the studio every now and then, believed that this scene did not happen over "Sweet Caroline," but later, when Neil recorded "Holly Holy.")

"In other words . . . Tommy let it be known that the songs weren't hits and he needed something better," said Glen. "Neil was upset because he thought he had shown his best work [an understandable reaction]. "[He] said, 'I have one started but it isn't finished yet,'" Mike Leech continued. "Tommy asked to hear it and he began playing 'Sweet Caroline.' We saddled up and nailed it in just a few takes." "We all loved that song," said Reggie Young enthusiastically. "We knew that 'Sweet Caroline' was a hit when we cut it," added Bobby Wood. The writer felt differently. "I don't think Neil was really pleased with the arrangement," Reggie reflected. Gene Chrisman recalled that the singer "didn't even want to cut 'Caroline.'" "Neil Diamond didn't like it at all," said Bobby Wood amusedly. "I remember him not liking the song at all and he didn't want it to be a single."

In 2008 Neil Diamond revealed that the inspiration for "Sweet Caroline" had been John F. Kennedy's daughter, an adolescent in 1969; he had seen a photo of her in a magazine when she was a child, riding a horse, and he had been struck by the hints even then of her eventual beauty and poise. The record commands the listener's attention from the very beginning, with a tense, slowly building horn line (originally a piano part, said Wood; "[Neil] came up with the . . . lick that the horns would eventually play") that bursts into an open sunlight of strings and horns leading into the song itself. Neil may have come up with the actual line, but the emphasis on a strong beginning is totally Tommy Cogbill. Roger Hawkins remembered that, as far back as the road trips, "Tommy was always one of the ones who'd stop a take and say, 'Let's get a good intro here.'" This introduction, and Tommy's gradual building the volume in the background, became so completely a part of the song that, as with "Angel of the Morning," no one has been able to set up the song without it, not even on the relatively underproduced version cut by Bobby Goldsboro with the former Shoals musicians in Nashville later in 1969.

"Sweet Caroline" is about a man looking back on the beginnings of a romance, not sure how it started or whether even to accept his good fortune: by the chorus, he shrugs and decides to be happy, and the triumphant sound of the music echoes his decision: "Good times never seemed so good." The second verse describes his loneliness before meeting Caroline, emphasized by the droning of the horns; again the background builds to the shouting

jubilance of the chorus. The repeating figure of the introduction begins again, this time overlaid with skittering strings, and when the chorus bursts into sunlight the title line is emphasized by Mike Leech's glockenspiel, implying that the speaker is so in love that he hears bells chiming when he mentions Caroline's name. The sound is elaborately layered, and the construction is such that the listener rides on the melody as Tommy Cogbill's emphasis on dynamics turns a good song into a great one.

Tommy's flair for the unusual is everywhere but in the string line, which at the singer's insistence was not done by the American arrangers. The final string and horn parts of "Sweet Caroline" were overseen elsewhere. "I'm not even sure how it was decided who would do the arrangements," said Mike Leech. "Neil decided that Mike and I did not have it so he did the overdubs himself in California," Glen Spreen observed. "Actually I really think that Neil was just a control freak and wanted to do things his way." If so, it would not be the only time that the independence of the American group would ruffle feathers, not only with artists but increasingly with record executives, who were not used to such independence from session players.

"We cut three hits from the get-go," Don Crews said proudly of the sessions. The songs established Neil Diamond not just as a writer, but as a singer and personality. "Brother Love" was released that spring, "Sweet Caroline" became the hit of the summer, and at year's end Neil was on the charts with a Top Ten single in "Holly Holy." It should have been a triumph for the group, but, as often happened in the world of American Studios, the musicians found that they had lost when they won.

Tommy Cogbill had negotiated not just the usual producer's royalty, but a percentage designated to go to the musicians, a policy that was gradually becoming a standard part of the AGP setup. Chips Moman had instituted the idea, and it was a feature of which he remained justifiably proud. "It was royalty sharing from the start. Not every project, but the ones I remember," said Bobby Emmons. The deal for this session had been worked out on an informal basis with the people close to Neil, including his regular producer, Tom Catalano. Bobby Wood related what happened from there. "They didn't want to pay us with that stuff," he said. "Tommy had made a deal with us for one percent. Somebody, from Catalano's office, told 'em they weren't gonna pay us. Tommy got a lawyer and they said there was no written contract."

It was not the first time that Southern boys, raised on handshake deals and word-is-bond business partnerships, found themselves at a disadvantage with New Yorkers, a fact of life with which they were all too aware. "A lot of guys were used to takin' advantage of us dumb Southerners," said Jimmy Johnson in the Shoals, using the term ironically. "I remember Tommy was telling me about working with Neil Diamond. Tommy told me that he got screwed by Diamond. . . . I was very saddened when Tommy told me Diamond didn't pay them for that." His normally easygoing drawl turned angry. "That's such a *rat*, y'know? To screw a guy like Tommy . . . anybody who would do that ought not to be let live. Every time I see or hear anything related to that guy, I cut it *off*." His voice became reflective again. "We were all very angry that Neil would have done Tommy that way. If he had ever called us to work with him, we would have said no. And never told him why." He sighed sadly. "I think Tom probably let it go, he didn't want the hassle."

Marty Lacker was surprised. "I'm not aware that Neil didn't want to do that," he said. By the time he took over from Don Crews as American's business manager the following year, the matter had been straightened out and Tommy and the group were receiving royalties from those records. "By the time I got there the deal had already been done and was handled for Neil by Art McKnow, his accountant," Marty added precisely. "Art is who I dealt with each quarter to make sure the check was sent. When I received it, I disbursed everyone's share in it to each of the musicians and Tommy." As an afterthought, he chuckled. "Neil's accountant really hated to hear from me."

Apprised of this, Jimmy Johnson was elated. "I'm so happy that took place!" he exclaimed joyfully. Had he known about it at the time, he would have seen it as further reason for jubilation. For at the beginning of 1969, despite many fears and misgivings, he and Roger Hawkins left the employ of Rick Hall, drew up incorporation papers, bought out the Fred Bevis studio on Jackson Highway in Muscle Shoals, and brought David Hood and Barry Beckett in as equal partners, looking directly to the American musicians for inspiration. "They just reaffirmed that 'hey, this could be done.' It was another slap in the face that opportunity was knocking," said Roger Hawkins.

The American group were unaware at the time of how much their work set the standard other session players wanted to achieve. They were stunned to learn, years later, that Motown musicians had followed what they were doing, and it was equally astonishing for them to discover how they all (not just Chips Moman, Tommy Cogbill, and Reggie Young, who had worked extensively there) were viewed in the Shoals. "We were trying to be what the American rhythm section was. . . . We looked up to 'em as guys who had a lot more experience than we did," commented Roger Hawkins. "The Muscle Shoals Rhythm Section, when it came to the American guys, we'd just stand back and say 'Gol-leee,'" said Jimmy Johnson respectfully. "When they walked in, everybody got the best from their music. It was real cool to look at them and figure out how to do it. They all had Cadillacs; they was in the big, big bread."

Jimmy always credited Chips with helping to give the Shoals rhythm section the self-confidence necessary to go out on their own. "We were so impressed that a guy as gifted and talented as him [would have] wanted us to take over their studio," said Jimmy, referring to Chips's offer from two years before. "We just didn't have the money to do it at the time, and we weren't ready." By now they were, and a loan from Jerry Wexler helped upgrade the studio they had bought so that Muscle Shoals Sound could become operational that April. It was rough going at first, and they were, as Jimmy put it, "scared chickens": "Before that time, no musicians had ever owned a studio. Friends of ours all over the country were takin' bets [on how long the business could last]; they gave us six months." But by the end of the year R. B. Greaves's "Take a Letter, Maria" had justified Atlantic's investment and launched another independent Southern studio. "When we started gettin' some things goin', Tommy was happy for us," Jimmy Johnson remembered.

The American group could also rejoice in the success of other friends. At the beginning of the year, Joe South made his breakthrough with the biting, cynical "Games People Play," about, among other things, the breakup of a marriage and the ways in which people waste time, money, and their entire lives (that it was eventually used as a jingle for the West Virginia state lottery is nothing short of obscene). And J.R. Cobb finally achieved his goal of composing a standard. "Traces" by the Classics IV was on the charts at the same time as Joe South's breakthrough, and by March it had become the hit of the spring. It is no surprise that this one appealed to so many people; it reworks the classic theme of love gone wrong, a man sorting through the photographs and mementoes that she left behind and hoping she will return. The melody is gentle and introspective, and the small details (the creased photos, a ring the woman had once worn) increase the song's intimacy. It was so far out of the Top Forty ballpark that J.R. and his usual co-writer, Buddy Buie, had misgivings: "We didn't know if radio would accept it," J.R. remembered. Not only was the Classics IV recording successful, but many other versions of the song were recorded, from a lilting instrumental by Billy Vaughn to the Lettermen's vocal which combined it with Mac Davis's similarly themed "Memories." After years of trying to write an entry for the great American songbook, nobody was more surprised than J.R. that "Traces" turned out to be the one. "It took a while for it to sink in," he reflected thoughtfully. "I've been stunned every time any song I've ever had anything to do with was successful. When you get so close to a song, you don't hear it the way other people do."

Another song composed by Buie and J.R. became the B-side of "Traces." "Sentimental Lady" did not become a standard, but should have: it features Cobb's most beautiful melody and a haunting lyric about a woman tortured by thoughts of a past love she could not forget. In just a few lines, J.R. sketches the outline of her memories; the "January snows" where the couple huddled together, and the height of a romance that flowered with the spring. In the chorus, Dennis Yost used his midrange to tender effect, pleading with the lady to keep on living. "Yesterday is gone, far away," he sighs sadly, his voice almost dwindling to a mournful whisper, "Far, far away." Even if one has never lost someone dear to them, the lyric evokes tears; to those who have, this song is solace. With its themes of sorrow and loss, it would have been an interesting ballad for the American group to record, but somehow it slipped past them.

That would be one of the few things to slip past them in the coming year. 1969 would be the high-water mark of the studio's fortunes. Much had been asked of them before, but from now on expectations would even be higher.

For it is not every group of good old boys who is called upon to restore the throne of a King.

### CHAPTER 17

# From a Jack to a King

Marty Lacker told the story over and over again: in a book of his own; in a set of reminiscences done with Lamar Fike and Elvis's cousin Billy Smith for the reporter and Elvis historian Alanna Nash; in a 1994 oral history compiled by Chips's then-secretary Rose Clayton; and in countless print and television interviews from those of Peter Guralnick to this account. Throughout the innumerable retellings, Marty's memory never wavered.

He was sitting in the Jungle Room at Graceland with Lamar Fike and George Klein one January evening when Felton Jarvis, the RCA staff producer who had replaced Chet Atkins in the studio working with Elvis, was there conferring with the singer on a recording session scheduled for Nashville. Elvis traditionally did not work until after January 8, his birthday; after that he would go into the studio and record a batch of songs, one of which would be scheduled for Easter release. This annual project, slated for the following week, was being discussed, and Marty could not stand it. Since that fall, when he began spending time at American during the waning days of his affiliation with Pepper-Tanner, he had seen for himself how good the musicians and Chips were. He was lobbying hard, as he had since he saw what was happening at American, for Elvis to record there. He knew that the television special that had just been aired was a big step in bringing Elvis back to his throne as the King of Rock and Roll, but he also knew that only a hit record would complete the restoration. Elvis knew it too: two Jerry Reed compositions he cut in late 1967, "Guitar Man" and "U.S. Male,"

and the song from the comeback special, "If I Can Dream," showed that he wanted to get back in the game.

Marty did not even want to hear about the upcoming Nashville session. "I knew it was gonna be the same old kerplunk kerplunk," he said, referring to the music of the older Nashville sidemen, "and I knew the songs were gonna be crap." He also knew why. Elvis was required to record material from the publishing company Hill and Range, whose executives administered a kickback scheme to give Elvis and his management a percentage of the writer's royalties. These kinds of deals were commonplace when Tom Parker had negotiated Elvis's contract in the fifties, but by 1969 it was an outmoded way to work. Marty knew it; so did everyone else. No songwriter was willing to give up the publishing rights anymore, not even for the honor of having Elvis do one of their songs. The outcome was predictable. "He'd pretty much just about drained the well dry," Don Crews estimated. "The recent stuff he'd had was these dumb old movie songs that didn't have any substance to it," said Reggie Young. And Felton wanted Elvis to go through the same motions. Just the thought of another session like that grated on Marty so badly he did not even go in the dining room and have dinner when the meal was served.

He got the shock of his life a few minutes later. Felton came racing out and telling him that Elvis wanted to go to American and do the upcoming session with Chips. They had four days to get ready. Could Marty set it up? He could—"I was outta that chair in a flash." He told Rose Clayton, "I didn't walk in there [to the dining room]; I ran in there." Elvis told him yes, he wanted to do it, and he said, "You and Felton work it out with Chips." Immediately Marty called the studio and asked for Chips; nothing was happening around the place, so the producer was home and Marty reached him there. He never forgot the conversation.

"I said, 'Chips, let me ask you something. Lincoln (I always called him Lincoln), you still wanna cut Elvis?' He said, 'Hell, yeah.' He said, 'Don't be kidding me.' I said, 'I'm not kidding. He wants to start Monday night.' I knew he had

Neil Diamond [scheduled]. Chips said, 'Screw Neil Diamond. We'll just have to bump some schedules around, but damn, we can do it. You know how much I want to do Elvis.' I said, 'I'll put you on the phone with Felton and he'll work out the details."

There were surprisingly few details to work out; the most important one was that Chips would only receive a producer's fee for the project, and no royalties. Marty noted that the fee was twenty-five thousand dollars, and added that the fee "was just for one album and if anything else was to be released [RCA released two albums' worth of material that Chips recorded with the King, plus innumerable reissues] then RCA should have rightfully paid Chips more." Felton had nothing to settle; Marty remembered, "Felton at the time worked for RCA Records and he was on a salary with them, which was totally different from Chips's deal." The second requirement was that the session would have no onlookers invited: the fewer people who knew about the project, the better. "All the musicians were asked not to tell anyone about the sessions and those of us with Elvis didn't tell anyone," said Marty.

There was a great difference in American's layout compared to that of RCA in Nashville, the studio to which Elvis was most accustomed. Marty described the difference: "American's door was right out on the street whereas Nashville RCA was in a bigger building and you had to go through other doors to get to the actual studio. RCA had control of the building." That being so, security at American would have to be a little tighter than usual. Chips was still astonishingly lax about such things, still leaving the doors unlocked during sessions, letting people wander in off the street and giving J.P. and his teenaged friends the run of the place. There was no other type of preparation, Marty insisted. "[People] think I told Chips how to talk to Elvis. That's a load of bull," he said flatly. "One of the reasons I wanted Elvis to record there was so he could work his magic and the only way Chips works *his* magic is by being Chips." Once things were set up, it was back to dinner at Graceland for the evening, and Marty

remembered, "Naturally, I sat there and ate a steak."

Marty wanted to prepare Elvis a little for what he would find at American, but he knew better than to begin drilling it into him right away. "With Elvis, everything was about mood," he reflected softly. "When he ate, you didn't wanna throw nothin' at him. It depends on how you put things to Elvis." But when Marty saw the opportunity, he took it, and again he never forgot what he had said. "You've got a great studio, great musicians, a great producer in Chips," he told Elvis. "And we all know you can sing, so can you get some damn good songs??!!???" The lack of decent material had been particularly frustrating to Marty, and to many other people who knew that Elvis had been squandering his voice on badly written songs made to order for the movie soundtracks. "What Elvis had done in the previous five years was trash," Marty said bluntly. When he told Elvis to get some good songs, his friend was silent for a moment, then said quietly, "I was gonna take you and show you this tape I got from Billy Strange."

Billy Strange was a respected Hollywood arranger and guitarist; he worked primarily for Lee Hazelwood at that time, but had been the original musical director on the comeback special and had introduced Elvis to his writing partner, a Texan named Scott Davis who went by the nickname Mac. Elvis had found Mac in a room with no windows, as the writer sat curled up on the floor and sang his tunes accompanied only by his acoustic guitar. The singer described Mac at the time as "the strangest guy you'd ever wanna meet," but was impressed enough with what he heard to record "Memories" and "A Little Less Conversation" for the show. The former was a deeply poetic song that, as with the Jerry Reed material, showed that Elvis was serious about relaunching his career; the latter became a posthumous hit in England when it was featured on the soundtrack to *Ocean's Eleven* and given a modern remix. Another Mac Davis tune, a witty treatise on hypocrisy called "Clean Up Your Own Back Yard," was awaiting release. Elvis had, halfway on his own, discovered a writer capable of strong lyrics and mature statements; his interpretations of Davis's work sent an important announcement that Elvis was now a grown man. Working at American, with its reputation for realistic music, would signal it, too.

This poetic realism was heard on the demo tape in Elvis's possession, in a song called "Don't Cry Daddy," about a man so devastated by the loss of his wife that he could hardly function, despite the knowledge that his children were as wounded as he. For Elvis, it evoked a memory of how lonely his father had been when Gladys Presley had died (although Elvis had never approved of the way Vernon had dealt with that loneliness, first by dating other women and then by marrying a woman Elvis never trusted). It was there in another song subtitled "The Vicious Circle," but better known by its repetitive phrase "in the ghetto." Again the view is stark, nearly hopeless: a boy on the South Side of Chicago feels the pressure coming down at him from all sides, he can't win, takes to crime and is gunned down by the cops in a shoot-out, and as he lies bleeding in the street another child is born who will repeat the story. It is the stuff that Bob Marley songs were made of, a story that gangsta rappers have also tried to tell, but they obscure the point by booming bass and gratuitous obscenity. Davis's melody is softly sorrowful, with undertones of almost pathetic grandeur as he documents the boy's struggles. The song seems to have triggered a sense memory in Elvis of his own humble beginnings, and to have expressed his compassion. These two songs were on his list from the beginning.

Once it was established that Elvis was coming in, the American staff scrambled to line up songs from the group's writers, although Glen Spreen recalled it amusedly as "sort of a casual scramble." Don Crews remembered, "I got all the fellas together—Mark, Dan, everybody— and I said, 'Y'all got anything?' They all looked at each other. I said, 'Mark, how about that song you just cut?'" Mark James had just been signed to Scepter and had done one record so far, something he had written about an aggrieved good old boy trying to explain himself to a

pathologically jealous woman; it featured an interesting string line and a romping bass part from Mike Leech. The story line was intriguing, and Crews thought "Suspicious Minds" just might work. "It's Only Love," Mark's new composition, was also a possibility (and Elvis did a softly rocking version of it the following year for the Nashville Marathon sessions). Don had faith in another new song that had been written by Johnny Christopher, who was still around on a part-time basis, pitching new material and attending sessions to learn and absorb as much of the atmosphere as possible.

The composition literally occurred to Johnny in a dream. He knew Elvis was coming in and naturally wanted to write something; he tried and tried, sitting in his Whitehaven apartment for hours with his acoustic guitar and not coming up with anything. Finally he stopped and went to bed so he would not wake his wife and baby daughter. "Half an hour later I woke up; this voice said, 'Mama Liked the Roses.' I always felt like that was a voice from God." He got the song down in twenty minutes, even the spoken part in the middle. "I knew it had a place in the middle for a recitation. I went in when no one was there and did a one-man demo," he said. "I was so nervous, I was twenty-five or twenty-six. I was askin' God to help me." It was the night before Elvis was supposed to come in; Johnny gave the demo to Crews, who passed it along to Chips. "A day or so later, he said, 'I played your song for Elvis and he cried.'" "We all knew he was thinking of Gladys," Bobby Wood remarked to Rose Clayton, and the spirit of Gladys Presley—her warmth, love of life, imagination, and deep religious commitment—seems to leap off the recording and into the hearts of the listeners. "And where would we all be without our mamas?" Johnny asked rhetorically (by 2006 he would be back in Georgia living with, and taking care of, his own mother, following nearly two decades of personal trials).

The only American group writer not asked to contribute songs was Wayne Carson, a surprising omission in light of his strong material and the number of hits he had already written. But then, he never aggressively pitched his songs, even at American. "I just figured Si would handle it for me," he growled ruefully. "I'm no damn song plugger. They kept it [the Elvis session] kinda hush-hush from us. I didn't know what it was about. Chips didn't really broadcast what he was doin'. I always felt a little left out of that deal but that's all right, shit, it's done, just move on," he shrugged. Don Crews said that the reason Wayne was not approached was that he had a single out at the time and Crews decided not to try for an Elvis release that might compete with Wayne's recording.

On the evening of Elvis's first appearance at American, most of the musicians were trying to play down the session's importance. After all, the king was the supplicant, coming to a place with a proven reputation for success. "I think everybody knew that he pretty much needed some songs and that this was the place where he might have a chance," said Ima Roberts. Security had been taken care of: "Security was simple, we locked the doors," said Marty Lacker. "Everybody who needed to be there was in the studio by the time Elvis and us got there. . . . If someone knocked on the door who wasn't part of the session they were not allowed in whether they worked at the studio or not" (though amazingly, J.P., the adolescent boy who hung around the studio, was permitted inside). Don Crews and Ima Roberts were upstairs in the office, available to answer the phone, type up lyrics, or do anything else that might be needed.

"I don't think anybody was scared, I think they were more in disbelief that he was actually coming," said Ima. "Why no, I wasn't scared at all," said Chips laconically. "He was just one more act." Mike Leech recalled that Chips actually was slightly nervous, like a person wanting to put their best foot forward when company was arriving at the house; he had asked that everyone be in the studio, ready to record, and got annoyed when he found Mike and Tommy Cogbill sitting in the front office working a crossword puzzle (Mike and Tommy just laughed).

"Were we scared?" asked Reggie Young rhetorically. "No. As a matter of fact, I know we were busy . . . we could see all the people we were recording. . . . I remember thinking, 'Oh, Elvis is gonna be here, cool.'" Bobby Emmons echoed the thought. "We were not awed to distraction even with Elvis because of the stature of some of the artists we'd been cutting," said the organist. "We were glad we had gained enough fame that someone of his stature would seek us out." Tommy Cogbill seemed unflappable as usual. "I'm sure he felt some excitement and pride when Elvis first arrived just as the other guys did but you'd never know it from watching Tommy," Marty Lacker observed. "I don't know that Tommy was a big Elvis fan, I don't know if I was," thought Reggie Young. Glen Spreen emphatically was not an Elvis fan; he had not really listened to many of his records since the first few hits back in the fifties. "I did not have an elevated feeling at all," he recalled.

Not even the horn section, who would be present for overdubs as Elvis was singing some of his final vocals on the tracks, seemed overly awed. Wayne Jackson, leader of the Memphis Horns, elaborated on his famous remark, "We were all thrilled at doing Elvis, but it wasn't like doing Neil Diamond." "Neil Diamond was heavy," said the trumpet player. "[Elvis] had been doin' stuff like 'Teddy Bear' and that was lightweight. . . . Elvis was not a top-chart rock and roll guy. All he did was those dipshit movies"—though Jackson went on to say that he personally had enjoyed many of Elvis's films and thought him a good actor and charismatic presence onscreen. "I said, Well, Elvis is coming here to get our sound, no use getting butterflies here," Bobby Wood told Rose Clayton. "But man, I knew when he was in the back parking lot!" "The night he got there and that back door opened, we were all taken," said Reggie. "I thought, Lordamercy, that's Elvis!" "He still had that same aura around him that he had had years before," said Bobby Emmons, who recalled seeing the King once standing outside the Memphian Theater.

"Reggie and I were sitting in the studio when Elvis and his entourage came strolling in the back door," remembered Mike Leech.

"First words I ever heard him say: 'What a funky, funky studio.'" "I was standing in the opposite corner by the piano," Bobby Wood remembered. "J.P. was sitting on the bass stool. He stood up and put his hand on his heart and followed Elvis with his eyes across the room. Elvis finally walked around the room and shook hands with everybody. It's hard to talk with your heart in your throat." "It felt like another session," Glen Spreen said offhandedly. "I shook his hand and said 'Glad to meet you,' it was as casual as could be." Everyone recalled that Elvis seemed relaxed, amused, and generally looking forward to working with this group of musicians.

Elvis had even more reason to be amused, Reggie Young added, because of a recent development: "Where the garbage cans were for the restaurant out back, they'd cleaned it up and all the rats from out back came in the rafters." They were running over the rafters and squeaking all through the sessions. "We don't want to forget the rat story," added Bobby Wood. "It was told for the truth but I don't know for sure. . . They were falling off the garbage bin out back and someone said one fell off the roof right in front of Elvis." It was a long way from the RCA studios in Nashville.

"We came in the back door like all of us always did," said Marty Lacker. "They spent an hour saying hello. They knew Elvis was special." "He made an entrance, there's no doubt about it," said Reggie Young. "He was decked to the hilt, he had on a blue leather jacket. He had that charisma. I just stepped back and said, 'Man, that's Elvis!' He came over and said something to me, kinda making a joke. All his entourage was with him." Marty Lacker had come in with him, of course. So had George Klein from WHBQ and Lamar Fike, Nashville's representative for the Hill and Range publishing company, with a stack of demos. Also present was Lamar's boss, Freddy Bienstock ("I could never find out who he was," said Reggie Young); Colonel Parker's representative, Tom Diskin; RCA staff engineer Al Pachuki (whose assignment to the console freed Ed Kollis to play some stunning blues harmonica), RCA vice president

Harry Jenkins (an executive assigned strictly to Elvis), and Felton Jarvis, whose role would be minimal but who nonetheless was there.

Reggie Young knew Felton from the early days of Muscle Shoals when the Felton-produced Tommy Roe hits had featured Reggie's lead guitar. He knew Felton to be a cheerful type and found him to be even more so now. "I just sensed that whatever Elvis wanted, Felton would see that he got it," Reggie observed. "He didn't want any waves at all." "May he rest in peace, he was a bit two-faced," was Marty Lacker's opinion. "Felton was there basically to keep Elvis happy and upbeat." "I didn't really have any direct contact with Felton. From a distance, he hit me as just the typical staff producer of a big record company, he was just there to do his job," said Bobby Emmons. "He was a reinforcement," said Glen Spreen. "I remember Felton sitting there and carrying on inane conversations with people who did not matter, and that inhibits your creativity," Wayne Jackson of the Memphis Horns noted sourly. Hayward Bishop was not there for these sessions, but he worked with Felton in Nashville later and, like Marty, always had mixed feelings about him; he recalled Felton as "a nice man . . . friendly . . . [but] kind of like a used-car salesman" (Felton's photos from the Memphis session and other places project that aura). "He was a *great* guy," Ima Roberts said enthusiastically of Felton. "Real easygoing, friendly, easy to talk to, unaffected by all that was going to happen. He was very unusual." "Felton was always nice to us," recalled Bobby Wood. "Felton was honest, had integrity, and was diplomatic when necessary," Glen Spreen added. "However, Felton was also a big-time party man . . . a joker and just loved to have fun. I liked hanging around him. I felt comfortable with Felton." Mike Leech did too; he took to Felton at once and began a friendship that lasted until Jarvis's death from a stroke in 1990.

An event as monumental as this session needed visual documentation, and history's most unlikely official photographer, Dan Penn, was there the first night, brandishing a boxy and by today's standards unwieldy Polaroid.

"I'd been gone a long time," he reflected. "Chips called and asked, 'Did I get you a camera for Christmas?' I said, yeah. He said, 'Why don't you come over and take a few pictures?'" Chips may have been looking for a chance to mend some fences; Dan was looking for that too, and so he went. "Dan taking the pictures . . . was a first for an Elvis session but Elvis had no problems with it because he was enjoying the guys and the sessions," said Marty Lacker. "It also just showed how happy the guys were to be cutting Elvis." The images from Dan's Polaroid camera have been shown around the world: Elvis and Tommy Cogbill sitting quietly in a corner; Chips, with a strangely blank expression, standing alongside Elvis; Felton wearing a plaid suit jacket; and most memorably of all, a group picture of the American musicians, including Dan, standing around Elvis, who is holding Tommy's Fender Precision bass. (Conspicuous by their absence were the late arrivals. Glen Spreen left shortly after preliminary work on the session began, and Johnny Christopher was not there at all the first night. It was symbolic of the way the latecomers would always be viewed by the musicians who had gotten there first.) "I took 'em all, except the one I was standing in. Everwho was standin' by took it," said Dan of his photographs, in a wonderfully Appalachian turn of phrase. "I don't recall who took that group picture," added Marty Lacker. "Obviously it wasn't Dan because he's in the picture. Might have been one of us who were with Elvis." Another photo, of Dan and Elvis, was obviously the result of someone else holding the camera.

During the time Dan was in the studio taking pictures, he and Elvis never spoke. "I didn't say a word to him; I don't never talk to stars, I figure they've been hassled enough," he explained. "I try to put the shoe on the other foot, I wouldn't want nobody sayin' nothin' to me. What you gonna say to a guy like that? 'Hi, Elvis'? He's only heard that forty-four thousand times. I don't go up to people who are anything. I'm not into the star thing. Stars are the most boring people I've ever seen. I like common folks, regular ol' people. [What could I say to Elvis?]—'Hey, I like the way you sing'—he's

only heard that fifty years ago. What're you gonna say to somebody like that? 'Hey, I'm pilled up too??'"—and he burst into chuckles at the thought.

There was also a home movie made on the premises that evening. The documentarian here was mainly Gene Chrisman, but some of the filming may have been done by Tommy Cogbill, who does not appear in any of the film (although Gene does).The rest of the group, and Chips, are highly visible; they clown, cuff and poke one another, and shove each other like boys in junior high (Dan even sticks out his tongue at the camera). Chips Moman mock-kicks Reggie Young and chases him down a hallway. Such horseplay, Mike Leech remembered, was common at American. "Yeah, just something to do," he said amusedly. "There were times when most of the guys would get into a little shoving thing, maybe sneak up and pull arm hairs, silly stuff like that. Nothing anybody did was ever enough to provoke anger.

"I teased Tommy a lot, and he took most of it in stride. He would say something like 'awright, you better cut it out or I'm gonna kick your ass.' . . . For all it would sound serious and he did have a serious look, but I knew him so well, and knew just how far to go before he got really mad, which he never did (at me for that kind of stuff). Of course I kept it up and he would finally jump on me and we would hit the floor or the old couch. . . . He would get me in an armlock or some such thing that hurt a little but he would let up after awhile and we would laugh, sweating and out of breath. It was actually good exercise. . . camaraderie at its best.

"I once walked up to Chips and slapped him on the back of his head—hard. And took off running. He chased me for awhile till I was finally caught and got smacked around. We were laughing the whole time."

Mike's specialty was the good swift kick, and he recalled delivering a few to some of the others. "Bob Taylor also had bruises on his shins. Why did I do that you ask? Same reason Cog and I got into wrestling matches. I would either pick on somebody or they would pick on me (good-natured—all done in fun) and we would wind up with sore spots or bruises. But we all laughed about it. If I had kicked Tommy in the shins he would have killed me. I would just give him a shove, something like that. You pretty much knew how far you could go with different personalities.

"I don't recall anybody ragging Tommy like I did. Certainly none of [the core group]. That's why I felt so close to him, that I'm the only one he allowed to pick on him."

Inevitably, the group teased some of Elvis's Memphis Mafia, and here also Mike Leech seems to have led the way. He began ribbing Marty Lacker on the subject of his Jewishness, using the phrase, "'Did j'eat yet?' 'No. Jew?'" Marty correctly read the teasing as a sign that he was "in," but Lamar Fike took exception to the one Mike pulled on him. "Lamar walked into the front office at American where a couple of us were sitting on an old couch," Mike explained. "When he sat down at the other end, we jumped up (my idea) like his weight bounced one end of the couch up." Lamar weighed four hundred pounds and Elvis, who wasn't heavy then, had always been sarcastic to him about his weight. Lamar had been on the receiving end of fat jokes for years, so, Marty recalled, "Lamar could hold his own with anybody even Elvis. . . [He] was used to it, but he didn't like it and *he* didn't think it was very funny when they did that, neither did I." The cutting up defused a lot of tension, particularly important for a session as monumental as this; but when the cutting up and kidding around were over, and Chips felt that the mood was sufficiently relaxed, he called for everyone to assume their places, and it was time to get to work.

Chips now had songs from the American repertoire; Lamar Fike and Freddy Bienstock had contributed several either from their own writers at Hill and Range or older songs on which they were able to get the publishing kickback. Knowing what was at stake for his friend, Lamar had found quality material, and Elvis began the session with one of the older selections, a classic that had been recorded by Glen Campbell in 1962, and later on by Jody Miller under Billy Sherrill's direction. "Long Black Limousine," as it emerged from these sessions, is a perfect slice of the American Studios worldview; unremittingly grim and sorrowful, but with wild dark beauty in the center of the pain. In telling the story of a country girl who left her hometown because she wanted to ride in a long black limousine and who came back in a hearse, Elvis was unknowingly telling his own story; and it is this as much as anything that gives the record its power. The same holds true with the slow ballad "This Is the Story," a prophetic look at how Elvis's life would be in merely three years' time. In just the first two songs Elvis demonstrated that he could address grownup subjects with as much passion as he had dealt with youthful concerns in the fifties, and the band was with him every step of the way. The Bix Beiderbecke of rock and country—self-taught, troubled, sensitive, eloquent, the voice of a generation—had finally found his Paul Whiteman Orchestra, musicians who knew best how to showcase his talent and frame it within the context of a large production.

And why not? Elvis's life had already seen a great deal of pain, from the privations of his childhood to the death of his beloved mother and his more or less indentured servitude to the army. The undercurrent of trouble in his marriage and the recent death of several relatives were factors in his life at the time of these recordings. What better outlet could he have had to express all the feelings he had kept inside him for years than to wrap his powerful voice around songs of suffering, sorrow, regret, and misery?

It is there on "Don't Cry Daddy," with the opening lines—"Today I stumbled from my bed with thunder crashing in my head, my pillow still wet from last night's tears"—that could have been a page from the diary of nocturnal melancholics such as most of the American group. It is there in the agonized, fruitless search of "Kentucky Rain." It is there in the doom-laden foreboding of Burt Bacharach's "Any Day Now" and the warning of "Inherit the Wind." The grief of "Mama Liked the Roses" and "It Keeps Right On A-Hurtin," the pained goodbye of "The Fair Is Moving On," and the sorrow of "Long Black Limousine": all are eloquent accounts of the despair and loneliness this man must have carried.

The music recorded on those January and February nights in 1969 is an embarrassment of riches. Small details jump out at the listener on the fourth, or fifteenth, or hundredth, listening that were not obvious before: the under-his-breath scat singing Elvis does on "You'll Think of Me," "Stranger in My Own Home Town," "My Little Friend," and several other tracks; the audible countoff between the spaces on "Inherit the Wind"; someone instructing Elvis "Yeah, one more time" at the beginning of "I'll Hold You in My Heart"; Tommy Cogbill's stunning work that almost leaps out of the speakers, particularly with "Gentle on My Mind" and his tour de force, jazz bass lines played with a pick, for "I'm Moving On"; the overdubbed backup singers, including Donna Thatcher (later Godchaux) groaning orgasmically on "Power of My Love" and Sandy Posey's ecstasy on "Rubberneckin'"; Ed Kollis's wild blues harmonica on "Power" and "Stranger," filling in between the lines of Elvis's majestic voice; Chips's revisions of the Dan Penn arrangement for "I'm Moving On"; the manner in which a string line fades out of one speaker and is immediately picked up by the next one, as if Mike Leech and Glen Spreen are having a conversation in spite of themselves; Bobby Emmons's swirling organ lines on "I'll Be There" and "Wearin' That Loved On Look," Mike Leech's chimes on "Long Black Limousine," Reggie Young's sitar on "You'll Think of Me" and Bobby Wood's ringing gospel piano on "Wearin'"; the metallic clang in the middle of the atmospheric "Kentucky Rain" (a sound made, according to Glen Spreen, when Tommy accidentally bumped into the speaker in one of the echo chambers).

These recordings, taken together, were Elvis's first cogent statement about his life, his personality, his interests, and his pain. "My Little Friend" evokes Dixie Locke, his first serious girl friend and the one he thought of marrying till his first record came out and the world changed. "Mama Liked the Roses" is, as Johnny Christopher hoped it would be, the tribute not only to Gladys Presley but to all inspirational mothers everywhere. If "Mama" and "Only the Strong Survive" evoke Gladys, and "It Keeps Right On A-Hurtin'" expresses his grief at her death, Elvis also worked on songs that spoke for Vernon: "Don't Cry Daddy," of course, but Vernon is represented also by two of his favorite songs: "From s Jack to a King" and Stan Kesler's "If I'm a Fool for Loving You," both of which could refer to his life after Gladys, and his marriage to a woman most who knew him thought was totally unsuitable. "Inherit the Wind" addresses Elvis's (and Chips's) legacy of hard luck and restlessness; "Stranger in My Own Home Town," as has been noted before, addresses Elvis's position in Memphis (but of course, it was true of Chips as well that his town would not accept him). The Gamble and Huff "Only the Strong Survive" is not only Elvis being comforted by Gladys but another position paper on stoicism: "There's gonna be, there's gonna be, a whole lot of trouble in this life / Ah, so listen to me, get up off your knees, 'cause only the strong survive." "The Fair Is Moving On" evokes both the carnival theme from some of Elvis's movies and the shadow of Colonel Parker, who after all these years, said Marty Lacker, was still "a carny con man." The Colonel was not at the sessions, nor did he have anything to do with choosing material ("Parker wouldn't know a hit if it slapped him in the face," Marty snorted indignantly), but he could count on his minions and representatives to be there, as they had been at all the RCA sessions, and structure the work being done to fit his agenda.

For instance, Bienstock and his crew pitched songs from their company and several of its subsidiaries. "Freddie Bienstock owned Bay [a European publishing company]," explained Marty Lacker. "Europe was five years behind us, musically." "They brought in all these demos," Reggie Young said. "We were standin' there and we had this little turntable in the studio." When they played the first song, Reggie added, "Elvis asked me, 'Do you like that?' 'No, not really.' He asked Bobby Wood, 'Do you like it?' Bobby told him in no uncertain terms. Felton then asked me and Bobby to stand out in the hall and he said, 'We've got all the material picked, please don't create waves.'"

"I don't remember the thing about Felton

and the hallway regarding the songs," mused the piano player. "I probably would have said that, I usually answer people when asked a question and if you don't want the truth don't ask.

"Elvis didn't ask me about the songs," Wood continued. "George Klein came over to the organ where I was standing and asked me what did I think about the songs they had been playing. I immediately told him I thought they were a piece of shit. He immediately turned to Elvis and said, 'Bobby Wood said those songs are a piece of shit.' I said, 'Thanks a lot, George.' That's when Elvis started laughing his butt off.

"I think that kind of broke the ice, for us as well as Elvis. I'm sure it made the suits unhappy but I didn't give a hoot about what they thought. We obviously knew more about what a hit song sounded like than they did."

It did not matter to Elvis. He knew he was finally getting to wrap his voice around important songs, and he was up for the challenge. "The final decision on the songs done was Elvis's but he did have input from Chips and I voiced my opinion on a couple of them," said Marty Lacker. "Whether Felton had any influence I do not recall." Marty and all the musicians said the same thing—that Elvis was relaxed during the sessions and that he worked as hard as everyone else. Both Mike Leech and Reggie Young said that, though they had no way to judge his attitude from previous sessions, they thought him committed to the material and eager to work. "He didn't want us to treat him any way other than as an artist there to work. Which we did," said Mike Leech. "Elvis was there to work and that's exactly what happened. Chips had been told by somebody 'don't tell Elvis he's sharp or flat' or something along those lines. Chips ignored the advice and treated Elvis (as we all did) just like any other (good) artist."

What trappings of royalty Elvis brought with him were met with amusement by the fiercely egalitarian musicians. "His entourage . . . was way overdone," Mike Leech observed. "You bet," echoed Glen Spreen. "That first day in Memphis, Elvis brought out one of his brown cigarettes and about four or five people were sticking lighters in his face." Reggie Young remembered the "brown cigarettes" as cigarillos (Tommy Cogbill tried them for awhile, in an effort to do without cigarettes) and Reggie also noted that if Elvis wanted to light one "he'd hold one of them up and there'd be more than one lighter" at his service. "To [the entourage] it was all one big party," said Mike Leech. The crowd packing the small studio may have had an inhibiting effect on Tommy, who was naturally reserved anyway. "Tommy's demeanor was always quiet, especially when around people who were not regulars," Marty Lacker recalled. Wayne Jackson remembered Elvis as "a great guy" but could not say the same about much of the entourage: "The only ones that weren't fun were his guys, who tried to walk around with their chests stuck out. They were all tryin' to talk to Elvis at once and we were tryin' to get a job done. . . . They were like about sixteen chickens cluckin' and pluckin' and we were serious about it. . . . All they wanted to do was entertain Elvis."

Chips Moman did not go in for that kind of thing, and he refused to bow and scrape. If Elvis had problems delivering a number, Wayne Carson remembered, the producer did not hesitate to say so. "Chips stood up and said, 'Hey, this ain't no fuckin' movie soundtrack. You need to *sing* that song!' . . . Hey, that microphone and that machine don't know who the hell [the singers] are." "Moman had more, what would it be, constructive criticism," mused Reggie Young. "He'd say, 'You were a little flat there.' I don't believe Felton would ever have said that." "If the take was good then Felton would say 'That's great, Elvis. Come on in and listen.' If the take was not acceptable then Felton would say 'That's good, Elvis. Come on in and listen,'" observed Glen Spreen. "I remember Moman told [Elvis] one time could he resing a certain phrase because his pitch was off," noted Reggie Young. "[Felton] about freaked when Chips told Elvis that he was a little pitchy. He seemed afraid to say anything to Elvis that might bring him down. That was not the way we worked. . . . We didn't care who we were working with, big or little, we would do whatever it took to help everybody," said Bobby Wood.

Far from being annoyed at that kind of treatment, the singer rose to the occasion and responded to Chips's perfectionism by singing as passionately and eloquently as a country Pavarotti. "He didn't give me any problems at all," said Chips graciously. "He really seemed to be trying," said Reggie Young. "Chips was trying to help get a performance out of him and I sensed that he appreciated it, at the time." "I think Elvis appreciated the output," Bobby Wood observed. "He was smart enough to be one of the guys." "Chips probably got the best out of Elvis since the Sun records or with Chet," Wayne Carson observed. Elvis always fed off the response of an audience, even a small one, so Felton was out in the studio, jumping around and dancing to get Elvis going, and Marty Lacker sat on a stool behind Chips in the control room, moving around in time to the music so that Elvis could see and respond.

When the first session's work ended at daylight, Elvis and some of his group piled in the car and went back to Graceland. Marty was there, and remembered Elvis sitting in the front seat of the car, reflecting on the night's work. "He said, 'Man, that felt great. I just want to see if I can do it again.' He could see the difference." "I don't know that he even knew he could come back," thought Reggie. "I had not seen Elvis happier," said Marty.

Elvis even got the chance to be a song plugger during the sessions. Barry Mann and Cynthia Weil had sent a demo of a ballad that had been recorded several times during the preceding two years, a story song called "Angelica." The American musicians, supervised by Chips and Tommy Cogbill, were doubling up during the Elvis sessions, recording Roy Hamilton by day and then, while he played an engagement at T.J.'s, working all night with Elvis. For once they were well-paid for their trouble: Reggie Young's session notes tell the story. "After midnight, it went to time-and-a-half," said the guitarist. "I was prime-time leader on one of the Elvis sessions—I made $195.00 [that night]. On January 18th, we started one hour regular time, two hours prime time, we made $87.68." The double shifts were rough on Tommy Cogbill especially, Ima Roberts remembered tenderly:

"Those little eyes used to be so swollen when he'd come in there. He didn't do well staying up." Dan Penn's photos of Tommy from the first night show a pale, slit-eyed, and exhausted-looking man.

No one had more respect for other singers than Elvis. He always had fondness for the big, soaring voices that had inspired him, everyone from Mario Lanza to Jake Hess of the Statesmen gospel quartet to Roy Hamilton. Meeting Hamilton was a chance he could not pass up, and Elvis arranged to come in early one afternoon. Hamilton turned out to be as admiring of Elvis as he was of Hamilton, and the two singers got along well. It was during this meeting that Elvis offered the other singer the chance to do "Angelica." At first, Hamilton demurred, but Marty Lacker recalled, Elvis was "bound and determined to give it to Roy." Eventually the singer accepted and recorded the song as the A-side of his first AGP single.

To hear "Angelica" is heartbreaking now, and it too must be classed as one of Tommy Cogbill's litanies. In the song, the narrator thinks there will always be enough time to do and say all he wants to do, but then in winter, when "the cold winds came," Angelica falls ill. The lyrics hint of a coma, where she cannot hear him, an eerie foreshadowing of Tommy's—and within the year, Roy Hamilton's—eventual fate. In the song, Angelica dies and the flowers never bought for her now torture the narrator. It was grim enough for Chips, spiritual enough for Tommy, and it remains one of their most haunting collaborations, as does the B-side, another Mann-Weil tune, "Hangups." It features a rolling figure from Reggie Young's guitar, a droning horn line courtesy of Glen Spreen, and the ironic closer, "Tired of living, but scared of dying."

The group recorded enough material with Roy for an album, and enjoyed every minute of it. "Roy Hamilton, one very nice guy," said Mike Leech admiringly. "I remember he was one of the few people who came in and filled up those big old theater speakers in the control room, not everybody could do that," said Reggie Young. "He was a very gentle person, nice man." "I don't remember how many days we worked with him, but for me, not nearly enough," said Bobby Wood. "I will have to say, every minute was a pleasure. Roy Hamilton was a dream, he was one of my heroes. What can I say about Roy Hamilton that hasn't already been said? He was a teddy bear. He and King Curtis were in the same boat. Gentleman, super artist, easy to work with . . . He made you want to play your heart out. He just blew everybody away." "He was professional, experienced, and knew what to try for," said Glen Spreen. "Roy was a genuinely nice human being." Reggie Young's session books indicate that one of the songs cut was a duet between Ronnie Milsap and Roy; that would be wonderful to hear, but the album was never released. "Angelica" became a moderate hit, but Bobby Wood thought regretfully that the group could have done better by Roy. "I think the only reason we didn't get a big ole hit with him was probably choice of material," Bobby reflected. "In hindsight, we just didn't have the right song for him."

Later that year, Roy Hamilton died of a stroke. When it happened, his manager, Bill Cook, who had befriended Marty Lacker during the sessions, asked Marty to speak to the press. Cook told Marty a story that would haunt him forever. "He said, 'Roy was in a coma.' He said, 'I was sitting beside his bed, all of a sudden Roy raised up in the coma, said 'Angelica, Angelica, I'm coming,' and he laid back down and died.'" Chips planned to release the album anyway, but, in a circumstance reminiscent of Frankie Lymon's the previous year, five or six women showed up demanding royalties and claiming to be Roy's real wife. Rather than face a protracted legal battle, Chips shrugged it off and let it go. The album tracks remained in Chips's tape vault, where all of the unreleased material was stored.

There were not many other songs from the double session that landed up in the vault. Only the Elvis song "Poor Man's Gold," from the Mac Davis tape, was never completed. And "never completed" is an accurate metaphor for this session; Elvis could have accomplished much more under Chips's direction, yet several things—as always at American, where you lost when you won and won when you lost—served

to cloud and sully what should have been the studio's greatest achievement.

The first and perhaps worst problem occurred during the third and fourth nights of the session. When Chips Moman heard the Mac Davis tape, with "Don't Cry Daddy" and "In the Ghetto," he naturally loved what he heard—so much so that he called out to the coast and requested that Mac come in person and sing the songs for him to see if they sounded as good. "I remember pickin' up Mac at the airport," said Ima Roberts, who was already familiar with Davis's writing. "He was a *nice* guy. I thought I was hot stuff, havin' him ride in my car, honey." "Only thing I remember about Mac Davis is, he seemed like a nice guy," said Mike Leech. "I noticed he sat off in a corner somewhere most of the time he was there. I think he wanted to butt out of everyone's way and just let us do our thing. I would say that was pretty wise of him—at that time." Bobby Wood and Reggie Young both remembered Mac in the control room, singing "In the Ghetto" for Chips, accompanied only by his acoustic guitar. "Mac was shakin' like a leaf," said Wood. "He did his songs well, he played good," was Reggie's estimation.

Elvis was as taken by the song when he heard it live as he had been when he had first encountered it on tape. "He said, 'That's a good song, but I don't know if I wanna do that,'" remembered Marty Lacker. "He said that because Parker had drummed it into his head, don't do a message song. Fortunately, Parker wasn't there. He said, 'Look, I dunno . . .' I said, 'If you're ever gonna do a song with a message, this is the one.'" He went home to Graceland that morning to mull it over.

When Elvis came in that night, Marty recalled that Chips asked him, "If y' ain't gonna do it, can I have it?' Elvis said, 'No, I'm gonna cut it.'" Chips had thought that Joe Simon or Rosey Grier could do the song, if Elvis had not wanted to; if he did, Chips was determined that the song would be an exclusive. And sing it Elvis did, in a recording whose significance, if anything, has grown over the years. "I played the exact same guitar part Mac played when he was pitchin' the song, it's built in," said Reggie

Young, who used the same old Gibson 440 he had played on Dusty Springfield's "Windmills of Your Mind" and Tommy had played on Sandy Posey's "I Take It Back," that Scotty Moore had traded to Chips. It gave the session continuity, as if Scotty were still represented in some way. "When we did 'Ghetto,' my hands were shakin'," the guitarist continued. "The whole front end of the song was me and him. It was nervousness, in a good way. Boy, he was just bigger 'n life. You definitely knew he was there." The song became a beautiful prototype of American at its best; Chips lays out the song as if he were a copy editor constructing a print narrative, with the bass figure and the booming tympani (Tommy Cogbill's idea, according to Mike Leech) serving as punctuation, signaling each new paragraph in the story.

Of course, what Elvis sang while Reggie and the others played was only a work vocal; he would come back later and do the definitive vocal with no musicians present except, occasionally, the Memphis Horns, augmented as usual by the players from Pepper-Tanner. Wayne Jackson, the horn section's leader, was impressed. "When I heard 'In the Ghetto,' I knew that would be a good one," he said. He told Rose Clayton that part of the impact was the strength of a song about the ghetto, being recorded literally in one of Memphis's seediest slums with the King assassination still fresh in everyone's mind. Elvis's reading of the song has dignity and understatement; he was at the top of his form as an interpretive singer, and the stark realism was, as always, an American group trademark.

The perfectionism of Chips and the core group was shared by the late arrivals. "I just wanted it to be perfect but not perfect in the sense of sterile," Glen Spreen explained. To that end, he felt that several of the recordings from these sessions were not as good as they could have been. "For instance, on the horn part for 'Suspicious Minds,' on the recording of the cellos and horns, one did it ahead of another by one beat, and that's because I wrote the part from memory. . . . I still cringe a bit when I listen to 'In the Ghetto.' At the end, when Elvis sings his final 'In the ghetto,' I have my hands

up, and when they come down, the strings are supposed to start the fade. They never came in together. I even tried using one hand. We kept punching in the fade. Finally Felton said 'that's good' (remember Felton's 'good?'), I complained but no one could hear the mess (in my mind at least). That's now on the recording." It is ironic that Glen had misgivings about the recording of "In the Ghetto," since the song wound up involving him in controversy.

The sequence of events is murky. Ima Roberts remembered Johnny Christopher coming up with a song similar to the Davis piece called "Sidewalks of the Ghetto." "I don't know if Chips commissioned him to do 'Sidewalks of the Ghetto,' but I could swear unless I'm losing my mind that he did," said Ima. Glen Spreen "vaguely" remembered the song but did not think Johnny had written it deliberately; he thought possibly Johnny had written it even before Elvis came in. Don Crews thought the song had been written later, although he remembered very little about the matter. Chips was fond of suggesting titles to his writers, but he always left the content of the song up to them; it was done in the spirit of experimentation, giving them an idea and letting them run with it. He may have regarded Johnny's tune as an insurance policy, a milder substitute that could be used in case Elvis felt the Davis piece made too much of a statement, and in fact it was recorded shortly after Elvis's sessions by the hippie-pop group Eternity's Children, who cut a few singles at American following the release of their California-recorded first album.

Flash forward one year, to January 1970. Elvis was playing Las Vegas to rave reviews and sellout crowds. He was going back in the studio again soon, and was wondering where to record. By then Marty Lacker had become studio manager at American, and was taking some time off to be at Elvis's show. "We're up in Elvis's suite," he remembered, when Elvis began to rant angrily about Chips. "'Y'know, so much for your damn buddy.' I said, 'Elvis, what do you mean?' and he said, 'I was told he tried to steal "In the Ghetto."' I said, 'Elvis, what're you talking about? Chips protected you. He was looking out for you.' The minute I heard it, I knew it had to be somebody from Nashville [who had said that to him, for reasons related to Nashville studio politics]. 'Whoever told you that is a goddamn liar,' I said. 'Now don't get smart,' he said. I said, 'My loyalty is with you.' 'Regardless, I ain't goin' back to that studio again.'"

Marty did not solve the mystery until much later. "I came to find out, according to Felton, Glen Spreen supposedly told Felton that Chips had called all the writers in and said, 'We need to write a song about the ghetto.' If I had found out before Elvis had died, Elvis would have known." In late 2004 he told Chips and Chips told the group what he had discovered.

The response was immediate. All of the long-held resentments about Glen finally found a focus. The late arrival was immediately cast as Judas Iscariot, and was considered persona non grata by the group from then on. "I like to think we're a forgiving little family, but some things go beyond the pale," said Bobby Wood. The American group suspected blowback, the possible avengement of some personal grudge against Chips, but Glen was so completely surprised at the entire story that this seems not to have been the case. Nor does the story he was supposed to have told sound characteristic of Chips, its subject.

No one thought to call him and ask what had happened. When he was eventually asked, Glen answered that he and Felton, whom he knew fairly well later on in Nashville, "talked casually now and then" about those landmark sessions, but he did not remember mentioning any songs, by name or otherwise, at all, and that mostly they had discussed "my little things that I could have done better" with the string sound. He added that he had never had either occasion or reason to discuss the songs with Felton: "There was no money in it for me, no glory in it for me. . . . If I had done anything supposedly that damaging, especially on purpose, I would have remembered it."

The likely conclusion is that if he said anything at all, it was a throwaway remark, tossed off inadvertently (when he was asked in 2006, he still seemed not quite to understand the implications of what he was supposed to have done). There was also the fact that Felton did

not even need to mention what he had learned: a similarly themed song recorded by an obscure hippie folk group weeks after the star had left the building is hardly plagiarism or a ripoff—it is not even worth discussing. It is no different from Ronnie Milsap, who was at the studio for some of the Elvis sessions, liking "Kentucky Rain" so much that he asked Kye Fleming and Dennis Morgan to come up with a song of that type, and they gave him "Smoky Mountain Rain," something with a completely different mood and feel. Marty Lacker was undoubtedly right in assuming that Nashville politics and income for the RCA studios where Felton set up shop may have been the motive for saying something to Elvis. Control of Elvis's sessions was also a factor, and the recording and publishing executives who had interests with Elvis's manager knew by now that Chips was no lackey. Once again Marty was right when he observed, "Parker was mad because he basically had lost control" when Elvis recorded with Chips in Memphis.

If anyone was at fault in the matter, it seemed to be Felton, playing here the role of village gossip and confirming Marty Lacker's original perception of him; but the siege mentality, so prominent at American and reinforced by Chips (who continued, despite his success, to view himself as being put upon by other people) had immediately kicked in. Chips was stunned, blindly uncomprehending, and deeply wounded by what he saw as a betrayal from inside, and to the core group, protective of their appointed leader as if they sensed some fragility in him, even a perceived harm to him simply would not do.

It could have ended there, with the musicians in the core group still angry and resentful and Glen Spreen going his way, but Glen decided that he should at least explain. In the fall of 2007, a year after he had retired from a successful second career as computer expert for a healthcare firm in California, he spoke directly with Chips and then contacted all of the members of the core group, telling them his side of the story. Not everyone responded favorably, but Chips seemed satisfied, and Mike Leech, Bobby Wood, and Reggie Young immediately apologized for having automatically assumed the worst of Glen. All three of them reached out, as if to make amends. Bobby Wood emailed Glen his phone number, and Mike Leech and Reggie Young also resumed intermittent contact after having been out of touch with Glen for many years. The imagined wound and all the other unspoken resentments went too deep for a total reconciliation, but at least some of the musicians were occasionally speaking to Glen, and the arranger was at peace knowing he had done all he could to bring that about.

Though the musicians in the core group, especially Bobby Emmons, were protective of Chips, he was tough-minded enough to look out for himself, as demonstrated by the way he handled another problem.

It occurred near the end of the first set of sessions. Elvis had been out for several days with a cold, and Chips and the group had cut backing tracks without him. "The night before we were supposed to go back," Marty Lacker remembered, "we listened to Hill and Range demos up in his office. I was sittin' on a chaise lounge over by the door. Elvis said, 'I ain't got any more good songs'" The Hill and Range representative, Lamar Fike, was in the room; so was Elvis's radio connection, George Klein. Marty was aware of the need for caution in approaching Elvis, but he figured the time was right for the second part of what he wanted to tell his friend. "I said to myself, hell, you've gone this far, go for broke. I said something to *Elvis Presley*—'They don't need you anymore.' He said, 'What?' I said, 'They don't want to give up the publishing anymore. There are lots of artists who write songs that sell a million records, but every time they come to us we have to send them to Hill and Range. There's no reason why you shouldn't have heard the demos first on every hit song for the past twenty years.' I didn't know if he was gonna throw an ashtray. I know Lamar wasn't happy because I was taking bread out of his pocket. Red [West] was smiling. George sat there like a bump on a log. George now tells Elvis fans and people that he's the one who got Elvis to record. Elvis started shakin' his leg. When he starts shakin'

his leg, he's either thinkin' or gettin' pissed off. Finally he said, 'From now on, I wanna hear every damn song I can hear. If we can get a piece of the publishing, that's just good business, but if not, I wanna cut it anyway.'" And he directed everyone in the room to get out and hustle, and find him some good songs. Lamar Fike found "Kentucky Rain," a song by Hill and Range's newest writer, Eddie Rabbitt. George Klein persuaded Neil Diamond to give Elvis a fairly explicit ballad for that era, "And the Grass Won't Pay No Mind" (Chips and Tommy would record an eloquent but wistful version with Neil himself). It was a continuation of the vow Elvis had made on the set of the comeback special: "I'm never going to sing another song I don't believe in."

That new resolve was put to the test as soon as he went back into the studio. "Elvis said, 'I ain't got any good songs.' Chips said, 'I got one song I cut on a writer.' Elvis didn't know Mark James from a hole in the wall," Marty remembered, but Chips played him the single of "Suspicious Minds" that Mark had cut a few months before. After several playings, Elvis still was not sure. "You think it's good?" he asked a few of the people close to him. "Joe Esposito convinced him to do it," Marty said.

While Elvis and the band were working on the track in the studio—Mike Leech told Rose Clayton that the slowed-down part in the middle was a bit tricky—the suits conferred among themselves. "Then entered the politics," said Reggie. "In walks Diskin and Freddie Bienstock," Marty Lacker elaborated. "They asked Chips, 'Can we talk to you?'" They led Chips into the little hall just off the control room and backed him up against the wall like a cornered animal, demanding a piece of the publishing for "Suspicious Minds." "I purposely went with them, because I didn't want them screwing up the session for Elvis," said Marty. "My interest was only in the session being successful for Elvis and Chips and the guys. I didn't want anyone screwing it up because it didn't fit their agendas."

To Chips's eternal credit, he refused to be part of the kickback scheme. In what may have been his finest hour at American, "Chips said,

'No, I'm not gonna give you a piece,'" remembered Marty. "They said, 'Well, then, Mr. Presley might not want to do this.' You don't back Chips down. He said, 'You can take your damn tapes and get the hell out of my studio. Don't ask me again.' Much to his credit, here comes Harry Jenkins and said, 'This boy's right.'" Chips stormed back into the control room, put his feet up on the console, and, Marty remembered, "was smokin' one of his damn unfiltered Camels, he was seething mad." (By 2007, Chips would be forced to quit smoking.) "I've seen Chips angry on many occasions," Mike Leech noted. "His eyes hollow out and his face pales. He was like that when we had the run-in with RCA." Tom Diskin, meanwhile, decided to go to Elvis in the studio. As he had previously, Marty followed Diskin out, to determine what the publishing executive was really saying.

"I 'm behind him, he doesn't know I'm behind him," said Marty. "And he said, 'Elvis, Chips is being obstinate. He doesn't want to give up the publishing on 'Suspicious Minds.' I'm shakin' my head now. And Elvis said to him, 'I know you're doing your job, but how about letting me and Chips handle the session.' I gave Elvis a thumbs-up." One myth that was widely circulated, said Marty, was that Elvis then supposedly asked Chips what could be done to make the session better and Chips suggested that the RCA executives and publishers from Hill and Range should leave. Wayne Jackson thought that Chips had even asked Felton to go: "I think he told Felton, 'Either you're producing or I am.'" "Nobody in the entourage was told to leave, that is a fallacy," Marty Lacker emphatically corrected. "The only one who left was Diskin and that was after Elvis told him to let him and Chips run the sessions." Diskin, of course, was Parker's man; he answered directly to the Colonel. The RCA and publishing executives, as well as Felton, stayed.

"Diskin got on the phone to the Colonel," Marty remembered, "and he said, 'Elvis wants to handle it without us.' Parker said, 'Give him all he wants. Let him do it and fall on his ass.' Diskin gets his coat and flew back to California. . . . Some falling on his ass. Thirty-six songs in twelve days. Four Top Ten [hits] and two platinum albums." "They cut forty-two songs [over the two sets of sessions], that's a lot of damn songs!" exclaimed Ima Roberts.

"Thank God there are people out there like Chips who will stand up to the suits and take them on," was Bobby Wood's fervent conclusion. And for standing up to them, not only then but during the overdub sessions when he was approached to turn over the publishing and he said what he thought, the executives never forgave Chips (not that he cared about antagonizing industry businessmen, his lifelong foes), and their interference probably had more to do with Elvis never working with Chips again than anything Glen Spreen might have accidentally said to Felton. "Lamar, every time I'd see him after that he'd give me the ol' cold shoulder, not that it bothered me because I didn't know him that well," said Don Crews. The atmosphere improved after Tom Diskin left in a huff. "After all his entourage left, he became one of us," said Reggie Young. "We sat around and it was very soulful and personal. . . . It just became a unit, we got down to business."

To make it worse for the executives, they were proven wrong. "Suspicious Minds" became a huge hit later in the year, becoming Elvis's first Number One in a decade. The story line is strong, and Elvis's voice veers between indignation and pleading vulnerability. "The Mark James recording of 'Suspicious Minds' was overdubbed at Phillips," said Mike Leech, who did most of the elaborate original arrangement for the piece. "I used the same arrangement on Elvis's version—same key."

The Elvis track is accentuated by an incredible bass line from Mike, so intricate and jazzy that many listeners automatically assumed it was Cogbill. The two developed specialties during their time at American. Tommy became known for complicated runs and Mike for four-beat simplicity, but Mike could handle intricate runs and rhythms as well as any bassist ever has. At times on this recording, he and the rest of the track part company—he is out there on his own, creating a countermelody on bass that serves to anchor the record.

It was Mike's last appearance at the studio for awhile. He recalled, "I had an insurance physical during which time the doctor who examined me said I had a condition which could be cancer. That scared hell out of me. I almost had a nervous breakdown up until I had surgery to correct the problem. After surgery I was told all was well, no cancer, so I breathed a huge sigh of relief, and went home to recuperate. When I hobbled to the studio a few weeks after, the Elvis sessions were all done, but I had managed to play and write arrangements on some of the biggest hits. I regret missing half the sessions, but at my age (29-ish) cancer was a word that was so scary that sessions lost their importance—even the Elvis sessions." The second half of the sessions, in February, when "Only the Strong Survive" and "Kentucky Rain" were done, were completed with Cogbill on bass and Glen alone handling the strings.

Nashville politics and the rivalry between Music City and Memphis did not end when the sessions concluded. Several weeks later, Marty Lacker remembered, "Fred Foster had this girl singer, we were sitting in the control room and Chips was listening to 'In the Ghetto.' Fred said, 'Damn, Chips, that's a hell of a song! Can I have it?' 'Hell, no!' Well, somehow Fred found out who had the publishing. Two days later Chips gets a call from Billy Strange, he starts yellin' at Chips." Billy apparently threatened to come to American and start a fistfight, Marty recalled further. "Chips said, 'Lemme know the flight you're on, I'll meet you there and save you the trouble.' He hung up." Billy never showed.

Felton Jarvis had deferred to Chips while he sat in the studio, but now that the tapes were finished he stuck an oar in here and there, perhaps as a not-too-subtle reminder of who really was in charge. "Chips was the producer and I think Felton had a feeling about that because he wanted to have more say-so especially in Nashville," observed Marty Lacker. "That's why when the sessions were over he took the masters back to Nashville and he almost screwed up 'Suspicious Minds' with that fake ending which is called a Fade and Bump. Many radio DJs and program directors didn't like it because it screwed up their timing on air. Felton thought that ending was clever, it wasn't for a record. That kind of fade and bump looks good

on stage but it doesn't work on a record." "You know, I guess I never knew Felton did the fade-out and back in," mused Bobby Wood. "I guess I missed that one. I always thought Chips did that one." Gene Chrisman did know, and was highly indignant.

RCA made further changes later on, when a release of all the songs from the session, *The Memphis Record*, appeared after Elvis's death; Chips's mixes were so altered as to be unrecognizable. Not until the box set *From Nashville to Memphis* was released did listeners get to hear all of the songs from the Memphis sessions in the order in which they were recorded and with the original sound (they are also available that way on a two-CD set, *Suspicious Minds*). Mike Leech observed something crucial: "[With remasters], sometimes vital overdubs were missing because they were done on the floor while going to the two-track. That was because on earlier stuff we didn't have as many tracks to work with and if we, as a last and final overdub, wanted to add a guitar or strings, we would go straight to the master two-track. Some of Elvis' remastered tracks [are] missing strings or horns for that reason."

Even the record's billing was subject to the demands of Nashville and the Colonel. "Here's a game I played on Parker that pissed them off," said Marty Lacker, who never had any use for the Colonel or for the publishing executives at Hill and Range. "When 'In the Ghetto,' the first record released from that session, got in *Billboard*'s Top Ten the first week it listed Felton as producer.

"I called *Billboard* and told them they had made a mistake, that Chips Moman was the producer. They asked who I was and I told them I was from RCA. The next week's chart, in the top five it had Chips's name as producer. I knew that would piss Colonel Parker and Felton off. The third week it had no producer credit, meaning they called and made *Billboard* do that.

"I called *Billboard* back and chewed them out for leaving Chips's name off, they asked who I was and once again, I told them I was from RCA. They then said, 'You guys need to make up your minds and we are leaving it blank unless we get the correct info in writing.' I then left it alone but I was happy to have pissed Parker off because I thought it was an injustice to Chips."

The musicians were pleased with the sheer number of songs that had been recorded during Elvis's two visits to American. They all knew the material was good and they felt that at least some of it might have commercial potential. "I thought 'Suspicious Minds,' 'In the Ghetto.' and 'Any Day Now' were strong. 'Don't Cry Daddy' surprised me," said Glen Spreen. Bobby Wood, on the other hand, loved "Don't Cry Daddy" because of its emphatic melody, and he felt that possibly it would be the hit from the sessions. When the Memphis newspaper conducted a joint interview between Elvis and Chips at the close of the sessions, Elvis had said rhetorically to the producer, "We've cut some hits, haven't we?" and Chips glanced over at Elvis and said warmly, "Maybe some of your biggest," although how prophetic a statement that was, Chips could not have known. Nor did anyone else involved with the Elvis sessions. "We didn't know we were gonna cut stuff that was gonna change his life," said Wayne Jackson. "I didn't [know its impact]," said Reggie Young matter-of-factly.

"I don't remember if anybody thought they had made a landmark recording," reflected Mike Leech. "Even if we did, it was no big deal since we had been accustomed to making those for awhile." It never occurred to the other string arranger either. "I can be very stupid from time to time," Glen Spreen said wryly.

Of all the musicians at American, none seemed to have more of an affinity with Elvis than Bobby Wood. "I think we hit it off because we were basically from the same neck of the woods," mused the piano player; his hometown was only a few miles from Elvis's hometown of Tupelo. They shared several other things as well: a farming background (Vernon Presley had been a sharecropper in Mississippi), and Bobby had had his slight experience as a teenage idol; though it was not on the same scale of Elvis's popularity, it gave him some empathy toward what the star had gone through. They had both been brought up in the church, both

played piano, and both still loved gospel music and quartet singing. They discussed these and many other things one night toward the end of the sessions, when Elvis came over during a lull in the recording and sat down beside Bobby on the piano bench. "We must have talked from thirty to forty-five minutes," Wood recalled warmly. "He told me he really liked our records and how much he loved working with us. He said it had been years since he had worked like that and he was obviously enjoying every minute. We talked about the church he went to and I told him about the church I went to. He told me that all were welcome to come out to the house any time we wanted when he was in town. He said just call George Klein. I never did. Wish I had later but when you were working the hours we were, all I wanted to do was go home and sleep.

"I remember one night in the control room I was admiring his ring. It was full of diamonds, rubies, and I don't know what else. He pulled it off and handed it to me and started talking about this jeweler who made stuff for him" (most likely the Memphis jewelers Harry Levitch or Lowell Hays, whom he even took on tour with him later). "He said 'It's yours.' Of course, it was a lot larger than my finger. I had to talk him out of giving me that ring. I guess it was my stupid pride but I don't know, I just felt that a lot of people would take from him and I guess I didn't want to do that. Looking back on it all that was probably one of the more stupid things I ever did. . . . I've wished a thousand times that I should have gone to Graceland and really got to know him better." Elvis talked with Bobby a little about California and making movies; the piano player who had once longed to be an actor felt that Elvis had placed himself unwittingly on a treadmill, as the singer talked about the pressure on the Coast, the pressure that could sometimes lead a man into breaking ethical rules that he knew were right.

"He seemed to connect with a Christian person that wasn't afraid to be honest, down to earth and still have a good time. . . . Elvis never seemed to care about money or tangible things at all," Bobby summed it up. "He was the kind of person that would give you his shirt. I'm just fortunate and thankful that I had a chance to work with him. What a talented and super person." "He was very real," said Marty Lacker softly, his voice still full of awe and regard for his longtime friend. And Wayne Carson spoke not just for the musicians at American but for everyone of Elvis's generation from the working-class South when he evoked Joseph Conrad's famous line: "He was one of us."

The musicians summed it up by saying that Elvis had been a pleasure to be around, even though many of them, like Gene Chrisman, "didn't talk to him much, just played the songs and listened to hear if the tracks were okay." Even those at American who had not directly participated in the sessions liked Elvis and were pleased that he was there. One evening Chips asked Ima Roberts to bring in some typewritten lyrics from the office. When she came down, Chips politely introduced her to Elvis. "He was real nice, very humble," Ima said of the King. "I'll never forget, he had a fever blister on his lip, I thought, wow, he's human. He was very nice, very shy. He didn't talk a lot."

Spooner Oldham had his Elvis sighting early in the sessions. He was in transition to California, deciding to move after a fire gutted his house in Memphis. He remembered being in New York that January with Jimmy Johnson and Roger Hawkins recording a few of the tracks that would appear on Aretha's *Soul '69* album when Chips called to tell him the news. "He said, 'Spooner, you might want to think about coming home.' I got home at dusk." His house was destroyed: "The roof looked like a Volkswagen had fallen out of the sky at the center of it." Spooner gathered a few odds and ends together and planned what he would do next. "I walked away with my suitcase and briefcase and went to the Holiday Inn. I was going to save the furniture because it had just had some smoke damage." He intended to go back early the next morning and retrieve everything. "I got there at eight o'clock. Everything was gone. Somebody had pulled a truck up there and made off with all the furniture." It was the last straw regarding Memphis, and he got married and moved to Los Angeles. He stopped by at American one day during this transitional time, although he was not looking forward to it. "I knew they were doing Elvis sessions, I was thinking, it's gonna be different here today, I'll have to answer questions and all the security questions that may ensue, I was gearing my mind." He was surprised to find no press coverage, no crowds outside (Ima Roberts recalled some people standing on the sidewalk toward the end of the sessions, but that was it) and the atmosphere in the studio much as usual. "There was Elvis sitting on a stool looking at a piece of paper that turned out to be 'In the Ghetto,'" Spooner remembered. They never spoke. "That's the only time I remember going back to American."

Wayne Carson, while not directly involved in the sessions, had a memorable encounter with the King. He was in the studio one afternoon overdubbing a background harmony vocal on B.J. Thomas's just-completed track of Mark James's "It's Only Love" when Elvis walked in. "I saw them gold-rimmed glasses when he came up behind me," Wayne recalled. "I thought, 'hell, I'm seein' things, I gotta stop doin' these pills!'" But it was no hallucination, as was proven when the singer introduced himself. "He stuck out his hand and said, 'I'm sorry, man, I'm Elvis.' I said, 'No shit.'" Wayne's unpretentiousness delighted the singer, who had been fawned over enough for several lifetimes, and the two began chatting. "It wasn't four minutes till lightning hit a transmitter and knocked out the station," Wayne remembered, and the result was a massive power failure. "We scrambled around and got some candles, I think Ed Kollis went to the drugstore and got some more. . . . The three of us sat there for about an hour. Eventually everyone got tired and left the studio. Even Chips left after awhile. A few of Elvis's boys came in, they said, 'D'you wanna leave now, boss?' He said, 'Go on out and get you a sandwich or something, I think I'm gonna hang here with Wayne.' There sat Elvis and I for about four hours."

It was just the two of them in the darkened studio, and Wayne discovered that talking to the King was "like talkin' to anybody else. He was a regular guy, rock and roll guy," although Wayne was aware of how remarkable it was that Elvis had taken to him since he knew that the reclusive singer "wasn't big on strangers." Elvis spoke at length about his ranch just over the Mississippi line, the Circle G, and he invited Wayne to visit him there. "He wanted to go fishin'. . . . He said, 'I'll send a private plane to come get you in Springfield, we can fly your motorcycle out on it, you can bring anybody you want.' I'll tell you something," Wayne declared emphatically. "If Elvis Presley ever needed one thing, he needed a friend who didn't work for him. He needed somebody out of that circle. He desperately needed someone to say, 'Cut that out,' just somebody to go get a hamburger with." With his no-nonsense manner and straight talk, Wayne would have been ideal for the role, and Elvis may have been looking for just such a person. "He gave me his bedside phone number. When I got home to Springfield, my wife said, 'I wish you'd quit havin' your friends call and tell us they're Elvis. There's somebody that keeps doing that.'" Wayne asked her if the caller had left a number; he had, and when Wayne checked the number against the one he was carrying on a slip of paper in his wallet he discovered it had really been Elvis. He tried to call back, but the number had been changed.

"I found out later that the Colonel had put the quietus on that," Wayne said of the terminated acquaintance. "Colonel Tom kept everybody away from Elvis; he ruled that Elvis kingdom with an iron fist," the songwriter added ruefully. The Colonel would have no new spheres of influence be brought to his boy. When the American musicians recorded with Elvis again at Stax in 1973, the studio was so full of people and he was so surrounded by his aides that the players could not even approach him; Reggie Young and Bobby Wood recalled that not one word passed between them and the singer.

"Those guys [on Elvis' staff] were always in competition with each other," said Bobby Wood. "I think that's why Elvis was looking for somebody to just be a friend. I'm sure that's why we talked for periods of time." "You have to understand that Elvis's life was not his own," was the sad observation of Jerry Carrigan, the drummer for the following year's Nashville Marathon sessions and several other Elvis sessions from the seventies, including those at Stax. Glen Spreen eventually came to feel sorry for Elvis because the singer was kept so isolated, and Wayne Carson regretted that his acquaintance with Elvis was so abruptly cut off: years after Elvis's death, Wayne kept saying in sad recollection, "He just needed a pal."

The consensus among both Elvis's close associates and the American group was that the sessions had been productive, even if no one felt at the time that a corner had been turned. The warmth and jokes continued after the official work was done. "I was told that after I adjourned the sessions to have surgery, that a banquet was held at the Ranch House next door to celebrate the end of the sessions," said Mike Leech. "During that time it was collaborated that when Lamar sat down, everybody would jump up, which I'm told they did. Lamar said, 'Mike Leech, you little SOB.'"

Mike's return following his convalescence was greeted joyfully by all. "When I came back, the mood was business as usual, except that I was greeted with smiles, laughs, and hugs. Made me feel really good," said the string arranger. "Chips played something and asked, 'How do the speakers sound to you, Mike?' (meaning I hadn't heard any music in awhile)."

Mike Leech was not the only one falling ill during the time frame of the Elvis sessions. The late hours and hard work, not only of these sessions but of the year and a half preceding them, were taking a toll on everybody. Bobby Emmons had been in the hospital for a collapsed lung the year before and had missed part of the Merrilee Rush sessions (hence Spooner Oldham's presence on a few album cuts), and now it was Chips's turn. Working around the clock, he collapsed from exhaustion. "I fell out in the mixing down of the Elvis sessions," he recalled. "Somebody put a wet rag on my forehead and when I came to, they asked, 'Can you finish?'" And Chips pulled himself up and completed the mix.

The effects of the Elvis sessions reverberated for years to come in the lives of all who were there. The sessions literally restored Elvis to his throne; by the end of the year he was on top of the charts once again. "I guess my proudest thing was to be able to step in and help a deserving artist held back by bad advice," said Bobby Emmons. "I felt that we had helped Elvis become what he was in the beginning, actually better, more quality in the songs," added Glen Spreen. And just as the American group put Elvis back upon the map, so he put them on the map as well. Though the credits were not listed on the album, everybody in the industry knew who had made the recordings, and it increased demand for the musicians and Chips, though they played down the impact. "I guess the Elvis things were highly visible, but we would have been okay without it," shrugged Bobby Emmons. Maybe so, but the Elvis sessions moved the American group into another level of success; when these sessions came out the group was mentioned in the same respectful tones as were the various Nashville session cliques or the players at Motown.

Elvis never returned to American, and adamantly refused to work for Chips again; yet he recorded with the rhythm section a second time in 1973, and beginning with the already recorded Mac Davis tunes like "Clean Up Your Own Back Yard" and some of the songs from the Nashville Marathon the following year, Mike Leech and Glen Spreen were on hand to write the string lines and give his records some continuity with the American sound. He continued to record material by American songwriters: Mark James's "It's Only Love," "Raised on Rock," and the last hit Elvis had in his lifetime, "Moody Blue." Red West gave Elvis a tape of the then-new Wayne Carson–Mark James–Johnny Christopher ballad "You Were Always on My Mind," and with its autobiographical theme of regret it was a natural for the singer, though Wayne Carson observed, "I thought he did it a little too fast. I still do," and Elvis never approached the wisdom that Willie Nelson gave the tune in its later hit version. Somewhat more effective was Glen Spreen's mournful "Holly Leaves and Christmas Trees," cowritten with Red West, that Elvis placed on his 1971 Christmas album, and Johnny Christopher's "If You Talk in Your Sleep (Don't Mention My Name)" was one of the King's last great rockers.

Even in concert, Elvis emphasized material like "Suspicious Minds" and "Steamroller Blues," which had been recorded by the Masqueraders under Mike Leech's direction. "What really got to me was, he knew how good American was," said Marty Lacker. "When he goes on tour, what does he start singing? American material." True enough, though the publishing and label executives made sure Elvis never again recorded with as much choice in song selection. There were songs from the group he never got to do. "Somebody told me that an acetate of 'Nobody's Fool' [a song Dan Penn had written with Bobby Emmons] was in his briefcase for the last ten sessions," said Emmons. "He was a big fan of 'The Letter,'" said Wayne Carson. "Somebody told me he wanted to do 'The Letter' and 'Soul Deep' both and then he up and died. He woulda sung the shit out of 'No Love at All.'"

Elvis's recording comeback had an impact in the immediate area, recalled Hayward Bishop, who had been mustered out of the air force and had moved to Memphis that spring. "Everybody in town was trying to talk like Elvis, you know, the mumbling, buzzing of the z's . . . 'Thankyouvir'mushfrmynex'nubberIllikead oalilso'thin'. Chips even did that for awhile. It got to be ridiculous." Tommy Cogbill remained unaffected by that trend, but he did go so far as to grow moderate-length sideburns, another fashion inspired by Elvis's return.

There are milestones in everyone's life and work, and the Elvis sessions were crucial for both the singer and the American musicians. The studio experienced success in the year ahead unlike anything the group had previously known.

American Studios in right foreground with Ranch House restaurant in rear, 1970. (Photo © Hayward Bishop)

Top: Bobby Emmons, 1970. (Photo © Hayward Bishop)

Bottom: Mike Cauley at the console, 1970. (Photo © Hayward Bishop)

Ad for American Studios, *Billboard* magazine, 1969. (Courtesy of Mike Leech)

Back parking lot at American, 1972. Left to right: Paul Davis, Sam Hutchins of the Masqueraders, Reggie Young, Mike Leech, Stan Kesler, and J.P. Richardson (Photo © Hayward Bishop)

Left to right: Gene Chrisman, Tommy Cogbill, and Mike Leech, 1970. (Photo courtesy of Mike Leech, © Hayward Bishop)

Hayward Bishop engineering, 1970. (Photo © Hayward Bishop)

Left: Hayward Bishop, 1970. (Photo © Hayward Bishop)

Mike Leech at work. (Photo © Hayward Bishop)

Mike Cauley, 1970. (Photo © Hayward Bishop)

Onstage at Memphis
Music Awards, 1972. Left
to right: Reggie Young,
Mike Leech, Stan Kesler,
Billy Burnette, Shane
Keister, and Hayward
Bishop. (Photo ©
Hayward Bishop)

"Aretha Now" session, New
York, 1968. Left to right:
Arif Mardin, Tommy Cogbill,
Roger Hawkins, Jerry Jemmott,
Aretha, Spooner Oldham,
Jimmy Johnson, and Tom Dowd.
(Courtesy of Jimmy Johnson
Music, Inc.)

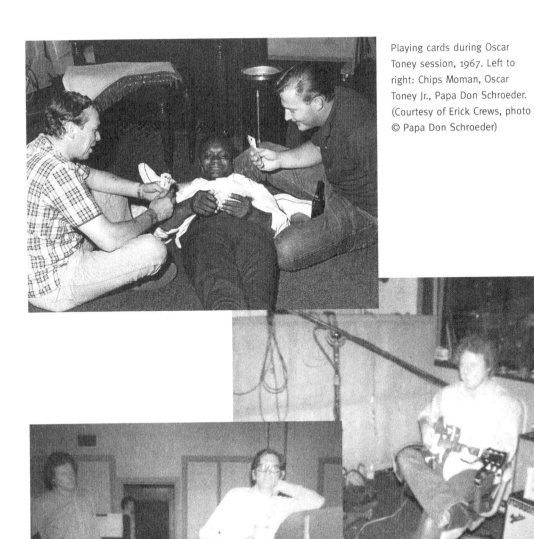

Playing cards during Oscar Toney session, 1967. Left to right: Chips Moman, Oscar Toney Jr., Papa Don Schroeder. (Courtesy of Erick Crews, photo © Papa Don Schroeder)

Reggie Young, 1972. (Photo © Hayward Bishop)

Above, left to right: Reggie Young, Shane Keister, Stan Kesler, 1972. (Photo © Hayward Bishop)

Right: Richard Mainegra, 1971. (Photo © Hayward Bishop)

Shane Keister, 1972. (Photo ©
Hayward Bishop)

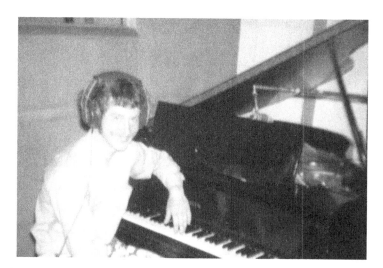

Above: Shane Keister playing
pool; Mike Leech and Reggie
Young playing ping pong,
1972. (Photo © Hayward
Bishop)

Right: Studio layout drawn by
Erick Crews.

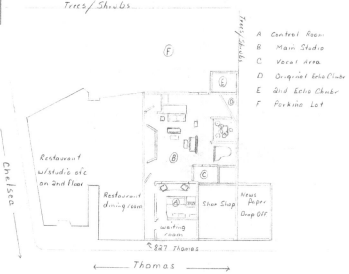

Glen Spreen, 1969. (Photo courtesy of Glen Spreen)

Wayne Carson on holiday in Acapulco, 1970. (Photo courtesy of Glen Spreen)

Reunion in Nashville, mid-1970s. Left to right: Gene Chrisman, Bobby Wood, Chips Moman, Reggie Young, and Billy Burnette. (Photo courtesy of Bobby Wood)

Mike Leech and Tommy Cogbill, 1970. (Photo courtesy of Mike Leech, © Hayward Bishop)

### CHAPTER 18

# Good-Time Merry-Go-Round: Life after Elvis

Post-Elvis, sessions were booked more steadily than ever, and if Atlantic's patronage was slightly falling off due to their involvement with Jimmy Johnson's new studio in the Shoals, there were more than enough outside accounts and old friends coming in to make up for it. Nor had the attitude of the group changed, at least on the surface, even though "they had made a little new history there," Ima Roberts noted fondly. "We knew [the sessions] were special, but so were many before Elvis," added Glen Spreen. "We were patting ourselves on the back (in our minds)." Bobby Emmons thought the studio atmosphere had been tense while Elvis was working there, and after the King had left the building, he recalled, "It was like, 'Let me get out of this tight corset and high heels'. . . a little less pressure, please."

The American group came close to being Elvis's backup band onstage, with Chips Moman handling the sound as Felton Jarvis would do later, although Chips dismissed the invitation. "There was some talk about it, but there was just some talk floatin' around," he said indifferently. According to Marty Lacker, it was more than that. Elvis was so impressed with Chips and the group that he had been quite serious about hiring them for the Las Vegas comeback shows he was planning. Marty remembered, "Elvis asked Chips about backing him in Vegas as we were standing in the control room. To my surprise, Chips at that moment said yes. However, on second thought later, he changed his

mind because Colonel Parker, on purpose, offered low money and Chips and the musicians were not going to give up more money than they could make doing sessions. Parker didn't want them to back Elvis because he was still pissed that he lost control of Elvis during the American sessions and he didn't want Chips influencing Elvis any further."

It was one of several fascinating near-misses the group had during the year. Throughout 1969, the studio phones rang almost constantly with people booking sessions. "There was a lot of calls—a *lot* of 'em," said Ima Roberts, who handled them. Though a great deal of attention was focused on the studio after the Elvis songs became hits, Ima maintained that those sessions had little real impact—"I don't know that business increased after Elvis, because we had been busy before." Glen Spreen saw it somewhat differently. "There'd been hits forever, but when Elvis came it really put us over," he estimated. Down in Muscle Shoals, Jimmy Johnson was pleased to observe the impact those sessions were having for Chips. "When Elvis came, he got all kinds of respect," said Jimmy.

"We had a ten-month waiting time," said Chips. Of course, not everyone who called could be accommodated given that schedule, and some people had to be turned away. "I turned down a lotta people I can't believe I turned down," Chips reflected, sounding amazed at himself. "I had to turn Dylan down—too busy. He wanted to go into the studio right away. I had a call about the Beatles, but I didn't have time to wait on them." Had he accepted those offers, Chips would have been the ultimate producer, the man who would have recorded all the acts in rock's Holy Trinity. Perhaps in the end, that would have been too much pressure for him; he could no longer have kept life as simple as he preferred, or maintained the illusion, even to himself, that he was just another good old boy picking on the back porch with his buddies.

Even when an artist could be slotted in, session starting times were casual, especially when compared to Nashville, where if a session was scheduled at two PM it began at two on the dot. "Some people, [Chips would] tell 'em to come to town and he'd be out at the farm or some-where and we'd have to just entertain 'em till he came in—it could be five minutes, could be five hours," said Ima Roberts. When everyone was there, all the jokes and small talk had to be run through before the musicians were in a mood to work, and Chips sat back and listened for them to adjust. When he thought the mood was appropriate, he would walk into the con-trol booth and announce, "Okay, this is the first song." On his productions, Tommy Cogbill sel-dom waited for the kidding to stop; the musi-cians knew to be on their toes the minute they came in and Tommy announced, "I'm ready." Even then, it sometimes took a run-through or two before the musicians were approaching a song as loosely as Tommy liked; they were used to Chips's methods and they had to unlearn what they were primarily used to.

There was still a strong Elvis connection at American, not just because of Marty Lacker but due to the addition of Bobby "Red" West, who joined the staff shortly after those monu-mental sessions. Like Marty a charter member of the Memphis Mafia, Red had also written songs; his idealistic "If Every Day Was Like Christmas" was a favorite among Elvis fans. He had left the employ of Elvis in 1967, hurt that he had been left out of Elvis's wedding; since then he had been out on the Coast, doing stunts and some acting for his pal Robert Conrad's TV show *The Wild Wild West*. But political pressure from Senator John Pastore of Rhode Island led CBS to cancel the show because of its fight scenes, and Red had returned to Mem-phis in search of something else to do. He had known Chips for a long time—"I helped him financially when he was struggling," said Red. Chips had also produced Red's original demo of the Christmas song, at Stax. He was aware that Red wanted to develop his music, and in his usual tradition of creating special places for people with something to contribute to his organization, he hired Red as a staff writer for Press. It was an assignment Red accepted with delight.

"I loved workin' with that whole buncha idi-ots, they were very productive people," he said warmly. "I had no problems." His down-home manner and no-nonsense attitude (personified in the character he later played on the TV show *Black Sheep Squadron*) was a combination that found favor at American. "Always liked Red—he would join us in little childish escapades around the studio, and seemed like he was en-joying himself," Mike Leech remarked. "Red had family in Corinth," said Bobby Emmons, pleased at the connection between Red and his hometown. "He was a big bouncer-type guy—but his performances on film and television proved he had more depth than that. He was always very friendly to me." "I already knew him pretty well," said Bobby Wood. "He used me and most of the guys at Phillips Studio to record his demos. I don't remember how many times I worked with him, but quite a few. We always seemed to get along pretty good as I re-member. I always liked him." "He was a *great* guy, I liked him, I liked his wife," said Ima Rob-erts enthusiastically. "Red West was a profes-sional," said Wayne Jackson of the Memphis Horns admiringly. "He was a big gruff lov-able old bear," said Hayward Bishop with fond amusement.

"He had a hell of a temper," said Richard Mainegra, an aspiring writer Red auditioned for Press Music. "He was definitely a charac-ter around there. . . . Loved to fight, and rarely lost one. He came in one day with his arms all bruised up. Said somebody had tried to kill him with a chair. Red smashed the chair . . . then smashed the guy. One thing about Red, if he said it, it was probably true. You always felt safe when he was around. Unless he was pissed at you."

"I liked the guy and thought his business, morality, and personal traits were pretty good," said Glen Spreen. "I remember, for whatever it's worth, that I had a Samoyed named Pascha. I lived in a smaller place [Glen bought a house in Whitehaven] and the dog would become lonely and eat things, like my couch, the books, the back door screen. . . . I was talking to Red about it, actually complaining but caring about the dog. Red had a ranch and offered to take Pascha. I think we were all better off." Red re-membered Glen's dog very well. "Big ol' white, lovable dog," he reminisced affectionately.

"Pascha passed away like ol' dogs do. She was a good dog, age fourteen when she died."

Red found the new job challenging but fun, and it gave him a chance to spend time at the studio. "Oh man, I was around there night and day for eight months," he said joyfully. "I was always over there. Whoever they were recording, I was there. I was tryin' to come up with something." Though he had been hired to write songs, as with everyone else at American his job description included a little of everything, learning to produce and running the control board while making demos. "The first time I worked the board, when you're overdubbing, you gotta change things around—the slides, the faders," he said, referring to Chips's settings. "I kinda had them messed up and Tommy came in and fixed it for me." Red created some interesting demos and a few master sessions at American, and his ear for talent was also astute, as was proven later in the year.

While Red West adjusted to his new job, the musicians and Chips worked on the sessions for B.J. Thomas that became the album *Young and In Love*, a work with an uncharacteristically exhilarated tone. There was a sense that the group could now do anything they wanted, try any musical experiment and somehow be able to pull it off. "I had many tools at my fingertips, tremolo glissandoing, voicing, dissonances, syncopation, and many more," said Glen Spreen, who did most of the arranging for the album. They had done the ultimate prestige session, and it had earned for them much freedom. The AGP label was kicking into high gear, and this too gave them some autonomy, since they were able to sign any act they liked and work with the artist undisturbed. They were like kids in the world's biggest candy store. "The album also taught me something," said Glen. "Pick your spots and take leaps. Be different." Even friends watching from a distance picked up on the new exhilarated mood: J.R. Cobb's midsummer hit for the Classics IV, "Every Day with You, Girl" (the title loosely borrowed from that of an old hymn) floats as effortlessly as a feather on the breeze.

The most memorable song from the B.J. sessions was the single, another Mark James composition, "It's Only Love." Credited to Mark and Steve Tyrell, Glen Spreen, who was present when the song was written on the piano in Steve's suite at the Holiday Inn Rivermont there in Memphis, recalled that Tyrell's only actual involvement was suggesting the title, which Mark chose after hearing several titles Tyrell had tossed out for his consideration. "Steve got part writer and, I believe, part publisher," Glen recalled. "Mark was not happy [about that. It] just really, really made Mark—I don't know if he was angry, but he was frustrated." At the time, Steve was making a pitch to become Mark's manager again and to record him in New York. (Tyrell made the same offer to Glen, who declined.) "Tyrell was all the time being a jive dude," Bobby Wood remarked. "Sometimes I didn't know when to take him seriously"—an observation with which even Glen, who had known Steve Tyrell for many years, agreed. Many of the others around American also did not know how to take him: Marty Lacker's impression was that "Steve was sort of a jiveass and he was really someone that used people. He was funny in a jiveass sort of way but you always had the feeling that you didn't want to turn your back to him in certain situations." "I never would have believed Tyrell would wind up where he did [as a crooner]," said Ima Roberts. "I thought he'd be an actor, he was so gorgeous." "Mr. Cool Man Tyrell," said Bobby Wood amusedly, in a phrase that neatly summed up the promotion man.

Though the circumstances under which "It's Only Love" were written suggest an almost businesslike way of composing, the results Mark came up with are not, and by the time Chips had gotten the song, it became a completely different statement. "I see the sunlight in her hair," B.J. softly declares over a chugging rhythm featuring Tommy Cogbill at his pulsing, James Jamersonian best. "I feel the warm smile that she wears." The woman seems to be a dream at first, and then the dream comes true during the singer's waking hours. The song is also about emotional vulnerability, describing what happens when one is already willing to fall in love and suddenly meets someone— "The clock that's ringing says it's time / to wake up to my destiny." The alarm clock's ringing describes both the literal waking from a dream and the fact that it was "time" to fall in love.

Chips Moman had for a long time been ready to fall in love; his wife Laurie, said Ima Roberts, was a quiet woman, frail and somewhat sickly, who stayed to herself on the farm for the most part. In some ways that was particularly suited to Chips, who was more shy than often assumed, but in other ways he had always been searching for something different. "[Laurie] was always nice to me but . . . kind of quiet," observed Mike Leech. "Chips and I went fishing together (at least once) and I rode with him in his jeep to his house to pick up our gear. Laurie was there and they exchanged some good-natured banter before we headed out. They seemed okay with each other—didn't notice any static between them—sure there had been, and was more to come—didn't see any of that." In his memoirs, Ronnie Milsap told a story that endowed Laurie with old-world wisdom; when he accidentally jammed a piece of metal into his finger and worried that the accident was severe, she advised him to take a piece of bacon with the fat still on and tie it over the wound, and the fat and salt would draw out the sliver of metal; he did as she suggested and saved his finger, for which he gave her all the credit and thanks.

Laurie's Southern ways would have made Chips comfortable; but like most introspective, melancholy people, he seemed to be looking for someone livelier to take him out of himself. For the most part he had been acquainted with women like Sandy Posey or Merrilee Rush, who were as somber and contemplative as he. By now he and Marty Lacker were occasionally listening together to the demo tapes sent him by the Screen Gems people in New York; on some of the songs they kept hearing a woman with a distinctive, somewhat nasal voice who sang off the beat, but there was something winning about her delivery. Chips was intrigued, and wondered who she was, and the warmth he seemed to be seeking flickers like a candle flame through the structure of "It's Only Love."

It was Glen Spreen's first official arranging credit, featured prominently on the back of the record jacket; he and Mike Leech had not been given label credit by RCA for their work on the Elvis material, at the insistence of the Colonel, who wanted the spotlight only on his boy. For "It's Only Love" Glen created an arrangement that, he said, worked better than he had ever imagined when he first heard the playback: "I got chills when the strings did that ascending line." The swirling crescendos leading up to the chorus were emphasized by the soft sounds of the Moman Tabernacle Choir, featuring Wayne Carson. "I was the utility man on a lot of those things," said the songwriter with gruff amiability, adding that he often did not appear on the album credits because his vocals were improvised at the last minute, after the list of participants had already been written up. "Chips and I spent a lot of time together and sometimes he'd say, 'Damn, that needs a harmony part.' I'd just go in and sing harmony on the mix." Another backup singer on the album had recently been added to the choir: Johnny Christopher.

On the strength of his guitar playing and his writing on the demo of "Mama Liked the Roses," Johnny began sitting in with the group and adding rhythm guitar to the proceedings; he was shortly asked to join the lineup permanently. "They were interested in me as a prospective talent; I don't know why," Johnny reflected. "I didn't think I had much to offer, but I enjoyed the company. I am honored to be in their company. I looked up to them." The admiration continued to be mutual. "I thought Johnny was the best rhythm guitar player I'd ever heard anywhere," said Bobby Wood. "Boy, you talk about talented, whew! God," exclaimed Rick Yancey, a local songwriter who signed on with American later that year." Chips said about Johnny's right thumb, "'That's the best thumb in the world.'" Chips was referring, of course, to the thumb Johnny used for strumming; Johnny played very low on the neck of the guitar, so that a standard acoustic almost sounded like an amplified twelve-string. "That style of acoustic guitar, when he played it, it set the whole B.J. Thomas sound," said Reggie Young respectfully. "[He] didn't consider himself a good player, but he was," declared Mike Leech. "Fantastic acoustic guitar player. Inventive, good timing."

The core group was adjusting, as much as they ever would, to the lately arrived hippies in their midst. By now they realized that Johnny Christopher's preppie exterior concealed as much of a free spirit as Glen Spreen's bell-bottoms and tie-dyed T-shirts displayed. "Glen was an L.A.-type hippie while Johnny was southern-style," Mike Leech said of the perceived differences between the two. "[Johnny's] eyes would widen along with a big smile when he was around [us]. He always asked things about licks and stuff, how or why Reggie came up with something. He was fun to be around, in the middle of everything, laughing, cutting up. Unlike Glen who sort of stood in the background, watching. Made everybody nervous."

Johnny's intensity commended him to the group—"That dude gives a hundred and fifty percent to whatever he is doing," said Bobby Wood—but Glen Spreen was no less passionate, especially about music, though he concealed it behind a deliberate manner and a soft monotone with no trace of Texas accent. In private conversation, the passion was apparent.

"[Tommy] said to me once that, in order to move anyone with music, you have to be moved yourself. Music has made me sweat and given me chills. I knew what he was saying was absolutely true," Glen commented. "To me music was more of a religion than a way of making a product. I was more emotional back then (a bit too passionate maybe). Having said that, I was still aware of the 'making a living' aspect."

Johnny Christopher's lifestyle in many ways may have been more unconventional than Glen's. "I remember that Johnny was a health-food nut, he might have been a vegetarian," said Reggie Young amusedly. "He was a vitamin freak," said Mike Leech. "He always gave advice as to how to keep your bod in shape. . . . He got on a vitamin kick—stopped eating fast food, only health food, lost a lot of weight—looked a bit unhealthy at times, but boasted that he felt great." He exercised and power-walked long before these things were fashionable. His then-

wife Jean, whom he had brought with him from Atlanta, had been married before, and Johnny happily played stepfather to her children. Several of the group remembered him driving an old Volkswagen, as opposed to the elegant foreign car Glen Spreen had chosen. Whatever he did, he did it all the way, from playing guitar to reinforcing Bobby Wood's yet-untapped ambitions. "Johnny was the first person to write with me and encouraged me," said Bobby. "We became bosom buddies. Think we were good for each other, strengths and weakness factor." But even Bobby had some reservations about the bounding enthusiasm of his new best friend when he looked back. "I guess every talented person I can think of has a screw or two loose," he sighed. "I think one hundred fifty percent is great, but the wisdom that only comes from God can point it in the right direction." For now, Johnny seemed to be on that right way up; his work during his first year at American would get better and better.

He contributed another dream-becomes-reality song to the B.J. Thomas sessions with his statement of déjà vu, "Fairy Tale of Time," which was not released on the album but became the B-side of the second single, "Pass the Apple, Eve" (which Johnny also put together, with help from Mark James and a title suggested by Chips). Set to the bouncy background of Mike Leech's springy bass and Gene Chrisman's precision drumbeats, B.J. tells the story of a couple who were destined to meet—and then meet again. "I knew you / when you were a dream to me," the story says. "You turned into a memory, and then became a part of me." The mood is joyful, almost giddy, as the couple rediscover one another; there is a sense that the connection between the man and woman will endure for as long as either one is alive.

Though Johnny Christopher came up with much of the music, the theme of "Fairy Tale" came from Mark James, who was writing about a literal reunion. Mark was married and his daughter was a little over a year old, but he had flown down to Houston for a class reunion the previous autumn and re-met his high-school sweetheart, Karen. She was as warm and open as Spooner Oldham's Karen, and though she too had married (to a prosperous doctor), she and Mark decided to get divorces and be together. It was an unfolding story that those of Mark's friends with a romantic temperament, like Mike Leech and Glen Spreen, observed with delight. "I think he got ["Fairy Tale of Time"] from Karen," Glen observed. "He always had that 'Fantasia' feeling about her." Karen is also the muse for "It's Only Love" and several of Mark's other memorable songs, even "Suspicious Minds," which Mark had written immediately after the reunion about attempts to appease his wife. Mark's songs at this point were directly autobiographical, with love song after love song flowing from his pen; love songs as such were not autobiographical for Chips Moman just yet, but a listener experiencing his records as they were released could sense that he was building up to something, that the pressure to experience "that Fantasia feeling" with someone was gnawing at him and would not be eased until it was found.

Innocuous pop hits of the day, such as Gamble and Huff's "I'm Gonna Make You Love Me" and the Brill Building selection (later revived by the Carpenters) "Hurting Each Other," comprise the bulk of the album. Only Mark James's experimental "Living Again," with its instrumental bridge borrowed from the one in Blue Cheer's "Summertime Blues," completely lives up to the promise of the single (which appears here in a remixed stereo version with some added string overdubs from Glen Spreen almost burying Bobby Wood's piano interval). A new version of "I Pray for Rain" is so slowed down that it almost sounds stoned. The musicians contribute wonderful touches here and there, most notably Bobby Emmons's introductory line for "Solitary Man," Reggie Young's sitar accents, and Bobby Wood's staccato piano. The most interesting songs from the session never made the cut for the album, making the follow-up to *On My Way* sound bland by comparison, despite B.J.'s flawless vocals and the empathetic playing.

There was an occasional item done in the style Chips preferred; the grimly realistic "Skip a Rope," "Solitary Man," the dragged-out "I

Pray for Rain" with its mood more of apathetic depression than of vengeance, and the B-side of "It's Only Love," which Mark James seems to have specifically crafted to suit Chips's inclinations. "You Don't Love Me Anymore" is unremittingly bleak, a brooding man walking down a railroad track and reflecting over a love gone bad. "Nobody knows the way I feel" is merely the opening line in this gloomy treatise, and it gets even more anguished: "The sky is gray with dark despair / The wind is blowing through my hair / I may be walking in the rain / My senses just don't seem the same," are the first four lines in the chorus. The narrator is either so preoccupied or depressed that he does not hear the train coming behind him, and Chips mixes in the sound of a rushing train with Gene Chrisman's relentless drum taps to imply either an accident or a deliberate suicide. It is a difficult record to listen to, and grim even for Chips.

The ability to wring every tear from a song that Larry Butler had noticed several years before had now become the musical style of American's leader. From now on, many of his productions would not make the Top Forty charts due to his variations on depressive themes. Even when he attempted a novelty record, as with Glen Goza's "The Box," it is nobody's feel-good song; Goza recites the horrifying tale of a lover's rage and vengeance in Boris Karloff tones. Chips preferred a layered sound, especially in contrast to Tommy Cogbill's slightly more spacious concepts; a Chips Moman mix is so intricate that if you listen to one of his records a thousand times, there is always something new leaping out that you have not heard before. American was about to enjoy its highest commercial success, but Chips chose to become more experimental; the records reflected the trends of the pop music world less and less as he delved into his thoughts and feelings for inspiration.

He instructed the group to do the same. Somewhere around this time, Chips began thinking of himself as a cracker-barrel philosopher similar to the ones he had worked with in the Shoals. He concluded sessions by calling the musicians in to the control room, sticking his feet up on the console, tilting back in his chair, and treating them to casual, rambling discourses they came to call his "lectures"—elaborately constructed thoughts on music and life he wanted them to heed. "He was trying to convert the world to Momanism," chuckled Ed Kollis. A soundman from later in the group's history, Hayward Bishop, said the same thing in almost the same words. Being four to six years older than most of his group, the oldest of them all except for Tommy Cogbill, Chips doubtless thought he was passing along hard-earned wisdom from his years of scuffling. "That may have been a little power play on his part, gathering the boys up to give them fatherly advice," Mike Leech speculated. Bobby Wood remembered that the lectures centered around music: "I think mostly they were about certain artists on songs that would be played for them, or if anybody had an idea of an old song that we could put a new arrangement to. I believe there were a few reprimands but nothing very serious."

"Our control-room lectures covered lots of ground," added Mike Leech. "One in particular I remember was 'don't buy foreign cars.' And he had a Rolls. . . . That was what was so funny about Chips's lectures. He would get on the bandwagon about something, and turn around and do just the opposite." The musicians listened attentively to what Chips had to say, but they claimed later not to have taken the suggestions as gospel. Mike remembered with undisguised amusement, "Lecture time was fun. We usually wound up telling jokes and having a good time. . . While we attended these lectures, after we all disassembled, we would laugh about it, and go on doing what we wanted." "I, for one, wouldn't take it too seriously," said Bobby Wood. "Most of the time we were kidding around with each other anyway. If things got too serious, someone would say something funny to break the ice. In those days I didn't take a whole lot seriously anyway. After all, if you can't have fun with what you're doing, it would get boring."

One of Chips's most oft-spoken tenets during the lectures was that they should not listen to the radio because they would wind up imitating the latest trends in music. "That was a theory I had for a long time," he said cheerfully, a theory he developed because he disliked copycat records. "That's what made me so mad about the Beatles—when the Beatles came along everybody wanted to play that kind of music." Not listening to the radio was fine for most of the group, since they were usually too tired to do much else anyway, said Bobby Wood. "When I left the studio, the radio would not be something I would turn on unless it was the classical station. At five o'clock in the morning I would have burned four or five packs of cigarettes and my mouth tasted like an ashtray smelled." It was okay with Wayne Carson as well, because he seldom held more than fleeting interest in what anyone else was creating. "I've never followed the trends, or had a hero to speak of," he said. "I mean, I liked Paul McCartney's work, but I figured out pretty quick there was only one Paul McCartney, so maybe there was only one Wayne Carson. . . . [Music] should be original, it shouldn't sound like everybody else," Wayne insisted. "The most important goddamn thing you'll ever have in your life is an original thought."

It was fine with Mike Leech for different reasons. "It was my choice to not listen to the radio—had nothing to do with whatever Chips might have said. One reason I stopped listening to the radio in Memphis, and this will sound a little like I'm bragging—not meant to be, is that most of the time when I turned it on it would be something we recorded, and I wanted to hear other things. The Muscle Shoals group felt the same way about their stuff." Nobody knew whether Tommy Cogbill listened to the radio—as with so many things going on in his life, he never said anything about it, but he was able to keep up with contemporary music to a certain extent through his habit of visiting the local clubs and listening to various bands at night when he was not at the studio.

Reggie Young did listen to the radio, bought contemporary albums, and analyzed them to see how other people made records. Occasionally he and Mike Leech played tapes in the control room at American. "We played tapes of stuff already recorded and we did have the *Magical Mystery Tour* album on tape by the

Beatles," Mike recalled. "That was a big hoot hanging out in the control room and listening on the big speakers." Surprisingly in light of his agreement with most of Chips's ideas, Bobby Emmons also listened to the radio. He approached his listening as any craftsman would, in the spirit of keeping up with the trends. "I've always thought that if you turned off the radio, you turned off your future in the music business," he said. "It's like pole vaulting in the dark. If you don't know where the bar is, how do you clear it? The thing about commercial music is, you've got to be different, but you can't be *too* different. You can't just jump as high as you can." Bobby's pole-vaulting analogy typifies his literary, metaphorical speaking style, which Bobby Wood dubbed "parables."

Tommy Cogbill did not stick around for most of the lectures, or for the tape listening; if he was not working he was not there. He was only occasionally in on the by-now frequent games that either interrupted recording or took place while the musicians waited around (even Wayne Jackson and the Memphis Horns took part if they were there to record an overdub). "Cog might play toss the line or flip the cards, but never took it seriously, as seriously as I or some of the other guys might have," said Mike Leech. "He would play for a few minutes, then find something else to do."

The rest of the group entertained themselves with poker sessions mainly, although Ed Kollis recalled, "We played hearts all night long with B.J. and his brother Jerry." "I do remember playing cards at the studio," said Glen Spreen. "Sometimes it was just because we didn't have an idea about how to approach a song so we cleared our minds by playing. . . . [If] we just couldn't come up with whatever it was, [we'd say], 'let's just stop and think about it.'" Bobby Wood added that sometimes the session breaks were due to sitting there for too long concentrating on one song. "[When that happens], your ears, your brain, your soul, is fried," he said. "If it ain't really happening group-wise, you take a break." At times Chips, sensitive to the mood in the room, would call for one of those breaks; when that happened, he left the control room and joined the musicians, reveling

in being one of the boys until it was time to take over and be the leader again. "We liked to play poker among ourselves because when Chips was involved it became 'us against Chips,'" Mike Leech reflected. "We felt intimidated by his gambling forte, and knew he could deal off the bottom if he wanted to and we would never know. [We] played small-stakes games and had a ball." When Chips joined the boys for a game, anything went. "I remember during one card game, I kept getting the same card each deal," Mike Leech recalled. "I made the comment, 'If I get that damn queen of spades again, I'll—' So next deal was Chips's, and sure enough the card showed up in my hand. I glanced at Chips and he was grinning at me."

Several other card games were favored by the musicians. "Don't know if you know how to do 'toss the line.' Or whatever it's called," Mike explained. "You can find a hard surface such as tile, locate a line, or you can toss closest to the wall. The bet can be whatever you want it to be and you can toss whatever coin you want. Whoever gets closest to the wall or line wins. The perfect toss is when the coin winds up leaning against the wall. That's hard to beat. Fun game that can get expensive.

"Also we played tossing cards into a hat or a container of sorts. That takes some skill and is also fun. Put a hat about four to six feet from where you are sitting, and a deck of cards. See how many out of the deck you can put in the hat."

Somehow they discovered a card game called "tonk," which had been familiar to blacks for many years but was just breaking through to white card players. The musicians played it by the hour while they were waiting for Chips to come in or when they were on the premises for overdubs. Mike Leech, Reggie Young, Bobby Wood, and Glen Spreen were especially fond of the game, and later on Hayward Bishop joined in (though Mike did not remember him as being a frequent player); once again, Tommy Cogbill was conspicuous in his nonparticipation. Nor did he take part in all the kidding that was an inevitable byproduct of the card-playing. "In the first place Tommy would never have been recipient of any banter. If he had been, he would have sneered, sighed, and disappeared," said Mike Leech.

"There was always something going on with us," Gene Chrisman remembered amusedly. When weather permitted, there were outdoor basketball games in the studio parking lot back of the building. Bobby Wood, Mike Leech, and Wayne Carson recalled these times fondly. "We had fun with basketball, playing different games," Wood reflected. "I had played high school basketball and was good at making goals even with one eye. Of course, Chips would want to bet on who could make a goal as usual. Johnny was pretty good at sports."

"We had a few pretty hot games with the Tennesseans against the Texans. It was Mark, Glen, Tyrell, against me, Johnny, Mike or Tommy, and maybe Chips. I think Ed Kollis was in on that too. It was pretty brutal. We also would play horse. It was a game of elimination. You would have to follow another person to a different location and if they made the shot and you missed, you would get a letter from H to O and if you went all the way to E and missed you were out." Wayne Carson participated in the basketball games whenever he was in town: "I played forward." "I can't remember who won but the Texans were taller," Glen Spreen said dryly.

As enjoyable as the B.J. Thomas sessions were, punctuated by cards and basketball, it was even more fun to see Bobby Womack again. He came back from his new life in Los Angeles to record his second album *Fly Me to the Moon*, and everyone remembered that he was as optimistic as ever. "Bobby and I would stay up all night during his album," said Glen Spreen warmly, remembering his first chance at arranging one of Womack's projects. "While working on string and horn parts we strayed from time to time to other subjects, like how he learned to play that right-handed guitar while being left-handed. Bobby was enthusiastic and enjoyable to be around. He had a lot of interesting stories and his view on things was very positive." The celebratory mood of the reunion is heard on their gleeful, just-after-midnight, romping version of "I Left My Heart in San Francisco"; in Womack's hard-charging composition "It's Gonna Rain," which features

a uniquely structured bass line from Tommy Cogbill; and in the fierce interpretation of the Motown classic "Don't Look Back." The jaunty mood carried through even in apparently pessimistic material like Womack's and Darryl Carter's compositions "Oh How I Miss You" and "I Can't Take It Like a Man," both with lyrics Chips would have loved—lines like "I haven't seen a good day since you know when" and "This is my third time down."

Only on "Everyone's Gone to the Moon" does the pace begin to slow, and Chips's vision completely dominates on only one track, a grim narrative set in an Arkansas prison that seemed to be inspired by a story then in the news about bodies discovered there (Bobby Darin's bluesy "Long Line Rider" dealt with the same subject at around the same time). As with the Mark James–composed flip side of the B.J. single, this song is not for frequent listening: it is one of Chips's bleaker productions. The album ends on a triumphant note, however, with Womack's tender "I Just Want to Thank You."

"You're my warm cup of coffee," Bobby declaims gently, and we feel we are listening to a morning moment between him and Barbara (one can almost see them seated at the breakfast table, with the sun shining through a window). The record flows effortlessly, sparked by the enthusiasm and passion of Reggie Young's guitar matching Bobby's, and toward the fade-out Bobby, as if entranced himself by what he is hearing, muses that he just wants to "let the music play awhile." "Womack and Reggie worked together so well," said Bobby Wood. "Reggie played [that] song that was so soulful and so burning and Womack said 'Play your guitar, Bobby.'" But it is Reggie who then completely takes charge of the song, playing chopped, choked guitar lines atop the long floating passages, carrying it on toward the fade. In that recording, Womack revealed himself as the easygoing, thoughtful man his friends had always known. But California had begun to change the guitarist, change him in ways most of the group did not yet understand. Ed Kollis knew what it was. "He was the first guy to introduce me to the funny white powder," the soundman said of Womack.

• • •

Spooner Oldham was also adjusting, in ways different than those of Bobby Womack, to life in California. His departure from Memphis had been reluctant, but with the increasing roughness of the neighborhood around the studio and with his house having burned, he saw no point in staying. "I think we had run our road, we had written and run the course. I knew in my heart and mind that American would never be the same as it was," he said somberly. "I was starting a new beginning." He joined the consortium of musicians, mostly from Atlanta, who wanted to found their own Los Angeles studio. "It was a good group of musicians that came out from the South," Spooner reflected; led by the Classics IV keyboardist Joe Wilson, the group also featured Emory Gordy on bass, Dennis St. John on drums, and Richard Bennett on lead guitar. They bought a small studio from Mike Curb's Sidewalk Productions and quickly began getting work as a group. Each member was also free to do outside recording. "I started listening to the names involved," said Spooner. "I was wondering what to do next anyway. The limelight was just gettin' softer. I was ready for a change, I think. There was no great money talk, but there was a salary talk. I decided to go try it for a weekly salary." It took a few months of preparation, but by August 1969 he was settled in.

Arriving in California, Spooner defined himself as he always had. "I was basically a songwriter for one, that was the way I could make my own music or noise, the second was that I was a keyboard player for hire," he said. Although he had a regular base of operations, the freelance work was disconcerting at first for a musician who had spent most of his career in house bands working out of one studio. "I was challenged again; I loved that. It was hard, but I loved it. I thrive on challenges, I used to not know that. I especially love to work with newcomers that are challenged themselves. It's the pioneer spirit, I guess. That keeps you young, I think, and of fresh mind."

In working the Los Angeles studio circuit, Spooner found all the challenges he could want. "It was challenging and daunting at the same time," he admitted. "[In Memphis and Muscle Shoals] we were used to knowing each other fairly well. I missed what I had gotten used to, knowing people better. I was thrown in with practically a different band every day. Each studio was different." He found many of his outside sessions through an acquaintance with Chris Ethridge, who had just left the Flying Burrito Brothers to pursue studio work. "I must give a lot of credit to Chris Ethridge for helping me find my way around," Spooner said gratefully. "We were a little bit disenfranchised together." After a time Chris refused to play bass on sessions unless Spooner was hired along with him. Ethridge was also a Southerner, from Mississippi, and he had always admired the work of the American group—"Chris was one of them boys that grew up on Memphis and Muscle Shoals," said Chips Moman with equal respect. "He sort of helped introduce me to a lot of Southern California pop, rock and roll, folk people," said Spooner. "I fell in right away with some so-called heavyweights."

The timing out of Spooner's arrival in town also contributed to his success. When he got there, "Leon Russell was probably the ace top session player," but Leon was writing songs and had his eye on a solo career. Next in line from him was probably Larry Knechtel, who was familiar enough with Spooner's work to occasionally ask him to play on dates when Knechtel was overbooked; within three years he too would be out of the studios, having signed on with David Gates's group Bread. By default, then, when producers needed a contemporary, soulful-sounding piano player, the choice was Spooner. "It was the timing, coincidental, my willingness to work and wanting to do well" that were the qualities to which he attributed his L.A. success. Even in such a competitive market, he did not aggressively push himself or parade his previous accomplishments. "I still wonder if they knew about me," he mused. "I never talked about what I'd done or the songs I'd written. And I never knew what they knew [about it]."

He even found another collaborator right away. "My memory says that for awhile, Karen and I moved into an apartment," he said. "I met Freddy Weller on the sidewalk, it turned out he lived there too." Weller was concluding his tenure with Paul Revere and the Raiders, and had just gotten his first hit on the country charts with his version of "Games People Play," written of course by his old Atlanta buddy Joe South. "We bonded as friends and writers," Spooner said of his acquaintance with Weller. "I think that Southern thing connected us right away; we were strangers in a strange land, so to speak." Spooner also saw a little of Bobby Womack occasionally, more from chance meetings than deliberate encounters, and the two of them eventually planned an album with Spooner slated to produce, but Womack's then-label never got back with them on the matter. Spooner could not comment about any changes in his old friend: "I didn't see Bobby often so I never knew what his lifestyle was like; I wondered, myself."

There was no danger of Spooner's changing to fit California. "A story reminds me of how subtle and unusual Spooner was," said Marty Lacker, who saw Spooner shortly after the move. "I had to go to L.A. on business and was staying at the North Howard Johnson's Hotel because it was close to where I had to go.

"One day I leave my room and walked down the hall to the elevator. While waiting for the elevator I heard a door open down the hall and a man and a woman came walking towards the elevator. I turned away not paying any attention until they got to the elevator and were standing behind me. When the elevator arrived I turned to let the lady get on first and when I turned I see Spooner standing there.

"I said, 'Spooner, how come you didn't say hello? I didn't know it was you standing behind me.' His answer, in his usual quiet and nonchalant way, was 'I didn't want to bother you.' I just shook my head and said to myself, 'That's Spooner!' Here we were over a thousand miles from Memphis. Coincidentally staying at the same hotel and meeting in the hallway by chance and he didn't want to bother me. I began to chuckle."

Los Angeles may have been new to him, but Spooner remembered feeling comfortable. "I don't know if it's my dual nature, but I

adjusted pretty well to the change." He found the city to be not at all what he had expected. "I'll give you a little picture of my first impression. . . . It wasn't that far removed from Memphis, in my mind. Drivers were courteous, there wasn't a lot of rush. It was just surprising to me that it wasn't as fast. Of course, when I moved out, there were three million people in L.A. County. Today it's something like twenty-five million, and that makes a difference." Even the fabled expensiveness of the city, Spooner discovered, was not quite true at the time. "People said, how you gonna live there, it's so expensive, it kind of puts the fear into going, but it was just the opposite. I found the prices, milk, bread, eggs, and so on, were favorable compared to Memphis. . . . Cokes were a little higher. . . . The only thing that was really expensive was a house." The quality of life, he thought, was good, and the people were friendly: "If you were gettin' on the freeway and had your blinker on, they'd move over for you." He was so busy adjusting to the new surroundings, he said, that he seldom had time to reflect on what he had left behind, although "I loved those people, still. I missed Tommy . . . I missed American Studios for a moment. Did I miss Memphis? I don't think so. I missed Dan . . ."

Back in Memphis, Dan Penn was adjusting, too. He had bought his new studio, Beautiful Sounds, and had hired Leon Sides to come in and set up the recording equipment. The studio was established with financial assistance from Jerry Carrigan. Carrigan even moved to Memphis for several years to help Dan get the operation going, thus forfeiting his position as Nashville's most successful progressive drummer. Kenneth Buttrey became the top-ranked player among the younger men in town, and even when Carrigan returned to Nashville he was never fully able to recoup the ground he lost. To everyone but Dan, Carrigan, and perhaps Herbie O'Mell, whom Dan had asked to be his operations manager and do for his place what Don Crews and Marty Lacker did at American, the idea of Dan running a studio did not seem to fit; his friends seemed surprised that he would even attempt it. "Dan was trying to be a mogul at one time," said Wayne

Carson amusedly. "Dan had never run a studio before; Dan just wasn't a businessman," said Norbert Putnam, offering one reason why Beautiful Sounds, despite Dan's idealism and intentions, never really went anywhere. Wayne Carson thought of another reason: "There just wasn't enough business. He'd have been better off to go to Muscle Shoals."

Wayne visited Beautiful Sounds occasionally, watched it being built, and carefully took notes on the details of running a recording studio, because he was starting one of his own back in Springfield. "I wanted a place to do demos where I didn't have to go four hundred miles," he explained. "I thought, hell, I can do this." Si Siman, of course, was Wayne's partner and main investor. "We were [also] in partnership with a fellow named Ralph Foster—he was the guy who owned the Ozark Jubilee," the songwriter added. In fact, the name eventually chosen for the studio, Top Talent, was taken from the management company Foster ran which had booked the Jubilee acts on the road. "That studio was my baby," Wayne said proudly; he was involved with everything from planning the building to buying the recording equipment. "[Ralph Foster] said, 'I'll put you in touch with an architect,'" Wayne recalled. "I designed the building and I told the architect what I wanted." He almost bought the four-track equipment from the old Fred Bevis studio in the Shoals, which Jimmy Johnson was reconverting with the help of the loan from Atlantic Records; he went down to look the equipment over but decided against the purchase on advice from Chips. "He said, 'Shit, don't do it. That stuff is obsolete. For the same amount of money you could put a little more with it and get something new,' and that's what I did."

The resulting studio did well in a city that had not been a music center for some years, although that was not Wayne's intention. "I never did want a commercial studio," he said. Nonetheless, when it was discovered what he had, a surprising number of clients booked time. "We did a lot of jingles, did a lot of radio shows, state conservation shows there, fifteen-minute radio shows. Unlike a radio station, we had the capacity of cutting eight-track tapes. Between myself and Juan Hoppe, we did some engineering." Two rock groups came out of the studio as well: Granny's Bath Water, which had been Wayne's road band at one time and lasted until the death in a car accident of the band's founding member; and, more substantially, the Ozark Mountain Daredevils. "They were like my kids," Wayne said fondly. "Those were kids who used to hang around the studio, went out on the road with me. And, as musicians will, they found each other, got together." Though Wayne was never directly involved in any of the Daredevils' recordings, he always spoke of the band with warm, proprietary pride, and he continued to operate the studio successfully until he sold it in 1974. "I'm probably one of the few people to have sold a studio at a profit," he observed. "Usually everybody goes tits-up—excuse me, belly-up." And though he adamantly insisted that he was not, never had been, and never would be, a businessman, the success of Top Talent Studios was another side of the gruff songwriter, and it proved that he could operate a business on the only terms he would ever happily accept—his own.

Because of Chips Moman's introspection and Tommy Cogbill's delightful adventurousness, the American group began working on a series of quirky, experimental records, many of them done either for their own AGP label or for Scepter. The financing by Bell and the enthusiastic boosting of Steve Tyrell practically guaranteed them a blank check to record anything they liked; their repertoire ranged from laid-back country-pop efforts by Mark James on Scepter and Wayne Carson on Monument Records to soul music by the Masqueraders on AGP, from the hippie sounds of Eternity's Children on the Capitol label to Ronnie Milsap on Scepter delivering the doom-laden and guilt-ridden Dan Penn and Spooner Oldham composition "Denver," with lyrics that both echoed the Bee Gees' "Massachusetts" and anticipated Dolly Parton's similarly themed and phrased "Down from Dover." Tommy Cogbill had been experimenting in the studio practically since he had begun producing; the carnival sound effects he had spliced in to the New Wave–sounding "Good-Time Merry Go Round" for Shadden the King Lears the year before were daring enough for a Top Forty record, but there would be even more adventurous works in the next few months.

Mark James and Wayne Carson remained the group's main writers, and both of them came up with memorable songs during this time. Mark's recording of his and Glen Spreen's "Candy" is a radical departure from Chips's usual gloomy productions: the rhythm is up-tempo, the horn section is prominent, and the phrasing calls forth thoughts of what B.J. Thomas's voice, stronger than Mark's pleasant tenor, could have done with the song. Glen Spreen said the song had been conceived as a deliberate departure from the standard American group style. "We always tried to get away from ourselves," he remarked. "I think we got into a little bit of bubblegum there. We wanted to make it a younger record. I know we wanted to make something commercial, but we also wanted to do the double entendre" (although "give me candy, Candy, baby" is nothing compared to some of the more suggestive material Johnny Christopher would later write). It apparently was a hit in Italy; Glen Spreen remembered receiving writers' royalties from BMI, which administered Press Music (later, when Chips's publishing was sold to EMI, Glen had to ask EMI for royalty statements).

Mark's solo composition "Dreamin' Till Then," recorded late in the year for the sharp-voiced R&B singer Joe Jeffrey, is another up-tempo song that made for a wonderful record (Reggie Young named it as a favorite). It is a song about missing someone, being content to dream until one sees them again, with obvious undertones of Mark's waiting for Karen. Glen created an elaborately sped-up, baroque string arrangement (classical music having been his first influence, from the time he had been emotionally moved by "Scheherazade" as a child) and Chips stacked countermelody atop countermelody, playing off the arranger similarly to his collaborations with Tommy Cogbill;

but there is a slightly unfriendly edge here, a sense of "can-you-top-this" that not present on those earlier productions. The string line tee-ters, wobbles, and crashes into Tommy's bass track and the backing voices softly intone the words of the chorus. It is a delight no matter how many times it is heard.

Wayne Carson was also working with interesting ideas. His "The Sunshine Belongs to Me" expressed a point of view not pessimistic enough for the American group, but it was perfectly interpreted by Eddy Arnold, who placed it on his album *Walkin' in Love Land* that year. Another one of Wayne's compositions from 1969 is startling. "The Grass Was Green," recorded by the Masqueraders under Tommy Cogbill's direction, anticipates the O.J. Simpson case by twenty-five years. "She was a woman of the world, although her years were just eighteen," the song begins, and indeed Nicole Brown was only a year older than that when she met her husband. "She was wickedly witty" (a delightful description in itself), "sinfully pretty," the narrative continues, and photographs of Nicole immediately come to mind. Tommy paces the record as deliberately as Alfred Hitchcock directing a thriller, leading the listener up to the denouement in which the jealous lover is as surprised as we are to discover what he has done, as if he has been in a trance. The ethereal backing vocals, set far off in the mix, contribute to the sense of unreality, and Lee Jones is still haltingly explaining himself (as in O.J.'s memoir *I Want to Tell You* and his other aborted book project) when the record fades out.

An incident involving the Masqueraders brought out the best in the atmosphere at American. Despite the differences with the late arrivals, it was one for all and all for one if an outsider came near—as with any family. Glen Spreen had written an arrangement for one of the records and the Masqueraders wanted copies of the arrangement to use for a concert. "I sent them, but somehow it did not make it there on time," said Glen. "These guys were very angry, blamed me, and threatened to come back to Memphis to mess me up. Everyone got the word. They all grouped together. When these guys entered the lobby of the American office they found Chips, Bobby Wood, Mike, Reggie, Chrisman, Tommy, Bobby E., and Chips's dog waiting. Everything then turned cordial."

The emissaries were lucky they had not also been met by Johnny Christopher, Red West, and Marty Lacker. Marty had played football in high school and knew how to handle himself. Johnny, of course, was an experienced athlete, and Red, who had been Marty's football teammate at Humes High, was so tough that he had regularly gone to bars in Germany, while he was there as security man and companion for Elvis during the King's military days, and cleaned the places out. Bobby Emmons and Glen Spreen were the most scholarly-looking of the musicians, but even they were redoubtable, and Tommy Cogbill and Gene Chrisman both possessed wiry strength. As for Chips Moman, his drawl, slight paunch, and pained eyes could be somewhat misleading. "Chips had an attitude, sort of that he was a badass," Mike Leech observed, with some puzzlement as to why Chips thought this necessary. "He always carried a pistol, and would brag a bit about individuals losing their nerve during a confrontation with him for some reason or another. While watching boxing, he would comment about the moves, what [the fighter] should have done, et cetera. Not that being a boxing fan makes one a badass, it just seemed to tie in with his attitude."

The Masqueraders composed much of their work and were somewhat limited writers, but Tommy Cogbill always made sure the backing was strong. "Tell Me You Love Me," one of the vocal group's compositions, is constructed by Tommy as a sweet jazz waltz featuring the humming of Bobby Emmons's organ and a warm bass line from Mike Leech. It relies on gentle persuasion, a theme Tommy often sought in his choice of songs, and nobody but Tommy would have thought to include a yodel in the chorus. "Love, Peace, and Understanding" is a tract on gradualism, disguised as an openhearted romp; to a compelling background track, Lee Jones declares, "A wise man

will change the things he can, and he'll leave the rest alone." Gradualism and patience in all things were principles in which Tommy undoubtedly believed; in fact, to one of the late arrivals, patience seemed to be the producer's most defining characteristic. "He was very mild, but very separated," observed Glen Spreen. "He knew a secret I don't think a lot of people know. Tommy had the fastest hands in the business when he played bass, but Tommy knew the secret to fast: Fast is never to try hard, but to relax and let it happen." If that analysis sounds almost Zen, perhaps that is accurate; there was something of the inscrutable Zen master about Tommy, a presence that was felt by the others even when he was not trying to assert himself. "Tommy was part of the group, he blended in, but he stood out as he blended in," Glen added.

Tommy was still recording Merrilee Rush, and her single from mid-1969 was no summertime frolic. If Bell had promoted it properly, Eddie Rabbitt's composition "Sign On for the Good Times" would have been one of the hits of the year. With its exhilarated mood, rapid pulse, churning twelve-string mixed and blended with John Hughey's steel guitar, and blaring horn section that pushes the entire track, it had more than enough to recommend it musically, and the lyrics were sociological journalism, a look at how courtship custom had changed. "One hundred years ago, wearing lace cuffs, you might have asked my father for my hand," Merrilee recites softly. "Today you just walk up wearing sandals, you say 'hi,' and you take my hand. You tell me what you need of me, I tell you what I need of you," Merrilee continues. "And we accept or we reject the terms and the conditions that we come to." Tommy injects nothing of his own view about it one way or another; he is reporting, letting the singer's voice and Eddie Rabbitt's words deliver the story. The steel guitar loosely qualifies it as a country song, but it has little to do with tradition: a hippie singer from Seattle and a bass player from Memphis kicking around a song about contemporary mores written by an Irishman from New Jersey. This is country music without limits, exactly the kind of thing Eddie Rabbitt and the newly arrived Combine staffer Kris Kristofferson, among other writers, were beginning to make popular.

The B-side of the single demonstrates how well the late arrivals fit, creatively if not in terms of personality, with American's reality-based approach. Nine writers out of ten could not have discussed mental retardation without sentimentality, but Glen Spreen's "Robin Mc-Carver" makes a more intricate point. We see McCarver trying to launch a toy boat on a river, and not understanding why he can't; the boat becomes a metaphor for all of us, sentient or not, trying to undertake tasks we do not understand and not comprehending why our dreams fail us. The symbolic use of the boat had been taken from a childhood experience of Glen's. "There was this newspaper, if you sold so many subscriptions they got you something," he recalled. "I got involved, and my prize was, they gave me a remote-controlled boat. I went down to the levee, maybe a block or two away from my house. The boat went out in the middle of the water, the remote got stuck, and I lost it. I still remember the feeling of almost being devastated. When that happens, you're much more careful next time." He superimposed that childhood memory over another one of having defended several retarded kids from bullies when he was in school. The memories were vivid, but the idea for the song came about slowly. He recalled that it took shape over several lunches at the Ranch House as he discussed the idea with Mark James. "I actually had a vision of writing the song," he said. "I know that we wanted to write something that portrayed a flaw in life. I do remember that it was unique for us. We grappled for a long time just to get it right, but Mark's that way." He had his own speculations on why Bell never promoted the single: "I think we didn't get pushed because no one had the time. Also, when Marty Lacker was hired to handle this area, maybe his head was turned to other things."

Glen was correct about Marty's priorities. Marty was less concerned with promoting individual recordings than he was with getting the entire name and reputation of American more widely known. He started a newsletter, written in a conversationally jocular tone, which he sent to radio stations informing announcers of upcoming AGP releases and about who was recording at the studio. There were promotional items: Bobby Emmons remembered a cigarette lighter with the AGP logo floating in the clear fluid at the base of the lighter. And Marty began laying the groundwork for the Memphis Music Awards, which focused attention not just on American but on the entire music industry in town. "I think he was just huntin' for something to do," Chips said with amusement at Marty's innovations. Marty liked Larry Uttal at Bell and worked well with him (he was himself a native New Yorker and understood the suits from that city as Chips never could), but AGP was not a priority for Bell; Uttal saw it as a vanity label, not as the means to an autonomous enterprise. Bell paid for all the production costs including studio time and payment of musicians, and their staff handled record promotion. Chips should have realized that Bell was not going to adequately promote a label that aspired to become its own possible competition; he said sadly, "I know that now. I didn't know it then."

The West Coast backup group the Blossoms were now signed to Bell, and they came to American for one of the more memorable sessions of the year. "In back of the studio was a garbage bin that was right outside the back door," Gene Chrisman remembered. "I guess I had put some rat poison in the bin to control them. On the day that we were recording the Blossoms, the back door of the studio was open, and a rat came down the steps. He just made his way into the studio, probably having eaten the poison, and was checking the place out. He made his way around to where the Blossoms were gathered at the mike, and when they saw him, they got up on a high footstool." "They started screaming," added Reggie Young amusedly. "There was this big ol' rat running on the floor. We never missed a beat. E took a broom, knocked him on the head, we never stopped playing." Gene continued, "Bobby

Emmons, having seen the rat, got the broom, hit the rat over the head, killed it, and dropped it into one of the ash tray cans and put the lid on it. Never a dull moment there. Always little things going on."

Several singles by the Blossoms were released on Bell, but nothing happened with any of them. Many of the recording experiments coming out on that label, as well as for others, were done by Chips Moman and Tommy Cogbill in collaboration; the two were still great friends and they and their families even took vacations together. Bobby Wood remembered that he and his wife Janice went to Disney World in Orlando that summer, taking their son there for a treat. Once inside the gate, they immediately spotted Chips and Tommy, accompanied by their wives and children. The piano player was amused—"I said, 'I came down here to get away from your ugly faces and you two are the first people I find!'" That closeness came through in the records Chips and Tommy made for their custom label; as they had done with "Soul Deep," they played off each other's ideas and constantly tugged the mood of the records back and forth between them. It is there in the pop singles they made with Eternity's Children and the Southern genre paintings they did with the songwriter Billy Wade McKnight, a Texas singer-songwriter with a foghorn voice whom Chips had signed to Press.

It is even there on the sessions they did featuring the American group and billing themselves as such on the label. Several instrumentals were recorded and released on the AGP label, and the 45 "Enchilada Soul" and "The High Times" illustrates the collaborative approach. "Enchilada Soul" is a moody collaboration credited to Bobby Womack and Rosey Grier; it features the hum of Bobby Emmons's organ and a dark, swirling string part from Mike Leech that Chips apparently liked so much he put it to use again on a King Curtis cut the following year. The fadeout showcases Bobby Womack playing a choppy guitar lead over Tommy Cogbill's intricate bass line; the two of them run a race as Mike Leech's string line rises like the sound of a strong wind blowing. "Always liked that record," Mike said with

quiet pride. "String arrangement is a mix of Bobby's ideas and mine." The song was cut in monaural as were all the American singles, so there is unfortunately very little separation between Bobby's lead and Tommy's rhythm line, making it difficult to pick out what each is doing. (The booming sound of a mono mix was a distinguishing characteristic of the American sound up until 1971, when they got a sixteen-track console and the sound became more separated and therefore lighter.) "The big boomy sound . . . is what I liked about American before they afforded new gear," said Mike Leech. "Before, the bass amp was miked, which gave it the punch you hear. Then came the direct boxes that you would plug into to go directly to the console. That took away some punch, but . . . it was necessary to go with the times."

The other side of the single, "The High Times," features Reggie Young's lead guitar playing a variation on a then well-known Pepsi-Cola jingle ("Taste that beats the others cold, Pepsi pours it on") over a galloping rhythm pattern set by Gene Chrisman and Mike Leech. Earlier, there had been an instrumental version of "Cry Like a Baby," the Box Tops hit of the year before. Though Dan Penn and Spooner Oldham were gone, the song they left behind was getting a workout. Chips cut a vocal version that summer with Arthur Alexander, who was taking a break from recording with the other former Shoals musicians in Nashville to try working in Memphis. Fred Foster masterminded that combination, and though it did not do anything, the singer would be back.

Because of their increasing involvement with Jimmy Johnson's studio, Atlantic no longer brought acts in as often as they had, but Billy Vera's "The Bible Salesman," recorded at American with Chips that spring, proved that the New York label could still match a good singer and a Memphis studio for an inspired recording. Though the song seems to have been triggered by the Maysles Brothers documentary about Bible salesmen working a windy, snow-laden territory up north, Chips altered the geographic focus to make it one of American's most classic Southern genre paintings. He gives the song an almost visual emphasis, underlining the salesman's pitch with Tommy Cogbill's relentless bass and Reggie Young's most sardonic guitar lead since "Working Girl."

The Joe Tex album *Buying a Book* is also a Southern genre painting, with Joe's songs creating a nuanced picture of working-class African American life. On this album, the horn section was even more of a motley group than the Moman Tabernacle Choir; it featured not only the Memphis Horns, but Glen Spreen trotting out his original instrument, the saxophone, and a few more surprise guests. The infusion created a rollicking sound that everyone enjoyed, Joe perhaps most of all. "Joe Tex liked a large horn section, so we augmented our core with Booker T [from the MG's at Stax, on trombone], and I can't remember who all, but it was a great section cut 'live,' going down with the track," said Mike Leech happily. "That was always a plus, having the horns along with the rhythm section. It sparked [us], and can be felt in the recordings."

And though old friends like Joe Tex were always welcome, American lost one of its most dependable patrons in the summer of 1969. Goldwax, after a five-year run that yielded few overwhelming hits but had always made a respectable showing, dissolved due to increasingly irreconcilable differences, both personal and musical, between Quinton Claunch and Doc Russell. "He had a good personality, but he didn't know anything about music," Quinton said of his former partner. Their Bell contract would expire in early 1970, and Quinton and Doc chose to sit out the remaining time and make no attempt to place the label elsewhere. And no one came looking for Goldwax, according to Quinton, which is surprising in light of their successes, especially with James Carr. There had been some interest from other labels initially. Said Quinton: "Jerry Wexler was over at Chips's studio one day. . . . He said he woulda liked to have done some business with us on the front end, because we had his kind of music, you know, the kind of things that Atlantic did." But by the time the Bell contract was up things were changing at Atlantic due to an upcoming merger with Warner Brothers–Seven Arts, Wexler was no longer as important to

the company as he had been, and Goldwax was through.

Quinton had no regrets and refused to speak bitterly of anyone. "I'm not gonna fuss about the past," he said gently of his differences with Doc Russell, who died of a massive heart attack in 1989. Quinton saw nothing of Doc after the label ended. He kept his hardware sales job until he retired and he remained close to James Carr until Carr's death from lung cancer. At the turn of the new century, when he was well into his seventies, he supervised the reissuing of the entire Goldwax catalogue on CD, first with an American businessman with whom he soon parted company, and then with Ace Records in England, to whom he sold the entire catalogue. And like all of the American group's patrons from the people at Atlantic and Bell to Buddy Killen, Fred Foster, and Papa Don Schroeder, he relished the time he spent with the musicians and cherished the contributions they had made to his records. "We enjoyed working with them so much," he said with warm enthusiasm. "I just take my hat off to 'em."

The year before, Goldwax had recorded Percy Milam's version of a country tune written in Nashville by Don Scaife (more evidence of Quinton's lifelong country leanings); "I Slipped a Little." Set to a skipping rhythm and a gentle hum on the Hammond organ, the story line is that of a man tempted by another woman; in the spirit of Billy Sherrill's and Glenn Sutton's "Almost Persuaded," he remembers his wife, stops the affair in progress, and goes home (although it takes him longer; he and the other woman spend the entire day together and they wind up in a tavern by sunset, where the denouement occurs).

It was a song about priorities, and by the end of the year, success and its perks brought about many changes in priorities, for Chips and for the entire band.

||||||||||||||||||||||||||||||||||||||||||||||||||||||||||||||

### CHAPTER 19

# Tommy Cogbill's Year

By the time of the Goldwax dissolution, many of the records the group had made the previous fall were either on the charts or about to be released, so that to the listening public American was entering a golden commercial period, although in actuality the musicians had left that phase behind in favor of experimental recordings. *Memphis Underground* was now on the jazz charts, and American continued that style with the Hubert Laws album *Crying Game*, engineered by Tommy Cogbill, who was also credited with the musical direction—to no one's surprise, since he remained the group's resident jazzman.

American's jazz and pop credentials increased when they recorded several singles with Buddy Greco, who had worked with Benny Goodman in the late forties but was now more of a lounge singer. Reggie Young remembered that "he was cool, he was like a Vegas kind of act, he was kinda taken with us." Greco brought in a demo of the Beatles' "Let It Be" that he wanted to do; the musicians had not heard the song before and Mike Leech remembered the band listening to it for the first time and running it down. The singer's preference for recording in the prearranged style common to New York or Los Angeles may have been a factor in the session's commercial failure. "I think Greco shot himself in the foot when he came down," Mike Leech reflected. "Most artists, when they came down, laid back and waited for the magic to arrive . . . but Buddy was so accustomed to running the show, so to speak, in the studio, that all we were allowed to do was what he wanted. And that was his selection of songs, to be recorded his way. Labels such

as Atlantic had to lean toward whatever these types of artists wanted. All the label could do was . . . cut a track or two, take it back to New York, mix it, release it, and move on to something else. They knew they didn't have a hit, but their hands were tied, probably by an agent."

Dusty Springfield now had the second hit from her album with "Windmills of Your Mind," featuring Reggie Young's contemplative acoustic guitar. "In the Ghetto" and "Don't Cry Daddy" put Elvis back in the front rank, and "It's Only Love" and the revamped version of "I Shall Be Released" by the Box Tops had been on the radio all spring. "Soul Deep" became a hit in September. Bell Records was so delighted that Larry Uttal personally offered the musicians and their families an all-expenses-paid vacation in Acapulco as a thank-you gift. With the exception of Mark James and Glen Spreen, both of them Houston boys for whom a trip to Mexico was commonplace, the group declined. "I could kick myself for not taking [it]," Mike Leech said later. Reggie Young added, "It sounded good, but to think about having to pack up and go was just too overwhelming. I just thought it would be more trouble than it was worth."

But why shouldn't everyone have had a holiday to enjoy their success? It was apparently a year of vacations; Chips Moman, Tommy Cogbill, and Bobby Wood with their trips to Disney World in Orlando, Mark James and Glen Spreen to Acapulco. Probably the most unusual holiday was taken by Wayne Carson and Dan Penn, who with their wives also took a trip to Mexico in early August 1969. The vacation itself was uneventful. They fished and drove, rode the motorcycles they had taken along, and souvenir hunted (Reggie Young cherished forever a hand-tooled leather wallet Wayne brought back for him). It was only on their return to the States that they ran into trouble.

"That was quite a deal," Wayne chuckled ruefully. "We'd been down to Mexico a couple of weeks. We come back to the border and our car was full up, the border guard said, 'You'll have to unload it.' Dan was tired, he said, 'If you wanna unload this SOB, do it yourself; I've unloaded it all up and down Mexico.' I talked to the guy then, I said, 'Look, we just came back from a vacation; we don't have any drugs, or guns, or anything illegal, we aren't those kind of people.' He said, 'Well, you got anything to declare?' I had a bottle of creme de menthe, a bottle of creme de banana, and a bottle of Jack Daniels, he just said, 'Ah hell, not enough to bother with' and let us on through. We'd been driving all morning; we got to Corpus Christi about four. Dan said, 'Let's get a motel, I want an American motel,' he was pissed off at Mexico. We spent the night."

The next morning, they awoke to a dazzling sight. "The sun was shining, the air was calm, the sky was a beautiful blue," Wayne remembered. "I said, 'Look at this day, it's beautiful, quiet and calm, we need to go out on the ocean and catch a big fish.'" Dan agreed, and the two of them sought the nearest marina. Wayne talked to the man behind the counter and established that everyone there could captain a boat; immediately he asked to charter one. "He said 'When for?' I said, 'This morning.' He said, 'You haven't been watching the news?' The way he said it, I thought there was an invasion. He said, 'Where do you live, anyway?' I said, 'Well, I'm from Springfield, Missouri, but we're going to Memphis.' He said, 'If I were you, I'd get my ass on the road and I wouldn't let my shirttail hit my ass. You're sittin' in the eye of a hurricane. That's why it's so calm and pretty.' This was Hurricane Camille. He said, 'Didn't you hear all the wind and rain last night?' I said no. He said, 'Well, if the front side didn't wake you up, the back side will.' I said, 'What will you do?' He said, 'We'll just sit tight and hope the insurance covers everything. This one is gonna take us out.' Dan and I went to the motel where our wives were, I said, 'Load 'em, we're getting the hell out of here.' Linda and Bridget were surprised, they thought we were going to charter a boat and they were going to do some shopping. I said, 'We're in the eye of a hurricane.' We got in that VW and battened down the motorcycles and all our shit and got out of there."

They were well into Texas when the storm arrived. "It caught us about a hundred and seventy-five miles inland. It about blew us off the road. It made Katrina look like a goddamn dust devil. We finally made it to a motel and watched it on television. The good news is, if we hadn't been down there chartering a boat we'd have never known, dumb as we are." Hurricane Camille was the worst hurricane ever in the United States until Katrina in 2005; the loss of life was huge and its pattern was relentless. "Hell, it never got out of there till it left Florida," Wayne added.

In a sequel of sorts, years later Wayne was vacationing in Gulf Shores, Alabama, with Bridget and their children. He stopped for gas, and in a vacant field next to the gas station there was "a great big Texaco sign, just out there all by itself." The station attendant told him the provenance of the sign. "It came out of New Orleans and blew up with Camille. It came sailing in there like a leaf."

Meanwhile, back in Memphis, Tommy Cogbill was proving once again that he did not need Chips to help him cut a hit record. "Sweet Caroline," the song Neil Diamond had not wanted to do on his first session, had made the public aware of the songwriter. It was inevitable that Diamond would return to American, and he was as much the maestro as everyone remembered. Mike Leech remembered with amusement that Neil stopped a take and complained, "The musicians are messing me up." Without even glancing up from the piano, Bobby Wood droned, "Well, get 'em outta here, we're trying to make a record."

As he had before, Neil presented the group with some newer material, and what a song he had for Tommy this time. "Holly Holy" is a dramatic love song with ancient, Old Testament overtones. Mike Cauley, who was hanging around the studio, remembered sitting in the control room with Glen Spreen after the rest of the musicians had gone out for lunch and hearing Neil somewhat shyly preview the half-completed song for them. Though the tone of the piece is dramatic rather than lyrical, word pictures are inevitably created; during the chorus, Neil Diamond asks that we "sing the Song of Songs," and we are immediately transported to ancient Israel. The lady in the song could have been one of Solomon's concubines, and she holds a powerful influence over the narrator, who when he sees her involuntarily "[runs] just like the wind will." She is less a woman than a creed, a way of life: "Where I am, what I am, what I believe in." The dynamic range so cherished at American is written into the melody, which rises as if one is climbing a staircase.

Against this backdrop, Tommy Cogbill set the music up quietly at first, slightly swelling in the middle verses, and then in the first chorus he seems to be signaling, "Full power!" As Bobby Wood plays a repetitive ascending figure, the strings counterbalance the melody. The choir, bursting in on the final line of the chorus and remaining a presence for the rest of the record, sounds as if Tommy assembled everyone he knew at three in the morning and told them to sing at the top of their lungs. The usual American formula would have been to bring the music slowly back down after that rousing chorus; Tommy keeps the mood going, building the second chorus to even greater heights of intensity and continuing from that height until the fadeout. It was his most passionate, intense, complicated production, and he never did another one like it.

Neil also brought in an uptempo number called "Ain't No Way" (no relation to Aretha's recording), vaguely reminiscent of his early work and structured something like his classic "Kentucky Woman." Tommy seems not to have heard anything in it initially; Neil's version comes off as a sketch with no overdubs or instrumentation. But when Tommy and Chips Moman reworked it for a Box Tops session, the song came alive. They worked on it in the manner they had by now perfected, feeding and tossing the lines to one another, and in this context as on many other records they produced together, the lyrics might well be self-referential. "You're all I'll ever need, and when I forget how good life is, you bring it home to me," Chips seems to be saying to his calmer friend, while out on the studio floor Bobby Emmons suddenly breaks in with a sinuous organ line immediately after Alex Chilton's vocal. Tommy's probable reply is in the second verse, filled with his optimism about the future: "Tomorrow sure looks something else no matter

where I sit" (whether in the bass chair or the control room), "and I can't forget that you're the why of it," the line continues, as if directly addressed to Chips. The Memphis Horns contribute blunt, punchy, almost nervous bursts at the end of each line to push the track along, and an instrumental bridge is propelled by Reggie Young's hammerlike lead, Bobby Emmons's subtle organ line weaving around and in between the lead, and a sliding, booming bass line from Mike Leech that Tommy chose to emphasize. It is a driving track, like many of those produced by Tommy.

In one respect, working with Neil Diamond had been easy because he was a writer; he could bring his own material to the sessions (and what did not work well could be adapted for someone else later). Finding songs for artists who did not write was more difficult. Screen Gems in New York sent demos from their music companies, and Marty Lacker recalled that Ira Jaffe, a vice president of the company, often came to Memphis with material he wanted to place. Chips Moman welcomed Ira's visits and actively sought material from him and from the Brill Building staff. "I stayed in contact with a lot of those writers," Chips said. More often than not Chips got the tapes first and used the songs for his solo sessions. He said that the tapes were usually sent directly to him because Tommy recorded more infrequently than he did and because Tommy was not as well known within the industry as a producer. (Chips seems to have disregarded the Catch-22, that Tommy was not well-known because he was not getting strong material to create hit records.) "Tommy was just starting out," Chips explained, sounding slightly aggrieved. "I can't help it if people send me songs, you know?" He kept the demos upstairs in his seldom-used office. "Anybody who wanted to could go in and listen to them," he shrugged. When they collaborated, Chips said, Tommy generally left the choice of songs up to him. Occasionally they went through the demos together, but Chips allowed Tommy and Marty only infrequent access—"I didn't want anybody around when I was listening," Chips explained. Chips maintained that he and Tommy never discussed the distribution of material, but it was clear that Tommy would have to cast a wider net as he searched for songs.

He found an source in Nashville, occasionally checking in to the Screen Gems office there, now being run by the promotion man Jack Grady. Jack remained one of American's important boosters, occasionally returning to Memphis with material, giving Tommy his choice of demos and proudly playing American's new releases for Nashville's younger players, more of whom were coming to town by the day. To these newcomers, the American group were the vanguard of advanced session playing. The attitude of Ron Oates, a piano player who moved to Nashville in 1969, was typical. "I noticed right away that Music Row was pretty much insular, only really interested in the Nashville Sound and the belief that we were state of the art in the recording business," he said. "In fact, we *were* the state of the art . . . in country music. Some of us newer players in town were Pop and R&B schooled, and we had great collections of other music. We were aware . . . of the wonderful records coming out of Memphis, but, early on, not so aware of the particular individual players involved. . . .[We] discovered a wealth of creativity and talent in those great players . . . [and] wanted to merge some of that great sound into our own records."

"We couldn't compare our skills to their skills," added Norbert Putnam. "They could take all day to cut one song and come back the next day and work on it if they weren't satisfied. We realized that what we played might not have the depth that they did." The assembly-line factor inherent with Nashville recording still limited the amount of time these musicians could spend working on songs. And the mysteries of the Memphis records were impenetrable even for those who knew a few of the players, as Putnam made clear. "All we heard in Nashville was the great Cogbill," he said (Reggie Young, of course, was also a known quantity to him and his friends). "I thought he did the most incredible parts. We never knew who did what."

"I did a terrible thing to Tommy one time," he chortled mischievously. "I was over at Screen Gems one Friday evening to play on some demos for Jack Grady, two sessions, back to back. I didn't wanna be there; I'd had a rough week. I wanted to have a drink, go home, get some sleep. Tommy was over there looking for songs. I asked him to play a run on my bass for a minute while I went to the bathroom. I never came back; I went home. The next day I got a call from Tommy: 'Norbert, you bastard, I was there till one in the morning playing on those damn demos!'" (Shane Keister, who became the primary synthesizer player in Nashville after the group's relocation there, placed that event not in Nashville circa 1969, but in the mid-seventies, and not at Jack Grady's but at Columbia during a Billy Sherrill recording session.) Some of Putnam's playing throughout 1969 was directly inspired by Tommy's work, most notably the galloping bass on Tony Joe White's "Polk Salad Annie" and his work on the Bobby Goldsboro album *Muddy Mississippi Line*, which showcased variations on Tommy's lead-bass idea.

Another source of material for Tommy was found at Fred Foster's publishing company, Combine, courtesy of Foster's main song plugger, Johnny McCrae, who was known as Dog to his friends. McCrae was an aspiring writer himself, and he and Tommy formed an immediate bond. "Johnny and Bob Beckham [Combine's administrator] used to come to Memphis to do demos, at which time we all did some hanging out together," Mike Leech recalled. "In Nashville they would pitch songs occasionally to Tommy from their Combine catalogue, but most of the stuff they tried to get cut were throwaways. In other words they kept the good-selling songs for the established artists (like Kristofferson's songs). That's not unusual or bad for publishing companies to do that—for obvious reasons—a little tacky because they were supposed to be good friends—and Tommy mentioned it to me on several occasions, having to listen to mediocre/bad songs they would pitch to him." Having to work with second-rate songs remained a sore point with Tommy, but just as he was able to produce "Sweet Caroline" and turn a good song into a great one, he could take a mediocre song and turn it into, at the very least, something good.

He did it for a California group called the Yellow Payges, recording several singles with them. "Vanilla on My Mind" became the best-known in retrospect, because of its teen-pop and psychedelia blend similar to his solo records for Merrilee, but Mike Leech's stomping bass line is pure R&B, and so is the intricate horn section Tommy used as icing to frost the cake. "Moonfire" predates the Eagles' "Witchy Woman" with its background harmony line, and the innovative fadeout features the voices floating hauntingly over Johnny Christopher's relaxed strumming. Though it has been said that the dance tune "Finger-Poppin' Good-Time Party" was recorded in New York, the biting lead guitar on the record is obviously Reggie Young. As with "Sign On for the Good Times," Tommy's production work on these singles is both ahead of its era and outdated: by 1969 the public tended to discount peppy teen-pop records.

One of the Yellow Payges singles had been written by Richard Mainegra, whom Chips Moman had signed to Press Music for the usual writer's "draw" on the recommendation of Red West. The money was not much, even for those times, but it was reward enough for Richard. "I just couldn't believe it . . . seventy-five dollars a week. I mean, how cool was that?" he said. To have Tommy finally choose one of his songs, after several months of Richard's trying to catch his ear, was the beginning of a dream come true.

Mainegra came from Slidell, Louisiana, an environment he tenderly recreated in the 1973 genre painting "Louisiana Love Song" (recorded by Doug Kershaw under the direction of Chips). The name Mainegra sounds Creole or Spanish, and Richard looked it: tall and dark, with thick curly hair, finely chiseled features, and piercing dark eyes. "He looked more like an athlete than a writer," recalled Glen Spreen. "I remember seeing him around American, I remember thinking this guy must be a real ladies' man," said Gary Talley, who still stopped by the studio occasionally.

Gary Talley was not the only one at the studio who came away with that impression, but nothing could have been further from the truth. Richard was, in fact, a teetotaling non-smoker whose helpful politeness seemed taken straight from a Victorian novel. "Richard is one of the good guys," said Mike Leech. "I can't think of anything he did off-color or the least bit aggravating. [He was] always upbeat, always complimentary." "I've never heard anybody say a bad word about him," added Hayward Bishop. "I thought he was a unique fit for the group, a good thing," said Glen Spreen. "He was a pleasant person . . . a friendly person, mildly outgoing." Bobby Wood found Richard to be "a little harder to get to know. He wasn't much of a conversationalist." Richard's gift for coming up with catchy hook lines and his smooth vocals on the demos he and Red West created were appreciated by everyone at the studio. "The guy had a great voice," enthused Ima Roberts. Mike Leech thought Richard's singing was almost operatic in volume and range. At the time he came to American, Richard had just dropped out of college to pursue his dream full-time.

Like most people who became serious about music, he had been fascinated with it since early childhood. "I used to read labels on records and try to figure out who did what," he said. Elvis was his starting point and early role model, and he began playing guitar when he was fourteen. By his middle teens, he was in a garage band called the Phyve, who made a few small-scale recordings. "By the time we were in college, we were catchin' on pretty good in Louisiana and some of the surrounding states. . . but I was the only one who really knew I was gonna try and make music my career . . . everyone else had a real job . . . we had some good times, though." He was writing songs, and he decided to see if he could place his work somewhere. He arrived in Memphis because Memphis was just a little closer to home than was Nashville.

"I couldn't have been more green when I showed up that first day," he recalled. "The first place I went was Stax Records. . . . I'd never heard of Stax. . . . It was just in the phone book. I believe it was Al Bell who took me in his office, politely listened to my awful tape, and suggested American Studios. To make a long story a little less long, Red West . . . saw or heard something in me and proceeded to try to find a place there for me. I believe Chips finally said to sign me just to get Red off his back." The two immediately began writing together, and Richard said ruefully, "Everything we wrote was turned down by Chips and Tommy. Red used to get so frustrated . . . he'd come back up[stairs] in the writer's room and throw the tape against the wall." For his part, Richard just felt lucky to be there, once he realized the impact of his location: "After all, I'm not one of the American group. I'm one of their admirers." This humility made him more welcome than ever, as the influx of new people had made many of the musicians embark upon a never-ending effort to determine if a newcomer's caste should be inner or outer circle. Richard remained in the outer circle, but he would also play a crucial role during some difficult times.

Red also recommended Rick Yancey, a Memphis native who had dropped out of Memphis State University and was writing for Hi when Red found him. He became another favorite around the studio, not only for his writing but his personality. Bobby Wood thought Rick was "different, more outgoing, and we talked, more than the rest of the guys" (the piano player was doubtless responding to Rick's awestruck enthusiasm at being there). "[He's a] good singer, writer," was Mike Leech's estimation. "Decent acoustic guitar player, great background singer with inventive harmonies. Talented, but never got the break he deserves." Some of that may have been Rick's own doing, but his talent was obvious and so was his ambition, and though he was on a draw at Hi he would not be satisfied until he was working for the studio that many people in Memphis now thought was the top of the line. "Everyone was aware that American was the best place to be, there were hits comin' out of there every day. Everyone wanted to be a part of it," he said eagerly. Unlike Richard, who when he came to the company had absolutely no idea who anybody was or what they had accomplished, Rick was well aware, and he was determined to become one of the staff. A neighbor arranged his chance. "I lived in an apartment, there was a fellow that lived upstairs from me, he was a tennis pro,"

Rick said. "He said, 'Well, guess what, you got an appointment with a guy named Red West.'" Red listened, liked what he heard, and immediately took him to Chips, who signed him.

"I was already signed with Joe Cuoghi," Rick remembered. "I went into Poplar Tunes and told him I wanted to go with American. He said, 'Come see me tomorrow.'" When he walked into Cuoghi's office the old man found his contract and tore it up in front of the astonished writer's eyes. Rick was free to go.

For him as for Richard Mainegra, working at American was a dream come true, and he was amazed at everything and everyone, particularly Tommy Cogbill and Chips. "He's somethin' else, there is nobody like Lincoln Moman," Rick affirmed. "Great writer, great guitarist. That's his greatest love, is talent. Talent presents so many possibilities. What he does is, he loves talent, and the beauty of talent is that something will happen you don't think of." If Chips's flair for improvisation delighted Rick, Tommy Cogbill impressed him even more. "He was quiet, a real classy guy, he dressed cool, one of the nicest guys you'd ever want to meet," he said. For Rick, being at American was the ultimate learning experience. "What it was for me was college," he said—the best place an aspiring writer could go to learn his craft. Rick said in an awestruck tone, "Some of the best writers from *everywhere* would come [by]— John Sebastian, Hal David . . . and in the house you've got Mark James, Wayne, Dan Penn. . . .'" Though technically that was not true—Wayne Carson's publishing was never administered by Press but by Rose Bridge Music, the company he and Si Siman established together to handle his songs, and Dan Penn was pretty much out of the picture by then—it is accurate in terms of the creativity.

The respect Rick gave them was returned by the musicians, who appreciated it when someone deemed them worthy of awe. Chips Moman almost immediately dubbed the new writer "Reckaifius," in a wonderful turn of phrase, and Reggie Young started calling him "Rickles." He immediately set out to tailor his songs to American's, and Chips's perfectionistic standard—"It was always my goal to write something they would like"—and he remembered getting a suggestion from Chips. "We went into the adjoining room where the guitars hung and he said, 'Listen, Reckaifius, I don't want you to write any three-quarter-time song. The guys in the band don't like it.'" There was no doubt in the minds of the two young writers. They had come home, and everyone felt that it was just a matter of time before they both created a hit.

CoBurt Records was an MGM subsidiary label run by the L.A. impresario Burt Sugarman and the television-special producer Pierre Cossette. They sent Tommy Cogbill a singer with enormous potential, the former Fisk University civil rights activist Angeline Butler. David Halberstam told her story in his book about the Fisk activists, *The Children*. By temperament, Angeline was a gentle, private woman, almost too shy for the public spotlight of the sit-ins that had helped to integrate Nashville. "We called her Ange*leen*," said Reggie Young warmly. "I can't tell you much about Angeline, except that she seemed very nice and was willing to work hard," Mike Leech commented. "She was a pleasant person with whom to work," said American's other string arranger. Her first love had always been acting, she still aspired to be on Broadway, and she sang in a dramatic wail like a country Bette Midler.

In making her album *Impressions* with Tommy, she became his equivalent of Sandy Posey, a female singer who interpreted his vision with tenderness and intimacy. Perhaps typically for Tommy, he structured the album differently from the ones Chips Moman had done with Sandy; on those records Chips and Sandy had seemed to be talking past one another at times, as if she were trying to catch his attention while he remained preoccupied with his own concerns. Throughout their album, Tommy and Angeline conduct a dialogue: the listeners are eavesdropping on two quiet, soft-spoken people intensely discussing pain, despair, guilt, success, failure, ethics, love, obligations, burdens, and consequences. The variety of themes and topics was arrived at partly by the confluence of the two personalities making

the record, but, according to Glen Spreen, partly by design—"Angeline was an attempt to do something different." The album observes the traditional conventions of singer and producer, but it is as much a conversation as any recording Tommy collaborated on with Chips.

We are pulled into the conversation with the first track of the record. Carole King's "Yours Until Tomorrow" is one of her most desperate songs, about a love affair that both parties know from the beginning is hopeless because one of them is married and will always be, and Angeline declaims with passion bordering on hysteria. Tommy sets up the backing tracks to guide her gently back into somewhat dispassionate calm, as he does throughout the album; her tendency to chew the scenery is balanced by his realism. This is not the same thing as being unaware of her pain; he shares it, and at times underscores it. "Tomorrow comes the real world," Angeline sings, looking at approaching daylight with dread. "It's crashing down on me," and Tommy brings up Mike Leech's mournful string line to emphasize the words, as if to tell her that the thought oppresses him too. There is no doubt that he means it. She finally goes into full-throated agony as she declares with the passion of an operatic heroine, "Tonight I see no boundaries, so I beg you, I beg you before my chance is gone, let me be yours until tomorrow," and this time he makes no attempt to restrain her. As if of her own volition, she calms down again, pleading reasonably for just one night of passion. "All I ask is one night," she says calmly, and the listener feels her desperation even more intensely than when she was yelling—and we understand the possible risks and aftereffects of her request as well as does she. When the track ends, one feels as if one has not heard a recording as much as one has been eavesdropping on a very private moment in time.

The same writing session between Dan Penn and Bobby Emmons that produced the musing, cynical "Nobody's Fool" also yielded the album's second track, the one CoBurt eventually released as a single. "Keep On Keepin' That Man" is Angeline alone, grappling with feelings of sexual guilt. The word picture Dan and Emmons paint of a woman "walkin' in the park all by yourself on a moody winter night, wonderin' 'bout what the home folks read in your letter" is stark and vivid, accented by Tommy's thoughtful production; it is easy to imagine Angeline, wrapped in a fur-collared coat, drawn into herself as she picks her wraithlike way among dry fallen leaves, stares up at the stars and the bare trees, and wonders how she got into the position of "keepin' a man without a ring on your hand" (an anomalous position for a South Carolina minister's daughter). Through the course of the song she comes to no conclusions, only deciding to go on as she is doing because no better course of action suggests itself. Tommy builds the music at exactly the juncture in which she arrives at this reasoning—in effect, she reaches a decision not to decide (in a song that was, not coincidentally, cowritten by one of the American group's most formidable procrastinators—Emmons's delays even in giving feedback during a session were the amused despair of the whole group, as everyone waited to see what he thought).

The Bee Gees became known in the seventies for riding the disco trend, but when they started out in the late sixties they specialized in ballads with a stately Victorian feel that nonetheless revealed deep despondency. A *Rolling Stone* writer described the interior landscape of their songs as one in which "the world flew or floated by in frightening isolation as everything dissolved into tears and rain." Tommy had captured that same rain-and-tears feeling on several of his recent productions, "I Shall Be Released" being the most notable, so it is no surprise that the Bee Gees' "Sounds of Love" from their album *Odessa* would have appealed to him. He set up a tinkling piano introduction to suggest actual raindrops on a window, and Glen Spreen's string line is less Victorian and more pessimistic than the original. The song's mood works so well with just the music that Angeline's vocal is almost a sidelight, but nonetheless a revealing one. "See the children playing the ball, see them playing along the wall / It makes me cry to see them smile," the song begins, evoking Tommy's five children at home, so innocently high-spirited in

their games that it depresses him. The song also captures a loneliness in Angeline that she seems to fear she will never escape. Tommy's portrait of emotional agony rings more true than do the nearly constant descriptions of this state of mind by Chips. This track is not about bearing life's trials with stoic resignation but rather about looking up from the bottom of a well, so far down that the way up looks insurmountable. Whereas in "I Shall Be Released" Tommy kept looking for hope and reassuring both Chips and the listener that some glimpse of it was possible, here he seems to see no way out of the painful dilemmas presented, either for Angeline or himself.

Tammy Wynette's hit "Ways to Love a Man" is next, and here again Angeline is talking not so much to the listeners as to herself, announcing that she intends to be there for her beloved if circumstances should ever change (but knowing all along that they never will, so that when she says "I've no way to hold him," it is with the sad, weary voice of inevitability). When she bursts forth with the final, climactic chorus— "With my hands, my heart, everything I can find, my time, my heart, my soul, my mind, I'll find the way to love him, if I can"—it is as if she has taken some sort of vow. But the listeners are aware of another connotation: it was hands, heart, ingenuity, time, soul, and mind that Tommy gave to the American group, and in the end we know that it is this vow and dedication that would take precedence. By now the group, and even many people outside it, had come to rely on Tommy absolutely. "My impression of Tommy was that he was smart. He read people well," said Johnny Christopher. Tommy's solid common sense was as well known as his musical ability, and people leaned on him in a way that made him uncomfortable at times. "Tommy really didn't like it when somebody wanted to treat him as this great wise man," said Hayward Bishop, one of those who did view Tommy that way initially but came later to know other facets of Tommy's still-waters-run-deep personality.

The Timi Yuro hit "What's the Matter Baby" is a romp, with Reggie Young leading the way; ironically, Timi Yuro came to American that year, recording some singles for Liberty that did not make an impression on the charts. Yuro also had a big voice, with projection similar to Angeline's; however, Angeline slips in a note of gleeful revenge in her version that was not there in the original. She almost gloats at the downfall of someone who would have nothing to do with her in times past: "The hurtin' is almost over, but baby, it's just started for you." The mood predates Toby Keith's "How Do You Like Me Now" but has the same effect; there is indeed life after high school (or whenever).

"Two Different Worlds," a song from Red West and Richard Mainegra, resumes the conversation between Tommy and Angeline; in fact, the mood of the song almost picks up the dialogue where it left off several tracks previously. It is a song meant for late nights, and rumpled beds in some motel. Tommy's jazz background comes into play, as he creates a setting that is both somber and cool. Angeline dispassionately tallies up the costs of a love affair doomed by a number of possibly insurmountable things—age, class, lifestyle goals, marital status, and possibly even race. "Two different worlds, so far from each other," she sighs. "If we ever make it, it's gonna be a struggle / It's a long long way, from your world to mine / It's uphill all the way, and so hard to climb." It reflected what was going on in Angeline's personal life so accurately that she requested its composers to make some changes in the lyrics; she felt that they cut too close. "Two different worlds are what we'll always find, you belong in your world and I belong in mine," she intoned resignedly. "I wonder if we'll really get together." Tommy underscores her message with the somber strings, as if he is listening intently to her and nodding his head, agreeing with her estimation of herself and her chances. In listening and nodding, he would have revealed little of his own view. "You couldn't tell what Tommy was thinking by looking at his face," said Marty Lacker. "The only way you knew it was if he expressed a thought at that moment. I never tried to figure him out because I liked him the way he was."

"Reaching for a Rainbow" was written by Larry Weiss, a Neil Diamond soundalike singer-songwriter who made his name several years later with "Rhinestone Cowboy." This is not a song about success, but about struggling for it in a quixotic way; it can be taken as Angeline's warning to someone, assessing the risks of a complicated endeavor better than he can. "You're reaching for a rainbow," she tells him, "on a carpet that won't fly." She so clearly perceives circumstances he cannot yet see that she almost flies into hysteria again, and once again Tommy pulls the music back to soothe and reassure her. But the topic of chasing success is only a part of this complicated song and track. Angeline reflects on what that success will mean to her—"My world will pass you by"—and what she is being given as opposed to what she wants. "What you're offering my way is a match that doesn't burn," she says somewhat accusingly. And she knows not only the price she will pay, but the price that he has— "I've seen your sunshine turn into rain," she observes forcefully, nearly chewing the scenery as Tommy tries to calm her with the rising, but still restrained, string line and the playing of the group. On the final chorus he is unable to be of reassurance, and she bursts into screaming anguish as he releases the string and horn line full-force behind her.

"Ladylike," Wayne Carson's contribution, features an unconventional premise, a powerfully pulling melody, and some interesting hook lines to make this another interior scene as Angeline talks to herself about her intentions. The song says that, in her world, seducing a man is not ladylike, not how she was brought up; but she is going to try it anyway because she is so deeply in love. On the surface, this song would seem to have contemporary parallels in the man-chasing genre of Beyonce, Britney, and their ilk; however, even in the art of seduction, Angeline remains a lady. "I've made my mind up to one thing," she recites, "I'll proudly wear his wedding ring." She is not putting herself out there for just anybody; she wants a home and family, and the implication is that she's going after a man of character and responsibility. The string line gives her words and delivery special dignity, and in her voice and Tommy's reflective setting, seduction can be and is a gentle art.

But if "Ladylike" is Angeline's point of view, what follows is Tommy's. His slowed-down, ironic, bluesy version of "When You Wish Upon a Star" says more in three minutes about the price of success than *The Bonfire of the Vanities* or the earlier *The Hurricane Years* did in their numerous pages. It is bitter, like wine turning to vinegar. Angeline's flat, deadpan vocal plays against the optimistic lyrics as if to jeer at them and mock them, agreeing with Tommy's cynicism even though she has not experienced success on his level. Come on, he seems to be saying, we know better than to think that "fate is kind" or that "when you wish upon a star your dreams come true." The ironic joke is underscored by a biting piano line that Bobby Wood said he did not play; obviously the keyboardist is Bobby Emmons, taking a rare turn at the piano.

A cruel twist to the fate of this obscure but innovative production is that the details of the backing track, from the emphatic piano line to the gliding strings to the trick ending and slowed-down tempo, were used almost verbatim for Reba McEntire's 1988 remake of "Sunday Kind of Love," although Reba did not seem to play the lyrics for irony. "So many people contrived the stuff that Tommy did naturally," Hayward Bishop remarked. This inappropriate recycling was not the first time the work of the American group was shamelessly copied. Guitarists in rock and country bands inserted into their work note-for-note versions of Reggie Young's guitar solos (for example, Glenn Schwartz's lead playing on albums by the San Francisco rock group Pacific Gas and Electric are notable for their Reggie-like phrasing and intensity, and Daniel Kortchmar's lead on Kate Taylor's 1971 recording of "Look at Granny Run" is Reggie from first note to last). The copying was carried one step further when the trio Blackhawk even imitated the *appearances* of American's homegrown writing trio featuring Richard Mainegra and Rick Yancey in their later incarnation as the Remingtons. "We knew," sighed Rick Yancey resignedly.

The final cut of the album, the Buffy St. Marie standard "Until It's Time for You to Go," is so direct, intimate, and personal that, as with the beginning of the album, a listener feels like an eavesdropper. Here the story told throughout the album ends, as Tommy, Angeline, and the listeners have all known it must; and as is inevitable for a story told by one of the American group, the ending is not happy. Angeline must say farewell to her beloved, and with only Bobby Emmons's stark piano as a witness, she mournfully, somewhat hesitantly at times, says goodbye. She emphasizes that her love affair has changed her, made her better, almost breaking the line "Now . . . I can bend" into a wounded croak, as if saying more would simply be too painful. And the line "until it's time for you to go" has been given an additional meaning over the years, given the early death that Tommy seemed to sense awaited him. If this farewell is not quite a litany, it is close; and in overhearing the last of the conversation, the listener gets the impression that neither of the people discussing these matters will ever be the same.

Tommy was so oblique that those who came late to American, like Marty Lacker, Glen Spreen, and Johnny Christopher, were unaware of everything that was going on with him, although Johnny in retrospect said, "I knew there were some things that troubled Tommy." Another late arrival, Hayward Bishop, recalled that Tommy "kept himself grounded, very much" but that "there were some insecurities he had that I didn't notice right away." Glen Spreen wondered about that too, years after the fact. "It's my personal opinion that Tommy was a little restless and not ever quite satisfied," he observed. "I can relate to that, and by relating, can understand the frustration, however silent it may be and however calm Tommy appeared to be." "Tommy was such a laid-back guy that he didn't have to be in control to be happy," said Wayne Jackson.

Mike Leech sensed that in some way Tommy was reevaluating, and that his priorities seemed different. "He was preoccupied a lot," echoed Ima Roberts. Success—he produced more of American's charted hits in 1969 even than Chips—had not spoiled him as much as it had altered his view of himself and where he fit into the world. "I don't think in the beginning he saw himself as a producer," said Ima.

"Tommy was quiet, but he didn't see himself as a great record producer," agreed Hayward Bishop.

On some level that remained true, but he was enjoying his success. Gone now was the battered Oldsmobile, and even the Cadillac he had first driven, which he passed along to his wife Shirley; he was now indulging himself with a Corvette, and after about a year with that, traded up again for a Jaguar—partly, one suspects, to tweak Chips, who bought a Corvette after Tommy had gotten his. (True to form, when Tommy bought his Jag, Chips got one too. "I'd have a real antique [car], and Tommy would have one about seven or eight years old," Chips said of the rivalry.) Tommy had always dressed well enough in an indifferent sort of way, but a photo taken at the studio shortly after this period of time reveals an almost dapper man with a suede jacket and slight sideburns.

Tommy never alluded to his slight change of direction and priorities, and he never said why or how it had happened, but a clue can be found in one of the last records he did on the Bell label for Merrilee Rush. Chip Taylor's "Got No Angel on My Shoulder" is in this context a man coming to terms with success, and what it means—one of the meanings being that the conventional wisdoms that had once worked for him could now be brushed aside as lightly as cobwebs. Set to an intricate background of twisting guitar passages, Merrilee almost whispers the lyrics that deal with the consequences of no more limits: "How long can I remain untouched," she asks, referring not to love but to the circumstances surrounding newfound fame. She sounds as if she is describing something that happened to her in the recent past, while the immediacy and drama of the music revealed that Tommy was discussing his present: "How can I do what's right for me, when there's no one to fight for me . . . Got no angel on my shoulder, to keep me hanging on." The slowed-down, anguished bridge seems out of place at first—Merrilee goes from a whisper to a scream as she recites four lines about missing and needing someone, under the current of Glen Spreen's dramatic-sounding strings.

"I wish you could touch me now," she intones, and then, volume rising slightly louder with each line, "I wish you could hold me now . . . I need you . . . Oh, how I need you." Repeated listenings make the meaning clear; as Joni Mitchell wrote the year before, something has been lost for something gained, there has been a renunciation. In retrospect those four lines are a litany, and when the track is played the anguish is still as chilling as a December day.

Tommy Cogbill never became well known outside the business, partly because almost all the attention given to American would focus on Chips Moman and partly because the Memphis music industry, where he made his reputation, was more low-key than was Nashville's. But a year's worth of hits—"Soul Deep," "Sweet Caroline," "Brother Love," "Holly Holy," "If I Never Knew Your Name," and "Turn On a Dream," as well as neglected masterworks such as the American group instrumentals, "Sign On for the Good Times," "I Shall Be Released," and Angeline Butler's album—was a list of accomplishments any producer could envy, and a set of recordings from which producers and musicians could learn for years to come.

CHAPTER 20

|||||||||||||||||||||||||||||||||||||||||||||||||||||||||||||

# Eyes of a New York Woman

If the music business outside of Memphis was taking little notice of Tommy Cogbill, they were beginning to recognize American Studios. In late 1969 Chips Moman was given his first important award when he was named the Producer of the Year by industry tipsheet the *Gavin Report*. "That was the biggest award in the business, the Gavin Report, because it was given by radio people," Chips said in soft tones of gratitude. "I cherish it." It was such an honor to the producer that when he went to Atlanta for their dinner, he took Marty Lacker and most of the musicians with him (although Bobby Wood did not go). "It was just an opportunity to get away from the studio together and, if I remember correctly, Chips paid for everyone," said Marty. "I was there because I was the one who always corresponded with Bill Gavin as I did with other industry publications, to let them know about the records we cut."

Away from Memphis, Tommy was almost another person. His mischievous side, fairly dormant in the day-to-day grind, emerged with a vengeance. "He knew what a good time was and could easily laugh," said Glen Spreen. "That was another side of him." "He was funnier than hell," said Marty Lacker fondly. "Around us, he was nuts. We were at the Hyatt Regency, and Chips, Tommy, and I were in the lobby when Tommy goes into his famous Tasmanian Fire Dance. . . . You've never heard of it? What he'd do was light up some newspapers, stick 'em in his behind and run across the lobby."

When Chips got up to accept his award, he was so genuinely touched and grateful that he acknowledged the musicians who had come down with him to cheer him on. He said that

the award was rightfully theirs, and that all he did was just turn a few knobs in the control room (Ed Kollis and Darryl Carter would have been amused to have heard that statement). The award was twice as gratifying to Chips because, unlike the musicians (who kept the *Billboard* chart in the control room with the position of their hits highlighted), he did not notice chart placings of his productions. "I never kept count, 'cause I didn't think I was in a contest," he reflected. So he paid no attention to how his records were selling? "Literally none," he said emphatically.

Chips may not have paid attention to the charts, but there was an indication of his success and his importance to Memphis music that would have been difficult to overlook: the New Year's Eve party hosted by Elvis ringing in 1970 at T.J.'s. As a thank-you to those who had restored him to his throne, the King invited the entire American group and Chips to celebrate with him. Not all of them turned up. Mike Leech did not go, for reasons he could no longer bring to mind. Glen Spreen recalled with amusement why he was not there. "This is probably hard for you, or even me, to believe . . . I forgot about it," he said. Bobby Emmons could not remember if he had gone. Bobby Wood attended but left so early he did not even see Elvis. "I had a steak and a couple of drinks and that was my utmost limit; I can table dance with two drinks," he said. "I just remember having a good time kidding around, laughing and talking." Richard Mainegra escorted Ima Roberts to the party, and he remembered Elvis's entrance into the club. "Sometime after midnight there was a commotion at the back door, and in the darkness you could see a line of dark figures makin' their way through the crowd. Someone held a large flashlight . . . it was the King of Rock and Roll himself. Later that night Red walked me over to meet him, and I can't begin to explain here what a feeling that was. It was a brief conversation. But I remember Red sayin', 'E, this guy's gonna make us a lot of money one of these days.'" Marty Lacker and his wife Patsy were there, of course; they came to the club with Elvis and Priscilla and "we mostly sat with Red West at the same table. Ronnie Milsap was

**247**

the regular performer at T.J.'s and he put on his usual good show," said Marty. At some point during the evening, the American musicians present took the stage and sat in with Milsap's band. "Tommy knocked everybody out on guitar," Marty added.

Chips was quietly pleased with his success and that of the group regarding the Elvis recordings. It proved that their way of making music was right: create a quality product and, without any need for hype, name acts who are also interested in doing good work will beat a path to your door. (This was proven again during Chips's Nashville comeback in the seventies and eighties, when Willie and Waylon, Merle Haggard, and Johnny Cash—all of whom were already among the most legendary names in music—sought him out.)

He was also preoccupied with business at this time. Throughout 1969 and his growing reliance on Marty Lacker, Chips had become disenchanted with the way Don Crews handled the management of the studio. It was a subject about which Chips, beyond a few broad hints here and there, later was reluctant to speak, but in discussing events with people close to him perhaps some of the reasons can be determined. "Chips felt that he was carrying the load of both ends of the studio, production and business," said Marty Lacker. "He felt that all Don did was just hang around." Chips also felt frustrated in some of his ambitions for the studio. Crews recalled, "Chips wanted to get rid of the old eight-track board. He said, 'Why don't you consider building us a sixteen-track board?'" Thoroughly familiar with his partner's ways by now, Crews said no. "I knew he wanted me to finance it." Tommy Cogbill was slightly more restless than previously, and he privately approached Crews about the two of them starting an independent label. Again Crews said no, out of loyalty to Chips. "I said, 'I can't cut a man in the back that way.'"

Crews was also still farming part-time, and Chips obviously preferred an office manager who would be there throughout the day and could devote full attention to the company. Marty Lacker alleged that he found important

letters and contracts unopened, jammed into the crevices of Crews's desk where he had misfiled or apparently forgotten them. Chips told Crews that he wanted to discuss this and other matters with him and called for a meeting at the Ranch House restaurant in mid-1969. Don recalled from there what happened.

"He said, 'I'd like to dissolve the partnership,' more or less. I said okay. He said, 'Well, I'll give you $22,000.00.' I said, 'Write me an agreement.' I backed out of the way to see what he was going to do, and of course, he did nothing. We drug it on for about six months." Finally, in early 1970, Chips filed a lawsuit against Don Crews to officially end the association.

"It drug on for quite some time," Crews remembered. The musicians had to answer depositions, which was difficult for them; they liked Crews but their main loyalty, as ever, was to Chips. "Don felt everyone was against him including us, which was not true," Mike Leech said sadly. "He made a remark after the deposition, 'I see Chips has the band in tune.'" Bobby Emmons recalled very little about the dispute. "I must block out stuff like that or something, because I don't remember any peaks and valleys," he said. "It was just a straight black line. It happened, but it was just laying there. I don't remember any of the details."

The lawsuit was settled out of court in 1971. Crews got fifty thousand dollars plus the smaller second studio, Onyx; Chips kept American and Press Music. Never again would Chips have a partner. Never again would he totally share responsibilities. "Boys will be boys and be possessive about their toys," was the wry observation of Glen Spreen, who left American in late 1970 before the suit was concluded. Marty Lacker continued the business end of the operation while Chips saw to the music; : neither Marty nor Tommy Cogbill had any financial ownership of the studio and consequently, little real authority. Chips was now the unchallenged king of the hill.

Don Crews continued—with great equanimity—small-time recording at Onyx until he finally scored a production comeback in the summer of 1975. A promotion man, Jack Gilmer, who sometimes worked out of the studio, led him to Bill Browder, the RCA man in charge of promoting the label's records in the Memphis area. Browder also had singing aspirations he'd harbored since the age of sixteen. Don recorded the basic tracks for a drinking-and-crying song called "Devil in the Bottle" at Pete Drake's studio in Nashville, using the American musicians, who had all resettled in Music City by then. Browder recorded his vocal at Onyx, and took the name appearing on the record—T. G. Sheppard—from the German shepherd dogs in the parking lot adjoining the studio. "Devil In The Bottle," one of the most tormented-sounding drinking songs since the Hank Williams era, became a huge hit on the country charts and launched a successful career. T. G. continued to record with Crews for several years thereafter until he came under the tutelage of another American Group patron, Buddy Killen. Most of his hits, whether produced by Crews or Killen, were done with the American group backing him, and later in his career he recorded with two other exemplars of Southern music, Rick Hall and Jim Ed Norman. The triumph of T. G. Sheppard was equally the triumph of Don Crews, and the American musicians were glad for him. For his part, he was happy to renew his association with them. "I had no problem with any of the fellas," he said warmly.

Don Crews and Marty Lacker, despite some outward differences in manner and style, shared many of the same ultimate goals for the studio. Both wanted to see American Group Productions progress, but Marty had wider contacts throughout the industry because of both his radio background and his years working for Elvis. When he had been the foreman for Elvis' group, Marty handled finances, budgeting, and organizing special events (he still occasionally arranged these for Elvis)—all of which could be valuable skills for the management of a high-profile recording studio. It was this diversity of skills and contacts, as opposed to the more local orientation of Don Crews, which seemed to be of interest to Chips. Crews in fact wondered if Chips had not been encouraged by Marty to dissolve the partnership, but evidence suggests that Chips reached that conclusion on his own.

He was at least partially ready to see what the next level of success would be like, and he was counting on Marty to help him get there.

Chips also began thinking about what he would do when the deal with Bell Records would end in early 1970. It was obvious that Bell was losing interest in Chips' kind of music, even though "Bell depended so much on what we did," said Bobby Wood. The label closed out its Goldwax deal at around the same time as Chips' contract was expiring. It was probably the first hint the group received that the record companies with whom they had successfully dealt up until now could just as easily find them expendable. Larry Uttal likely sensed that Southern R&B-based recordings were losing their mass appeal, and like all industry executives Uttal was looking for the next big thing. He found it in Britain, where a few producers were developing a half-Fifties revival, half-bubblegum style of rock. The emphasis on novelties gave Bell a couple of hits later in the seventies with Sweet, Gary Glitter, and Suzi Quatro, all of which were far removed from Chips Moman and Quinton Claunch. So where would Chips get the financing he needed to continue with his American group idea?

Capitol Records provided the answer. They had signed Rick Hall in late 1968 and given him more money than he had gotten from his earlier arrangements with Atlantic; this deal had yielded much for Rick but very little for the musicians, which provoked Jimmy Johnson and Roger Hawkins into leaving Fame and starting up their studio. Though Rick's deal was not the kind Muscle Shoals was used to getting, it was apparently typical for Capitol at the time. In early 1972, the songwriter Tim Rose spoke of his recent Capitol involvement to *Rolling Stone*: "You know Capitol. The producer got the money." Obviously a producer's company, the suits there petitioned Chips, and he said, "It was just a deal we couldn't turn down." In late January 1970, when the contract with Bell expired, Chips signed with Capitol.

Marty Lacker was involved with the contract negotiations, as was Tommy Cogbill. "I worked alongside of our attorneys Walter Hofer and Arnold Rich, from Hofer & Rich in

New York," Marty recalled. "They would come down and we would have meetings with the five of us or at times Chips and Tommy would answer questions I asked that Walter and Arnold wanted answered. Then we had a final meeting before the attorneys finished the negotiations with Capitol."

In some ways the new contract offered better terms than Bell had given them. Chips would continue with a new label, named for himself (the logo featured stacks of poker chips spelling it out in capital letters). For the first time Tommy Cogbill would have a custom label of his own; his would be called Trump, and he could sign and record acts independently of Chips. By now Chips was so used to having been taken advantage of by labels that he had become a tough negotiator for himself; he demanded, and usually got, a substantial amount of money before he began a project or signed with any company. "They called me the Front Money Kid," he laughed. It was no different now; Marty Lacker remembered some of the terms eventually agreed to by Capitol. "I believe it was a three-year deal and yes, both Chips and Tommy got front money and further quarterly or semi-monthly payments," said Marty, his near-encyclopedic memory for details still calling the terms of the deal to mind. Marty did not know if the musicians were all supposed to share in any record royalties. "That would have been between Chips and the musicians, not Capitol," he said. Mike Leech added that the musicians did not get anything beyond payment for having played on each session, but the musicians would have a chance to produce records on their own. It was an important next step toward making American Studios a self-contained musical empire.

To commemorate the signing, Capitol Records paid for the entire American group to come to Los Angeles for a celebration party, at the request of Chips and Tommy, who both felt that everyone should be there. Bobby Wood remembered the trip as an overnight journey and then back; Mike Leech thought that the adventure took several days. "We called [that trip] the L.A. Turnaround," laughed Bobby

Wood, adding that the name came from "a famous pill people used to take." "Sal Iannucci was the president of Capitol at the time and he made a big deal out of the signing," said Marty Lacker, who accompanied the musicians out to the Coast for the occasion. Several friends also flew out for the event, including Herbie O'Mell from T.J.'s and Dan Penn's studio, Angeline Butler, who was still in town for awhile following the completion of her album, and Jimmy Kingsley, a reporter for the *Memphis Commercial Appeal* who regularly did stories on the city's music scene. "It was such a long flight, I think everybody was bored by the length of the flight, just enough to buy too many of those little-bitty bottles," said Bobby Emmons. "Negotiating the check-in at the hotel became a real challenge."

Also accompanying the group was Campbell Kensinger, a Vietnam veteran who was now on the American payroll as Chips Moman's bodyguard, although why the informal and unpretentious Chips needed the beginnings of an Elvis or Phil Spector–style entourage is unclear. "Campbell was one of the baddest guys in Memphis, he could tear your head off with one punch," said Marty Lacker. "I think his family owned a section of Memphis that included some bars and restaurants," Mike Leech reflected. "He was a bartender at one place for awhile. Also not positive but I think he was due a sizeable inheritance, which he would get at some point. But the deal was, he had to be straight up until that time, which he was."

Robert Gordon devoted an entire chapter of his book *It Came from Memphis*, his account of the bohemian life of the city, to Campbell, and details about Kensinger's life and death (a shootout in 1974) can be found there. Gordon and several of the American musicians were under the impression that at one time Campbell had been a member of the Memphis Hell's Angels chapter, but Chips Moman adamantly said no (not that Chips, with his fondness for rough characters, would have minded if Campbell had been). "He was like a little elf, he was such a small guy. Short and small. He wasn't that kind of person at all. He was more like a mild salesman," the producer recalled warmly. "I remember him being a *big* guy," Bobby Emmons said with some surprise. "I understand he was a . . . shall we say . . . he had plenty of credentials necessary to be a bodyguard . . . but he was a sweetheart to us." Marty Lacker recalled that Campbell was not really either a bodyguard or security man, but just there, in another one of Chips's places especially created for somebody he happened to like. "He had a purpose," Chips maintained.

Campbell's tasks and duties were loosely defined but varied. By now, the Rolls-Royce functioned as a company car, and Campbell drove it to the Memphis airport to meet important acts coming in town to record. When the acts wanted to go clubbing, to T.J.'s or the Rivermont after sessions, Chips, who had no taste for night life, would head back to his farm and dispatch Campbell to escort the artists and be security for them. The biker also served as security man for Chips's daughter Monique on occasion, because Chips, high-profile in Memphis since the Elvis sessions and feeling vulnerable about it, feared for her safety. "Y'know, when people think you've got a lotta money, they might try and do something to your children," he said sadly, as if he had reluctantly dealt with a regrettable by-product of his notoriety.

Far from being afraid of the biker, most of the musicians and office staff enjoyed having him around. "Campbell Kensinger was my buddy," Marty Lacker recalled with amused pleasure. "I used to call him Freak." "He was a bad, bad dude," said Bobby Wood with amusement, adding, "He was definitely a bad dude, but he was always our friend. He woulda fought for us just like we were brothers." "He was a huggable biker, he looked like Fabio on steroids," said Hayward Bishop, who met him later. "He was really a softie on the inside." "We all knew Campbell could easily take us on," added Mike Leech. "He knew it also but apparently liked us. The feeling was mutual, and we had some fun taunting him at times. He thought that was very funny." "I liked being around Campbell even when I wasn't worried about gettin' beat up," chuckled Bobby Emmons. Tommy Cogbill

also got along well with the biker, from all accounts, and Campbell proved a cheerful companion on the California excursion.

The trip was memorable in many ways. Bobby Wood and Mike Leech both remembered that the group was sitting at a large table in the hotel restaurant eating a meal (Wood said breakfast, Mike said lunch). Mike related what happened. "The waiter came by and said he was told to give us a note. Reggie accepted it, read it, paled, and passed it around. It said (something like) 'you whiteys from Memphis better get the hell out of our town. Signed, The Black Muslims.' After a few minutes of nervously absorbing this, we heard laughter from the other side of the restaurant. There sat Bobby Womack and Rosey Grier in a booth laughing their heads off." "Big ol' laugh," added Bobby Wood.

The celebration lasted for several days, in the recollections of most. "We went to that round building you see in all the TV shows, the Capitol Tower, for the signing," said Bobby Emmons. "L.A. was party time. . . . After we took care of business, we had a couple of days to goof off, and that we did," said Mike Leech. "There were several episodes I didn't attend. Reggie and I stayed together most of the time and did our own thing, which was mainly hit the hotel bar. Gene Chrisman never came out of his room." Reason being, said the drummer, that he was skeptical from the beginning about the whole thing. "Capitol, forget that," he said dismissively. "We was cuttin' a lot, people were comin' in. You can't nail one company down. I got bombed on the plane going out there." There was a private party for everyone in one of the hotel suites, but Mike Leech and Reggie Young missed out on it, "having stayed too long at the bar," the string arranger added with amusement. It was a great blowout bash and a good way to let off steam but, as all things do, it ended and it was time to fly back to Memphis and get to work.

By now "work" was an elastic term. They remained in the studio for hours, either recording or waiting on Chips to come in; he was not above ordering the musicians to be at the studio at a certain time and then not showing up himself till hours later, with no explanation. While waiting, they had to have something to do. The card games increased, and so did the pranks with which everyone filled the hours by playing.

Even Tommy Cogbill, who had been at one remove from the cutting up when it started, now joined in the practical joking. "Tommy was mostly the no-nonsense type," Mike Leech remembered. "He would get squirrelly sometimes, but it had to come from him. He could start some mischievousness and be as crazy as we all were, but as I said, his call, not ours. If he was angry, stay away, or just don't mess with him." Johnny Christopher remembered Tommy's "little impish smile" and added, "He could be quite hilarious sometimes." The hijinks in which Tommy and the others participated were also a release of tension, because by now anything could happen in the slowly deteriorating area around the studio. The petty crime wave that Spooner Oldham foresaw and cited as one of his reasons for leaving had indeed come to pass, although Mike Leech recalled that there were relatively few incidents when considering how rough the neighborhood was becoming. Bobby Wood disagreed with Mike (as he often did; the two interpreted many events differently): "All our cars had been broken into, you couldn't leave nothin' in your car. . . . [There were] headlights broke out, convertible tops slashed, the guy who had the print shop next door got robbed and shot at a couple of times. It was just a bad area. North Memphis was rough," the piano player sighed. Most of the musicians now carried guns as a matter of course, on the advice of the Memphis police chief. Don Crews gave everyone shotguns as a Christmas gift one year. Tommy and Chips both had collected guns for years, but now even the outwardly amiable Bobby Wood had taken to bringing a .38 with him as he came to work.

One night that winter they were upstairs in one of the offices while they were waiting to do some overdubs. Mike Leech explained, "There were offices upstairs over the Ranch House restaurant, and the stairs leading up were metal grate and a little noisy. We were (me, Wood, Reggie, Gene, Emmons) all . . . sitting on the floor playing poker. Wood shushed everybody, stood up, pulled his gun and eased over to the door. He whispered that he heard somebody coming up the steps. He aimed his gun head-high at the door then jerked it open. There was a cop standing there...the gun was aimed right at the middle of his forehead. He said 'whoa whoa whoa' while stepping back. Bobby put his gun away and the cop proceeded to chew him out. Bobby explained that he didn't have any idea who it was, but the cop was pissed." "He said hold it hold it hold it and I said I'm sorry sorry sorry," Wood recalled ruefully. "It scared my socks off and his too. The cop said, 'You'd better put that gun away before I recall I saw it.'" "I personally thought the cop shouldn't have sneaked up the stairs," added Mike Leech. "The neighborhood was known for theft, break-ins. If it had been a cop up there with us he would have done the same thing [as Bobby]."

At other times they could count on the cops to help them with their pranks. "The cops liked us, and many nights they would gather in our parking lot out back," Mike Leech remembered. "We had a few nice chats here and there. So one night while the chief (can't remember his name) was inside the studio, Tommy sneaked back and put . . . rocks in the hubcaps [of the chief's cruiser]. Hilarious! *But* . . . the funniest part is, the chief had Tommy arrested and hauled off to jail. They kept him a few hours just to let him sweat. When he was finally brought before a judge in night court, we were all gathered in the judge's chambers trying to stifle our laughter. The judge 'threw the book' at Tommy until we all decided it was enough, and then we all walked out of the chambers laughing. The look on Tommy's face was priceless."

The look on Marty Lacker's face was probably priceless too, when he became the recipient of one of the group's more adventurous stunts. Mike Leech and Reggie Young were still continuing the "J'eat yet? No. Jew?" that had become a running gag. The two of them picked the lock on Marty's briefcase and sneaked in a sign, written in huge capital letters: "JEAT??" They recalled that Marty had not been amused, and he had behaved as if there was something in the briefcase he did not want them to see, but

Marty cherished the memory. "Yes, I remember that briefcase deal," he said. "I laughed when I saw it and I immediately knew who did it."

And then there was the matter of the cars. It started, as much of the kidding seemed to, with Bobby Wood. "I had this 1960 big ol' blue Cadillac parked on the street over at Sun," the piano player laughed. "I had made the mistake of telling Tommy that almost anybody's key would fit my ignition." Tommy started the car and drove it several blocks down the street, leaving Bobby to search for it. "I thought my car was stolen and picked up the phone to call the police, he started laughing. Then I knew I'd been had."

The piano player got him back. "We grabbed a couple of Coke crates and put 'em under the back wheels of his car," Bobby chortled. "The back parking lot was pretty dark and scary late at night. There were at least four of us, I think including Campbell. We picked the back of his little sports car up and one of us inserted two Coke crates underneath the rear axles so Tommy couldn't see that his rear wheels were just about an inch off the pavement. When Tommy came out we all got in our cars like we were leaving. We slowly were pulling off waiting to see what Tommy would do. When he cranked up and put it in reverse, nothing happened. . . . He jumped out of his car going 'Wait, wait, wait,' . . . and shouted at us not to leave." "Those back wheels wouldn't do nothin' but spin," laughed Gene Chrisman, who was one of those in on the joke. "We got out of our cars and came over and asked what was wrong. Somebody broke out in laughter as somebody shined a flashlight under the car to reveal the Coke cases," Bobby Wood continued. "Tommy just laughed with us and said something like, 'You turkeys.'"

If the pranks between Wood and Tommy seemed to have an edge, it is partly because there was one, although Bobby was understandably loath to play up those differences later. He had not been at the studio very long and he and Tommy still had to adjust to each other musically. "I always knew we had different heroes when it came to music. In those days Tommy was playing old-school jazz. That stuff was on another planet for me."

Chips Moman recorded Bobby as a solo singer, just as the piano player had hoped he would. None of the songs were released, and Bobby found working with Chips as an artist rather than as one of the band to be disappointing compared to his earlier experiences with Stan Kesler. "The material Chips chose was not me and I was very uncomfortable," said Wood, who considered it just as well because if he had gotten a hit he would have had to leave the band to tour. "I was not a happy road puppy anyway. After awhile I felt content in being a good session player." Stan Kesler had done several singles with Bobby, including the Tom T. Hall story song "Margie's at the Lincoln Park Inn," that were more to the taste of the piano player than the pieces he recorded with Chips.

The Tom T. Hall song was Bobby's kind of country music, progressive and realistic, and he would have liked to have had success with things like it. "I had some records that were regional hits," Bobby stated with quiet pride. "'Break My Mind,' on which the guys played, was number one everywhere it was played, which wasn't a lot of places. I actually was still recording with Stan and Jim Vienneau after I went to American." He attributed his lack of success on the charts to the fact that "We just didn't have the right song to follow 'If I'm a Fool.'"

Though Bobby Wood was philosophical about the fact that he would probably be a studio musician for the rest of his life, Mike Leech wondered if the spotlight still pulled Bobby a little. "When he was reduced to the status of a mere session player, it was, I'm sure, more than a little disappointing to him," Mike observed empathetically. Not so, said the piano player. "Mike is wrong about me being pulled into the spotlight. Just the opposite," Bobby stated firmly. There was an unspoken caste system at work both in Memphis and Nashville, which judged the studio players to be on a lower social level than were the stars, and that could have theoretically bothered the once-aspiring singer, but Bobby maintained that he never let it. "I just never cared if anyone looked down on me as an artist or a musician or as a person," said Wood with quiet independence. "When you have the peace God gave me, what someone else thinks is their problem, not mine. That's just the way I've looked at life as far back as I can remember."

"Anytime some artist would show up at the studio, Bobby felt and exhibited a camaraderie toward that person—like, 'I know; I've been there,'" Mike Leech continued. "I thoroughly enjoyed being in the studio and actually looked up to all the people around me," Bobby elaborated, making his feelings more clear. The piano player still sang when he could, becoming a mainstay voice of the Moman Tabernacle Choir along with Johnny Christopher; in analyzing his attempt at a singing career, he speculated that he had the same problem as Dan Penn—his voice was not easily categorized by the strictly formatted radio playlists of the day. To quote the title of a song written by Dan in 1994, the way these writers sang was "too rock for country, too country for rock and roll."

Tommy Cogbill wasn't sure Bobby could have been a success. "Cog and Wood clashed a few times," recalled Mike Leech. "Tommy didn't like Bobby's voice for some reason. I always kind of liked it. But one time for something I don't remember he was putting Bobby's voice on something and he got very angry. He looked at me and said something like, 'Who does he think he is, B.J. Thomas?' He didn't finish the overdub, and it seems like he just walked out. Not positive, but he stood up and looked very exasperated." "While we didn't see eye to eye on songs and the way they should be recorded, I think we still had a respect and love for each other," said Bobby. "All I know is we got really close after we moved to Nashville [later on]. We even began to think more alike. I think when you put your heart and soul into what you are doing, you finally reach the same goal."

As with the personality clashes between the core group and the late arrivals, these things were temporarily set aside when everyone got down to work. At the start of the year, recording seemed light. B.J. Thomas was in doing some vocals for his breakthrough album that featured the Burt Bacharach theme from the movie *Butch Cassidy and the Sundance Kid*.

"Raindrops Keep Fallin' On My Head" had taken the Texas singer to a new audience, people who were not familiar with Chips Moman or Hank Williams Sr., and with the success of that single he proved that he could handle sophisticated songs. The resulting album seems thrown together in retrospect; Florence Greenberg apparently wanted to release something quickly to capitalize on the success of the Bacharach song, so B.J. sang over some tracks that had first been used for other singers on the label. Many of the backing tracks came from an album Buddy Greco had done in New York earlier that year under the direction of two arrangers, Pete Dino and Florence's son Stan Green; the remaining three tracks, produced by Chips, featured two songs previously recorded by Ronnie Milsap and a pounding, stomping gospel-style version of "Suspicious Minds" that went on even longer than the Elvis version (with no trick ending). B.J. had actually recorded it before Elvis came in, but the track had been held back because Elvis would not record anything if he thought someone else was trying it out. It featured some call-and-response singing between B.J. Thomas and Johnny Christopher, and by the end of the track the entire Moman Tabernacle Choir leaps into the mix, providing a shouting, joyful free-for-all.

Of the tracks originally recorded by Milsap, the Jim Webb composition "Do What You Gotta Do" works best. It is set to a rolling, syncopated organ line from Bobby Emmons and a churning bass track from Mike Leech that thenceforth would be a recurring feature in much of the group's work. B.J.'s tone is conversational and warm at the beginning of the song, slowly working up to a full-throated wail in the final chorus—a masterful display of dynamics, not just with the music but with the vocal. The string track features Mike Leech's trademark cloudy somberness, and the backing vocals bounce off his bass line like leapers on a trampoline. Mark James's "Mr. Mailman" seems at least in part borrowed from his waiting-for-Karen real life storyline; although Mark changes the plot a bit toward meeting a woman on vacation rather than a class reunion, he (through B.J.) speaks of his anxiety as he awaits more news from her, and asks the mailman, "Won't you bring me just one letter, and everything will be all right."

The song also features Reggie Young's skittering electric sitar—by now the electric sitar was a standard part of Reggie's arsenal—over multilayered electric guitar parts. "It almost didn't matter what guitar he used, it still sounded like Reggie," observed Jimmy Johnson, Reggie's friend and kindred spirit down in the Shoals. "Reggie Young plays those golden guitar licks," observed another Shoals musician, Jerry Carrigan. "Reggie and I played off each other often," said Mike Leech. "Once a track was nailed down, it would then become the 'Reggie show' because that's when he would overdub the finishing touches that became masterpieces, with or without Chips's manipulating."

At a time when rock guitarists were going into pyrotechnics and involved solos, Reggie's brevity was welcome; no line or riff from him lasted one moment longer than the listener wanted. That was somewhat due to Reggie's deliberately unassuming attitude: "I've never got into the me-me-me part," he laughed. To Donnie Fritts, who still came to American occasionally to pitch songs and visit with everyone, Reggie's approach put him in a class by himself. "If anybody has any right to be cocky, it is Reggie, but he's not," said the songwriter with warm regard. Mike Leech, who knew Reggie best in those days, thought he could identify the source of the calm shown by the lead guitarist: "[Reggie's] celebrated cool is a result of a stream of praise he steadily receives (from everywhere)"; so much so that after awhile Reggie became indifferent to it and just continued to do what he did best.

This understated approach was what made the whole thing work, said Bobby Emmons. "Part of it was, we didn't show off a lot of musicianship, basically," the organist reflected. "I'm going to preach a little here, [but] that's where a lot of . . . and tastes and times change . . . in those days, the urge to show off your talent was very bad for the record. That was one of the things that made sixties music, the simplicity, it was not overplayed. We were not called in to cover up and distract from a hit song, we were

there to extend it." While Emmons felt that understatement helped the records artistically, it hurt the reputation of the group among rock musicians of the time. "It's hard to impress somebody with simplicity, musician-wise, so we didn't get the respect." Of course, that professionalism was due to the group being studio players, by definition part of a cooperative enterprise.

The musicians still sought commercial success for each and every recording they did, although Chips Moman increasingly seemed to prefer making records that were about art for art's sake. One of the most revealing recordings he made during this time was a single with Sonny Charles, a singer featured with the L.A.-based Checkmates, Limited (ironically, the Checkmates had recorded Toni Wine's masterwork "Black Pearl," a song best described as an updated and more passionate version of Fats Waller's "A Porter's Love Song to a Chambermaid"). "It Takes a Little Longer," written by Gary Wright, is one of the most hard-hitting of Chips' productions; it features words advising the listener to trust no one—"You try a little harder, and get a little smarter," the chorus declares. "Till you find out in the end, that you haven't got a friend." It also showcases a pounding beat (although Mike Leech and Gene Chrisman are uncharacteristically buried in the mix). Mike's soaring string line, Glen Spreen's blaring horns and Reggie Young's sitar all emphatically drive home the dour, cynical message—but at the same time, the music instills in the listener the heart to carry on in spite of everything, soul music in the truest sense of the word. Stoically carrying on despite the odds was one of the most important tenets of Chips's philosophy; he had stressed it before in records he had done, and he would again. But unlike Norman Whitfield's "Smiling Faces" of a year and a half later, here Chips seems not quite to believe the truth he is telling; the person he is trying to convince is himself.

The B-side of the record, Johnny Christopher's "Mr. Welfare Man," is somber in a different way. It is outwardly a conventional story song, narrated in the voice of a ten-year-old boy asking the family's caseworker if this is the day the check arrives (the boy is trying to be stoic about it and sometimes failing). It must be a winter day, because the boy says it is cold; he and his mother and sister have been living on bread and cheese for the past five days, so it is obviously toward the end of the month, when the check has gone to pay other bills and their food stamps have been exhausted. The boy's father has been in prison for a little over a year, and that very day the family got word that the oldest son, the narrator's brother, has been killed in Vietnam. Johnny's acoustic guitar playing on this track is uncharacteristically sharp, and Mike Leech's bass underlines the story with a simple accent line here and there. "Mr. Welfare Man" is—like "Nine-Pound Steel," "In The Ghetto," "I've Been Down This Road Before" and "I Shall Be Released"— music for the forgotten; it describes the lives of those whom good fortune never visits. If you have ever lived that way, or known those who have, Johnny's song and Chips's skill in framing the story will ring true at once; if not, it is a valuable beginning lesson about what those on the bottom go through just in the course of *one* day—a series of humiliations and agonies endurable only by the kind of stoic resignation Chips described.

The cold realism and the biting anger of both these songs carried over into the next album Chips was slated to produce. Once again, the American group were asked to revitalize the work of a talented singer who had stopped having hits with the old formula. Brenda Lee, "Little Miss Dynamite" to her many fans, had been recording with Owen Bradley and his Nashville Sound A-team; her 1969 release, "Johnny One Time," was an elegant torch song that had been more successful in Europe than in the United States, so clearly it was time for a change. Working with the American group might add a new dimension to her on-record persona of cutesiness mingled with Patsy Cline torchiness (it is no coincidence that Patsy had also been one of Owen Bradley's acts).

"I remember, she was a little bit of dynamite—adorable, *adorable*," said Ima Roberts. "Brenda is one of my favorite people, always has been, and she was very cooperative and great in the studio," said Marty Lacker warmly. Chips Moman remembered her with delight, and Mike Leech described her as "A pleasure to work with. She was studio savvy and we all got along just great. She had a great sense of humor and we really recorded some nice things on her. I always liked Brenda." "I was very pleased to work with Brenda Lee because she was, as far as I could tell, my daddy's favorite recording artist," said Bobby Emmons happily. "And 'I'm Sorry' was always very easy on my ears, as well. Just a *joy* to work with." "She thoroughly enjoyed working with us," added Bobby Wood. "She said for years that that album was one of her favorites because it was more funky and soulful than anything she had ever done. While the album was not a big success she [considered] it to be one of her best efforts." Brenda herself, speaking in 2003, said that she had enjoyed the sessions and had loved working in such an intensely creative environment. Clearly she was trying things out on the album, titled *Memphis Portrait*, that she had never tried as a singer before, with the full encouragement of Chips.

Probably because of the experimental nature of the record, Chips was also pleased with the sessions, but its doubtful even he could have known what a statement the album as a whole would make. It can only be ranked with the Elvis sessions, the B.J. Thomas albums *On My Way* and *Most of All*, Joe Simon's *No Sad Songs*, the Box Tops' *Dimensions*, Townes Van Zandt's *Flyin' Shoes* and the two Highwaymen albums from later in Chips's career as the most coherent statements of the philosophy that life is an unending series of misfortune that can be redeemed only by endurance and determination.

There was now a division of labor among the members of the group whose tasks overlapped. Tommy Cogbill, who was now concentrating more on production and getting his custom label going, was completely absent from the album. Mike Leech played bass but did no arrangements, leaving the field to Glen Spreen's despondent-sounding strings. Johnny Christopher played acoustic guitar but contributed no songs, although the album was full of compositions from the group and their friends; "Walk a Mile in My Shoes" and "Games People Play" from Joe South and Paul Davis's "I'll Keep on Lovin' You" are done in a vinegary style that permeates the whole album. The characteristic that Chips seemed to feel was missing from Brenda Lee's previous recordings is *anger*, and he gave that emotion full rein.

Chips was also paying attention to the female voice that had caught his notice on demos he received from New York. By the end of 1969 he had requested that Marty Lacker call Ira Jaffe at Screen Gems asking about her, and he now knew who she was. The record-buying public did too, although they did not know her name. Toni Wine sang the female lead on the novelty hit of the year, "Sugar Sugar" by the Archies. (Ron Dante, lead singer with the studio-assembled Cuff Links, was the male vocalist.) "I'm gonna make love so sweet," cooed the singer, and a listener's immediate reaction was that this woman was too talented to sing such fluff.

She was indeed talented: Toni had been a piano scholar, a Juilliard graduate who was now, in addition to her Archies work for Don Kirshner, the top jingle singer in New York City. She had been a Brill Building writer since the mid-sixties, when she composed "Groovy Kind of Love" with Carole Bayer Sager. It had been a British Invasion hit for Wayne Fontana and the Mindbenders in 1966 and her best-known work until 1969, when she wrote her passionate, soulful masterwork "Black Pearl." Phil Spector made that song into an immediate classic when he recorded it with Sonny Charles and the Checkmates. A lesser-known composition chosen by and partially credited to Spector, "You Came, You Saw, You Conquered," was an elegant comeback record for the Ronettes. Chips had grown enamored of her voice, and he told Marty Lacker he would like to record her.

It was a time for scouting female vocalists. Petula Clark had not had a record on the U.S. charts since "American Boys" in late 1968; presumably aware of the critical prestige Dusty Springfield's album had garnered, she sent word that she would like to record in Memphis, and Marty Lacker went to New York for a meeting with her. Neither he nor Chips remembered exactly how Petula chose American instead of Stax or Hi, but Chips emphatically recalled why she wanted to be in town. "She found her way to Memphis 'cause we were *hot!*" he exclaimed.

Marty continued the story: "[Petula] wanted to meet someone from the studio before she would agree to come. Before I flew to New York I called Toni and told her that Chips would like to meet her and that I was coming to New York to meet Petula and would she like to fly back to Memphis with me. She said yes.

"My meeting with [Petula] was at the NBC-TV studios in Brooklyn where she was taping a variety special with Anthony Newley. That's why we met there. After her taping, she, her husband Claude, and I went to the Brasserie to have a late meal. I told her about Chips, the musicians, and the history of the studio and the hits we had cut.

"We talked awhile to try to put her at ease . . . We talked at both places about what to expect when she came to Memphis and after I assured her she'd enjoy it, she asked if I would stay close to her and Claude when they were here for the session. [She said], 'I don't know anyone there.' I said, 'Well, now you know me. . . .' She said she felt comfortable with me during our meeting. She agreed to come to Memphis a few weeks later."

It was also imperative that Marty Lacker find Toni Wine. She had sent some demos down to Memphis as part of the Brill Building package of songs they regularly received, but, Chips recalled, "I was gonna cut one of her songs on Brenda Lee and I had lost the demo. I was gonna cut that night." When Marty located her, he explained the situation and she eagerly agreed to bring a replacement demo down in person. "The next day Toni met me at the Essex House where I was staying and we went to the airport and flew to Memphis," said Marty. We went straight to the studio. I introduced her to Chips, he was mixing some records. I left them and went home."

In 1968 Chips had suggested to Mark James

that a song be written using the title "Eyes of a New York Woman," in an apparent tribute to Eileen Burns of Bang Records, who had become a loyal booster of the studio. Chips could not have known how significant to his life that line would become.

His courtship of Toni Wine at first seemed to be a strictly professional one. With his emphasis on songs, he had devoted much of his time to building a stable of writers, and he had already signed a group as enviable as the signings of Buddy Killen at Tree or Fred Foster at Combine. And he wanted Toni to become part of that stable: with her Brill Building background, track record of hits, and Juilliard education, he felt that she would be a valuable addition to the company. He tried to sign her as an exclusive writer for Press, but she resisted, because she was making more money on her own. Bobby Wood remembered, "When she came to Memphis, she told Chips, 'I go to my mailbox twice a week. And I have checks from sixty to eighty thousand dollars in the mailbox'"—her royalties from songs she had written and jingles on which she had sung (though she received no royalties from the Archies records, which led her to break with Don Kirshner before the year was out). In time, however, Toni's vivaciousness turned the courtship into a personal one as well.

Perhaps it was to be expected that a man who spent his life painting pictures and mood statements with sound could have been so captivated by a voice. Toni talked the way she sang, with warmth and more than a trace of a New York accent. It was an exotic quality to Chips, who still spoke with his slow Georgia drawl overlaid at times with an Elvislike snarl. He was also impressed with her musicianship; her classical training and Juilliard education never ceased to astound him. "She gave a concert at the age of ten at Carnegie Hall," he said with awe, still the Georgia farm boy astonished that he had won his city girl. Neither he nor Toni had ever seen anyone like each other before.

"I didn't really know who she was. Foot, I barely knew who the Beatles were," said Bobby Wood. She attempted to make a good impression, although in some ways she seemed to be

trying too hard. Glen Spreen remembered her saying and doing things "that just didn't strike a chord." She even made an effort to join the prank-playing in the studio. "I remember her playing a joke on Chips when she first came down from New York," Bobby Wood recalled. "She told all of us not to laugh. She sat down at the piano and started to sing some of her songs and made out like she had a lisp. Chips was looking at her and didn't know what to say. We finally broke out in laughter; Chips then knew he had been put on."

Another eyewitness to the joke remembered it well, although Mike Leech said it happened somewhat differently. He recalled that Toni arrived at the studio slightly before Chips did and that she was demonstrating on the piano a song she had written when Chips walked in. One look at her and the producer's eyes glazed over as if he had been poleaxed. "Chips stood there with a silly grin," Mike said. "She looked at him and did the same. . . . He was smitten from that day on."

"The eyes of a New York woman," Mark James wrote, "are eyes that can hold a man." Photos of Toni Wine taken at the time show that she had beautiful eyes: large and round, dark, expressive, with more than a slight hint of sadness in them—a hidden knowledge of pain that would have appealed to a melancholy man. She was petite and willowy, with long dark hair and a radiant smile that widened when she looked at Chips. "I wouldn't say Toni was strikingly beautiful, by no means," Mike Leech observed thoughtfully. "She was cute. And she knew it. She had that little bashful smile. I'll never forget the first time I saw her and she sat down at the piano and sang a song. Chips was just one big grin.

"She would turn around during the song and smile at him and her eyes would be just a little out of focus, almost crossed at times; and she sang with a slight lisp that I thought was going to send Chips through the ceiling. It was love at first sight. . . . Chips just stood there with a grin from ear to ear," continued the string arranger. For Chips, the lines Mark James had written now clearly applied to him: "She swept me off of my feet, made my world seem so complete.

I'll never have to look no more, I've found what I've been looking for." After years of restless searching for "that Fantasia feeling," Chips had finally run across a woman who seemed to embody it.

"I think she possessed every physical and mental attribute that Laurie didn't have," Mike Leech reflected, contrasting the difference between Toni and Chips's then-wife. "Laurie was tall, thin. . . . She just didn't flaunt her looks or intelligence, like Toni did. Toni was short, cute, bubbly, talented, and was eager to show it off. Brought Chips to his knees." Mike was protectively aware of how emotional and open Chips could be beneath that hard-boiled exterior, and he felt that Toni exploited that quality. "She showed up at a time when he was terribly unhappy with his marital relationship," observed the arranger. "Her cutesy little wispy voice caught him at a very vulnerable time and he fell head over."

"In the beginning, Toni was nice and she and I hung out a lot when she wasn't with Chips because I was the one she knew best," said Marty Lacker. There was a decided culture clash between the soft-spoken Southern boys and the New York lady. "Here's this Jewish princess, very aggressive, and all the guys were so laid back," said Ima Roberts. "None of us were accustomed to that fast-paced personality." "The band couldn't accept that hurry-up New York session style that had been a way of life for Toni for so long," observed Bobby Emmons. Since Marty Lacker had spent the first fourteen years of his life in what is now the South Bronx, he understood her attitude more than did most of the staff, but he later thought her "conniving and controlling," a sentiment echoed by Glen Spreen. He had served in the army with New Yorkers and knew from that experience what they were like, so her aggressive manner did not bother him; her apparent motives did. "I didn't have a positive feeling about her even if I had a slight grasp on what she was all about," he said. "She made one friend . . . Chips. That was it."

"I won't lie—I resented her being there, and I think all the other guys did, too," said Mike Leech. Not quite: Reggie Young thought well

of her, and she trusted his considerate manner enough to confide in him when she was concerned about or having troubles with Chips. "I felt like she was extremely talented," said Bobby Emmons of his first impression. "Her track record appeared to be earned." As she became more familiar with the premises at American, she began to behave as if she were a combination of the group's unofficial mascot and the official first lady, much to the musicians' surprise and occasional annoyance, especially since that was the way Chips seemed to see her. To many of them it seemed as if Chips was reliving his adolescence, and increasingly distracted as he fell more deeply in love. He worked closely with Toni in the studio during the Brenda Lee recordings, and the opportunity to make full use of her writing and her background vocals seemed to delight him.

He began the album with one of the Bee Gees' most affecting songs from their sorrowful period, the gospel-flavored "Give a Hand, Take a Hand." The song begins with a statement of idealism and innocence lost, underscored by Bobby Emmons's solemn line on the organ: "Wish the world was made for all little children / We'd be happy once again." Having established a longing for the impossible, the verse continues: "And we won't hurt when we're all like little children / We won't ever feel the pain," and the strings and horns burst in with one long sustaining line, as if Glen is in agreement. As Chips's interpreter, Brenda Lee seems almost to be fighting the lyrics; she is forced to put across a gloomy melody with lyrics out of character for her style. The second verse is a treatise on death and dying, featuring such cheerful lines as "When my fight at last on earth is over" and offering a hope of reunion with friends: "We'll all join hands another day." It is only in the chorus that the will to self-assertion and hope breaks through: "Everybody's got to give a hand."

The rousing effect of the chorus is marred by some seemingly inappropriate handclapping, and the reason it is there can be explained by the lyrics of the final verse: "I love you, I've told you a million times / Do you believe what I say? / You know my love belongs to you hereafter."

Toni Wine was singing backup, obviously off the beat, dragging slightly behind the others and clapping her hands whenever she found a space in the music. According to Mike Leech, the whole effect was out of place, though Chips seemed not to notice. "Toni drove us crazy when she was on a mike," sniffed the exasperated bassist. "For one thing, she had to have her voice so loud in the headphones that it was difficult to hear ourselves. And during a take, when she wasn't singing, like during an instrumental passage, she would make noises, and clap her hands, which was very disconcerting, to the point of having to stop the take. . . . I did, however, especially like the stuff we did with her and Brenda Lee."

"Toni was okay at times on the sessions, and then at other times she could, to me, get a little out of hand," Gene Chrisman thoughtfully assessed. "A little arrogant at times." Bobby Wood recalled: "I think everybody appreciated her talent. I loved her piano playing," but he also recalled her as "Typical New York—talked a lot." In the opinion of Glen Spreen, "She was talented, smart, professional," but he added that she brought little to the table compared to what Chips and the group could do. "I had a lot of respect for her talent, but even there, there was something wrong with it—it was too well schooled. Chips was a guy to be respected and a guy to learn from. I didn't learn anything from Toni except 'Don't listen.'"

Toni brought several songs from New York down with her, most of them written with her then-collaborator Irwin Levine (who later became famous for writing "Tie a Yellow Ribbon 'Round the Old Oak Tree"). And though most of the songs were written before her involvement with Chips, many of them seem to be oddly prescient of their connection. Her songs for this session, and for the Petula Clark session that followed it, are the first of half a dozen songs she and Chips wrote separately and together, commenting on their courtship and marriage like scenes from an Ingmar Bergman movie. "Sisters in Sorrow," the first cut introducing the sessions' dominant theme of anger, is addressed directly to someone's wife, offering her empathy even though the woman speaking

defiantly refuses to abandon the competition. "Hey, broken heart, I know exactly how you feel," country music's most girlish torch singer snaps and snarls. "I've had a ride on that same Ferris wheel." Chips allows Toni to restate the chorus's hook line—"Sharing his bed and sharing his name"—immediately after Brenda Lee sings it. The track does not appear on the LP, but was later released as a single; the music is as biting and harsh as the words, and if it was meant to show radio programmers and listeners another side of Brenda Lee, they obviously did not want to hear it.

"Leavin' on a Jet Plane," the second song on the album, was on the charts while Chips was recording it. It was a hit for Peter, Paul, and Mary featuring Mary Travers's delicate vocal lead; just as their versions of Dylan songs had established him as a writer, so now they were establishing the compositional strength of a former Chad Mitchell Trio vocalist, John Denver. Here, Denver's penchants for sentimentality and overwrought phrasing borrowed from Victorian poetry are kept under control, as he wrote in a quiet, conversational style about a man whose traveling kept him away from his sweetheart. It was obviously an autobiographical song, since he was frequently touring; but the song could apply just as well to people like Chips and Toni, lovers meeting and then having to say goodbye for awhile. It could apply to a draftee about to fly off to Vietnam, or a draft evader heading for Canada. It could apply to a salesman who was too much on the road, or a corporate CEO who traveled a lot looking for smaller companies to acquire. "Leavin' on a Jet Plane" is universal in its tone of sweet regret, and Chips expands the regretfulness into sorrow, underscored by Glen Spreen's contemplative string line, which swirls upward in the last chorus as if the plane is taking off. The delicate acoustic guitar lines of Johnny Christopher are prominently featured, and Bobby Emmons also comes to the fore with his subtle, yet emphatic organ line beneath the vocal. Brenda Lee sings the lyrics with good cheer shading into deep tenderness, Gene Chrisman inexplicably reprises his "Hooked on a Feeling" percussion part in the second verse, and Mike Leech is the perfect anchor throughout, keeping the romantic dreams and the music firmly rooted in common sense.

Common sense has nothing to do with the next selection, "So Close to Heaven," written by Toni Wine's Brill Building colleagues Weinstein and Stroll. The two New Yorkers were fond of composing songs with obvious drug references, as their Chips-produced album several months later would prove, but this time they were writing about the most addictive drug of all, falling in love unexpectedly. The story line, though not written specifically about them, describes what literally happened to Chips Moman and Toni Wine on the day they became locked in their *folie à deux*. "Lightning flashed, thunder roared," the lyrics described the effect. "And all the future I depended on / In a moment, it had come and gone." Now, each alone and bereft without the other, the couple were sorting through the pieces and trying to figure out exactly what it was that had happened to them. Whether it was good or bad, neither could yet say; they only knew they had been "so close to heaven / I was so high off of the ground / You brought me so close to heaven / And I think I may never come down." The trick ending, Bobby Wood's pounding piano, Mike Leech's springboard of a bass, and Glen Spreen's blaring horn line, symbolize the sudden stops and starts of an affair just beginning. The second verse describes what could possibly for Chips have been an added benefit of a new romance: "Someone I could tell my troubles to" (when everyone else was tired of hearing his myriad grievances).

"Games People Play" is as angry and bitter in the American Studios version as it was when Joe South had written and recorded it, even though Brenda Lee's high-pitched voice is not really suited to such an indictment of the world. Again she seems to be fighting the lyrics, although her gospel-style rendition is in keeping with the song's Jeremiah-like tone. Reggie Young's electric sitar is prominent, weaving around elaborate filigree lines from Bobby Emmons. Though Joe South had long been a distant acquaintance, and of course had worked with Tommy Cogbill and Spooner Oldham on

some of the Aretha records, his most famous song seems an odd choice for the session until one listens to the second verse, and realizes that it is about a dissolving marriage.

The next track on the album, "I Think I Love You Again," was written by Toni Wine and Irwin Levine in New York but aired here as a scenes-from-a-courtship sequence. The speaker seems to be taking the measure of the man who has so overwhelmed her, and fully aware of what some of the risks were; "You're your own person just the same way that I am, so sometimes we get each other down," says the second line of the song. Later, in the second verse, she mentions his chronic restlessness and inability to ever be satisfied. Her solution, at least in the song, seemed to be that she would try to wean herself away from him; she goes looking for someone with "a perfect body, a pretty face, but no mind." But all her running does not work, and she faces the fact that for all the difficulties she might confront, she is helpless: "Feelings are coming back to me and I think I love you again." Toni can be heard shouting that key line over the rolling beat; she is not quite in sync with the rhythm and her voice sounds shrill.

Side two begins with one of the strongest position papers ever done by Chips, and probably the most startling song on the album. "Lord Never Makes a Burden Too Heavy to Carry," by the New Jersey songwriter Benny Mardones (who would have a 1979 pop hit with a dramatic power ballad called "Into the Night"), anticipates his fellow Jersey boy Bruce Springsteen with a gritty, realistic song that lays bare some inconvenient truths and feelings. The first lines sound as if it will be a simple Southern genre painting—"Tarpaper shanties on an old dirt road / Seeing my mama working made my blood run cold." For the first time Brenda Lee, who had endured childhood poverty in Atlanta, seems to understand what is expected of her, and she delivers the lyrics with fierce conviction born of experience. The recitation of facts in the first verse turns in the second verse to the sociological insight that poverty provokes feelings of anger and self-pity: "People making fun made me wonder and doubt / Why the

Lord chose our family to have to go without." The precarious existence makes her "a child stricken with fears" who cannot comprehend why her beloved mama is so accepting. But her mama replies in the chorus, as Mike Leech thunders on the bass to underscore the message: "Lord never makes a burden too heavy to carry / He ain't gonna put a challenge where it can't be won / Some people have to try a little bit harder / Before their life's work is done."

A key tenet of this piece, as with so many of the songs Chips recorded, is that if one is unhappy and plagued by bad luck, one is simply marked from birth to suffer, and the only way that pride, dignity, and even beauty can be salvaged from all the meaningless pain is to bear it stoically. In the end, according to this view, the stoicism reaps dividends in terms of character development: "My strength built of rock from what I thought was sand." The song concludes with a prescient line about passing the philosophy of stoicism on to a son—several years after Chips and Toni Wine finally married, Toni did indeed give him a son, Casey, to whom Chips was devoted and to whom he taught the recording engineer's trade. "Lord Never Makes a Burden" would have been a strong song no matter who was producing it, but in the hands of Chips, it became something special.

Reggie Young had begun writing songs again, with the help of a buddy who had known him since high school, Red Williams. Red began turning up at American sometimes, and he and Reggie occasionally worked on something they thought might interest Chips. "Hello, Love" was their latest work, and it became a standard around the studio for awhile; many of Chips's acts recorded it. B.J. Thomas recorded the best version almost a year later, but Brenda Lee's was the first, and it is set off by some intricate guitar work from its writer and a softly flowing string line. In ordinary times it might have been out of character for Chips to choose such a happy song to record, but here he includes one about a life full of previously unexplored possibilities.

Anger returns on a version of "Walk a Mile in My Shoes," and from there the album leads into "Proud Mary." Less than a year after the

John Fogerty song had been on the charts, by 1970 it was hackneyed, though it had not started out to be, and the American Studios version restores some of its original freshness. Credit for the innovative version must go prominently to Bobby Emmons, who offers a thick, sheet-of-sound organ line in the bridge and then makes way for Mike Leech's deliberate pacing. "Do Right Woman," another standard by this time, is trotted out in a slow, deliberate version featuring Reggie Young's incisive guitar fills and bursts of emphasis from Glen Spreen's horn arrangement.

The album closes with a song from Paul Davis, the Mississippi songwriter who occasionally showed up at the studio to pitch his work to Chips. "I'll Keep On Loving You" is an insubstantial song, but Chips seemed drawn to its heavy, doom-laden melody and theme of crying yet staying strong. Mike Leech anchors the recording with a six-note bass figure that became a trademark of his sound; he would use it to effect on several other recordings over the years, most notably on John Prine's first album, where he played it on several songs. Glen Spreen's string line rises in a slow, twisting curlicue around the melody in the bridge, and the horn section blares another repeating figure as Brenda improvises a spontaneous, soulful fadeout. Toni Wine can be heard humming loudly underneath Brenda's vocal in the chorus, an example of what seemed to some of the musicians like showing off—with the full consent of Chips, who was giving Toni carte blanche to contribute anything she wanted to the recordings. None of them knew what to do about it, or even how long Toni's tenure with Chips would last; as with the presence of the late arrivals, everyone tried to shrug it off and endure it.

They endured it again on the next important recording, made immediately following Brenda Lee's. Petula Clark and her husband, the French impresario Claude Wolf, came to town for her scheduled session, and a photograph of Petula and Claude posed at the control board with a somewhat stunned-looking Chips reveals that the elegant British singer and her husband were still not completely comfortable on this new turf. It was another example of culture clash—Glen Spreen, whose clothes were so unconventional by American group standards, remembered forever the floor-length lion skin coat Claude wore. Her presence was noted in town, said Reggie Young. "She was [still] very good and very, very 'propah,'" he laughed. "James Kingsley came in to take a photograph of her for the paper and he asked her to put her foot up on a chair or on stool or something and she said [Reggie slipped into an imitation of Petula's British speaking voice] 'No—it isn't proper.'"

The musicians were hardly a help in easing the differences, totally committed to their style of teasing and practical jokes. Some of the cutting up was for deliberate effect, to throw the out-of-town artists off balance; then, according to plan, the singer was supposed to be twice as amazed that these japesters could settle in to do some serious work. It may have been intended to put the singers at ease, but the group sometimes forgot that such a strategy did not work with everyone—one of whom, at least at first, was Petula.

"She was lovely, and her husband was nice," said Ima Roberts. "I was proud to be working with Petula, because I considered 'Downtown' to be one of the icon records of that era," said Bobby Emmons. "Plus I was always a sucker for the English-accent girls on the folk-rock tracks. They were the new power vocalists after the big-finish torch songs of the forties." "I remember Petula as being a kind of formal person when we first met," said Glen Spreen. "She, being the reserved English lady, didn't quite know how to take our sense of humor," recalled Bobby Wood. "She was very uptight because of our shenanigans before any actual recording took place," Mike Leech added. "She quietly stood in the vocal booth for some time, waiting to record, while we totally ignored her and played our 'games,' which is what we always did before work." "I mean, you had Bobby Wood standing there taking out his glass eye and popping it in his mouth, then taking it out and putting it back in his eye socket," added Glen Spreen amusedly. "She got very upset and

started crying," Mike Leech continued. "We were surprised and settled down to work."

By the early years of the twenty-first century, recording involved hours of sifting through material. It is astonishing that even for such an important client as Petula Clark in 1970, Chips Moman's methods of selecting songs were as improvised as in the days when he operated on a shoestring. Bobby Wood remembered that even as the sessions were taking place, Chips was still in the process of deciding what to cut. "We would hash over old songs to do and discuss which ones would work for her," said the piano player. As Dusty Springfield had been before her, Petula was nonplussed. "She was used to having everything being arranged with full orchestra and singers and everything planned out," Bobby Wood continued. "She thought she had dropped off the planet."

"I don't think we ever found the right songs for her, we just recorded some trial and error stuff," Wood added, although the finished album *Memphis*, released in the summer of 1970, sounds like anything but a thrown-together project. In the end, Chips relied mainly on work from his own staff and from Toni Wine; it was a wise decision, because the album provides a showcase for all the writers and maintains a unified vision. The mood throughout is warm; Chips tapped into the soft midrange in Petula's voice and utilized it for good effect. The liner notes to the CD release of the album mentions that, on a BBC interview show in the nineties, Petula cited it as her all-time favorite of the records she had done—perhaps because of its departures from her usual style.

For instance, she had never sung anything as sensual and explicit as the Toni Wine composition "I Wanna See Morning with Him," which opens the album. This was one of the songs Toni had written in New York with Irwin Levine; in this context it becomes another scene from a courtship, capturing the tumultuous moment in a love affair when one knows that physical consummation is near. Petula's voice is affectionate rather than deliberately sexy, and Toni cries out in full-throated, ascending cadences behind her. "I'll smile, as he wins my heart away," Petula croons. "Lips pressed on lips until the break of day." The fact that Petula sings so understatedly gives the song even further power, as if she is speaking of a deep and devastating attraction. Wayne Jackson's Memphis Horns, scored by Glen Spreen, carry the weight of the melody, offsetting and accenting it all the way through the song and into the fadeout.

Johnny Christopher's thought piece "Nothing's As Good As It Used to Be" is next, and his light, slightly swaggering acoustic guitar runs anchor this track and the remainder of the album. By now his playing and his background vocals had been thoroughly integrated into the core group's sound, and he had staked out a territory in the mix midway between Mike Leech and Reggie Young, who graciously stepped back and let him be featured here. The song had originally been recorded by Ronnie Milsap, who delivered the lyrics in a stentorian bellow to a shuffle beat. Petula declaims in a soft, contemplative voice atop the jauntiness of the acoustic guitar run and the flowing string line. "Wonder why you gotta have something new," she reflects in a tone suggesting that restlessness is the essence of the human condition. "It seems like you think what you have'll never do . . . Looking back, do you really think you could do so much better, when nothing's as good as it used to be?" "It came from the heart," Johnny Christopher said passionately about the song's creation. "The melody and words were real. When it's not from the heart it becomes normal commercial mass-produced stuff."

"Good Night, Sweet Dreams" features surrealistic lyrics and an impassioned melody, courtesy of Weinstein and Stroll: "Down a green-embroidered stairway, through a manhole in the wall / Left to wallow in the sewer, hearing echoes down the hall"—and that is only part of the first verse. Petula's voice is soft, reassuring, as if she is the one calling out to the listener from somewhere in that abstract dreamscape, while Chips builds the melody to a chorus encouraging the person wandering through the senseless dream to hold on and hope, because "the mighty sun is calling." Quite another word picture is painted in Chips' version of "Neon Rainbow," complete with a new horn arrangement from Glen Spreen. Mike Leech's original string arrangement is mixed with less echo here, and as a result it sounds slightly thinner than the Box Tops original. Wayne Carson's lyric unintentionally offers echoes of Petula's standard hit "Downtown," which also dealt with the magic of a city by night (the two songs can be heard as a suite when played consecutively). Characteristically, Wayne shrugged off the fact that a singer as internationally prestigious as Petula had recorded one of his compositions. "Songs get cut if they're good songs," he said matter-of-factly. "They're like old cars, they don't give a shit about who's drivin' 'em."

It is doubly ironic that Petula recorded "Neon Rainbow," because the Motown-sounding "Right On," written by Petula herself under a pseudonym, echoes the sentiments of a song Wayne Carson used to close out his own solo album two years later. Both "Right On" and Wayne's later "Good People" make a point lost in those days of obsessive hipness: that awareness was a by-product not of how you dressed or what lifestyle you espoused, but of what was in your heart. To a warmly sophisticated Englishwoman, married for many years to the same man and the devoted mother of two children, psychedelia must have seemed odd indeed, and here she was serving polite notice that she was not going to be relegated to the back burner of music or life by people who thought themselves groovier than she because she dressed neatly and preferred to live conventionally. Her lyrics make her claim explicit: to be on the side of the light, you don't have to protest, be a groupie, dress sloppily, or do drugs—"All you gotta do is say what you mean and mean what you say . . . once you decide that love and peace is the only way for you." Reggie Young's electric sitar delivers acerbic commentary, and Glen Spreen's string line muses thoughtfully beneath her vocal. This track, as well as the similar song later done by Wayne Carson, gave comfort to a lot of people who were sympathetic to peace and love but who found themselves too square for the times.

Ira Jaffe of Screen Gems brought Chips a new song by an Oklahoma writer now based out of Los Angeles, David Gates. Gates was in the process of recording "It Don't Matter to Me" with his own soft-rock group, Bread (which featured a later colleague of Richard Maine-gra's and Rick Yancey's, Memphis's own Jimmy Griffin). In an apparent attempt to lay the groundwork for Bread's first album, Jaffe was trying to place some of Gates's songs, and the one he chose for Chips was a classic, describing the attitude of a generation at least attempting to do away with traditional possessiveness. The speaker knows that the lover addressed is eager to have a fling, and the speaker makes no attempt to stop it, realizing that only through exploration will the beloved ever be free to come back: "There'll always be an empty room waiting for you / And an open heart, waiting for you." Petula's voice is warm with wisdom and soft with compassion, and the piercing sound of Reggie Young's sitar emphasizes the freshness of the sentiments. Wayne Jackson contributes one of his bright trumpet lines and Gene Chrisman is extremely effective with both drums and overdubbed percussion. Chips was so justifiably pleased with the results of this recording that he wanted to release this as a single, and the musicians were certain that they would have a hit if he did, but David Gates ultimately refused permission, fearing that Petula's release would block his own band's chances of success with the song. Bread made the charts with it in the fall of 1970.

"How We Gonna Live to Be a Hundred Years Old" is pure vaudeville, a nod to Petula's background in British music halls, with a kazoo in the instrumental bridge (Toni Wine does a shrill, nasal "nyah-nyah-nyah" underneath the noise) and a hokey, Guy Lombardo–style saxophone. Chips repeated this concept on several songs Jackie DeShannon recorded with him later; apparently he thought that older styles in music meant exclusively the so-called "sweet" bands that had been popular around the time he was born in the mid-thirties. The record begins with a bit of audio vérité: one of the group counts it off in a mock-British voice and Petula giggles winningly. By now she had loosened up considerably, to the point where, Glen Spreen remembered, "She would carry a small bottle of brown liquor, maybe bourbon, with her. I

remember that she would take it out while she was in the singer's booth and sip it between her lines." "Gene is solely responsible for easing the atmosphere," Mike Leech praised the drummer. "He began calling her 'Petunia' and would say before counting a song off, 'Here we go, Petunia' . . . Broke the ice and all was cool from that point. See, there's more to being a session player than just playing." "She would just look at him like, 'What a dummy.' We would laugh," said Bobby Wood. Mike Leech added, "She would giggle each time and from that point on she and us became friends and we did some very nice things."

Red West and Mark James's "When the World Was Round" is one of those "very nice things"—a soft, meditative song addressed to someone slowly losing touch with reality, either through denial or drugs (the reason is unspecified): "When the sky was blue, it wasn't good enough for you / You wanted to change it, so you rearranged it / Feeding it with colors from rainbows in your mind." There was a real-life irony to the song, because Red West's longtime friend and former employer Elvis was slowly slipping into dependency on sedatives and diet pills, and Red was one of the people who challenged Elvis about it from time to time (Marty Lacker was another). "Red told us that every little bit you had to straighten him out for awhile," said Wayne Carson. "You could tell him, 'You may be *a* king, but you ain't *the* king.'" "Can't you see you're dreaming your life away?" Petula, speaking Red's thoughts, pleads softly, as if she is not expecting a change in behavior but feels the need to express her feelings about it anyway. Johnny Christopher's relaxed groove on acoustic guitar, a presence more felt than openly audible, amiably paces the song, and Glen Spreen's horn and string arrangements meander lazily.

Johnny Christopher's good-natured playing continues on a song he wrote, "That Old-Time Feeling," a melodic piece about rediscovering an old lover and falling back into the attraction. "All of a sudden I'm in a dream," says Petula bemusedly. "Just looking at you has made it begin." Bobby Emmons adds some thick asides on keyboard and leads the group into the rolling, syncopated beat that was rapidly becoming one of their specialties. Reggie Young's electric sitar adds piercing commentary and the listener can ride the beat like a whitewater rafter until discovering all too soon (the song only has two verses and a two-line chorus) that the song is over.

From Johnny Christopher's musings about an old love we are pulled into the story of a love affair just beginning: another scene from a courtship, Toni Wine's and Irwin Levine's "That's What Life Is All About." It is very much a morning song, and one can almost picture sunlight streaming through curtains. A woman awakens, watching her new lover asleep beside her, and she wonders if she should wake him but decides against it, lying back down as she reflects on how fortunate they are to have found each other. It was a song that would have had resonance for the solidly married Petula, and her happiness is reflected in the joy with which she sings. "Always you, always me, always us, always we," she declaims in an ascending spiral with Toni joining in on the key words, and together both women shout the entire title line. Toni's nasal voice sounds harsh set against Petula's dulcet tone, and their timbres do not blend well, but that did not prevent Chips from using the dissonant sound for effect. Bobby Wood contributes a soft swirling piano line near the fadeout.

The album concludes with yet another American group version of "People Get Ready," featuring Reggie Young's sitar. Delivered by the wrong voice, Curtis Mayfield's lyrics about the (gospel) train having "no room for the hopeless sinner" could sound self-righteous, but Petula sings it so sweetly that she seems to be the voice of reason itself.

The Brenda Lee and Petula Clark albums were recorded with a slight change of staff in the control room. Chips was producing and still doing much of the engineering, but both of his original assistants on the sound crew were gone. Darryl Carter had left when Bobby Womack did, and Chips said "I don't think he left on a good note," though he was at a loss to remember other details. (Darryl was still in Memphis at the time and later produced several Masqueraders singles for the label.) Ed Kollis had accepted an offer from Columbia Records in Nashville to work as staff engineer at their studios, an unlikely pairing given Columbia's emphasis on union rules and restrictions and Ed's instinctive loathing of anything resembling authority, but it offered Ed a chance to advance himself. "I saw the writing on the wall," he explained about why he left.

Kollis was replaced by Mike Cauley, who had begun hanging around American through an acquaintance with Bill Allen, a pilot Chips sometimes hired to fly his plane. Cauley was an Arkansas boy, a college dropout interested in songwriting; he had also taken an electronics course in high school, and that knowledge became his entree to American. His initial responsibilities were much the same as Darryl Carter's and Ed Kollis's had been: "Basically, I started out running the tape machine, stopping and starting it, going for coffee," he said. "The eight-track did not have an automatic rewind, so they needed somebody to sit there and run it." He became so used to sitting there alongside Chips that he could almost read the producer's mind; he instinctively knew when and why to stop the tape or rewind it. Cauley almost drifted into engineering; by his own admission he was immature then, emotionally younger than his twenty-two years, and it was easy for him to fluff off the opportunity he had. For several months, he dropped out of the picture; he maintained he was not fired, although why he left the first time is unclear. But the outcome was not. Chips needed a new assistant engineer. It was largely due to Tommy Cogbill that he found one.

"I was greener than Kermit the Frog." So said Hayward Bishop, the third of the American group late arrivals. If a TV sitcom were based on the personalities of the American Studios musicians, Hayward and the even later arrival Shane Keister would be cast as the mischievous, bumptious younger brothers.

He came from Norfolk, Virginia, the first person in his family to be born below the

Mason-Dixon line. His father and grandfather owned and operated a towboat company on the Delaware River. "During the Second World War, they ran gasoline to the military ships at Norfolk," he said. His father, for whom he was named, died of kidney failure when the boy was four months old, and his mother worked in a furniture store to support him and his older sister. He claimed not to have missed having a father around; his environment in Norfolk was so close-knit that his family and many of the neighbors took group vacations, a custom that continued for years. "You know how they say it takes a village to raise a child?" Hayward asked rhetorically. "Well, I was raised by that village." He knew every family on his street; even neighbors without children his age had toys with which he could play when he visited them. He would search for that lost sense of warmth and community for the rest of his life. The only disadvantage, he said, was that a slight, fatherless boy was required to learn how to handle himself: "I had to fend off bullies. I can spot bullydom in its early stages."

Among his first memories was music. "I started wanting to be a drummer from the time I was three." His mother had wanted to be a drummer, and he had vivid memories of her tap-dancing in the house. The percussiveness of the tap beat fascinated him, and at the age of eleven he formed his first band on the porch of his best friend's house across the street. Hayward played drums, inspired both by the records done at Cosimo Matassa's studio in New Orleans and by the Los Angeles drummer Hal Blaine. "Hal Blaine could drive the band when he played, and that's what I always tried to do," he said. "Gene Krupa set a style of flamboyance that I liked—that razzamatazz, that lilt. . . . Xavier Cugat had a band, I learned that Latin feel, I loved it. I liked uptempo, I was learnin' groove as a baby and didn't know it." After his first band, he and a guitar-playing friend organized a rock group originally called the Halfbeats; after mergers with other bands and several name changes, the group evolved into the Fourivis Four. This quartet played the naval bases, downtown dives, and NCO clubs

in the Norfolk area. "I was supporting myself from the time I was fifteen years old," said Hayward. "I was paying my own bills, making my own decisions."

His first recording session was in October 1962 at the age of sixteen, when he played drums on a Gary "U.S." Bonds recording called "I'm in Love with the Girl Next Door." Bonds, one of the first musicians on the Norfolk scene to gain a national audience, was recording for the local producer and promoter Frank J. Guida. "Gary was hot at this particular time," said Hayward. "Gary had had two hits with Frank already... he had had the hit 'Quarter to Three' and 'New Orleans' by this time. . . . The studio was actually about a mile and a half from where I lived and was in the neighborhood where I went to high school." When he was not working, he and the other members of his band attended every show they could; the Bill Black Combo passed through Norfolk at that time, and Hayward was in the audience, transfixed by Bobby Emmons's virtuosity and his solemn demeanor on stage. To Hayward, high school and the social games played by the preppies who dominated that environment was "a fantasy world": his mind was elsewhere, concentrating on the career in music he planned to have.

After he and the others left high school, the Fourivis Four toured up and down the East Coast, though like many bands of that region they played many of the coastal summer resorts and specialized in the genre later to be known as "beach music" because of its popularity in those towns. It was a style of music indigenous to the Carolina and Virginia coasts, a style for which Hayward maintained a lasting affinity. "R&B bands were good. They were different from the way the white guys played music. The white kids loved the black music because it was so danceable," he explained. "And that is the key . . . originally certain music was selected to incorporate a dance form called the shag, which basically a slowed-down version of the jitterbug. That developed a whole new genre unto themselves. The music had to have certain danceable qualities so they could dance the shag." Later, beach music grew from the early forms of R&B and took on much broader tempos and feel, encompassing recordings from Fontella Bass in Chicago, Chuck Jackson in New York, and many classic Memphis and Muscle Shoals recordings. Performers could be black, white, or integrated groups, but the music was predominately soulful R&B. By the time the Fourivis Four became a part of the style, the scene had regional bands and singers such as the Embers, the Showmen, and Bill Deal and the Rondells. "It had to have horns in it, a Hammond B3, and it had to sound black and anthemic," Hayward said.

In 1965, Hayward's band made a small-scale recording in Cleveland, Ohio, at Audio Recorders in the basement of the same television studio where the Mike Douglas talk show was being broadcast live. "There's a cool story that goes along with our arrival," Hayward said amusedly. "Freddie and the Dreamers were scheduled to appear on the Mike Douglas show the day we were there. We had just driven across country from New York where we had signed with an agent, we'd made a trip thing of this. We arrived with two carloads of instruments, maybe three, and looking like musicians. Upon getting out of the car, we were mobbed by . . . screaming teenage girls. They thought we were Freddie and the Dreamers." (Cleveland obviously had not diminished its rock and roll fervor since the days when Bobby Wood had gotten similar treatment there.) With a New York booking agent and a small-time record already appearing on the charts in some places, it appeared that the Fourivis Four were just about to make the next step from a regional to a national band when Hayward and several of the others were drafted.

"It's funny—I was in Canada, on tour, when I got my notice," he recalled. "I could have stayed up there, but I didn't want to. For some reason, I thought, when I was older and my children would ask me 'What did you do in those days?' I didn't want to tell them that I had not honored my obligation." Though at first the draft looked like a bad twist of fate, interrupting a promising career, his time in the Air Force led him to the discovery that changed his life.

He was stationed at the Air Force base in Blytheville, Arkansas, and frequent listening to local radio led him to a powerful FM station broadcasting from Memphis, just over the river. "The DJs would play all the records coming out of Memphis and talk about all the studios—Stax, American, and Hi," he recalled. "They seemed to have a lot of inside information. They'd talk about the big-name artists who were cutting in town—you know, they'd say 'Wilson Pickett is in and he's cutting at American' or 'Paul Revere and the Raiders are here,' and they'd talk about American and Chips Moman. I'd say, 'When I get out of the service, I'm going to Memphis and get involved at a studio somewhere. I don't care if I have to sweep the floors, I just want to work in a Memphis recording studio and be a part of that.'" In the meantime, he organized and led a band called the Little Green Thing which played Top Forty and soul hits at some of the local clubs; though Hayward was unhappy with the level of musicianship in the band, tapes of it reveal that it was much better than the usual groups that could have been heard in roadhouses of the era. "We played locally, and in the boot heel of Missouri, they knew about us too. It was a pretty hip band for the area, it was a fairly country-ized area but we had a white R&B band, we could just about guarantee a full house in any nightclub in the area we played at because of the hipness of the band. The clientele came from the base and they were just anxious to hear anything other than country music. Country music wasn't too hip at that time."

Day trips to Memphis made him familiar with the city. "It was big; it looked like a city, and there were symphonies and museums and things like that which are offered by a city, but it felt like a small town. It really had this kind of rural feel." On one of those trips he met Stan Kesler, standing outside the Sun studios on Union, and he and Stan struck up a slight acquaintance. His occasional conversations with Stan further heightened his desire to become a part of Memphis music. Being stationed near Memphis when so much was happening there, he had a chance to observe bits of history in the making, as he did one night in December 1967. "I was at the American Airlines freight terminal when I saw all these broken instruments coming in—and the guy said it was Otis Redding's band's instruments, the plane had crashed." His communications group patrolled the streets of Memphis for several days following the spring 1968 riots after Martin Luther King was killed.

At around the same time, he took the Little Green Thing into Sonic Studios and, with Roland Janes presiding, cut an inexpensive demo just to document the work of the band. Watching Roland Janes at work in the control room was as inspiring to Hayward as listening to records had been. He had always been fascinated by electronics and the dimensions of sound, and now he aspired to become a record producer. "I was a record buyer, a producer from a listener's standpoint," he said. He was and would remain a voracious collector: of records, books, electronic equipment, guns. And all the while, he was eagerly counting the days until he could be out of the service and get on with his ambitions.

He was transferred to Guam in mid-1968, a year he spoke of forever after as "the worst of my life." He had been separated from his band and from access to what was going on in Memphis, and the love of his life had just broken off with him, plunging him into an uncharacteristic depression. "I don't think many people understand how heartache can devastate one," he reflected (at times he himself seemed not to understand it). His new assignment in a supply unit which sometimes involved driving transport allowed him to see the ravages of war up close. "I was in a military situation where we were support for Vietnam. I was getting the realness of the war, as close as you can come without being in the front lines," he said somberly. He requested and received a transfer back to Blytheville to finish his hitch. Upon being mustered out in early 1969, he worked for a few weeks as a disc jockey in Monette, Arkansas, launching him on a lifelong fascination with radio announcing, and in June of that year headed with his new wife Donna for Memphis.

His trips to Memphis music shops had acquainted him with a stereo store owned and operated by the Stuber family, and he had often chatted with the owner when he stopped by there. "It was on Union Avenue, a respected business in the Memphis community . . . it was a father-and-son operation, and the father sold pianos on the lower level of the store. The lower level was a grandiose hall, about halfway back was a staircase that went up to the upper level." Ernie Stuber, who handled the stereo side of the operation at the upper level of the store, mentioned in a casual conversation with Hayward that he would like to add a recording studio setup to his business, cashing in on the boom in Memphis music. "I was sort of aspiring out loud what I really wanted to do and as I was aspiring to him, I think he saw me as somebody who could make his dream come true. He said, 'Could you do it here?' I thought for about two seconds and I said, 'Sure.'" Hayward clerked in the stereo store while he worked on the building, turning three empty rooms originally used for storage into what he remembered as a "decent little recording facility." It attracted the notice of the electronic shop's frequent customer Bill Cantrell, who had founded Hi Records and still bought stereo equipment for its operation. Cantrell befriended the young studio designer and served as an unofficial mentor. "He liked the idea that I was taking that venture on," said Hayward. "He kind of took me under his wing."

With suggestions from Cantrell and his own ingenuity, Hayward remembered, "The studio came together in three months. It worked beautifully." But then Stuber decided he did not want a studio after all. The store proprietor had not reckoned with aspiring players coming to his setup and hanging out until all hours, and he felt they were disrupting the business. He closed the studio and let Hayward go. "There was this shyster in Memphis, he came from a radio background, he convinced Ernie that he could make them more money than I could.... That was kind of like my Stax experience," the drummer recalled, referring to Chips's having developed a promising business for an owner only to be summarily fired. But as he so often would do, Hayward landed on his feet.

He took a day job at York Arms, a sporting goods store in Memphis. "That was the store that sold James Earl Ray the rifle with which he killed Martin Luther King," Hayward noted sadly. Nothing of note happened while he was there; he stood behind the counter and observed. "I was not enjoying working at the store at all. I just wasn't a jock and never had been... I did find out where high-school coaches go in the afternoon," he laughed. "They go to sporting-goods stores and hang around and tell stories." He found a better job at W&W Distributing, another Memphis electronics store. Through Bob Tucker, who came to that store now and then—"He was professorin' at Memphis State," said Hayward—the aspiring musician found out about the Bill Black Combo. To ever-diminishing notice following the departure of Reggie Young and Bobby Emmons, Tucker was still releasing instrumental recordings under the Bill Black name for the Hi label. To the surprise of Tucker and practically everyone else, the Combo had just recorded an instrumental version of Paul Simon's "Keep the Customer Satisfied" that was on the charts, and the group was in demand for weekend shows at small clubs and theaters in Arkansas and Mississippi. Hayward landed a job as drummer with the Combo and even played on the album quickly assembled to capitalize on their hit. The album was recorded at Lyn-Lou, and from that experience Hayward became acquainted with the studio head Larry Rogers, whom he remembered warmly.

As did Bill Cantrell, Bob Tucker and Larry Rogers both gave Hayward encouragement at a time when many people were laughing at the newcomer's open desire to become a part of the Memphis scene. During the time he had been putting the studio together for Ernie Stuber, Hayward had bought several Neumann microphones at a shop owned by a man named Weldon Jetton, and Jetton had told him point-blank to forget about working in music. "He said, 'Do yourself a favor. Get out of the business right now. You'll never make it.'" (Two years later, at the Memphis Music Awards, Hayward walked past Weldon Jetton's table with the rest of the American group, as they accepted an award for outstanding musical contributions.)

Bob Tucker mentioned to Hayward that Tommy Cogbill was scouting about for an assistant engineer at American. For all that he had heard American Studios mentioned over the radio for years, Hayward had no idea who Tommy Cogbill was; Chips Moman had gotten all the attention. Bob Tucker called Tommy and told him that he had met a young man who wanted to work in a recording studio; Tommy said, "Send him over."

"The first night me and Tommy met, we were arguing—I was implying and he was definitely stating," said Hayward. "Tommy hadn't met me before and I didn't have any background on Tommy. The evening I went over to talk to Tommy, Red West was recording Richard Mainegra on a song called 'Feelin' Bad.' And Red West monitored louder than I had ever heard in my life, there had to be 120 decibels coming out of that monitor system. . . . Red had those A7s blistering in the control room and Tommy had to yell to make himself heard." Tommy and Hayward were talking in the small anteroom on the other side of the control room: they could hear the music thundering through the walls. "Tommy and I were talking above our normal voices so it sounded like we were yelling at each other anyway, just to hear each other," the drummer continued. "Tommy was trying to explain what 'feel' was, trying to get me to understand . . . that this was the most important thing on a record . . . and I was talking about sound—Tommy and I were talking about the same thing. Tommy thought I was arguing with him. Tommy and I laughed at this later on." Hayward left the studio believing that his interview had gone badly—"I thought I'd lost the case"—but much to his astonishment, Tommy called him back and said that Chips would like a word with him. When he went back to American, however, he found not Chips waiting for him, but Marty Lacker, whom Hayward described as being "very intimidating."

"He said, 'Why do you want to work here?' I said, 'Well, I used to be intimidated by you record people, now I want to be one of you.' I think he got a kick out of that." Marty talked to Chips, Chips gave his consent, and Hayward was in. "I started at American on March 20, 1970."

The first people he remembered seeing, aside from Tommy Cogbill and Marty Lacker, were his fellow late arrivals. "Johnny Christopher stuck his head in the door of the studio and I thought, 'Where did this preppie come from?' He had the madras shirt, the loafers, all of that." He met Glen Spreen came in the control room when Glen came in to play back a tape of a track he was arranging. "Glen was like absolutely the stereotypical hippie, he wore sandals, a tie-dyed T-shirt, and bell bottoms, and he wore little round wire-rim glasses." The core group seemed blurred to him at first, though Mike Leech quickly emerged as a friend and ally, in the same way he had been to Ed Kollis. "Hayward's arrival on the scene was fun," said Mike warmly. "He was one funny man. We hung out quite a bit together and had some good times."

Bobby Wood devised the stunt for Hayward's official welcome (although he did not remember). "It was the first day. The first day was kind of a floating thing. They were sorta pattin' me on the back, 'Hey, welcome,' that kind of thing. They invited me to have lunch with them at the Ranch House restaurant," Hayward recalled. "We were sittin' at one of those big round tables. I picked up my glass of tea and there was Bobby Wood's glass eye. I think Bobby said, 'Here's lookin' at you.' I think I drank the glass of tea, I don't remember. . . . It spoiled the whole joke. That might have been my downfall." Hayward may have overstated the case; the turning point for him, when he became the second black sheep of the American family, did not happen until several years later, after the group had moved to Atlanta. But he was right about the wariness with which the group regarded him—a wariness that, as with Glen Spreen, would never go away.

"They had an impression of me, which was a non-impression," he recalled. From childhood he had been aware of bullying and slights, so he was more conscious than Glen or Johnny Christopher had been about the way the core group (except for Tommy Cogbill and Reggie Young) regarded latecomers to their scene. The American group were used to people being bowled over on first meeting by their reputation and their ability; they did not know how to take the attitude of a soundman who was respectful but not cowed. "I did not feel sub-prestige at the time," Hayward said. "The one person I would have been intimidated by would have been Tommy Cogbill. . . . Tommy right off the bat was a kind of mystery man. I grew to see that Tommy was cool, there was this cool presence that I noticed right away. I had to fight off an awestruckness every time I was around Tommy." Hayward had, of course, already been around Memphis music a little when he arrived at American, and "I wasn't quite as intimidated as I would have been"; rather, from the beginning he looked about for the chance to see what he could contribute. "I wasn't a threat to anybody, but wherever I go, I have to be somebody that people will know," he said.

His first assignment was to sequence, in the order Chips requested, the tracks for B.J. Thomas's album *Raindrops Keep Falling on My Head*. He also served as tape editor. "It sounds like a bigger job than what it is," he explained. "I just took a razor blade and sliced off the countdowns and things. [Another] one of my engineering duties was to set up demos when the writers wanted to do something." His first demo was for the writer Billy McKnight. Writers' demos would be "sometimes just guitar/vocals, sometimes a full band," said Richard Mainegra. "Sometimes a song was pitched live, sometimes the demo was played. In the early years I was in Nashville, it was very common to walk across the street with your guitar and play live for a producer who was lookin' for songs for an artist. Today most writers record elaborate demos of their songs, sometimes creating better demos than the eventual records themselves. But you'd never tell the producer that.

"The demos we did at American were for the most part just guitar-piano-vocals," Mainegra continued. "And sometimes one or two of the American group would be walkin' through the studio, hear somethin' they liked, and out of the goodness of their hearts, run out and play somethin' neat." For his own demos, he continued, "Red West was usually in charge behind the board," but Hayward would be engineering, and through setting up writers' demos Hayward came to know and be familiar with the vocal skills of both Richard Mainegra and Rick Yancey.

Another of Hayward's tasks was, as it had been for his predecessors, simply to run the tape recorder, keeping it operating while Chips concentrated on the music. Chips signaled his engineers with hand gestures and, of course, it took a little while for a newcomer to read his signals properly. Mike Leech recalled an incident while Hayward was learning. "He sat on a stool, and when you looked into the control room, Chips was in the middle at the controls, and Hayward on the left, at the tape machine, poised, ready to record, play back, flag takes. . . We were in the middle of a take, when I glanced up to see Chips grinning, like he did when something good was happening. He looked up over at Hayward, and nodded, like 'ain't this cool.' Hayward thought he was signaling to him to stop the tape, which he did. The ensuing conversation between them from what we could gather looking through the glass was, 'why did you stop the tape?' 'I thought you said for me to.' And back and forth. Very very funny. Don't know if Hayward remembers that or not." "That did happen," Hayward recalled with amused exasperation. "Chips was indoctrinating me into his hand signals. His hand signals were all the same—whatever he meant for it to mean. He'd just stick his hand up halfway in the air. Mike fell out laughing, he thought it was hilarious."

To ease his way into the new environment, Hayward behaved as he had done throughout his life, playing the class clown in order to get noticed and accepted. "That Hayward was a character," Gene Chrisman chuckled. "I thought he was hilarious as a comic," chortled Bobby Emmons. "He had some of the funniest routines I've ever seen." "Sometimes to get things going in the studio, Chips would have him do one of his routines," said Richard

Mainegra delightedly. "One of the funniest was to see this tall, lanky fellow stoop upon the top of one of the big studio speakers and act like a big disgusting vulture. . . Wings flappin', jumpin' from foot to foot and screamin' his head off. You just had to be there . . . and fortunately, I was." Hayward also did a pantomime routine imitating a window washer. "The window washer routine was great!" Mike Leech exclaimed happily. "He would pretend there was a window, spray some imaginary Windex on a cloth, begin wiping, and as the imaginary spray dried, would start squeaking. Hilarious!" "Everybody really got into it," Hayward recalled. "I'd act like I was gonna fall and you'd hear everybody in the room gasp and go 'oh,' they were so into it with me." He also did a routine about a dog getting a bone caught in its throat, complete with sound effects.

"One night it was just me, Chips, and Hayward [who were there]," Mike Leech remembered. "Chips and I were in the control room listening to something when a small American flag appeared on the left side of the glass (between the booth and the room), waving. Chips and I cracked up. Then, a few minutes later, it appeared on the right side, which we also thought was funny. Then, several minutes later, it appeared at the top, in the center of the glass. Now that was hilarious! We never knew how he managed to get up there, because we never saw him, just the flag. That's the kind of stuff Hayward pulled all the time, which I loved. Hay and I also had a slow-motion 'boxing match,' that was funny. I would slo-mo 'hit' him on the jaw, and it would take him minutes to fall." Another time running the tapes in the control room, Chips ordered the new soundman to "flag that take," meaning mark it for later use. Hayward produced from somewhere a miniature American flag and stuck it in the reel of tape.

According to the soundman, much of his clowning was deliberate, designed to break the ice and get everyone in the mood to work, which is why Chips often utilized that skill before sessions began. "Some of these guys have baggage on the session, wife, girlfriend problems," Hayward explained, adding that the musicians needed to be disarmed and brought together on the same page to make the best recording. Occasionally he overdid it; his brashness made some of the musicians at American think twice. "It was funny at first, but then it got old," said Gene Chrisman. "He was probably right," Hayward conceded. Still, he was where he wanted to be, handling the sound for one of the top studios in Memphis. It was like giving a child his own key to a candy store.

His position as assistant engineer gave him a vantage point unlike any other at American, and though he never showed it, he was in awe of Chips and Tommy from the beginning. "I got as close to pedestalizing as I ever had in my life," he said of his initial impressions. "The band were just old country guys. I thought they were all smart. There was kind of an unspoken consensus that the smartest person around there was Wayne Carson. There didn't seem to be any grandstanding anywhere. If there was any grandstanding to be done, it was probably me. They didn't get in each other's way, they were all so respectful of each other."

His job also gave him a chance to observe Chips Moman at close range. "Being Chips's assistant engineer, I watched the man for eighteen hours and I could hear a different side of it," he observed. "Right at the very front I was amazed at his being King Chips and then I wondered how he got to be that way." One reason, he concluded, was the technical and engineering skills Chips possessed. "When it came to tape editing with a blade, Chips Moman is the absolute best there is!" Hayward exclaimed admiringly. "I've been with him when he had as many as eight to ten one-eighth to one-fourth slivers all laid out next to the chopping block—he knew what was on each tiny piece. He would assemble, disassemble, reassemble, until he had what he wanted. I saw the splices, but could not hear or detect them on playback! An amazing talent."

Chips, Hayward discovered, was a man very aware of himself and of the effect he created, even though the producer appeared not to be. "I always picture Chips wearing a white or blue T-shirt with a cigarette pocket. He was always smoking, and sometimes he'd bum a cigarette off me. I can still hear him, 'Got a cigarette, Haywit?' [the drummer lapsed into an imitation of Chips' Elvis-influenced mumble]. He was proud of his reputation, proud of that gambling thing." Glen Spreen agreed with that assessment. "Chips told us one time about a guy he knew back in Georgia who would go to the outskirts of town and say, 'I'll bet that five-mile marker sign is wrong, it's really a four-mile marker, what do you want to bet?' Somebody'd bet him about five dollars. He'd go out then and move the signs. Chips was happy to know that guy." "Chips, a gambler? You bet, hence the name," assented Mike Leech. "For a living? Not really, but I think during some of his 'down' times he hustled pool. . . . Chips once told me that he would never go a day without earning or winning at least one dollar." "That's how Chips got his nickname, he was in the money," Don Crews said in a valedictory to his former partner. Many of the gambling stories centered around the private racetrack at Chips's farm and the events he hosted there. "I had people from thirteen states comin' in every Sunday afternoon to race," he said nostalgically. Hayward had never been much of a gambler, and the stories Chips told as the two of them sat in the control room offered him another outlook on life entirely.

But from the beginning, Hayward's touchstone for the group, as it would be for so many, was Tommy Cogbill. "I don't know what Tommy saw in me," he reflected. "He encouraged me and lifted me up from the start. Our relationship was a unique combination of fatherly, big-brotherly love and one of close personal friendship." It was a role Tommy filled for many of the others as well. "Tommy was the undisputed papa of us all," added Hayward. "Tommy was a good person. Tommy could get things done because he had the good reasons and the heart." Johnny Christopher, who was himself still in wide-eyed awe of everyone after his first year there, agreed with that assessment. "That was the thing about Tommy, he had such a great heart," said Johnny fervently. "Tommy was one of a kind—I loved the man. I feel like Tommy was God's gift to music." Donnie Fritts, who was still a frequent visitor at

American when he came to town, echoed the thought. "He was such an innovative cat on the bass. Very easygoing guy. . . . It was all just like a family."

The Don Crews lawsuit was hurting the family environment of the studio quite a bit, Hayward thought; he was sensitive to the tension around the place and the feeling that something was not right, even though he did not fully understand what it was. Most of the others knew no more details of the lawsuit than Hayward (although, being the new kid on the block, he thought for years that they knew something he did not). Chips seldom talked business with any of the musicians other than Tommy Cogbill, and neither he nor Tommy were exactly the type to confide. "Working for Chips, we were never made privy to any of the higher-ups' activity. Like it wasn't any of our business," said Mike Leech. "On several occasions there would be honcho meetings in the control room. We weren't told to keep out, but we were never invited in, and we were supposed to be stockholders in the company (never happened)." Both Hayward Bishop and Mike Leech recalled that the siege mentality was in high gear around the studio at the time, and that Crews was routinely demonized. Bobby Wood conceded the siege mentality and the groupthink that was commonplace among the musicians but passed it off as naïveté. "We just basically did what Chips suggested, we were young bucks and didn't know about the record business," he said.

Chips was making it all up as he went along, too, although the musicians did not seem to be aware of that fact due to the authority with which Chips carried himself, as a king among equals. "You know what I followed???? My nose," Chips said emphatically. "Wherever it took me, that's where I'd go." He had gotten far on his gambler's instincts, and he had no reason to think his instincts would not serve him well now. He had a new business manager, a new record deal, a new soundman for the studio, and even a new love as a new decade began.

And, Chips and the group were all sure, things could only get even better.

### CHAPTER 21

# Just Can't Help Believing

B.J. Thomas had come to American during a lull in his career, but was now one of the top singers in the country due to his hit recording of the Burt Bacharach movie theme, "Raindrops Keep Falling on My Head." According to Glen Spreen, Chips Moman was more than a little miffed that the man he considered to be *his* singer had gotten his biggest hit with someone else. The pairing of Scepter's best-known male singer with the label's staff arranger/composer made sense from the viewpoint of the suits, however. "Scepter also ran the management company that managed B.J., it was win-win-win," observed Glen Spreen amusedly. "Chips was very possessive, and he was also very insecure." B.J. Thomas was also insecure, and his work with Bacharach in New York ceased abruptly. In B.J.'s memoirs he said that the collaboration fell apart when Bacharach made a comment in the studio about the way recording was done in Memphis that B.J. took as a slur against Southerners. The signs of trouble had been apparent even during the recording of "Raindrops," when B.J. sang his lilting run on the final line of the song. It was improvised, and according to Glen Spreen, "Bacharach gave him a dirty look."

Chips Moman would not have; he would have been delightedly caught up in the moment and loved the creativity, which is why B.J. was happy to return to American. "Everybody's Out of Town," featuring a Hal David fantasy lyric about being the last person alive after some unnamed disaster, was the last record from the team of Bacharach, David, and Thomas. "We knew it wasn't a hit; too negative," said Glen Spreen flatly. It was also the title track of B.J.'s spring 1970 album from Scepter, though the bulk of the album's recording was done at American, with only two of the tracks from the Burt Bacharach session in New York. (A third Bacharach recording, "Send My Picture to Scranton, PA"—featuring an effective how-do-you-like-me-now lyric from Hal David—appeared on the B-side of "I Just Can't Help Believing.")

B.J.'s return to American was not auspicious. "They all came down with some sort of flu," Glen Spreen remembered. Mike Leech and Gene Chrisman were there throughout the sessions, but Reggie Young and Bobby Wood missed a few days, and Bobby Emmons was out altogether. Glen Spreen played the Hammond B3 in Emmons's place, and he remembered Spooner Oldham being temporarily back in town and coming in to substitute for Wood. (Spooner himself did not remember, but he did recall flying back to Memphis a time or two during that period, during which time he and Dan Penn finished writing their classic "A Woman Left Lonely.") Glen also thought that Wayne Carson had filled in for Reggie Young, though the songwriter had no memory of it. Although Mike Leech played bass for the entire session, Tommy Cogbill was also present as a listener. A photo taken at the sessions shows Tommy and Reggie Young looking through the glass into the control room, both leaning on the small control-room ledge like patrons at a bar. Reggie is in the foreground, his elbow propped up on the ledge as he glowers into the camera; with his curly hair, aviator glasses, and thin face, he resembled an annoyed Jerry Lee Lewis. Tommy is further away from the camera's view; he was wearing a suede jacket and had begun to grow thin sideburns. He is staring down at his folded arms and appears to be listening intently to the playback; he looks small and preoccupied.

The Bacharach influence carried over into the B.J. sessions, said Glen Spreen. "Bacharach really inspired us to step it up a notch," and despite the absence of a few key people, the mood seemed confident. The album begins with "Everybody's Talking," another movie theme, featured in that winter's hit *Midnight Cowboy* and

given a thoughtful treatment by Chips; it features incisive piano fills and an uncharacteristically somber tone in B.J.'s voice. At the end of the recording, Toni Wine is barely audible, humming the melody that had been the string line in the Harry Nilsson version. Chips had always used this technique but began to rely on it more and more as the sound of the American group became defined: stray bits leap out of the mix, whether from Toni's voice, Reggie Young's guitar, or Bobby Emmons's Hammond B3, so that no matter how many times one listens to a Chips Moman production, a new sound can be heard to delight the ear all over again.

The album is sequenced so that the Bacharach title tune follows "Everybody's Talking," and then returns to the American sound for Mark James's dramatic "The Mask." Gene Chrisman's whipcracking drums and Mike Leech's ominous rumble on the bass signals that we are in dark, brooding territory, as B.J. delivers the tale of a man who knows his lover is seeing someone else; he knows because she is suddenly cold to him, going through the motions in love and life. Only Loretta Lynn's "When the Tingle Becomes a Chill" addresses the topic of emotional and physical frigidity as openly; and as with the Lynn composition, there is a grimness that evokes mechanistic lovemaking. To listen to this record is to shudder; once again Chips and the American group had described cold, harsh reality for all time.

It is a tribute to the quality of the songs on this album that even a song as well written as "The Mask" sounds like filler when compared to the next track. Barry Mann and Cynthia Weil's "I Just Can't Help Believing" was already a great pop song, but the combination of B.J.'s expressive voice, Chips Moman's elegant production, and the inventive playing of the musicians made it special. Glen Spreen remembered that it had been done in two nights' worth of work. "Sometimes we did three takes and that was it. 'Cause we knew. Musically, you can tell, and musically means emotionally," he said.

The result is one of the most euphoric, optimistic tracks ever produced by Chips, and the song shimmers with the incandescent glow of newfound love. Toni Wine underscores her intentions in the album version when she echoes B.J. on the line "This time the girl is gonna stay": significantly, Chips edited out her comment when he tinkered with the single, changing the mix a little and overdubbing some intricate classical-sounding countermelodies over the string line.

The creation of the string line is somewhat obscure, with the memories of both Mike Leech and Glen Spreen not fully weighing in on the matter. Mike believed at first that he had written the arrangement alone, then in further reflection was sure that at least some portion of it had fallen to Glen. Glen said that he conceived the original string line around Spooner Oldham's three-note keyboard run, heard immediately after B.J. Thomas sings, "And my heart beats with the rhythm of her sighs"; the keyboard run is a leitmotif through the remaining verses as well. The original string arrangement, heard on the album version, is smooth, sounding almost effortless; the overdubbed version heard on the single is dark and complicated, more melodically interesting, as Glen was aware. "It had some build, the first one just laid there," he said. The new string line offers the one hint of melancholy in an otherwise optimistic and bright production.

The single release also featured, for the first time, percussion from the American group's new sound engineer. When Hayward Bishop was hired, Chips initially did not know that he was a drummer; the fact came out in casual conversations when the two were simply running tracking sessions as Chips played the song and decided where the overdubs should go. "I'll tell you the story, and it's a short broad story," Hayward said. He could not recall the exact sequence of events, but at some point they were listening to the piece and Chips said casually, "Can you play a tambourine? Why don't you put a tambourine on it, Hayward?" The question may have been raised as simple curiosity, a way of finding out what the new man could do; with no direction other than that, Hayward picked up a tambourine and walked into the studio. "The little back bathroom is where the percussion overdubs always were," he said. "The acoustics were all concrete. It was little,

dingy, with a twenty-watt light bulb way up high." With the track being fed to him over the earphones, Hayward played, and Chips made it apparent he liked it and wanted Hayward to contribute to a few more of the already finished tracks. "Gene and I shared percussion parts and sometimes played together," said Hayward, and that would be the case from then on.

Hayward is featured on the American Group's version of the Junior Walker hit, "What Does It Take." The original Motown version of the song was slow, elegant, bewildered-sounding; here, the group stays close to the pattern of the original arrangement but speeds up the tempo a little, capturing a rush of feeling. B.J. shouts the lyric as Hayward's tambourine rattles spiritedly behind him, keeping pace every step of the way with Gene Chrisman's racing rhythm, Mike Leech's bouncy-sounding bass, and the hard-driving saxophone solos by Andrew Love of the Memphis Horns. Hayward said he had been specifically trying for a Motown sound on his early percussion efforts, and his Detroit stylings fit perfectly with an actual song from Berry Gordy's organization.

"Oh Me Oh My" was a spontaneous recording, according to B.J. Thomas. "Chips was late, we got bored, and said, hell, let's do something." The song they chose while killing time is one of the most underrated Bee Gees ballads, originally recorded in Muscle Shoals by Maurice Gibb's then-wife, the Scottish singer Lulu. It features a sophisticated lyric worthy of Bacharach and David, evoking elegant restaurants and intimate conversations, staging a ballet on a table top and the genies evoked by the wisp of cigarette smoke. It is meant to be played on a Sunday night after a good meal and a little wine. The record as finished, with Chips Moman overseeing its final construction, evokes both Glen Spreen's admiration of the work written by the Gibb brothers—"I used to like the Bee Gees back then, I did a lot of their stuff. I don't know why I never got a hit with any of it"—and the giddy delight of a new love affair.

For all the beauty of the recording, Glen Spreen was unhappy with the results when he listened to it again years later. His string line, he opined, was less than perfect. "My strings, number one, were not syncopated. I fell into a boring groove," he said critically. "There just weren't any dynamics." He considered the track a misfire, although B.J. gave the lyric a passionately heartfelt sound, ranging from a tender whisper in the verses to a full-throated gospel wail on the chorus. Glen's high standards for an arrangement were identical to the standards already touted by Tommy Cogbill and Chips: "My goal was to complement, create, elevate, but, as the oath says, first do no harm." In retrospect he did not view Tommy Cogbill as especially exacting. "He was subtle and pretty much laid back when we were in the studio," mused the arranger. "I think he expected a lot, like the very best. As long as he was convinced that this was the very best he was quiet. Although, even if it wasn't he would be subtle and take a teacher-like approach. He would question me into arriving at a conclusion that showed I knew what he was looking for." Mike Leech found Chips to be "teacher-like" in a different way: "He had a commanding personality that made you feel like you were being sent to the principal's office when certain things came up." Chips could be formidable, but he preferred a relaxed environment in the studio; even as he sat behind the board directing the musicians, he laughed and joked with them, and gave free rein to his natural mischievousness.

Mark James's "Created for a Man" is another piece evocative of Mark's muse, and its subject matter, a loving woman, likely held special resonance for Chips at this time and may have influenced his selecting the song. The song also calls to mind the steadfast loyalty of B.J.'s beautiful wife Gloria, who stood faithfully by him throughout his struggles with drug addiction. (Gloria was photographed with B.J. on the album covers for both *Young and In Love* and *Raindrops*, the latter re-creating the bicycling scene between Robert Redford and Katherine Ross.) Chips recycled Wayne Carson's "Sandman" from 1968, and again it is no accident. This time the lyric about a ferociously independent man toppled like a mighty oak by love has less to do with Wayne's passion for his then-wife Bridget than it does Chips's utter devastation at one look from Toni Wine: "As strong as

stone, I stood alone, depending only on myself / And suddenly my eyes fell on you / And with a smile, you conquered me."

If Toni has been a shadow presence on several of the songs, she emerges clearly in the album's finale, "Bridge over Troubled Waters." With its themes of sorrow, redemption, and pain, this Paul Simon masterwork should have been a natural for Chips to record; there are infinite nuances of melody and countermelody in the song that he could have brought to the fore (as he later did in a majestic version for Willie Nelson). Instead, he does not seem interested in the content at all. He allows Bobby Wood, on electric piano, to race through a melody line that begs for an acoustic grand. The track sounds perfunctory and distracted, as if Chips is only in the studio because he has to be. Nothing seems to take hold of his imagination until the introduction to the final verse, when all of a sudden he connects startlingly with the song; he is in focus, and it is such a change that the listener sits up and takes notice.

One soon learns why. "Sail on, silver girl," B.J. croons softly, and he is answered by an immediate wordless, semi-operatic vocal from Toni Wine. She becomes the silver bird of hope, hovering over Chips and gently guiding him away from his eternal despair. It is both touching and heartbreaking to hear.

If Chips's feelings for Toni are stunning on record, they were no less so for the group and its support staff to watch in person. "God, I hate to even say it; you'd better let the guys tell that one," said Ima Roberts ruefully. "That was a train wreck waiting to happen." Marty Lacker felt that Chips was put through many emotional changes during his time with the songwriter, and added, "Toni turned out to be the typical domineering Jewish woman—and I can say that because I'm Jewish." From the beginning, Chips gave Toni the power to sway his moods; Hayward Bishop, in the control room, remembered Toni calling the studio from New York, reaching Chips in the middle of sessions, and Chips putting his feet up on the console and tilting back his chair to talk to her, not even bothering to signal to the musicians out on the studio floor to stop playing and take a break. The conversations could last an hour or two, and during that time the musicians busied themselves with endless rounds of poker or tonk. "We played tonk for quarters. I [once] won five dollars in quarters. We were tonkin' our butts off," laughed Hayward. Then Chips would emerge from the control room, pleasantly distracted and unable to concentrate, not willing to plunge himself into the despondency from which he created his best work. After talking to her, recording music about despair was an emotional trip he could not bring himself to take, so the sessions were called off and everyone ordered to reassemble another day.

She could be just as distracting when she was there. Both Hayward Bishop and Mike Leech remembered that when she was in the studio, she behaved toward these Southern exotics with whom she worked as if she were Dorothy in Oz. She had obviously never seen anything like this group of good old boys before—Hayward Bishop remembered that she even brought her mother down from New York on one occasion so that her mother could meet them. Everything that the musicians did or said was amazing to her. If she heard one of the group come up with something funny—Bobby Emmons, for instance, whose specialty was indirect wordplay—she yelled delightedly about it in her New York–accented voice that struck these soft-spoken Southern boys as a macaw scream. "Ohmigawwd," they recalled her proclaiming, "ohmigawd, Chips, did you *heah*, did you heah what Bobby just said? He's brilliant, I tell you, he's *brilliant*—" Chips, of course, was used to Bobby's asides, so he would shrug it off. "No no *no*, Chips, you gotta *lissen*, you gotta *heah* what Bobby just said, he's brilliant."

"I think her 'brilliant' observations were used to make us think we were really something," said Mike Leech. Hayward Bishop concurred. "Toni's role was to be The Spotter Of Brilliance. And if she could identify the brilliance when she saw it, then that made her brilliant too." It's likely that Toni saw her astonished praise as another way to ingratiate herself. If so, said Glen Spreen, it was not working. "Everyone caught on to what she was doing—even me," he chuckled wryly. "Drawing conclusions is one thing she did not do well. She said things that the rest of us wouldn't. She was just too blunt." The musicians took a diplomatic approach, for example, to the shortcomings of the songs, but Toni, in keeping with the way these things were reviewed in New York, would burst out with, "That song is a dog!!"

"I think Toni was taken with the fact that she was formally trained and used to working with people who were highly educated in music, who had put in so much time and worked so hard to become qualified, and that she walks in on a bunch of guys who seemed to be totally unarmed, yet had this amazing track record," observed Bobby Emmons. "The reason I can discount some of the other theories of her intentions is that hey, she married the leader of the outfit. If she was laughing up her sleeve at us, she would never have done that."

"I don't think Toni was intentionally doing things to bring out the negatives; however, the effect was noticed," Glen Spreen observed. "For example, if we were in a social place, like a restaurant, and someone would say something in a kidding way about another person in the group, Toni would latch on to that and conclude that all was not paradise at American. In other words, [she thought] that we were acting out a charade of friendship and group admiration." Glen and Hayward Bishop, independently of each other, both suspected that Toni was reporting to Chips what was said or done when he could not be around. "If we said something, she would analyze it, and then go back to Chips with her analysis, and I could see her doing it," said the arranger. "I thought she was fast, I thought she was intelligent, but she was aiming at the wrong things." Tommy Cogbill was not around her very often. "I don't have a mental image of ever seeing Chips, Toni, and Cogbill in the same room—ever," said Mike Leech. "Not that he wasn't but it would be a rare occasion. Tommy, after digesting what he saw, not just Chips and Toni, would pay attention for awhile till he made a decision as to whether or not it was worth his time, then give a little inhale, sniff or snort, close his lips tightly, gather himself up and head out (fast). That's the best description I can give of his disappearing act."

Tommy developed a new part of his persona at the beginning of 1970. From somewhere, and for reasons he never explained, he began incorporating duck quacks into his conversations. The quacks became so closely identified with the bassist that after Tommy's death Bobby Emmons kept a toy stuffed duck on his desk at home as a remembrance of his friend. Hayward Bishop thought the idea may have come from a record by the jazz trio Young-Holt Unlimited in which each line of the song was punctuated with a slurred "wack-wack." The quacks became one of the things everyone remembered most about Tommy, noting how he would look into the studio, see that nothing was happening and try to stir things up with a low "Waaack." If no one looked up, he would quack slightly louder. If he got no response, he would quack very loudly, and if there was still no response, he'd chuckle, "Well, you guys are no fun. I'll see you later." And off he'd go. Occasionally, Mike Leech remembered, Tommy stopped in again early in the morning to see what was happening. "We looked rode hard and put up wet sometimes," said Mike amusedly. "And I remember Cog coming in the back door, clean clothes, fresh, bright-eyed, sassy, and ready to rock. We, on the other hand, looked (and probably smelled) like we had been up all night (and probably had been)."

Several projects were ongoing at the time; work was scattered among several artists. Chips was still working on overdubs for the Petula Clark album. Tommy Cogbill was recording Shadden the King Lears for his new label. And most prominently, the New York songwriters Bobby Weinstein and Jon Stroll, who had written "Sweet Cream Ladies" and "Goodnight Sweet Dreams," came down to do a record of their own on Chips's new label. Capitol was eagerly awaiting the first recordings from Moman and Cogbill, and Chips came out of the gate first like one of the fast sprinters he raced out at his farm.

As with all of the most recent recordings, Chips produced and Glen Spreen was handling the string and horn arrangements. Mike Leech was now the main bass player, Tommy Cogbill having turned his interest more and more to the production and business side of the studio. "He was relieved, I think, because there was someone (me) who could play on hits also and take some heat off. I would play on almost everything unless, sometimes, a song came along that wasn't my cup of tea and Cog would come to the rescue," said Mike Leech. "That was cool because then I could kick back and enjoy watching Tommy. . . . When I played something he liked he would look at me and laugh." Hayward Bishop was still in the control room for the most part, helping Chips with the engineering, but he also overdubbed percussion on several tracks. By now he was not limited to the tambourine; he began bringing his percussion kit bag with him when he came to the studio, and Chips granted him complete freedom to add overdubs with any percussion instruments he wanted. He loved having the chance to experiment, and tailored his percussion parts to fit what the group had already done. "I was trying to not interrupt the formula and be part of the formula," he said of all his work at American. He also now sang backup with Bobby Wood and Johnny Christopher (their voices can be heard on "Roll It Down the Hill," with Hayward doing the high tenor harmony).

It was just as well, thought Hayward, that he could do a few odd chores, for by now he feared his job on the sound crew was in jeopardy. "I was never implanted as an engineer-who-did-all-the-projects kind of engineer," he said. Mike Cauley, whom he had replaced, had been an electronics repairman; although Hayward had educated himself in electronics fairly well by that time, he was no technician, and he only knew how to run the board. He recommended a friend of his from W and W Distributing, Dale Smith, who knew something about equipment repair, and Chips agreed to hire him. "Dale Smith was a good friend, he was real astute at amplifiers," said Hayward. "Dale was hired to do basically what Hayward did, which was to pull some maintenance and file tapes, etc. He was a very nice guy," said Mike Leech. Dale came on board during the Weinstein and Stroll project.

The percussion overdubs Hayward contributed were not apparent on the album opener, the title song "Cook Me Up Your Taste." The title, as well as the remainder of the lyrics, was heavy with double-entendre on the subject of drugs: no surprise, said Glen Spreen with wry sarcasm, because Weinstein and Stroll were "both smokin' a lot." "They sang like they were stoned," added Bobby Wood. It was the first real exposure to chronic stoners the American group had experienced, and most of them found it unsettling but curious, in the same way much of middle America was interpreting pot-smoking by that time. "Around 1970," Hayward Bishop said with a historian's precision, "drug use began to be respectable."

The New Yorkers overlaid their preferences for Cheech and Chong–style in-jokes for dopers atop an already existing Tin Pan Alley sensibility. Unfortunately, the Tin Pan Alley of Weinstein and Stroll's imagination was not the Brill Building of their contemporaries Goffin and King, Mann and Weil, or even Toni Wine; they reverted back to the Alley of 1912, with jerry-built lyrics and flimsy construction. All of that and more is present in the title song. Bobby Weinstein delivers the lyric with inflections reminiscent of Rudy Vallee at his most mannered. On the surface, it seems to be a mock hymn to domesticity: "Cook me up your taste, I've heard that you've become a specialist / Creating peace and harmony," Weinstein intones slyly. After a few bars of this, the song changes into a slow, bombastic declaration of exactly how domestic and devoted the speaker wants the lady to be: "Bake your cake for me / Sleep and wake for me." Following this, Glen Spreen suspends the string line delicately above a soft piano run; he would make an entire generation familiar with that effect when he used it again on Dan Fogelberg's "To the Morning" two years later. From there, the tune segues from a piano lead into a horn-driven, pounding riff featuring Reggie's adventurous, spinning lead line, and the writers, backed by the Moman Tabernacle Choir, shout statements that may or may not be hallucinations before returning to the original "cook me up your taste" theme. Though the shifts of tempo and mood show how quickly the group could change pace, it is

doubtful they would have chosen a song like this if left to their own devices.

Some of them enjoyed the adventure of it. "We've always been on the cutting edge of reaching out and stretching out to expand," Bobby Wood said amiably. "It was another batch of unusual material," mused Bobby Emmons. "It was inspirational to find anything to contribute to it, but I was proud of the finished product." Reggie Young, always the most musically open-minded of the core group, thrived on the challenge of making the record, as he had on the earlier psychedelic album by Joseph Longoria. "I liked them, it was certainly different; they were different," Reggie said with pleasure about the two writers. "It was kind of a shot in the arm." "I liked Weinstein and Stroll. Didn't really get into their music but went along for the ride," said Mike Leech amiably. "These guys ended up being nice folks," Bobby Wood added warmly (Weinstein eventually became an executive with BMI in New York). "At the time, they were a couple of New York hippies." Gene Chrisman remembered them warily as "strange." Chips Moman disagreed, thinking them to be "great people." Glen Spreen found the New York writers to be interesting but he was not happy with the work. "Weinstein was a bit of a business type and Stroll was more of an artist," he said. "I liked the way Jon Stroll played piano. . . [but] some of those songs were way out there." Hayward Bishop had no use for the music at all, scorning the endless drug references in the songs as the "typical nudge-nudge, wink-wink" innuendo that characterized many records of that time.

"The Cat Was a Junkie" takes the innuendo and brings it out into the open in a piece that, with its grim subject matter, fit better with the American Studios style. It is also more structured, with a strong melody and a strictly narrative story line. Ronnie Milsap liked it so well when he heard it that he went into the studio with Chips and did his own version. The song is about a man who discovers that a friend of his has died of an overdose: "I didn't know that the cat was a junkie / He never led me to believe he was anything else but the son of a banker."

The second verse led to a misunderstanding in the studio. Weinstein and Stroll recited some of the symptoms of heroin addiction that should have tipped the narrator off about his friend: "You've got to be highly suspicious / You must be aware of the pupils in size / And food becomes highly delicious." The song's melody is structured in such a way that to sing this line properly it must be slurred, and the reference baffled Bobby Wood. "When they sang they had this drawl that was hard to understand," he remarked. "I was sitting in the control room listening to the playback. . . . After the playback was over I asked, 'What's a froobie?' The guys looked at me like, 'What are you talking about?' I said, 'It sounded like they said, 'Froobies come highly delicious.' Everybody fell out laughing." "I was there when that happened," said Hayward Bishop. "Bobby was sitting on the back of the sofa and he was saying, 'I still don't understand what froobies are.' We let him go on for awhile, you know, what?? I think Mike straightened him out about the lyric. We all just guffawed."

"La Juin" has echoes of the Johnny Christopher instrumental he composed in apparent homage to his wife," "La Jean," but for Weinstein and Stroll it is not a love song to a woman but to a summer's day, as fleeting as it is beautiful. It is the reverse of the Shakespeare poem that begins "Shall I compare thee to a summer's day," and it is a pity that the lyric they devised, with lines such as "Lady life is lead me where I'm led," does not match the originality of the idea. Glen Spreen's string line literally takes the piece from a whisper to a scream, as the soft tones beginning the song give way to the louder, Serge Gainsbourg–influenced chorus (Gainsbourg's fondness for shock and outrage obscured the fact that he had superb melodic gifts) and a neo-Tchaikovskyan crescendo straight out of the classical music the arranger had always loved. Glen said that he, like Mike Leech, never had any trouble getting the sound he sought from the Memphis string players. "I could relate to 'em, yeah, they were easy to talk to, easy to understand," he said reflectively, although he was less formally educated

in technical musical terms than was Mike. "I was lucky because I was self-taught. . . . There were a couple of terms . . . tremolo glissando, I used that a lot. They knew what it meant, what I wanted."

On the Alex Chilton–style rocker "You Can Never Go Back Anymore," Chips guides everyone through the breakneck pace he and Tommy Cogbill perfected for the Box Tops recordings, and the writers come up with some beautiful harmony vocals that are rather wasted on lyrics like "How do you like your vanilla . . . coconuts? / Brother and sister gorilla. . . in a rut." It is especially wasteful because the chorus is rousing and strong; with the addition of some coherent verses, it could have possibly been a hit. The first verse refers to, of all things, bananas, which may have been what Glen Spreen was thinking about when he described the effects of all the pot the writers were smoking: "Everything was just great with them, bananas were just great with them," he said sardonically. "They could be eating a banana and it was the best banana in the world." The musicians had seen strangeness among some of the artists before: Dionne Warwick was interested in psychic phenomena even then, and Timi Yuro had ordered her life by the alignment of the stars, but, Glen observed, "They at least had the ability to make choices. These guys . . . ," and his voice trailed off with a disbelieving chuckle.

"Aunt Birdie Came to Croton" is somewhat incomprehensible; It is ostensibly about an old lady from Pennsylvania who arrives "with her Amish bag of tricks" to do an intervention on her ne'er-do-well nephew, but one is unsure whether Birdie will correct him or whether he will corrupt her. Although Bobby Weinstein says with special glee that Birdie is arriving to "fix what she can *fix*" (the last word uttered with emphasis), we know that she is at least somewhat innocent of what her nephew and his friends are up to; one of them, apparently the narrator, says that she "set fire to my window garden and almost blew her mind." Hayward Bishop was not sure even Weinstein and Stroll knew what any of it was supposed to represent. "They probably wrote halfway and got so stoned they tripped over their own double entendre," he said. "They probably were happy to get two or three drug references in and that was it." The backing track is anything but stoned-sounding; it is focused, sharp, and to the point, featuring some stinging guitar leads from Reggie Young.

"One Long Day" is a slight joke (the title is actually the name of the song's hero) but a charming song. Its locale of Shanghai and its tale of a peasant girl in the big city echo Tin Pan Alley songs of the thirties set in exotic places (such as the 1939 "On a Little Street in Singapore," one of Sinatra's first recordings with Harry James). The musicians respond to the happiness implied here with glee of their own, turning the song into a joyful romp too compelling to resist. Also in the novelty category would be the campy "Movie Star Song" and the quizzical "Falling from Fatigue," which holds echoes of the ragtime days of Tin Pan Alley, repeating the title line with a thousand flat variations, structured the way Irving Berlin once described as the way bad songs are written. One can imagine Eddie Cantor struggling through something like this. It was not really anybody's cup of tea, but they all accepted it and did the best they could.

"Roll It Down the Hill," a phrase sung over and over throughout the piece, seems to be the precursor of a more important song for Chips that became something of a self-portrait some months later. Reggie Young's feedback-laden guitar is again reminiscent of the work Tommy had him do for Alex Chilton, and for the first time on the record Bobby Emmons makes his presence felt. "He's been chose to roll it down, to roll it down the hill," the song says, and asks the question, what was success worth? It may have been a question Chips was asking himself, in light of his new priorities; all of a sudden it seemed rather beside the point to be spending all those endless hours processing his misery in the studio.

He had taken on yet another assistant now, a fellow by the name of Walter Hanson, who did carpentry work for the building. Hanson's carpentry skills were much needed, because at

this time Chips acquired the Ranch House restaurant next door. Why he bought it was not clear, but everyone seemed to think it had to do with an expansion of the studio. "The impression I had was that it was going to be a second studio," said Hayward Bishop. "That was gonna be a demo studio, it was gonna be the B room." For the time being, Chips used an antechamber between the main dining room of the Ranch House and the studio as a combination rec room and storage area, and moved some of the instruments there. Mike Leech described the ambience. "There was a door from the studio into a room just this side of the restaurant. The immediate room through that door was where we kept the ping-pong table, pool table, [the] tympani I'd used on 'In the Ghetto' . . . Tile floors, tacky wood paneling, bright sound, good for acoustic guitar, apparently good for tympani and congas. . . . That eventually expanded to include more of the old restaurant. I think they even installed an old console, but I don't remember us ever using it."

With the addition of the pool and ping-pong tables, the atmosphere became less one of a recording studio than it was of a fraternity house with an ongoing party. The studio almost literally never closed; someone was always there even if sessions were not scheduled. Hayward Bishop would be in the control room listening to tapes; Richard Mainegra or Rick Yancey or Mark James would be upstairs in the writer's room, crafting something; Bobby Emmons might be below in the studio perfecting licks and runs on the Hammond B3; three or four of the other musicians might be in the new annex, playing games or just hanging out. Mike Leech and Johnny Christopher were the undisputed ping-pong champions, aggressively contesting one another and everyone else for hours at a time. "[Johnny] was a very good player and taught me some shots, but I could never beat him," said Mike warmly.

Sometimes Tommy Cogbill joined the madness for a quick game of pool, although Mike Leech added, "He wasn't a 'hanger-outer' like we were." Mike also remembered the night Bobby Emmons played pool opposite Bobby

Wood—Emmons wound up embedding a pool cue in the Celotex wall. "Wood had never played pool in his life, and E was an avid player," laughed the bass player. Bobby Wood remembered, "There was quite a bit of pool playing going on. I wasn't bad for a one-eyed guy. I could cut the hair of the ball but couldn't seem to shoot a ball straight in." Mike Leech was also a fairly good pool shark.

I was pretty good at . . . games, but Chips usually took everybody's cash eventually. As he did with almost all the betting games. He was the worst pool shot I ever saw till somebody bet him a dollar. . . . When you played a game with Chips, get ready to be hustled. That's an old ploy—even in golf. I've actually done that, played fair to bad until the bet gets right, then hit a 260-yard drive down the middle of the fairway. That can actually be dangerous, depending on how much money is involved. Like in the movie *The Hustler*, when Paul Newman got his thumbs broken.

Chips and I played ping-pong some together but he wasn't great and I could always beat him. One day he decided to take me on and bet a dollar a game and with each loss would double the bet. We played all day and the bet was up to a hundred sixty-seven thousand dollars till I finally got so tired and he finally quit. We never played again.

It is surprising that there were no fistfights during any of the games, but the musicians had other ways of letting off steam. Mike Leech recalled one incident shortly after Walter Hanson got there. "One time Reg and I rolled in late after having had a few, and got into a friendly scuffle. In the process we trashed some things, like when he shoved me into the Celotex wall in the control room, and we ripped up some baffles. In the adjacent room that used to be part of the Ranch House where the pool table, ping pong table was, there were wall-sconce lights about every four feet or so along the walls. Reggie took a pool cue and walked around the room popping out each light with the cue.

"The next morning I received an early call from Reg. He suggested we call Walter to try

and get things repaired before the bosses showed up. When we got to the studio later, Walter was there, with a big grin on his face. Not a word was said."

Hanson had once been a policeman, and he still maintained the air and attitude of one; everybody recalled him as being big and tough. Marty Lacker remembered that Hanson "had the reputation of being somewhat of a badass," but also recalled, "I had no problem with Walter." Toughness was a quality Walter sought in others, and tested them for it, according to Hayward Bishop. "Walter was somebody who thought a man's man went around grumbling all the time. . . . He wanted to see how much man was in all the people." Mike Leech described him as "a big meanish redneck," but added, "We got along fine." "I believe Walter Hanson was a dark individual and he appeared to me to have a sociopathic instinct," said Hayward. "You could tell the man had been around the block a few times. . . . He was a rough-looking man." "Walter was also a pilot, and one evening we took a little flight around the city together. He let me fly the plane," said Mike.

Because of his pilot's credentials, Hanson was assigned such jobs as going to the small private airport near Chips's farm in Raleigh and flying Chips's private plane to a larger hangar at the Memphis airport so it would be ready when Chips wanted to take an excursion. One day Walter came into the studio and asked Hayward if he would like to ride out to the Memphis airport, pick up Chips's plane, and fly it back to the small airfield in Raleigh. The trip out was fairly routine, Hayward recalled, and then "When we got to the Raleigh airport, he buzzed the field once. He was at a high altitude, we were a couple of thousand feet up. He put it into a steep dive, and he looked at me like, 'Heh heh heh, do you wanna die.' Dumbass Walter didn't know I'd been with the Strategic Air Command the year before. . . . I was interested in airplanes because I was an ex-Air Force guy. I was interested in airplanes and being able to talk to people about aircraft. What he didn't realize was that Chips had talked ad nauseam about the safety of this plane. It was just a small airplane, but it was solid as a rock. . . . He had this look on his face like, 'Am I scarin' you?' He was thinkin' I was some kinda teenager goin' [lapsing into the shriek of a terrified teenage girl] 'Oh, don't crash the plane, don't kill me, don't kill me.' I knew he was tryin' to scare me, so I said, 'Can we do that dive again?' He looked at me kinda puzzled and he said yes. I think that was when I got on Walter's 'man' list."

Dale Smith never did: Hayward's buddy was forever loathed by Hanson. "He thought because Dale didn't serve in the military, he was a wimp," said Hayward. The antagonism culminated when Walter suddenly and inexplicably punched out Dale at Red West's birthday party in the Thunderbird Lounge some months later; Dale quit on the spot. "I heard a few months later (could have been a year) that [Dale] died, I think of a heart attack," said Mike Leech sadly.

Before he left American, Dale Smith was witness to an amazing scene. He was in the control room with all of the musicians listening to a playback. Toni Wine was also there, seated on the console watching Chips, who had his back to her while he was working. She was wearing close-fitting, high-cut denim shorts—hot pants, they were called in those days—and she casually reached over, took one of the razor blades used for editing the tapes, and whacked off a stray hair peeping from the leg opening of her shorts. Mike Leech, Hayward Bishop, and Dale Smith, who were in direct line of observation, looked at one another in astonishment. Chips never knew it had happened, and Dale made rather a production of dropping the razor blade in the wastebasket later.

Even if Chips had seen it, he might not have noticed; he was becoming oblivious to almost everything except her presence. He was traveling more, using his out-of-town trips as a way to be with her, flying her off for excursions in his plane. "Looking at Life," the closer of the Weinstein and Stroll album, is a thought piece that probably typified Chips's state of mind at this time, and is the track on the album most in keeping with his established style. Bobby Wood provides one of his standard chiming intros,

on electric piano this time, Mike Leech anchors everything with an outwardly simple but melodically intricate bass line, and the strings swirl upward as though the curtain is rising on a scene from a play. But it is a tableau vivant that the listeners experience; we see a man in solitude as he speculates about "where is up, when we're feeling down, and nobody comes around." The mood changes quickly, and the next question arises: "Where is down when we're feeling up?" It was a relevant question for Chips, since when Toni was near he could no longer find the elevator button marked "down." It was a short step from astonishment at suddenly having become a winner to taking the viewpoint that losing was somehow more honorable than winning . . . and to setting things up to lose once again.

Reggie Young, Bobby Emmons, and Mike Leech thought their second attempt at psychedelia worked well, and they had enjoyed the experiment. Hayward Bishop thought the instrumentation was great but that the songs were inferior. Glen Spreen agreed. "It really turned me off to do it," he said. "We were not doing those songs because we felt like doing them."

The late arrivals, although none of them at that time knew that the others were also aware of the same thing, saw something else. The attitude of the group was changing. They had become more conscious of their position, it seemed to Glen Spreen. "We were starting to talk about 'Last year we had twelve records in the charts, this year we have only three.' That's when I knew we were starting to reach and things were not the same." Bobby Emmons in particular seemed to pay close attention; everyone recalled him walking into the studio announcing how well their current releases were doing. The musicians clung more and more to their group identity; the private jokes flew among them thick and fast, so that a newcomer like Hayward Bishop was baffled by some of the interchanges he heard. He curiously asked Tommy Cogbill about it—if anyone in the group wanted an explanation for anything, they sought out Tommy—and Tommy shrugged it off. "Don't pay any attention to it," the older man advised. "I don't understand half of what they're talking about myself."

Part of the reason was that Tommy was still only at the studio when he had to be: he was careful to maintain a life, and friendships, outside of American. "He never let himself get so embedded in the American thing that it controlled him," said Hayward Bishop. For this, Hayward increasingly respected Tommy. Hayward had been observing both Chips and Tommy carefully as he formulated his own ambition to become a producer. He asked Chips for permission to come in the studio and practice mixing on nights no one else was there, playing with the already recorded tapes in the control room. Chips consented, and Hayward spent hours in the studio by himself, listening, remixing, analyzing the records, and learning. Sometimes Tommy happened by the studio, just to check in and see if anyone was around, and he formed the habit of stopping by the control room to chat with the assistant engineer he had, in essence, hired. The chats were casual at first, and then grew longer and longer as the two began to discuss music, recording, and many other aspects of life.

"To this day I don't know what kind of friendship we had," Hayward observed, adding that they seldom saw one another outside of a work situation. "There was a point in time when Tom knew I was his friend. I think he could feel my respect for him. All I needed to know about Tommy was that he was a superior human being. He was a light." The fact that Tommy was so willing to talk with someone was something of a surprise, especially given the older man's reputation. "The impression was that Tommy never talked," said Hayward, adding that in his own experience nothing could have been further from the truth. "He was a durn magpie! . . . Tommy didn't mind philosophizing with people if they didn't dominate the philosophy." When he and Tommy talked, Hayward said, "It was always call and response. It was always a true sharing of our feelings and philosophies."

According to Mike Leech, Tommy related to him in somewhat the same way. "Tommy was to himself, but if you asked him a question, like 'would you like to get a bite to eat?'

he would answer right away. He would talk to you if you asked him something, no hesitation. He was good about giving advice to me like 'Watch yourself,' 'Take care of your money,' etc. We had some very good conversations late at night, about anything and everything. In looking back, I wish I had asked more and remembered more."

Glen Spreen also knew where he stood with Tommy. "Tommy matched my view of what the great classical composers would be like," said the arranger, noting that "I never had any in-depth conversations with Tommy, [but]. . . we did talk a few times. I remember discussing the Hofner bass that Paul McCartney played. Tommy described the guy's playing in detail, and, having the same kind of bass that day, he demonstrated by playing the same way. Tommy picked up on things very quickly." By now the string arranger, if not completely accepted, was irritatedly endured (except for Tommy Cogbill and Reggie Young, both of whom continued to treat him graciously), and he was even included on some late-night listening excursions at clubs with a few of the others. It was on these rounds that he realized Tommy seemed curiously adrift. Tommy was waiting for the Capitol deal to completely take hold, and he was recording acts almost as quickly as Chips, but he seemed unsure of other priorities. "He was having a pleasant time with life," Glen recalled. "We were all at T.J.'s one night, we were having a good time. Tommy thought he was giving the doorman a dollar, he gave him a hundred-dollar bill—he didn't know it. Mike noticed it and told Tommy the next day. He didn't remember it."

Tommy's records during this time sound anything but unfocused. In fact, he was forging miles ahead, taking the sound of the American group where it had never gone before. For example, Sunshine Trolley's "Central Park Days" is a delight: from the time the chime-like chorus of voices begin this gentle song, the last thing anyone would imagine is that it came from a run-down studio in Memphis known for despondent music. With its references to red balloons and sunny days, meeting by the rock in the park, and fleeting moments too soon gone, the song stakes out a middle ground between hippies at a love-in and the famous series of ads for Drambuie set in Central Park with images of carriage rides and romantic evenings.

It also displays a simple elegance, a previously neglected aspect of Tommy's personality that was not lost on Hayward Bishop, who was avidly studying Tommy's style. "The thing I noticed right off the bat is that Tommy's work had a sheen to it," he said. "I'd look around me and say, 'Well, it's the same microphones, the same room—it was a crummy room—and Tommy made it sound like a dag-gone palace!'" In the view of another late arrival, the subdued elegance was one of Tommy's most outstanding characteristics. "Tommy's just a notch above—he always was," said Glen Spreen with admiration. "When he talked, he said something very pointed. He was one of those sort of leaders by doing, he led by example. Chips led by his uniqueness, but then also dictated." "Tommy was a fiery personality," said the third late arrival, Johnny Christopher. "There was nobody like him. He was always a bright spot. You wanted to go behind him and go where he went. . . . He had standards of excellence; he wasn't selfish. He had a beautiful approach to music and working with people."

The easy-listening lilt of "Central Park Days" makes it clear that Tommy was reaching for the widest possible audience. "He had more of a grasp of how everything fit together," Glen Spreen said. "He wanted the continuity of the song but he still wanted the surprise" of interesting runs or innovative chords. Tommy had similarly spoken to Hayward Bishop, whom he had told that when he produced he liked to tweak the music. "Tommy would get bored after thirty seconds—I'd watch him changing things," Hayward said. The effect for a listener was a ride on an aural roller coaster. It was this element, borrowed from Tommy's years as a jazzman, that made his productions such a feast for the mind, and it was a musical strategy with which Glen agreed: "I thought, if you do things more than one time, you're boring."

Chips Moman was also responsible for some of their less formulaic songs during this time frame. He seemed to be tired of the melancholy music he had been making. The first single he sent out to radio from his new label was an exhilarating work: Ronnie Milsap's version of a Mark James composition, "Loving You's a Natural Thing." "Can't think of no one else I would rather be with," is the opening line of the record, following a cyclonic-sounding introduction that catches the listener up into the full-force hurricane of a love affair. In many ways the production is out of character for Chips. There is an extremely cluttered midrange, layered with keyboards and overdubbed instruments and dominated by Reggie Young's fuzz tone guitar. The rhythm careens as Ronnie Milsap shouts the lyrics with more than a hint of blues and Southern-gospel phrasing.

And yet as stunning a work as it is, Chips was uncomfortable with it. He was in the control room with Hayward Bishop as the musicians were playing and Milsap was singing in the studio when he turned to the younger man and said, "I don't think Ronnie Milsap has a commercial voice." To the novice engineer, who sensed a certain potential in the sharp wail and conversational precision of Milsap's range and intonation, it was like a light going on— "What's wrong with this picture?" Granted that Chips had been trying to get a hit record with Milsap for two years and had not succeeded, but that could have been due to many variables, including the possible unwillingness of Steve Tyrell and the Scepter promotion team to push the releases. It was not clear at the time whether Chips felt that Capitol's larger promotion staff could do better for a Milsap single. But it made Hayward wonder. "There I was, Mr. Green," he said, "and here was Chips telling me he didn't think this voice had any commercial potential."

It was the first of several mistakes in judging music that the young soundman saw Chips make, which seemed odd to him given Chips's reputation as a man with an uncanny ear. "I believe I was in the control room when he turned down 'Candida,' but I'm not really sure," said Hayward, referring to the comeback song for Tony Orlando that made the charts later in the year. "Chips said, 'No, I don't think it's a hit.' . . . I'm hearing that and thinking it's a dag-gone smash, maybe I should trust my own instincts more." Apprised of the fact that Toni Wine had written the song (and sang backup on the eventual recording), Hayward howled with laughter. "She never let Chips forget that she'd written it," added Bobby Wood with obvious amusement. "I remember her rubbing it in his face that he didn't think it was a hit."

Toni contributed the B-side of Ronnie Milsap's single, with another one of the songs she wrote with Irwin Levine in New York (she can be heard wailing away in the background). Set to a softly chiming electric piano, "So Hung Up on Sylvia" is a first-person account of a boy in love with a girl who at first listening seems unwilling to return his affections, or maybe just stubborn; it is only through repeated listenings that we realize the narrator is white and that Sylvia, the object of his affections, is not only black but a fairly militant one, in the era of separatist militancy. It is structured so subtly that its intent gets lost on the listener, leaving one baffled at lines like "I cried when she said, 'How I wish you all were dead'" (Toni hisses Sylvia's remark), or "Colors are a drag." Reggie Young loved the song and found it an interesting piece with which to work. "I thought it was just too cool," he said thoughtfully. Hayward Bishop thought it pretentious, a deliberate attempt to cultivate well-meaning white liberal sentiment. Of course, the Brill Building writers had grown up in the fifties and had always identified with the rhythm and blues they had heard from sources like Alan Freed's late-night radio show. Toni sang best when she gave free play to the soulful intonations in her voice, as she does on the background vocal here.

The strongest compositions recorded by the American group in early 1970 belonged to Wayne Carson. Alex Chilton still came into the studio now and then, growing more and more disillusioned with the idea of the Box Tops but committed to finishing his contract with Bell. To that end, Chips and Tommy Cogbill collaborated again on two memorable records that featured Wayne's songs. "You Keep Tightening Up on Me" is an uptempo piece; Wayne recalled "I just wrote it one morning; there's no real story." But there is truth in the verses,

Wayne (and perhaps Chips) falling in love in spite of himself, trying to keep the feelings at arm's length by waiting for the other shoe to drop: "I keep waiting for you to do something I don't like." That's just the opening line in this remarkable song, set to a crawling organ line by Bobby Emmons that eventually fades into the mix as Chips and Tommy attempt to play off the piece in their standard style, tugging the dynamics of the song back and forth between them. "You gimme love when I want to, leave me alone when I don't," wrote Wayne of the ideal woman, fully aware that even unobtrusive devotion could be a trap: "You keep tightening up on me, and I can't break away." A sense of fear may well have been overtaking Chips as he realized how deeply in love he had fallen; whatever his intentions had been when he first met Toni, his vulnerability was getting the best of him.

"King's Highway" can now be seen as one of Tommy Cogbill's litanies, since it is all about life after death, though Wayne Carson intended it as more of a meditation than a prophecy. "That was just a little religious statement; that's kinda my take on all that," Wayne shrugged. In his view, death is like peacefully falling asleep and waking up to be "thumbing a ride down the King's Highway" (the perfect concept of heaven for a Jack London type such as Wayne). He—and by extension now, Tommy Cogbill, speaking to Shirley—asks his wife not to grieve. "Cash my life insurance in," he asks (and Alex Chilton takes on some of the characteristics of Wayne's Ozark growl when he sings the line), "Maybe go to Mexico with friends." She can do this safe in the knowledge that he will be all right as he travels down the King's road. Wayne's characteristic tough-mindedness is expressed when he states that he's prepared for dying: "After all, I knew I would someday." Apprised that a listener felt this was one of his strongest songs, Wayne replied: "So did Chips."

It is also reflective of the spiritual search Tommy Cogbill continued for the rest of his life; Hayward Bishop, Papa Don Schroeder, and the later arrival Shane Keister were among those with whom he shared that journey and his insights, discussing it with them at length and on many occasions. According to Hayward Bishop, Tommy purposely looked for a spiritual component in many of the songs he chose for his sessions. "Tommy looked for his relationship to a song. Every producer does. If they can't emotionally connect with it, they realize it will go into mechanicalness. . . . He always tried to find a song that had a hopelessness and gave it a happy ending." The shading of sorrow evolving slowly into hope had been characteristic of Tommy's productions from the beginning, but this theme was becoming more apparent as Tommy further developed his style.

Wayne Carson was not on hand for the recording of "King's Highway," uncharacteristically done at Onyx. Hayward Bishop recalled discussing with Mike Leech the fact that Chips had apparently chosen the locale as a safe place to continue meeting Toni. He also recalled transporting a carload of microphones over to the second studio to get it ready for the session. This record was one of the last ones made at Onyx before the lawsuit against Don Crews eventually gave the studio to Chips's former partner. Mike Leech had acquired Bill Black's old stand-up bass, and he brought it in to play an intricate line behind the song's chorus (on the record it sounds as if he later strengthened the part by playing electric Fender atop the existing figure). But he had not played acoustic bass in awhile, and his fingers had not completely developed the calluses necessary to get the slapback effect. Hayward Bishop resurrected the "Big Noise from Winnetka" strategy by tapping his drumsticks on the strings of the bass—and at the same time, getting good-humored revenge. "I was gunning for Mike on that one," he chortled. "We'd pick on each other all the time. He started kicking me almost from the first day I got there." For "King's Highway," added Hayward, "I played the slap part with drum sticks on the bass while Mike strummed it. A couple of times I'd crack Mike across the knuckles. He was gracious about it, though."

Chips's siege mentality was working overtime about the ongoing Crews lawsuit, and for legal reasons he seemed to fear taking on any additional activity, although Marty Lacker recalled that Chips was not specifically enjoined from so doing. Marty remembered, "Everything remained the same except that it got really better as far as production and the business end." Marty's promotional efforts were bearing fruit, although some of the musicians like Bobby Wood and Glen Spreen, who both preferred a more laid-back atmosphere, looked askance at the necessity for promotion. There were still contractual obligations to be honored and new clients coming in, but Chips appeared to be working reluctantly. Reggie Young's session books tell the story: from June 1970 until the end of the year, there are gaps in the calendar listings for up to three weeks at a time, and nothing at all in November.

What sessions there were seemed doomed to misfire. Bill Medley came in to work with Chips for two days in May, having become familiar with the studio through his involvement with one of the Blossoms at the time they recorded there. Everyone was eager to work with him, knowing that his presence added even more to the studio's prestige. "I really enjoyed it because he was a very soulful singer," said Reggie Young appreciatively. Toni Wine was around, singing backup and contributing songs, and Hayward Bishop recalled, "[She] was a big influence on the sessions." Bobby Wood found Medley to be "gracious" but a little ill at ease, and Mike Leech concurred. "Almost all established artists were a little bewildered at our method of recording. Like playing corkball for two days with B.J. before ever playing a note," said Mike amusedly.

Gene Chrisman thought some of the bafflement of the big names recording at American came from the group's determined egalitarianism. "We never had to shine anybody's shoes to do their sessions," he said with unassailable dignity. "We never treated one of the artists any better than the other. It did not matter if Joe Blow came to record, we would treat him just the same as we did Elvis when we cut him. We would be friendly to all, but not to the point that we were somebody to pamper them. We never had time for that, and I don't believe in doing it and never will do it. Call me, I'll work, but I am not buying you dinner or rubbing your shoulder trying to get work from you. Later for the politics."

Gene did not even remember seeing Bill Medley, which is surprising because the drummer is prominently featured on a record that, with a little more work and preparation, could have been one of American's best. Toni Wine had brought in a story song called "Smiling in My Sleep" about a couple on their wedding night, reflecting on their elopement; with its theme of passion on the run, it indirectly calls to mind the story of herself and Chips. Chrisman and Mike Leech begin with a chugging, explosive rhythm track that is a musical description of scorching passion, topped with fiery wordless vocals from Bill Medley and Toni, who play off one another's voices so beautifully that it sparks the finest background track Toni recorded at American. In just four bars, the sound accelerates like a runaway train—and then Chips inexplicably stops the forward motion cold, bringing the backing down to just the soft sound of electric piano as Bill Medley begins the story: "Yesterday in Rapid City / Thought you wouldn't be leaving with me."

Toni joins in with softly passionate assent as Medley sourly delivers the watching world's opinion of the absconding couple's romance: "They said 'He's no good, she's no better.'" The song's momentum ascends to another fiery chorus with a vocal blending so intimate one almost feels compelled to avert one's ears, and then comes another inexplicable descent and a line on which Bill Medley seems understandably to stumble.

It was meant to be a soulful touch: the narrator is talking about the preacher who married them and asks, "How'd you like that sweet old reverend?" Bobby Wood recalled that Medley was uncertain how to deliver the line, despite repeated instructions by Chips. Hayward Bishop, seated beside Chips in the control room, cringed throughout the whole second verse: "When I first heard husky-voiced Bill Medley sing the line 'How'd you like that sweet old reverend,' it struck me as a flagrant song-lyric-to-artist mismatch. But two lines later, when he sang 'Kiss a kiss to build a dream on'—that was all just too unrighteous for this particular

brother to be singing." Hayward had a point: Bill Medley was possessed of the most masculine baritone since Vaughn Monroe, and "kiss a kiss" seems to be a line that would have been better uttered by a woman (and a very young woman at that). "Another thing I didn't like is that [the track] tore down too much. It kept tryin' to start. Bill didn't comment on it, but he was struggling the whole time he was there," Hayward continued. But the final blazing chorus, kick-started with some crackling drums from Gene Chrisman, in which Toni and Bill Medley lock into a rapid-fire recitation about the love between a woman and a man, kept the complaining soundman riveted to his chair.

The remainder of the session found Medley working through yet another American Group version of "People Get Ready". The song is a natural for him, and he delivers it with sonorous dignity reminiscent of his own "Peace, Brother, Peace" of two years earlier. He struggles again on Chips's recycled version of "Dark End of the Street," finally giving it a doom-laden reading that has less to do with his voice and everything to do with Chips. It is a dense, claustrophobic-sounding recording, and Medley sings like a man trapped in the middle of something surreal. It was an accurate portrait of Chips, now living out the song he had helped to write. This new recording was colored with a sense of strangeness, as if describing a dream that actually happens, in which the protagonist is never at any moment sure what is real.

For Chips, it may have been a dream. For many of the musicians, it was slowly becoming a nightmare.

# CHAPTER 22

IIIIIIIIIIIIIIIIIIIIIIIIIIIIIIIIIIIIIIIIIIIIIIIIIIIIIIIIIIIIII

# Going in Circles

Even the late arrivals were settling in now, and the players had grudgingly gotten used to them—Johnny Christopher, in particular, was a fixture. Hayward Bishop, the most recent arrival, still seemed to be an unknown quantity, but the group was becoming familiar with his abilities as percussionist, and they even liked his work as engineer—Mike Leech remembered Hayward's mixes as being thoroughly arrived at and "very, very clean." The distribution deal with Capitol Records was a particular prestige note for the company—they were now on the same label as the Beach Boys and the Beatles.

In the studio, the rapport the musicians had with one another when they were recording seemed uncanny even to people who were familiar with it—people like Rick Yancey, who was attempting to make the transition from promising writer to solo artist with a record deal of his own. "You wouldn't believe it, they could communicate with each other across the room with Morse code," Rick said, still awestruck after years had passed. "Gene would listen to the demo and write the charts down." The group used the Nashville system of numerals symbolizing the chord changes, but due to their style of deconstructing the songs to insert their own creativity they were not as dependent on the system as comparable players in Music City would have been.

Decisions on whether the approach at any given time was working were made by consensus. "Most of the time when we are working on a song, blatantly spoken ideas are snubbed," explained Mike Leech. "Somehow in the finale, the product is better than it would have been [had] the outspokenness been heeded. That's just [our] way of doing things. Stall as long as possible till something magic appears, all on its own." "We always respected each other's input,

which I think made for an extra effort on our part," said Bobby Wood. "If Reggie or one of the guys heard something that would be a good musical hook for the song, we would jump in."

The final arbiter was the producer; at this point in the group's history the producer was almost always either Chips Moman or Tommy Cogbill. But even Chips often left the decisions about song construction up to the group, who mostly preferred the consensus approach (Bobby Wood was usually the most outspoken). "We were a plethora of feedback," declared Mike Leech. "Emmons didn't say too much, because so much was being said and done by everyone else, me included. I was right smack in the middle of helping put it all together, and I loved it." "My theory has always been that if you just shut up and listen, the song will tell you what it wants put on it," said Bobby Emmons. If a recording conveyed stoic suffering, Chips was apparently satisfied, and the fact that he did not seem to know that he sought such moods gave the records their power.

Although Marty Lacker had observed the musicians a great deal by this time, he would never cease to be amazed at what he saw. "I have long believed and have often stated on numerous occasions to others that those seven musicians, the American rhythm section, are the most creative and innovative studio musicians I have ever heard or know of," he said emphatically. "I often think and believe that some mediocre records by artists cut somewhere else, including some of Elvis's so-so records, would have been hits to some degree if they had been cut at American with this group. They were, and still are, phenomenal creative talents. There are individual musicians just as talented, but as a group, in my opinion nobody touches their creativeness." Glen Spreen agreed wholeheartedly. "You know, the fact is that they all were better, by far, than almost any of the players who were considered very good to the best of breed," he reflected. "They created. Most of the others did not create that much or consistently."

It was all the more astonishing because each man was equal in talent to the others. "They were all just stalwarts in their position," was the admiring estimate of Jimmy Johnson, who by now had become established with his own Muscle Shoals Rhythm Section. That was not the case with rhythm sections in cities like Nashville, or with rock groups of the day; in those situations, it was common to pad out the proceedings with one or two excellent musicians covering up three or four bad ones. But with Chips Moman's commitment to excellence, anyone who could not play and think like a pro would not have lasted long.

But by the summer of 1970 the musicians, with their solid professional work ethic, were watching as Chips increasingly seemed to be losing focus, at the very time—with the Capitol deal and the expansion of the studio facilities to include the Ranch House restaurant space—when the business needed his total concentration. To a certain extent the studio could run itself without him—Marty Lacker was taking care of bookings and handling the distribution of money, and Ima Roberts was there in the office to assist if need be—but that did not seem to be what Chips wanted, either. The studio and all the responsibilities that went with it were like a child he had so carefully reared that he couldn't stand to see it grow up.

Since the ascent of an African American, Al Bell, at Stax Records, the label had taken a more militant turn, fitting in to the mood of Memphis following the King assassination but alienating the label's pioneers, many of whom began drifting away because they did not like working at the studio under its new ambiance. The atmosphere of guards and guns was alienating not only to the Memphis Horns but to Steve Cropper (who left to start his own short-lived studio, TMI), Booker T Jones, and the label's undisputed queen, Carla Thomas. Booker and Carla began turning up at American every now and then, like children escaping an oppressive family, and it was no surprise as to why. Booker had played in one of Chips's early club bands when he was getting started, and of course Chips had given Carla her first hit, the one that had solidified the Stax label and interested Jerry Wexler. It is unclear why Chips did not make more of the reconnection with the Stax artists; it would have been the ultimate

triumph over Jim Stewart, but somehow Chips could not avail himself of an opportunity that had landed right at his door.

Carla Thomas had placed several hits on the soul charts since 1961's "Gee Whiz," using the sparse formula that Stax had perfected. She had a pliant, passionate voice that was slightly lost when she competed with blaring horns but that flowed naturally with soft, gentle strings, as exemplified by the supple grace of "Gee Whiz." Her arrival at American after having been displaced at her home studio seemed logical.

The musicians were delighted to see her. "I just remember she was nice," said Reggie Young enthusiastically, a sentiment echoed by Mike Leech. "She was just a sweetheart, she really was," was the warm assessment of Hayward Bishop. "I remember meeting her father, Rufus," said Glen Spreen; the old man, who had always taken a proprietary interest in his daughter's career and even recorded some duets with her, was apparently there for some of the sessions. "That was a thrill for me. Even though his records were not what I would call my favorites, they were still entertaining and I respected his sense for business. Anyone that could make a career with a chicken record was probably a smart dude" (Rufus's record of "Funky Chicken" was the dance song of the year, reviving interest in the senior Thomas after several years of his not having hits). "Carla was an easy person to work with from what I remember," Glen continued. "I thought on the whole it was a nice atmosphere" when she was at the studio.

The session proved to be a focusing point for Chips. In three important sessions done that year, including Carla's, he proved that when his mind was on his work, he could still create music of astonishing beauty and substance. During Carla's sessions, in part because Toni Wine was on hand and singing backup in the studio, Chips seemed to be his old self again, and the sessions took flight.

An incident early in the Carla Thomas sessions illustrates the clarity of his focus and his ability to catch the moment. Toni Wine was demonstrating a ballad she had written, playing it on the piano for Carla, when the mood of intimacy on the studio floor struck a spark in Chips." I was setting the mikes up for the demo," Hayward Bishop recalled. "Chips signaled to me to put the microphones around them without disturbing them. [He] signaled with his finger to his lips and gave me a 'shh' sound. Carla was gettin' into it so much." When Hayward had unobtrusively set some microphones up around them, Chips rolled the tape, capturing a tender basic track with just Toni's delicate, classical-sounding piano and Carla's heartfelt voice.

And no wonder Carla seized upon the song, even though it was supposed to be only a run-through. "I Loved You Like I Loved My Very Life" is less a song than it is a diary entry, a late-night confession so sorrowing that the listener does not hear the singer's anguish as much as live it with her. Speaking directly to a lover who has left or perhaps even died, the song doesn't use any of the cliches constructed to hide inconvenient feelings; there is no talk of "healing," "achieving closure," or "moving on." It acknowledges the dark truth that death or leaving is *loss*, and that loss can create a wound so deep it will never stop hurting, a wound almost too deep for words or tears. It is as if the singer is petitioning heaven itself to help her live with the terrible burden of her pain, knowing all the while that she must shoulder it alone. The despair is so profound that enduring seems futile: "Did you ever wake up wondering why you ever woke up at all?" Carla pleads softly, and then later, railing against fate, she asks, "And how will my soul ever find a place?" This is the voice of one small person, lost in a universe that seems to be either indifferent to or mocking her grief, weeping for one human being who meant the entire world to her. "I loved you like I loved my very life / now there's no reason to go on," she says, and a mournful string line overdubbed later by Mike Leech sweeps through the song like a cold gust of wind bearing down upon her soul. Listen and you hear the sound of one heart breaking.

Not since "I Shall Be Released" had Chips done a record so stark, and as always, at the center of the pain is a wild melodic beauty, spelled out by Toni's piano and Mike Leech's

strings. It is a difficult record to hear because of its agony, and a listener either understands its emotional truth immediately or will never be able to grasp it. Carla's voice had always had an undertone of girlish vulnerability, but on this song she gave it free rein, sounding like a woman-child dealing with pain a thousand years old. The contrast between her girlishness and the adult agony is stunning, just one of the many contrasts to be found in this recording. It is, simply, a masterpiece.

Of course, Chips had always understood melancholy best, and throughout his career had brought forth thousands of nuances, shades, and variations on that theme. If "I Loved You Like My Very Life" is about grief, so another memorable song from the Carla session deals with both stoicism and self-pity. "Carrying a Heavy Load" may at first hearing seem an unlikely piece for a Memphis producer and a female soul singer to attempt, since it was written by the Englishman Paul Rodgers (who later founded the group Bad Company) and originally sung by him in his first band, Free. Like most of the songs written by Rodgers, it was both strong and simple, with a melody that rumbled and trudged in the tradition of "Volga Boatman" or "Marche Slav." And that is exactly the treatment Chips gave it, with a plodding rhythm emphasized by the crash of Gene Chrisman's drums, a screaming ascending guitar solo from Reggie Young, and the most elaborate piano solo ever placed on record by Bobby Wood. With fiery conviction, Carla begins the tale of "a young man . . . on his own . . . hearing ancient songs" and a listener is reminded of the young Thomas Wolfe, hearing the "lost voices in the night" of his ancestors and carrying in his soul a sense memory of their suffering as well as his own. One wonders for a moment if Carla is also speaking of oppression, of the "heavy load" of racism she and her generation must continue to bear.

And then realization sets in: the young man wandering far from home, believing in music, and born carrying a heavy load, in this context likely refers to Chips himself. The song implies that there is nothing to do but to continue shouldering the burden without complaint, because misfortune will find anyone who is marked for sadness. "Carrying a Heavy Load" was one of several remarkable recordings Chips made in 1970. None of them reflect the pitiless impartiality of "I Shall Be Released"; there is no blindly seeking a way out of misery, as the earlier piece seemed to be, but embracing it, wearing it almost as a badge of honor. Losing was seen as somehow more virtuous, more proof of strong character, than was winning—so how could a man with that viewpoint live with himself if he was winning? It was a question, like so many other interesting ones, that Chips raised but was never totally able to resolve.

"Hi-De-Ho," the Carole King song also recorded by Blood, Sweat, and Tears that year, is about challenging that fate, and announcing that the speaker is at least going to get "a piece of the sky" even though he has usually been "so far down the bottom looked like up." It is no accident that Toni Wine, so central to Chips's happiness, is prominent on the song, supplying a gospel-tinged harmony vocal to Carla's and providing enthusiastic handclapping. One can almost see her in the studio, joyfully playing off Carla's voice. Her presence, while not as audible on the other Carole King tune chosen, "Sweet Sweetheart," is subtle; from the backing vocal we get another glimpse of the meaning and warmth her voice implied.

Any description of Chips Moman must take into consideration the dreamer's restlessness that seemed to be one of the things driving him: the dissatisfied conviction that things had to be better somewhere else, that "pioneer spirit" that Spooner Oldham described. Up until now, few songs he had done addressed this, but he found the perfect vehicle in James Taylor's "Country Road," which was a huge hit for the singer-songwriter at around the time several of the Carla Thomas sessions were done. Taylor's writing of that era was often accused of despondency and even self-pity; his mournfulness made his work a natural for Chips to interpret.

In "Country Road" Chips does not emphasize the contemplativeness of the original; his version races, as if he is running away from something—or towards someone. Gene Chrisman is at his most emphatic since the jazz of *Memphis Underground*: his snare-drum accents are placed exactly where the listener anticipates them. It is a perfect illustration of Gene's view—a view he shared with Hayward Bishop and the Shoals' Roger Hawkins—that drums are not just timekeeping noise, but an inherent part of the musical statement. Hayward Bishop handles the percussion overdubs, and the tambourine dovetails perfectly with Gene's work on drums. "I had no problems at all with Hayward," Gene said with gracious warmth. "Whatever he wanted to do was fine with me." Drummer and percussionist provided a solid underpinning for Reggie Young's guitar solo, as biting and aggressive here as he had been on "Carrying a Heavy Load," and he and the rhythm instruments are responsible for pushing the track forward.

And then there was one of the most warm and soulful tracks the group ever recorded, "I'm Getting Closer to You." It is almost Stax-like in its earthy simplicity, and as such was a fine vehicle for Carla, whose girlish vocal had a ragged, hoarse edge here that implied sexual awareness. "I was surprised at how well she could really sing," commented Glen Spreen, who was on hand mainly as an observer while Carla worked effortlessly though all the moods of the songs. "I don't think that came through enough." The setting here is on board a train heading for Memphis; she is four hours away from a reunion with her lover, and joyfully anticipates their being together. It could have been the subtext of the stunning 1992 Deborah Allen video "Rock Me," in which a character evoking the one in Alex Harvey's "Delta Dawn" runs away from home to catch a bus bound for Memphis to meet up with a man. And as is usually the case with their multilayered works, there is something new, a fresh perspective on all the voices, each time the listener approaches the song.

Chips made some of his most definitive statements in the course of the Carla sessions; now, in late June 1970, it was Tommy Cogbill's turn. His sessions with a young singer named Nanette Workman, signed by Capitol that year, were as evocative as the Carla Thomas sessions had been for Chips, and listening to them today reveals a producer in full command of his talent. Nanette had spent most of her career in Canada, but according to Wikipedia, she was born in New York and grew up in Mississippi. At the time she recorded with Tommy, she had achieved some success as a background singer, contributing harmony vocals to several Rolling Stones songs including "Honky Tonk Women." Her voice on these recordings is elegant and warm, fitting well with the jazz-inflected nuances Tommy increasingly blended into his productions.

"One of Us Should Have Been There" is a delicate, highly structured song about regret: the woman is addressing her kind, faithful, but boring lover after she has left him for a sweet-talking man who arbitrarily threw her over. An offhanded grace covers up the heartache, and Glen Spreen's horn line supplies sharp assent. Mike Leech is rock-solid here, his playing so anchored that it seems to simulate the lover's voice as Nanette lists her regrets.

Tommy's take on sorrow had always been slightly different from that of Chips, and "To Be Loved," with its soulful, stretching melody that reaches out to the listener like a pair of beseeching arms, is one of his most agonized works. He allows Nanette to act the role of "a lonely heart that cries out to be loved," capturing the inner landscape of a human being in an emotional hell. The narrator has fallen in love and will never have the love returned, and somewhere in the back of her mind she knew all along that it would be so. She assails her lover for his indifference to her but in the end she gives up, refusing to blame him, instead despising herself for the very loneliness that led her to him. It is simply worded on the surface but with complicated emotions beneath, and the listener wants to weep along with her as she says she knows she will never see him "with a longing look in his eyes for me." The string line builds, in the same style as did the horns on "I Shall Be Released," from a whisper to a swelling scream of agonized passion, as full as a heart bursting.

"Let Me Be the One" is the most jazz-tinged selection, with a trumpet solo flickering like a candle atop a softly sophisticated string line. The Paul Williams song about providing strength and understanding was a summation of Tommy's role at the studio, and he gave it a quiet assertiveness missing in most treatments of the song. The standout of the sessions, however, is a piece that is not the story of a person, but of a group.

"Going in Circles," the Friends of Distinction hit from the previous fall, is about being baffled by someone's confusing behavior, perhaps akin to the bewilderment common to many of the musicians that summer as they adjusted to the studio's increasingly confused atmosphere. It is as if Tommy, the soul of the band in so many ways, channeled all the unspoken frustration and directed it into the creation of a startling work with a tense, brooding string arrangement that is more polished than and in many ways superior to the original. The musicians certainly seemed to feel that they were "going in circles"; Hayward Bishop remembered Mike Leech and Reggie Young coming in to the control room after hours and discussing the situation, going around and around the topic and never finding an answer, Reggie banging his fist on the console in frustration as he shouted, "Why? Why? Why?" But there was no answer, in part because Reggie was applying logic to a situation that had none.

If the direction of the studio seemed to be veering precariously off the rails, it was apparent to at least one of the musicians that the Carla and Nanette sessions were allowing the group to resume what it did best. "I remember being encouraged," said Glen Spreen after listening again to Tommy's version of "Going in Circles." "They became who they were again. They didn't have to force themselves to be psychedelic or something."

There were other signs that the studio might yet pull out of the curious drift in which it seemed to be immersed. After Dale Smith left, Chips reluctantly hired Mike Cauley again. "Cauley was hired as assistant engineer, light troubleshooting," said Mike Leech. It was a move that seemed inevitable, with Hayward Bishop increasingly featured as percussionist, sometimes working beside Gene Chrisman in the studio as the basic tracks were recorded. Cauley immediately tried his wings not only as engineer but producer: his one finished work, "Blue Horizon" by Bob Meyer, shows that he carefully studied and mastered the sound of Chips and Tommy's "third way" to the point where he could duplicate it, striking that middle ground between Chips' melancholy and Tommy's passion. "It landed Pick of the Week in *Billboard*," Cauley remembered. "My problem was that I did not have the experience to promote it."

The two assistant engineers immediately disliked each other, Hayward Bishop recalled, and he became convinced that Cauley would have liked to see him fired. The hostility emerged openly during a summer excursion. "I had a ski boat back then and took Hayward on an outing," Mike Leech remembered. "He was funny in the studio, but you should have seen him on water skis. He lost one ski at some point and it took him ten minutes to fall. My side hurt from laughing so hard." According to Hayward, the routine was deliberate. Mike Cauley was with them, steering the boat, and he zigged and zagged it dangerously. But Hayward, growing up in Norfolk near the water, had always been at home on water skis, and he treated the two Mikes to an exhibition of stunt skiing that had him—and both of them—still chortling about it years later.

And after only four months at American, Hayward was getting his chance at becoming a record producer.

It happened as a by-product of his control-room talks with Tommy Cogbill. The bassist had promised to record Piccadilly Circus, a local rock band that was under the direction of a drummer named Bubba Williams, brother of Shadden Williams from Shad and the King Lears. Tommy recorded one song with them, "New Orleans Ruth," a rocker about a boy sent to look up one of his father's old lovers. He had filled out the sound with the American players, and "They thought it was too slick," said Hayward. "Tommy planned on using the American group but they [Piccadilly Circus] didn't like the idea. It got to the point where they

were beginning to argue with Tommy about it because they wanted to play on their own records. Tommy didn't really want to deal with it; he was afraid he wouldn't be able to create the kind of quality record he could with the American group." He offhandedly discussed the problem with Hayward, "in one of the nights when I was doing my practice-mix situation. He had just talked to that drummer. He'd go 'Whew' when he was in an intense situation," and he did it now, telling Hayward that he really did not know what was best. "He was trying to stall until he could figure out what he was going to do. I said, 'Well, Tommy, I'll do it, if you don't want to.' He perked right up and said, 'You will?' He'd already cut 'New Orleans Ruth.' . . Tommy knew [that if he used them on the record] there would be a contrast in the sound. 'You want me to?' [I asked.] 'Shoot, yeah.'"

"We made arrangements to have a meeting with Bubba Williams," Hayward continued. "His reaction was, 'Great.' They wanted a chance to show off so they didn't mind a lesser producer. Tommy let me pick the song." The piece he chose for his debut, "Come On Down to Earth," is a reprimand, a man self-righteously upbraiding someone for affectedness and snobbery. It fit with a censorious aspect of Hayward's personality; to the group, he was eventually viewed as a common scold. But with his experience as a disc jockey, he also sensed something besides a reproach in the song. "I thought it had a bounce to it. To me, it had a commercial appeal to it," he said. "I wanted a national hit—I didn't want something that only fit Memphis. It just had to be a good record."

The resulting sound is best described as "radio-friendly": the Top Forty stations were playing hard-driving horn bands like Blood, Sweat and Tears, Ten Wheel Drive, and Lighthouse. Piccadilly Circus fits perfectly into that tradition and its record could have been easily slipped into any playlist featuring those acts. "They had a horn section," Hayward remembered. "The horn players weren't good at doing head arrangements, but they had a Memphis sound in their horns." The swirling organ line that begins the record, the aggressive, hoarsely shouted vocals reminiscent of David Clayton-

Thomas, and several additional overdubs were done by the band's guitarist, Jack Holder. "I found out that Jack Holder was an enormous talent," said Hayward enthusiastically. "[The record] is about ninety percent Jack Holder. I cut it in two nights, including overdubs. The [middle] part, where it shuts down all of a sudden? That's a board fade. You take your arm and run it to the left [of the console switches] and shut everything down." The band was still playing on the studio floor, but Hayward faded everything out after the second chorus except the drums; "Then I built it up and did another fade" to close out the record. In retrospect the aspiring producer thought the finished product too raw, and in fact it still has a few rough edges here and there. But it accurately captures the sound of a band and a trend.

Now it was time to play what he had done for Tommy. "I was scared to death," Hayward said, but several nights later, during another one of Tommy's visits to the control room, he played the tape for his mentor. Tommy listened, head down as usual when hearing a playback, leaning on the console with his hands as the music echoed through the speakers. When the tape was over, Tommy looked up. Hayward never forgot the reaction.

"He said, 'Damn. I like it better than mine,'" recalled Hayward with awestruck amazement. The younger man was incredulous. "Tommy said, 'No, I really mean it. It sounds natural. It doesn't sound contrived.'" And then came the most astonishing remark of all. "He said, 'I 'm gonna release it. And I'm gonna put our names on both sides as co-producers.' I couldn't stand it. And he was true to his word." The record came out on Tommy's custom label, and Hayward held a copy in his hands by autumn. "When I saw that record, that was my ticket," said a still-astonished Hayward. "*My . . . gosh.* This came out in September and I got there in March. I'd been there six months and had a co-production credit with Tommy Cogbill. What a blessing that was."

The record did not do very well in the charts, but for Hayward Bishop that was beside the point; his ambitions had been supported by the man whom the musicians all respected.

"Tommy was so willing to share," Hayward said gratefully. "I took a raw group and did something Tommy liked with it. From then on, Tommy and I had a different kind of bond." At least for the moment, Hayward no longer felt that he was going in circles along with the others. He had a direction. He was a record producer now.

Hayward would have some new equipment with which to work later that year. After one equipment breakdown too many—it may have happened during Wayne Carson's "No Love at All" session—the decision was made to go to a 16-track control board, and for awhile, once Chips put out the word that he was looking to upgrade, the studio was inundated with electronics salesmen. Eventually Chips chose to order a control board, one he said that he just simply liked. "I might be wrong, but I think Chips got a deal on it and that's why he got it," observed Marty Lacker Chips had been wanting to go to 16-track for quite some time, since it was state-of-the-art technology; some Nashville studios had featured 16-track consoles for roughly a year and a half. "After laying down his lead guitar, Chips felt the console to be his instrument, and he always tried to get more than just utility work out of his axe," said Bobby Emmons, referring to Chips's determination to acquire the latest and best equipment possible for his studio. Installation of the new board fell to the outside technician Leon Sides, with soldering and plugging-in responsibilities from Hayward Bishop.

The old control board was placed at Onyx, whose ownership was still in dispute, though Chips may have anticipated keeping that studio. The absence of a board of any kind at American was making Chips edgy, Mike Cauley noted. "He was like a wasp without anything to sting. He was just walking around the studio, saying, 'It's gonna take two weeks to take that board to Onyx.'" Of course, Chips had reason to worry about the amount of time it would take to get everything going, because he had sessions booked over the course of the next few days.

Cauley told him it was fairly easy to install, and that he could do it within twenty-four hours. Chips offered him five hundred dollars as a bonus if he could, and he accepted the challenge. Mike Cauley, Richard Mainegra (whose pickup truck had been commissioned for the transport), Rick Yancey, and Hayward Bishop took the 610 board there one evening. "Later that night, after literally kicking the 610 (while on its side) through a tight control-room doorway, Cauley and I wired it into Onyx," Hayward said. "Four hours later it was up and running without a hiccup. Cauley was a good electronics guy." Cauley said it was Red West, accompanying the aforementioned troupe, who kicked the console through, and he recalled that, even with his know-how, it took longer than anticipated. "We got Leon to come and look at the wiring," he recalled. "We got it going in twenty-three hours." Cauley asked Chips if he would pay Hayward extra as well for helping. Chips agreed, and Cauley got his money (Hayward said that for some reason, the bonus never reached him).

Installation of the updated equipment at American was just as eventful. Chips said that the new equipment got installed "probably in three or four days." Hayward Bishop recalled the new machine. "The second board was an Electrodyne," he said, adding the detail that it was "a twelve-input, eight-bus console, with more equalizer per input, and [we] added an Ampex MM1100o sixteen-track, two-inch recorder with Dolby A noise reduction. I assisted Leon Sides in the upgrade."

"They had to widen the back door," he continued, "so that the new console could pass through it and be taken to the control room. "We had a couple of days of no door on the back." Security remained nonexistent at the studio whether a door was attached or not, in keeping with Chips's preference for informality. "I always had an open-door policy, people just came in and walked around till they found me," he said. That was admirable, but risky. By now the half-grown J.P. still had the run of the place and was occasionally bringing in his friends. Microphones and other bits of crucial equipment turned up missing. (Patsy Hill, a new secretary at the building, apparently suspected Hayward Bishop was the culprit; when

it was discovered years later that J.P., the teenager who hung around the studio, had been the thief, no apology was extended.) People would walk in the back door straight into the studio in the middle of recording, apologize when they saw what was going on, and leave.

"One time some idiot came in and said he knew karate," related Bobby Wood. "Chips said, 'How fast are you? See if you can beat this .38 to the door.'" And once a man strolled in and thought he was in a bar (presumably he had heard all that sad music drifting out from the studio). Mike Leech remembered amusedly that Tommy, who was rummaging around behind the long counter at the end of the room, straightened up and asked the straggler, "Can I help you?" "I'd like a Scotch on the rocks with water," said the man, and when Tommy had finished sputtering with laughter, he explained the situation and sent the man on his way. It was against this backdrop of strange characters rambling in and out of the building at all hours that the new console was installed.

Hayward Bishop was beneath the console soldering and running wire while Leon Sides was working above when through the open space that had been the back door, "There was a black guy comin' in with a gun," Hayward remembered. "Leon heard a sound, he was up and lookin' through the control-room window. I'd never seen anyone move that fast. Leon drew a bead on this guy with a .357 Magnum." Though Leon was mild-looking enough—Hayward recalled that he "looked like Mr. Dithers in *Dagwood*"—he was also "a crack shot. He and his son both were. He could literally shoot an aspirin out of the air with a revolver. If that guy had taken one step into the studio he would have been one dead guy."

The musicians who had left seemed to be finding their direction. Ed Kollis was adjusting, though reluctantly, to the rules and protocol of engineering at Columbia Studios in Music City. "Once I was in Nashville, I was in the Nashville deal," he said with cynical amusement. "I was the hippie guy; [Billy] Sherrill didn't like me." For his part, he did not like Columbia Studios, finding even the building itself to be inferior to American. "I hated it. Studio A was a joke, the ceilings were too big, too tall." The time-serving aspect of the Nashville assembly line was also offensive to Ed: "Those folks would punch the clock." Being marooned on the Columbia premises for eight hours a day meant that he was not free to pursue an alternative career as a harmonica player, in the town where Charlie McCoy was king. He landed a few sessions' worth of work with his old Tulsa friend J.J. Cale, but he could not launch a career on three or four songs when most of the city was unaware of what he had done even on recordings that everyone in town knew and liked. Essentially one of his functions at Columbia was to act as bait, a resident hippie to persuade the singer-songwriters coming to town in the wake of Kris Kristofferson that the studio was not outmoded.

To that end, the company assigned him to travel north and seek out one of the label's most important acts, a woman whose hoarse Texas voice gave her a feel for contemporary country songs and phrasing. It was his job to convince Janis Joplin to record in Nashville. "I ended up going to Woodstock, found Janis in the hotel, banging the drummer," he said. He talked to her about Nashville and she was not unwilling to try working there; her friend Kris had just gotten established in town after several years of scuffling, and if the rules of the city were bending enough to accommodate him it could probably manage to handle her, too. Yes, she would love to try it, Janis said, but first she was due to go out to California and record her next album at Sunset Sound, in Los Angeles.

Spooner Oldham met her there, in late September. Several months before, he had been working with her producer, Paul Rothschild, on a session for the Everly Brothers, and Rothschild was familiar with Spooner's writing. "Rothschild said, 'Are you and Dan still writing together?' I said, 'There's one song, Dan and I have one verse,'" Spooner replied. Rothschild's answer was, "I'd love to hear anything you're still writing." The song described for Rothschild had been started in Memphis when Spooner was still living there; it had been inspired, he said, by the atmosphere at T.J.'s. "Seems like

Herbie O'Mell said something about—he had a girlfriend named Jane and he was thinking about 'a woman left lonely.'" It sounded like a good hook line, so the two writers started work. "I think we wrote a verse and let it lay for awhile." It was still unfinished at the time Spooner had talked with Rothschild, but the producer liked the premise and said, "If you'll finish that, we'll do it with Janis." Spooner was in touch occasionally with Dan by phone, and the two of them agreed by long distance to finish the song. "I booked a flight to Memphis, called Dan," he said. "I think we were over at the Carriage House," where Spooner was staying, when the second verse, about "the fevers of the night," was put together. Spooner took the tape back to Rothschild, and that was it.

Or so he thought. But one day he got a phone call. "I heard this real efficient, secretarial voice . . . cheerful, secretarial-type voice. She said, 'I understand you've got a song written for the Janis session, we'll be at Sunset Sound, what do you like to drink?'" When Spooner walked in, he recalled, "She was playing acoustic guitar and singing 'Bobby McGee.' I just basically went up behind the control board and sat with Paul Rothschild." They discussed the demo tape, which Rothschild had liked, and he told Spooner, "I'll probably get a studio musician to do the piano part." Eventually Rothschild decided that Richard Bell, piano player for Janis's backup band, could handle it, and Spooner was pleased with the results. "What a great part he played," said the keyboardist with warm enthusiasm.

When Janis spotted him, she issued an immediate challenge. "She did say when I walked in, 'I understand you're a big-time songwriter.' I said, 'That would truly be my pleasure.' There she was in her Minnie Pearl costume. It struck me, that voice [I'd heard on the phone] had been Janis. It dawned on me, it was two people with the same personality." He saw enough from just one session to know he far preferred the girl on the phone. "It was ridiculous, the role she played," he muttered.

"I remember another thing strange about that evening," he noted. The musicians were standing around listening to the playbacks and he had an opportunity to talk to Janis alone. "I said, 'You've had a great career, Janis; I'm proud of you.' She looked at me like I'd stuck a knife in her stomach. She looked at me like I'd hurt her, looked real cold in the eyes, and she said, 'Spooner, I think it's gonna end any day.'" The next night, October 4, 1970, Janis died of a combination heroin and alcohol overdose.

Janis's label had been informed that the sessions were going well, and they had triumphantly been expecting a new single. Exactly what that release should be was much discussed in the days ahead. "A very few days later, Paul called me and said, 'I'm happy to inform you that 'A Woman Left Lonely' will be Janis's last single,'" remembered Spooner. But of course, that was not the case when the final decision was made; Clive Davis, then head of Columbia, decided that the already proven "Me and Bobby McGee," previously a country hit for Jerry Lee Lewis and Roger Miller, could cross over into the rock charts and find a new audience among Janis's fans, many of whom did not listen to country music. Spooner also suspected that "the powers that be needed an 'up' song." Davis was right, and the Kristofferson release became Joplin's best-known and best-selling single.

Janis also recorded (with Bobby Womack on guitar, though Spooner did not remember seeing him) "Trust Me," and, along with the crossover hit from Kristofferson, it seemed to indicate that she was returning to her roots as a folk-country singer who belted out Rose Maddox songs accompanied by the strumming of her autoharp. Had she lived and continued on that path, a visit to American Studios, given her fondness for their kind of material and her desire to prove herself as a Memphis singer, looks from this distance as if it would have been inevitable. It is to wonder, with one of those sad looks at what might have been, what Tommy Cogbill, with his innate sensitivity and his awareness of anguish, could have made of her.

Chips Moman was in the studio more frequently than he had been in awhile, and the musicians clung to a shred of hope that this was a positive development. There was even a road trip to New York that fall, a session involving Dionne Warwick with Chips producing and Campbell Kensinger acting as bodyguard and general factotum. (Hayward Bishop had not been informed that the others were going, and so remained in Memphis.) The record made during the trip was another slice of realism in the same style as the *Soulful* album. "Give a Damn" had been recorded by Spanky and Our Gang in 1968, and to narrate this grim description of inner cities Elaine "Spanky" McFarland had muted her usually sparkling voice to give it a brittle edge. Dionne did not change her delivery at all, so she skips through lines like "If you take the train with me, uptown through the misery" as if she is gliding through a Bacharach-David song about an office romance. Chips, emphasizing as he always did the strength of a song, did not see that it was clearly a mismatch of artist and material.

The musicians found Dionne as idealistic as ever, much to their occasional amusement. Bobby Wood recalled dismissively, "Dionne came into the studio one night in New York. [She was talking], she was on this binge of peace, lovey-dovey . . . Campbell just spoke up and he said, just as a joke, 'I don't think there's enough *blooooood* in the streets.'" Mike Leech remembered a shopping trip in the city. "Emmons saw a jacket he liked, and bought it. It was one of those 'Buffalo Bill' things with the leather tassels hanging from the sleeves. He really liked the jacket until . . . Bobby Wood showed up in the hotel lobby wearing one exactly like it. Emmons pitched a fit, and tossed his jacket into the garbage. Now I know E didn't think it one bit funny, but the rest of [us] howled." "I think I fished it out later, traded it to my brother-in-law for a lumberjack checked model later on," chortled Bobby Emmons. "It was a J.C. Penney special."

Upon returning to Memphis, Chips was in the process of supervising sessions for B.J. Thomas throughout the year that comprised the *Most of All* album, released in late 1970. By now B.J. and his brother Jerry were such good friends with the group that there was a great deal of hanging out, not only in the studio but after hours in the Memphis clubs. "We attended a club in Memphis once where B.J. was performing," said Mike Leech. "Jerry had a mustache at the time, and some guy sitting at the next table began making wisecracks about it. We were all sitting together at several tables which were pushed together. About twelve to fifteen of us. The guy wouldn't leave Jerry alone—kept smarting off. I was seated next to Jerry when he got up, walked over to the guy, and slapped him in the face about five times. The guy jumped up, grabbed Jerry, and . . . fell across our table, hit the dance floor fighting. B.J. jumped offstage and right in the middle of it. It was a big mess. People screaming, others joining in the fight, owner-managers trying to cool it while cops rolled in."

The atmosphere in the studio was not quite as rough, but B.J. was feeling a certain pique at not being offered what he considered to be the best material. It would be hard to quarrel with Chips's choices—some James Taylor compositions, Bill Medley's "Brown-Eyed Woman," Reggie Young's "Hello Love" (the definitive version), a Wayne Carson song or two—but B.J. doubtless surmised that he was becoming just another instrument in Chips's version of the Wall of Sound. Never had B.J.'s innovative wail been as submerged in the mix as it was for these songs; never had his voice been treated as if he were just one component in an already existing formula.

Nonetheless, the results include some of the singer's most expressive vocals, combined with some of Chips's greatest musical statements. For instance, there is the portrait, most likely a self-portrait, painted by Chips through James Taylor's "Rainy Day Man," a clear statement about preferring losing to winning. Everything that had been implied in "Roll It Down the Hill" and "Looking at Life" was out in the open here. "All you wanted from the start was to cry," says Taylor's lyric, with its implication of deliberately setting things up to fail, forcing the issue until defeat came crashing down. "It does you no good to pretend / You made a hole much too big to mend And it looks like you lose again, my friend," the second verse continues, almost but not quite sympathetically, and the string line is thoughtful and reflective.

"Rainy day man don't like sunshine / Don't chase rainbows, he don't need good times," says the second chorus. Here Chips is on familiar territory, the "black hole." And yet the production is so full of melodic touches, so full of depth and strange beauty, that the listener understands instinctively why Chips seemingly wants to stay there.

The other James Taylor composition, "Circle 'Round the Sun," structured almost like a classic twelve-bar blues, continues and extends the mood of wild, dark beauty found at the center of existential pain. Taylor's images of geese flying in the night wind and a restless mind overextending itself are echoed in Glen Spreen's evocative, swirling strings. Here a slight amount of hope is extended, in the ascendant strings and in the second verse's declaration that "the sun is gonna shine on my back door someday" (another borrowing from classic blues, as is the title). At the end of the second verse is a remarkable fadeout featuring the overdubbed and multi-layered guitars of Reggie Young, Wayne Carson, and Johnny Christopher, weaving around, over, and through the strings. Even after repeated listenings, some of the guitar lines are indecipherable, but the mood is not; the screaming of the guitars and the strings sound a haunted threnody.

Bill Medley's "Brown-Eyed Woman" was originally a subtle song about an interracial affair (perhaps inspired by Medley's romance with one of the Blossoms); in this version and context it seems yet another look at a roller-coaster romance. B.J.'s wail becomes as much a part of the band as is the solemn grand piano of Bobby Wood and Mike Leech's quiet strings. This version of "Brown-Eyed Woman" becomes a song of pure despair, as if Chips is trying to communicate with someone he loves desperately, and all that Toni can manage is the bitter "Stay away, baby," as he fades her out on the final refrain.

Chips Moman and Toni Wine went through several breakups before they eventually married in the mid-seventies; all of this took an emotional toll on Chips, who could be moody even at the best of times. Richard Mainegra was particularly understanding of Chips's attitude during this time, and considered the mood swings he saw to be "[what] most people believe comes with the territory of being an extremely talented person. We generally stayed clear when he was in a bad mood. But when in a good mood, he was the life of the party."

If "Brown-Eyed Woman" reflects turbulence, "Hello Love," from Reggie Young and Red Williams, seems to describe roller-coaster romance on the upswing. It is the most upbeat of several versions Chips recorded; Bobby Wood's piano is jaunty, almost but not quite swaggering, and Wayne Jackson's bright trumpet solo embodies good cheer. "Good-bye misery, hello love," B.J. sings in a mellow fadeout. The two James Taylor songs and "Brown-Eyed Woman" are about finding beauty and acceptance even in the deepest pain; "Hello Love" is about transcending pain, at least for awhile. For anyone seeking to determine the message of the American group, these works are essential listening.

By contrast, the Burt Bacharach song "Close to You," already a hit for the Carpenters by the time Chips got around to it, is something of a misfire; it is not an inherently sad song, and Chips seemed not to know how to interpret it, handing it over to Bobby Wood on piano. Possibly Chips was in one of his absent-minded moods when he recorded it. Much to the dismay of the musicians, his pattern was reasserting itself, and he was staying away for weeks at a time, which at this point meant no sessions—and hence, no money—for the players unless Tommy Cogbill assumed the load and created work for them (as he frequently did).

When Chips was around, the others were tense, unsure of what to expect from him. Some of them preferred that he stay away if he were only going to take them on his trip. "Actually, I kind of enjoyed [his absences] in a way, because he was so controlling," said Glen Spreen. "His influence wasn't that good anymore." The arranger made the best of the situation while Chips was gone: "Steve and Wayne were both in town and we decided to go to Mexico for awhile." The others, not blessed with quite as much money as Wayne Carson's songwriting royalties and Steve Tyrell's staff position with Scepter gave them, sat around waiting for Tommy Cogbill to call a session or showed up at the studio as usual. To Glen Spreen, the atmosphere had changed completely from when he arrived two years before. "I remember that the control-room conversations were more about concerns," he observed. "The actual session output was less creative. . . . We were also doing and being less of who we were and copying rather than leading. . . . When you went into the studio, it was different. It was like a ghost town. There were people there, but no one was there." It was a demoralizing atmosphere for the musicians, but Chips seemed oblivious, hoping as usual that things would somehow straighten out on their own.

Wayne Carson's "Table for Two for One" works better than had the Bacharach tune, its melancholy mood tempered by elegance: "Give me a bottle of wine for two / and I'll just drink half and leave the room / Without my baby." Wayne played guitar on the session, filling in for an ailing Reggie Young. Reggie was in the hospital with pneumonia—an incident he did not remember later—and the nervous songwriter visited him there, asking what the approach to playing lead should be. Reggie's advice: "Don't play nothin' till you have to." The song itself was inspired by a remark. "I heard Sammy Davis Jr. say on the *Tonight Show*, 'I wanted to be a big enough star to go in and order Chateaubriand . . . for two.'" Wayne changed the mood of triumph to a somber one, the man entering the restaurant where he and his "girl with the golden hair" had once gone; now he enters, and leaves, alone, missing her but pretending she is still there. He laughed ruefully about having made the change: "You don't want to be singin' to a steak! . . . although several times, I thought I was." He was proud of the song and the fact that for awhile it became a studio standard—Chips recorded it with as many artists as he could. "I live by two things and always have and always will: endeavor and results," said Wayne assertively.

The other song Wayne Carson contributed to the sessions, "No Love at All" is a contemporary version of the classic "Pictures from Life's Other Side": a look at loneliness and how it affects people, from a bewildered old man to a homeless child to a young girl standing on a bridge and thinking of ending it all. Although the final version is credited to Wayne with Johnny Christopher, Wayne recalled Johnny functioning merely as transcriptionist. "I wrote it in Chips's Cadillac goin' across town," he said, en route to one of his own recording sessions. "We were goin' over to Hi Studios 'cause American had blown up." Johnny sat in the back seat writing down the lines to the song as fast as Wayne could toss them out, up to and including the bridge that B.J. left out of his version. Wayne, who recorded the song before B.J.—"Everything them guys had a hit on, I recorded first"—was somewhat puzzled that the bridge was omitted; he includes it in both his original version and a new one he recorded in 2000. The omitted lines are as timely today as they were at the height of Vietnam, about a soldier coming back from the war, suffering from post-traumatic stress, taking to drugs and crime to ease his torment; in Wayne's original version he growls at the end of the verse, "Don't that beat all?" with an anger not heard on record since Johnny Cash had snarled "Like you throw a dog a bone" about the treatment of Ira Hayes.

Glen Spreen was credited for producing "No Love at All," and the title song of the album, "Most of All," was his final work under the umbrella of the American group. B.J. Thomas was so tired by now of getting what he considered to be warmed-over material and of being used as a vehicle for Chips's mournfulness that he was no longer willing to record at American; he wanted to finish the album in Atlanta under the direction of Buddy Buie, backed by J.R. Cobb and the Atlanta Rhythm Section. Glen was one of the few people the singer, overworked and confused by pill-fed paranoia, still trusted. "B.J. had a lack of confidence. He was always insecure," said Glen. When he asked Glen to come along to Atlanta with him to produce and arrange, the string man could not say no. "B.J. called and said 'I'm in Atlanta, I want to do these albums.' He was my friend, so that was that . . . and I believed

in his voice." The song J.R. Cobb came up with for the session, "Most of All," was yet another attempt from this underrated writer to contribute to the great American songbook. It is written in first person: a man on the road, calling home from the train station in St. Paul, missing his wife, and reflecting on his life with her versus his travels. It is tender, romantic, and lonely all at once, and B.J.'s voice together with Glen Spreen's dynamic strings catch and reflect every nuance of the lyric and the melody like prisms reflecting light. Mike Leech said that B.J. had a timeless voice; in "Most of All," he also had a timeless song.

Absconding to Atlanta had consequences Glen had half hoped would happen (and, had they known the details, the band back in Memphis definitely would have). "Chips's whole rule was, 'If you do anything at any other studio without asking, you're gone.' . . . [But] there was no way I could refuse B.J. I guess I coulda tried to hide it." He called from Atlanta to let Chips know. "Chips wouldn't talk to me. I called Marty, he said, 'You know what this means.' He talked to Chips for a minute and then Chips said, 'You're outta here.'" Glen had anticipated it, thinking he would follow Ed Kollis to Music City. "Nashville was like my Plan B. I think I was ready for an adventure, that's what music is all about, at least it was back then."

He provoked his own firing knowing that he had at least some assurance of work elsewhere. Felton Jarvis had been actively courting him since the summer, when the Elvis camp had flown him and Mark James out to Vegas to see the show. Felton seemed to want Glen to come on board as resident string arranger even as he himself was the exclusive producer, though Mike Leech disputed the premise that Felton wanted an exclusive arranger. Mike's assertion can be proven by noting that Mike and Glen both had been tapped to write some string parts for the Nashville Marathon sessions of June 1970. Glen was also getting nibbles from Jack Grady at Screen Gems. "Screen Gems were trying to romance me, give me an office. They were trying to hire Mark." With these more-or-less promises before him, Glen sold his house in Whitehaven—the day before he left for Atlanta, knowing in advance what was coming—and took off for Music City.

Nashville required some adjustments for the string arranger, but not many. "I remember getting an apartment there," he reflected. "Nashville was still not that formal, but it was. The union was a lot more adhered-to; there was more method." Felton Jarvis proved to be as good as his word, taking the newcomer around on sessions he produced to meet other musicians: "Felton bragged about me, 'Glen was in Memphis, he did forty or fifty hits.' If Felton liked me, they would at least give me a chance." Through Felton, Glen met the Muscle Shoals expatriates, who had been operating Quadraphonic Studios for a little less than six months, quickly making it the most progressive studio in town. Glen settled in there as more or less resident string arranger and occasional producer until he left Nashville for good in the middle seventies.

He brought to Nashville a widely expanded concept of the producer's role in the making of a hit record, a concept learned directly from watching Chips and Tommy.

I can't remember how many times I've been asked what a producer does or is. I think that was the most-asked question that came my way.

People don't understand that the producer is the person responsible for making the recording, the singer, the songwriter, the musicians, and more, a success. For example, if it weren't for Chips, Elvis never would have cut "Suspicious Minds." I doubt if Neil Diamond would have had more than a mediocre hit, "Brother Love," if Tommy hadn't said to Neil, "Is that all you got?" Then Neil had to come back with "Sweet Caroline."

Producers motivate, make the tough decisions about when things are right (and wrong) and sell the record company on the product so that company will promote it. . . . Sometimes the producer will even come up with ideas for the songwriters, like Chips did, or show the musicians how it should be played, like Tommy [sometimes] did.

The producer is the most important person in the room. The musicians can go to another session or another producer. The producer is stuck with that piece of work. The songwriter can write another song for someone else. The producer has to have a hit in about one out of every three recordings or he can have a serious career crisis.

Producers are the people that take the chances and gamble their careers. They also plan the logistics, come up with the budget, hire the right people for the project, and convince other people to take chances. Their role is primary.

Glen's post-American work as producer, arranger, writer, and musician is beyond the scope of this study, but it ranges from the mellow chamber music arrangement backing Domenic Troiano's "Getting Old" to the Bobby Emmons–influenced organ and harpsichord lines on Eric Andersen's "Florentine"; the lonely, solitary vision of his composition "Holly Leaves and Christmas Trees," the prayerfulness of Joan Baez's "Weary Mothers," the euphoria of Jose Feliciano's "Magnolia," the bored cynicism of B.J. Thomas's "Sweet Cherry Wine," the playful eroticism of Katy Moffatt's "Kissin' in the California Sun," the driving rock of Rusty Weir's "Don't It Make You Wanna Dance" and the soaring, exuberant string lines of the J.R. Cobb composition "Mighty Clouds of Joy" (another Atlanta recording with B.J.). His peak year was 1974, when he produced "Please Come to Boston" with Dave Loggins and became, as Tommy Cogbill and Chips Moman had been before him, a producer who made a recording for which he will be remembered. He also did the string arrangements for the Dan Fogelberg albums *Home Free*, *Captured Angel*, *Twin Sons of Different Mothers*, *Phoenix*, and *The Innocent Age*, and he named Fogelberg as his all-time favorite of the artists with whom he worked.

The American group was, on the whole, not sorry to see him go, feeling that he had never fit in the first place. But Hayward Bishop regretted that he had not had the chance to work more closely with the string man. "Glen was the quiet lion—he'd keep all of his roars to himself, but his well-appointed opinions would show up in his work," said the percussionist. And

Glen's departure left ripples in the pond. Six of the American group were gone now. Dan Penn was still floundering with his independent studio. Darryl Carter was not doing much. Bobby Womack was adrift in California, but Spooner Oldham was thriving there. Ed Kollis was managing well enough as staff engineer for Columbia in Nashville, and Glen Spreen would make remarkable strides at Quadraphonic in the same city.

It was enough to cause the more restless members of the group, especially Johnny Christopher and Bobby Wood, to think twice about coming in to the same studio day after day, finding either no work at all or an increasingly detached and disconnected leader. The musicians were beginning to realize that there was a larger world out there, and that it was a world operating by somewhat different rules—a world in which Chips Moman was not automatically the king.

### CHAPTER 23

# Right Can Be So Wrong

The setup at American seemed to be coming apart despite the continuing deal with Capitol, which guaranteed the studio a certain number of accounts, and the annexation of the Ranch House restaurant next door to expand the facilities. The lawsuit with Don Crews had yet to be resolved, and it created a numbing atmosphere, Ima Roberts remembered, because "nobody wanted to take sides." "I hated it when that court thing came up, we were caught in the middle," said Bobby Wood. "Nobody knew who was on Chips's side or who was on Don's, and everybody thought I was on Don's side—I really didn't care," said Mike Cauley, who had returned in the interim. "Everything was up in the air over there," said Stan Kesler, looking on from the sidelines (though he would not be a disinterested observer for long). Chips Moman was preoccupied not only by the lawsuit, which he seemed to view as just another aggravation he did not need, but with his consuming passion for Toni Wine.

"On Toni's arrival, everything was changed to fit her needs," Mike Leech groused, and he recalled one subtle change as an example. "Sometimes between cuts, [we] would play silly stuff, just to break the monotony, sometimes it was really fun and funny, sometimes just silly. Session players have always done that, and it's a nice breather after concentrating so hard hour after hour. After you-know-who arrived (and was always sitting in the control room), we were told by Chips not to cut up between takes anymore. [We] just looked at each other like, 'Okay, it used to be fun, I guess now it isn't.'"

Some of the resentment was natural . Reggie

Young saw through it and named it for what it was. "If there was a negative, she broke up the good ole boys' gang," he reflected. For a group of traditional Southern boys, brought up in the fifties with the conventional view of a woman's role, it was a shock to see some of the women associated with group members take an equal place with them. Judy Spreen had been difficult enough for them to deal with, but Glen had been so seldom in their midst that she did not represent a complete problem. It was not possible to evade Toni's presence as easily. Though she was used to the musicians by now, Toni still tried to ingratiate herself by talking about the big time as she had experienced it in New York (never mind that she had not been a top-tier Brill Building writer). "She told us stories about people in New York; she said Rock Hudson was gay, long before that came out," Hayward Bishop remembered. "She started taking on the control-room braggadocio. Her Juilliard thing was always brought out somehow, in some form." One of her favorite stunts was to demonstrate her perfect pitch; if Reggie Young or Johnny Christopher were tuning up in the studio, she called out the proper note to them over the talkback, although neither needed to be told. "Chips got a kick out of that, as I recall," said Hayward Bishop amusedly. "It was amazing because when she sang backup, I thought she sometimes sang off-key." "Toni was very good at stacking parts," said Bobby Emmons of the singer's overdubbed backup vocals. "She could come up with another harmony before you could rewind the machine."

To be with her, Chips sometimes had to make the excuse of calling everyone together for a session. Gene Chrisman recalled one such time. "Chips called a midnight session on a Saturday night," Gene said matter-of-factly. "He wanted to get out of the house because Toni Wine was in town. . . . I went and picked Mike up and we were both pretty ticked off about having to go in at midnight to record." The two of them stopped off at T.J.'s. "We ordered us a fifth of whiskey, drank it, and went to the studio," continued Gene. "We were both out of it. I don't remember getting fired, which I probably

did, but I was so mad I didn't care." But if they were fired, it did not last; two days later both were back in the studio.

Not only were there impulsive firings, but key people were walking. Glen Spreen's leaving for Nashville had been the most spectacular. The group as a whole did not suffer (the departure only gave Mike Leech more to do, since he was now both featured bassist and string arranger for all the sessions). But up in the office, Ima Roberts decided she had also had enough. During her transition—she would work at Onyx for several months and then she too went to Nashville, eventually becoming an executive at BMI—she shared office duties with another lady, Patsy Hill. Patsy had been hired to replace Ima doing clerical work for the studio, but before long she seemed to behave as if she were Chips Moman's exclusive private secretary (which in turn made Ima even more fiercely protective of Tommy Cogbill's interests).

No one save Chips in either the office or downstairs warmed to Patsy. Marty Lacker instinctively distrusted her from day one, and felt that Chips had made a mistake in hiring her. From the vantage point of the musicians, who seldom ventured up to the offices, there seemed to be a change in the business atmosphere. Hayward Bishop thought the new routine was "cold and strange," and Marty Lacker, who was there every day working with Patsy, concurred. Both Marty and Hayward, independently of one another, felt that Patsy spread rumors, turning Chips against certain people in order to consolidate her power. The mood of the office became one of intrigue, further hastening Ima Roberts's departure. Ima kept in touch with Tommy Cogbill about what went on at the studio after she left, and the reports he gave her made her not sorry to have gone. "In my mind, I was there during the good times," she said.

The deal with Capitol Records kept anticipation almost to a boiling point among the musicians. They were sure that one more hit record would solidify the plan of which Chips dreamed, and that his idea of a musicians' collective would become a second Motown. With the sense of pacing and crescendos he used to such effect on his records, Chips in his control-room talks spun visions of what the enterprise would become when it was properly launched. In the meantime, everyone sat around waiting, increasingly treating the studio as the fraternity house they had never been part of. Tommy Cogbill was seldom around during this period; he was curious to see how things might turn out but unwilling to spend as much time in the studio doing nothing as were the others. In his view, a recording studio should be a place to work, not a recreation hall.

Chips often expressed the hope that once his new label was established, everyone who worked at the studio would eventually want to produce (an idea that was fine with Hayward Bishop and Mike Cauley, but of not much interest at the time to Bobby Wood or Gene Chrisman), and in a grand, expansive mood he decided that eventually they all should even have offices. Tommy Cogbill was granted the rear office upstairs, back of the writers' rooms and the larger room where Ima and Patsy worked. There was one problem: Tommy did not want an office. He did not like offices, was uncomfortable sitting behind a desk, and if he had business to transact he preferred to do so from the Memphis clubs, meeting friends and talking with aspiring acts and writers. By now even the "third way" of production he had achieved when he collaborated with Chips was happening less and less. Chips was concentrating on the acts he wanted for his label, and Tommy with his. The two agendas were diverging.

Since Tommy did not want an office, he allowed Reggie Young and Mike Leech to take the room and do whatever they liked with it. Reggie Young did not know what to do with an office either, but he came up with an original idea. From somewhere, he found yards and yards of parachute silk and draped it over the ceiling, creating a tentlike appearance. "I think the walls were carpeted and all that stuff," said Bobby Wood amusedly. "Plus, we burlapped the windows so no light would stream in during late partying or listening," added Mike Leech. The Parachute Room became an upstairs nest for the writers, creating a soft ambience. "The

two of them really made a nice atmospheric lounge out of the room," Hayward Bishop remarked. It also became a refuge for Reggie and Mike when somebody else would be occupied down in the studio.

Usually the control-room occupant would be Hayward Bishop, still working with practice mixes and documenting the sessions on which he recorded percussion overdubs. He had also taken it on himself to label the unmarked tape boxes, which he did in his own inimitable way. "I began with artsy lettering, then it soon progressed into lettering with cartoons and caricatures of the artists, and so on," he explained. "Chips liked it, but after about two weeks of Toni declaring it was 'brilliant,' I lost interest."

The control-room occupant just as easily could have been Tommy Cogbill, playing something, or Chips himself, listening for what he might want to add to an already finished basic track. "He gave me some great advice once when I asked him how he knew when the record was finished," said Mike Leech. "He said the song/playback would tell you, when you reached the magic mix." And when Chips was in focus, working with a name act, there was more than enough creative fire.

Jackie DeShannon, newly signed to Capitol, first came to American that fall. She had been working out of Los Angeles for most of her singing and writing career, but at heart she was still a girl from western Kentucky, and with her long blonde hair, thin face, and large melancholy eyes she had a specifically Appalachian beauty. The combination of stoic strength and heartbreaking vulnerability—at times when she wrote and sang she seemed almost too open, acknowledging sentiments most people would not admit to holding—was very much from her region as well, and it was a combination she shared artistically with the American group. The pairing was so perfect that listeners who were familiar with both her work and theirs had only one question—"What took you so long to meet?"

Of course, she was not an unknown quality to the musicians. Everyone knew that long ago on the Beatles tour she had dated Reggie Young, and there was much curious watching to see how they would now get along. Jackie was cordial to her old friend, and for Reggie's part, he was happy to be working with her again, as he had always admired her talent. "She was cool, I enjoyed seeing her," he said happily. Marty Lacker had also known her from before. "Jackie was a longtime friend of mine because she was connected to Elvis in the early sixties," he said, referring to the movie days when Elvis usually had a bevy of young women visiting him. "At his L.A. house she would refer to herself as 'Jacqueline Jackie, Child of God.' We had a great time while she was there. I had assigned Campbell to take her around and I have a strong suspicion they hooked up while she was in Memphis. They both had some of the same likes and personalities. Jackie also performed at the '72 Memphis Music Awards show for me. She was a sweet person." Bobby Wood agreed (perhaps the only time he would have agreed with Marty Lacker on anything). "Everybody liked her, she was very likeable; she just worked with everybody like a charm," he said warmly. "She is just a sweet person," Hayward Bishop said enthusiastically, echoing Marty. "I really just loved her to death." Mike Leech admired her composition that had been a hit the year before, "Put a Little Love in Your Heart," and in his recollection she got along well not only with Campbell Kensinger but with Johnny Christopher, in whom she discovered another kindred spirit. She and Johnny spent many hours at the studio writing and auditioning songs for one another, and the musicians became as used to her as if she had been there since the studio's inception.

Johnny's composition "Show Me," a warm song inexplicably given the full Guy Lombardo treatment from Chips, was the only song ever to emerge from these sessions, giving the remaining tracks the status of a great lost album. The tracks, done in a series of sporadic sessions from late 1970 through early 1971, are as powerfully emotional and melodic as her release a year later with the group on Atlantic, and Chips concentrated enough on making music to raise the hopes of his band. Lost album or not, these selections comprise some of Chips's finest work.

Some of the tracks misfire—Jackie alters "For the Good Times" so much that she practically composes a new melody to accompany Kristofferson's words, and she surprisingly misreads Carole King's "Child of Mine," the New York writer's love letter to her daughters. But then there is the plodding, prayerful version of George Harrison's "Isn't It a Pity," from early 1971; the dreamy sensuality of "Sleeping with Love" and the chantlike quality of "Makes You Beautiful"; the folk-gospel of "Gabriel's Mother's Highway," with its chorus of "Come on, children, come on" evoking the classic spirituals; the gentle remake of "Sweet Inspiration" with Jackie's a capella chorus; the bluesy version of "You Don't Miss Your Water," with Reggie Young's completely empathetic backing; the Gallagher and Lyle composition "International," which anticipates the early twenty-first century melding of religion and global expansionism ("Hey . . . Jesus . . . / We'll make them be international / Like you and me"); the hippie celebration of "Johnny Jo from California" with its instrumental hook borrowed from Los Bravos' "Black Is Black" and freewheeling lyrics about hitching a ride on a truck and counting telephone poles down the highway; the thoughtfulness of "Now That the Desert Is Blooming," the Southern genre painting "Stone Me," and the meditation on a troubled marriage, "Seven Years from Yesterday." Bobby Emmons is a shining standout through all the recordings, inserting solos and runs that emphasize and underline the melody in fresh, innovative ways. Reggie Young and Johnny Christopher imbue their guitar lines with their awareness and understanding of both the music and the lady. Hayward Bishop is thoroughly blended into the group as percussionist by now, and he, Gene Chrisman, and Mike Leech are a formidable rhythm team that create flawless grooves. And yet as magical as all these selections are, three songs from these sessions stand out as classics.

Jackie recorded two versions of her own "West Virginia Mine" with Chips and the American group (the song eventually surfaced on her 1971 album *Songs* with yet another version, done in California with backing by Dick

Rosmini on guitar and her future husband Randy Edelman on piano). Jackie returns to her Appalachian roots, playing the part of a miner's widow living among "cardboard houses and coal-dust-covered vines" who cautions her son not to take up the trade of his dead father and work until "all your good health has been robbed." It was a timely song in 1970 and 1971; a series of mine disasters over the previous three years and attempts to collect black-lung benefits for miners had placed the coal industry in the news and on the defensive, and the president of the United Mine Workers was under investigation for having murdered an opponent who sponsored reform. Against that backdrop, Jackie sings passionately, "Keep on cryin' about the West Virginia mines"—keep telling the story of America's forgotten people. Chips did one version with the Memphis Symphony's Noel Gilbert playing a fiddle run that evokes but does not imitate the high-lonesome sound of bluegrass, and the full, rich chords played by the group bring this recording closer to traditional music than anything they had done since the departure of Dan Penn. The second version, similar to the more subdued treatment given the song by the California musicians, features the ringing acoustic guitars of Reggie Young and Johnny Christopher, who are such an integral part of the sound that they almost serve as narrators in tandem with her.

"Stone Cold Soul" is a classic of another kind, a ballad of unrequited love that talks back to the beloved rather than caving in beneath the anguish. An uptempo weeper seems to be a contradiction in terms, but this number's spirit and sass anticipates Jackie's later "I Won't Try to Put Chains on Your Soul" for the Atlantic label. The bass line is intricate enough to have been played by Tommy Cogbill, but its bouncy rock and roll style suggests the presence of Mike Leech, who also contributed the stinging yet mellow string line. Hayward Bishop's tambourine work evokes Motown's percussionist (especially on the choruses) and Jackie's voice strikes a blend of anger and vulnerability as she reproaches her indifferent lover. "I tried so hard to know you," she declares sadly, discovering that she is left "standing in the ashes of my fire." She reluctantly concludes that her lover is inaccessible, that he simply has "a stone-cold soul." Feeling bad never felt this good.

Perhaps best of all, there is an American Studios position paper. "Live Till You Die" embodies the stoic elements of "Momanism," with a bit of the uptempo rocking flavor that Mike Leech later gave the Dobie Gray recordings in Nashville when he played bass and arranged the strings. The song, dealing with staying afloat in a rapidly changing world, has a strong gospel feel. "I have to spin the spinning wheel," Jackie declares fervently, acknowledging her duty as a writer to keep chronicling her times. Bobby Emmons handles the Hammond B3 like a classical virtuoso, embellishing the melody line with a precision and confidence belying the insecurity he sometimes revealed in comments such as "Open mouth, insert foot."

The American group were certain that at least several of the cuts would be hits, but Capitol didn't agree and didn't release them (two of the songs, "International" and "West Virginia Mine," were re-recorded). It was a huge disappointment, considering how much creativity had gone into the sessions. To the despair of the musicians, the company seemed to be trapped more than ever in its downward spiral. Toni Wine got much of the blame, but she was acting with the full consent of Chips, who allowed her much latitude. His carelessness, combined with his preoccupation with Toni and the lack of work, was starting to get to everyone. "Even the most loyal band members were beginning to show signs of mutiny," Hayward Bishop remembered. Mike Leech and Reggie Young complained vociferously to each other, and sometimes to anyone who would listen, though both remained basically loyal. Bobby Emmons, the closest to Chips by this time, was puzzled, but seemed to hope things would get better. Tommy Cogbill kept a reasonably low profile, concentrating on production and trying to sort out his still uncertain priorities. Bobby Wood and Johnny Christopher said nothing yet—although they assuredly would later.

Possibly the most irritated member of the group at this point was Gene Chrisman, who with his organizational skills and precision was furious at what he saw as the sloppiness of the operation. It was another sign of just how bad things really were, for Gene was phenomenally slow to anger. "The only time I saw him ready to kill somebody was once on the golf course when somebody in the group behind us hit into us while I was putting," said Mike Leech. The drummer had several meetings with Chips in Moman's upstairs office, letting his complaints be known. Chips shrugged it off. Gene began showing his resentment by staying away for weeks at a time, sometimes even missing scheduled sessions—he knew that Hayward Bishop could fill in for him if necessary, and he saw no reason to be there just sitting around. Always proud and dignified even in anger, Gene dealt with his difficulties privately while he tried to decide what to do.

Hayward's first sessions as drummer were somewhat surreptitious, because he was non-union at the time. Gene Chrisman's name was on the time cards turned in to the musicians' union, and Hayward was given the money, so Hayward recalled. He estimated that he did several sessions this way before Mike Leech, who by now had become the percussionist's advisor regarding the intricacies of the music business, and Johnny Christopher both suggested that he go ahead and fill out the necessary forms to join the union.

Shortly before Christmas, Chips brought in a gift for the band, a portable Magnavox color TV set they could watch while they were waiting around for him; he placed it in the Ranch House annex. "It stayed in the Ranch House area for one week, then disappeared," Hayward Bishop recalled. "When I asked where it was, Reg and Mike said, 'Haven't you heard? Chips took it back and put it in his barn lounge.'" ("Haven't you heard?" was a phrase to which Hayward would forever be allergic—nobody told anyone else anything at American, and seemed to think everyone knew how things were almost by telepathy.)

All of the growing resentments came to a head at the office Christmas party. Chips was scheduled to attend, and at the appointed hour the musicians—except for Tommy Cogbill, who was off somewhere, and the two Bobbys;

"I was home enjoying my kid, I didn't see him for the first three years of his life," said Bobby Wood—assembled in the small office reception area, which had been decorated with Christmas cards strung up around the room and a five-foot high, fully decorated tree.

"On the desk, wrapped in green cellophane, was a fruit basket complete with two brick-sized fruitcakes," Hayward Bishop remembered. "Beside it were two room-temperature bottles of cheap wine—and no corkscrew, plates, napkins—nothing! We waited about thirty minutes, then started digging the cork out of the wine bottles. We really made a mess of it. Chips hadn't shown up. Then, Campbell Kensinger walks in and tells us that he had just delivered Chips and Toni to the airport." Chips had not even officially sent a message of apology back to the group; Campbell had just volunteered that piece of news. Everyone stewed about it for awhile. Somebody was sent out for more booze. The party quickly turned rowdy.

"We all tried to beat up Campbell while he delightfully threw each of us across the room, laughing like a Viking ruler," continued Hayward. He and Mike Leech bashed the fruitcakes over Campbell's head, while the biker "just lightly bear-hugged me for it as if to say 'Thanks for including me.' We wrestled, punched each other, and who knows what until we were out of breath. Then, while catching some air, we all spotted the Christmas tree at the same time. This arrogant little sparkling trimmed-out bush that seemed to be thumbing its pristine branches at us."

The group mind they so celebrated among themselves had never been stronger. At one and the same time, the musicians all looked at each other "as if we were World War II G.I.s about to charge out of a foxhole," laughed Hayward. "We all decided to attack that tree in the same second." They kicked and stomped the tree to flinders, and then set about looking for other things to demolish.

They wound up vandalizing the whole office space. "Furniture was overturned, pictures were askew, trash cans turned upside down, cheese dip from the basket smeared all over the walls," Hayward Bishop recalled. Tommy

Cogbill arrived in the middle of the madness, shook his head disapprovingly, and left. By now everyone—even Patsy Hill, the new secretary who was so devoted to Chips—had had too much to drink, and almost all the musicians were determined to inflict damage. "After it was all over, I took pictures of the aftermath," said Hayward Bishop, ever the amateur historian. "It was so trashed that the studio cleaning lady threatened to quit over it." Repairing the damage to the walls alone cost a considerable amount of money, and yet, recalled the percussionist, "Chips never referred to the incident, which was probably a very wise choice."

The beginning of 1971 continued the cycle of hope and disappointment to which the musicians had grown accustomed the year before. Hope, because the group was still trying new things out in the studio on the chance that something might really succeed. For example, there was the accident of Reggie Young's becoming a solo artist—and a vocalist, at that, even though Reggie did not usually even sing in the Moman Tabernacle Choir.

"Pencil," a composition from Reggie and his lifelong pal Red Williams (who made a solo recording of his own at American), was originally a two-man demo, with Reggie playing all the guitars and the bass in a folk-accented style, and Hayward Bishop on percussion. Red Williams engineered the demo, and the ideas for the multitracked arrangement came from Reggie. It is an accomplished enough demo that it could have gone out as a master, with Reggie singing about taking a pencil to write someone he misses, rendered in a thoughtful, expressive tenor pitched several tones higher than his measured speaking voice. Chips Moman liked it so much that he chose to re-record it with the entire band, adding slight echo and smooth background vocals. He also worked on the lead vocal to ensure that Reggie sang every note correctly, and gave the entire production an uncharacteristically light touch that he would bring to bear on a more famous recording soon afterward. He inveigled Scepter to release it, much to Reggie's surprise. "I'm kind of a shy guy, back then, anyway," the guitarist

reflected. "I never thought of myself as becoming a star." He was probably relieved that the record did not sell, so he could remain in the background.

Tommy Cogbill was also doing what he did best in early 1971—producing and trying to hold the group together. Chips Moman was gone most of the time following the last of the Jackie DeShannon sessions. The musicians were sitting around with no work, which since they were not on salary meant no money, and all of them had families to feed; Hayward Bishop's wife was pregnant. They tried to follow their established schedule anyway. Bobby Wood remembered the routine. "We'd all get up around eleven, we'd show up at the studio around noon and go have lunch at Porky's across the street." Porky's had become the local eatery (it specialized in barbecue) after the Ranch House had met its demise, and Mike Leech remembered it as "just a greasy old diner. . . . They once had a fire, and Reggie said, 'The dishwater caught on fire.' That's where Bobby Wood put his glass eye in his coffee and summoned the waitress that 'something is in my coffee.' The black girl paled."

After lunch, the group would straggle back to the studio and see if anything was going on, if Chips had shown up yet or if Tommy Cogbill had something for them to do. Hayward Bishop was certain that Tommy paid for many sessions out of his own pocket, just to keep the group working and making records. The bassist traveled frequently to Nashville during this period, looking up Johnny McCrae and other friends, and asking them to bring any act they might know about to Memphis. Wayne Carson, up in Springfield, felt the same sense of responsibility, and he often referred acts to American who had originally shown up at his small studio.

Tommy created some of his finest work in 1971, and a series of sessions he supervised during the three weeks of Chips's absence in February tells the story. He was developing a subtle, intricate sound centered on the interplay of acoustic guitars and his trademark use of mood and tempo changes, with the kickers, surprises, and strong hook lines that were also characteristic of his production style. Reb

Duncan seems to have been an act found for him by the people at Combine; a pleasant-sounding light tenor, Duncan's "Angel" unwittingly refers back to "Angel of the Morning" in its portrait of a woman slowly waking up from a one-night stand; she thinks of her passionate lover and wonders if he will even remember her. It is a scene that is elegant, sensuous, and melancholy all at the same time. Tommy establishes the backdrop of her morning awakening with emphatic, jazzy acoustic guitar from Reggie Young. "I Still Love You" takes the listener to Mexico with its strong Latin mariachi feel, accented by percussion from Hayward Bishop, who had loved the Latin sound since his fascination with the percussion of Xavier Cugat's orchestra. Jazz, the music of Tommy's heart, also has a strongly Latin cast (as in the use of percussion by Stan Kenton's big band and by Dizzy Gillespie's "Manteca" and other works featuring the Cuban conga player Chano Pozo), and Tommy undoubtedly enjoyed bringing this concept to a group of good old boys.

Skip Rogers also seemed to have turned up as a result of the connection with McCrae at Combine; nobody knew for sure. There was no pre-production at American of the kind that is commonplace today (the Elvis session was the only one that had come even close to that standard), and Tommy played his cards close to the vest anyway. What is known is that the 45 released on Trump in early 1971 turned out to be one of the finest of Tommy's career.

"He Sang a Good Song" is another of the litanies, a hard-hitting tune with obvious spiritual connections. It is about the life of Christ and the standards thus set that represented what Tommy apparently wanted to do with his own time on earth: "He sang love, he sang peace, love one another." Cogbill set up the tune with acoustic guitar work from Reggie Young and Johnny Christopher that is melodically gentle but biting in attack. The backing vocals, played down in an earlier version but accented as Tommy drew up the final arrangement, are from a three-man singing group Hayward Bishop had been working with featuring the songwriters Richard Mainegra and Rick Yancey. The warm harmonic blend is reminiscent of the Beatles,

and Tommy highlighted the singers to emphasize the "peace and love" aspects of the song.

The other side of the single, a ballad called "I'm Going Back Home," is a masterwork. If Capitol had promoted it properly, it would have been the "Detroit City" of a new generation. The theme is the same; small-town Southerner comes to the big city (Chicago, in this case), feels alienated and alone, suffers from homesickness and plans to go back as soon as he has the money (though it is implied he never will). Tommy put the feel of late winter, when the recording was made, into his production; the somber pacing and Mike Leech's strings evoke the bare trees, gray skies, and barren brick buildings referred to in the lyric. (In an earlier run-through, Tommy placed the emphasis on Reggie Young's updated version of the Grady Martin "growl" guitar heard on "Detroit City" and on Bobby Emmons' Hammond B3 line that ran through the music like a swirling wind.) As a statement of homesickness, it can be placed alongside the 1969 Roger Miller recording of "What I'd Give to Be The Wind." The men of a previous generation, ensconced in the factories, dealt with their loneliness by hitting the bars; the younger narrator walks in the park, looks at the birds huddled together, and wishes he too could fly south away from the cold. Like all of Tommy Cogbill's work, it had special resonance for one young girl, a Southerner in exile somewhere in the Midwest, wrapped in a long brown overcoat as she ventured on solitary walks through the "cold gray streets," observing along with the singer, "Man, this town has really showed me what lonely means." To those like her, Tommy's genre painting of Southerners up north was a description of the feelings they endured every day, and the lament "I can't seem to find any down-home people" was not a line in a song, but the story of their lives.

For those missing the down-home, Tommy offered one of his slightly askew hoedowns on his next production, "Old Joe Clark" (yes, the fiddle tune), done by the vocal group Montage (featuring Michael Brown, who had written "Walk Away Renee"). The backing track features the suspended chords Tommy loved from his jazz days, with supple but biting guitar fills from Reggie Young, Bobby Wood's barrelhouse piano, and Hayward Bishop joyfully clanging a cowbell. The B-side, "Orange Juice Commercial," is one of Tommy's teen-based rockers, charging ahead at full tilt with several intricate tempo changes, bridged expertly by Bobby Emmons playing a series of thick, commanding lines on the Hammond B3.

John Stewart, late of the Kingston Trio and composer of the Monkees' hit "Daydream Believer," was next up, having been brought to Memphis by Capitol, the label he shared with the group. He had recorded in Nashville slightly under two years before, and the work he had done there was a critical but not a commercial success. Most likely Capitol hoped that the Memphis groove would keep him true to the country roots he espoused but would make the results slightly more oriented to Top Forty. "Never Going Back" seemed the most obvious choice to accomplish that, but Capitol chose not to promote this nor the experimental "Appalachian Lady" with its multitracked lead vocal, an almost percussive bass line from Mike Leech, and its wheezy harmonica overdubbed by the singer. "Swift Lizard" is a Southern genre painting worthy of John Fogerty, whose work seems referenced here; it is a Tom Sawyer scene about barefoot boys walking beside the highway in the heat of the day, while the lizard sits in the sun and seems to be mocking them. With its thudding beat and droning melody, it would not have been out of character for Waylon Jennings to have sung, and is probably the rawest track ever created by Tommy, who generally preferred a certain gloss on his recordings—for instance, his later work for the Masqueraders that year on the Brill Building "How Big Is Big," written by the Kasenetz-Katz novelty singer Joey Levine, is pure Broadway.

The incident of the Shell-Shocked Marine was typical of the strangeness beginning to pass for ordinary life around American. In February 1971, Mike Leech was on the premises (Mike remembered it as being late at night; Hayward Bishop said it was in mid-afternoon) when "a guy just walked in off the street, and told us he had a song he wanted us to hear," Mike said.

"We were always curious when things like that happened—you never know so we let him in." The decrepit-looking man walked in carrying a tape recorder under his arm, and he promptly plugged the machine into the nearest electrical outlet and began playing his reel of tape. Hayward recalled that he was sitting in the control room talking with Tommy Cogbill, who had entered while the tape was playing out in the studio, and they did not know what was going on with the tape to which Mike was listening. "This poor guy was singing about a love he had lost, Carol from Coffeyville," Mike Leech continued sadly. "He rambled on and on, had a look on his face like he was out there somewhere, and he had a bad cold. Anyhow, it was a very long song, Carol this, Carol that, and right near the end of the song, it went something like 'And I'll always love you . . . Mary.' Hayward and I almost fell on the floor but tried to hide it till he left." "We didn't realize how much time had gone by, it was like forty-five minutes," Hayward added. After the man left, Mike came into the control room holding the tape. Hayward never forgot the look on Mike's face. "His eyes were like big and round and he said, 'I cannot believe it. I can't believe it was happening.' I mean, we were putting each other on so much, with something like that you almost thought Tommy or somebody was gonna pop out of the woodwork and say 'Gotcha!'"

Of course, the Shell-Shocked Marine could not have wandered in off the street with his battered tape if American had not maintained its open-door policy. Chips wanted the environment to be that of a family in a house, living in a place of truth and creativity all the time—the good-old-boy version of a commune. And it was working; despite the occasional setbacks, innovation still seemed to be the norm among the writers and musicians at the studio. The year before, the political activist Abbie Hoffman had praised the Beatles for being "organized around the way they create" (with the musicians themselves as the inner circle, musicians associated with them as the next circle, and then their wives, children, and friends outside the business), and he looked to this as the foundation for an alternative to the nuclear family. Hoffman obviously knew nothing about session men, because whether in Nashville, Hollywood, or Memphis, that had been the standard structure of studio players' lives for years.

The most interesting combination such an atmosphere produced was neither an established act, although in a way, it was—or something new, although in a way it represented that, too. It was an act that had developed right there at American when no one was looking. Neither Chips nor anyone else seemed to know fully what to do with Richard Mainegra and Rick Yancey; they were still on the premises, writing and occasionally singing backup. When an artist did one of their songs, they were in the control room, looking on as the recording evolved; Richard Mainegra compared that feeling to "watchin' your child bein' born." Both had cut a few solo singles, but nothing had happened with any of the releases. "The tracks just didn't come off," thought Hayward Bishop. There was a strong feeling around American that the writers had enormous potential if it could be harnessed. Both were accomplished vocalists and good guitar players, with Richard's twelve-string being the most versatile.

Richard had one hit to his credit now, a piece he had written with Red West called "Let's Give Adam and Eve Another Chance," eventually recorded by Gary Puckett and the Union Gap. It is a gospel-style song with a message of brotherly love that seemed ironic in the wake of the Kent State University killings that occurred around the time the song was all over the airwaves. The title was inspired by a bit of men's-room graffiti Richard had seen in college. "I have some great memories that really stand out from back then, and hearing the intro to that record for the first time, late one night on the radio, was definitely one of them," he said. Another song that he and Red West wrote together, a piece called "Separate Ways," was lying fallow after Red returned to Elvis's employ in the summer of 1970 ( following a death threat in Vegas, the King had decided he needed the extra security).

Richard and Rick Yancey started singing, at first informally, with a friend of Rick's, a farm boy from Buford Pusser country in West Tennessee named Sherrill Parks. "I knew Sherrill from some other bands and stuff," said Rick Yancey. Mike Leech remembered Parks as "A little guy with a Neil Young voice. Shy, quiet, funny—frail stature. One of the good guys, [with] seemingly no ambitious side." The harmonic blend of Sherrill's growl, Rick Yancey's slightly nasal delivery, and Richard's smooth tenor atop created something unique. What was neat was that we sounded so good together," said Rick Yancey. Tommy Cogbill had already used their harmonic blend on one of his productions, as previously noted, and to supplement the staff writers' weekly draw Richard and Rick were getting from American the three singers began gigging around Memphis as Cymarron, a name taken from a short-lived Western series on CBS called *Cimarron Strip*.

They landed a weekend gig at a Pizza Hut just outside Memphis on Highway 61, a job arranged by Sherrill Parks. "He called and said, 'D'you wanna play a little pizza place for fifteen dollars?'" remembered Rick Yancey. He and Richard Mainegra came into the control room one night soon afterward and asked Hayward Bishop, who was doing practice mixes as usual, to play drums for them at the show. He agreed, and they made arrangements to meet at Richard's apartment, near the Memphis airport and in the general area of Onyx Studios, to rehearse. When he arrived, Hayward sat on the sofa listening while they ran through a song they wanted him to learn, a Rick Yancey composition that was meant to be a sequel to "The Letter." "This was the first time I had heard them as a group, and blending with each other and singing harmony parts with each other," he said. "I stood up from the sofa right after I'd heard them sing. I could hardly contain myself. I said, 'That's it.' 'That's what?' 'That's the sound.'" Ever on the lookout for new acts to produce, Hayward heard a vocal blend that would stand out on Top Forty radio; there were already hits by harmony groups like Crosby, Stills, and Nash, the Carpenters, and America out there, with the Eagles soon to follow.

He took them to American after hours and cut "Thank You for the Letter," with two guitars, Sherrill Parks's harmonica, and himself on drums. They enlisted a friend, Butch Carter, to play bass. "We were just wingin' it, as I recall," said Richard Mainegra. "Gettin' in the studio at odd hours when it was free, experimenting with instruments and sounds. We were all pretty green around a studio. Had no engineer either. I remember Hayward hittin' the 'record' button, then runnin' out in the studio to play drums. It got pretty funny, and we had a ball." The result is a record so polished, so accessible, and so commercial-sounding that it is hard to believe it was put together by a new group and a novice producer. The harmonies have a soft confidence that sounds as if it comes from years, rather than months, of the writers singing together. Rick Yancey's lead is slightly hoarse, but the other voices smooth it out, and Richard's acoustic twelve-string lead is distinctive and compelling.

The idea in the minds of both producer and group was to present Chips with a fait accompli, a completed single with A and B sides that he could release on his label. "We just wanted to pleasantly surprise him with this project," said Hayward Bishop. They started looking through songs to find one for a B-side, and they came up with another composition of Rick Yancey's, a brooding ballad called "Like Children." It features Sherrill Parks' fuzz-toned harmonica, a hammering guitar lead reminiscent of Crosby, Stills and Nash, and the three-voice blend, triple-tracked by Hayward Bishop to further thicken and sweeten the sound. "'Like Children' was the only song of mine that ever appeared on a [released Cymarron] recording," noted Rick Yancey in an aside.

They had been recording "Like Children" at American, taken the track to Onyx, had just finished it up and were working on some overdubs (including Richard Mainegra on organ) when those who were intending to surprise received a surprise. Chips Moman walked in the studio with Toni Wine. Hayward Bishop remembered the reaction. "Chips went 'Wow!' He liked what he heard." "I loved the sound," said Chips enthusiastically. Richard Mainegra remembered that Chips pulled him aside and said, "I think we've really got something here." "He was so astounded by what he heard that he

literally pushed me off the console," Hayward Bishop continued. And just like that, Hayward was out, Chips was in, and Cymarron had become his new pet project. "This was about eleven at night, he called all the American musicians, got 'em out of bed, he said he wanted to cut," said Hayward. Chips ordered everyone to assemble at American within the hour; that stunning vocal blend had energized him more than he had been for awhile. "Cymarron was good artists," Chips reflected.

That night, they listened to the finished tracks Hayward had cut but wound up not doing anything memorable. Chips did record an experimental version of Rick Yancey singing his "Letter" sequel alone, but there is a nervous tension both from Rick's jittery vocal and from the American group themselves. A few days later, Chips came in and presented the musicians with the song he wanted them to record for Cymarron's first official session, an Alex Harvey tune called "Rings."

The song had come to him through Marty Lacker. Several months previously Marty had attended the California wedding of Bob Hamilton, the author of a music-business newsletter and tip sheet called the *Hamilton Report* and one of Marty's contacts within the industry. Hamilton shared the same lawyer, Walter Hofer, with American, and Marty sat next to Walter at the wedding while the songwriter Alex Harvey played something he and Eddie Reeves had written especially for the event. "Rings" poetically structures a ringing phone, a ringing doorbell, a ring around the sun, and the golden ring of marriage with its promise of happily ever after. Marty told Walter Hofer that he was sure the wedding song sounded like a hit.

The theme begins with lovers reconciling after a period of estrangement—a saga somewhat mirroring the roller-coaster affair of Chips and Toni Wine. By now Toni had taken a suite at the Belleview Towers, an exclusive high-rise in Memphis, and she used it as her base of operations when she was in the city. Marty Lacker had one experience of going to the Towers while Chips was ill and retrieving some belongings Chips had left there, telling

Toni that Chips was reconsidering their situation. Some of the problems seemed to come from Toni's expectations of Chips. She apparently hoped that he would begin associating with people outside of the studio, attending formal industry functions, and getting to know label executives—all of the things he had thus far steadfastly refused to do. The group often heard him in the control room, pleading with Toni over the phone, asking her not to drag him to another black-tie affair. Eventually he gave in and purchased a denim suit, which he wore (with no tie) to the functions at which Toni wanted him to appear. But such differences are the stuff of romances, and in the end they always got back together. "No use fightin' about things we can't recall," said the lyric of "Rings." "It don't matter now at all."

Bob Hamilton eventually moved his business to New York, where he worked out of Hofer's office, and when Marty Lacker came to New York soon afterward he stopped by. Toni Wine was also along. She was on her way down to Memphis and was flying back with Marty, and she stood by patiently as Marty asked Bob Hamilton about the song that had been played at Bob's wedding. Marty requested a tape of the song so he could take it back to Chips. "On the plane to Memphis, Toni asked me if I would let her give it to Chips. I said okay, I wasn't looking for any credit," Marty recalled. "A few years later I learned from Chips that she had told Chips that she got the song for him. People never cease to amaze me, what they'll do to score points with someone."

Chips had been excited about the song from the minute he heard it, and several weeks later when conferring with Marty Lacker and Cymarron about material for their session, Marty suggested it again. The singers were not so sure. "I don't think they particularly liked the song until it was finished," reflected Chips. "We weren't exactly thrilled with it," said Richard Mainegra. "The demo was really country-soundin' and slow, and we were writin' our own stuff and sounding a lot more Eagles-ish. But [Chips] told us to go upstairs and work it up the way we'd be happy with it. So we changed a chord or two and livened it up a bit."

Though Chips denied that "Rings" was meant to be a valentine for Toni, its theme of reconciliation, love, and happily ever after might have been in part a reason for his having been so strongly affected by the song. He gave it the same light touch with which he had been experimenting on Reggie Young's "Pencil." Of course, to others who were in love or falling in love, "Rings" had the same resonance, and when it was released Top Forty radio played it right away. It is arguably one of Chips's most commercial and accessible recordings; not since "Hooked on a Feeling" had he produced a work so infused with both happiness and elegant grace.

Working with Chips on the track of "Rings" was Cymarron's big chance, and they were awed at their sudden leap into the major leagues. Richard and Rick had recorded with him before, of course, but never in a group situation, and being relatively inexperienced they were and would remain awestruck at the firepower surrounding them at that first session. A name producer, a song everyone thought was a hit from the pen of a hot writer, the American group in their places. Richard Mainegra described it as "the kind of setting recording artists all over the world would kill for. And it was all for us three guys who had just been rehearsin' for a Pizza Hut gig."

The changeover was not accomplished without bad feelings. Hayward Bishop felt that he had had the chance of a lifetime stolen from him. Cymarron themselves felt a certain loyalty to Hayward and were not sure if accepting Chips's offer to record them was the right thing to do. "They had the courtesy, all three of them, to come in one night when I was in the control room and semi-ask me if it was all right," Hayward said. Richard did not recall that, but did remember that Hayward "gracefully took a back seat." Not only did he step aside, but he encouraged them to work closely with Chips; he knew that a record with a well-known producer had more of a chance at success than one bearing the credit of a percussionist starting out in the business. He had already had it out with himself about what was best. "I had to make the decision, whether I was going to quit over it or make a big fuss about it," he reflected. In the end, and throughout the Cymarron saga, Hayward opted for professionalism.

"I had a lot of involvement, even after Chips took over the project," Hayward reflected thoughtfully. "I engineered almost all of Mike Leech's string arrangements," blending them in with the ringing voices to heighten the effect. Chips also asked Hayward to help him set up and arrange the voices so that they sounded like the harmonic blend Chips had first heard in the studio. "My first response was, 'Boy, you got a lotta nerve.' But there was something in me said, wait . . . there was something that was gonna emerge from that." He recorded and triple-tracked the voices, making them sound like the three-man chorale of his own productions.

Hayward was never the type to suffer in silence, though, and after mulling it over for a few days he went into Chips's office. "I went into his office and told him I didn't like what he did. I thought it was pretty crummy. . . . He didn't care. He didn't feel apologetic. I said, 'It's like you and I are in a pie-eating contest and you're one of the judges.'" The question of the B-side was under debate at this time, and Hayward met with Chips again and asked if one of the tracks he had already cut could be used as the flip side of the single. "He said, 'You can have the B-side and you will get production credits, but you won't get royalties.'" When asked if the demo producer had received back royalties for the B-side of a hit record, Chips replied, "It don't work that way," implying that there were different rules of payment for the use of a demo as opposed to a completed master. Hayward didn't mind; he wanted to have his name out there on a recording far more than he wanted the money, and once again he agreed to the ultimatum. Some discussion went on about which of Hayward's two completed tracks would be best to use. Chips suggested "Like Children," because it was a showcase for Rick Yancey's writing, but he wanted it remixed.

Hayward submitted a new mix, in which the vocals were sharply defined; Chips rejected it. Another mix was tried, this one echoing and booming, accentuating the pessimistic mood of Rick Yancey's lyric and giving the record a somewhat darker sound; this was the mix to which Chips agreed. When the record came out, the high sounds had been flattened, for reasons never discovered. The effect was dull and diminished, but it did not obscure the essential radio-friendliness of the cut. To further confuse the issue, the mix that appears on the Cymarron CD reissue is the mono mix rather than the stereo mix appearing on the 45. Nonetheless, Hayward Bishop had the B-side of a Chips Moman 45 all to himself, and only Tommy Cogbill (with "Reap What You Sow" for Merrilee Rush) had ever accomplished that before.

Hayward believed the timeline for the Cymarron adventure happened in mid-1971, but Reggie Young's session books make the date clear: Cymarron's first recording with Chips, the one featuring "Rings," was done on March 3. Work on the album continued intermittently throughout the summer.

"Intermittently" is an accurate term, because for the early part of June Chips was gone and there were no sessions. Chips maintained that during this time he often came in when he did not really want to, just to keep the group working and the studio in operation, but the musicians disagreed, universally saying that it was Tommy Cogbill who propped things up. Dan Penn helped, too; although he was almost completely estranged from the group by now, he gave them some session time when he produced Ronnie Milsap's first album that summer. But Dan and Tommy could only do so much, and for the most part "We were lookin' at the walls," said Bobby Wood. 'We probably had way too much time on our hands in '71. Chips and Toni went to Florida, they had a house there at the time, they were gone for three months. . . . They were spendin' a lot of time in Florida and we were sittin' around lookin' at each other. Several months went by and we weren't makin' nothin'. Chips, he made beaucoups of money. He wouldn't do an album unless he made eighty grand."

"Naah," said Bobby Emmons dismissively. According to Emmons, Chips was not well;

the organist was in Chips's confidence but had been asked not to relay that information to the rest of the band. "Chips's doctor said he would not put him in the hospital if he would promise to stay away from the studio for a month," said Emmons. "He was serious about it, he said 'If you don't, you're gonna die.'" Emmons felt honor-bound to keep the secret, but, as in every family, where there are no explanations forthcoming, the "children" draw their own conclusions. Why didn't Chips say anything about it? "You don't necessarily tell anybody when you're sick," he explained. "The doctor ordered me to stay out of the studio for ninety days." Of course, if word had leaked out that the studio's biggest drawing card was ill, it would have been extremely bad for business.

Though Bobby Wood was quick to say, "I'm not blaming nobody, him or us or anyone else," he was not exactly the suffering-in-silence type either, and he let his complaints be known to the rest of the band. "Wood was the first of our group to express his desire to make a change," said Mike Leech. "We sort of resented that at the time." "They looked at him like he was some kind of anarchist," said Hayward Bishop; it was a response Hayward received when he voiced similar grievances some time later. Nobody wanted to see the dream die; it had been too important to all the musicians, and to Chips. "Individually, *all* these guys loved American, and so did I," said Chips emphatically.

But Wood had an ally in Johnny Christopher, who had some of the same misgivings. The two of them took refuge in the Ranch House basement, and they sat there by the hour together, not only working on songs but discussing the problem and hardening in one another the desire to leave. "We felt our situation had maybe peaked out," said Johnny. "There were long being-on-call hours that you weren't paid for. We struggled with long hours, we were keeping families together." Johnny had been idealistically happy to be part of a collective where he was asked to unselfishly give; now he was taking a second look at what that meant. "In trying to be giving, generous people, nobody looked out for us," he reflected. "That maybe not being taken care of was a blessing." It was

making both him and Bobby Wood wonder if there were greener pastures elsewhere, and since both of them were now songwriters as well as musicians, settling in the writer's paradise of Music City seemed to make more and more sense. As Bobby put it, "I told Johnny in our discussions, we knew a lot of people in Nashville. . . . I said, Foot, I can starve to death in Nashville as well as I can here."

For now, though, there was the Cymarron album to record, and everyone was happy for the homegrown act. "Rings" was the hit of the early summer, surprising the singers perhaps most of all, but especially delightful to Chips, who would remain proud of the record. Chips was now taking his custom projects to Columbia Records, starting a new label, Entrance ("I was makin' my entrance onto the CBS label," he said of the name; Bobby Emmons joked that the label should have read "Entrance and Exit"), following the end of the Capitol agreement by mutual consent. (Tommy Cogbill continued his Trump label at Capitol until that agreement was terminated early the following year.) In a 1996 interview, the singer Steve Alaimo, who was also back recording at American around this time, said that he brokered the Entrance deal on the strength of "Rings," inveigling the Epic label (itself a Columbia subsidy) to take a chance on Chips. "Rings" gave the label a solid hit right out of the gate, so doing an album should have been easy.

Some of it would be recorded without Gene Chrisman, who was increasingly staying away and letting Hayward Bishop play the drums, much to the new man's reluctance. All of it would be done without Mike Cauley, who had been fired for the second time shortly after the new recording console was installed. Cauley was sacked due to an inadvertent misadventure on the part of Mike Leech and Reggie Young, whose relation to Chips and the company at this point could fairly be considered that of guerrilla insurgents. As pure escape, the two also continued to play Beatles tapes in the control room and discuss them, getting a kick out of hearing George Martin's intricate production values boom out over the control-room speakers. "Those were great times. I loved that.

Some of the most fun I can remember," said Mike Leech warmly.

One night he and Reggie Young entered the control room during one of their late prowls, only to find the console locked and inaccessible without the use of a key (which quite obviously neither of them had). "It was a key switch mounted on the wall—it's just like a light switch, it even has a plate," Hayward Bishop explained. "Before that we'd go to a central place on the console, flip a switch and the whole board came on. We generally left it on, though." The new setup "highly pissed me off. Reggie left, and later Mike Cauley came in," the other Mike remembered. "He had had a few also, and he told me he knew how to hotwire the board." Mike issued a terse command—"Do it." Hayward Bishop was there that night but made a point to stay far away from what was going on. "I knew no good could come of it," he said. Cauley began tinkering with the new wall switch—and blew every amp in the recording console." He told me to shut down the main power supply, which was in the back of the studio," Mike Leech added. "With screwdriver in hand, he took the casing off the lock assembly, did some rewiring, and told me to turn the power on at his signal. He eventually said, 'Okay, turn it on.' I did, and he immediately yelled, 'Turn it off! Turn it off!'"

The next morning, as the outside technician Leon Sides was under the console making repairs while a stunned and guilty Mike Leech looked on, Tommy Cogbill came in. Mike told him what had happened. Chips did not know about it yet, and Tommy's response was "I'll take care of it." When Mike owned up to it some time later, he and Reggie Young were severely reprimanded, but Cauley was sacked following a confrontation with Chips. "He wanted to go to the parking lot and fight it out," the soundman recalled, and that put an end to what Hayward Bishop called "the second Mike Cauley administration." Cauley's personality had never really been a good fit with either Chips or the musicians; no one, with the exception of Mike Leech, had gotten to know him really well, and even Mike, with his policy of extending goodwill to anyone new who came to the studio,

eventually broke with Cauley, finding him too eccentric for comfort. Cauley joined Don Crews at Onyx and worked there for about six months; finally, frustrated by the lack of good musicians elsewhere in Memphis and having been spoiled by working with the best, he left the music business entirely. He spent the next thirty-five years as a drifter, making a living in a way Chips would have envied. "I made it my mission to play cards in every casino in Vegas," he said; living on his moderate gambling income, he traveled to California, Arizona, Key West, even Nashville, staying in none of them very long. In 2007, at the age of sixty, he resurfaced as the compiler of an online writer's thesaurus.

Though the studio had lost a potentially great producer when Cauley was fired, work on the Cymarron album continued as though American was not squandering its resources. But the waste is apparent on the Cymarron album. "Cymarron was an unfinished symphony," said Hayward Bishop. "What you hear on the album has little to do with how we started out," Richard Mainegra added regretfully. "We were heavily influenced by Crosby, Stills and Nash, Neil Young, Creedence Clearwater. . . . The album had to be thrown together in two weeks to take advantage of the single. And we ended up recordin' some things that really took us away from how we originally heard ourselves."

It begins, as the album properly should, with a remixed "Rings," on which Mike Leech's melodic string line and Reggie Young's bell-like guitar on the fadeout are featured almost as prominently as the voices. Billy McKnight's composition "In Your Mind" and Sherrill Parks's "Across the Kansas Sky," the next two tracks, are the ones Richard Mainegra and Rick Yancey cited as being the most fully realized and the most true to Cymarron's original concept. Both feature strong lyrics and stunning harmonies. "In Your Mind" also showcases a stately, gliding string line by Mike Leech, who was at the peak of his arranging creativity in 1971, turning out string line after string line that not only accentuates the messages in the song but in some cases adds to them. "I always tried to make a record build, unlike keyboard string players who usually enter a song wide open with no place to go," Mike explained. "I will play a simple line, then as it appears again add either harmony or go up an octave, or both." Reggie Young's sharp fills ending each line of the second chorus sound like a soul screaming in pain.

Sherrill Parks's beautiful "Across the Kansas Sky," with its almost standard country melody, begins with the memorable image of a young bird sailing high over the prairie, and goes on to address the drifting, spirited lover who evokes the soaring bird: "You say you aren't looking for a life that will tie you down / So if you want out, it's all right with me / How long it will take you to get to nowhere, I cannot say / But you've burned another bridge along the way." The lover concludes that he cannot hide his sorrow (a line that would have decided Chips on doing the song right there and right then) but that in the end the drifter "put me through some changes for the better at the time." Mike Leech contributes an assertive bass part, playing a flurry of thunderous notes at the end of each line, a technique he called "doodling up." Both works are classic American Studios recordings as much as they belong to the singers, and both are a pleasure to hear. Sherrill Parks's writing in particular was strong; he also wrote the Paul Revere and the Raiders soundalike "True Confessions" that closes the album (and provided the Mark Lindsay–style vocal).

Richard Mainegra's equally countryish "A Good Place to Begin," as well as his melodic "Valerie," also showcases the writing talent of Cymarron. Richard characterized "Valerie," which became the follow-up single, as "just a pretty melody with an amateurish lyric. Did name my cat after the song, though . . . and I loved the way the record turned out. Of the three of us, Sherrill and Rick tended to write the coolest songs." He was dismissive of his own vocal, although it sounds warm and listenable. "I personally didn't know what the hell I was doin'," he said. "I sounded like a choirboy influenced by the Bee Gees." All the album tracks discussed up to this point feature the musicians providing capable backing—Mike

Leech's ascending string line on "Valerie" is superb—and Chips doing what he did best. "We had a good time cuttin' 'em; Chips scared the fire out of 'em," Hayward Bishop said amusedly. "Chips was like a magician," said Rick Yancey respectfully. "He would just listen to it as it came through the speakers. He just had this ability to direct." Listening to the songs in order as they appear on the CD, up through "Valerie," is to hear Chips producing great music almost effortlessly. After "Valerie," however, the album falls apart.

For much of the remaining album tracks, Chips concentrates on older songs rather than new material, not necessarily a wise thing to do when showcasing the work of new artists. Most likely he wanted to display the group's versatility on songs they didn't write, but "Break My Mind" does not fit Cymarron's choral-style voices at all. The American Studios standards "Hello Love" (prominently featuring Hayward Bishop on castanets) and "Table for Two for One" also misfire. The misfires are not the fault of the musicians, who contribute some beautifully intricate basic tracks (such as the acoustic guitar interplay on "Table for Two"), or even Cymarron, who handle the songs they are given as best they can, but of Chips for leading the voices in a direction opposed to their style. The idea of recording "Tennessee Waltz" as a slow blues, for example, is brilliant, but it is a concept that should have been given to another singer to handle. Its application here is only partly salvaged by the three-voice chorale in the middle. "I'm pretty sure it wasn't one of us who suggested 'Tennessee Waltz' for the album," said Richard Mainegra. "I kinda remember thinkin', 'this is just not us!' I guess it was just a favorite song of Chips." Richard described the problem exactly: Chips was trying to shoehorn the singers into a predetermined concept rather than relying on the vocal blend to dictate material (thus violating his own cardinal rule of letting the music decide how a production should go).

Some indication of that concept came from their version of the Bee Gees' "How Can You Mend a Broken Heart," in which Cymarron sing beautifully but serve only as vehicles for Chips's themes of sorrow and self-pity (Mike

Leech's string line is reminiscent of Mantovani and tilts the track even more in the direction of melancholy). Reggie Young sensed the vocal resemblance to the Bee Gees but added that the trio had gifts all their own: "They were totally different than anything else we had done at American," he reflected dispassionately. "To find someone who can write their own material, that's really something."

It is possible that Reggie was right, and that the singers' own material should have been featured more. Richard Mainegra thought so. "In hindsight, maybe things would have been different if the cool stuff had seen the light of day," he said. Some of the "cool stuff" included "Right Can Be So Wrong," a song about a romance going sour for reasons baffling to both parties, with crescendos carried not by the strings but by the keyboards and the voices creating an almost unendurable tension. A promotional version of it was released, featuring a stentorian guitar overdub from Reggie Young and an added harmonica line from Sherrill Parks, but radio stations unfortunately did not notice. "What's a Little Dirt" showcased the full harmonic blend and featured a great line: "Who wants to be the best-dressed solitaire player in Memphis?" Another recording with commercial potential was Johnny Christopher's "Keep Me Warm" (when she returned to California, Jackie DeShannon recorded it); Bobby Emmons and Bobby Wood played an instrumental break that blends the keyboards and sounds like a Bach chorale. And then there was the beautiful "Shores of California," which shares with Jim Webb's "Galveston" and the Dells' "Does Anybody Know I'm Here" the perspective of an unwilling—and homesick—soldier in Vietnam. For all the lofty sentiments of protest music, much of it forgot that the soldiers themselves did not want to be there, as Chips and the American group reminded us. "That one should have been released," Hayward Bishop said bluntly; he named it as his favorite Cymarron recording.

Hayward also believed that the strength of Cymarron lay in their vocal blend, and that Chips had the concept of one lead singer—Richard, who had the smoothest voice of the three—and the other two singing harmony. Cymarron would have the same problem in the middle nineties, when they had a Nashville recording comeback as the Remingtons, with the California import Josh Leo producing and the late Jimmy Griffin replacing Sherrill Parks. Leo did not understand the harmonic blend—and Richard Mainegra thought that Leo felt such a combination was not commercial enough for country radio—but the old-time disc jockey Ralph Emery understood it. Every time they appeared on his *Nashville Now* television show he insisted that they perform an intimate acoustic set as they sat in the conversation area. Perhaps Emery should have been their producer.

"Rings" got as high as seventeen in the charts. "We were on cloud nine for awhile there," Richard Mainegra said about it. He later wrote a blithe tribute to those days on the Remingtons' first album: "Well, things looked good a time or two / I made a little noise." He had—but with the uniqueness of Cymarron's vocal blend, to listen to the CD reissue now is to get a depressing sense of an opportunity sadly wasted and formidable talents squandered. By 2007 Jimmy Griffin was dead of lung cancer and all three of the original Cymarron were out of the music business after having been involved for many years as successful writers—Richard Mainegra did particularly well, composing songs for Tanya Tucker ("Here's Some Love") and Crystal Gayle's "Let's Do It Right," with its lyric that love is "more than just holdin' hands in the moonlight / It's reaching out and taking a chance." They also worked, individually and collectively, as jingle singers, something they had done since the Cymarron days, when they recorded jingles for an advertising agency and for the First National Bank in Memphis.

Jingle singing paid the bills, as it did and does for many background singers, but it is a tragic waste of talent when one considers that this was a group with a harmonic blend that could have kept them at the forefront of the soft-rock style for many years. Even more tragic than the termination of several good careers,

Rick Yancey and Richard Mainegra, who had been like intertwined fingers since the beginning of Cymarron and all through their second phase as the Remingtons, are no longer in communication with one another. Richard said it best as he paraphrased his own composition: "There's nothing left to do but go our separate ways, and pick up all the pieces left behind us."

||||||||||||||||||||||||||||||||||||||||||||||||||||||||||

### CHAPTER 24

# Wasted Doing Nothing

The wasted opportunity with Cymarron was another demoralizing experience for the American musicians, all of whom were rooting for the trio and felt that their own creativity was highlighted by the fact that these singer-songwriters had been found and nurtured by their studio. At about this time, in the summer of 1971, three other singer-songwriters came in to record. One of them became a generational icon; one was a writer and vocalist of strong promise who was held back by the resegregation of the music charts; and one had been a singer-writer before the term was fashionable.

The writer who became an icon was a first-generation Chicagoan with strong roots in Jackie DeShannon's western Kentucky. Inspired by Roger Miller and Bob Dylan, John Prine had been writing songs for some time, but was unknown until Kris Kristofferson heard him in a Windy City club after hours one night at the behest of Steve Goodman, another songwriter who had just completed work on his first album. Kris pulled some strings; another early patron—Paul Anka, of all people—pulled a few more, and before long Prine had a contract with Atlantic and Arif Mardin was bringing him to Memphis for his first recording session. (After a brief lull—perhaps awaiting the outcome of the Crews lawsuit—Atlantic Records again began bringing acts to American by mid-1971.) "John Prine was (admittedly after I talked to him many years later) scared to death," said Mike Leech. "It was his first studio experience and we made him very nervous."

Some of Prine's songs had a country flavor, so it may have been assumed by the Atlantic team that their standbys could get more out of him than could musicians in New York. The tectonic plates seemed to be shifting within the country music industry; Waylon Jennings and Willie Nelson, backed on records at this point by many of Nashville's renegade younger musicians (including, by now, Glen Spreen on occasion), were creating a demand for the kind of melodic playing and hard-hitting lyric content that the American group had been featuring all along (Wayne Carson, in fact, placed a song with Jennings that year, the narrative "Don't Let the Sun Set on You in Tulsa," although Wayne's recording of it is better). John Prine's work fit perfectly with this rising demand, and his album, with the American musicians backing him, became a rallying point for the movement.

Not that the musicians were aware of the trend: their job was to concentrate on whatever was brought to them to record, and no one discussed with them why certain acts were there or for what the artists and producers were looking. "Motown had meetings, Stax had meetings, to discuss things like that," Hayward Bishop noted. "We never had meetings. We never even discussed the groove [when we were recording]. I tried, a couple of times, and then I got these looks like, 'Oh, he's going to make us think about it; he's going to make us *analyze* the groove.'" The group preferred to arrive at recorded perfection almost by magic; this was good in the emphasis it placed on spontaneity, but bad in that no attempt was made to look at the whole picture.

The fact that publishers and producers in New York and Nashville saw Kristofferson's success as a template was even more obscured in Memphis, where for the most part the studios were making the kind of music they always had. Willie Mitchell was having a phenomenal recording comeback with Al Green, as well as lesser hits with Syl Johnson, Otis Clay, and Ann Peebles (who had married Don Bryant, Reggie Young's and Bobby Emmons's acquaintance from their days at Hi); Stax continued to make solid R&B records (though more often than not, no longer in Memphis but at Jimmy Johnson's Muscle Shoals Sound),

and the lowest studio on the totem pole, Ardent, began to get some attention in mid-1971 due to their reputation as an overdub facility. Ardent went mainstream that year as Led Zeppelin's and James Taylor's third albums gave it instant prestige. Noel Gilbert and Wayne Jackson overdubbed string and horn parts by the California arranger John Andrew Tartaglia for a Kate Taylor album released on Cotillion that summer. That an Atlantic subsidiary would have signed an artist like James Taylor's sister, who was not a singer-songwriter but whose voice had strong country inflections and could be marketed as part of the new Nashville, was an indication that the softer, more poetic trend borrowed from folk music was entering the mainstream, and that even rhythm and blues labels like Atlantic were seeking such acts.

The American musicians were not sure they wanted to be the support system for such a songwriter-oriented trend (and even after they had become exactly that in Nashville some years later, most of them disowned the concept). "I hated folk music. I thought it was lyric on lyric," said Bobby Wood. "I wouldn't pay any attention to the lyrics; the feel was life to me." Nor did he like the folk audience. "I call 'em 'brain people,' College Joe types," he said. "I couldn't relate to that music." The new style may have been fine for Chips Moman, who was himself a writer and thus sensitive to a strong lyric, but the group thought of themselves as groove players first and foremost, and there seemed little to run with in such word-oriented work, with its roots in Dylanesque folk rather than R&B. "I didn't know where to put him," Bobby Wood said in bafflement at Prine. "Folk and piano never worked for some reason. I had not a clue where to put him." Hayward Bishop recalled his reaction when Prine came into the studio and began running down his songs accompanied only by his acoustic guitar. "I remember thinking, 'How are we gonna get anything musical out of *that*??' There was no evidence of groove whatever, and I was hungry for groove. Prine came off like a folk poet. This guy was nasally, he didn't have any tone to his voice, and all his songs are in the same key! I thought, this is gonna be like milking a dag-blasted *dog*!"

Reggie Young and Bobby Emmons both took another view. "John was the most different writer I had ever heard in my life," Reggie said happily. "Yes sir, really, he was really unusual." In his first major interview with the rock press, a *Rolling Stone* piece from early 1972, Prine recalled Reggie saying to him: "I've been playing music for fifteen years, and your songs are either the worst I've ever heard or some of the best. I kind of think they might be the best; I can't tell yet. They sure are different." The album proves Reggie correct on both counts; selections run the gamut from pieces that eventually became standards to hideous throwaways. "He was deep into his music," Bobby Emmons added with thoughtful admiration. "He was not just reading it off the next Post-It note. I liked it that he had the ability to look at all these subjects that other writers wouldn't touch."

"Illegal Smile," about marijuana, of course, is another "nudge-nudge, wink-wink" drug-reference song, with the drug being touted as a way to escape everything from the doldrums to raving paranoia. But in the thicket of the topical references to Chicago's Judge Julius Hoffman and the throwaway lines tossed out in apparent homage to Roger Miller, a couplet stark enough for imagist poetry—"Bowl of oatmeal tried to stare me down / And won"—demonstrates precisely what is so maddening about Prine: the realist hiding behind the smartass, the poetic urge lurking behind the impulse to show off, the wisecracks delivered in a flat Dylanesque nonvoice. Though Bobby Wood may have assumed that folk music does not do well with keyboards, he and Emmons are the standouts here, punctuating Prine's in-jokes with blurts of sound that function almost like a coffeehouse audience laughing on cue. And there, thought Wood, lay the challenge: "Those songs that might have had good lyrics but nothing else to hang your hat on were the hardest to get going, unless we came up with something rhythmically on our own."

"Spanish Pipedream" is undoubtedly the song to which Reggie Young referred when he said amusedly, "He was singin' somethin' and the title didn't pertain to nothin' he was singin' about." At no time do the words "Spanish pipedream" appear in the body of the song, a tale played for laughs about a draft evader meeting up with a stripper who advises him to "blow up your TV" (a line often used by media critics in the twenty-first century). The group essentially plays backup here not to Prine but to the former Bakersfield steel guitar player Leo LeBlanc, who was featured at the time on many Muscle Shoals sessions. LeBlanc did not have the poignancy of John Hughey's crying steel, but he had a strong rhythmic sense, and his accents here provide a pattern for the American players to follow.

In the engineering chair while Arif Mardin from Atlantic directed the session (the entire album, except for the classic "Paradise," was recorded at American) was an old friend that the players were happy to see. Stan Kesler had signed on with Chips following the collapse of his Sounds of Memphis studio. Chips approached him, so the studio head recalled, because "I kinda liked him; I knew what he could do." "He asked if me and B. B. Cunningham would be interested in working at Onyx," Kesler recalled, but by the time Stan was ready Chips had lost that studio in the Crews lawsuit and Stan became the engineer at American. Stan's hiring was never discussed in advance with the musicians; one day he just turned up among them and announced, "I'm working here now."

Reggie Young was delighted at Kesler's presence. "I felt good that he was there, just to help our group get stronger," he said. Mike Leech found not only Stan's engineering skills but his personality to be a positive addition. "I love Stan because he kept his opinions to himself, never forcing a thought on anybody, unless you asked him. . . . He was always level-headed, maybe sort of no-nonsense, but he didn't mind jumping in the middle of any controversy. We were up for some kind of an award once, and Chips was expected to make the acceptance speech. He conned Stan into doing it, which he did, and did a fine job."

For Chips, it was a chance to finally stop engineering so many of the sessions. "I needed somebody, y'know, if I was gonna have any time off," he explained. "I could have time to write. We used to be booked months and months in advance." By now Hayward Bishop was doing practically no assistant engineering; he had become the full-time percussionist, which he enjoyed though he missed the chance to experiment with sound, and hoped he would get it again when he became a producer. He was also no longer a salaried employee, but taking his chances on the availability of sessions with the rest of the band. To the musicians—who were still unaware of the larger picture—Stan's arrival seemed another piece of the puzzle falling into place; if someone as respected in Memphis music circles as Stan Kesler was now involved with the studio, it must be more proof that American was headed for big things. Having Stan there meant that the studio could now schedule sessions without Chips; Stan could not only engineer but produce if necessary. His mixes were even cleaner than those of Hayward Bishop: from now on, American Studios recordings would have a light, spacious sound in which almost every instrument was clearly audible. That worked particularly well with the Prine recordings, since Prine was a writer in the folk tradition where every word was intended to be heard. Kesler liked Prine's writing and thought him "real easy to work with," the perfect beginning to his career at the studio.

The keyboards dominate two more Prine standards, "Hello in There" and "Sam Stone." Bobby Emmons provides understated accents to Prine's narrative about lonely old people, with a structure in the chorus that seems to bear down even more harshly than Prine's already harsh voice.

"Sam Stone" is one of the definitive songs of the Vietnam years. It begins with a terse opening verse that works as would the beginning of a short story: "Sam Stone came home / To the wife and family / After serving in the conflict overseas." Wounded in the war and suffering from PTSD, Sam develops a drug addiction that results in petty theft to support his habit, and finally dies of an overdose: "Climbing walls while sitting in a chair." The keyboards and Reggie Young's sitar emphatically underline the

sentence describing the powerful grip in which heroin kept Sam: "And the gold roared through his veins / Like a thousand railroad trains." The chorus switches to the first-person perspective of one of the children: "There's a hole in Daddy's arm, where all the money goes," and emphasizes the emotional damage a dysfunctional family can inflict: "Little pitchers have big ears . . . Sweet songs never last too long on broken radios." "Sam Stone" is a grim slice of life that fits the already established tradition of American Studios, and in its no-nonsense realism it remains one of the group's classic recordings.

If all of the songs on the album up to this point were rough-cut jewels of storytelling, honed and polished by the American group until they glowed, "Pretty Good" marks the beginning of the throwaways. It starts out promisingly, as a laconic satire of small talk ("Pretty good, not bad, I can't complain / But actually, everything is just about the same") and quickly degenerates into an unrelated series of Prine's jokes and fillers ("Up in the sky, an Arabian rabbi/ Fed Quaker Oats to a priest") as if he has a verse to occupy and he does not particularly care how. The Roger Miller influence is there, but Prine seems to have forgotten that even the most outrageous of Miller's jokes had elegance and context; he was not just doing wordplay for its own sake.

Mike Leech sticks to a six-note bass line throughout the recording, and would use that figure on three other songs during the session, apparently because he saw no space to be inventive. It may have been his protest about being handed such material, but that six-note riff became a signature; producers and listeners alike realized he could get more out of six notes than many bassists could out of twenty. "I thought what I played was boring on most of that album, but I did like the overall product, what everyone else played," he observed. Bobby Emmons and Reggie Young rise to the challenge inherent in the song, Emmons with a swooping organ line that singlehandedly saves (and sparks) the entire track, and Reggie Young by a completely anarchic display of feedback-laden slide guitar at the end, as if he is saying to Prine, "Okay, you bring us a crazy song? Well, we can get crazy, too." Of course, since their responsibility was to embellish, it was easier for Reggie and Emmons to find spaces in the songs than it was for Mike Leech, Gene Chrisman, or Hayward Bishop, who had to establish a rhythm and be supportive with material that seemed to have no internal beat and nothing to support.

The disaster of "Pretty Good" is followed by three compositions that show Prine again in control of his talent. "Your Flag Decal Won't Get You into Heaven Anymore" is a satire that works. At the height of the Vietnam War, its supporters pasted flag decals and stickers on their car windows in the same spirit as the "Support the Troops" signs on cars during the war in Iraq, and *Reader's Digest* even included flag decals in issues of their magazine. Prine's song takes a good-natured poke at this, including only one serious line to make his point; "Now Jesus don't like killing, no matter what the reason's for." It is ironic that the American group should be the ones to have recorded this; there is an assumption that musicians of the era were liberal, but most of the American group made a typically Southern transition to conservative politics, a journey typified and summed up by Bobby Wood. "My family were Democrats years ago," he said, and although he later became a conservative voter and even donated to the Republican party, "I'm still not a Republican; I'm a common-sense person. I guess I'm a Reagan Democrat."

"Far from Me" is Prine being serious again. There is some wordplay involved, but it is really an Edward Hopper painting come to life; the story line details a love affair slowly running out of steam. Stan Kesler's spacious mix symbolizes the emotional distance between the couple, and even the final scene closes out non-committally: "I said, 'Will I see you tomorrow?' She said, 'No, I've got something to do.'" Mike Leech reprises his six-note bass line as the melody is predominately carried by Leo LeBlanc (who toured with Prine for awhile). The chorus slips into pure poetry, with the line "an old broken bottle looks just like a diamond ring" accented by Hayward Bishop's metallic-sounding triangle.

The six-note bass line turns up yet again in a selection destined to be a standard. "Angel from Montgomery" is such an exemplar of compressed, cynical writing that its merit was obviously immediately after the album was released. Bonnie Raitt picked up on it immediately and the song became identified with her. Its sharp, bluesy pattern (doubtless the element that drew Raitt to the song) is probably Prine's strongest melody. Raitt's version keeps the song's vulnerability without the rage; on Prine's original recording, it is jarring to hear a man singing the opening line, "I am an old woman," and the bitterness of the song is so palpable that it leaps off the record, "If dreams were lightning, and thunder were desire / This old house would have burnt down a long time ago," Prine snarls in his angry nonvoice. He is even more biting in the final verse: "How the hell can a person / Go to work in the morning / And come home in the evening with nothing to say?" The conclusion, reached in the chorus, is an extension of what the American group had been saying in their music all along: "To believe in this living is just a hard way to go." Bobby Emmons only realized this connection with their previous work years after the fact: "That's where 'In the Ghetto' belongs, in the same scene as Prine wrote," he said with some surprise. In addition to all its other treasures, the recording features the finest Hammond B3 solo Bobby Emmons ever contributed; he commands the intro forcefully., giving it an almost gospel emphasis, and he imbues the long fade-out with graceful swoops, swirls and curlicues that suggest a wild bird taking flight. "I wish I could remember that," laughed the organist.

"Quiet Man" is another throwaway, punctuated by the six-note bass line Mike Leech had by now played on four songs. "I guess crawl inside this crazy brain of mine, maybe you can tell me why I played the same bass line four times," Mike said ruefully. "Not trying to pass the buck by any means, but for me (or other good session men) to play the same thing even twice on the same album is unusual. Of the thousands of songs I've played on, on each and every one I try to come up with something different. There's an old studio joke I've heard a few times when somebody plays a lick that isn't working, and says, 'That's funny, that lick worked on the session I did yesterday.' Probably the hardest time for playing something new or different is on standard country sessions, where there is a formula for what is played." To a certain extent, Prine's work fit the country formula of which Mike spoke; the new wave of Nashville writers seized upon the album and claimed it as an inspiration. One irony is that this track, which features Mike's plodding bass line, has an introductory verse that could have been spoken by the bassist to describe himself: "I don't talk much, I'm a quiet man / Beauty and silence both run deep / and I am running like crazy while you are asleep." Between the string arrangements he was doing for most of the sessions, his bass playing, his increased discontent with the behavior shown by Chips, and a personal life that featured a crumbling marriage, Mike was indeed "running like crazy" during this time; his salvation was his work, and in hanging out at the studio.

"Donald and Lydia" is another novelistic vignette, sounding almost cinematic in its descriptions of the fat girl and the young soldier who longs for her. It is hardly a conventional love story, and the affair between them seems to be consummated only in their solitary fantasies, but we are left with the sour conclusion that it is better than nothing. LeBlanc and Bobby Emmons give the closeout music a swirling feel evocative of roller coasters, carousels, penny arcades, and the bright lights of the midway movie where Lydia worked as ticket-taker and young soldiers like Donald wandered in from the nearby Army base. "Six O'Clock News" is another grim ballad, culminating in a suicide: "The whole town saw Jimmy / On the six o'clock news / His brains were on the sidewalk / His blood was on his shoes." The denouement immediately calls to mind the soliloquy on an unknown "C. Green" in *You Can't Go Home Again*, where Thomas Wolfe does an entire riff on the probable life, dreams, and purpose of one unknown man who leaped out of a New York hotel window.

Uncharacteristically for a recording made at American Studios, the album ends on an upbeat note. The sentimentally unsentimental "Flashback Blues" features an experimental trade-off: Gene Chrisman on percussion and Hayward Bishop playing drums. It was one of several instances when that occurred, much to the enjoyment of both. "I had my own percussion section, right next to Gene," Hayward recalled happily. That group of percussion instruments—tambourine, cabasas, all sort of exotic things—had been purchased for the studio by Gene, once he realized there was someone on staff who could handle the chore. "We had a good time," Gene said warmly. Stan Kesler mixed Hayward's percussion tracks at a lower level than did Chips, blending them with the rest of the music for a less intrusive effect.

The Prine sessions featured other tracks with Hayward Bishop playing drums; this was at around the height of Gene's absences. They were too similar in musical interpretation to have a two-drumset situation, as was popular at the time (used by the Allman Brothers, the Grateful Dead, Lynyrd Skynyrd, and others); nevertheless, the two drummers enjoyed taking turns at setting the beat and adding embellishments with percussion, reading each other instinctively and staying out of one another's way. As with Mike Leech and Bobby Emmons, who also experienced their duties being shared by someone else, neither man in the drum chair saw the other as a rival, but as a contributor—an approach that embodied the spirit of the group at its best.

No one from the Atlantic crew was along this time save Arif Mardin, and the musicians who had worked with him before found him slightly different this time, more reserved and removed. Hayward Bishop remembered playing drums and running down a song that he thought would work better if he changed the rhythm accents slightly. Arif was standing directly across from him, and "He looked me right in the eye and said [lapsing into Arif's heavily Turkish accent] 'No experimenting, please.'"

If the Cymarron album had been a brilliant failure, the John Prine album was a signpost, pointing in the direction the group would travel from then on. Nobody had a name for this kind of music yet. A few people were calling it "progressive country," but that did not seem to fit. Nonetheless, the success of Kristofferson and the underground prestige of the Prine album, with its hard-hitting songs that were recorded by other artists, was proof that a new generation was in town, and that their way of making country music was the way ahead.

"That album came off real well," said Stan Kesler with quiet satisfaction. Despite its immediate impact when it was released in early 1972, Bobby Emmons for one felt that "It has yet to be recognized for what it is. It was country music as far as taking on those subjects, kinda reporting." He was fully aware of the craftsmanly enhancement the group had given the recording. "A lot of the rock groups would try something like that, but they would turn down the volume and turn up the guitars," he observed. "A lot of people like to do a thing where they pull the curtain and show a silhouette. We left a lot of room for the story to stick out." At the other extreme, Hayward Bishop, with his roots in the more uptempo sound of beach music, found the whole Prine session to be really trying. "We were tired by the time we got halfway through it," he said. "It was a drudgery. I was glad when it was over."

In the studio as the Prine album was completed, watching Arif Mardin wrap up the session, was the newest act on the Entrance label, an aspiring singer who had been an eighteen-year-old schoolboy not long before. Billy Burnette had been a week out of high school in Los Angeles when his father Dorsey, who was now a respected songwriter and who had known Chips Moman since the days of the Rock and Roll Trio in Memphis, had mentioned that his old pal happened to be in town and that Billy should look him up. "Chips was staying at the Hyatt Regency," Billy remembered laconically. He played Chips some of the material he'd been working on and he was immediately signed to Entrance "as a writer and an artist," Billy said.

Billy flew to Memphis and with Chips's help found a small apartment off Overton Square and settled in. Chips assigned him yet another of those specially created places at the studio while he learned the ropes. "I worked running the tape machine. It was a good time to be down there; it was a good time to be in Memphis," he recalled. "Overton Square was really rockin'. The people I met through Chips was amazing." Of course, Chips knew people all over the city, from the upper echelons to the seediest (though he seemed to prefer the seediest ones). The roughness of the area in which the musicians worked was made apparent. "I had an old Chevy Nova," Billy recalled. "I think it was my first car. . . . My car got stolen one day and the guys let it go in the middle of the street because it stalled." Memphis itself was a known quantity to Billy, because he had always had ties there. "I had family all in Memphis—aunts, cousins," he said. And in coming to American, he discovered a family all his own.

"It was an amazing journey," he said. Billy grew up around music business professionals and was no stranger to the business himself. He toured with Brenda Lee during his thirteenth summer, and when he had been a child, "Herb Alpert produced a couple of Dr. Seuss records with me." But the amount of talent he discovered at the studio was astonishing, especially since he was learning what all of them had accomplished. It surprised him that they themselves seemed not to completely know. "I don't think they knew the power they had; they didn't act like it," he said. He had heard his father and his uncle Johnny often speak of Chips, and he was vaguely familiar with some of the releases the studio had done because "My dad had mentioned a few names. I was a big fan of the Elvis records," he said, but he added, "I didn't know the depth of who they were."

He was granted a warm reception. "They accepted me really good, for being a kid," he said. "They were amazing, they were so nice to me." In Billy, the group found a lot to like: a quiet but amiable sort who seemed serious about his work but always willing to have fun with them. Bobby Wood and Johnny Christopher connected immediately with him, as fellow writers, and he and Johnny almost instantly began working up songs. Mike Leech thought Chips had signed an artist of practically unlimited potential. "I've always thought of Billy as super talented," he said with admiration. "He's good-looking, sings great, pretty good guitar player." Stan Kesler had known Billy's father in the early days. "Billy, he was a talented boy," said the soundman. "I don't know if Billy inherited his talent from Dorsey or his style was created personally, but when he combined his singing and his guitar feel, he was truly electric," said Bobby Emmons admiringly. "He had a wonderful feel."

The arrival of Billy Burnette seemed to be another indication that the new label would take off at any second. Billy was only eighteen and already seemed poised to become an artist with real chart longevity. The presence of Billy Burnette and Stan Kesler, two people with impeccable Memphis music pedigrees, looked to the group as if Chips was in a position to virtually take over the town. American now had links all the way to the beginning of the city's rockabilly scene. The studio was staking its claim to both the recent past and to the future, and this further raised the musicians' hopes, creating an air of excitement around the place that Billy vividly remembered.

Marty Lacker was involved at the time with a project that helped to spotlight the group's accomplishments. He wrote, produced, and staged the first annual Memphis Music Awards, a spectacular intended to draw international attention to the city's music industry. It began, said Marty, with a casual conversation. "The biggest bank [in Memphis] was the First National—Lyman Aldrich wanted the music industry's business," Marty recalled. "He said, 'I'd like to throw a dinner for all the studio people.' From that came Memphis Music Industries. I came up with . . . the Memphis Music Awards." At the 1971 ceremonies, five of the American players were nominees for musician of the year, and "Chips won the Producer of the Year award," Marty added proudly. Though Chips claimed that awards meant nothing to him, to be honored by the city he loved had to have been one of the highlights of his life. "At that time, Memphis was my heart and soul," he said with deep emotion.

Recognition from the Memphis Music Awards filled the studio atmosphere with renewed possibilities—but on another level, the mood was deflated and confused, almost listless. No one was really talking to anyone else; no messages either from Chips or from the upstairs business offices seemed clear. And it was precisely at this time, when the musicians did not need any other distractions, that a new element became commonplace at the studio. For the first time, the players understood what Weinstein and Stroll had been talking about. Now many of them occasionally wore illegal smiles.

"I correlate weed arriving at the same time Billy Burnette did," said Mike Leech. Billy brought his California customs with him, and before long many of the American group, their curiosity provoked by the example, began turning on to Jamaican Gold. The only two musicians who were willing to speak for the record about that time period recalled it as an adventurous experiment. "There were some funny, funny times spent with each other," said Mike Leech. "I've laughed at Hayward's nonsense till my sides hurt." Bobby Wood claimed that at first the drug sharpened his awareness. "I think at an early-on point, it did help me hear things I wouldn't have ordinarily heard," he reflected thoughtfully. "But there's a cutoff point, and I didn't know when I had gone past it."

Not everyone went along with it. Gene Chrisman limited his smoking to cigarettes. Bobby Emmons continued to be his abstemious self, consuming nothing stronger than his usual enormous amounts of black coffee (caffeine, of course, is a stimulant, working almost like uppers on the nervous system), although he too began hanging around the studio more, curiously watching the others giggling and reeling and being playful under the influence. Richard Mainegra also avoided it. Stan Kesler, older than the musicians he recorded, had always stayed away from that sort of thing, and did so now. "You get on that dope, it cuts out your thinking process," said Stan. "I always thought I could do better if my brain was clear. . . . I'd say 'Well, if I can't hear now I don't think I wanna hear' when they'd pass the joints and say 'Aw c'mon, it'll help you hear better.'" Tommy Cogbill's attitude was "Big deal"; marijuana had long been a fact of life in the jazz world and he was already bored by the concept, though it amused him that his younger friends thought they had made the discovery of a lifetime.

Chips Moman was no stranger to getting high either, although the musicians did not realize that at the time. "We were so naïve we didn't realize he was already doing it," said Mike Leech. "Our thing was, don't use it when working. We held onto that pretty good, depending on the artist and the importance of the session. Also we had to be careful because the cops were friends and they were apt to stroll in the back door at any time. Weed was a big taboo back then."

The rule, Mike added, was "made up ourselves—not enforced by anyone," and it seemed to work. They approached recording with the same focused professionalism they had always shown. "We didn't believe we could perform as well under the influence," Mike commented. If the group preferred to stay unstoned while working for the most part, what they did in the off hours, waiting around for a session or just hanging out at the studio was another matter. "Almost all of us enjoyed it from time to time, and especially after work during playbacks," Mike recalled. They discovered favorite places to smoke—the echo chambers were one, and they also toked up on the roof of the building. (The musicians were not the only ones who had discovered the building's roof. "We used to hear noises on the roof and not know what it was," Chips Moman said amusedly. They found out later that the fourteen-year-old girl who lived next door to the studio was climbing up there with some of her friends. "They would listen to the music through the roof," Chips added. "If I'd known that, we could've written 'Up on the Roof'"—a comment that provoked one of his most contented cackles.)

The musicians did not need herbs to stimulate grand visions. The scenario of what would happen when the new label really got under way was a particularly delightful dream. They expected, and Chips encouraged them to think, that the new label would in time become a one-of-a kind musicians' cooperative that would be a beacon and an example to the rest of the music business, with everyone in authority of some kind and everyone taking part in production and administrative decisions. Hayward Bishop said of the unspoken assumptions:

It was expected that Tommy was going to be made a partner and then the succession of band-member/lieutenants would follow. I personally expected the order of command to be Chips and Tommy as equal partners, then Stan Kesler, and then Reggie (because of his age), then Bobby Emmons. And maybe Reg and Bobby would share an equal position. . . . To this day, that pecking order, with Marty Lacker on board the team . . . making up the board of directors, would have been a killer combination of talent that in many ways resembled Motown's and Atlantic's. . . . Especially since we were already being used by Atlantic. Also, Stax's chief talents were willing to come over with us.

For now, they had to live in the present, and the present was less than gratifying. Chips was still frequently absent, and many of the 45s he produced when he was on the premises did not sound as if they would set the world on fire. "Long Distance Kissing," a song written and recorded by Toni Wine about her romance with Chips and produced by him, was forever viewed by Mike Leech and Hayward Bishop as the antithesis of everything American Studios had stood for. The group that had made its reputation with no-nonsense realism like "Nine-Pound Steel," "In the Ghetto," and even "Sam Stone" was now reduced to backing a female voice crooning, "Long distance kissing / don't make the missing go away." Such a record also rubbed salt in the wounds of several musicians who were enduring troubled marriages (Mike Leech's marriage ended at around that time, and he sorrowfully surrendered custody of his daughters) and who were understandably sour about the couple's passion being thrown in their faces.

Even when he was focused, Chips was almost always selecting material that explored the theme of infidelity. The soul singer Mittie Collier's Entrance single was a two-sided treatise on the subject: the angry "I'd Like to Change Places with His Part-Time Lover" (a tacit admission that Laurie, waiting at home on the farm, was not having an easy time of it during this period) with the impassioned, desperate "If This Is the Last Time" on the B-side. Johnny Christopher's solo 45, an Isaac Hayes–influenced single written by the acoustic guitarist and called "Love Stuff," emphasizes the steamy side of an affair. It made the others, who prided themselves on not having to resort to double entendre to get across their messages, very uneasy; even Bobby Wood, the person closest to Johnny at the studio, had some misgivings about the song. Its message did not seem to trouble Chips.

When Toni Wine occasionally went back to New York, Chips stopped by the studio even when he had no scheduled sessions, just to see what was going on and be part of everything—much to the confusion of the musicians, who did not know whether he was appearing among them as leader or brother. At times, Chips himself seemed not to know. Invariably, the good-natured games wound up in a betting frenzy when Chips was there. For instance, there was the Night of the Great Race. Recalled Hayward Bishop:

On this particular Toni-less hangout evening, Chips turned every competition into five-dollar bets. Red Williams was there shaking his head in amazement at our childishness. After [Chips] winning several thousand imaginary dollars racing everybody around the parking lot and changing the rules to his advantage, and spouting these words: "Youth is no match for an old man with speed," which I thought was hilarious, Red Williams, who took the remark as a pompous declaration of near deification, took me aside and whispered a challenge I should use on Chips. I hadn't been involved in the competition yet. . . . I said, "Chips, I'll race with you around the parking lot one lap for five dollars." Chips said, "You're on." Red counted down and said, "Go!" Chips came out of the chute like a year-old stallion and gave it his all—while I just barely trotted around to the finish line where Chips was bent over panting from his burst of glory. I said, "Give

me the five dollars." He said, "*What*??!! I won the race, dummy." Then I said the exact words that Red had instructed for me to say: "Yes, but I said I would race with you for five dollars—I didn't say I would beat you." Everybody laughed. I believe that created a lasting bad impression on Chips. Red was the winner that day.

That was the kind of hustle Chips appreciated, and it is easy to imagine him using the same trick on somebody else later.

When Toni was available, Chips stayed away from the studio as much as ever, and though the band had little to do at this point they kept hoping for a turnaround. Something—perhaps a new artist, perhaps the presence of Stan Kesler and Billy Burnette, perhaps the opportunity to write something—would rekindle Chips's interest and everything would be as before. "No one knew when he was gonna show up," said Hayward Bishop. In the meantime, while they waited, there were the games. The ping-pong playing was nearly compulsive. They invented a "cup game" which involved trying to bat an empty Styrofoam cup all over the studio without ever letting it once touch the floor. "I had forgotten about the cup game," said Mike Leech amusedly. "You wouldn't think that would be much exercise but it was huge fun. It was actually one of those Styrofoam coffee cups. When you hit it up there was no telling which way it would fall so it kept you jumping around." Reggie Young remembered a billiard game they called "wompy-doo."

"In full game mode now, because of Chips's absenteeism and the band's boredom, we were running out of challenges," recalled Hayward Bishop. One night most of the group were there waiting for something to happen, even Gene Chrisman, who was seldom around for the hijinks. Hayward continued:

He got caught up in the heat of hyper-gamism. He was the Guru of Games. . . . He came up with a ball game where the individual would have to bounce a ball off a series of objects with one throw in a particular sequence. This particular episode had the studio tympani drum up against the metal back door. An empty wine bottle . . .

was placed on the drum head. The ball had to bounce off a panel, the door, and the tymp without knocking over the bottle. Gene could do it! Nobody else could.

Can you imagine the variety of sounds this bounce sequence produced??? "Bap, slap, bong, and thud." Billy Burnette threw the ball too hard and knocked the bottle over and broke it. That sound was, "Bap, slap, bong, and thud CRASH!" After we had laughed uproariously, Gene said he thought he heard someone outside.

The Memphis police regularly patrolled the parking lot, because of the high-crime area and because by now almost everyone's car had been broken into. Billy Burnette was the only one of the musicians who did not carry a gun. Hayward continued:

We all thought maybe somebody might be breaking in our cars. So in a testosterone rush, I volunteered to check it out. We got very quiet. I got my gun out, cocked it, eased up to the back door, then flung it open and struck an Audie Murphy–like stance, holding the gun straight out. Immediately, a cop yelled "Drop the gun!" from a half-hidden position behind the dumpster about four feet away. Dumb me, instead of being scared, was relieved and said, "Oh, thank God. Hey guys, it's the police." Never realizing how close I came to being shot by a cop who was aiming a .357 Magnum at me, at point-blank range of approximately two and a half feet and who had to make the instant determination of whether I was a good guy or a bad guy. To this day I shiver at the stupidity of my action and am thankful for the training that officer had had. We didn't play that game again.

There were still occasional sessions, and the one immediately following Billy Burnette's arrival was done for a client Buddy Killen brought from Nashville, an African American singer-songwriter named Paul Kelly. Kelly and his companion (later wife), a superb backup singer named Juanita Rogers, wrote impassioned soul ballads and Southern genre paintings with equal skill. ("Jezebel," written by Kelly

and Rogers, is a near-perfect portrait of gossipy Southern biddies and their reaction to a sexy younger member of their church congregation: "Hide my son.") Killen seems to have viewed him as a more serious version of Joe Tex, and selections like "Dirt" (as in "he ain't nothin' but") and "The Day After Forever" are as melodic and soulful as anything the group had ever done. Hayward Bishop, however, was feeling a slight carryover from the Prine sessions, as he also sensed little in Kelly's songs for the musicians to grasp. "The stuff he presented to us came off like African chants," he said (a quality most audible in the album's title song and opener "Dirt," featuring Hayward 's moody, rattling percussion and his attention-commanding cowbell). "The sessions seemed stiff," Hayward added. "It seemed like everything came off the same, to me. Of course, Buddy Killen didn't tell you if you were going in the right direction or not." "Yeah, I remember on several occasions where we would do a great-feeling take and afterwards Buddy would come out in the studio with this scrunched-up face and say, 'It just doesn't . . . just doesn't . . . feel right . . .'" added Mike Leech. Stan Kesler contributed a warm, immediate mix that sounded as if Kelly and Juanita were directly in the room with the listener, and everyone was more sure than ever that, with Stan on board, good things were just bound to happen.

But it seemed to be always the case with this group that even as one door opened, another closed. Marty Lacker had become thoroughly disillusioned and disappointed with the studio operation by mid-1971. He refused to discuss many of the details, saying only that the reasons were "between Chips and I." Certain reasons can be deduced, however. Marty was unhappy with Patsy Hill's attempting to develop her own power base through Chips, and the studio was not progressing as rapidly as Marty had doubtless hoped it would at the time he came on board. It was time now to move on, and Marty did, leaving to establish his own marketing and promotion firm, which he called Mempro. "We represented worldwide music publishers and placed their songs with producers and artists," Marty recalled. "We also promoted records for airplay to radio stations for all the major record companies and others in the country. That plus we handled all the Memphis Music, Incorporated business and then for the Memphis and Shelby County Music Commisssion that I founded with the city and county governments in late '71, for which I was the first chairman of the commission." Between that and developing the Memphis Music Awards, Marty was busier than ever, and seldom went back to American due to what he saw as the increasingly poisonous atmosphere there.

Tommy Cogbill was not involved in the new commissions and groups set up to codify the institution of Memphis music. In August 1971 he began work on an album that revealed his production talent in all its complexity. The Ronnie Milsap album had begun an involvement that Warner Brothers, then considered the most experimental and artist-oriented record label, was taking in Memphis (Paul Kelly's album also came out on Warner), and Tommy was asked to do an album for a long-underrated and sadly-neglected talent.

Arthur Alexander's career had been languishing practically from the time of his first hit ten years before. "You Better Move On" had been a revelation when it came out in 1961; its simple story line, plain-spoken lyric, and easily accessible tune, together with Arthur's soft vocal delivery, revealed the country side of R&B and was the first big hit for Muscle Shoals. But Rick Hall, who had produced the record, and the session players who had participated (Dan Penn's Pallbearers, no less) had established more solid careers than had Arthur, who was perhaps one of the first and certainly one of the most original singer-songwriters in the music business. He had recorded (in the Shoals and elsewhere) all through the sixties, but nothing ever happened with the songs he cut, some of which he remade and reconstructed for these sessions.

Because Arthur had a history of depression and other difficulties, his closest friend, Donnie Fritts, came up from the Shoals to look after him while work was going on. "To be honest, they felt like they couldn't trust Arthur," Donnie said of the label executives. "My wife

Donna and I took him over" (though Donna Fritts did not remember and said she was not involved). Of course , that was no hardship for Donnie, since he loved visiting there. "Some of my best memories are of being at that studio in Memphis," he said.

And no one need have worried. Arthur handled everything very well while he was there, and the musicians remembered him warmly. "Right off the bat, he had the respect of everybody," Donnie recalled happily. "He was the biggest, meanest-looking man I ever saw," said Mike Leech. "But he was one of the gentlest, nicest guys I ever met. Liked him a lot." "He had the biggest hands I'd ever seen," recalled Hayward Bishop. Spooner Oldham had worked with Arthur since the Shoals and from his vantage point in California he watched the developments happily, because he had always liked Arthur. "I'm sure it's hard to get a whole-person overview, because I never knew Arthur outside the studio," he observed, adding that whenever he and Arthur had worked together, he had always found him to be "friendly, no static. I always wondered what he was like when life situations occurred." "I liked Arthur," said Bobby Emmons happily. "Since 'You Better Move On' had always been one of my favorite records, every time we worked together, I felt under pressure to cut something in the league with that."

"It was funny watching Tommy as [Arthur's] producer because of their stature," chuckled Mike Leech. "Tommy would come out [of the control room] to suggest something to Arthur and have to look straight up. Funny. The other amusing thing I remember is, we did a song of his where it's called for a single pitched note to be sung whereas it's held across a few measures. Sort of a chanting thing. Arthur had a tendency to sing a little sharp, and when this part of the song came up, Tommy's head would cock a little sideways, like a dog hearing a siren."

The CD reissue some years later has the songs out of sequence, ruining the effect of the album, so the Ace Records 1988 reissue on vinyl is the most essential pressing of the work. It followed the original track listing, and the songs shall be discussed in the order presented there. "I'm Coming Home," the album opener, features a memorable (if somewhat clunky) groove and a blaring horn section throughout. Tommy framed the songs with strong intros to capture the listener's attention, and the horn line makes this one an immediate success. "He could *cut*! Wonderful, wonderful tracks for those songs," exclaimed Donnie Fritts. This one is a celebration of a man leaving work, in perhaps the same mood Tommy might have felt when he pulled off another of his late-night escapes, heading for Whitehaven in his Jaguar, ready to forget the increasingly depressing atmosphere of the studio for the time being ("Just let the good guys sing their song / And let the villains do their wrong"). Its closest parallel is Ian Tyson's "Be There When I Get Home," recorded in Nashville around the same time; the scene is roughly the same, a man on his way home late at night after having been "worn to a frazzle" at work, but the speaker in Tyson's song is not at all sure anyone will even be in the house waiting for him; in Alexander's version, there will be a light in the window, a bed in which to rest, and no clamorous responsibilities demanding that a tired, worn man should shoulder them alone.

"It Hurts to Want It So Bad" is the album's second track, and from the opening notes of the tightly woven acoustic guitars (Reggie Young, Johnny Christopher, and possibly Tommy Cogbill himself; Hayward Bishop recalled that Tommy overdubbed some parts) the listener enters the song's mood of despondent longing. At first, attention focuses on the lyrics as Arthur simply and effectively tells the story of how the longing for love affects different age groups, but closer listening makes one realize that the guitars sound as if they are cutting you in two, and it takes slightly further listening to realize that this is exactly the intended effect.

"Go Home Girl" is slightly reminiscent of "You Better Move On" both in melody and song structure; Tommy sequences it as a bridge between "It Hurts" and his other important statement about despondency. "I'm in the Middle of It All" strikes a quiet, stoic mood, evoked by its distant-sounding horn line. Where Chips Moman would have pulled out

all the stops and played the agony in this song for all it was worth, Tommy downplays the anguish. "He was always very understated, which is the grace of a producer," said American Studios keyboard player Shane Keister. It is a skillfully written song with a strong melody, and Arthur Alexander's naturally soft voice talks as much as it sings. The song seems to come from a place of inexhaustible sorrow, which on the surface would have made the song a better fit for Chips than for Tommy, but Cogbill treats the lyric and Arthur's voice with understanding and compassion, never letting the track overwhelm the story. The chorus and the final verse are completely given over to Arthur's suffering: "I ache with heartache and pain / And I've got a hurt / Lord knows that I can't explain." The track is a less anguished version of Tommy's earlier "Sounds of Love," with its similar expression of confusion.

"Burnin' Love," recorded several months before Elvis found it, expresses the other side of Tommy, the partygoer and prankster the musicians knew, the one who took over the upper suites of the Holiday Inn Rivermont for some memorable bashes when his song-plugger friend Johnny McCrae was in town. (Hayward Bishop recalled attending one such party and seeing Tommy carefully picking his way through the madness, greeting the percussionist as jauntily as if he were saying hello to him in the park.) During one of those events, Chips paid the local police a goodly amount of money to take Tommy's Corvette and park it in the lobby of the Rivermont—and no one found that funnier than Tommy himself. "I only remember Tommy once or twice being anything but jovial and happy," observed Shane Keister, who did not know Tommy in Memphis but became a good friend when the group had relocated to Nashville. "Burnin' Love" expressed the upbeat side of Tommy, but as a recording it somewhat misfires; Tommy races through it with seemingly little regard for its rhythm, emphasizing instead a deceptively smooth horn section. Theoretically, a Tommy Cogbill recording of "Burnin' Love" could have been one of the great recordings of all time; the actual track did not completely pan out.

That can never be said of the ballad written by Dan Penn and Donnie Fritts that closes side one of the album. Volumes could, and maybe someday will, be written about the greatness of "Rainbow Road." Mike Leech said of the song, "I loved [it]." "Rainbow Road" is arguably Dan Penn's finest contemporary story song, written, as is always the case with him, from the gloomy side of Clinch Mountain. He and Donnie expressively narrate in first person the tale of an aspiring singer eventually sent up for murder, and Arthur Alexander assumes the voice of the old black bluesman in the story so convincingly that most listeners believed every word in it had happened to him. Not so, Donnie Fritts insisted. "'Rainbow Road' was written *for* Arthur, and not *about* him," the writer declared adamantly. "It was a song I wanted to write for Arthur's voice." Tommy surrounds the simple eloquence of Arthur's vocal with a production so Southern and atmospheric that the trailing string line, as weary-sounding as a sigh, evokes falling-down small houses and cotton fields strung along dust-covered roads. There is also a surprise ending, the light trickle of Bobby Wood's piano introducing Mike Leech's somber string line and Reggie Young's biting, bluesy guitar asides to fade out the record. It is interesting that Glen Spreen's dark-and-stormy-night arrangement of "Rainbow Road," done in Nashville for Joan Baez the following year, begins with his piano, as if he is continuing the story where Bobby Wood left off.

If one is listening on vinyl, one now hears the rollicking A-side of a 1973 single, "Lover Please," and quickly flips over for several songs in a row that can be heard as a suite, a mediation on life and love. "Love's Where Life Begins" was an older song; Alexander had first recorded it in the mid-sixties, but Tommy smoothed it out from the somewhat rough first version, using Mike Leech's reliable bass as punctuation for the story he wanted to tell. The song's first four lines are so pessimistic that it is surprising Chips Moman never tried a production of it; lines like "Yesterday I was happy, I was / Full of life and full of love / Everything was going my way / But then again, that was yesterday"

seem custom-tailored for him. Tommy placed the emphasis elsewhere; he seemed particularly to highlight the Beatlesque "yeah yeah yeah" refrain, giving the backing vocals by Charles Chalmers's family group (the Joint Venture) prominence and allowing them to do some delightful call-and-response with Mike Leech's bass line.

Steve Cropper's "Down the Back Roads" features Reggie Young playing terse, Cropper-style guitar, a beautiful unbroken string line by Mike Leech, and Hayward Bishop playing a family heirloom, a pair of castanets his parents had bought on their honeymoon. Tommy utilizes the melodic gifts of the group to emphasize the lyrics, self-descriptive in the beginning—"Take this road, on my own / There's only me to hold on": no one to tell him when he was making a mistake, no one to advise him, it was all up to him. "Make my bed, where I lay my head / and travel on down the back roads." For Tommy, the back roads were better than the highway; he was seeking a place "where the simple life is found / That's where I'll lay my troubles down." Unlike Chips, who did not seem to believe he could ever shed it, Tommy apparently sought a way to "loose myself from this heavy load." And as was stated in the song, the way to do that was to find your place, know it, and remain there, and once that happened a man could live in peace with himself: "Whippoorwill sings a song / This is where you belong. / Find a friend, and you'll begin / Traveling down the back roads." In an era of attempts to pack too much philosophy into the fragile weight of a three-minute song, "Down the Back Roads" is profound without even trying to be; Henry David Thoreau would have understood the song perfectly.

"Call Me Honey" is from Dennis Linde, the man who wrote "Burning Love" (he also wrote "I'm Coming Home"); Linde's work was undoubtedly brought to Tommy by Johnny Mc-Crae, since Linde was a staff writer for Combine. In taking this work to Tommy, McCrae found Linde's greatest interpreter; the writer had a real feel for both R&B and Southern vernacular songs which brought out similar inclinations in Tommy. "Call Me Honey" is a mixture of those two styles, evoking front porches on cloudy spring days and a good old boy's remorse after a quarrel. The horn arrangement alone is a classic of Memphis music, and Tommy creates from the raw material a recording that is funky but tuneful, and as always with him, completely original.

"Come Along with Me," a song written by Arthur and Donnie Fritts, closes out the suite of songs with boundless tenderness; to hear the song, then and now, is to weep. "Most of my songs come from ideas," said Donnie, and this song is an expression of both Donnie's extraordinary sensitivity and the warm goodwill of Arthur Alexander's voice. Add to that Tommy Cogbill's gentleness, and it becomes a remarkable recording. It is addressed directly to a young girl, perhaps a girl like the one who had been emotionally moved by Tommy's records; the speaker, be it Arthur, Donnie, or Tommy, is so aware of her pent-up and inchoate longings that it seems he shares them: "Little girl, I know that you are young / You're listening for a song, but it ain't been sung / You're looking for a love, well, I'll show you one." No promises are offered, or given, simply a note of reassurance: "Just come along with me."

From there the song becomes a genre painting, highlighting a feature of Southern courtship that not often commented on: the dire warnings issued to a couple beginning their involvement. Life below the Mason-Dixon line has always been more communal than the more isolated and individualistic lives up north, and it is understood in the South that any romance affects not only the couple involved but their families and the community; consideration must always be given to the collective. Mike Leech weighs in with a string line that is one of the more beautifully eloquent of his career, as if it is he who delivers the dire warnings: "Now I know people say, I've been around / And I can hear them say 'Don't let him tie you down.'" The speaker asks the young girl to judge for herself, and delivers a line in the chorus that is classic Muscle Shoals: "We can make it, baby / Just like grits and gravy." He concludes by saying

once again that he knows she is both longing for a physical experience and starving for affection: "Your young life is hungry, but it will be fed." The effect is reassuring, and the tentative promise of "Come Along with Me" offers more than a thousand songs promising undying love and eternal devotion with nothing to back up the words. A young girl could put her trusting hand in the hand of a man speaking this way, and never for a moment fear.

"Call Me in Tahiti," yet another winner from Dennis Linde, describes being aggravated, annoyed at everything, and wanting to get away. It was a mood Tommy would have understood; the musicians all remembered his shake of the head and his "Whew!" if something was too stressful to be talked about. It is implied that this is only a thirty-second flash and that the speaker will remain in harness, even if he would dearly love to escape and "not worry about that junk at all." A good-humored song, almost boisterous, "Tahiti" satirically dismisses any idealistic hope of changing the world: "I've tried it too, but now I'm saving me / Only me." For the kind of realism preferred in the American Studios view of life, the world can only be saved one person at a time, and Tommy outlined the way such a process takes place in the next track on the album.

Donnie Fritts's and Arthur's "Thank God He Came" is one of the most specifically religious of Tommy's litanies, and it closes out the original Warner album, "Hey, all you sinners," announces Arthur, not in the fire-and-brimstone style of an evangelist but as someone relating to a fellow human being. "I'm talking to you. And I want you to listen, 'cause I am one, too." And quietly, softly, with reverence and awe, as Tommy supports his message, Arthur begins to tell the story of Christ, and repeats the lessons that His life has to teach: "When evil surrounded Him, He overcame / He knew no strangers / Every man was the same." The lessons of forgiveness and egalitarianism, said Arthur and Donnie—and by extension, Tommy—were the priceless gifts that Christ had to give the world, even though that gift was rejected: "The world didn't want Him, but thank God He came."

According to Donnie, the song was written in such an awkward way that even he and Arthur were not sure it was going to work in the studio. "It changes time, and Tommy put it together where it absolutely made sense."

The Warner album ends here, but the Ace reissue closes out with "They'll Do It Every Time," recorded with Arthur at Chip Young's studio in Nashville during a session in 1973. Though it was recorded later, it s worth noticing because its theme is a metaphor for life itself: "When you think you've got it made, that's when your heart will break / Every time." The "they" of the title is on one level a politically incorrect reference to women, but in the context Tommy gives it, "they" means anyone from the suits to the fickle finger of fate, everyone dedicated to pulling the rug out from under someone. "Look out, brother," Arthur—and Tommy—ruefully advises. "You'd better run for cover, 'cause / They'll break your heart / Every time." Tommy imbued the track with flippant cynicism. "I've been here before," he seems to say, "and I'll probably be here again, so I 'm not taking it all that seriously."

The Arthur Alexander album was released unnoticed in January 1972; although it did not become a huge seller, it slowly emerged as a classic recording strictly by word of mouth, partly because the songs and the production steadily grow on the listener. It exhibits Tommy's varied production approach the way a gallery display does for a painter. (It is also a great showcase for the variety and depth of Donnie Fritts's writing.) From all accounts, Tommy himself, seldom inclined to look back at his own work, knew what he had accomplished. "The Arthur thing was his baby, y'know," said Donnie. "I was so proud of Arthur and the way Tommy brought out those songs."

"Tommy was wonderful, one of the best, and a gentleman, too," he added. "He was just such a wonderful person, sweet person." Richard Mainegra offered a revealing snapshot of Tommy from about this time.

One of my thoughts of him was wakin' him up from a deep nap one afternoon to meet my fiancée. At 827 Thomas Street, recording could start at three in the afternoon and go continuously for two days. People would be droppin' like flies and end up dead asleep on the couches in the offices upstairs. That was where I found Tommy this particular afternoon. My fiancée pleaded with me not to wake him, but I was excited that she was in town and I wanted her to meet Tommy. Tommy, bless his heart, sat straight up on the couch like he was about to meet royalty, tryin' his best to act like he was just restin' with his eyes closed for a moment. He sat there and talked to us for a few minutes, with his eyes practically crossed from bein' so tired. He smiled and tried to look like he was coherent, but I'm sure that after Suzie finally pulled me from the room, he fell flat back on the couch and was snorin' before we had reached the bottom step.

Tommy said the least of everyone regarding what he wanted to accomplish if the new label developed as planned. "He'd talk if you talked to him, but he wasn't a big talker; kinda like me," Stan Kesler said with a chuckle. "One on one he'd talk pretty good. We just discussed different sessions. Musician talk , more or less. We'd talk about everything, certain artists, certain songs. We just discussed different sessions." The others could sketch out a reasonable idea of what he expected. If it happened, the situation would be perfect for a man who did not like to knock on doors looking for accounts; if the studio was affiliated with a major label, as it had been throughout much of its history, the record company would automatically send him clients with whom he could work and he could leave all details of promotion and distribution alone. Not enough about the anticipated setup seemed defined yet in the fall of 1971, and so Tommy continued to bide his time.

The other musicians were even more fervently anticipating the future which Chips assured them lay ahead. "We were really talkin' about, 'Boy, this is really gonna be something,'" said Hayward Bishop, remembering the sense of building momentum. At last there seemed every reason for the musicians to feel that way: Stan Kesler was there, Billy Burnette was a talented and prestigious addition to the staff, and Cymarron's one hit record, though none of them had composed it, had focused attention once again on American's writing talent.

The most enduring song composed at American Studios surfaced in the fall of 1971, although it took a little over ten years to find its audience. The story of how "You Were Always on My Mind" was composed is contradictory at times. Wayne Carson wrote the first two verses almost a year previously; Glen Spreen recalled the song being practically a finished entity during his final days at the studio. Wayne wrote the verses for no specific reason except that it seemed to express a universal feeling. (His co-writer Johnny Christopher said, "It came from a real-life situation." Johnny may have been inspired by incidents from his own life, but Wayne adamantly insisted he had not thought of the song in autobiographical terms.) Wayne had been wanting to record the song for some time. It had a plaintive melody and its lyric tenderly expressed regret for things left undone. He played the new composition for Chips, who immediately saw its merit but suggested that it needed a bridge. Wayne could not think of one at that time, so the song was placed on the back burner.

It took on finished form one night while Wayne was recording at American, the songwriter recalled. "Chips said, 'We need one more song—how about that 'mind' song?'" Chips still thought it needed a bridge, so Wayne took a break from recording and went upstairs to Chips's office to work on it, hammering out the melody on an old upright piano Chips kept there. "Pretty soon, Johnny Christopher walked in," said Wayne. The two of them worked on composing a bridge, but, Wayne remembered, "Nothin' stuck. 'Bout an hour into it, Mark James walks in and says, 'What're you workin' on?' I said, 'We're workin' on this ol' song.' Mark said, 'Shit, sounds like y'all got it finished.' He said, 'If you're gonna add anything, it needs to be real simple. It needs to be something like, 'Don't let your love die.' The rest of it just fell out." "I said, 'Mark, you're the piano player.' Mark sat down and sang the bridge," said Johnny Christopher. "We finally got it through in three minutes," continued Wayne. "Johnny'll tell you we worked and

worked on it, which was horseshit." They went back down and played what they had come up with for Chips and the band. "The guys were downstairs, waiting to record," said Wayne. "They were kind of pre-rehearsing. Merrilee Rush was in and they were doing some things with her." That night Wayne and Chips recorded what Wayne felt was one of the definitive versions of "You Were Always on My Mind"; though Wayne had harbored no real desire to be an artist, he was sure that this record would make his reputation not only as a writer, but as a singer.

He was signed to Fred Foster's label, and he and Chips were so sure of what they had that they took the tape to Foster the next day. "Chips and I got on his airplane and followed I-40 in the fog all the way to Nashville," Wayne recalled. Foster met them at the private airfield in Henderson and drove them to his office. They played him the tape. "I couldn't get arrested," Wayne said ruefully. "Fred said, 'I don't think the world is ready for it.' Chips and I just looked at each other." They went back to the airfield, got back on Chips's plane, and neither said a word all the way back to Memphis. Then, when the plane touched down and they climbed out, Chips finally spoke. "Chips said, 'I won't forget that son-of-a-bitch, and I won't forget that song.' I said, 'He'll rue the day he turned it down,'" Wayne recalled. At the time, it looked like another missed opportunity. Wayne knew it would have made his career, and as for Fred: "He missed out on a label-saving thing at a time when he desperately needed it. He just flat-out missed it."

Others knew the worth of the song. Red West saw to it that Elvis got a copy, and it fit so perfectly the things Elvis wanted to say to Priscilla as their marriage was falling apart that he immediately recorded it. A year or so after Elvis's version, Brenda Lee, still impressed by American and its writers, did a version. And in 1981, when Chips was recording Willie Nelson and Merle Haggard at the Pedernales studio he and Bobby Emmons had built for the Texas writer, Johnny Christopher suggested that "You Were Always on My Mind" be tried. "That day was destiny," said Johnny. Haggard did not imagine the song would make a good duet, so he bowed out and Willie ended up singing it alone, backed by the American musicians and an edition of the Moman Tabernacle Choir including Johnny Christopher, Toni Wine, and Bobby Wood (voices overdubbed in Nashville, said Bobby).

"Forty-five minutes later, when we heard the playback, we knew," said Johnny Christopher. From Bobby Wood's gentle grand piano intro (played on a Bösendorfer that kept going out of tune, Wood remembered) to the compassionate wisdom of Willie's vocal to the deliberate underplaying by the American musicians and Reggie Young's plaintive electric guitar line immediately following the bridge, "You Were Always on My Mind" as recorded by Willie Nelson stands as perhaps Chips Moman's greatest—and certainly his best-known—production. It swept the Grammies and the CMAs not only that year but the following one as well, and won for all three of the writers and for Chips some long-deserved recognition. (And when Chips walked up to the CMA podium in the fall of 1982 to receive his award for having produced the record of the year, he was wearing the same old denim suit he had had since the Memphis days.)

The success of the song also meant that Wayne Carson was responsible for writing the two biggest hits American had released, "You Were Always on My Mind" and "The Letter." Of course, Mark and Johnny had contributed to "Always on My Mind," but the dominant writer was Wayne, who remembered an unlikely analogy. "Chips put it best; 'Mark and Johnny killed the bear, Wayne shot it'"— an unfortunate simile to direct at Wayne, for whom brown bears were an enduring symbol of the independence and tough-mindedness he prized. "It left a lot of people with varied tastes in their mouths," Wayne added amusedly. The most notable person eating ashes, of course, would have been Fred Foster. "You talk about a sore spot," said Wayne with justifiable glee. "He never even wanted to talk about it."

Neither Wayne Carson nor Johnny Christopher guessed that the song would have the impact it did—almost taking on a life of its own. "I don't think any of us ever knew how that song would continue to play out in our lives," said Johnny Christopher. "I've found that expecting something out of a song usually means that the song will fall way short of that," Wayne growled knowingly. He got a glimpse of what might happen, though he did not take it seriously, when he played an advance copy of Willie's version for Combine's plugger, Tommy Cogbill's pal Johnny McCrae. "McCrae said, 'Shit, it's a Grammy,'" Wayne said disbelievingly. "When it became Willie's mantra, I said, 'Jesus Christ.' Then in 1989, when the Pet Shop Boys recorded it, I thought, 'It's never gonna end.'" "You Were Always on My Mind" became the song that wouldn't die; in 2007 yet another artist, the French-Canadian singer Michael Bublé, had a hit with it.

If the writers could not explain how it happened, they thought they could explain why. To Wayne Carson, the song was successful because it reflected a part of the human condition. "It seems to say what everybody has known or felt at one time," he reflected thoughtfully. "We've all been guilty of it one way or another. We've all been on one end of that stick at one time or another. It's as universal as 'Happy Birthday.'" Johnny Christopher thought the song bore a larger spiritual message than just guilt and regret. "It's an apology. It's concern, consideration for your fellow man," he said intently. "I've sung this song in hospitals, prisons, ministries, in AA meetings. . . ." Wayne expressed the reason for the song's enduring significance and longevity more succinctly when he was interviewed about it by Connie Chung. He told her, "You just can't fuck up a great song" (it would have been interesting to have seen her expression when she heard that).

In artistic terms, if not commercial ones, the fall of 1971 had been one of American's finest. Two prestigious albums had been made, their significance and quality only increasing with time, and one superlative song, arguably one of the greatest standards ever composed, had been completed though not yet known to the general public. If word of mouth is the best advertising, the studio and the musicians could count on one of the strongest campaigns for their work.

But albums that gain prestige over time and songs that do the same are not enough to keep a troubled business going.

||||||||||||||||||||||||||||||||||||||||||||||||||||||||||||||

### CHAPTER 25

# Broken-Hearted Rock and Roll Band

By late 1971 the lawsuit with Don Crews was finally settled out of court; Chips Moman kept American while Crews now had ownership of Onyx. The first John Prine album, released on Atlantic, was an enormous prestige success. The hiring of Stan Kesler to engineer sessions and to produce already looked to be one of the best decisions Chips ever made. In a remarkable turn of events, Chips proved that, had he been so inclined, he could have been the leader of the entire Memphis music industry. For although Chips and the American musicians stayed removed for the most part from the administrative side of things, that fall they were the organizers of an important musicians' union meeting due to a conflict with Andy Ledbetter, the president of the local.

Bobby Wood remembered the circumstances, describing Ledbetter as a man "who didn't fit in to the session thing, you know? He was already dillydallying around with the New York people; he could give a flip about Memphis. He was a Mr. Stiff, one of those guys that looks down his nose at everybody." "He was the longtime head of the union and most musicians were tired of his ways," added Marty Lacker. "This guy was interferin' with our work," continued Bobby Wood. "The union is supposed to be there to help the musicians, not work against them. He started comin' down on us—"

"A lot of it had to do with the length of sessions," Bobby Emmons explained. "We were royalty-driven co-producers of the projects we were playing on as musicians. We very early on in the American sessions, as far back as '68, even before we had a name for what we were doing, were earning royalties. We were earning royalties on that first James and Bobby session. The union by-laws were behind the times to even visualize that type of situation. The union had a strict three-hour limit on master recordings. We set our time limit at five hours because we figured that of that five hours, two of it was directed at our production responsibilities. They weren't *all* fifty-five hours, as rumor has it." Chips, never one to flinch from a confrontation, decided to call a special union meeting to discuss the problem. "Andy Ledbetter didn't know what was in store for him," Marty Lacker observed.

"We went over [to the musicians' union building] about six-thirty, seven at night," Bobby Wood recalled. "Chips had called everybody, we had the symphony guys; we all knew them and had used them a lot." According to Hayward Bishop, who was in attendance, those gathered in the upstairs meeting room were a Who's Who of the Memphis music industry. All of the American players were present, from Tommy Cogbill to Billy Burnette. Booker T and the MG's, Isaac Hayes, and the Memphis Horns all were there from Stax. Elvis sent representatives, and Marty Lacker was there as an independent observer. Chips also brought along Campbell Kensinger, just in case. "We had Campbell up there to make sure Ledbetter didn't leave or that nobody would start trouble," said Marty.

From Bobby Wood's recounting of events, it was shrewd of Chips to have brought Campbell. Bobby recalled the union president. "He tried to roughshod us, it almost came to blows. . . . Chips got up and said, 'I think we've got a quorum, we've got the right to kick your ass.' It got pretty rank. I guess [the president] made a couple of threats. . . . Chips is Mr. Card Player, he's the maverick gambler of all time, and he called the guy's bluff, he said, 'You don't need to be threatening me, man.' Campbell walked up to [the union president] and said, 'I think it's time for you to leave. I'd get my hat and coat and go. Walk out the door before you get thrown through it.' The guy left and we never saw him again."

"They voted Ledbetter out and Bob Taylor in," said Marty Lacker. Bob Taylor was the horn player who had known the American musicians since the days when he and Reggie Young had shared the Haunted House; he visited the studio often and was highly sympathetic to Chips. "He was one of us," said Bobby Wood. From then on the American group was more or less left alone by the union for the remainder of their time in Memphis. "We could do whatever we wanted to and not have to worry about somebody drivin' by the building, you know, tryin' to catch us at something, somebody goin' in to play who wasn't entered on the time card," Bobby Wood added. "In later years, the national union actually made a separate category for self-contained groups," added Bobby Emmons. It was quite a triumph for Chips, and he seemed rejuvenated by the coup he had led. His creativity was sparked. It was time to go into the studio again. Billy Burnette had an album to do.

The record should have worked. All of the right elements were in place. Billy Burnette was eager and happy to be there. He had been writing some with Johnny Christopher and several of their collaborations found their way onto the album. Chips was in the control room and Toni Wine was in her place out on the floor of the studio, ready to sing backup along with Bobby Wood, Johnny Christopher, and Hayward Bishop. The musicians were eager to play. "The arrival of Billy Burnette gave me new hope in really getting a label going," said Bobby Emmons with quiet emphasis. "Billy's music was different, solid, and exciting. I was thinking, 'Boy, if we are going to have a shot at a label, this is the guy, this could be it.'"

But from the very first track, "Always Wonderin' About You Babe," something is missing. Chips seemed to quickly lose interest, perhaps when it became apparent that Billy's songs were what could be expected from an eighteen-year-old Los Angeles hippie. The lyrics are fragmented; there is promise, but nothing connects. "I was musically, kinda like all over the place," Billy admitted. Interesting ideas begin, only to meander into unrelated subjects. This was the standard for pop music in the twenty-first century, but it was a fairly new style in late 1971. Chips seemed drawn to its experimental value even if he did not quite know how to showcase it. In the end he proved to be as absent for the sessions as he had been for the earlier psychedelic work with Joseph Longoria. Occasionally he injected a medicinal dose of sorrow into the proceedings—as in the sobbing fiddle directly behind a line that said "I feel so fine" in Billy's and Johnny Christopher's double-entendre "Get On Down and Love Me All the Way," or the choir, sunk in full echo, sighing "I'm . . . sorry" on the ballad "Just My Love." (One can even hear the clicking of the dial as Chips turns the echo up full blast on the singers). It was essentially up to the musicians and Billy to choose the direction for the album, and the work became the third psychedelic recording done by the group.

"They loved doing that record, it gave everybody a chance to stretch out," Billy recalled. "Stretching out" is a mild description of his and Johnny Christopher's composition "Twenty Years Ago Today"; in retrospect it seems more appropriate for the twenty-first century than for 1971, with its hints of global warming, population decimation, and the Second Coming. The song is embedded in an instrumental track featuring passages from Reggie Young's guitar, Bobby Emmons's Hammond B3, and Hayward Bishop's congas that sound as if they are whirring together in a blender; this whirring-blender effect would be used on several tracks in the future and should have been developed further. Atop the apocalyptic lyrics and the thick instrumental track are shrieks and shouts from the Moman Tabernacle Choir, with Hayward Bishop doing a series of chilling falsetto screams. The effect is bloodcurdling, and is perhaps the most chaotic depiction of apocalypse after the Beatles' "Revolution 9," with guest performer Yoko Ono whispering "Number nine, number nine" throughout the recording, in a style almost as foreboding as Hayward Bishop's horror-movie yells.

A few of Billy's tracks are little more than demos, although the bluesy "Riff Raff Man" and the plain-spoken "I'm Getting Wasted Doing Nothing," with its two-guitar intro lifted directly from the intro of "Suite: Judy Blue Eyes,"

would have been excellent songs if they had been fully developed. Chips seems literally not to care; his usual perfectionism is missing. If he had been in form, he would have instructed his protégé to do rewrite after rewrite until the lyrics were stronger; as it was, Chips seemed content to give each unfinished song a pass or two and let them be. He stuck them experimentally between more finished tracks, referring to them as "inserts."

Two tracks show what a carefully supervised and polished album by Billy Burnette could have been like—and they were produced by Reggie Young. "Billy was good, he enjoyed writing," said Reggie. "Goin' to a Party" is a delight from beginning to end; Billy's lyric tells in a few compressed verses the story of some evening revelers, and Bobby Emmons's racing keyboard line captures the feel of a group tearing through the streets late at night to get to another party as the first one breaks up. The track also features some amazing interplay between Tommy Cogbill and Hayward Bishop, teamed for the first time as a rhythm unit. Tommy heard the song, liked its groove, and asked to play bass on the track. The new man could not have been happier. "Tommy got behind me and under me like a bulldozer and pushed me with the simplest of licks," said Hayward with pleasure. "Tommy Cogbill and Mike Leech are the only two bass players in my career that could do that so uniquely." Mike Leech tried for a similar-sounding groove with Tommy Cogbill's conga drums—Tommy occasionally sat in on percussion when he felt like taking part—on the Chips-produced "Too Bad I Missed You," even reprising a bit of the riff from "Goin' to a Party." They create a loose, jazzy feel but the song does not support them; it sinks under the weight of an excellent premise poorly stated.

The other track produced by Reggie, the Billy Burnette composition "The Last War Song," is an unjustly neglected piece, serious where John Prine's "Flag Decal" is sardonic. Bobby Emmons embroiders Billy's thoughts with gentle, delicate curlicues of sound, and Stan Kesler's open-sounding mixes create plenty of space for him to be heard (he had been almost obliterated in the mixes prior to this). According to

Stan, letting everyone be heard was exactly the point. "That was one of our main objectives—nothing was overproduced," he said. "When it got to be full, we quit. It would be full, but not overcrowded."

If Reggie Young had been in charge of the entire album, it is likely Billy would have had a solid career; as it was, the intermittent albums he released over the years, many of them produced by Chips, remained curiosities more than essential listening. Mike Leech thought of producing some work with Billy at one point; he went to Bell Records' promotion man, Dave Carrico, who had been so friendly when Chips was signed to the label, and asked if he would be interested. Much to Mike's disappointment, Carrico brushed him off. But for Billy, making that first album (titled simply *Billy Burnette*) remained a once-in-a-lifetime thrill. Billy remembered flying up to New York with Chips and meeting Columbia Records executives Clive Davis and Ron Alexenburg; the album photo, showing him huddled in the snow wearing jeans and a thin denim jacket, was taken on that visit. That trip, in which Chips and Billy were meeting on equal terms with Chips's long-hated opponents, the suits, represented a triumph of sorts.

In another triumph of sorts, Cymarron were invited to sing for Elvis at his private 1971 New Year's Eve party, once again held at T.J.'s. Ronnie Milsap and his band, still featured at the club, would also entertain. It had not been a good year for the King; his marriage was falling apart, and once again, after a promising resurgence, his recording career seemed temporarily in abeyance. Hayward Bishop was there to back Cymarron on drums, and he recalled Elvis's entrance, timed impeccably to coincide with the stroke of midnight. "Elvis came in all dressed in black, wearing two pistols," he said. "He came in through the kitchen, with a big entourage. The first thing he did was mill through the audience, kissed all the women and shook hands with the men." Richard Mainegra wondered why he and his friends were onstage at all. "I felt like a complete fool," he cringed. "I mean it felt totally ridiculous to be singing up there with Elvis Presley in the audience. I

remembered hearin' about him shootin' out television sets when singers he hated were on. I was half expectin' to hear a loud pop and see a flash any moment."

The new year, if not exactly promising, initially did not look as if it were going to be as bad as 1971 had been. Atlantic had scheduled sessions three months into the new year, and they began by bringing Herbie Mann back to Memphis, this time accompanied by another one of the label's mainstays, the former Ray Charles saxophonist David "Fathead" Newman. The series of sessions lasted four days, and Atlantic was able to wring two albums out of the pairing: *Mississippi Gambler*, released that June, and *Memphis Two-Step*, which came out later in the year. "The Herbie sessions were laid back, no heat," recalled Mike Leech (Stan Kesler disagreed, finding the flutist to be very exacting). "The Atlantic entourage was there en masse, and though I always considered them to be a little New York jive, they did supply direction. Conversations with Tom Dowd always made me feel I wasn't near as smart as he. Same with Arif although he seemed a little shy at that time. Ahmet was cool, and Wexler was okay, but they didn't have as much musical input," Mike reflected. Stan Kesler, working with the entire Atlantic group for the first time since he had been behind the control board (he had been around Arif Mardin for the Prine sessions) admired what he saw from them. "They impressed me as knowing what they were doing, they had it pretty well together," he said warmly.

The material was good, and the group played behind Herbie as solidly as ever, but the albums lacked the adventurousness that had sparked *Memphis Underground*. "Herbie did some things with the Stax crew also," Mike Leech noted; it seemed to him that the flutist was getting as much as he could from Memphis music before it finally exhausted itself. But *Mississippi Gambler* is important for another reason than music: It is the final album fully credited to Gene Chrisman as the drummer for the American Studios rhythm section. (He was credited for some songs on the Atlantic-supervised sessions for Danny O'Keefe several months later, but no one remembers him being there for them; and, although Gene himself was inexact about the date, he was certain he had gone by then.)

During this time, Chips Moman decided to concentrate on Entrance artists such as Billy Burnette, Cymarron, and Steve Alaimo to the exclusion of some accounts who had been associated with the company for awhile, though he denied that he had closed the studio to anyone. It is unclear how his decision was relayed. Hayward Bishop did not remember it ever being discussed; one day some of the clients were coming in as usual, then never being heard from again. Mike Leech and several of the others thought Chips had let them know about it during one of his control-room talks with the band.

Gene Chrisman remembered it that way. "I remember when Chips said, 'What we gonna do, we gonna cut out the accounts.' I turned to Bobby Emmons and I said, 'Buddy, you can start to *hang . . . it . . . up*. It's *over*.'" Bobby Emmons confirmed the details of the meeting and added that the emphasis on in-house acts had a method behind it. "See, this is all after realizing the writing on the wall, realizing that house bands did not get credit. Back then, people did not notice studio bands but now people are more interested in pulling the hood and finding out what made it run," he said. "We were trying one more time to get a label off the ground." "I think we all knew it was the beginning of the end, Gene especially, and probably Cogbill," Mike Leech reflected (perhaps the others knew but could not admit it to themselves). For Gene Chrisman it was the last straw; he was not going to wait around for the end.

"I had . . . had . . . *enough*," Gene said emphatically. "I was already fed up, I had spent enough time at that studio. When you're not working, what can you do?" He left the music business entirely, taking a nine-to-five job at a collection agency. Later he worked for a filter manufacturing company where he had been briefly employed in the late fifties before he had signed on with Jerry Lee Lewis's band. "I did work a few things in later years after I left American," he said. Most of those projects were either under the auspices of Sam Phillips's son Knox in Memphis or occasional commutes to Nashville doing sessions for Fred Foster, who was using the American group as his unofficial house band. In 1979 Gene moved his family to Franklin, Tennessee, rejoined the others, and became their indispensable drummer once again, proving further that you could check out of the American orbit anytime you wanted but you would never be able to leave. He remained amusedly nostalgic about his time in Memphis—"It was some good days and some crazy days"—but he seemed more contented with the career of freelance session musician that Nashville offered. He even experimented with production and touring, supervising some of the recordings of the gospel artist Betty Jean Robinson and playing shows occasionally both with the core group and as a member of the backup band for the Patsy Cline soundalike Mandy Barnett. His wife Mary died in the nineties, and within a few years he married a lady named Louella who delighted in domestic pleasures just as he did. He cooked, golfed, gardened, remained active in his church, and scarcely looked even a day older than he had when he was the mainstay of the American house band.

Gene Chrisman's departure was a shock, but at least the group had an immediate replacement. Hayward Bishop had been filling in for Gene on several occasions while Gene arrived at his decision to leave. Now Hayward was the studio drummer, much to his own surprise—he could not imagine anyone but Gene Chrisman occupying the American drum chair. It had never occurred to him that he would be anything but a percussionist and occasional substitute if Gene could not be there, and he had not wanted anything else. He still hoped to become a successful producer eventually, and was informally working with a local band called Junction.

His involvement with Junction seems to have begun with a chance encounter at a music store. "It was the Amro music store in Whitehaven," said Jim Davis, the band's leader. "To the best of my recollection, that's where I met Hayward. Perhaps it was simply, 'What are you doing?' 'This is what I'm doing.' We were kind of instant friends." Jim Davis had another connection with American; his girlfriend sometimes baby-sat Reggie Young's children, and Reggie occasionally stopped into the store to buy strings. In the view of Jim Davis, Reggie's matter-of-factness was a great advertisement for the unaffected atmosphere of American. "I was impressed that he drove his Volkswagen to work," said Jim. "His environment was so much the middle-class working man's environment. Reggie would wear his blue jeans and his blue-collar shirt, no tie of course, he was just the epitome of a simply dressed, immaculate, but unpretentious man. I have never discounted the influence of Reggie Young on me."

Jim Davis admired the eloquent simplicity of Reggie's playing, but his own work leaned toward the more intricate style characteristic of lead guitarists at that time. "I have been a jazz-rock player since Jeff Beck did something different with the Yardbirds," said Jim. At the time Jim and Hayward met, Junction had been together as a band for a little over a year, working around the city at various gigs Jim recalled as "schools, parties, maybe fraternity parties." Junction was experimenting with the jazz-rock style that Hayward had already tried recording with Piccadilly Circus, although Junction was more advanced with the concept. Hayward still felt that it was a style with commercial potential, and so, as had been the case with Cymarron, Junction began coming in to the studio during off hours or late at night when nothing was booked, trying to capture their essence on tape. Hayward preferred working with self-contained bands from the beginning; the sound of the American group was already a known quality to him, and he still hoped to make a recording that did not sound like typical Memphis music when it was played on the radio.

Developing Junction into a recording group did not cushion the shock of the next blow. It was several weeks into the year by now, there was a lull between sessions, and Gene Chrisman had left. However, there was still hope for the future of the studio, because Tommy Cogbill was present.

And then Tommy was gone, too.

One January evening, Chips and Tommy met upstairs in Chips's office to discuss matters related to the development and progress of the company. "Tommy was probably the only one who could have a difference of opinion with Chips," B.J. Thomas observed. The results of that meeting were never discussed or made public by Chips, but the outcome was clear.

Hayward Bishop remembered the denouement. "I don't remember how it was that the few of us who were there in the studio knew about the topic of the meeting," he said. "There were only a couple of us hanging out in the studio that evening and it was fairly early. I was in my usual nest, which was the control room. Tommy came down and came in to where I was. He seemed sad and disappointed. We started talking about the meeting and Tommy informed me he had been cut out of his position . . . and that Reggie would be named vice president." Reggie Young had never asked for or lobbied for such a position, and when Chips offered it to him he did not want it; when it was later inquired of Chips why he had offered a vice-presidency of the company to Reggie, he replied with quiet dignity, "Because he was my friend." Did that make Tommy Cogbill less of a friend? At this point, no one was sure, and both Tommy Cogbill and Reggie Young were shocked.

So was Hayward, when he heard. "Man, you could hear my heart hit the floor," he said, still stunned. "Not that Reggie wouldn't have done a good job, but we *all* thought of Tommy as second in command. . . . So here's Tommy with this bewildered look on his face and his head down—like he was still in shock. I don't think it was about the position as much as it was the gut-punch from Chips and the reality of the coldness." Tommy had been closer to Chips at times than anyone. Chips had always relied on Tommy's judgment to pull things through. But none of this had kept him from making that decision, which outraged Hayward now.

The younger man tried to console Tommy for the loss, as Tommy had done for him when he had lost his chance with Cymarron, but "I was just adding misery to misery. All I could do was to tell him how sad and mad that made me." Tommy did not say much else, and left soon after. No one ever learned where he went that night.

"I believe that meeting was the straw that broke the camel's back because Tommy quit soon after that meeting," Hayward said. But it may not have been the only reason. Marty Lacker, who did not see Tommy before he left the studio, was certain that Tommy disliked other things as well. "I think he was tired of the influence Toni was having and how it was changing the atmosphere at American," he said. "He never talked to me about it, but I knew why he left," said Stan Kesler. "No work and no sign of any, it looked like things were going down rather than going up." Chips Moman was vague about the reason Tommy gave his notice: "I imagine he told me, but I don't remember all of our conversations," he said offhandedly. There was in any case little incentive for Tommy to stick around; he had been hanging on for awhile, waiting to see what would happen. He had been the one holding the group together; if there were no American Group Productions, and sessions were becoming few and far between, his job at the studio was done, and he could go. He had always been good at knowing when to leave, and he knew now.

At least the first sessions done under this set of circumstances were for someone in the family, and thus a supportive environment for beginning anew. Bobby Womack and Darryl Carter came back for a session in late January 1972. Hayward Bishop had never met Womack or Darryl before and enjoyed working with them. He recalled with amusement the tan leather Superfly suit that Darryl Carter wore each and every day, and the scent of Carter's heavy musk cologne. The increasingly seedy world outside the studio encroached upon the musicians as well. Billy Burnette remembered there being trouble somewhere in town and having to drive Womack to the place where the guitarist was staying.

It was Hayward Bishop's first session as full-time drummer, a situation full of pressure; he knew he would have to play as solidly as Gene

Chrisman had done while bringing his own style and creativity to the recordings. He had, of course, filled in before, but he had been secure in the knowledge that Gene would return. "I didn't even consider that I would be permanently occupying his space," he said. As was usual with the studio procedure, there was no preliminary announcement and no preparation for the new role he would have to assume. "It was just being called for a session—and to be on drums," Hayward said. "I have to commend Emmons, Mike, and Reggie, though. They never openly grumbled or acted smug toward me at any time. In fact, Reg and Mike seemed just fine. I could never really tell how Emmons felt."

"Hayward's style was definitely different from Gene's," mused Bobby Emmons. "That old saying 'marching to the beat of a different drummer' definitely had basis in fact. I'd been working with Gene almost day and night for four years. My internal clock was *set*. But the bottom line was, Hayward was a fine drummer. I eventually adjusted and we made some good recordings together." For his part, Hayward knew he had to make sure that his contributions had the same precision and quality with which the others were familiar. "Playing in that rhythm section was a great honor and challenge," he said respectfully.

Mike Leech thought that Hayward succeeded brilliantly, reflecting that he liked working with the new drummer's "open sound." "He doesn't jam a lot of notes into a fill," Mike said. "As a result, what he plays is effective. Most drummers doing fills will play every note Mel Bay taught them, mainly to impress the client. But the fills don't make any sense, as Hayward's do." Hayward was awestruck that Mike would have held his playing in such esteem, and he more than returned the compliment. "Mike Leech's duration on his notes are perfect," said the drummer.

Three interesting songs were recorded during Womack's two days in the studio; a remake of "Sweet Caroline"; a mellow version of the Beatles' "And I Love Her," featuring Mike Leech's tender string passages and a softly-spoken introduction from Womack: "You see,

I've always believed . . . that to give, ya gotta get, y'know. And if you don't give it . . . you don't get it, that's right." These tracks are sparse and spare, as if there is emptiness in the studio; listening, one could almost sense the musicians slowly, reluctantly leaving. But the sessions yielded one of American's strongest hits, and one of Mike Leech's most memorable performances: that descending bass line (*Rolling Stone* described it as "warm") which was the hook for the Womack and Carter composition "Woman's Gotta Have It."

In *The Billboard Book of R&B Hits*, Darryl Carter said he had based the concept on a couple he knew in Memphis; the wife was feeling neglected and it was obvious that if the husband was not more attentive to her—and soon—she was going to bolt. It was written as a cautionary tale, a reminder that women need affection: "A woman's gotta have it, I believe / She's gotta know that she's needed around." It is the best statement of female emotional needs since the Depression-era "Try a Little Tenderness." But that song had been about overworked and overstressed women in hard times; this was about women dealing with prosperity, with husbands and lovers who had no time for a private life and very little to give emotionally. In 1972, the watchword of the day was fulfillment, and if a woman could not get it from the workaholic man she was with, she would find someone else. Just to repeat the message for all the success-driven yuppies who missed it the first time around, James Taylor, in his continuing fascination with soul music, recorded the song a few years later.

The message was strong enough, but what made the record an instant delight was the presence of Mike Leech. "I believe Mike Leech's descending syncopated bass line on 'Woman's Gotta Have It' was the groove signature that brought that record to Number One," said Hayward Bishop joyfully. Mike was genuinely pleased to think that something he had played had made an impact on the public. It was surprising that he could discuss work that moved the listener emotionally as commercially significant, but once his meaning was

understood the definition was better appreciated. "Commercial music, the way I mean it, is music . . . that has an appeal to the public. The more appealing, the more gratifying," he explained. "If a bass line I played was on a million-selling record, then I've accomplished my purpose and am very happy. In other words, I played something (however dark, buried in the background) that was appealing to the masses, sold records, and I've reached my goal. If it only sold ten thousand, something was wrong." "Woman's Gotta Have It" was a rallying point at a time the musicians desperately needed it (and even more so when it was released in June 1972, rapidly ascended to the top of the R&B charts, and crossed over into pop as the group were struggling in Atlanta), and it seemed to prove that the craftsmanship and integrity that had seen them through the roughest times would do so yet again.

If "Woman's Gotta Have It" proved that the group could rally, the next set of sessions for Atlantic gave the group five days' work and a brilliant album so effortless-sounding that a listener would never guess how seriously awry things were at the studio. Again, it helped that the artist was like family. Jackie DeShannon was returning after a year and a half away from Memphis; she was now signed to Atlantic following a chance meeting with Jerry Wexler on a plane. There was no question where Wexler intended to take her for recording, and that was fine with her; when the time actually came, Wexler was ill and could not attend the session, so Tom Dowd and Arif Mardin supervised. Hayward Bishop recalled that Jackie came down almost a week before the Atlantic producers. "She was an equal to the other veterans," Hayward said. "I thought she was a professional and a delightful person. She certainly and rightfully had my respect and admiration." As when she had been at the studio before, there was much time spent hanging out and trying new material before anything was captured on tape. Though Chips was not on the premises while the recording was going on with the Atlantic crew, hours before the session began he took a calculated risk that could have cost everything. "He was playing pool with a guy named Williamson and he had me take the studio microphones and pile them up and use them as collateral," said Hayward Bishop. Fortunately, Chips won.

For Hayward, it was a stressful occasion even without the risk incurred by last-minute gambling. He had proved himself as a replacement for Gene Chrisman, but that was only for several songs; now he would be asked to sustain those skills through the creation of an important album. It was also his first association with Tom Dowd, and Hayward found the New York engineer to be so brilliant and interesting he wished he had gotten a chance to have worked with him more. "He was a fascinating man, but he had the ultimate—common sense," said Hayward. He casually mentioned one day to Dowd that he had heard a rumor about Dowd's being such a good engineer that he was able to deliver a perfect stereo mix without listening to the monitors. "I asked him to do it, he smiled at me and said sure, and he turned all the faders down." After a few minutes, Dowd calmly turned up the faders again and played back the track that he had mixed; it was letter-perfect. "I said, 'Well, it's no longer a rumor, is it?'"

Though the new drummer felt tense and concerned about his work throughout the sessions, he need not have worried. His playing sounds relaxed and casual; this album is one of his finest showcases both as drummer and percussionist. He and the other featured musician on these tracks, Reggie Young, both reach an inventive and creative peak, together leading the group into areas of music they had not yet tried. Jamaican music was beginning to get some attention after having been an occasional curiosity on the charts for the last few years; now it seemed poised for a huge breakthrough. Jackie's album *Jackie* is the closest thing to a reggae (or was it "Reggie") album that the group ever made.

It starts with her version of John Prine's "Paradise," ironically the only song from his first album not recorded at American. The group more than makes up for having missed out on it, though; from the song's introduction

Reggie Young is assertively at ease, and Hayward Bishop never falters. His timekeeping and accents are placed perfectly and easily on the ear; he achieves his lifelong ambition "to drive the band," and he proves himself the equal of his own drum heroes, Roger Hawkins and Hal Blaine. He sounds as if he is hitting the drums more lightly than did Gene Chrisman; an illusion, Hayward said, because of the way Gene had been miked and because of the settings for him on the control board. "I play with one stick turned around," he said. "My backbeat stick, I play with the end, not the tip. I did that to get the low-end impact. . . . When you hit drums hard, it doesn't necessarily make them louder." Jackie's vocal is gentle and empathetic; Prine was writing about her own native area of Kentucky, and she reasserts her roots with quiet strength. If the group had never recorded another song, this version of "Paradise" would stand as a classic.

The John Hurley and Ronnie Wilkins composition "Heavy Burdens Me Down" further demonstrates Hayward's versatility as he negotiates skillfully between the bluesy passages of the verses and the more driving tempo of the choruses. The title and the first verse sound as if the track will be similar to "Born Carrying a Heavy Load," but the focus switches in the second verse from personal self-pity to empathy for the whole world, wondering why "the old men lie / and the young men die." The bitter, blueslike emphasis is accented by Reggie, who once again is the second standout; the entire track is polished and precise.

Equally graceful is Jackie's own "Brand New Start," one of her classic weepers. She begs and pleads for her lover to return, saying that she is "half a woman" without the man who taught her "loneliness and pain," hoping that he will let her back into his heart and his life. For those who have never known overwhelming passion, Jackie's habit of wearing her heart on her sleeve in song is almost embarrassing; for those who have known it, the feeling she describes is painfully real. Reggie Young embellishes her woeful voice with intricate curlicues of sound, and Tom Dowd's string overdubs (recorded in New York) soar and sail like a spirit determined to overcome the agony. It is what the American musicians had always done best: direct communication, without drama or sentimentality—just a soul talking to another soul, and hoping he or she will hear.

"Only Love Can Break a Heart," Neil Young's standard from his classic album *After the Gold Rush* of two years before, is given a gentle treatment emphasizing Bobby Emmons playing the rolling, syncopated rhythm which by now was one of the standard runs in the American group repertoire. Hayward Bishop's congas add an unusual flair, as do the ethereal voices of the Joint Venture engaged in some flowing call-and response background lines set against Jackie's Appalachian wistfulness.

Her own "Laid-Back Days" is a meandering celebration of country pleasures: whole-wheat bread and apples and falling asleep on a blanket on the grass. At any rate, one assumes it is going to be a quiet celebration; and then, immediately after the listener thinks he has heard the final chorus as Jackie sings "You're all around . . . You're all around me," the track takes off. Reggie Young and Hayward Bishop lead the others on a jam that would not be out of place on a recording of progressive jazz, with Reggie's lead, Hayward's drums and overdubbed percussion, and Bobby Emmons adding assertive, attention-getting fills from the Hammond B3 as the three musicians slide into the whirring-blender effect with which they had experimented on Billy Burnette's apocalypse song. As the whirring slows down, with only a millisecond to decide what to do, Jackie leaps in again and sings the refrain: "La la la la lovely, laid-back days." Hayward described it as "Us taking her vocal cue when she was ready. We certainly had no problem with her calling that one. It was her song!"

"Full-Time Woman" came from the San Francisco guitarist and songwriter Alice Stuart; Jerry Wexler was enamored of the song and inveigled every female artist on Atlantic to cut it (though not all of them did). It is understandable why Jackie did; it is as emotionally vulnerable a song as one she could have written. From its opening lines, "I hear you've got a full-time woman now / Does she love you like I never could? Does she try and understand you / Does she help you, like I never would?" the listener is hooked, pulled into the speaker's confusion and heartache. Alice Stuart herself thought Jackie's version worked best because of its understated grace; she said in a 1973 *Rolling Stone* interview that the other women who had covered the song "insist on screaming it." Credit for the brilliance of this version goes not only to Jackie but to Tom Dowd's glossy, polished string line and to the incisive tastefulness of Reggie Young's guitar lead.

"Vanilla O'Lay" is the one everybody remembers now, not so much because the song was a success when it came out (it wasn't) but because it was licensed for Oil of Olay lotion commercials on television. In its original form it is another of the Jamaican-sounding tracks; although it sounds on the surface like another celebration of country pleasures (gathering wood, caring for an aging cat, loading up the car for a traipse down "the gypsy turnpike"), Reggie Young's thick, blurry lead, Hayward Bishop's prominent drums and percussion, and Bobby Emmons's whirring organ lines make the listener wonder if Jackie had set her story in the country outside of Kingston.

Steve Goodman's "Would You Like to Learn to Dance," both romantic and playful, was another Wexler suggestion. Bobby Wood's piano assumes a Victorian formality; however, apart from Reggie Young's lead, the dominant instrument on the track is a harpsichord, overdubbed in Miami, where Wexler and Dowd were now predominately based. Perhaps the Atlantic producers thought the instrument added to the semi-formal mood of the piece, but to the listener it is a distraction; it would have been preferable to hear the American group alone.

All of the tracks so far are prelude to the album's highlight, the most agonized song of all. Hayward Bishop named this one as his favorite. Donna Weiss and Mary Unobski were one of the most formidable writing teams to have emerged from Memphis. They had composed the beautiful, aching "That Kind of Woman"; Weiss in particular seemed to write songs that cut straight to the center of female anguish. On

"I Won't Try to Put Chains on Your Soul," they scored another direct hit on the heart, a song of mingled pain and anger that seems to be a wife speaking, but could be a spurned mistress as well: "I was your shadow till the night came falling / Then it's her / Go on and go, if you've made up your mind / and it's her / You prefer." Tom Dowd accents the chorus with his finest string arrangement, building and building an unbroken line in a passionate but more open style than the similar writing of Mike Leech. *Rolling Stone*, reviewing the album, called the track an "all-stops-out barroom weeper," forgetting that women, for whom the song speaks for and its natural audience, for the most part were not prominent customers at beer joints back in 1972. This was a song to be listened to over and over again in the privacy of a room, soothing and assuaging a woman's pain. To Hayward Bishop, the effect was "a finished, New York sounding record . . . that fit Jackie's vocal style and delivery. I would've liked to have seen Atlantic follow up 'Vanilla Olay' with that. It just sounded rich, full, and commercial to me." Donna Weiss later collaborated with Jackie on the Grammy-winning "Bette Davis Eyes"; for women who had loved and lived every note these two had ever written, the response to the 1981 award given to these long-neglected talents was, "Finally."

Van Morrison's "I Wanna Roo You" was another harbinger of the future for Jackie; the Irish singer became one of her closest collaborators later in the year. Johnny Christopher's acoustic guitar establishes the song's mood as Reggie Young's lead swirls like snowflakes glimpsed through a window on "the twenty-third of December." Reggie's guitar line is so much a part of the song that it can be sung as part of the melody, in the same way that Louis Armstrong's trumpet figures used to be when he backed singers like Bessie Smith, and despite Hayward Bishop's Jamaican influence and Johnny Christopher's scuffling acoustic strum Reggie is such a dominant figure that the listener is immediately transported to Whitehaven, watching the guitarist gazing out his living-room window at the snow. Jackie has never sounded more plaintive than in the chorus when she almost

whispers the line, "Y'know . . . I'm lonely"; it is unclear whether she is speaking to someone in her past or her future. As with many tracks cut at American, the meanings and implications here are multilayered, and the musicians are in fine form.

"Peaceful in My Soul," one of Jackie's own compositions, ranks with "Bread and Butter" and the later "Warm Winds and Sweet Wine," recorded with the Joy of Cooking vocalist Toni Brown in Nashville, as among the American group's greatest meditations on serenity. Happiness is not a concept the musicians could describe very well, but they were masters at describing the absence of pain, that calmness known as contentment. This is a reflective, autumnal song, from the "painted fields and diamond hills" to the "burning gold" of the lover's hair; the back cover of the album, which features Jackie seated on the wood rail of a small footbridge looking at a stream, comes immediately to mind as one listens to the gentle inflections of Reggie Young's guitar and the soft footfall of Bobby Wood's piano.

The final track, Jackie's tribute to Anna Karina, the French actress she admired, is laden with hooks that should have delighted any radio program director, from Reggie Young's introductory lead figure (another of his lines that would be widely copied) to Hayward Bishop's scattershot conga drums to Bobby Emmons's assertive keyboard asides. That Atlantic Records itself was not the operation it had been is apparent when realizing that this was never released as a single. When looking at the album credits, much to the new drummer's crestfallen surprise he was listed as "Bishop Heywood" (he had also been listed that way when he was cited as percussionist on the John Prine album). Atlantic in the old days, when Chips and Tommy Cogbill first worked for them, would have certainly taken the trouble to learn the names of the backing musicians.

It had been six years since the first road trips to record Wilson Pickett had cemented the studio's ties with the label—six years and a lifetime ago. Atlantic Records and the American group had made many important records together. At times it was debatable who had benefited most from the collaboration. Wexler remained a partisan of the rootsy sound that Southern music had to offer; Arif Mardin did some of his finest arrangements supporting work recorded in Memphis; and in many interviews he gave throughout his lifetime, Tom Dowd described the American musicians in the same superlative terms as he did those of the Stax and Muscle Shoals studios, and for the same reason—he found them to be talented, cooperative, cheerful people whom he greatly respected. "I overheard two of the Atlantic people saying one time, 'A studio is nothing but bricks and boards. The people make records,'" said Bobby Emmons.

But the time would come when this mutual admiration would no longer matter. And it came when the studio desperately needed Atlantic the most.

### CHAPTER 26

# From Atlanta to Good-Bye

The second set of sessions with Jackie DeShannon were the last completely coherent work the American group recorded in Memphis. Though Atlantic had another several days of sessions booked in February, reserved for another singer-writer in the John Prine mold named Danny O' Keefe, Jackie's were the final ones in Memphis for Johnny Christopher and Bobby Wood. "I wouldn't have left that situation if it was still happening. I basically left because of work," said Bobby Wood. "By this time I was getting a little frustrated, me and Johnny both." By the middle of the O'Keefe sessions, they were gone.

They traveled to Nashville for one day in the interim between the Jackie and O'Keefe sessions, on what Hayward Bishop termed a "search-and-destroy mission." They were seeking work, and they wanted to know if any of their Memphis accounts would help them get established if they moved. One of the first people they saw was Tommy Cogbill, there on a similar mission. "He said, 'Don't tell anybody I'm here.' We said, 'Don't you tell anybody we're here!'" Bobby Wood laughingly recalled.

Fred Foster had been wanting the whole group to move for quite some time, and he said he would guarantee them some work. Buddy Killen also said he would be glad to book them for his sessions. It was all the musicians needed to hear. Tommy Cogbill settled in just off Music Row, within walking distance of all the studios, at a cinderblock apartment building called the Americana; he planned to send for his family when he had gotten established and sorted things out. Johnny Christopher found an apartment in town and later purchased some acreage north of the city, in Goodlettsville. Bobby Wood returned to Memphis just long enough to put his house up for sale. On the road outside of Jackson, Tennessee, he called his wife Janice on the CB radio he now used in his car. His message: "Start packing."

"We hated to leave, it seemed to me the clients had left," said Bobby Wood. "I said, I've gotta support a family here, like we all do. . . . Nobody was makin' anything." "We were driven out," said Johnny Christopher emphatically. "We would have stayed! We were the kind of people, unless we had been driven out, we never would have left." Both knew that in the four-session-a-day grind in Nashville, they would never have the opportunity to work so closely with a group of musicians again. "We lived together in the studio for about four years," said Bobby wistfully. "I don't think we saw our kids as much as we saw each other." It was if they were children leaving home, departing the nest to try their luck. But Nashville offered new opportunities for songwriters, and of this they were well aware. "I said, 'Bobby, you haven't even tapped into what you are gonna do yet,'" said Johnny Christopher.

"I went through a terrible thing when I resigned with Chips," Bobby recounted. "I said, 'I really hate to go.' Boy, he put such a guilt trip on me, he blew his stack, he said, 'You don't know what you're doin' to me, you're leavin' just as I'm gettin' things rollin'!' He just made me feel like dirt. I told him I'd stay awhile longer. I thought about it for three or four hours but something in my gut said *no*." He called Chips back and told him that he was gone and that the decision was final. "By March of '72 we were living in a house," said Bobby. The house was just outside Nashville, in the then-fashionable area of Brentwood; both country music stars and session players often settled there.

The group may have been falling apart in Memphis, but that could not have been determined from a look at the charts. In March 1972, Joe Tex's "I Gotcha" went to Number One on the soul charts, Number Two on the pop. It had a thick but danceable groove, and the Memphis Horns played big-band riffs atop. According to Mike Leech, it had been recorded as Joe's

sessions always were, horns and rhythm instruments live in the studio. "The hardest part was hearing the arrangement the way Joe heard it. He wasn't musically trained, but he had the arrangements worked out in his head and would convey that to us," Mike said. "Working for Joe, all you had to do was try to read his mind. The cool part was, once you had what he wanted, he would get excited and grin. The rhythm section would work with Joe till we got it right, then the horns would come in. They had to work with him just like we did. When it was finally all worked out and we played together it was phenomenal." "Joe was a smart cookie when it came to R&B," added Bobby Wood.

For the album, Joe did several songs with the same groove and style as its title song "I Gotcha." "You're in Too Deep," featuring Bobby Wood's pounding piano and Hayward Bishop's relentless cowbell clanging, works best, because it flows a little more smoothly. "For My Woman" is a soul classic that would not have been out of place in 1967; the treat here is the band, calling out "Right on brother, right on" in the middle of Joe's spoken chorus. The Motown soundalike "God of Love" and the melodic "Taking a Chance" are strongly dominated by the horn section, and "It Ain't Gonna Work" is a treat from beginning to end, with Joe playing the part of a working man confronting the collapse of his marriage. On one of the final tracks he cut as a bass player in Memphis, Tommy Cogbill pushes the track along, and the song's punch line is worthy of classic blues: "When you got your body one place, and your mind somewhere else, it ain't gonna work, baby."

Occasionally Buddy Killen was reluctant to use some of the American sidemen. In a way, it was understandable; he had first met Hayward Bishop when the drummer was crouched atop one of the amps doing his imitation of a vulture, complete with sound effects. "Because of my comedic side [some people] had a reluctance to look at my serious side," said Hayward. "I had to watch Buddy Killen look all over Memphis for a drummer on 'Give the Baby Anything That the Baby Wants'—it was Steve Holt and I had to *endure* that." Though the musicians corralled Killen in the control room and lobbied intensely for Hayward, with Mike Leech, Reggie Young, and Bobby Emmons being the most emphatic about his ability, Killen used Holt only for that track. Hayward said that he actually loved what Steve Holt had done on the record, and felt that he had done a great job.

The group seemed as prominent on the Top Forty as ever. But at the studio, the damage done in the last few months was too severe to deny any longer. Gene Chrisman was now out of the business. Bobby Wood, Johnny Christopher, and Tommy Cogbill were working on demo sessions in Nashville. The musicians remaining in Memphis were demoralized and stunned, hanging on one day at a time; they still did not know what was happening, but this rapid exodus was telling them things could not go on this way much longer. It would take a miracle to hold things together now.

Fortunately, a miracle was waiting in the wings.

It was Hayward Bishop who discovered Shane Keister. Perhaps a more accurate word was "rediscovered": the nineteen-year-old keyboard player had been in town for the better part of 1971, working on jingles at the Pepper-Tanner company and recording as a session musician . . . for Stax.

John Shane Keister's involvement at Stax is not well known, but he was a bit player, occasionally contributing piano alongside or filling in for Carla Thomas's brother Marvell, who had moved up to studio keyboardist when Booker T departed in 1970. Shane had first attracted the label's attention when he had been a member of a Texas rock band they had signed that year. Southwest FOB introduced the world not only to Shane Keister but to the vocal and writing talents of Dan Seals and John Ford Coley. The band came to Memphis to record, and Shane stayed on, making use of his classical training and sight-reading skills to land the Pepper-Tanner staff job. Jim Stewart, who was less involved with Stax but still able to make suggestions and recommendations, had been impressed with the young keyboardist at the time of the album and caught up with him again when Shane was playing "cocktail piano

from five to seven PM" in a lounge where Stewart had stopped in to have a drink. Between sets, they chatted, and Stewart learned more of Shane's history.

He came from Huntington, West Virginia, a small city on the Ohio River (about an hour south from Janice Wood's hometown across the line), and when he was seven his father, a car salesman, moved the family further west to Portsmouth, Ohio, where the elder Keister opened a Ford dealership Shane had studied music since he was three, and he spoke gratefully of his first piano teacher. "That's where I really received my best training," he said with enthusiasm. "She kept me in classical music." By the time he was twelve, "I was playing jazz with the junior high stage band. Other than classical music, jazz was the first music I was exposed to—playing charts by Neal Hefti, Henry Mancini . . ." He also gigged with local rock bands and absorbed influences from Top Forty radio, but "the teacher told me, 'Make sure you play classical music all your life,' and I still do. I've tried to keep my hands in good condition." There was a small college in Shane's hometown, Marshall University in Huntington (famous for a 1970 plane crash that killed most of its football team, a tragedy depicted in the movie *We Are Marshall*), where he studied for a year, but Marshall was more of a sports-centered school than a music school, and so Shane transferred to North Texas State University, which featured a music department with a reputation equal to that of Berklee College of Music back east. There he fell in with his colleagues in Southwest FOB, left school, and set out on the path to Memphis.

Jim Stewart expressed a low-key interest. "He said, 'I'm doing a session on the Emotions,'" Shane recalled. Stewart invited Shane to come and observe, and when he got there he saw for the first time all the greats whose names he had noted on records. "There was Al Jackson, Duck Dunn, Steve Cropper, Bobby Manuel," he said in awe. "I remember it was wintertime, it was early '71." Marvell Thomas was late to the session; no one knew why at the time, but he'd had "a minor fender bender and was down at the station house for about two hours." In the great tradition, a star was born when a fill-in was desperately needed. Jim Stewart asked if Shane could play a song through on such short notice, and he sat down at their piano and gave it a try. "They liked what I was playing, and from then on they used Marvell and myself."

Working at Stax taught the classically trained piano player the rudiments of R&B. Soon after his arrival, "Al Jackson came over to me one day," Shane recalled. "He said, 'Shane—you're playin' like a white boy. Let me show you where the groove is.' He put his hands on top of mine" and tapped out the beat. "It left a deep impression on me," the piano player remembered. "[After that] I had a semblance of rhythm pocket." Between sessions at Stax and his staff job at Pepper-Tanner, "I was making a good income," he added. At only nineteen, he seemed to be settled. He was already married, to a red-haired girl from Florida named Alice who was an aspiring lyricist; the couple hoped to write songs together someday. For now, there was not only the regular work at Stax and Pepper-Tanner, but occasional engagements at restaurants and clubs in Memphis, playing jazz and standards. One of the clubs he sometimes played was obscure then, but like Federal Express and Holiday Inn, it was one of those Memphis companies that eventually went national: TGI Friday's.

Hayward Bishop heard him there. He liked the atmosphere at TGI Friday's and sometimes stopped off at the club before going to the studio. Going into TGI Friday's gave him his "daily dose of crowd"; he needed the contact with people, keeping him in touch with the larger world that the small, inbred life at American tended to close out. "I believe it was a Sunday night," Hayward recalled. "Shane was playing with this combo that I believe was put together just for this gig." Shane remembered that he was working, as he often did when he played clubs around town, with a flute and saxophone player named Edwin Hubbard who was well known in Memphis. "It was a group, Edwin and me and a great drummer named Donnie Patterson—I don't know what ever happened to him," Shane said.

"I came in a few songs before the end of the next-to-the-last set," Hayward recalled. "Shane was obviously the most polished musician in the band and his playing attracted my attention, and I'm sure, everyone else's as well. They took a break and I somehow got involved in talking with Shane at the corner of the bar." They chatted briefly before the next set, and though Hayward had originally been intending to stay a short while and then get to the studio and work with the Junction band, he stayed over for the last set. "When he began playing 'Eleanor Rigby' fairly rapidly and in triple time as if to emulate a tap echo . . . I saw true virtuosity." At the end of the set, Hayward told Shane about the vacant piano chair at American and asked if he would like to audition for Chips, and Shane enthusiastically said yes. The next step was to inform Chips of his discovery. He reached Chips, asleep out at the farm in Raleigh, and told him, "I've found your piano player."

Chips arranged to meet them at the studio when Shane's set was done, Hayward recalled. He said he would be there in thirty minutes, but got there in fifteen. In Shane's recollection, Chips came directly to the club and he did not remember Hayward being there at all. In Chips's recollection, he met Shane when "he just walked in [to the studio] and said hello." Both musicians immediately registered Chips's reaction. "He said, 'I like the way you play,'" said Shane. In Hayward's memory, Chips was more enthusiastic; he had said, "Damn, son, have you got a third hand or something that we don't know about?" In either case, he told Shane that he was used to working with a two-keyboard lineup and that his regular piano player was now in Nashville. Shane, in turn, mentioned that he was working at Pepper-Tanner and doing some sessions at Stax. "Being only nineteen, I didn't know the political implications," said Shane; he knew nothing of Chips's history with the Stax label and Jim Stewart. "He said, 'I'll pay you twice what he is,'" recalled the piano player, who added that Chips did not mind his doing occasional sessions for Pepper-Tanner if he chose.

"I came in in the middle of the Danny O'Keefe sessions," said Shane. "That was enough for my young blood." He was walking into the middle of a session organized and produced by Arif Mardin for Atlantic's subsidiary Signpost label; he was replacing a pianist who had a track record of playing on hits; and he had to come in cold. As usual for personnel additions and changes, no announcement was given to the rest of the band.

"Seems like one day he just showed up," said Mike Leech. "Shane rolled in, nobody knew who he was, where he came from, nothing. But all he did was play piano (and play the hell out of it). . . . He is a very good player, great chops, but he always deferred to our ideas, though he probably had some better ones. I think that was the new kid on the block mentality." "I thought it was good," Reggie Young said of the change. "I always enjoyed working with Shane, he was a real asset to the group." "Shane's a good boy, he's a good guy, very talented musician; they were lucky to get him after Bobby left," said Stan Kesler. Hayward Bishop thought that Shane's virtuosity revitalized the players. "Shane not only *never* dropped the ball, but he gave us all the hope that we didn't have to miss a step, and that sessions could go on," said the drummer. "Bobby Wood had proven his exemplary musicianship with the American group—now, it was Shane's turn."

The last late arrival had strong memories of his first day at work. "The first time I met Toni Wine was the first day I went to the studio," he said. "It was at one o'clock in the afternoon." He immediately sat down at the Baldwin grand piano located in the main studio (a smaller Baldwin was now in the Ranch House annex) and began to play, at the behest of Chips. "Chips said, 'Play something. Play anything you want to.'" He ran through some of his favorite works and when he paused for a second, he looked up to see Toni standing beside the piano, watching him intently. "'Do you play?' I asked. She said, 'No.' Chips said, 'She's lying.' I didn't put it together that she and Chips were together romantically. I thought she was just someone employed by the studio." Shane liked Toni and spent a lot of time talking to her. "She was very nice, very friendly," he recalled. "I remember talking to her a lot about New York, it really whetted my appetite to see it." It was

the beginning of a dream that finally came true for Shane when he moved to New York as staff producer for Atlantic Records in the nineties.

Mike Leech and Hayward Bishop both recalled that the self-taught Bobby Emmons seemed to be extremely intimidated by Shane's technical skills and classical training. "Intimidated I don't think is the right word," Emmons reflected. "I was very *impressed* with Shane's chops, but had mixed emotions on whether or not he would be able to tone down that kind of power to the approach we had been so successful with. My fears proved to be unfounded, however, because he became a top session man in no time." Shane said that for awhile he did not know if the musicians liked his playing or not, because they never told him. Mike Leech conceded the point. "He is probably right about not knowing if anybody liked his playing. . . . That was just our way with newcomers, Shane included. Probably a stuffed-shirt attitude, but that's the way we were. He seldom was complimented for what he most certainly deserved, but he didn't mind." The other late arrivals had handled their reception by becoming even more of what they had always been (Johnny Christopher friendly and ingratiating, Glen Spreen quiet and watchful, Hayward Bishop as the class clown); Shane dealt with it by being, Mike recalled, "overcomplimentary . . . [he] over-laughed at jokes that weren't particularly funny."

For Shane's part, he did not feel he could compliment his colleagues enough. "These guys were the reason I was successful," he said. "They had a track record a mile long. . . . I was nineteen, almost twenty, and here I am working with giants. I wasn't intimidated, but I was awed." He was impressed by their informal demeanor most of all. "Nobody had any attitude," he said. "I felt a little distant because I didn't know anybody. But in just a week or so, we were all hanging out."

There was only one discordant note, he thought. Reggie Young and Bobby Emmons knew Morse code, and Shane recalled that during breaks between songs the two of them would be holding a private conversation on their instruments, making the "dots and dashes" sounds while he, Mike Leech, and Hayward Bishop looked at each other in puzzlement. "I was always paranoid that they were talking about me," he laughed. Not quite, according to Emmons, who said that most of the time he was actually spelling out a common four-letter word. "I knew it would get Reggie tickled and it would ease the tension," he chortled, adding that everyone had their ways of defusing the intense concentration needed while they were working on a song. "Tommy used to put his hands over his face and scream. If somebody had missed the intro about five times in a row and the tension was really building, he would put the palms of his hands up to his mouth and scream as loudly as he could. It would always break everybody up. Bobby Wood would make a sound like a typewriter, with the bell carriage return after each burst. Shane just hadn't learned the language yet."

The newcomer learned his craft by emulating the professionalism he saw from the others. "Mike Leech was really responsible for tutoring me and teaching me," he said gratefully. "I didn't know the art of arranging for pop records. I really admired what he would write—he would let me study his scores. He was very patient with me. Mike taught me, always listen to the lyric.

"I remember Stan Kesler, too, was real encouraging. He was such a soft-spoken, mild-mannered, warm engineer. Stan was the first person to get me interested in audio." The older man told the newcomer a little about engineering in Memphis, and later in Atlanta, Shane recalled, "He gave me Audio 101." As with the others no longer affiliated with the group, he held warm memories of his former colleagues. "They were always gentlemen and gracious people," he said. "If it hadn't been for them, I'd probably still be playing at the Holiday Inn."

The late arrivals were all younger and bolder than the core group had been. They were city boys on one level or another rather than the unassuming country boys of the central unit; the first two had even been hippies. Shane was no hippie, but he too brought with him the new concept of female equality in the person of his wife Alice, who like Judy Spreen and Toni Wine before her, became a fixture in the studio. "I was kind of collared at that point," Shane admitted. "Alice was quite insecure about me." She insisted on accompanying him wherever he went, and she had talent, in the tradition of Judy Spreen's piano playing and Toni Wine's Brill Building experience. "When she was writing, she was an excellent lyricist," Shane said of Alice. (An example of her gift appears on the 1982 Florence Warner album *Just Believe It*; "Pirate" features wildly romantic lines that read like a poem by Christina Rossetti over a lushly cinematic melody created by Shane, all of it given an elegant polish by Norbert Putnam's production.) Shane rationalized Alice's presence at American, saying that proximity to so many top writers would help her gain further knowledge of her craft.

The new musician entered the group in the midst of their endeavors for another singer-songwriter type whose music they did not fully understand. Danny O'Keefe came from the Pacific Northwest by way of the same Minnesota coffeehouse scene that had first sparked Bob Dylan's career. He had been writing for awhile, and had even recorded his first album up in New York for Atlantic's Cotillion label the year before. Bobby Emmons described him as "focused on taking advantage of his opportunity to get his music out. He was all business." "I remember him being a quiet person, laid back and rolled with the flow," said Stan Kesler. Both Reggie Young and Bobby Wood, who had played piano on the first few songs they had done with O'Keefe, liked working with him, although Reggie Young recalled him as "serious" and Wood said as he had of Prine, "We didn't know where he was."

"He was into Native American stuff," Reggie Young added amusedly. Bobby Wood recalled the writer's unusual vocal warmup. "We were in the control room and he let out this God-awful scream. . . . He started screaming in the control room at the top of his lungs, scared us to death. He said he'd gotten it from the Indians. I said, 'Do it again and I'll scalp you.' He said, 'That clears out your vocal cords.' I said, 'I thought we were gonna have to take you to the emergency room.'" Possibly it was incidents like these which led Mike Leech to conclude that the songwriter was a bit strange; then again, perhaps it was his material. "He could have had a brilliant career if he had had sense enough to stay commercial," concluded the arranger. "How 'Good-Time Charlie' came out of his brain along with all the other stuff is beyond me. 'Good-Time Charlie' is a great song."

"Good-Time Charlie's Got the Blues," the song to which Mike Leech referred, became a standard, and one of the songs most closely associated with the American group (after they had moved to Nashville, by which time the song had become a hit, almost every record producer in town hired them to cut yet another version of "Good-Time Charlie." Even Chips Moman did one, which accentuated and underlined the song's obvious self-pity). It is the track that opens O'Keefe's album, even though the version recorded in Memphis is not exactly the same one that everyone heard on the radio the following fall. O' Keefe went back to New York and changed a few things, playing down the grimness of the original arrangement and accentuating the slide-guitar passages that made Reggie Young famous in Nashville. "They thought I was playing a steel guitar on that one," said Reggie amusedly. "I was using a volume pedal, sort of squeezing out notes." O'Keefe also substituted the line "Said they're moving to L. A." for the original line, which was "I believe this time they're gonna stay." "I don't think he liked 'Good-Time Charlie,'" Reggie Young said with some surprise. "He wasn't doin' cartwheels over that song."

A generation before indie music, "Good-Time Charlie's Got the Blues" became the slackers' national anthem. It speaks for a generation of small-town drifters who watched their high-powered friends grow up, flee their hometowns for college and jobs, find mates, become successful, and leave them behind, stuck in the same boring jobs and boring lives or living off their parents. "They said this town'll waste your time," the narrator morosely concludes. "I guess they're right, it's wasting mine." Reggie Young's famous slide-guitar accents are sharp and acerbic; O'Keefe sings in a mopey whine that was perfect for the self-pitying angst of the song. The jaunty whistling at the end is the final graceful touch, implying that Good-Time Charlie will endure and probably still be a slacker twenty years hence.

"Good-Time Charlie" is an instant classic, and almost any song would sound lesser by comparison; nonetheless, two of O'Keefe's most incoherent ones, riddled with incomprehensible allusions, obvious puns, and drug references follow. "Shooting Star" seems to refer to a funeral wake, though it is somewhat hard to tell; there are "dumplings giggling," a woman's lover talking in a corner and "eating the holey sole of his shoe," and an elephant sitting in a chair. "He quoted a famous poet, 'The morning is waiting for Electra,' or something similar," said Mike Leech. "When that lyric came by, we all exchanged glances." One line almost redeems the mess: "A rainbow rises from a frozen cup of coffee," but even this one blurs poetic allusion into hallucination. "The Question (Obviously)" is more of the same, the only bright spots being Reggie Young's bluesy lead and some interesting atonal piano that could only be Shane Keister, buried beneath O'Keefe's snarl. The listeners have not been properly introduced to Shane yet, but they will be.

Two excellent songs follow the horrible ones. A version of Hank Williams Sr.'s "Honky-Tonkin'" is superb; sparked by Leo LeBlanc's steel and Mike Leech's upright bass, the group manages a first-class re-creation of traditional country, a style nobody was enamored with except Stan Kesler, who seems to imbue the recording with special care. Since O'Keefe whined when he sang anyway, his voice did a creditable Williams imitation. His composition "The Road" is a reflective look at life on tour, sparked by Reggie Young's slide guitar playing a similar figure to the one on "Good-Time Charlie."

Two other songs, one poorly written and one slightly pretentious but effective, serve as the listener's introduction to Shane Keister. "Grease" attempts to be a rocker but fails, though it features some barrelhouse piano in a more intricate style than the way Bobby Wood handled it; whereas Bobby stayed pretty much to the lower and middle ranges of the keyboard,

Shane is all over the place. "American Dream," an antiwar song, is overwritten, but the group makes it stunning: it begins with Shane's classical piano, rippling as befits Vladimir Horowitz playing Chopin. In the lyric, O'Keefe looks out the window at the rain and borrows a metaphor from the 1920s: he sees war as the Big Parade and imagines all the soldiers in all the wars, straggling in line, with their wives and families walking alongside and wondering if the sacrifice was worth it. In the chorus he changes the perspective to the first-person hopes of a returning soldier, who wants nothing more than to settle down peacefully on a plot of land with a family and a "funky old pickup truck." This section is underlined by the whirring-blender effect now perfected by Reggie Young, Hayward Bishop, and Bobby Emmons; Mike Leech has now found a way to enter the mix, playing an intricate bass line that adds even more spice to the blend. There is a reprise of the first verse and Shane's keyboard takes on the impressionistic sound of the raindrops trickling on the windowpane as the track ends—a stunning introduction to Shane's virtuosity.

"Valentine Pieces" is not as overwrought, but it is beautiful, even if it is nobody's idea of a conventional tribute to February 14. The speaker is staring out the window at the sunset as torn fragments of old valentines litter the floor. Bobby Emmons's organ line evokes a cold wind sweeping through the room and stirring the scraps, though once again Reggie Young's slide guitar predominately carries the piece. Disillusioned love is also the theme of the stately, slow "I'm Sober Now," an intelligent mix of traditional country (courtesy of Leo LeBlanc's steel guitar) and the modern theme of anger rather than sorrow at the ending of a romance, capped with a memorable line: "They say some folks can make it, livin' on their own / But the only ones I've heard of was either saints or stones." These songs all have merit and are worth hearing.

"Roseland Taxi Dancer" was the one both Reggie Young and Bobby Emmons enthusiastically named as their favorite song from these sessions; they seemed drawn to its unusual subject matter and its changes of mood

and tempo. It is one of several compositions with nostalgic themes O'Keefe wrote over the years: his 1975 "Delta Queen," a tribute to the famous paddle-wheeler, is similar in both melodic structure and intent. In "Roseland" we go back in time to the mid-1930s, when ten-cents-a-dance girls were waltzing around the famous Roseland Ballroom in New York to the tune of Clyde McCoy's "Sugar Blues"; a ghostly trumpet, overdubbed in New York, simulates McCoy's sound. (Arif Mardin would have been better off to get a saxophone for the big-band simulation; Charlie Parker worked on the Roseland bandstand for a short time when he first came to New York around 1939.) The final song on the album, "I Know You Really Love Me," is only a sketch, featuring Shane Keister's vaudeville piano and a brief lyric referring to the British comic strip *Andy Capp*, which also had a following in the United States over the · years.

As with the Weinstein and Stroll album, the drug references and inside jokes referring to drugs are numerous: the "cocaine afternoons" of "The Road"; the "gotta get off, gotta get off" harmonies on "Grease" (overdubbed in New York by Felix Cavaliere and Eddie Brigati of the Rascals); the hustler "searching for a crumb" from the dealers who will "make you bleed before they sell you some" in "The Question"; the substance that will give "a brand new lease" in "Grease." Probably the best of the drug songs, and one of the funniest and most cynical ever in the genre, was the talking blues "Louie the Hook Vs. the Preacher." Punctuated by Reggie Young's sharp guitar comments, O'Keefe tells the story of the junkie Louie, who would have "reached his destination / if hell had been his goal." Going through withdrawal and needing money, Louie meets a well-dressed, prosperous-looking preacher "hustling for the Lord," and from there it is a matter of who can run the biggest con, as both of them extort and exhort each other. Louie wins, claiming to have been saved, and takes up a collection from the onlooking crowd; he gets sixty dollars, enough to get him by till he can hustle again. O'Keefe concludes near the close of the song: "Preachers and junkies, a man don't need for friends," and sums it all up in a bitter line: "If Jesus Christ was a preacher, He got the short end of the take."

Such vinegary songs may have been a departure for Arif Mardin, but Shane Keister, observing the Atlantic producer for the first time, found him to be quite at home with the material and with working in Memphis. "I remember I was awed by his musicality," said Shane. "He suggested something to me [that] only a master would understand or even conceive. . . . Arif was a great admirer of Reggie's sound. He crossed all bridges. . . . He was always a gentleman. I never heard a cross word from him, I never even heard him curse. I think he recognized my classical ability. He was brilliant—intellectually a brilliant man. Arif was one of the giants of the record industry."

Shane might have made more of the connection with Arif at that time, but the Atlantic group and American came to a parting of the ways. The O'Keefe sessions were the last ones the New York label would make at the studio. For years the musicians did not know why Atlantic suddenly stopped coming down to make records with them. Stan Kesler did not find out until later, either, but he recalled what he thought the problem had been. "Atlantic and Wexler and Chips and all of 'em got kinda crossways," he said. "I think Chips got to charging too much, he wanted a piece of everything that was cut there. He wanted an override, a percentage, plus studio time and pay for players. . . . I think that surcharge was one of the things that broke up the deal." Bobby Emmons thought the surcharge had little or nothing to do with it; he felt that Wexler preferred working out of Atlantic's new operation at Criteria in Miami. "Everybody's always looking for a way to do it cheaper," he said, adding that Atlantic had been a delight to work with right up until the end. "They were just sweethearts, really," he said enthusiastically.

Stan could not recall where and how he found out about the studio's most important client withdrawing their account, but he was sure he did not learn about it from Chips. "I didn't hear him saying a word about it, I just heard little bits of information around," he said

vaguely. He was also unclear if Chips had informed the musicians. "He might have told them something, see, I don't know," he said. "It would be more normal for him to keep it quiet." Reggie Young said that the players were not consulted about any additional percentages or charges. "Most of that business I really didn't know," he said. Chips Moman denied closing the door to the Atlantic account; he felt that there had never been a problem between the label and himself, and he always remained in cordial touch with Jerry Wexler. But something changed, and with the loss of the Atlantic account there was practically no business left. "The sessions came to a screeching halt," said Reggie Young. So what were they to do? Well, in that downtime, the last of the late arrivals found his instrumental voice.

"I started becoming interested in electronic music at North Texas State," said Shane Keister. That was during the era of the *Switched-On Bach* albums by Walter Carlos, classical music played on synthesizer, which by definition would have provoked the attention of a predominately classical keyboardist with some inclinations toward pop music. His interest was further piqued by the large synthesizer owned by Pepper-Tanner. "Pepper-Tanner had a huge Moog, it was so unstable," said Shane; it seemed a bit intimidating, so the piano player had never tried it. But one day, walking into the studio for a routine jingle session, he saw a smaller Moog that the studio had just bought. "I fell in love with this mini-Moog," Shane recalled. "I went back [to American] all excited." He wanted to buy one of his own and work with it, but "I couldn't get the financing, and Mike Leech co-signed for that mini-Moog. I still have it: it's a classic."

It was at this time, when he acquired the synthesizer and began studiously working with it, that his greatness became apparent to everyone at the studio. "The word 'genius' has been falsely overapplied in this industry," said Hayward Bishop. "But in my opinion, Shane Keister is one of the very few that really qualify for that title. He also has a decent amount of humility. . . . Tommy and Shane were the two most genuinely charitable people I've ever met.

Shane really had a genuine depth. He's got a brilliant sense of humor, his mind is right there with you.

"When he got the Moog synthesizer, he woodshedded in the control room with it until he really got brilliant," Hayward continued. "He'd come up with sounds and give 'em funny names, like 'pffft'—that's 'a seagull hitting the side of a battleship.' I asked him where he came up with his [ideas] and he said, 'In dreams.'" ("I also dreamed music," said Glen Spreen, adding that he had been careful not to let any of the censorious American group know. "My mind would put me in a control room, looking at the speakers and hearing this unusual but beautiful music.") Shane whooped with laughter when he was asked about the sound effects. "I do remember that!" he exclaimed delightedly. "I'm amazed that Hayward would even remember." He also happily recalled the hours he spent learning the instrument on which he eventually made his professional reputation. "Pete Peterson at Pepper-Tanner taught me how to program a synthesizer," he said, adding that although he worked a time or two with the cumbersome large machine at the jingle factory, he had never really been comfortable with it. "The mini-Moog was so fast," he said.

The same sense of humor that led Shane to caption his sound effects also led him to become one of the prime instigators of mischief around the place. "Musicians, they're a breed all their own, most of 'em have a subtle sense of humor," observed Stan Kesler. With practically no session work at the time, there was not much to do at the studio but hang around, and the pranks became more intense than ever.

For instance, there were the hot-air balloons. Mike Leech thought Hayward Bishop had first come up with the idea, but the credit must go to Shane, who idly mentioned one afternoon that he knew how to make hot-air balloons from clear plastic laundry bags. "I learned to make those in college," he said, laughing uproariously at the recollection. "You take a laundry bag that goes over clothes. Then you take a couple of drinking straws and put them together with thread. You cut a slit in the straws with a razor blade and put birthday candles in the slits . . . It's

sort of a self-contained hot-air balloon." Mike Leech decided that some should be crafted, and immediately the group laid in a supply of laundry bags, birthday-cake candles, straws, and thread. "We started in the afternoon, we went over to the drugstore and got the supplies, they must have thought we were nuts," laughed Hayward Bishop. They spent the remainder of the day assembling the balloons. "We took sticks and made an 'X' and hooked the open end of the bag to them," Mike Leech explained. "We then put birthday candles on top of the sticks." "We looked like a dag-gone hobby shop, like an assembly line," Hayward Bishop chortled. Then, with the balloons having been manufactured, Shane, Mike, Hayward, Reggie Young, Billy Burnette, and Rick Yancey all climbed to the roof of the building that night—Shane estimated the time at about eleven PM—and set one of the contraptions alight. "It was a real still night, there wasn't a breath of wind," said Shane—or anyway, not until they were ready to launch the first balloon.

"The bag began to fill with heat and started to rise," said Mike Leech. "We stood in awe as it went higher and higher. It was great! Then at about three hundred feet, the plastic bag caught on fire. As it was falling, the wind picked it up and started blowing it down the street, heading right for a gas station about three blocks away. Our mouths dropped open, we looked wide-eyed at each other, and ran back down and hid in the studio, expecting to hear an explosion and sirens at any moment." "Our mood changed from exhilaration to absolute panic," said Shane. "We were expecting a Mrs. O'Leary's cow situation," said Hayward Bishop, referring to the legend of how the great Chicago fire began. "We could see the headlines: 'Memphis Rhythm Section Burns Down North Memphis.'" "Nothing happened, thank God, but what a rush!" exclaimed Mike Leech. "Wonder how many UFO reportings there were that night?"

It was also Shane who contrived the blowguns. "He made thirty bucks showing how he could make a rolled-up *Billboard* magazine into a dart . . . using a mike stand as a blowgun," said Hayward Bishop. "That thing was a

FAST—conical-shaped dart." "Oh, the blow-gun!" exclaimed the instigator. "I think my cousin taught me that. I've been making those since I was twelve or thirteen. You take a half-inch piece of pipe and magazine paper that has a gloss on either side. You basically make a cone out of [the paper], a long streamlined cone." When one end of the cone was licked, the gloss of the paper sealed it shut. "Then you drop it in the half-inch pipe," Shane continued humorously. "I'm tellin' you what, it'll do a good seventy to eighty yards and land point first. You dare not shoot somebody with 'em because they'll go in somebody's skin." At Marshall University he and his friends had embedded Blue Diamond matches, which ignited on contact, in the cone tips of these homemade darts and they blew them out the upper windows of the high-rise dormitory, Twin Towers, watching the darts catch fire when they landed on the sidewalk below. Shane demonstrated the blowgun for the American musicians—and embedded the *Billboard* magazine deep into the studio wall.

He was an observer of one bit of silliness that occurred when Billy Burnette's eighteen-year-old California girlfriend, Liz, was visiting in Memphis and accompanied Billy as he stopped by the studio one evening. Shane was a skilled marksman (he, Hayward Bishop, and Tommy Cogbill regularly went out to a field in Murfreesboro and practiced target shooting during the later Nashville years) and now he, Billy, and Hayward were shooting Hayward's BB gun, which had been "specially altered for impact," into the studio wall. Target practice in the studio had long been a common custom; there was a special piece of tape on the studio floor behind which the musicians often stood and emptied their guns into the wall when the tension from hours of concentration on a song seemed to be too much. "The guy in the print shop learned to duck," Hayward laughed. Shooting into the wall was fun at first, but something else was required to really demonstrate the velocity of the souped-up device. "This little toy was now almost lethal!" Hayward continued. "This thing would bury a

BB into a plank of wood so far you couldn't see the BB!" The musicians adjourned to the parking lot, where they could aim at objects further away.

Billy Burnette noticed that a few of the neighborhood's back porch lights were slowly being turned on. "Wanting to further demonstrate the distance [the gun could shoot], I chose the light five houses down," Hayward continued. "One could hear the BB hitting metallic objects on the porch, but I couldn't hit the light. We all had a turn at it. Liz went last and instead of targeting the distant light, chose the immediate one next door and hit it at first shot! We all dashed inside and waited to hear police sirens. Sure enough, we heard sirens coming down the street about five minutes later—but it was the usual Memphis Fire Department responding to another call." The sirens and rumble of the fire trucks as they passed the studio were so common that it became a standing joke among the musicians that the Memphis Fire Department had been heard (however obscurely) on more hit records than anyone in town. Billy's girlfriend and her aim at the porch became another legend in the lore of the American musicians, and long after she and Billy had parted company she would forever be known to the players as "Liz Oakley."

All of this was fun, but nothing was getting anything accomplished. With Atlantic no longer coming to the studio, "sessions had dropped off quite a bit," recalled Stan Kesler. Melba Moore came in for some work and she was warmly received, but no other name clients followed her. The musicians were reduced to recording instrumentals under the name the American Group just to give themselves something to do. There was practically no more work in town. It hardly seemed worthwhile to stock the studio; Reggie Young recalled that when the Ampex distributor came in to resupply the studio with its usual order of reel-to-reel tapes, "Bobby Emmons said, 'Here's another load of sand for the desert.'" "That was one of those holdin' on for dear life periods," said Cymarron's Richard Mainegra. Chips Moman was wealthy, but everyone else had houses to pay for and families to feed, and nobody knew what was going to happen next.

Exactly when the idea of moving to Atlanta was first considered as an alternative by Chips is not clear. The largest city in Chips's home state had been a background factor of life at American for awhile. J.R. Cobb, of course, remained a friend of the group, and so did Paul Davis, who came up occasionally for sessions at American but was more or less based in Atlanta. Shack White, a songwriter who wrote "Amerikan Music" (pronounced AmuREEcan) for Steve Alaimo, was also living in Atlanta, and began turning up at the studio now and then. American had already been represented in Atlanta a little more directly when Glen Spreen had recorded with B.J. Thomas there and done some string arrangements for Joe South. That summer the Atlanta-recorded "Mighty Clouds of Joy," with its theme referring to happiness both spiritual and temporal and Glen's arrangement evocative of the sun bursting through clouds, was a hit on the pop charts for B.J.

Slowly the idea of relocating took root in Chips's mind, and it was not long before what at first may have been idle speculation became the Next Big Thing. Shane Keister remembered it happening exactly that way, a rapid evolution. "It started as a rumor, over a few days it spread into a fact," he recalled. "Somebody else in the band told me, 'Chips wants to move to Atlanta.'" "We were sittin' around and Chips brought it up. He was serious, I don't know how serious we were," said Reggie Young. "I think they would have always stayed in Memphis, but Chips got that roamin' fever and moved to Atlanta," observed Jimmy Johnson, watching from the sidelines and thinking that the sudden uprooting left the group "heartbroken." All of a sudden there was a new dream to chase.

Nor is it clear why Chips wanted to leave. "I'm not sure I ever knew the real reason," said Richard Mainegra. Stan Kesler added, "I don't know what possessed him." Chips himself gave several reasons, all of them obscure. "He thought there was a lot of talent down there, he said Atlanta is full of talent," Stan Kesler

recalled. Shane Keister recalled the same thing. "He thought it was an untapped market," said Shane. "He felt like Memphis was dying, which it was." Hayward Bishop had the impression that Chips wanted to go down and compete directly with Bill Lowery's empire; Reggie Young agreed with that impression. "The idea was to go down and take over Atlanta," he said.

Chips said that the deciding factor was the nominations for the Memphis Music Awards, which were announced that spring. Although the group would be cited for the collective accomplishment of having played on 122 chart records since the studio's beginnings in early 1965, in the individual song, producer, and instrumentalist categories not one American staffer was nominated for anything. "That hurt all of us' feelings," Chips said, his voice a mixture of sadness and indignation. "I felt that Memphis music had insulted all of us. That's what made me want to get the hell out of there. . . . We had more hits than the whole town! I think anybody'd consider that a slap." Bobby Emmons agreed that the Memphis Music Awards had slighted them. "The FBI couldn't have found us among the listings of nominees that year," he said. "The lesser achievers [in town] turned out to get more glory out of the deal. We were just a bunch of hired guns; the city didn't care anything about us." Dan Penn also gave assent to the apparently universal view among the American staff that they had never gotten proper recognition or acknowledgment for their creativity. "In America and Europe and all over the world, nobody ever gave these guys credit," he said disgustedly.

In the interpretation of Bobby Emmons, the city fathers, who did not know much about the Memphis music industry to begin with in spite of the endeavors of people like Marty Lacker, wanted to honor city-based record labels such as Stax and Hi rather than recording studios. "They couldn't find any benefits to a Chicago boy cuttin' [in Memphis] for a New York label," he added, in an obvious reference to John Prine's sessions the year before. It was apparent that new acts were not coming to Memphis as often as they had, and American unfairly caught blame for something over which the studio had no control. "People, in retrospect, started saying that American's leaving had killed Memphis music," observed Bobby Emmons thoughtfully. "I don't see how we could have done that because, to hear Memphis tell it, we were never there."

There was another factor involved for Chips. Georgia, and particularly the area surrounding Atlanta including LaGrange, was a place from which he felt he had been too long away. "I had kind of a longing for home, you know?" he said wistfully. "It had been a long time since I'd been home." He went back to LaGrange, looked at some property, and ended up buying a house. It was from here, almost forty-five miles from Atlanta, that he hoped to commute every day when the studio got established.

The move seems to have been another pipe dream, about which Chips was convincing himself as much as he was convincing the musicians who believed in him. Being in a house band was a security blanket for a group of meek country boys who were not totally sure they had what it took to succeed in the larger world (because they had no idea of how that world viewed their talents). No one was completely sure that the move was the right thing to do, but everyone was determined to give it a try.

Even the loyal Bobby Emmons was somewhat skeptical. "I didn't want any part of it," was his first reaction, but he added, "I was kinda like a prune picker, I was ready to follow the fruit." After all, Emmons knew as well as anyone else that "sessions were down to nothing." "We weren't doin' that much in Memphis," said Reggie Young. "Memphis had kinda dried up." "Things were going downhill fast," said Stan Kesler. "We all were wondering about our future, and I guess he was too. We figured he was such a hot producer, he could make it wherever he went. . . . He was just ready to get out of Memphis because if you're falling it's hard to get back on top." Stan himself didn't want to move, to Atlanta or anywhere else, but, he reflected, "Chips was pretty good at enticing you to do something." In Stan's case, Chips asked him if he would come to Atlanta with the others and stay until the studio was built and operating,

then he could come back if he wanted. Stan eventually agreed to go. "All of us, what else are we gonna do, y'know?" he asked resignedly.

"Shane and Hayward were new, they didn't have any name and they might not have made it," Stan continued. That was precisely the feeling of the new piano player, who figured he had nothing to lose by making the move. "My security was challenged," he said of the sudden announcement. "My thoughts were, well, if he's gonna move, I'm gonna move." The alternative was Nashville, which Shane did not feel ready for. He had tried the place once and not been successful. "After I graduated from high school, I went down to Nashville with a trio—we starved to death," he said. Hayward Bishop also felt he had nothing to lose. "I was young and I felt I could afford one more move," he said. He also was waiting on some money Chips had promised him for the masters to Junction. If everyone else was going to try and stick it out a little longer, he figured he could, too.

Chips could have started over with musicians in Atlanta—the town was full of them—rather than uprooting the American players, but he preferred to cling to his "boys," in part, thought Mike Leech, because of a well-concealed but painful lack of confidence. "Chips is insecure musically in the fact that he surrounds himself with musicians who can understand what he is trying to put across," the string arranger observed thoughtfully. "That's one main reason we always got along, we could figure out what he was trying to say. He always said he hated working with other pickers because he couldn't talk their language. Especially the string players."

There were a few more sessions scheduled before everyone could pack up and leave. Mike Leech was producing a country songwriter who had grown up in the Lauderdale Courts with Elvis and had gotten a song he had written, "Miracle of the Rosary," recorded by his old neighbor and classmate the year before. Of the tracks Mike recorded on Lee Denson, "Let the Big Wheels Roll" is best; its theme of a trucker on the road fits Denson's wobbly voice and stilted, traditional style. Judging from these selections, Mike would have made a fine producer; the material is suited to Denson's old-fashioned singing approach and the mix has a solid clarity typical of both Stan Kesler's engineering and of Mike's own deliberate, precise personality.

As retro as Denson was, another artist out of the past for whom Chips initially had high expectations was the rockabilly legend Billy Lee Riley. Billy Lee had been hanging around Memphis since the demise of his kind of music; he had narrowly missed his chance back then and he knew it, and he badly wanted that crossover hit. In coming to American as the last even remotely important act to record there, he was aiming for the largest possible audience, and Chips Moman had signed him to Entrance with that kind of success in mind.

The musicians liked Billy Lee and enjoyed working with him. "I been knowin' Billy Lee since back in the fifties," said Reggie Young; Billy Lee came from Reggie's Arkansas hometown. Stan Kesler, too, had known him a long time, from those days when they were both at Sun. "He was long recognized in the area as a soulful rock-blues man," said Bobby Emmons. "He always had a good feel, it was rewarding to accompany him." Hayward Bishop seemed to view Billy Lee as somewhat sad, a man whom time had passed by. Shane Keister respected the faded star. "I remember being very impressed by his roughness of voice and the character that came out of his voice," said Shane. "He was a very nice man, very well mannered, but his voice was gruff. He reminded me of Tony Joe White. He was very nice, fun to work with, he worked real hard. I never sensed a problem with him."

The new piano player had begun his career at American working with Arif Mardin; he was now learning how to take direction from Chips. "The one major difference, I would say, Chips, being from the South, was more informal," Shane observed, contrasting the two. "Chips always had great ideas. Chips was really good with specific things at the right time. He'd give general direction, and then he'd say, 'Play that again and leave the organ out of the first verse,' or whatever. [He] was really good about letting the playback tell its own story."

Chips gave Shane specific directions for what he wanted on a Tony Joe White composition called "I've Got a Thing About You, Baby." "Chips said, 'Get a steel drum sound on the mini-Moog.' It was the blind leading the blind." (Chips seems to have tried something similar on the Steve Alaimo recording "Sand in My Pocket," which sounds like a cross between reggae and beach music; the producer was apparently unaware that in Hayward Bishop he had a beach-music expert in his midst.) The finished product is a pleasure, from Mike Leech's deliberate bass line to the piano flourishes of Shane Keister atop the solid organ lines of Bobby Emmons. But the real star of the record is Hayward Bishop, who is playing not only drums but several layers of overdubbed congas and assorted percussion. "Chips pretty much gave me carte blanche on percussion overdubs on that record," he said in astonishment. "I can remember being pretty amazed at how far he let me go. I was looking for that old black train-porter shuffle feel from those thirties and forties black-and-white movies. Chips seemed to envision Jamaican islands."

Whether imagining islands or a musical with the Nicholas Brothers tap-dancing, the worth of "I Got a Thing About You, Baby" is demonstrated by the fact that, according to Shane Keister, the Memphis radio stations picked up on it immediately and gave it a great deal of airplay, though it failed to sell. "We used to call those songs 'turntable hits,'" said Bobby Wood—records that caught on with disc jockeys but not the general public. The group re-recorded it a little over a year later with Elvis at the Stax sessions in 1973; for the second version, Tommy Cogbill played bass and Glen Spreen contributed a pleasant string line. There isn't much percussion on the second version of the song (Hayward Bishop wasn't there) and it sounds somewhat smoother; the fact that it was Elvis performing it made the public aware of the song, and it belatedly became a hit.

The B-side of the Billy Lee Riley 45, "You Don't Love Me (Yes I Know)" is pure Chicago blues, an old Bo Diddley classic that had been an R&B hit for Willie Cobbs in 1960. (Gayle McCormick had recorded a version in 1969.)

"Fannie Mae" is more of the same, another track that Hayward Bishop for one thought one of their best. It would be hard to dispute that claim, but a case could also be made for the Little Willie John standard "Fever." This version takes the song away from the supper-club sultriness with which Peggy Lee famously endowed the tune and brings it all back home, with one of the most textured, layered productions Chips had done since "Circle Round the Sun" two years before. The Hank Williams Sr. standard "You Win Again" has a rough, scarred beauty, from Mike Leech's unobtrusive string line to Billy Lee's vocal, which gives the record more than another touch of the blues. Tony Joe White's "Even Trolls Love Rock and Roll," the second single, is probably meant to seem amusing, but in Chips's hands it comes off as ominous and spooky as did Glen Goza's "The Box." There is real work of merit here, sparked by Reggie Young and Shane Keister throughout. Richard Mainegra and Billy Burnette were now occasionally sitting in on acoustic guitar as informal replacements for Johnny Christopher, although with typical modesty Richard never for a moment considered himself to be a member of the band. With this new mix of session veterans and teenagers learning their trade, Chips was still able to lead and direct a great group of players and get the best out of them.

The Billy Lee Riley sessions were for the most part unheard by the general public. "There was some enmity between him and Chips," remembered Shane, and most of the recordings were never released, remaining in the tape vault (although Chips talked for awhile about resurrecting a private label and making them available). It was one more in a series of quarrels and failed opportunities that marred Chips's career, both in Memphis and later.

By now Chips was thinking of his future in Atlanta, although he made it clear that he was leaving Memphis more in sorrow than in anger. "The entire city council stood in my front yard and begged me not to leave," he remembered. "I told 'em it was too late." Marty Lacker also tried to talk Chips out of going. He paid one of his infrequent visits to the studio to try

and persuade his old friend. "It didn't work," Marty said of his effort. "I basically talked to him about the contributions they had made to Memphis and how it would be a shame to throw all that money away just to move to Atlanta." But all of the Atlanta people who had been coming to the studios had made an impression, and Marty understood that. "Atlanta did a good selling job on Chips and I'm sure the prospect of being close to LaGrange played a part in it," he observed. "Atlanta paid more attention to him than the city of Memphis did. They gave him a studio all wired and ready to go plus they sent trucks up to move him. They laid the red carpet out for him and he liked that. He really felt unappreciated in Memphis by the powers that be." (The studio was not actually wired and ready: David Wright, who owned a small studio next to the warehouse Chips found for his, came up and helped unwire the console and rewire it at American Atlanta. "We stripped the mike lines out of the wall, took everything," said Bobby Emmons.) Stan Kesler did not even try to talk Chips out of it. "I could see he had his mind made up," said Stan.

The musicians were not about to go without some commemoration. In what they all admitted was a sentimental gesture, they and Stan Kesler wrote their names on the echo chamber in the studio. Even Tommy Cogbill, back visiting Memphis for a few days to see his family, stopped by and signed. They also spray-painted a note on one of the walls: STAND HERE AND FEEL THE ECHOES FROM A THOUSAND HITS OF AGES PAST. Mike Leech took a photograph. He also came up with another idea. "Shane and I decided to leave a little note," Mike said. "The outer wall of what was the Ranch House, facing Chelsea Avenue, was white painted bricko block. We took spray paint, got a ladder, and wrote ATLANTA OR BUSTED on the wall. In big black letters. Chips saw it and hit the ceiling. His comment, 'You guys get me in more shit' . . . he told us the place was rented and that we had to get it off. We took the same black spray paint and covered what we had written, leaving a huge block of black. I expect we drove Chips crazy with some of our antics."

Not everyone was going. Campbell Kensinger stayed in town, and when the Memphis music scene he had loved and been part of died, Campbell died too, his official death only a formality. Rick Yancey cited family responsibilities as the reason he could not leave. "Everybody went but Sherrill and me," he said. "My mom and dad were elderly. They needed me in town. My wife and new baby were there and her family were there. I ended up staying in Memphis till I was forty-one, till my mother died. What upset me was that Richard moved and that was like the death blow to Cymarron." Richard would take an apartment in a subdivision called Windy Hill Village; he had sung an advertising jingle for it only a year before. Billy Burnette was young and footloose; he decided to go along for the ride. Reggie Young and Bobby Emmons planned to commute for awhile, until they could find houses and send for their families; Stan Kesler did the same. Mike Leech was more or less homeless at that point; he would live in the studio during his Atlanta tenure. Hayward Bishop and Shane Keister took apartments across the hall from one another, just outside of the city in Marietta. Watching from the sidelines, Gene Chrisman noted that if he had not already left the studio, he would have quit when those plans were announced. "I wasn't about to make that trip. I *hate* Atlanta," the drummer said vehemently. "I just don't like big towns."

The last official session at American, according to the session books of Reggie Young, was for their songwriter friend Paul Davis, on May 15, 1972. On June 1, the Memphis Music Awards were held, and the group received a special plaque honoring their contributions to the Memphis music industry. The next morning, June 2, Hayward Bishop went in to the studio early and worked on some overdubs for his nearly completed Junction project. "I was finishing the vocal lead overdub on the last song of the Junction LP while the movers were waiting for me to finish and shut down," said Hayward. "We were overdubbing the very last vocal on the very last song. We had been there since early the night before, we had been there all night long. American Studios in Memphis finally ended at 9:27 AM on that day. The next

day, June 3rd, we led the moving van on to the Atlanta studio location."

It was literally "good-bye, good-bye to everything." Chips was leaving the farm in Raleigh, leaving the studio he had built and spent so much time working in, leaving the city he had loved and called home since he was fourteen. If he had initially planned to rent out the studio, in the end he did nothing with it; "I just left it," he said. The story of the studio does not quite end with Chips's departure from Memphis. A fellow named Bill Glore, who owned a small gospel label called Prophecy and a rockabilly label called Glo-Lite (whose big artist was the Sun alumnus Malcolm Yelvington) took over the building in the late seventies, and he proudly printed the studio's famous address on the labels of his records. In 1986 American was opened to Chips and the group once more, when they recorded Johnny Cash, Roy Orbison, Jerry Lee Lewis and Carl Perkins there for the *Class of '55* sessions. For awhile, the Elvis estate took people on tours of the studio, but their interest in it seemed to stop there. Glore tried to involve them in properly repairing the building, as he was operating on a shoestring. With the short-sightedness typical of Memphis, no one came forward to preserve it, and in 1989 American was torn down. It was an example of the lack of respect for history and accomplishment that had driven Chips away.

As he left for Atlanta, Chips took as many of his toys as he could, especially the cars and motorcycles; because of his chronic distrustfulness, he preferred to have someone he knew take the cars down. "I volunteered to drive the Ford Maverick," recalled Hayward Bishop. "He rode with me and we talked like we were brothers. The last thing I remember him saying to me was, 'Gimme a cigarette, Haywit.'"

There would be other triumphs for Chips, and for the musicians, following the six-month disaster that was the move to Atlanta; relocation to Nashville, recording comebacks with the likes of Waylon and Willie, Merle Haggard, and Johnny Cash among the clients; there was even a personal triumph for Chips, since by the time of his relocation to Nashville he had married Toni Wine. The marriage ended in the mid-nineties, and both Toni and Chips re-married, she to a retired music -industry ex-ecutive (sufficient revenge on a man who had spent his entire life fighting the suits), he to a warm, down-to-earth woman named Jane who enjoyed his horses and his country pleasures. Toni resumed her career as a backup singer and occasionally toured with Tony Orlando. Chips settled down on a farm in Georgia and raised horses, although he could still be coaxed out now and then for a project. He suffered several health problems as he aged, but an interview with the *Memphis Commercial-Appeal* in mid-2008 revealed him to be as sharp and as melancholy as ever at the age of seventy-one.

For the group without Chips, there would be hits with Dobie Gray, Larry Gatlin, Crystal Gayle, Billy "Crash" Craddock, T.G. Sheppard, and even Elvis. There would be Grammies and CMA awards for Chips and for all of the American writers, most notably for Wayne Carson's, Mark James's, and Johnny Christopher's "You Were Always on My Mind," when that song finally got its due. Tommy Cogbill returned to producing with his 1974 remake of "Everlasting Love" featuring Carl Carlton. Glen Spreen created his masterpiece in the same year with "Please Come to Boston." Reggie Young became the top session guitarist in town when Grady Martin abandoned the field to tour with Willie Nelson. Stan Kesler worked as the staff engineer at Pete Drake's legendary Nashville studio before moving back to Memphis, directing the custom recording operation at the Phillips studio, and briefly operating a florist shop. Hayward Bishop made a name for himself as the drummer on the recordings of country music's best-selling group of all time, Alabama. Bobby Emmons collaborated with Chips on the composition of two progressive-country standards, "Lukenbach, Texas" and "The Wurlitzer Prize." Bobby Wood emerged as a songwriter and session player, famous for his piano intro on Garth Brooks's "The Dance." Shane Keister became Music City's foremost synthesizer player, and from there pursued a career first as a gospel keyboardist and arranger and later as staff producer for Atlantic Records in New

York. Richard Mainegra and Rick Yancey had a recording comeback as the Remingtons and Billy Burnette became a short-term guitarist for Fleetwood Mac. Dan Penn and Spooner Oldham were elevated to semi-legendary status, revered as living relics of the long-forgotten era of soul music.

And yet, for all of them, Memphis was where the story began, and American in Memphis would always be their point of reference. "That was a good studio and it had a certain air, but the real thing was the musicians," said Stan Kesler. There was, of course, even more to it than the musicians' skills, utilized on record with the philosophy stated by Bobby Wood: "Play your soul and make it real and put some embellishments on it to give it the groove." "We tried to leave something better than we found it, musically," said Bobby Emmons. "We did our job, and hoped we had cut a hit somewhere along the line," said Gene Chrisman. There was the fortuitous combination of personalities involved; "[It took] a lot of luck, a lot of talent and a lot of great songwriters hangin' around," offered Dan Penn. "It's called talent and good songs—songs that made a difference," said Wayne Carson from his writer's perspective. There was the direct communication between the players and the listener: "I once had the opinion that if I could be a successful communicator of music, I would consider my life as an achievement of my goals," said Glen Spreen. It was the camaraderie and loyalty among the musicians themselves: "It was just a bunch of brothers makin' music," Chips Moman said casually. "It was like family, everybody was for the family," said Johnny Christopher. "We were genuinely concerned about each other and our families and lives." "We had so much wonderful fun, not only making wonderful music, but with each other in other venues. My dear friends who I miss working with and hanging with," added Mike Leech. And it was the enduring significance of the music they chose to make—strong, melodic songs that addressed the real-life situations of the listeners. "Did we pass the stress test?" asked Spooner Oldham.

Tommy Cogbill answered that question in

a conversation with Bobby Wood in Nashville shortly before Tommy died. "Tommy said it was fate that had put this group together," said Bobby Wood. "I asked him, 'Well, who was in charge of that?' He kind of smiled at me and said, 'You know.'"

This list is an attempt to cover as many of the recordings mentioned in the book as possible. Most of these are available on CD, purchasable online from Amazon, CD Universe, or other such places. For those looking for the out-of-print works and obscure 45s mentioned in the text, or who are simply vinyl purists, there are also some good online sources: probably the best is Gemm.com, which works as a clearinghouse for music stores all over the world. The Roots and Rhythm website is also invaluable.

Gentrys: The only one of their Chips-produced recordings available on CD is the all-important first album, *Keep On Dancin'* (Collectables) The reissue also includes the Doug Sahm soundalike "Spread It on Thick" as a bonus track. *Gentry Time*, the second album, appeared on a CD with the first one several years ago but that combination is now out of print. It is worth hunting for, though, if only to find Dan Penn's and Spooner Oldham's exhilaratingly beautiful "Sunshine Girl," or the raucous stomp of "Giving Love Never Hurt Nobody." The second album's liner notes by George Klein are, in and of themselves, a classic of the era. For those willing to locate some of the later singles, two in particular are a must: "Woman of the World"/"Two Sides to Every Story" (MGM—this is the one possibly augmented by Jimmy Johnson and Roger Hawkins from the Shoals) and the 1968 "Can't Go Back to Denver"/"New Girl in Town" (Bell) with Dale Hawkins (yes, the one who sang the original version of "Suzie Q") as guest producer.

Sandy Posey: There are several reissues of her work around, but the one to get is *Born to Be Hurt: The Anthology 1966–1982*, an Australian import from Raven Records. This one includes all the important monologues, as well as the lesser-known work such as Wayne Carson's incisive "Shattered" and

the later Tommy Cogbill–produced singles from Nashville in the seventies. For those interested in tracking down old vinyl, her 1968 *Looking at You* LP on MGM, with thoughtful versions of the Mann-Weill "Shades of Gray," Wayne Carson's "Meadow of My Love," and "Handy," featuring Bobby Womack's lead guitar, is well worth having.

Jumpin' Gene Simmons: *Haunted House: The Complete Jumpin' Gene Simmons on Hi* (Hi UK) is a two-disc set that includes both his 1964 album, featuring songs like Brook Benton's "Hotel Happiness," and assorted singles, including Reggie Young's compositions "I'm a Rambling Man" and "Go On, Shoes." The version of Jesse Stone's classic "Down in the Alley," featuring Reggie's blazing slide guitar, is also included. A must-listen for anyone wanting to hear the way it sounded when Mike Leech, Reggie, and Bobby Emmons were just beginning to work together.

Ace Cannon/Bill Black Combo: This is tricky, because few of the original albums have been released on CD. A double set from Bill Black that has appeared on CD is a two-album set, *Bill Black's Greatest Hits/Bill Black Combo Goes West*, so if you are looking for "Smokie" and "White Silver Sands," this is probably the one to have. Ace Cannon's work seems to be repackaged only on insubstantial "greatest hits" collections, so the listener will have to be resourceful and find the old vinyl. The two best Ace Cannon LPs on Hi are *Ace Cannon Live* (which offers the listener a chance to hear Mike Leech, Reggie Young, Bobby Emmons, and Tommy Cogbill working in a live-in-the-studio setting) and the innovative, Reggie-arranged *Sweet and Tuff* from mid-1966.

Additional Hi: The place to begin would be with the CDs released in the late nineties, *The HI Records Story: The Early Years, Vols. 1* and *2*. In addition to instrumental tracks from Ace Cannon, the Bill Black Combo, and Willie Mitchell, the two-CD sets feature work from Jerry Jaye, Murray Kellum, and even lesser lights of Memphis music such as the vocalist Charles Hines, who worked with many of the Hi musicians at the Hi Hat Club. There are several Don Bryant compilations, all issued by Hi UK; of these, *The Singles Collection* and *Comin' On Strong* provide the best sample of this underrated singer. The latter CD offers up "Clear Days and Stormy Nights," and even several covers of Buck Owens material!

Goldwax: There have been several repackagings of the Goldwax singles and James Carr material over the years, all of it supervised by Quinton Claunch; *The Goldwax Story, Vols. 1 and 2* on Kent are a good beginning. Volume One has most of the essential singles, including the Ovations' Chips-engineered "It's Wonderful to Be in Love" and Dan Penn's "I'm Living Good," the first song of his recorded by Chips at American. It also features the James Carr classics "Dark End of the Street" and "Pouring Water on a Drowning Man." A Japanese import, *The Goldwax Collection, Vols. 1 and 2*, released on Vivid Sound in the late nineties and now out of print, covers much of the same ground but also includes "I Slipped a Little" and some of the later work with James Carr and with Quinton's other acts. For James Carr, *The Singles* remains the essential CD, including everything from "Dark End of the Street" to the Reggie Young–featuring "You Got My Mind Messed Up" and the later, gospel-influenced "Freedom Train" with the Dixie Flyers. CD Universe offers another James Carr compilation, *A Man Worth Knowing*.

Wilson Pickett: All four relevant albums are available on CD: *The Exciting Wilson Pickett* (the first road trip album, featuring "Land of a Thousand Dances"); *The Wicked Pickett* (in which Tommy Cogbill permanently assumes the bass chair and not only "Mustang Sally" but "Uptight Good Woman" are featured); *The Sound of Wilson Pickett*

(featuring "Soul Dance Number Three" and "Funky Broadway"), and the Tommy Cogbill and Tom Dowd–produced *I'm In Love*. For out-of-print vinyl fans, there's the RCA album *Miz Lena's Boy*, recorded with the American group during the seventies in Nashville and featuring some amazing musical interplay between Tommy Cogbill and Hayward Bishop.

Aretha Franklin: Atlantic has done well by reissues from the Queen of Soul, making available on CD everything she recorded during her peak years. *I Never Loved a Man, Aretha Arrives, Lady Soul, Aretha Now, Soul '69* . . . every one essential listening, with *Lady Soul* probably her best. As if that were not enough, Atlantic/Rhino has also issued a double CD of *Rare and Unreleased Recordings* that give us further insight into the masterful combination of a great singer with equally expert musicians. One complaint: the astonishing "My Song" is on none of those reissued CDs nor the two-volume greatest-hits package. It is the B-side of Atlantic's 1969 single, "See Saw."

More from Atlantic: Both the Sweet Inspirations' first LP, recorded at American, and the two Arthur Conley titles recorded there, *More Sweet Soul* and *Soul Directions*, are available on CD. King Curtis's work is fairly well represented on CD as well, with a two-album disc, *King Curtis Plays the Great Memphis Hits* (the New York road trip album) paired with *King-Sized Soul*, the Tom Dowd and Tommy Cogbill–produced album which gave the world "Memphis Soul Stew." The Tommy Cogbill–engineered work, *Sweet Soul*, begun at American just before the King assassination, can also be found on a Spy/Rhino CD; the Chips Moman–produced *Instant Groove*, which features Johnny Christopher's lush instrumental "La Jean" and Duane Allman overdubbed on several cuts done in New York, was finally reissued on CD in 2008. Find the LP; you will never be sorry.

Herbie Mann's *Memphis Underground* is, of course, available on CD, and so is *Dusty In Memphis*, although the anniversary issue of that landmark album is unnecessarily bogged down by irrelevant bonus tracks from Gamble and Huff and Jeff Barry that should have been compiled separately. A similar mistake is made with the bonus tracks on the reissue of Jackie DeShannon's Atlantic album, *Jackie . . . Plus*. A smaller label, Hacktone Records, has taken it upon itself to release the Dynamics' *First Landing*, highly recommended work from the American group at its peak, with two of the later arrivals on hand and a crisp sound courtesy of Tommy Cogbill. And speaking of small labels, in 2006 Wounded Bird released the Danny O'Keefe album, *O'Keefe*, with "Good Time Charlie's Got the Blues" (Shane Keister's introduction to the studio). The first Prine album, *John Prine*, is available through Atlantic/WEA. Steve Alaimo's work on Atco, including the Dan Penn and Spooner Oldham–produced "Watchin' the Trains Go By," can be located on a CD from his own label, Hot Productions, and though it is hard to find, the search is worth it (the liner notes, however, are maddeningly incomplete).

Joe Tex: Thankfully, a British label called RPM is releasing two-album CDs of Joe Tex's best work, and the place to begin is with *Live and Lively/Soul Country*. That one features not only the Chips-engineered "Skinny Legs and All" (featuring Ed Kollis) but the astonishing bass work of Tommy Cogbill on versions of "Engine Engine Number Nine" and "Dark End of the Street." And even better, it makes available the previously neglected, single-issued-only cuts "Men Are Gettin' Scarce" (done in the same style as "Skinny Legs") and "I'll Make Every Day Christmas for My Woman." *Happy Soul/Buying a Book* offers more pleasures, two of the most specifically Southern-referenced albums ever made by the group—absolutely delightful genre paintings. For now, listeners will

have to find the Atlantic vinyl pressing of the Chips and Tommy–engineered *Joe Tex Sings with Strings and Things*, from early in 1970, *I Gotcha*, featuring Tommy Cogbill's last bass work recorded in Memphis, but it is well worth the search.

Papa Don Schroeder: James and Bobby Purify didn't record very often, and their first album, recorded in Muscle Shoals with Chips Moman on lead guitar, included "I'm Your Puppet" and several other Penn-Oldham tunes. Neither it nor the second album, recorded at American, *The Pure Sound of the Purifys*, has been released in its entirety on CD, but European Sony BMG has a *Best of James and Bobby Purify* compilation featuring the best tracks from both, up to and including "Shake a Tail Feather." Mighty Sam McClain has fared even worse: of the CDs by him now in print, not one covers his Bell recordings done at the Shoals and American. Charly Records in England did issue a Mighty Sam compilation LP in the eighties, *Papa Don's Preacher*, and this is the one that people will have to track down. Sundazed did better by Oscar Toney Jr., releasing his album *For Your Precious Love* and including all the remaining Bell singles on one CD. If you are looking for "Never Get Enough of Your Love," "Moon River," or "Down in Texas," they are here.

Joe Simon: The place to get his American classics on CD is RPM's compilation *Monument of Soul*. The pun is intended, because the anthology provides a look at most of his Monument recordings from Memphis and Nashville. Both "You Keep Me Hanging On" and "Nine Pound Steel" are here. Vinyl collectors would be better served going directly to the source: the Monument LP *No Sad Songs*.

Masqueraders: There is a heroic attempt at a compilation Masqueraders CD, *Unmasked*, released in 2006; unfortunately, it omits two of the group's most important works:

Wayne Carson's composition "The Grass Was Green" and the Mike Leech–supervised (though credited to Chips) "Steamroller Blues," the cut that directly inspired Elvis to feature the song in concert. The tracks are not presented in order, either, so the listener will have some trouble sorting out the years each recording was done. That said, the rest of the good work is here: Chips's masterful "On the Other Side"; Tommy Cogbill's "I'm Just an Average Guy" and the beautiful jazz waltz "Tell Me You Love Me."

Psychedelia: The Joseph Longoria *succes d'estime* has been reissued—*Stoned Age Man*, originally on Scepter, is available now on CD from Radioactive Records. The other two experimental psychedelic albums—Billy Burnette's self-titled first album on Entrance and Weinstein and Stroll's *Cook Me Up Your Taste* on Capitol/Chips—are out of print and available only through second-hand stores specializing in vinyl.

B.J. Thomas: There is no end to the greatest hits compilations, some re-recordings, of the many hits B.J. Thomas has had over the years, but three packages stand out. Varese Sarabande reissued the original gold-packaged *Greatest Hits, Volume 1* that appeared on Scepter: it is important not only because of the Moman-produced hits but because of the earlier recordings done in Texas under the supervision of Huey P. Meaux, with several tracks arranged by Glen Spreen. Ace Records in England carried the idea slightly further with their *Scepter Hits and More;* this CD includes "Most of All" and "Mighty Clouds of Joy." *Have a Heart: The Love Songs Collection* (Varese Sarabande) ties up a few further loose ends, gathering all the remaining Atlanta-recorded tracks including the CD's title song (and Reggie Young's composition "Hello Love"). But for such masterworks as "Rainy Day Man," "Circle Round the Sun," "Sandman," and the stunning "I've Been Down This Road Before," a search for the out-of-print albums

on Scepter is necessary. *On My Way, Young and In Love, Raindrops Keep Falling on My Head, Everybody's Out of Town*, and *Most of All* are all essential listening. And get *B. J. Thomas' Greatest Hits Vol. 2* for the neglected Glen Spreen composition "Life," a reflective thought piece.

Box Tops: Also essential are the Sundazed CD reissues of the four Box Tops albums on Bell: *The Letter/Neon Rainbow, Cry Like a Baby, Nonstop*, and *Dimensions*. Each CD is presented with painstaking care, and each one features outtakes and singles never before appearing in any Box Tops compilation. For some reason, however, the compilers overlooked the 45 of "I Shall Be Released," which differs in many ways from the version heard on the CD; search for the single on Mala/Bell.

Other singers: Dionne Warwick's complete 1969 *Soulful*, along with all the outtakes from the sessions and her tracks from the 1970 New York road trip, can be found on a CD from Rhino Handmade. Merrilee Rush's *Angel of the Morning: The Complete Bell Recordings* is also on CD as an import from England's Rev-Ola label (but you will have to track down the Bell 45 with the original, pain-ravaged version of "That Kind of Woman"—only the second, softer version is available on the CD).

Some of the early Ronnie Milsap singles can be found on a Collectables CD, *A Rose By Any Other Name*, and his Warner Brothers self-titled first album, produced in 1971 by Dan Penn and featuring both the American and Muscle Shoals musicians, is also available on that label. An obscure CD on the Country Stars label, *Kentucky Woman*, is incomplete but has many of the Chips-produced recordings from Scepter. Petula Clark's *Memphis* CD suffers from a muddled remix; despite the presence of an outtake here and there, listeners are better off finding the vinyl version with its crisper, clearer sound.

Brenda Lee's *Memphis Portrait* is unavailable on CD; listeners are advised to search.

Although the Arthur Alexander album produced by Tommy Cogbill appears on a CD reissue as *Rainbow Road: The Warner Brothers Sessions*, listeners are recommended to get the original album sequence on Ace Records LP reissue from 1988, simply called *Arthur Alexander*.

Angeline Butler's agonized, soulful album *Impressions*, on CoBurt Records, is out of print and available only through searches for used vinyl; nonetheless, it is essential listening.

For some of Tommy's and Chips's finest collaborations, Collector's Choice has a Roy Hamilton compilation CD, *Tore Up: The RCA and AGP Singles*. "Angelica" alone is worth the price.

Neil Diamond: The two albums on which the Memphis-recorded tracks appear, *Sweet Caroline* and *Touching You, Touching Me*, are on CD through the auspices of MCA.

Elvis: There is no lack of RCA/Sony BMG reissues to choose from here, but the two-CD set *Suspicious Minds*, featuring all the Chips-produced recordings, is the one to have. The complete recordings are also to be found on the equally essential box set *From Nashville to Memphis: The Complete '60s Masters*. BMG/Follow That Dream released a limited-edition CD of outtakes and studio conversation, *Memphis Sessions*, that is out of print now but essential for anyone wanting to hear how Chips carefully but casually sculpted his sessions. Additional unreleased Memphis Sessions tracks can be found on the set *Platinum: A Life in Music*. Purists are cautioned to avoid *The Memphis Record* at all costs: the mixes are so altered as to be unrecognizable.

In-house artists: Bobby Womack, of course, is perhaps the best known of these, and his first two albums, *Fly Me to the Moon* and *My Prescription*, are available on a two-CD set from EMI. A smaller label, The Right Stuff, has reissued *Understanding*, on which "Woman's Gotta Have It" appears.

Cymarron's album and most of their randomly issued Entrance singles are to be found on the Collectables reissue *Rings: The Very Best of Cymarron*.

Most of the writers did solo albums at one time or another, and most are out of print now. Vinyl collectors should find Wayne Carson's Monument album *Life Lines* and Mark James's self-titled 1973 solo album on Bell. Wayne recorded extensively on MGM during the early part of his career, though his work for that label has never appeared on CD. His MGM 45s are all worth tracking down; all are highly musical, featuring classic and elegant production from Chips. There are also assorted Mark James, Richard Mainegra, and Rick Yancey singles on Scepter; for historians, Mark's original version of "Suspicious Minds" is the most interesting of the lot.

Donnie Fritts has done three albums, all fortunately on CD; although they are not within the time frame cited here they are a valuable introduction to an underrated writer. His latest, *One Foot in the Groove*, and the late-nineties *Everybody's Got a Song*, which was released on John Prine's Oh Boy! label, are both good overviews. Even better is his 1974 *Prone to Lean*, available, though with difficulty and at great expense, as a Vivid Sound Japanese import.

Dan Penn has several CDs available, though like Donnie's, all were recorded beyond the scope of this history: his 1973 *Nobody's Fool*, done at his own Memphis studio, offers a portrait of the writer in transition. *Do Right Man* (Sire/London/ Rhino) is a confident Dan in the nineties, with backing from the American and Muscle Shoals musicians. To hear him and Spooner Oldham together (including rare harmony vocals from Spooner), the classic live recording *Moments from This Theater*, on the Proper Records label, is the one to have. Spooner Oldham's own instrumental 1972 LP, *Pot Luck*, is out of print but well worth finding, as is Bobby Emmons's solo work for Hi (with Reggie Young and Mike Leech rounding things out), *Blues with a Beat and with an Organ*. Bobby Wood's self-titled 1964 album on Joy is of course out of print and difficult to find, but recommended for historical purposes, and his later singles on the Joy and Bell labels are delightful.

Assorted Singles: There are any number of singles that have never been compiled into a CD collection, most notably the work that came out on AGP/Bell. Whatever the original intentions for the label may have been, it quickly became the experimental laboratory for Tommy Cogbill, and acquiring the singles he produced is essential to an understanding of his talent. Key pieces include Jumpin' Gene Simmons's "Home Again/Don't You Worry 'Bout Me"; Shadden the King Lears' "Good Time Mary-Go-Round," and the American Group instrumentals co-produced with Chips, "The High Times"/"Enchilada Soul."

The serious collector of American Group recordings will find much of the Memphis material, ironically, more easily obtainable than most of the later recordings done in Nashville: for every celebrated record, every "I Can Help" or "You Were Always on My Mind" done there, twenty albums seem to have fallen through the cracks. The Nashville recordings made by the group are beyond the scope of this survey, but the listener can begin by gathering the mid-to-late-seventies and early eighties work of Waylon Jennings, Willie Nelson, Merle Haggard, Larry Gatlin's work on the Monument label, and Crystal Gayle.

## NOTES

The following notes indicate interviews referenced in each chapter.

### Introduction
Bobby Emmons, Bobby Wood, Hayward Bishop, Reggie Young, Shane Keister, Glen Spreen, Marty Lacker, Spooner Oldham—June 2008; Chips Moman—February 2004 .

### Chapter 1
Bobby Wood—September 2002, January 2004; Fred Foster—October 2002; Gene Chrisman—September 2002, October 2002; Mike Leech—August 2002, September 2002, January 2003, June 2004, July 2004; Shirley Cogbill—October 2002; Stan Kesler—October 2002, January 2003; Wayne Jackson—March 2007; Wayne Carson—February 2007; Reggie Young—*Guitar Player*, October 1986; January 2004; June 2003; Hayward Bishop—January 2003; Bobby Emmons—September 2002, June 2003; Larry Dean Stewart—October 2002.

### Chapter 2
Mike Leech—September 2002, June 2003, January 2003; Ed Kollis—September 2002; Hayward Bishop—May 2003, January 2004; Dan Penn—January 2004; Don Crews—February 2004, March 2004, June 2008; Chips Moman—February 2004; Wayne Jackson—March 2007; Jimmy Johnson—June 2003; Quinton Claunch—February 2004; Bobby Wood—January 2003; Gene Chrisman, October 2002; Spooner Oldham, March 2004; Bobby Emmons—January 2003, June 2003; Reggie Young—June 2003; Fred Hester—October 2002; Stan Kesler—January 2003; Sandy Posey—March 2004; Larry Butler—January 2003, John Hughey—January 2003.

### Chapter 3
Dan Penn—October 2002, January 2004; Spooner Oldham—March 2004; Jimmy Johnson—February 2004; Norbert Putnam—March 2006, April 2006; Chips Moman—February

2004; Reggie Young—January 2004, May 2004; Larry Butler—February 2003; Bobby Wood—January 2003; Don Crews—April 2004, February 2004; Mike Leech—June 2002; Hayward Bishop—May 2003; David Hood—April 2006; Roger Hawkins—April 2006.

### Chapter 4

Mike Leech—August 2002, September 2002, January 2003, March 2004; Reggie Young—June 2003, May 2004; Bobby Emmons—October 2002, June 2003, March 2004; Hayward Bishop—May 2003; Stan Kesler—October 2002, January 2003; Gene Chrisman—October 2002; Larry Butler—February 2003; Bobby Wood—February 2003; Spooner Oldham—July 2003, March 2004; Jimmy Johnson—February 2004; Don Crews—February 2004; Chips Moman—February 2004; Roger Hawkins—April 2006; Dan Penn—October 2002, January 2004; Larry Butler—February 2003; Don Schroeder—February 2003; Quinton Claunch—February 2003.

### Chapter 5

Mike Leech—September 2002, October 2003, April 2004; Bobby Wood—April 2004; Stan Kesler—October 2002; Reggie Young—May 2004; Dan Penn—October 2002; Jimmy Johnson—April 2004, February 2004; Spooner Oldham—March 2004, April 2006; Chips Moman—February 2004, November 2007; David Hood—April 2006; Hayward Bishop—September 2006; Roger Hawkins—April 2006; Gene Chrisman—October 2002.

### Chapter 6

Hayward Bishop—May 2003, March 2005; Stan Kesler—February 2005; Jimmy Johnson—February 2004, April 2005; Dan Penn—October 2002; Roger Hawkins—April 2006; Bobby Emmons—January 2003, April 2005; Mike Leech—September 2002, May 2003, January 2003, March 2003, September 2003, February 2005, April 2005; Chips Moman—September 2004, February 2004; Don Schroeder—February 2003, March 2005, April 2005; Reggie Young—May 2004, September 2004; Don Crews—May 2004, September 2004; Gene Chrisman—October 2002; Bobby Wood—September 2004, March 2005; Sandy Posey—April 2003, February 2005; J.R. Cobb—March 2004; Spooner Oldham—March 2005.

### Chapter 7

Don Crews—September 2004; Chips Moman—February 2004, November 2004; Reggie Young—May 2004, September 2004; Dan Penn—October 2002, January 2004; Wayne Carson—June 2005; Mike Leech—September 2002, January 2003, May 2003; Jimmy Johnson—April 2006, September 2006; Don Schroeder—April 2005; Glen Spreen—September 2002, May 2005; Spooner Oldham—March 2005; Hayward Bishop—May 2003, October 2004; Bobby Wood—September 2004; Johnny Christopher—June 2005; Gene Chrisman—October 2002; Bobby Emmons—April 2005.

### Chapter 8

Bobby Wood—January 2003, September 2004; Jimmy Johnson—February 2004; Bobby Emmons—June 2003, October 2007; Chips Moman—February 2004, October 2005, November 2005; Gene Chrisman—October 2002; Reggie Young—May 2004; Mike Leech—August 2002, September 2002, June 2003, October 2003; B.J. Thomas—July 2005; Hayward Bishop—May 2003; Spooner Oldham—March 2005; Dan Penn—January 2003; Don Crews—September 2004; Glen Spreen—September 2002, May 2005; Wayne Carson—June 2005; Ed Kollis—October 2002.

### Chapter 9

Dan Penn—October 2002, January 2004; Mike Leech—July 2002, September 2002, January 2003, August 2005; Gary Talley—February 2006; Chips Moman—April 2003, February 2004; Spooner Oldham—March 2005, February 2006; Wayne Carson—June 2005; Bobby Emmons—April 2005; Reggie Young—January 2006; Gene Chrisman—October 2002; Jimmy Johnson—February 2006; Fred Foster—October 2002.

## Chapter 10

Reggie Young—May 2004, January 2006; Chips Moman—November 2005, September 2006; Bobby Emmons—June 2003, October 2007; Fred Foster—March 2006; Bobby Wood—January 2003, September 2004, May 2007; Mike Leech—August 2002, September 2002; Wayne Carson—June 2005; Dan Penn—January 2004; Don Schroeder—April 2005; Jimmy Johnson—February 2006; Roger Hawkins—May 2007; Ima Roberts Withers—September 2003; Spooner Oldham—March 2005; Gene Chrisman—October 2002; Ed Kollis—October 2002; Gary Talley—February 2006.

## Chapter 11

J.R. Cobb—May 2005; Bobby Emmons—April 2005, October 2007; Mike Leech—February 2003, August 2004, June 2006; Don Crews—September 2004; Spooner Oldham—September 2006; Bobby Wood—January 2003, June 2003, September 2004, July 2006; Chips Moman—February 2004, September 2006; Reggie Young—May 2004, January 2006; Wayne Jackson—September 2002; Ima Roberts Withers—September 2006; Ed Kollis—October 2002; Wayne Carson—February 2007; Dan Penn—October 2002.

## Chapter 12

Mike Leech—September 2002, August 2004, June 2006; Ima Roberts Withers—September 2003, June 2006; Don Crews—June 2006; Hayward Bishop—May 2003; Reggie Young—May 2004, January 2006, July 2006; Wayne Jackson—January 2006, March 2007; Bobby Wood—September 2004, January 2003, June 2006; Norbert Putnam—July 2006; Chips Moman—July 2006, September 2006; Stan Kesler—August 2007; Spooner Oldham, February 2006, April 2006; Glen Spreen—May 2005; Gary Talley—May 2006; Gene Chrisman—October 2002; Roger Hawkins—July 2006, December 2006; Jimmy Johnson—February 2006, September 2006; Bobby Emmons—October 2007; J.R. Cobb—August 2006.

## Chapter 13

Mike Leech—April 2003, October 2003, June 2006; Reggie Young—May 2004, July 2006; Bobby Wood—January 2004, September 2004, June 2006; Spooner Oldham—September 2006; J.R. Cobb—January 2003; Sandy Posey—February 2005; Chips Moman—February 2004; Billy Robinson—March 2006; Gary Talley—May 2006; Jimmy Johnson—April 2006; Donnie Fritts—April 2006; Norbert Putnam—March 2006, June 2006; Johnny Christopher—June 2005; Spooner Oldham—May 2006; Hayward Bishop—June 2006; Bobby Emmons—October 2007.

## Chapter 14

Jimmy Johnson—September 2006; David Hood—April 2006; Chips Moman—February 2004, April 2003, September 2006; Mike Leech—July 2003, October 2003, November 2003; Gene Chrisman—October 2002; Bobby Emmons—October 2007; Ima Roberts Withers—September 2003; Hayward Bishop, May 2003, March 2005; Bobby Wood—July 2006, November 2006; Spooner Oldham—September 2006; Roger Hawkins—December 2006; Reggie Young—July 2006; Don Crews—June 2006; Donnie Fritts—April 2006, July 2006; Ed Kollis—October 2002; Glen Spreen—September 2002, August 2006, November 2006, February 2008; Dan Penn—January 2004; Jerry Carrigan—March 2004.

## Chapter 15

Chips Moman—September 2006; Roger Hawkins—December 2006; Ed Kollis—October 2002; Reggie Young—May 2004, July 2006; Bobby Emmons—April 2005, October 2007; Mike Leech—August 2002, September 2002, July 2005, January 2007; Wayne Carson—January 2007; Bobby Wood—January 2003, January 2006, September 2006, January 2007, May 2007; Gene Chrisman—September 2002; J.R. Cobb—August 2006; Ima Roberts Withers—August 2006; Marty Lacker—January 2007; Dan Penn—October 2002; Ed Kollis—October 2002; Jimmy Johnson—February 2003; Don Crews—June 2006; Hayward Bishop—May

2003, September 2006; Glen Spreen—September 2002, December 2006, October 2007; Norbert Putnam—May 2006, October 2006; Wayne Carson—August 2007; Gary Talley—November 2006, December 2006; Stan Kesler—January 2003.

## Chapter 16

Dan Penn—January 2004; Wayne Carson—February 2007; Glen Spreen—December 2006, January 2007; Mike Leech—February 2007; Reggie Young—May 2004, February 2007; Hayward Bishop—September 2006; Chips Moman—September 2006; Marty Lacker—March 2007; Bobby Wood—September 2002, November 2006, March 2007; Bobby Emmons—October 2007; Reggie Young—February 2007; Wayne Carson—June 2005; Don Crews—June 2006, May 2004; Mike Leech—September 2002; Mike Cauley—October 2007; Gene Chrisman—October 2002; Bobby Wood—November 2006; Roger Hawkins—July 2006, December 2006; Jimmy Johnson—May 2004, September 2006; J.R. Cobb—August 2006.

## Chapter 17

Marty Lacker—January 2007, March 2007; Don Crews—January 2007; Reggie Young—February 2007; Glen Spreen—December 2006, January 2007, March 2007; Johnny Christopher—June 2005; Wayne Carson—January 2007, February 2007; Ima Roberts Withers—February 2007; Chips Moman—September 2006, October 2007; Mike Leech—August 2002, September 2002, June 2004, February 2007; Bobby Emmons—April 2005, October 2007; Wayne Jackson—March 2007, February 2007; Bobby Wood—September 2002, March 2007, April 2007; Hayward Bishop—May 2003, September 2006; Dan Penn—January 2004; Spooner Oldham—April 2007; Jerry Carrigan—March 2003.

## Chapter 18

Ima Roberts Withers—February 2007; Glen Spreen—December 2006, January 2007, May 2007; Bobby Emmons—October 2007; Chips Moman—February 2004, April 2007;

Marty Lacker—January 2007, June 2007; Jimmy Johnson—October 2006; Hayward Bishop—September 2007; Red West—May 2007; Mike Leech—August 2002, September 2002, January 2003, October 2003; Bobby Wood—July 2006, March 2007, May 2007; Wayne Jackson—March 2007, May 2007; Richard Mainegra—January 2003; J.R. Cobb—August 2006; Wayne Carson—February 2007; Johnny Christopher—June 2005; Rick Yancey—March 2003; Reggie Young—February 2007; Ed Kollis—October 2002; Spooner Oldham—April 2007; Norbert Putnam—October 2006; Quinton Claunch—August 2007.

## Chapter 19

Reggie Young—July 2007; Mike Leech—February 2003, May 2003, July 2005, June 2007; Wayne Carson—May 2007; Mike Cauley—October 2007; Marty Lacker—January 2007, May 2007; Chips Moman—April 2004, November 2005, October 2007; Norbert Putnam—January 2006, October 2006, March 2007; Ron Oates—September 2002; Shane Keister—October 2007; Richard Mainegra—January 2003; Glen Spreen—May 2007, June 2007; Gary Talley—November 2006; Hayward Bishop—May 2003, September 2007; Bobby Wood—June 2007; Ima Roberts Withers—February 2007; Rick Yancey—March 2003; Bobby Emmons—April 2005; Johnny Christopher—June 2005; Red West—May 2007.

## Chapter 20

Chips Moman—February 2007, August 2007, October 2007; Bobby Wood—May 2007, July 2007, August 2007, September 2007; Marty Lacker—January 2007, June 2007, July 2007, August 2007; Glen Spreen—January 2007, May 2007, July 2007; Mike Leech—June 2005, January 2007, July 2007; Bobby Emmons—April 2005, October 2007; Richard Mainegra—January 2003, February 2003; Don Crews—June 2007, August 2007; Bobby Wood—September 2007; Hayward Bishop—May 2003, September 2007; Gene Chrisman—September 2002, October 2002, August 2007; Johnny Christopher—June 2005; Jimmy Johnson—October

2006; Jerry Carrigan—March 2003; Donnie Fritts—April 2006, August 2007; Ima Roberts Withers—August 2007; Brenda Lee—March 2003; Reggie Young—October 2007; Wayne Carson—February 2007; Ed Kollis—October 2003; Mike Cauley—October 2007.

### Chapter 21

Glen Spreen—December 2006, January 2007, May 2007; Hayward Bishop—September 2002, May 2003, January 2007, March 2007; B.J. Thomas—June 2005; Mike Leech—August 2002, October 2002, March 2003, May 2003; Ima Roberts Withers—August 2007; Marty Lacker—January 2007, June 2007, August 2007; Bobby Emmons—October 2007; Reggie Young—February 2007, July 2007; Bobby Wood—May 2007, June 2007, August 2007; Gene Chrisman—October 2002; Chips Moman—February 2004; Johnny Christopher—June 2005; Wayne Carson—May 2007.

### Chapter 22

Mike Leech—August 2002, September 2002, November 2005; Rick Yancey—March 2003; Bobby Emmons—October 2007; Marty Lacker—October 2007; Glen Spreen—December 2006, January 2007, September 2007, February 2008; Jimmy Johnson—October 2006; Reggie Young—July 2007; Hayward Bishop—May 2003, August 2007; Gene Chrisman—September 2002; Mike Cauley—October 2007; Chips Moman—September 2007; Bobby Wood—January 2004, September 2005; Ed Kollis—October 2002; Spooner Oldham—April 2006, August 2007; Richard Mainegra—February 2003; Wayne Carson—February 2007, May 2007, August 2007.

### Chapter 23

Ima Roberts Withers—August 2007; Mike Cauley—October 2007; Stan Kesler—August 2007; Mike Leech—September 2002, January 2003; October 2003; Reggie Young—July 2007, October 2007; Hayward Bishop—May 2003, August 2007; Bobby Emmons—October 2007; Gene Chrisman—September 2002; Marty Lacker—January 2007, September 2007; Bobby Wood—January 2003, June 2003, July

2007, August 2007, September 2007; Richard Mainegra—January 2003, February 2003; Rick Yancey—March 2003; Chips Moman—November 2005, August 2007, October 2007; Johnny Christopher—June 2005; Mike Cauley—October 2007.

### Chapter 24

Hayward Bishop—August 2007, September 2007; Bobby Wood—January 2003, September 2007; Reggie Young—May 2004, August 2007; Bobby Emmons—October 2007; Chips Moman—April 2003, September 2007, October 2007; Mike Leech—May 2003, June 2003, November 2004, February 2007; Stan Kesler—August 2007; Gene Chrisman—October 2002; Billy Burnette—August 2007; Marty Lacker—January 2007, September 2007; Donnie Fritts—April 2006, August 2007; Spooner Oldham—August 2007; Shane Keister—October 2007; Richard Mainegra—February 2003; Glen Spreen—January 2007; Wayne Carson—September 2007; Johnny Christopher—June 2005.

### Chapter 25

Bobby Wood—September 2007; Marty Lacker—September 2007; Bobby Emmons—October 2007; Hayward Bishop—May 2003, August 2007, September 2007; Billy Burnette—August 2007; Reggie Young—August 2007; Stan Kesler—January 2003, August 2007; Mike Leech—May 2003, July 2003; Richard Mainegra—February 2003; Gene Chrisman—October 2002, September 2007; Jim Davis—June 2005, Chips Moman—April 2003, October 2007.

### Chapter 26

Bobby Wood—January 2003, September 2004, September 2007; Hayward Bishop—September 2002, May 2003, August 2007, September 2007; Johnny Christopher—June 2005; Mike Leech—August 2002, August 2003, November 2004; Bobby Emmons—October 2007; Reggie Young—May 2004, August 2007, October 2007; Shane Keister—October 2002, September 2007; Chips Moman—August 2007, September 2007, October 2007, Stan Kesler—January 2003, August 2007; Jimmy

Johnson—October 2006; Richard Mainegra—February 2003; Dan Penn—October 2002; Marty Lacker—September 2007; Rick Yancey—March 2003; Gene Chrisman—October 2002; Glen Spreen—July 2007; Spooner Oldham—April 2007.

## BIBLIOGRAPHY
|||||||||||||||||||||||||||||||||||||||||||||||||||||||||||||

### Books

Booth, Stanley. *Rythm Oil.* New York: Vintage Books, 1989.

Bowman, Rob. *Soulsville USA: The Story of Stax Records,* 2nd ed. New York: Schirmer Trade Books, 2003.

Bronson, Fred. *The Billboard Book of Number One Hits.* New York: Billboard Books, 2003.

Clayton, Rose, with Dick Heard. *Elvis Up Close.* Atlanta: Turner, 1994.

Dickerson, James. *Goin' Back to Memphis: A Century of Blues, Rock and Roll, and Glorious Soul.* New York: Macmillan, 1996.

Franklin, Aretha, with David Ritz. *From These Roots.* New York: Villard Books, 1999.

Gillett, Charlie. *Making Tracks: Atlantic Records and the Growth of a Billion-Dollar Industry.* New York: E. P. Dutton, 1973.

Gordon, Robert. *It Came from Memphis.* New York: Faber and Faber, 1995.

Guralnick, Peter. *Dream Boogie: The Triumph of Sam Cooke.* Boston: Back Bay, 2006.

———. *Careless Love: The Unmaking of Elvis Presley.* Boston: Little, Brown, 1999.

———. *Sweet Soul Music: Rhythm and Blues and the Southern Dream of Freedom.* New York: HarperCollins, 1996.

Halberstam, David. *The Children.* New York: Random House, 1998.

Hopkins, Jerry. *Elvis.* New York: Simon and Schuster, 1971.

Hoskyns, Barney. *Say It One Time for the Brokenhearted: The Country Side of Southern Soul.* London: Bloomsbury, 1998.

Houston, Cissy, with Jonathan Singer. *How Sweet the Sound.* New York: Doubleday, 1998.

Jackson, Wayne. *In My Wildest Dreams, Volume One: A Collection of Rock and Roll Tales.* (self-published): Nashville, TN: Sweetmedicinemusic.com, 2007.

Jorgensen, Ernst. *Elvis Presley: A Life in Music—The Complete Recording Sessions.* New York: St. Martin's, 1998.

———. *Reconsider Baby: The Definitive Elvis Sessionography.* New York: Pierian, 1986.

Lacker, Marty, with Patsy Lacker and Leslie Smith. *Elvis: Portrait of a Friend.* Memphis, TN: Wimmer Brothers, 1979.

Lacker, Marty, with Billy Smith and Lamar Fike as told to Alanna Nash. *Elvis and the Memphis Mafia.* New York: HarperCollins, 1995.

Thomas, B.J., with Jerry Jenkins. *Home Where I Belong.* Waco, Texas: Word, 1978.

Thomas, B.J., with Gloria Thomas. *In Tune: Finding How Good Life Can Be.* Westwood, NJ: Fleming H. Revell, 1983.

Tobler, John, with Stuart Grundy. *The Record Producers.* New York: St. Martin's, 1983.

Wexler, Jerry, with David Ritz. *The Rhythm and the Blues.* New York: Knopf, 1996.

Womack, Bobby. *Midnight Mover: The True Story of the World's Greatest Soul Singer.* London: John Blake, 2007.

Zanes, Warren. *Dusty in Memphis.* New York: Continuum Books, 2003.


### Periodicals and Other Sources

*Bass Player.* "Mike Leech" (May 2000); "Tommy Cogbill." February 2006. (Both articles available on line at bassplayer.com)

Benmclane.com/alaimo (interview with Steve Alaimo)

Dahl, Bill. "Papa Don Schroeder Reminiscences." Sundazed.com. 2003.

Elvispresleynews.com. "How Chips Moman Revived Elvis' Recording Career."

Georgiarhythm.com. "Chips Moman Talks about His Life in Music," 2003. "American Way," .pdf 2005.

Hutton, Joss. "Dan Penn and Spooner Oldham." Perfect Sound Forever (online music magazine), 1998.

*Journal of Country Music* 12, no. 3 and 13, no. 1. Rob Bowman and Ross Johnson. "The Flip Side of Memphis: Stan Kesler Interview." 1990.

Norton, Cathi. "Dan Penn—A Shade Tree Guy." 1995 (Box Tops website: Boxtops.com).

*Memphis Commercial-Appeal.* Bob Mehr. "Chips Moman: The Missing Man of Memphis Music." July 13, 2008.

Properamerican.com. Interview with Dan Penn and Spooner Oldham. 2008.

*Rolling Stone.* "John Prine, A Folkie Comer." Issue 97 (December 9, 1971): 16–18.

### Web Sites

Bobbyemmons.com

Chipsmoman.com

Danpenn.com

Memphisboys.com

Pnwbands.com (info and photos of Merrilee Rush)

Soulfulmusic.blogspot (a fan site for the group featuring links to other sites and articles)

Spooneroldham.com

49; Diamond sessions and, 193, 195; *Dimensions*, 186; "Don't Forget About Me," 165; "Don't Let Me Lose This Dream," 100; "The Door You Closed to Me," 134; "Do Right Woman," 55; "Do Unto Others," 130; "Down in Texas," 115; "Down the Back Roads," 334; downtime and, 226, 252, 282–83; "Dreamin' Till Then," 231; drugs and, 66, 328–29; "Drown in My Own Tears," 60; Dynamics sessions, 183; early career, 5–6, 11; editing and, 60; Emmons and, 7; "Enchilada Soul," 234; "Everlasting Love," 366; "Every Day I Have to Cry Some," 31; "Everyday Living Days," 191; "Every Man Needs a Woman," 124; "Every Time," 136; *The Exciting Wilson Pickett*, 35; "Fa-Fa-Fa-Fa-Fa," 59; "Fair Lover," 185; family of, 152; "Fields of Clover," 136, 137; "Finger-Poppin' Good-Time Party," 240; Franklin sessions and, 56–57, 61, 89, 109; Fritts and, 273–74, 336; "Gentle On My Mind," 206; Gentry Time, 31–32; "Glory Road," 194; "Go Home Girl," 333; "Going Down Slow," 91; "Going in Circles," 294; "Goin' to A Party," 341; at Goldwax, 53; "Good Morning Dear," 136; "Good-Time Merry-Go-Round," 230–31; "Good to Me As I Am to You," 109–10; "Got No Angel on My Shoulder," 246; "The Grass Was Green," 231; "Green Onions," 59; guns and, 360; "The Happy Song," 189; "Happy Times," 103; Hayes and, 16; "Hello Sunshine, 85, 140–41; "Here I Am," 94; "He Sang a Good Song," 311; Hi Records and, 18–19, 37, 53; "Hold On, I'm Comin'," 58; "Holly Holy," 237, 238; "House of the Rising Sun," 192; "The House That Jack Built," 141; "How Big Is Big," 312; "Hurtin' Don't Come Easy," 195; "Hush," 130; "Ice Cream Song," 185; "If I Never Knew Your Name," 195; "I'll Hold Out My Hand," 189; "I'm a Midnight Mover," 145; "I'm Coming Home," 333; "I'm Drifting," 35; "I'm Going Back Home," 311; "I'm in the Middle of It All," 333; "I'm Just an Average Guy," 185; "I'm Movin' On," 151, 206; *Impressions*, 242; "I'm Sorry," 76; "I'm Sorry about That," 73; "I'm Your Puppet," 106, 178; "I Never Loved a Man," 55, 100; influences on, 54, 85; "In the Pocket," 99; "I Saw Pity in the Face of a Friend," 171; "I Say a Little Prayer," 139; "I See Only Sunshine," 190; "I Shall Be Released," 113, 188, 243; "I Still Love You," 311; "It Ain't Gonna Work," 351; "I Take It Back," 70; "It Hurts So Bad," 333; "It's Gonna Rain," 227; "It's Only Love," 221; "It's Wonderful to Be in Love," 17; "I've Come a Long Way," 85; "I've Got a Thing About You Baby," 363; "I Wanna See a Change," 141; "I Was Made to Love Her," 100; jazz

and, 161; "Juliet," 195; "Jump Back," 59; "Keep on Keepin' That Man," 242–43; "Kentucky Rain," 214; King assassination and, 142; King Curtis sessions and, 57, 58, 144; "King's Highway," 287; "Knock On Wood," 58; "Ladylike," 244–45; *Lady Soul*, 108, 109; "Land of a Thousand Dances," 34; "Last Night," 59; Leech and, 140, 183, 203, 205, 279, 285; leisure time and, 91, 174, 234; "Love Is a Beautiful Thing," 73; "Love, Peace and Understanding," 232; "Love's Where Life Begins," 334; "Loving You Is Sweeter Than Ever," 179; Mainegra and, 336; Mann sessions and, 162, 163; Masqueraders and, 121, 122, 231; "Memphis Soul Stew," 87; "Midnight Angel," 188; "Midnight Hour," 59; Milsap and, 153–54; Moman and, 30, 42, 120, 173, 344; "Money Won't Change You," 109; "Moonfire," 240; "Moon River," 114; "Mr. Businessman," 170; "Murder in the First Degree," 185; Muscle Shoals and, 36, 54, 72, 115; musician pay and, 196–97; musicians union and, 340; "Natural Woman," 62; new material and, 238–39; "New Orleans," 162; "New Orleans Ruth," 295; New York and, 110; "Nikki Hoeky," 109; "Observation from Flight 285," 129; "Ode to Billy Joe," 99; office of, 306; "Old Joe Clark," 311–12; "The Old Man at the Fair," 155; "Only the Strong Survive," 214; "Orange Juice Commercial," 312; "People Gonna Talk," 152; "People Gotta Be Free," 178; Picadilly Circus sessions and, 295, 296; Pickett sessions and, 34–35, 42, 84, 86, 88; pranks and, 333; Presley sessions and, 202, 204, 207, 208; producing and, 84, 102, 127, 146–47, 149, 160, 185, 196, 220, 310–11; Putnam and, 239; quacks and, 279; "Reaching for a Rainbow," 244; "Reach Out," 94, 191–92; "Reap What You Sow," 129; Rich and, 38; "Robin McCarver," 233; "Rock Me," 186; "Rollin' in My Sleep," 150; Rush sessions and, 127; Samudio and, 21; "Save Me," 61; "Seesaw," 140; "She Knows How," 104; "Sign On for the Good Times," 232, 240; "Since You've Been Gone," 109, 152–53; sitar and, 133; "Slip Away," 159, 160; solo album by, 51; "Son of a Preacher Man," 165; "Soul Serenade," 60, 187, 234; "Sounds of Love," 243; spiritual search by, 287–88; Spreen and, 168, 169, 182, 277, 285; "Sunshine and Roses," 129; "Sweet Caroline," 195–96, 303; "Sweet Cream Ladies," 189; Sweet Inspirations session and, 93; "Swift Lizard," 312; "Tell Me You Love Me," 232; Tex sessions and, 144; "Thank God He Came," 335–36; "That Kind of Woman," 160–61; "They'll Do It Every Time," 336; "Think," 139; B.J. Thomas sessions

Rider," 20; "Cheater Man," 75; "Cherry Blue," 19; Christopher and, 155; Clark sessions and, 263; Cogbill and, 11, 19, 32, 51, 100; Conley sessions, 145; "Corina, Corina," 20; Crews and, 248; "Dark End of the Street," 48, 49; DeShannon sessions and, 307; Diamond sessions and, 194; "Donald and Lydia," 326; Dowd and, 83–84; downtime and, 282; drug abstention and, 328; early career, 7, 10, 12; "86 More Miles," 19; "Enchilada Soul," 234; "Every Man Needs a Woman," 124; family of, 152; Foster and, 111; "Games People Play," 261; "Give a Hand, Take a Hand," 259; "Goin' to a Party," 341; Goldwax and, 53; "Got to Hold On to You," 152; Harris and, 38; "Haunted House," 21; Hi records and, 8–9, 38–39, 53; "Hooked on a Feeling," 170; "House of the Rising Sun," 153; "I Can't Make It Alone," 166; "I Don't Want Nobody to Lead Me On," 121, 184; "If I Never Knew Your Name," 195; "I'll Be There," 206; "Illegal Smile," 323; illness of, 217; "I'm Going Back Home," 311; "I'm Sorry," 76; influences on, 54; "I Shall Be Released," 188; "I've Got a Feeling About You, Baby," 363; jazz and, 161; "Keep Me Warm," 320; "Keep on Keepin' That Man," 242–43; Keister and, 354; on Kensinger, 251; King assassination and, 142, 143; "Laid-Back Days," 348; "The Last War Song," 341–42; "Leavin' on a Jet Plane," 260; Lee sessions and, 256; Leech and, 326; "Let's Face Facts," 122; "Live Till You Die," 308; Longoria sessions, 192; "Love the Time Is Now," 145; "Lukenbach, Texas," 366; Mann sessions and, 162, 163; Mardin and, 83–84; Masqueraders and, 121, 231; "Mattie Ree," 19; Memphis Music Awards, 361–62; "Memphis Soul Stew," 87; Mitchell and, 38; Moman and, 73–74, 102, 120–21, 316–17; musician's union and, 339–40; newcomers and, 181; in New York, 299; "Nine-Pound Steel," 113–14; "No Sad Songs," 113; O'Keefe sessions and, 355; "Only Love Can Break a Heart," 348; "On the Other Side," 122; "Orange Juice Commercial," 312; Parker and, 39; Paul Revere and the Raiders and, 123; "Peg o' My Heart," 20; on Penn, 73–74, 102, 107; "People Gotta Be Free," 176; Pickett sessions and, 86, 88; Posey and, 71, 95; Presley and, 247; Presley sessions and, 202, 203, 218; "Pretty Good," 324; Prine sessions and, 323, 327; "Proud Mary," 262; Purify sessions and, 66, 67, 68; race and, 143; Rich and, 38; Riley and, 363; "Roll It Down the Hill," 282; "Roseland Taxi Dancer," 357; Rush and, 129; Samudio and, 20; Schroeder and, 64, 68;

"Sentimental Journey," 20; "Shake a Tail Feather," 68; "Shilo," 157, 158; Simon and, 112; "Sittin' Home," 19, 20; "Solitary Man," 224; Springfield sessions and, 166–67; success and, 173; Sweet Inspirations sessions and, 94; "Tell Me You Love Me," 232; Tex sessions and, 117; "That Old-Time Feeling," 265–66; B.J. Thomas sessions and, 275; "Twenty Years Ago Today," 341; "Until It's Time for You to Go," 245; and using horns, 124; "Valentine Pieces," 357; "Vanilla O'Lay," 348; Warwick sessions and, 179; "Wearin' That Loved On Look," 206; Weinstein/ Stroll sessions, 280, 284; West and, 220; "What'd I Say," 19; "When You Wish Upon a Star," 245; "Whiter Shade of Pale," 100; "Windmills of Your Mind," 166; Wine and, 259, 278, 305; Womack and, 84; "The Wonderful World of Summer," 148; "The Wurlitzer Prize," 366; "You Keep Tightening Up on Me," 287; Young and, 18, 185; "You're All I Need to Get By," 178

English, Bill, 9
English, Ronald, 40
Entrance (label), 317, 327
Epic (label), 317
Ertegun, Ahmet, 161, 342
Ertegun, Nesuhi, 161
Esposito, Joe, 212
Eternity's Children, 234; "Sidewalks of the Ghetto," 210
Etheridge, Chris, 228
Evans, John, 105, 107. *See also* Box Tops, the

Faith, Percy, 52
Fame studios, 28, 29, 44, 45, 54
Farlow, Tal, 19
Feliciano, Jose, "Magnolia," 303
Felts, Narvel, 9, 17; "86 More Miles," 19
Fernwood Recording Studio, 3, 16
Fike, Lamar, 199, 203, 205, 212
Fisher, Toni, "The Big Hurt," 8
Flash and the Board of Directors, 74, 123, 147
Flatt and Scruggs, 106
Fleetwood Mac, 366
Floyd, Eddie: "Fair Lover," 185; "Knock on Wood," 58
Floyd, Ralph, 5
Fogelberg, Dan: "Captured Angel," 303; "Home Free," 303; "The Innocent Age," 303; "Phoenix," 303; "Proud Mary," 262; "To the Morning," 280; "Twin Sons of Different Mothers," 303
Fogerty, John, 262
Foley, Red, 78

157, 211–12, 224–25, 248, 274, 282, 291, 296–97, 301, 316–17, 330, 343, 361, 362, 364, 365, 366; American musicians and, 17, 21, 46, 91, 131, 132, 196; "And the Grass Don't Pay No Mind," 212; "Angelica," 208; Atlantic Records and, 35, 58, 84, 358; awards, 247, 328, 338, 366; "Baby, Baby, Baby," 60; Beatles and, 219; "The Bible Salesman," 234; in *Billboard*, 190; Bishop and, 268, 273, 316; "Born a Woman," 25–27; "The Box," 224; Box Tops sessions and, 104, 186, 187; "Bridge Over Troubled Water," 277; "Brother Love's Traveling Salvation Show," 194; "Brown-Eyed Woman," 300; Burnette and, 327, 341, 342; Butler and, 30; "Can't Find No Happiness," 114; "The Cat Was a Junkie," 280; "California Dreamin'," 146; "Candy," 231; "Can't You See," 157; Capitol Records and, 249–50; Carr and, 47–48; "Carrying a Heavy Load," 292–93; Carter and, 159; Cauley and, 318; "A Change Is Gonna Come," 61; Chilton and, 186; Chrisman and, 309; Christopher and, 222; Clark sessions and, 263; Claunch and, 17, 18; "Close to You," 301; Cogbill and, 30, 42, 90, 187, 344–45; "Come the Sun Tomorrow," 192; compared to great bandleaders, 120; "Country Road," 293; "Created for a Man," 277; creative philosophy of, 77; Crews and, 17, 288, 339; "Cry Like a Baby," 234; Cymarron and, 314, 319, 320; "Dark End of the Street," 47, 48–49, 289; "Deep in Kentucky," 135; Diamond sessions and, 193, 194; *Dimensions*, 186; "Don't Cry Daddy," 209; dogs and, 158–59; "Do Right Woman," 54, 55, 61, 63; Dowd and, 35, 91; downtime and, 226, 227, 283; "Dreamin' Till Then," 231; drinking and, 150; "Drown in My Own Tears," 60; drugs and, 66, 329; *Dusty in Memphis*, 167; "Dusty Roads," 15, 194; Dylan and, 219; Emmons and, 7, 8, 120–21; "Enchilada Soul," 234; engineering and, 91, 272; "Even the Trolls Love Rock and Roll," 362; "Everybody's Talking," 275; "Everyday Living Days," 191; "Everyone's Gone to the Moon," 227; *The Exciting Wilson Pickett*, 35; "Eyes of a New York Woman," 169, 257–58; family of, 152; "Fever," 364; "Fly Me to the Moon," 146; "For Your Precious Love," 67–68; Franklin sessions and, 54, 55, 56–57, 63; "Funky Broadway," 72; gambling and, 46, 226, 273, 283, 330, 346–47; Gentrys and, 22–23, 28, 31; *Gentry Time*, 32; "Give a Damn," 288; "Give a Hand, Take a Hand," 259–60; "Glory Road," 194; "Gone," 170; "Gonna Build a City," 192; "Good Night Sweet Dreams," 264; "Good Time Charlie's Got the Blues," 356; "Good Times," 61; Hamilton's death and, 209;

"Hello Love," 262, 301; "Hey Jude," 177; "The High Times," 234; "Highwayman," 155; Hill and, 305; "Hold on I'm Coming," 58; "Hooked on a Feeling," 170; "House of the Rising Sun," 53, 192; "How Can You Mend a Broken Heart," 319–20; "Hurtin' You Don't Come Easy," 195; "I Ain't Never Loved a Man," 55; "I'd Like to Change Places with His Part-Time Lover," 329–30; "If Every Day Was Like Christmas," 220; "If I Never Knew Your Name," 194–95; "I Found a Love," 72; "I Just Can't Help Believing," 275, 276; "I'll Build a City," 192; "I'll Hold Out My Hand," 189; "I'll Keep on Lovin' You," 262; illness of, 217; "I Loved You Like I Loved My Very Life," 292; "I'm Moving On," 206; "I'm Sorry about That," 73; "I Need a Lot of Loving," 72; influences on, 54; "Inherit the Wind," 206; "In the Ghetto," 209, 210–11, 214; "I Pray for Rain," 224; "I Saw Pity in the Face of a Friend," 170–71; "I See Only Sunshine," 190; "I Shall Be Released," 113, 188; "I Stayed Away Too Long," 82–83; "It Don't Matter to Me," 265; "It's Not Easy," 148; "It's Only love," 221; "It Takes a Little Longer," 255; "I've Been Down This Road Before," 171–72; "I've Got a Thing About You, Baby," 363; James and, 82; "Juliet," 195; Keister and, 353, 363; Kensinger and, 250–51; Kesler and, 323–24; King assassination and, 142; "King's Highway," 287, 288; "Knock on Wood," 58; Kollis and, 118; Lacker and, 233; Laxton and, 56; "Leavin' on a Jet Plane," 260; Leech and, 187, 277; Lee sessions and, 256; leisure time, 167, 234, 236; "The Letter," 81, 102; "Light My Fire," 170; "Long Distance Kissing," 329; Longoria sessions and, 192; "Looking at Life," 284; "Lord Never Made a Burden Too Heavy to Carry," 262; "The Love of My Man," 179; "Love Stuff," 330; "Loving You's a Natural Thing," 286; "Lukenbach, Texas," 366; Mainegra and, 241; Mardin and, 58; marriage of, 222, 230; "The Mask," 275; Masqueraders and, 231, 275; material selection and, 238; "Meadow of My Love," 147; *Memphis Portrait*, 256; "Midnight Angel," 188; Milsap and, 153–54; "Mojo Woman," 73; "Money in My Pocket," 146; "Moonlight in Vermont," 146; "Moon River," 114; "Most of All," 299; "Mr. Businessman," 170; "Mr. Welfare Man," 256; "Murder in the First Degree," 185; Muscle Shoals and, 33, 54, 72, 115; musical style of, 224; musicians union and, 339, 340; "Natural Woman," 62; "Neon Rainbow," 264; "Nine-Pound Steel," 113; "No Sad Songs," 112, 114; "Nothing's As Good As It Used to Be," 264; "Observation from Flight 285," 129;

Chilton and, 104, 107; Cogbill and, 33, 36, 102, 103, 130; Coke ads and, 149; Conley sessions and, 145; "Cry Like a Baby," 133, 134, 135, 234; "Dark End of the Street," 47, 48, 49; "Deep in Kentucky," 135; "Denver," 230; "The Door You Closed to Me," 134; "Do Right Woman," 54, 55–56, 61, 63; "Dreamer," 82; drinking and, 107; drugs and, 66, 144; early career, 28–30; "Everyday Living Days," 106; "Everything I Am," 106; "Every Time," 136; Fame and, 83; "Fields of Clover," 136; on Franklin, 54–55; Hall and, 47, 75; "Handy," 130; "Happy Times," 103, 104, 106; "Hey Mister," 95; on hippies, 191; "If You Need," 136; "I Met Her in Church," 152; "I'm Living Good," 30; "I'm Movin' On," 151, 206; "I'm Your Puppet," 45–46, 106, 178; "I Need a Lot of Loving," 72; influences on, 28, 74; "In the Same Old Way," 114; "I Pray for Rain," 106; "Is a Bluebird Blue?," 29; "I Stayed Away Too Long," 82–83; "Keep on Keepin' That Man," 242–43; King assassination and, 142, 143, 144; Leech and, 103; "The Letter," 68, 78–79, 80, 81, 102, 103; "Lost," 136; the Mark V's and, 29; McClain and, 45; on Memphis, 74; Mexico trip and, 236–37; Moman and, 30, 31, 33, 73, 74, 75, 78, 120; *Moments from This Theater*, 28; Muscle Shoals musicians and, 115; "Neon Rainbow," 104, 105; in New York, 57, 149; "Nine-Pound Steel," 113, 114; "No Sad Songs," 113; Pallbearers and, 29; "Oh What a Fool I've Been," 93; Oldham and, 41, 55; "One Night Stand," 125; "On the Other Side," 122; overdub sessions and, 137; "People Gonna Talk," 151–52; "People Make the World," 106; Pickett and, 34; Presley and, 203–4; producing and, 77–78, 107–8, 127, 133, 149; "Rainbow Road," 334; "Respect," 60; "Rock Me," 186; "Sandcastles," 130; "Sandman," 171; Schroeder and, 64; "727," 137; "She Ain't Gonna Do Right," 44; "She Shot a Hole in My Soul," 151; "Since I've Been Gone," 153; singing backup, 178; sitar and, 133, 134; songwriting and, 31; "Standing in the Rain," 95; Stax Records and, 76, 101; success and, 174; "Sunshine Girl," 30–31; "Sweet Inspiration," 92; Sweet Inspirations (group) sessions and, 93; "Take Me," 83; Talley and, 104; "Thank You for the Sunshine Days," 157; Thompson and, 78; "Trains, Boats, and Planes," 106; "Uptight Good Woman," 44; Vienneau and, 27; "Wang Dang Doodle," 135; "Watching the Trains," 156; "Weeping Annaleah," 136; "Whiter Shade of Pale," 100; "A Woman Left Lonely," 275, 298, 299; "Yesterday, Where's My

Mind," 152; "You Keep Me Hangin' On," 135; "You Left the Water Running," 44; Young and, 33

Penn, Linda, 106, 113

Pennington, Wallace Daniel. *See* Penn, Dan

Pepper-Tanner Jingle Company, 3, 134, 189, 352, 358

Perkins, Carl, 3

Perkins, Luther, 16, 115

Perkins, Thomas Wayne. *See* Wayne, Thomas

Pet Shop Boys, "You Were Always on My Mind," 338

Phillips, Esther, "Cheater Man," 74, 75

Phillips, John, 52

Phillips, Knox, 343; "No Not Much," 164

Phillips, Sam, 3, 12, 20, 101

Phillips Studio, 43, 52, 53, 164, 213, 366

Phyve, 240

Picadilly Circus: "Come on Down to Earth," 295–96; "New Orleans Ruth," 295

Pickett, Wilson, 139; "Bring It On Home to Me," 86; "Don't Cry No More," 85; *The Exciting Wilson Pickett*, 35; "Hey Jude," 177; "I Found a True Love," 145; "I'm a Midnight Mover," 145; "I'm Drifting," 35; "In the Midnight Hour," 35; "I've Been Good to You," 145; "I've Come a Long Way," 86; "Jealous Love," 85; "Land of a Thousand Dances," 34; "Let's Get an Understanding," 145; Muscle Shoals sessions, 33–34; "Mustang Sally," 42; "Something You Got," 35; "Stagolee," 85; "That Kind of Love," 85; "That's Where It's At," 145; "We've Got to Have Love," 86

Poplar Tunes, 241

Porter, David, 94

Posey, Sandy: American and, 24; "Are You Ever Coming Home," 70; "Blue Is My Best Color," 27; "Born a Woman," 24–25, 26–27; "Bread and Butter," 95; "Caution to the Wind," 27; Coke ads and, 149; "Come Softly to Me," 95; "Deep in Kentucky," 135; early career, 24; "Handy," 130, 148; "Hey Mister," 95; "I'm Your Puppet," 69; "I Take It Back," 70, 71; "It's All in the Game," 27; "It's Not Easy," 148; "It's Wonderful to Be in Love," 95; "Just Out of Reach," 27; "Last Day of Love," 95–96; "Love of the Common People," 95; "Meadow of My Love," 147; Moman and, 94, 148; in Muscle Shoals, 33; "One-Man Woman," 148; "Out of Tune," 147; "Patterns," 95; "A Place in the Sun," 96; "Rubberneckin'," 206; "Satin Pillows," 27; "See You on the Rebound," 95; "Shades of Gray," 147; "Shattered," 95; "Silly Girl," 148; *The Single Girl* (album and song), 26, 69–70, 95; "Something I'll Remember," 147; South and, 148; "Standing in the

Penn and, 30, 33; "People Get Ready," 266; Pickett sessions and, 86, 88; Posey and, 94–95; pranks and, 252, 283; Presley sessions and, 202, 203, 204, 206, 207, 208, 217; "Pretty Good," 324–25; Prine sessions and, 323; Purify sessions and, 65, 66, 67; "The Question," 356; race and, 143; "Rainbow Road," 334; "Ram-Bunk-Shus," 39; on recording with road bands, 104; Rich and, 38; "Right Can Be So Wrong," 320; "Right On," 264; Riley sessions and, 363–64; "Rings," 318; "The Road," 356; "Rock Me," 186; "Roll It Down the Hill," 282; "Roseland Taxi Dancer," 357; Rush sessions and, 127, 128; "Sam Stone," 324; "Sandman," 171; Schroeder and, 64, 68; "727," 137; "Shake a Tail Feather," 66, 67; "Silly Girl," 148; Simon and, 112, 114; "Since I've Been Gone," 152; sitar and, 133, 134; "Sittin' Home," 20; "Skinny Legs and All," 117; "So Hung Up On Sylvia," 287; "Son of a Preacher Man," 165; "Spanish Pipe Dream," 323; Spreen and, 181; Springfield sessions and, 166, 167; success and, 114; "Sweet Caroline," 196; Sweet Inspirations session and, 94; on T.J.'s, 154; "Table for Two for One," 301; Tex sessions and, 116, 117; "That Old-Time Feeling," 266; B.J. Thomas sessions and, 97–98, 275; C. Thomas sessions and, 291; Thompson and, 78; "Together," 188–89; Toney sessions and, 114; "Twenty Years Ago Today," 341; "Valentine Pieces," 356; "Vanilla O'Lay," 348; Warwick sessions and, 179; "Watching the Trains," 156; "Weeping Annaleah," 136; "The Weight," 179; Weinstein/Stroll sessions and, 280, 284; "West Virginia Mine," 308; "We've Got to Have Love," 86; "What's the Matter Baby," 243; "When a Man Loves a Woman," 88; "Who Will the Next Fool Be," 53; "Why Am I Treated So Bad," 94; "Wild Side of Life," 157; "Windmills of Your Mind," 166, 236; Wine and, 259, 304–5; "Working Girl," 129; "Would You Like to Learn to Dance," 343; Yancey and, 241; "You Don't Miss Your Water," 307; "You Got My Mind Messed Up," 48; "You Keep Me Hangin' On," 112; "You'll Think of Me," 206; "You Were Always on My Mind," 338

Youngstown (label), 22

Yuro, Timi, 281; "What's the Matter Baby," 243–44

CPSIA information can be obtained at www.ICGtesting.com
Printed in the USA
LVOW03s1600211014

409813LV00008B/194/P

9 781617 031991